Intelligence and
Information Policy
for National Security

SECURITY AND PROFESSIONAL INTELLIGENCE EDUCATION SERIES (SPIES)

Series Editor: Jan Goldman

In this post–September 11, 2001, era there has been rapid growth in the number of professional intelligence training and educational programs across the United States and abroad. Colleges and universities, as well as high schools, are developing programs and courses in homeland security, intelligence analysis, and law enforcement, in support of national security.

The Security and Professional Intelligence Education Series (SPIES) was first designed for individuals studying for careers in intelligence and to help improve the skills of those already in the profession; however, it was also developed to educate the public in how intelligence work is conducted and should be conducted in this important and vital profession.

1. *Communicating with Intelligence: Writing and Briefing in the Intelligence and National Security Communities*, by James S. Major. 2008.
2. *A Spy's Résumé: Confessions of a Maverick Intelligence Professional and Misadventure Capitalist*, by Marc Anthony Viola. 2008.
3. *An Introduction to Intelligence Research and Analysis*, by Jerome Clauser, revised and edited by Jan Goldman. 2008.
4. *Writing Classified and Unclassified Papers for National Security*, by James S. Major. 2009.
5. *Strategic Intelligence: A Handbook for Practitioners, Managers, and Users*, revised edition by Don McDowell. 2009.
6. *Partly Cloudy: Ethics in War, Espionage, Covert Action, and Interrogation*, by David L. Perry. 2009.
7. *Tokyo Rose / An American Patriot: A Dual Biography*, by Frederick P. Close. 2010.
8. *Ethics of Spying: A Reader for the Intelligence Professional*, edited by Jan Goldman. 2006.
9. *Ethics of Spying: A Reader for the Intelligence Professional*, Volume 2, edited by Jan Goldman. 2010.
10. *A Woman's War: The Professional and Personal Journey of the Navy's First African American Female Intelligence Officer*, by Gail Harris. 2010.
11. *Handbook of Scientific Methods of Inquiry for Intelligence Analysis*, by Hank Prunckun. 2010.
12. *Handbook of Warning Intelligence: Assessing the Threat to National Security*, by Cynthia Grabo. 2010.

13. *Keeping U.S. Intelligence Effective: The Need for a Revolution in Intelligence Affairs*, by William J. Lahneman. 2011.
14. *Words of Intelligence: An Intelligence Professional's Lexicon for Domestic and Foreign Threats, Second Edition*, by Jan Goldman. 2011.
15. *Counterintelligence Theory and Practice*, by Hank Prunckun. 2012.
16. *Balancing Liberty and Security: An Ethical Study of U.S. Foreign Intelligence Surveillance, 2001–2009*, by Michelle Louise Atkin. 2013.
17. *The Art of Intelligence: Simulations, Exercises, and Games*, edited by William J. Lahneman and Rubén Arcos. 2014.
18. *Communicating with Intelligence: Writing and Briefing in National Security*, by James S. Major. 2014.
19. *Scientific Methods of Inquiry for Intelligence Analysis, Second Edition*, by Hank Prunckun. 2014.
20. *Quantitative Intelligence Analysis: Applied Analytic Models, Simulations and Games*, by Edward Waltz. 2014.
21. *The Handbook of Warning Intelligence: Assessing the Threat to National Security—The Complete Declassified Edition*, by Cynthia Grabo and Jan Goldman. 2015.
22. *Intelligence and Information Policy for National Security: Key Terms and Concepts*, by Jan Goldman and Susan Maret. 2016.

To view the books on our website, please visit https://rowman.com/Action/SERIES/RL/SPIES or scan the QR code below.

Intelligence and Information Policy for National Security

Key Terms and Concepts

Jan Goldman and Susan Maret

ROWMAN & LITTLEFIELD
Lanham • Boulder • New York • London

Published by Rowman & Littlefield
A wholly owned subsidiary of The Rowman & Littlefield Publishing Group, Inc.
4501 Forbes Boulevard, Suite 200, Lanham, Maryland 20706
www.rowman.com

Unit A, Whitacre Mews, 26-34 Stannary Street, London SE11 4AB

British Library Cataloguing in Publication Information Available

Library of Congress Cataloging-in-Publication Data

Names: Goldman, Jan, author. | Maret, Susan author.
Title: Intelligence and information policy for national security : key terms
  and concepts / Jan Goldman and Susan Maret.
Description: Lanham, Maryland : Rowman & Littlefield, 2016. | Series:
  Security and professional intelligence education series ; 22 | Includes
  bibliographical references.
Identifiers: LCCN 2016013304 (print) | LCCN 2016024779 (ebook) | ISBN
  9781442260153 (cloth : alk. paper) | ISBN 9781442260160 (pbk. : alk.
  paper) | ISBN 9781442260177 (electronic)
Subjects: LCSH: Intelligence service—Dictionaries. | Intelligence
  service—United States—Dictionaries. | National security—Dictionaries. |
  National security—United States—Dictionaries.
Classification: LCC JF1525.I6 G65 2016 (print) | LCC JF1525.I6 (ebook) | DDC
  327.1203—dc23
LC record available at https://lccn.loc.gov/2016013304

Printed in the United States of America

Contents

Series Editor Foreword

Jan Goldman

It began with the scribbling of the words "analysis" and "assessment" over twenty-five years ago. I was working in Washington, D.C., for the government, and there seemed to be a misunderstanding among my readers. As a young intelligence analyst, I took for granted that my readers knew the difference between these two words. For the record, "analysis is what you know" and an "assessment is what you believe." As we would later find out in our decision to go to war for weapons of mass destruction, miscommunication can have deadly consequences.

Nevertheless, these simple definitions stuck with me throughout my career as an intelligence analyst and later as an educator in higher education. I began to keep a notebook with words that I thought were instrumental in assisting in the analysis and communication of intelligence reports to policymakers. My first booklet in 2001 was just over seventy pages long, which I gave away to other members of the intelligence community. In 2006, I established the Security and Professional Intelligence Education Series (SPIES) at Rowman & Littlefield. This series has the sole purpose of supporting "professional intelligence training and educational programs across the United States and abroad." One of the first books to be the series was my 175-page lexicon, *Words of Intelligence.* This book viewed national security from beyond borders, which unfortunately is no longer true.

In the post-9/11 era, terrorism has become *the* prevalent transnational threat. We can no longer rely on our borders for security. In the "war on terrorism," front-line fighters include local and state officials. Consequently, the book was expanded to include law enforcement and emergency management, as well as military terms. That book was published in 2006: *Words of Intelligence: An Intelligence Professional's Lexicon for Domestic and Foreign Threats.*

Today, national security concerns at home and abroad have become further complicated and enhanced with the cyber threat. Terrorists seeking to destroy, incapacitate, or exploit critical infrastructure can cause mass casualties from halfway around the world. Additionally, foreign intelligence services can use cyber tools to gather information and conduct espionage activities. In the mix to collect, monitor, and report on the cyber threat for national security is the role of civil liberties. Thus, can we maintain our civil liberties while seeking to maintain security? In the course of this debate, do Americans need to sacrifice some liberty in order to ensure their safety? In the age when all "information" can be transformed into "intelligence," with unlimited access to everyone and everywhere, how do we understand and prepare for a threat?

This book is an attempt to understand information and intelligence in the realm of how it is used, how it is protected, and how it is understood in national security policy.

It is with great pride that this groundbreaking book is included in the series.

Acknowledgments

Intelligence and Information Policy for National Security: Key Terms and Concepts was a demanding project in terms of not only the selection process but also the sheer number of terms that required verification. Thanks to Eric Baker, John Linford, Juli Parrish, and Pat Walls, who supplied technical guidance; Tiffin University student researchers Zoe Livengood, Brian Turner, Sara Zambo, and Nicholas Klawitter, who provided research support; archivists David Clark and Randy Sowell at the Harry S. Truman Library and Museum, who assisted in verifying historical details; and Hamilton Bean and Chris Hables Gray, who provided valuable observations on the introduction. Finally, we wish to thank family, friends, and colleagues who provided support throughout the lengthy research and editorial process.

Introduction and Overview

Intelligence and Information Policy for National Security: Key Terms and Concepts

Susan Maret

This book owes an intellectual debt to Raymond Williams, who forged the way in understanding how human beings, language, and society are inextricably linked. In his influential text, *Culture and Society: 1780–1950*, Williams ([1958], 1960) identified significant "keywords" noteworthy for their widespread use in Western society and, scratching the surface, certain words that are important signifiers of historical change. According to Williams ([1958], 1960: xi), keywords such as *industry, democracy*, and *culture* serve as barometers in

> thinking about our common life, about our social, political and economic institutions; about the purposes which these institutions are designed to embody; and about the relations to these institutions and purposes of our activities in learning, education and the arts.

The singling out of these particular words as hallmarks of historical developments, or "historical formations," is, as Williams (1976: 15) notes, "the record of an inquiry into a vocabulary." Williams went on to expand his study in a later, highly regarded work, *Keywords: A Vocabulary of Culture and Society*. In naming particular words as mile markers, Williams (1976: 15) explains:

> I called these words Keywords in two connected senses: they are significant, binding words in certain activities and their interpretation; they are significant, indicative words in certain forms of thought. Certain uses bound together certain ways of seeing culture and society, not least in these two most general words. Certain other uses seemed to me to open up issues and problems, in the same general area, of which we all needed to be very much more conscious.

The gallery of approximately 128 words that make up *Keywords* enabled Williams (1976: 15) to peer into what he described as "particular formations of meaning—ways not only of discussing but at another level of seeing many of our central experiences." Finding inspiration in Williams, *Intelligence and Information Policy for National Security* is a documentary record of the culture(s) that create and follow those "binding" and "indicative" words that

1

drive information—national security policies. This language might be termed institutional, administrative, or bureaucratic;[1] it is at once specialized, technical, and ideological.[2] Bureaucratic events "take shape" through language (Sarangi and Slembrouck 1996: 6, 9). The information-rich language of national security is also discourse as "practices obeying certain rules" (Foucault 1972: 138)[3] and a "shared way of apprehending the world" (Dryzek 2005: 9). In the case of the information and national security, language and discourse reveal subtleties in institutional values, mission, rules, culture,[4] politics, knowledge, and, ultimately, power relations, or the network that "traverses and produces things" (Foucault 1980: 119).

The objective of this introduction is to introduce a framework for thinking about the language and discourses of the national security information policy system. This language—and discourse especially—allows for the construction of "meaning, and relationships, and [to] define legitimate knowledge" (Dryzek 2005: 9–10). In the following sections, I discuss the intersection of information and national security policies. I also outline those bodies responsible for agenda setting and carrying out policies related to information and national security. I then offer a window into how we might think of this specialized language and related discourses: as a *codified language*, *rational language*, *cultural language*, *secret language*, and *anticipatory, evolving language*. I conclude this introduction with a brief explanation of how words and concepts were selected and compiled for inclusion into *Intelligence and Information Policy for National Security*.

INFORMATION AND NATIONAL SECURITY: A MERGING OF WORLDVIEWS

Intelligence and Information Policy for National Security is a discovery tool providing insight into the words and ideas that form the foundation of information and national security policies. This "tool" is a guide to the language and discourse that fuel policies, with policy generally understood as a "series or pattern of governmental activities or decisions that are designed to remedy some public problem, either real or imagined" (Stewart, Hedge and Lester 2008: 6). Further, this book expands on the current research literature of information policy, as types of "policies which govern the way information affects our society" (Domestic Council Committee on the Right to Privacy 1976: xi). The broad character of information policy is "interrelated so that actions taken in one area may impact others" (Feldman and March 1981: 184) and, as such, is a "set of interrelated principles, laws, guidelines, rules and regulations, directives, procedures, judgments, interpretations, and practices that guide the creation, management, access, and use of information" (McClure 1996: 214). Information policy also concerns "doctrinal positions—and other decision making and practices with society-wide constitutive effects—involving information creation, processing, flows, access, and use" (Braman 2011: 3). In addition to these views, information policy includes inquiry into the creation of language and discourses that occur during the public policy process or "policy cycle" (e.g., identification of problems, agenda setting, policy making, budgeting, implementation and evaluation).

Information policies take on a more involved, perhaps even labyrinthine quality when affected by national security, or what is characterized as the National Security State.[5] National security, as it is defined by one policy-setting member of the U.S. government, is characterized as the

> collective term encompassing both national defense and foreign relations of the United States with the purpose of gaining: a. military or defense advantage over any foreign nation or group of nations; b. A favorable foreign relations position; or c. A defense posture capable of successfully resisting hostile or destructive action from within or without, overt or covert. (U.S. Department of Defense 2013)

In 1956, political scientist Gabriel A. Almond (1956: 372) observed that national security policy has two interrelated characteristics: first, the technical character of problems coupled with "specialized competence required to make intelligence judgments," and second, secrecy, "for much of the essential information necessary to appraise national security policy decisions has to be withheld from public knowledge and discussion. Without it public discussion is helpless, or often positively misled by leaks and rumors." By its very nature, national security policy deals with issues of grave significance,

> for national security policy does deal with the issues of life and death— not of "expendable" proportions of societies and these resources— but in the contemporary world with the very life and death of whole societies and their cultures. (Almond 1956: 372)

Included under the umbrella of what might be seen as simply *national security information policies*, or those policies that in some way concern information and national security, are Freedom of Information Act *exemptions* (e.g., national defense or foreign policy information properly classified pursuant to an Executive Order), *redaction* (blacking out of sensitive information), and *reclassification*, or the classification of information previously declassified (Executive Order 13526: 2009). Information policy also intersects with national security in the rules concerning security classification of information. With its tiered level of access to information (TOP SECRET, SECRET, CONFIDENTIAL) and distinct markings that restrict accesses to "special" information (e.g., *Controlled Unclassified Information*, or *CUI*), this type of national security information policy is labeled as *classified information policy*. Classified information policy includes "security classification policy and classified national security information policy" (Kosar 2010: 2). Classified information policies, or national security information policies, are historically well established through Executive Orders and various public laws (Quist 2002).

National security information policies also include the professional practice of intelligence, where "information that has been analyzed and refined so that it is useful to policymakers in making decisions—specifically, decisions about potential threats to our national security" ("Intelligence," this work). The practice of intelligence, a highly analytical process, consists of transformative steps that take data to (usable) knowledge in order to support the national security policy process.[6]

National security information policies also include technology development and applications (e.g., algorithms, databases, cryptologic systems, hardware, software), which range from identifying and protecting critical infrastructure to cyberwarfare, datamining, and individual and mass surveillance. For example, in 1997, the President's Commission on Critical Infrastructure Protection identified disruption to, and vulnerabilities of, the U.S. communications infrastructure and global networks. Denial of service attacks (DoS), information warfare, hacking, and cyberthreats were singled out as potential threats to U.S. national security. The Commission (1997: 4) noted that "major disruptions (*sic*, of any infrastructure) could lead to major losses and affect national security, the economy, and the public good." In a Department of Homeland Security commissioned study, unmanned vehicles and associated control and communications infrastructure were found to be "vulnerable to spoofing, hacking, and jamming" (Fleming et al. 2015: 1, 47). Of late, doxing is also identified as a threat to infrastructure *and* official credibility.[7]

Stretching an idea from Sandra Braman (1995: 4–5), national security information policy as it is proposed in this introduction concerns "self-reflexive and constitutive roles for the state, creating the conditions under which future activity (including policy-making) will take place." On occasion, these policies are the product of "compromises and conflicts between political institutions that are bent on protecting their own power and maximizing their own political benefits" (Zegart 2010: 213).

WHO CREATES NATIONAL SECURITY INFORMATION POLICIES?

The global "national security system" (Whittaker, Smith, and McKune 2011) is highly dependent on data, information, and knowledge.[8] This system is really a federation of governments, intelligence agencies and law enforcement branches that participate in global information sharing, courts, corporations, expert-specialists, IGOs (intergovernmental organizations), and civil society (e.g., NGOs or nongovernmental organizations, networks, associations, advocacy groups, social movements). Think tanks such RAND and federal bodies such as the Public Interest Declassification Board (PIDB) are also components of the national security information policy system. The PIDB, for example,

> advises and provides recommendations to the President and other Executive Branch officials on the systematic, thorough, coordinated, and comprehensive identification, collection, review for declassification, and release of declassified records and materials of archival value, including records and materials of extraordinary public interest. (Public Interest Declassification Board n.d.)[9]

The U.S. State Department's (n.d.a) Advisory Committee on Historical Diplomatic Documentation, which "monitors the overall compilation and editorial process" of the *Foreign Relations of the United States* (*FRUS*) series, is another example of a federal body actively engaged in interpreting and carrying out national security information policies. The Advisory Committee oversees "all aspects" of the preparation and declassification of the *FRUS* series, the "official documentary historical record of major U.S. foreign policy decisions and significant diplomatic activity" (U.S. State Department n.d.a, n.d.b). Government-created nonprofits are also an integral part of the national security information policy federation. Two well-publicized examples are In-Q-Tel, an "independent, not-for-profit organization created to bridge the gap between the technology needs of the U.S. Intelligence Community (IC) and emerging commercial innovation" (IQT 2016), and the UK government–Nesat partnership, which funds the Behavioral Insights Team (BIT). BIT is the "world's first government institution dedicated to the application of behavioural sciences" (Behavioural Insights Team 2016).

A principal element of this federation is the Intelligence Community (IC), who "tasked themselves with creating formal and informal ties with the nation's academic, nonprofit, and industrial communities" (Johnston 2005: xvi). The IC often relies on contractors and what are termed *highly qualified experts*, or HQEs. HQEs are defined by the Office of Director of National Intelligence (2008) in Intelligence Directive 623 as follows:

> A Highly Qualified Expert (HQE) is an individual, usually from outside of the Federal Government, who possesses cutting edge skills or world-class knowledge in a particular technical discipline or inter-disciplinary field beyond the usual range of expertise; other experts regard the individual as a leading authority or practitioner of high competence and skill in their common area of

expertise. The expertise and skills of an HQE are generally not available within the ODNI and/or the IC and are needed to satisfy an emerging and non-permanent requirement.

Through their contribution to classified work products, HQEs and contractors directly influence national security information policies (Halchin 2015).

THE FEDERATION AS MACHINE, EPISTEMIC COMMUNITY, PARAPOLITICAL SYSTEM

The bodies involved in the national security information policy cycle might be thought of in several theoretical ways. First, the "national security policy machinery" is a metaphor devised by the Subcommittee on National Policy Machinery (1960: 2) in its review of the U.S. "national security policy process." The Subcommittee (1960: 2), often referred to as the Jackson Committee for its leadership by Senator Henry M. Jackson, reported that the Cold War brought the "obliteration of time-honored distinctions between foreign and domestic policy . . . and witnessed a multiplication of the resources required for national security." Writing in 1960, Chairperson Jackson recognized the moving parts of government operations and their influence on policy implementation:

> The plain fact is that good policy demands both good men and good machinery. And though it may be true that good men can triumph over poor machinery, it is also true that they are more effective when they work with good machinery. It has been almost 13 years since the Congress took a look at the organization of the government for making and executing national security policy. The National Security Act of 1947, which created the National Security Council, was essentially a codification of the lessons of World War II. (447)

It is interesting to note that the United Kingdom's Cabinet Office (2010) also refers to "national intelligence machinery" and "intelligence machinery" in its description of those elements of UK government charged with protecting national security, conducting intelligence work, and performing oversight of intelligence-related activities. Both the Jackson Subcommittee and the Cabinet Office's reference to "machinery" bring to mind Max Weber's (1946) ideal type of bureaucracy.[10] In his classic work *Economy and Society (Wirtschaft und Gesellschaft)*, Weber sought to explain the historical rise of bureaucratization as an organizing force. But Weber went further than merely sketching the evolution and structure of the bureaucracy and its connections with capitalism,[11] utilizing an Industrial Age metaphor to capture the machine-like nature of the hierarchically structured organization focused on technical superiority.[12] Throughout *Economy and Society*, Weber (1978: 973) characterizes the bureaucracy as a "bureaucratic machine":

> The fully developed bureaucratic apparatus compares with other organizations exactly as does the machine with the non-mechanical modes of production. Precision, speed, unambiguity, knowledge of the files, continuity, discretion, unity, strict subordination, reduction of friction and of material and personal costs are raised to the optimum point in the strictly bureaucratic administration.

With its division of labor, emphasis on specialization, and "expert training" (Weber 1946: 198), Weber's bureaucracy is exemplified in what is termed the "intelligence bureaucracy" (Johnson 1985: 1). The intelligence bureaucracy, comprising expert actors from the Executive Branch, the National Security Council, National Intelligence Council, intelligence agencies, law enforcement, corporations, and the private sector (e.g., HQEs), has a distinct role in not only producing data, information, and knowledge but also acquiring, analyzing, prioritizing, storing, and controlling these forms of social capital.

The bedrock of this bureaucracy is *intelligence*, which Sherman Kent (1950: ix) defines as a "kind of knowledge," a "type of organization that produces knowledge," and an "activity pursued by an intelligence organization." In connecting intelligence to a form of knowledge and knowledge-based organization and activity, Kent set the proverbial stage for several theories that capture the essence of intelligence as knowledge. First, the national security policy machinery/intelligence bureaucracy might be considered an *epistemic community*, or a "knowledge-based experts-epistemic community," that plays a significant role in

> articulating the cause-and-effect relationships of complex problems, helping states identify their interests, framing the issues for collective debate, proposing specific policies, and identifying salient points for negotiation. (Haas 1992: 2)

In their work on international policy coordination, Peter Haas and colleagues suggest that an epistemic community is one of diversity, made up of individuals from a variety of backgrounds, fields, and disciplines who "bond" through shared beliefs, "or faith in the verity and the applicability of particular forms of knowledge or specific truths" (Haas 1992: 3). This community—which Haas describes as a network—is somewhat cohesive in terms of a "shared set of normative and principled beliefs, which provide a value-based rationale for the social action of community members" (Haas 1992: 3).[13] Most important, epistemic communities share causal beliefs, which are "derived from their analysis of practices leading or contributing to a central set of problems in their domain and which then serve as the basis for elucidating the multiple linkages between possible policy actions and desired outcomes"

(Haas 1992: 3). Perhaps the most distinct feature of an epistemic community is the emphasis on "shared notions of validity—that is, intersubjective, internally defined criteria for weighing and validating knowledge in the domain of their expertise" (Haas 1992: 3). United through what Haas (1992: 3) terms a "common policy enterprise," an epistemic community thrives on data, information, and knowledge in order to address uncertainties, problem solve, and shape institutional outcomes and policies. Certainly the intelligence "machinery" or bureaucracy can be considered an epistemic community under these conditions; certain knowledge-laden policy documents such as the *National Intelligence Estimate (NIE)*,[14] *National Security Strategy (NSS)*,[15] and the U.S. Department of Defense's *Quadrennial Defense Review (QDR)*, and other documents in this "review" series,[16] are but a few examples where particular epistemic communities negotiate complex problems to forecast trends and assess risk from a security and defense perspective.

In addition to being considered a bureaucracy, a machine, or an epistemic community, the federation of bodies involved in the national security information policy process might also be considered a *parapolitical system*, which David Easton (1965) defines as the "internal political systems of groups and organizations." Parapolitical systems "are subsystems of subsystems," whose members either accept or are expected to accept the "responsibilities for dealing with the major problems generated by the fact that an aggregate of persons live together as a society, share some aspects of life and are compelled, thereby, to try to resolve their differences together" (Easton 1965: 52).

Whatever theoretical frameworks are used to capture the organization and structure of the national security information policy system, it is important to note that "democratic objectives would be impossible to attain in modern society without bureaucratic organizations to implement them" (Blau and Meyer 1971: 165).

THE CODIFIED LANGUAGE AND DISCOURSES
OF NATIONAL SECURITY INFORMATION POLICY

In a sense, words and concepts terms included in this dictionary might be labeled as *jargon*, loosely defined as a technical language of a particular group. The language and discourses of national security information policy are certainly specialized, and they represent a distinct worldview held by experts that includes "syntax, semantics, document design, schemas, and perspective-taking" (Shuy 1998: 177). However, the language and discourse of national security information policy, primarily codified in law, statute, official doctrine, and standards, not only forms a basis for cohesive institutional action but also, in doing so, communicates complexity.[17] This language and related discourses are more than mere jargon created by subalterns in Weber's bureau. Codified language as discourse acts to "construct meanings and relationships . . . define common sense and legitimate knowledge" (Dryzek 2005: 9); moreover, discourse "blur[s] distinctions between *what is said* (language) and *what is done* (practice)" (Hall 2001: 72–73).

Weber's (1978: 642) bureaucracy, with its focus on the concrete product of the "power of command," suggests the language and discourse of national security information policy derives its authority (and power) from the "legality of enacted rules and the right of those elevated to authority under such rules to issue commands" (Weber 1978: 215, 217). As recorded in *Intelligence and Information Policy for National Security*, many terms and concepts have their roots in Executive Orders (e.g., Truman Executive Order 10290, 1951; Eisenhower Executive Order 10501, 1953), National Security Council Intelligence Directives, Presidential Directives, statutes (e.g., National Security Act of 1947, P.L. 80–253; the Intelligence Reform and Terrorism Prevention Act of 2004, P.L. 108–458), and internal policies of agencies and departments (e.g., Intelligence Community Directives). The codified language and discourses of national security might also be thought of as a historical record of presidential actions, sessions of Congress, judicial decisions, and the policy actions of government bodies.

Words and concepts often run the risk of containing multiple meanings in legislation, public laws, statutes, and regulations. For example, the term *weapons of mass destruction* has five definitions listed in the *U.S. Code* (Carus 2012). Multiple definitions lead to a diversity of interpretations and regulatory actions by those entities engaged in policy. As Carus (2012: 35) discovered, "U.S. government agencies have developed at least 14 alternatives since the 1960s . . . and 21 U.S. states and the District of Columbia have adopted definitions, as have a number of other countries and international agencies."

Codified language and related discourses are typically devised by governments and bodies other than the United States. For example, in the United Kingdom, certain laws (e.g., Official Secrets Act; Regulation of Investigatory Powers Act 2000) and internal rules of agencies (e.g., MI5 and MI6) create a codified language. Treaties, international agreements, and conventions also designate certain "keywords" and concepts for use on an international scale. Informally, IGOs such as the North Atlantic Treaty Organization (NATO), established in 1949 by the United Nations, communicates with its multinational membership through the *Glossary of Terms and Definitions* (AAP-06); the United Nations Office for Disaster Risk Reduction (UNISDR) established a standardized terminology to "promote a common understanding" of terms used in disaster-response, warning, and risk (United Nations Office for Disaster Risk Reduction 2009).[18]

A "RATIONAL" LANGUAGE

On one hand, the terms and concepts reported in *Intelligence and Information Policy for National Security* are "rational" in the sense that they result from the rule-directed (codified), calculable nature of the bureaucracy as it addresses a multitude of challenges. The words, concepts, language, and discourses of national security are replete with distinctions between types of individuals and groups (e.g., *Citizen Corps, human source, insider threat, unprivileged enemy belligerent*) and the naming of panoptic technologies that profile individuals and predict behavior (e.g., *biometrics, Terrorist Identities Datamart Environment*).

The rational language of national security information policy suggests that the "most pressing problems of social life do involve the clash of ends and values and thus, according to Weber, cannot be solved in an objectively rational manner" (Brubaker 1984: 5). This scenario holds true when deliberating on social problems of an intractable, global nature. For example, the struggle to define terrorism (e.g., "one man's terrorist is another man's freedom fighter"), predict the risk of adverse events (e.g., *horizontal scanning*), categorize individuals who may be responsible for "terrorist" activities (e.g., *detainee, enemy combatant, extremist*), and effect their removal from society (e.g., *rendition*) and subsequent questioning by authorities (e.g., *enhanced interrogation*) presents enormous ethical and moral challenges to the rule of law, civil liberties, human rights, and integrity of policy decisions. Moreover, this particular language and discourse points to the "violence that we do to things, or, at all events, as a practice we impose upon them" (Foucault 1972: 229). "Rational language" is not unprejudiced or disinterested.[19] As illustrated by many of the terms and concepts included in this guide, the rational language and discourse of national security suggests that "organisations compete, they have moods, they can sulk, they can have nervous breakdowns, they can show all the symptoms of paranoia" (Omand 2009: 418).

In sum, the highly diverse language and discourse reported in *Intelligence and Information Policy for National Security* cannot be divorced from the events that brought them into existence[20] and the institutional texts in which they appear. As Dorothy E. Smith (1984: 70) explains, texts are "constituents of a social course of action in which they are first produced and then become active in the ordering of phases and relations."

A CULTURAL LANGUAGE

As an expression of culture, numerous words and concepts reported in *Intelligence and Information Policy for National Security* convey official doctrine. Doctrine, as the "fundamental principles by which the military forces or elements thereof guide their actions in support of national objectives" (U.S. Department of Defense 2015), standardizes communications and coordinates joint military actions. Language and associated discourses of doctrine may be considered a manifestation of national security information policies at their most essential level, as doctrine (as a form of directive language) can be "understood as a cultural and political guidance system in which values are handed down from the past as deposited" (Mueller 1973: 18). This "guidance system" provides an individual or a group with "the means to identify within a given culture or political entity" (Mueller 1973: 18). In other words, as Robert W. Shuy (1998: 176) remarks, "bureaucratic language is a mark of membership."

Examples of specific cultural guidance systems are the Office of the Director of Intelligence's (ODNI) *Intelligence Community Directives (ICDs)*, *Intelligence Community Policy Guidance (ICPG)*, and *Intelligence Community Policy Memorandums (ICPMs)*. These documents not only give the members of the IC a roadmap in terms of guidelines and protocols to follow but also establish a common language in which the seventeen federal agencies and affiliated intergovernmental bodies that comprise the IC communicate. For example, the ODNI's 2015 *Principles of Intelligence Transparency* is pure national security information policy in that it "includes not only sharing information about the rules that apply to the IC and its compliance under those rules, but also sharing information about what the IC actually does in pursuit of its national security mission" (Office of the Director for National Intelligence 2015b: 1).

What might be thought of as a clash of cultures occurs when similar words and concepts created by institutional bodies have differing meanings. For example, *critical information*, defined by the Office of the Director of National Intelligence (2015a) in its Intelligence Community Directive 190, and used by the U.S. Department of Defense (DoD) in its *Dictionary of Military and Associated Terms* (JP 1-02), illustrates contrasting worldviews[21] (see table 1).

Table 1. Contrasting Definitions between ICD 190 and the DoD *Dictionary*

ICD 190	*DoD Dictionary*
Critical information (CRITIC) is information concerning possible threats to U.S. national security that are so significant that they require the immediate attention of the president and the National Security Council.	Specific facts about friendly intentions, capabilities, and activities needed by adversaries for them to plan and act effectively so as to guarantee failure or unacceptable consequences for friendly mission accomplishment.
Critical information includes the decisions, intentions, or actions of foreign governments, organizations, or individuals that could imminently and materially jeopardize vital U.S. policy, economic, information system, critical infrastructure, cyberspace, or military interests.	

ICDs and the DoD's *Dictionary* establish a shared language and "guidance system" within the IC and U.S. Department of Defense, respectively. However, contrasting meanings of identical words and concepts reflect divergent worldviews held by these two bodies. Sociologist C. Wright Mills (1940: 322) sized up the problem of distinct worldviews when he observed that

> in acquiring a technical vocabulary with its terms and classifications, the thinker is acquiring, as it were, a set of colored spectacles. He sees a world of objects that are technically tinted and patternized. A specialized language constitutes a veritable a priori form of perception and cognition, which are certainly relevant to the results of inquiry . . . different technical elites possess different perceptual capacities.

A LANGUAGE OF SECRECY

In its report on pre-war intelligence and the National Intelligence Estimate process, the Senate Select Committee on Intelligence (2004: 483) found "functional flaws in the Intelligence Community include the absence of any or adequate 'red teaming' and peer review—a procedure to reconcile differing departmental and analytical views in the formation of the NIE."[22] This scenario points to the more secret aspects of the national security information policy system, for, as Richard Jenkins (2010: 14) suggests,

> The bigger and more complex the organization, the greater the potential and opportunity for the disruption of its rules and structures, the more dark corners

exist in which to escape surveillance, and the more difficult it may become to rationalize and communicate procedures or monitor adequately their execution.

In his ethnographic study of the CIA, anthropologist Rob Johnston (2005: 11) found that "more organizational emphasis is placed on the secrecy than on effectiveness." Whether we brand secrecy as a product of the Jackson Committee's national security policy machinery, Weber's bureaucratic machine, the "dual state" (Morgenthau 1962), "invisible government" (Smoot 1962; Wise and Ross 1964), a "parallel form of government" (Commission on Protecting and Reducing Government Secrecy 1997), a parapolitical system (Cripp 2009; Easton 1965; Scott 1996; Wilson 2009), a "shadow governance" originating from the depths of the deep state (Wilson 2009), a display of the "double government" (Bagehot 1895: 235, 255; Glennon 2015), or the second world (Simmel 1906; Maret 2011), the language and discourse of hidden actions as policies carry the weight of Weber's (1978: 215) "legitimate domination." That is, shielded policies, just as public policies, are warranted on the "rational grounds of providing security" (Weber 1978: 650).[23] Classified memoranda (e.g., the Department of Justice Office of Legal Counsel or OLC Opinions[24]), the "controlling interpretations" of the Foreign Intelligence Surveillance Court (Subcommittee on the Constitution of the Committee on the Judiciary 2008), and "torture policies" as outlined in the declassified Senate Select Committee on Intelligence (2014) probe on the CIA's detention and interrogation policies are but a few cases where secrecy trumps publicity and transparency.[25]

AN ANTICIPATORY, EVOLVING LANGUAGE

Language is not only a "simple representation" of the world but also an "intervention within it" (Lecercle 1990: 47). As an "intervention," the Intelligence Reform and Terrorism Prevention Act of 2004 (IRTPA) overhauled the IC to establish the Information Sharing Environment (ISE). The ISE provides "for the sharing of terrorism information in a manner consistent with national security and with applicable legal standards relating to privacy and civil liberties" (Intelligence Reform and Terrorism Prevention Act of 2004, Sec. 1016, "Information Sharing"). The bedrock of the ISE is *terrorism information*, defined as follows:

(A) means all information, whether collected, produced, or distributed by intelligence, law enforcement, military, homeland security, or other activities relating to—(i) the existence, organization, capabilities, plans, intentions, vulnerabilities, means of finance or material support, or activities of foreign or international terrorist groups or individuals, or of domestic groups or individuals involved in transnational terrorism; (ii) threats posed by such groups or individuals to the United States, United States persons, or United States interests, or to those of other nations; (iii) communications of or by such groups or individuals; or (iv) groups or individuals reasonably believed to be assisting or associated with such groups or individuals; and (B) includes weapons of mass destruction information.

In addition to IRTPA's creation of the ISE, information policies as national security policies manifest through "national investment in terrorism-related information sharing." The national investment is detailed as the development of policies, systems, and standards that enable the nation to address related priority threats, including physical and cyber threats to our critical infrastructure, transnational organized crime, human trafficking, drug trafficking, and illicit financial networks. Leveraging the processes and tools we have already developed and integrating information on a wider range of threats will strengthen the ISE, accelerate the delivery of new capabilities, and improve decision making and program effectiveness (Program Manager Information Sharing Environment 2014: iv).

The national security information policy system establishes distinct meanings for words and concepts in response to global change, threat, risk, and conflict. The concept of *indications and warning* (I&W) is a case where definitions shifted between editions of the DoD's *Dictionary of Military and Associated Terms*. In the April 2001 amended through October 17, 2008, edition of the DoD's *Dictionary*, I&W had the following definition:

> Those intelligence activities intended to detect and report time-sensitive intelligence information on foreign developments that could involve a threat to the United States or allied and/or coalition military, political, or economic interests or to US citizens abroad. It includes forewarning of enemy actions or intentions; the imminence of hostilities; insurgency; nuclear/nonnuclear attack on the United States, its overseas forces, or allied and/or coalition nations; hostile reactions to US reconnaissance activities; terrorists' attacks; and other similar events. (U.S. Department of Defense 2008)

An epistemological shift occurred in the 08 November 2010, as amended through 15 December 2015, edition of the *Dictionary*; the I&W concept is distilled:

> Those intelligence activities intended to detect and report time-sensitive intelligence information on foreign developments that could involve a threat to the United States or allied and/or coalition military, political, or economic interests

or to US citizens abroad. It includes forewarning of hostile actions or intentions against the United States, its activities, overseas forces, or allied and/or coalition nations. (U.S. Department of Defense 2015)

We can only speculate as to the reasons for the change in meaning between the 2008 and 2010 editions of the *Dictionary*. The language shift perhaps indicates a refinement of institutional goals and, more important, how one contingent of the intelligence bureaucracy views its (evolving) mission and objectives within the U.S. national security policy system.

Another case is with the word *harm*, noteworthy for its association with damage and threat. Harm, a term used within the U.S. Department of Defense and an agency within the DoD, the Defense Security Service (DSS), is used unevenly. In Department of Defense Instruction 3216.01 *Use of Animals in DoD Programs*, harm is defined in a singular way, while harm does not appear in the current edition of the *Dictionary of Military and Associated Terms*. In the DSS *Glossary of Security Terms, Definitions, and Acronyms*, harm is equated with damage but not defined in its *Glossary* (see table 2).

In his review of specialized (cultural) words used exclusively within AF-SPC (*battlespace characterization, space effects*), Flood (2008: 31) argues for "integration with the rest of the Air Force to a share a lexicon—a common language." Flood (2008: 31) found that the Air Force Space Command (AFSPC) "was largely a separate entity from the rest of the Air Force. Thus, like an isolated culture on a remote island, AFSPC's language developed to a point that it became a separate dialect, sometimes incomprehensible to the parent Air Force culture." Flood recommends a remedy to fix the use of "exclusive" terms used by AFSPC: to standardize language in DoD's *Dictionary of Military and Associated Terms* and within Air Force doctrine.

In an example that brings to mind Almond's thought that "national security policy does deal with the issues of life and death," Starr, Collins, Green, and Regehr (2015) argue for resolving semantic disputes over "nuclear terminology." The terminology in question is the uneven use and understanding of the

Table 2. Association of the *Term* Harm with *Damage*

Department of Defense Instruction No. 3216.01, Use of Animals in DoD Programs	Defense Security Service, Glossary of Security Terms, Definitions, and Acronyms
Harm: Any procedure that either causes lasting detrimental physical, behavioral, or psychological damage, or exposes an animal to potentially perilous situations (e.g., releasing a nocturnal animal during daylight hours).	Damage: A loss of friendly effectiveness due to adversary action. Synonymous with harm.

concepts of nuclear first strike "Launch Under Attack" (LUA) and "Launch on Warning" (LOW). According to the authors, LUA was previously defined in the DoD's *Dictionary of Military and Associated Terms*, but the term was removed; no official definition for LOW is "apparently published." The solution, as Starr, Collins, Green, and Regehr (2015) recommend, is to "create a new, mutually understood set of terms, which would reduce ambiguity (and thus disagreement) when describing how the United States and Russia might respond to a perceived or confirmed nuclear attack."

ORIGINS AND ORGANIZATION OF INTELLIGENCE AND INFORMATION POLICY FOR NATIONAL SECURITY

The core of *Intelligence and Information Policy for National Security* is constructed on two works: Jan Goldman's (2011) *Words of Intelligence: An Intelligence Professional's Lexicon for Domestic and Foreign Threats* and Susan Maret's multi-revised *On Their Own Terms: A Lexicon with an Emphasis on Information-Related Terms Produced by the U.S. Government.*[26] *Intelligence and Information Policy for National Security* greatly builds on these publications.

Words and concepts were selected for their significance to information and national security policies, and they were visible in mainstream news, alternative media, and film (e.g., Laura Poitras's *Citizenfour*). Historical and contemporary declassified and open-source U.S. and UK government publications, IGO and NGO publications, scholarly articles, books, congressional hearings, legal briefs, and Freedom of Information Act documents were consulted in order to capture the language and discourse of national security information policy. An "in their own words" approach was taken, where definitions of terms and concepts are, for the most part, direct quotes from a wide range of official publications.

As a finding aid to the language and discourse of national security information policy, this book is an attempt to capture the often-differing interpretations assigned to words and concepts by numerous bodies. For example, some words such as *national security* contain multiple definitions so as to present differing perspectives. In addition, many terms in common usage within the Intelligence Community are not attributed to any one source, and some definitions may have been refined by either Goldman or Maret and are cited as such. Terms and concepts are in alphabetical order; to assist researchers, "see" breadcrumbs are included to direct researchers to related words and concepts. Within formal definitions, potentially unfamiliar acronyms are spelled out in order to further translate official definitions.

In following these methods, readers are encouraged to think of words and key concepts as more than a measure of group identification, mode of communication, barometer of institutional vitality, and delivery system for hidden policies. At its heart, *Intelligence and Information Policy for National Security* is a guide to the origins and contexts of the words and ideas that drive institutional actions as products of national security information policies. Above all, this guide demonstrates the pivotal, dynamic role language and discourse have in shaping the policies that intersect national security and information. As Jean-Jacques Lecercle (1990: 47) observes, words "do not only do things, *they are things.*"

NOTES

1. In this discussion, *institution* is employed in order to capture the various bodies that produce language as a reflection of policies and actions. It is interesting to note that Weber (1978) used organization and institution in an undifferentiated way throughout *Economy and Society*. However, sociologist Philip Selznick identifies a critical distinction between organizations and institutions. Selznick (1957: 17) observes that "institutionalization is a process. It is something that happens to an organization over time, reflecting the organization's own distinctive history, the people who have been in it, the groups it embodies and the vested interests they have created, and the way it has adapted to its environment." Institutional theory is also attractive, as it "highlights cultural influences on decision making and formal structures . . . holds that organizations, and the individuals who populate them, are suspended in a web of values, norms, rules, beliefs, and taken-for-granted assumptions, that are at least partially of their own making" (Barley and Tolbert 1997; also see Berger and Luckmann 1967; Giddens 1995: 265; Keohane 1988; Nee 1998; Peters 2005; Powell and DiMaggio 1991; Robertson 2010; Selznick 1957, 1996; Workman, Jones, and Jochim 2010; Zegart 1999).

2. In the sense that thought or knowledge is socially situated and collectively shared.

3. See Foucault (1972, 1978) for an examination of discourse and its relationship to power.

4. As "socially located forms and processes of human meaning-making, whether they occur in specialized institutions, and whether or not they are confined to one clearly bonded group" (Spillman 2011).

5. The national security state, or NSS, has the following elements: control of the public sphere; covert actions and the rise of secrecy regarding state actions; federal (and local) law enforcement metamorphosing into security enforcement and surveillance; limiting or undermining individual rights; nuclear weapons; and organizing for war, cold war, and limited war. See Marcus G. Raskin and Carl A. LeVan (eds.), *Democracy's Shadow: The Secret World of National Security* (New York: Nation Books, 2005).

6. The intelligence cycle (the collection, processing, analysis and production, and dissemination of data and information), this work.

7. Dox (doxx) or doxing (doxxing) refers to hacking and releasing personal identifiable information, including private details of one's life, to social media platforms in an attempt to harass, embarrass, and discredit an individual. Doxing can be politically motivated; see Bruce Schneier's (2015) commentary on the doxing of CIA director John O. Brennan.

8. Roughly, *data* is information in raw form, such as numbers and statistics; *information*, from the Latin *informare*, gives form to knowledge; and *knowledge* is a "set of ideas and acts accepted by one or another social group or society of people pertaining to what is real for them or others" (McCarthy 1996: 23). It is interesting to note that Truman Executive Order 10290 (1951) links information and knowledge as "information . . . means knowledge which can be communicated, either orally or by means of material."

9. The PIDB was established by the Public Interest Declassification Act of 2000 (P.L. 106–567, 114 Stat. 2856).

10. Although Weber's use of ideal type "may appear to place him in the epistemic dark ages" (Turner 2007: 43), an ideal type is variously defined as a framework, an interpretive method, a model, and "partial pictures of culture" that pertain to a certain type of social action and social reality (Mommsen 1974: 10, 50). Weber thought of ideal types as "particular concepts employed by social scientists in order to formulate rigorous explanations" (Segre 2004: 91–92).

11. Weber (1978: 224) speculated that capitalism is the "most rational economic basis for bureaucratic administration."

12. Perhaps there is a risk of overplaying the bureaucracy in the age of the "new institutionalism." We take Alvin W. Gouldner's (1950: 59) observations to heart, as they are useful in pointing out the limitations of the bureaucracy as laid out by Weber: "if we are indeed living in an epoch of 'the bureaucratization of the world,' then it may be that we have all the more need for theoretical tools which will point up distinctions among bureaucracies and bureaucrats. A single type of bureaucracy is not adequate, either for scientific purposes or practical political action, in a bureaucratized world. A type which includes within itself as much as Weber's does leaves no room for the discriminations without which choice is impossible, scientific advance difficult, and pessimism probable."

13. See the special issue of *International Organization* 46, no. 1 (1992), on the subject of "Knowledge, Power, and International Policy Coordination."

14. Suggested by the National Security Act, P.L. 80–253. NIEs are classified but undergo declassification and can be found in the CIA's CREST database.

15. Mandated by the 1986 Goldwater-Nichols Defense Department Reorganization Act, presidents must submit a NSS to Congress. The NSS identifies and outlines global security issues. The Taylor Group's National Security Strategy Archive contains pdfs of the NSS since the Reagan administration. See http://nssarchive.us/.

16. The *QDR*, *Nuclear Posture Review*, *Ballistic Missile Review*, and *Space Posture Review* are mandated by various laws. See the U.S. Department of Defense at http://www.defense.gov/News/Special-Reports/QDR.

17. Taken from Luhmann (1989, 1995).

18. Created by the United Nations General Assembly Resolution 56/195 in 1999, UNSDIR expanded in 2001 to "ensure coordination and synergies among disaster risk reduction activities of the United Nations system and regional organizations and activities in socio-economic and humanitarian fields" (United Nations Office for Disaster Risk Reduction n.d.).

19. Note that official language and discourse as reported in this work is at odds with scholarly investigations into language and discourse. See, for example, Bolinger's (1980) investigation of agency interpretations of words such as *assassination*; Butcher and Atkinson's (2001) review of language, metaphor, and power; Cowan and Cull (2008) on public diplomacy; De Beaugrande's (2004) discussion of patriotism and different types of terrorism; Gibson and Lutz's four types of doublespeak; Gray's (2005) extensive discussion of "what is terrorism?"; Merton's ([1969], 1995) essay on the language of power, escalation, and war; and Weaver and Pallito (2006) on the legal language of extraordinary rendition.

20. See Foucault's (1991) "Politics and the Study of Discourse."

21. The DoD *Dictionary* contains DoD and NATO terms currently in usage, and it is the "primary terminology source when preparing correspondence, including policy, strategy, doctrine, and planning documents and applies to the Office of the Secretary of Defense (OSD), Services, Joint Staff, combatant commands, DOD agencies, and all other DOD components" (Hock 2011: 139). Hock reports that terms removed from each edition of the *Dictionary* are archived in the DoD's Joint Terminology Master Database (JTMD).

22. Red teaming "can mean role-playing the adversary, conducting a vulnerability assessment to determine weaknesses, or using analytical techniques to improve intelligence estimates and intelligence synchronization" (Longbine 2008: iii).

23. Although Weber discusses "rational grounds" in terms of torts ("bone fide purchasers"), there is relevance to this discussion of security.

24. See Goitein (2015).

25. Other examples are outlined by Aftergood (2015).

26. On the Web at the Federation of American Scientists since 2005.

2X The *2X Staff conducts mission and RM for all HUMINT and CI entities located within the designated AOIR (area of intelligence responsibility). It coordinates, deconflicts, and synchronizes all HUMINT and CI activities in the designated AOIR. ("*2X" indicates 2X functions at all levels.)[1]

4D STRATEGY Defeat, Deny, Diminish and Defend; principles outlined in the 2003 *National Strategy for Combating Terrorism*.[2]

5 EYES SURVEILLANCE SYSTEM Beginning in 1946, an alliance of five countries (the United States, the United Kingdom, Australia, Canada, and New Zealand) developed a series of bilateral agreements over more than a decade that became known as the UKUSA (pronounced yew-kew-zah) agreement. This established the "Five Eyes" alliance for the purpose of sharing intelligence, but it primarily signals intelligence ("SIGINT").[3] The marking FVEY designates distribution to "Five Eyes" countries.[4]

97 ECHOES (97E) The official classification number for the interrogator course taught at military colleges, including Fort Huachuca, Arizona.[5]

100 PERCENT SHRED POLICY Every airman, civilian, and contractor on base is responsible for destroying paper they create or use in their workspaces when they no longer need it. The 100 percent shred policy requires a 3/8-inch crosscut shredder or better. People who do not have a shredder in their work center should work with their unit's OPSEC coordinator and resource advisor to find or procure one.[6]

201 FILE The CIA opens a 201 file on an individual when it has an "operational interest" in that person.[7]

NOTES

1. Department of the Army. *Human Intelligence Collector Operations.* FM 2-22.3 (FM 34-52). September 2006. Accessed February 26, 2015. https://www.fas.org/irp/doddir/army/fm2-22-3.pdf.

2. Executive Office of the President. *National Strategy for Combatting Terrorism.* 2003. Accessed February 26, 2015. https://www.cia.gov/news-information/cia-the-war-on-terrorism/Counter_Terrorism_Strategy.pdf.

3. Nyst, Carly and Anna Crowe. *Global Information Society Watch 2014: Communications Surveillance in the Digital Age* (51). Accessed January 4, 2015. http://giswatch.org/sites/default/files/unmasking_the_five_eyes.pdf. Also see Borger, Julian. "NSA Files: What's a Little Spying Between Old Friends?" *The Guardian*, December 2, 2013. Accessed January 4, 2015. http://www.theguardian.com/world/2013/dec/02/nsa-files-spying-allies-enemies-five-eyes-g8.

4. Greenwald, Glenn. *No Place to Hide.* New York: Henry Holt, 2014.

5. Chatterjee, Pratap. "Meet the New Interrogators: Lockheed Martin, from Missiles to Intelligence." *CorpWatch*, November 9, 2005. Accessed January 4, 2015. http://www.corpwatch.org/article.php?id=12757. Also see Department of the Army. *Human Intelligence Collector Operations.* FM 2-22.3 (FM 34-52). September 2006. Accessed January 4, 2015. https://www.fas.org/irp/doddir/army/fm2-22-3.pdf.

6. United States Air Force, Malstrom Air Force Base. *Getting into the Habit: 100 Percent Shred Policy Begins March 17.* March 10, 2009. Accessed January 4, 2015. http://www.malmstrom.af.mil/news/story.asp?id=123139099.

7. Assassinations Records Review Board. *Final Report of the Assassination Records Review Board* (45). September 30, 1998. Accessed January 4, 2015. http://www.archives.gov/research/jfk/review-board/report/arrb-final-report.pdf.

ABLE DANGER In summer 2005, news reports began to appear regarding a datamining initiative that had been carried out by the U.S. Army's Land Information Warfare Agency (LIWA) in 1999–2000. The initiative, referred to as Able Danger, had reportedly been requested by the U.S. Special Operations Command (SOCOM) as part of larger effort to develop a plan to combat transnational terrorism. Because the details of Able Danger remain classified, little is known about the program. However, in a briefing to reporters, the Department of Defense characterized Able Danger as a demonstration project to test analytical methods and technology on very large amounts of data. The project involved using link analysis to identify underlying connections and associations between individuals who otherwise appear to have no outward connection with one another. The link analysis used both classified and open source data, totaling a reported 2.5 terabytes. All of this data, which included information on U.S. persons, was reportedly deleted in April 2000 due to U.S. Army regulations requiring information on U.S. persons be destroyed after a project ends or becomes inactive.[1]

ABOVEGROUND Used to describe extremist groups or individuals who operate overtly and portray themselves as law-abiding.[2]

ACCELERATOR Any event, action, or decision by an influential person that becomes a catalyst to an impending threat scenario.[3]

ACCEPTABLE LEVEL OF RISK An authority's determination of the level of potential harm to an operation, program, or activity that the authority is willing to accept due to the loss of information.[4]

ACCESS In counterintelligence and intelligence use, a. a way or means of approach to identify a target; or b. exploitable proximity to or ability to approach an individual, facility, or information that enables target to carry out the intended mission.[5]

ACCESS AUTHORITY An entity responsible for monitoring and granting access privileges for other authorized entities.

ACCESS CONTROL 1. The process of granting or denying specific requests for obtaining and using information and related information processing services. 2. To enter specific physical facilities (e.g., federal buildings, military establishments, and border-crossing entrances).[6]

ACCESS ELIGIBILITY DETERMINATION A formal determination that a person meets the personnel security requirements for access to a specified type or types of classified information.[7]

ACCESS TO CLASSIFIED INFORMATION The ability and opportunity to obtain knowledge of classified information by persons with the proper security clearance and a need to know of specified classified information.[8]

ACCIDENTAL HAZARD Source of harm or difficulty created by negligence, error, or unintended failure.[9]

ACCOUNTABILITY Assignment of a document control number, including copy number, which is used to establish individual responsibility for the document and permits traceability and disposition of the document.[10]

ACCOUNTABILITY REVIEWS The accountability review process is designed to assist the DNI (Director of National Intelligence) in assessing the roles and responsibilities of the IC elements and personnel related to the activities under review and developing pertinent findings and recommendations.[11]

ACCREDITATION The formal certification by a Cognizant Security Authority (CSA) that a facility, designated area, or information system has met Director of National Intelligence (DNI) security standards for handling, processing, discussing, disseminating or storing Sensitive Compartmented Information (SCI).[12] *See* COGNIZANT SECURITY AGENCY; COGNIZANT SECURITY AUTHORITY

ACCREDITING AUTHORITY Customer official who has the authority to decide on accepting the security safeguards prescribed or who is responsible for issuing an accreditation statement that records the decision to accept those safeguards.[13]

ACCURACY 1. Extent to which an evaluation or assessment is truthful or valid. 2. An attribute of the credibility of a source of evidence; refers to the ability of a source to make required discriminations or distinctions among possible objects or states being sensed. *See* CREDIBILITY

ACCURACY OF FIRE Precision of fire expressed by the closeness of a grouping of shots at and around the center of the target.[14]

ACKNOWLEDGED SPECIAL ACCESS PROGRAM (SAP) Existence is acknowledged but its specific details (technologies, materials, techniques, etc.) are classified as specified in the applicable security classification guide.[15]

ACOUSTICAL INTELLIGENCE (ACINT OR ACOUSTINT) Intelligence information derived from the collection and processing of acoustical phenomena.[16] *See* SOURCES OF INTELLIGENCE

ACTIONABLE 1. Information that is directly useful to customers for immediate exploitation without requiring the full intelligence production process; actionable information may address strategic or tactical needs, support of U.S. negotiating teams, or actions dealing with such matters as international terrorism or narcotics. 2. Intelligence and information with sufficient specificity and detail that explicit responses based on that information can be implemented.[17]

ACTIONABLE INTELLIGENCE 1. Intelligence information that is directly useful to customers for immediate exploitation without having to go through the full intelligence production process.[18] 2. Although there is no "official" definition for this term, it is considered Information that will force the consumer to initiate action as the result of a mitigating or impending threat. For example, President Bush said that an intelligence memo he read shortly before September 11, 2001, contained no actionable intelligence that would have helped him to try to prevent the 9/11 attacks. According to the officials in the Bush administration, the August 6, 2001, memo "Bin Laden Determined to Strike in US" stated there was no indication of a terrorist threat because there was no time or place of the attack. National Security Advisor Condoleezza Rice said, "It wouldn't have done any good to have the FBI director, CIA director and other top law enforcement and anti-terrorism officials meet regularly in the summer of 2001 to sift through the several warnings that preceded the 9/11 attacks." Rice said there weren't enough specifics or actionable intelligence to justify such meetings. However, according to White House Counter-Terrorism advisor Richard Clark, "'When you're told there's going to be a major terrorist attack, but oh, by the way, we don't know where or when, that's all the more reason to put down whatever else it is you're doing . . . roll up your sleeves and get involved in trying to find that actionable intelligence.'" [19] *See* HOLY GRAIL; MURKY INTELLIGENCE

ACTIONABLE MEDICAL INFORMATION REVIEW Since 2006 U.S. Army censors have scrutinized hundreds of medical studies, scientific posters, abstracts and PowerPoint presentations authored by doctors and scientists at army medical research centers—part of a little-known pre-publication review process called "Actionable Medical Information Review." The program is intended to deny Iraqi and Afghan insurgents sensitive data such as combat injury and death rates. But dozens of studies reviewed under the program did not involve research directly related to combat operations. Instead, they described controversial topics like the effects of war on soldiers' children, hospital-acquired infections, post-deployment adjustment issues, refugees, suicide, alcoholism, vaccines, cancer among veterans and problems with military health care databases.[20]

ACTIVE CELL SITE SIMULATORS (ACSS) 1. One form of increasingly pervasive technology masquerading as a 1980s pen register is the active cell site simulator, technically known as an International Mobile Subscriber Identity (IMSI) Catcher and colloquially known as a stingray, a triggerfish, or a dirtbox. First developed in the 1990s, an ACSS mimics cell phone towers, and tricks cell phones into connecting with it and its location and at most routing calls and text messages through the stingray to law enforcement officers. ACSSs are now operational by everyone from the National Security Administration in Afghanistan to the Gwinnett County Police in Lawrenceville, Georgia. Despite their operational breadth, however, law enforcement agencies at all levels have failed to disclose their use of ACSSs to the courts, resulting in only a handful of cases where a judge was even given the opportunity to consider whether the devices are constitutional (3–4).[21] 2. The CIA and the U.S. Marshals Service, an agency of the Justice Department, developed technology to locate specific cellphones in the U.S. through an airborne device that mimics a cellphone tower, these people said. Today, the Justice Department program, whose existence was reported by the *Wall Street Journal* last year, is used to hunt criminal suspects. . . . The program operates specially equipped planes that fly from five U.S. cities, with a flying range covering most of the U.S. population. Planes are equipped with devices— some past versions were dubbed "dirtboxes" by law enforcement officials— that trick cellphones into reporting their unique registration information.[22]

ACTIVE DECEPTION Measures designed to mislead by causing an object or situation to seem threatening when a threat does not exist. Active deception normally involves a calculated policy of disclosing half-truths supported by appropriate "proof" signals or other material evidence. The intelligence network of the deceived must pick up this information. The deceived must "discover" the evidence and work hard for it to be more convinced of its authenticity and importance. Information that is easily obtained may seem less credible and of doubtful value.[23] For example, during World War I, Great Britain used active deception in the form of dummy airfields and flare paths. These phony installations had a dual purpose of attracting German strafing and bombing raids and consequently diverting the enemy airplanes away from the real Allied airfields. Additionally, these bogus installations exaggerated the number of operational airfields, which deceived the enemy about Allied military strength in the sector.[24] *See* A-TYPE DECEPTION; DECEPTION; DENIAL AND DECEPTION; PASSIVE DECEPTION

ACTIVE SHOOTER An individual actively engaged in killing or attempting to kill people in a confined and populated area; in most cases, active shooters use firearms(s) and there is no pattern or method to their selection of victims. Active shooter situations are unpredictable and evolve quickly. Typically, the immediate deployment of law enforcement is required to stop the shooting and mitigate harm to victim.[25]

ACTIVITY BASED INTELLIGENCE (ABI) 1. An emerging—and critical—methodology that applies advanced analytic techniques to "Big Data" so we can provide "Big Value" to decision makers. That is, we identify patterns, trends, networks, and relationships hidden within large data collections from multiple sources: full motion video, multispectral imagery, infrared, radar, foundation data, as well as SIGINT, HUMINT and MASINT information. An operational example of this could be using wide-area motion imagery to process, capture, and store object identification data (2).[26] 2. A high-quality methodology for maximizing the value we can derive from "Big Data"; that is, making the new discoveries about adversary patterns and networks that give two crucial advantages—unique insights and more decision space—to policy makers, military planners and operators, intelligence analysts, law enforcement and first responders. ABI also teases out subtle behaviors and relationships between the "known" targets, objects, and network.[27]

ADAPTIVE RISK Category of risk that includes threats intentionally caused by humans.[28]

ADEQUATE SECURITY The security commensurate with the risk and the magnitude of harm resulting from the loss, misuse, or unauthorized access to or modification of information.[29]

ADJUDICATIVE PROCESS An examination of a sufficient period of a person's life to make an affirmative determination that the person is an acceptable security risk.[30]

ADVERSARIAL APPROACH The view that the other side or party in a conflict is an enemy that must be defeated and destroyed without compromise.

ADVERSARY Individual, group, organization, or government that conducts or has the intent to conduct detrimental activities.[31]

ADVERSARY COLLECTION METHODOLOGY Any resource and method available to and used by an adversary for the collection and exploitation of sensitive/critical information or indicators thereof.[32]

ADVERSARY THREAT STRATEGY The process of defining, in narrative or graphical format, the threat presented to an operation, program, or project. The adversary threat strategy should define the potential adversaries, the courses of action those adversaries might take against the operation, and the information needed by the adversaries to execute those actions.[33]

ADVERSE INFORMATION Any information that adversely reflects on the integrity or character of a cleared employee, that suggests that his or her ability to safeguard classified information may be impaired, or that his or her access to classified information clearly may not be in the interest of national security.[34]

ADVISE (Analysis, Dissemination, Visualization, Insight, and Semantic Enhancement) The term "ADVISE" has been used interchangeably for two different stages of research and development: the first refers to a toolset or development kit—a set of generic tools to gather, link, and present information. The second refers to a collection of deployed systems to test the effectiveness of the toolset in specific settings. Since each of these references to "ADVISE" raises a different set of privacy protection risks, it is important to distinguish between the risks presented by a development kit and the risks presented by a deployed system. This report uses the following separate terms: The terms "ADVISE technology framework" or "Framework" refer to the first stage of research and development: the toolset/development kit. The term "ADVISE deployments" refers to the second stage of research and development: implementations of the ADVISE technology framework.[35]

ADVISORY COMMITTEE ON HISTORICAL DIPLOMATIC DOCUMENTATION Established by Public Law 102-138, the Foreign Relations

Authorization Act, Fiscal Years 1992 and 1993, signed by President Bush on October 28, 1991. Section 198 of P.L. 102-138 added a new Title IV to the Department of State's Basic Authorities Act of 1956 (22 USC 4351, et seq.). The statute sets the membership of the Committee at nine members drawn from among historians, political scientists, archivists, international lawyers, and other social scientists who are distinguished in the field of U.S. foreign relations. Six members represent the American Historical Association, the Organization of American Historians, the American Political Science Association, the Society of American Archivists, the American Society of International Law, and the Society of Historians of American Foreign Relations; there are also three "at large" members. The members are granted all necessary security clearances. The legislation requires that the Committee meet four times a year. The Historian of the State Department serves as executive secretary of the Committee.[36]

ADVISORY SENSITIVITY ATTRIBUTES User-supplied indicators of file sensitivity that alert other users to the sensitivity of a file so that they may handle it appropriate to its defined sensitivity.[37]

AERIAL RECONNAISSANCE *See* AIR RECONNAISSANCE

AGENCY In intelligence usage, an organization or individual engaged in collecting and/or processing information. Also called collection agency.[38] *See* AGENT; INTELLIGENCE CYCLE; SOURCE

AGENDA-SETTING THEORY News or other information made available to the public by the media ultimately defines what is considered significant. *See* CNN EFFECT

AGENT 1. In intelligence usage, one who is authorized or instructed to obtain or to assist in obtaining information for intelligence or counterintelligence purposes.[39] 2. A person recruited, trained, controlled, and employed to obtain and report information and controlled by a case officer.[40] 3. "AGENTS have access to important information and pass that information secretly to their case officer."[41] An agent may also be known as an "asset" but never referred to as a "secret agent" (a term relegated to popular culture in books and movies). Agents are not professional intelligence officers. Also a term used to describe a U.S. special agent of a counterintelligence agency. *See* AGENCY; CASE OFFICER; SECRET AGENT

AGENT HANDLER *See* CASE OFFICER

AGGRIEVED PERSON A person who is the target of an electronic surveillance or any other person whose communications or activities were subject to electronic surveillance.[42]

AGNOTOLOGY Attributed to linguist Ian Boa, the study of ignorance, from *agnoia*, "want of perception or knowledge," and *agnosia*, "a state of ignorance or not knowing, both from gnosis meaning knowledge."[43]

AIR FORCE OFFICE OF SPECIAL INVESTIGATIONS (AFOSI) We are a federal law enforcement and investigative agency operating throughout the full spectrum of conflict, seamlessly within any domain; conducting criminal investigations and providing counterintelligence services. (AFOSI's mission is) to identify, exploit and neutralize criminal, terrorist and intelligence threats to the Air Force, Department of Defense and U.S. government.[44]

AIR PHOTOGRAPHIC RECONNAISSANCE The obtaining of information by air photography, divided into three types: (1) strategic photographic reconnaissance; (2) tactical photographic reconnaissance; (3) survey/cartographical purposes and to survey/cartographic standards of accuracy. It may be strategic or tactical.[45]

AIR PICKET An airborne early warning aircraft positioned primarily to detect, report, and track approaching enemy aircraft or missiles and to control intercepts.[46] *See* AIRBORNE EARLY WARNING

AIR RECONNAISSANCE The collection of information or intelligence interest either by visual observation from the air or through the use of airborne sensors.[47] *See* RECONNAISSANCE

AIRBORNE EARLY WARNING The detection of enemy air or surface units by radar or other equipment carried in an airborne vehicle, and the transmitting of a warning to friendly units.[48]

ALERT Readiness for action, defense, or protection; a warning signal of a real or threatened danger, such as an air attack; the period of time during which troops stand by in response to an alarm; to forewarn, to prepare for action.[49]

ALERT CENTER A site for the review of all incoming current intelligence information that possesses, or has access to, extensive communications for alerting local personnel. An additional responsibility may include the ability to task appropriate external collection assets within the system.[50] *See* INDICATIONS CENTER; WARNING CENTER; WATCH CENTER

ALERT FATIGUE A condition that exists when a constant state of alert is enacted, resulting in the deterioration of readiness for action. For example, "When the Israelis launched their sudden attack into Lebanon in 1982, Palestinian surprise was due in part to alert fatigue or the cry-wolf syndrome. This phenomenon results from the desensitization of an entity's warning capability because the threatened attack or event did not occur. On possibly as many as four occasions prior to the June attack, Palestinian forces predicted and prepared for the expected Israeli attack. Each time the attack never came. It is not surprising, therefore, that the PLO saw the events in early June as a repeat of previous Israeli saber rattling. Arafat's presence outside of Lebanon on the day before the attack dramatized this point."[51] *See* CRY-WOLF SYNDROME

ALERT MEMORANDUM Correspondence issued by high-level intelligence officials to policymakers to warn them about developments abroad that may be of major concern to the country's national security; a memorandum coordinated within the intelligence community if time permits.[52]

ALIEN Any person who is not a citizen of the United States.

ALL HAZARDS A threat or an incident, natural or manmade, that warrants action to protect life, property, the environment, and public health or safety, and to minimize disruptions of government, social, or economic activities. It includes natural disasters, cyber incidents, industrial accidents, pandemics, acts of terrorism, sabotage, and destructive criminal activity targeting critical infrastructure.[53]

ALLIED PRESS INFORMATION CENTER *See* JOINT INFORMATION ENVIRONMENT

ALL-SOURCE INTELLIGENCE 1. Products and/or organizations and activities that incorporate all sources of information, most frequently including human resources intelligence, imagery intelligence, measurement and signature intelligence, signals intelligence, and open-source data in the production of finished intelligence. In intelligence collection, a phrase that indicates that in the satisfaction of intelligence requirements, all collection, processing, exploitation, and reporting systems and resources are identified for possible use and those most capable are tasked. 2. In the NICE (National Initiative for Cybersecurity Education) Workforce Framework, cybersecurity work where a person: analyzes threat information from multiple sources, disciplines, and agencies across the Intelligence Community. Synthesizes and places intelligence information in context; draws insights about the possible implications.[54] *See* SOURCES OF INTELLIGENCE

ALTERNATIVE ANALYSIS Rigorous and systematic analytic consideration of differing viewpoints, explanations for observed or reported phenomena, or possible future outcomes. The Intelligence Community (IC) Analytic Standards, implemented in June 2007, require analytic products to use alternative analysis where appropriate. Analysis 101, the ODNI's joint course for new analysts, provides in-depth instruction in critical thinking and structured techniques to facilitate alternative analysis. How can this help us? Alternative analysis helps bound, clarify, and convey analytic uncertainty while minimizing the risk of analytic surprise. It facilitates examination of various explanations for reported phenomena, underscores differences in interpretation of evidence and links them to differing assumptions, extrapolates data to consider "alternative outcomes," and identifies key drivers expected to shape the direction of future events. Why do we need this? Alternative analysis helps bound, clarify, and convey analytic uncertainty while minimizing the risk of analytic surprise.[55]

ALTERNATIVE COMPENSATORY CONTROL MEASURES Used to safeguard sensitive intelligence or operations and support information (acquisition programs do not qualify) when normal measures are insufficient to achieve strict Need-to-Know controls, and where Special Access Program (SAP) controls are not required.[56]

ALTERNATIVE MEDIA Various information sources that provide a forum for interpretations of events and issues that differ radically from those presented in mass media products and outlets.[57]

AMALGAM OF FIEFDOMS The efficiencies project also showed that the current apparatus for managing people and money across the DoD enterprise is woefully inadequate. The agencies, field activities, joint headquarters, and support staff functions of the department operate as a semi-feudal system—an amalgam of fiefdoms without centralized mechanisms to allocate resources, track expenditures, and measure results relative to the department's overall priorities.[58]

ANALYSIS A systematic approach to problem-solving; the process of separating intelligence data into distinct, related parts or elements and examining those elements to determine essential parameters or related properties. Often the word *analysis* is incorrectly interchanged with *assessment*. To understand the difference, it is usually said, "analysis is what you know and an assessment is what you believe."[59] *See* ASSESSMENT; OPINION

ANALYSIS AND PRODUCTION The conversion of processed information into intelligence through the integration, evaluation, analysis, and interpretation of all source data and the preparation of intelligence products in support of known or anticipated user requirements.[60]

ANALYSIS OF COMPETING HYPOTHESES Identification of alternative explanations (considered hypotheses) and the evaluation of all evidence that will disconfirm rather than confirm the hypotheses. This method involves eight steps:[61]

1. Identify the possible hypotheses to be considered. Use a group of analysts with different perspectives to brainstorm the possibilities.
2. Make a list of significant evidence and arguments for and against each hypothesis.
3. Prepare a matrix with hypotheses across the top and evidence down the side. Analyze the "diagnosticity" of the evidence and arguments—that is, identify which items are most helpful in judging the relative likelihood of the hypotheses.
4. Refine the matrix. Reconsider the hypotheses and delete evidence and arguments that have no diagnostic value.
5. Draw tentative conclusions about the relative likelihood of each hypothesis. Proceed by trying to disprove the hypotheses rather than prove them.
6. Analyze how sensitive your conclusion is to a few critical items of evidence. Consider the consequences for your analysis if that evidence is wrong, misleading, or subject to a different interpretation.
7. Report conclusions. Discuss the relative likelihood of all the hypotheses, not just the most likely one.
8. Identify milestones for future observation that may indicate events are taking a different course than expected.

ANALYSIS PRODUCED A disseminated or un-disseminated product, assessment, study, estimate, compilation, or other report created and reviewed or validated by an IC element. It also includes databases comprised of information that may inform analysis.[62]

ANALYST YELLOW PAGES Derived from the Analytic Resources Catalog (ARC), a searchable directory of expertise and contact information for intelligence community analysts. It was intended to facilitate collaboration among analysts by enabling them to search across the IC for their counterparts.[63]

ANALYTIC MISSION MANAGEMENT (AMM) An office established by the Deputy DNI for Analysis with the responsibility for knowing how analytic resources are arrayed across the community. AMM is also tasked with identifying the gaps in the analytic community's understanding of critical targets, and for collaborating with the collection community to close those gaps. In addition to developing a staff cadre that can accomplish this mission, the office has also developed processes to gather key information from the analytic community to support mission management.[64]

ANALYTIC RESOURCES CATALOG (ARC) A database containing information about the skills, experience and expertise of the analysts in the IC. The ARC provides management information, such as the numbers of analysts currently working specific intelligence topics. The ARC is also the basis of the Analyst Yellow Pages, a directory available on JWICS providing contact information for analysts working certain countries and topics.[65]

ANALYTIC STANDARDS In June 2007 the DNI implemented an Intelligence Community (IC) Directive mandating that specific analytic standards guide the writing of intelligence analysis in all IC analytic elements, be the basis for evaluation of IC analytic production, and be included in analysis teaching modules and case studies for use throughout the IC. These standards, which emerged from a collaborative effort between the ODNI and representatives from the analytic elements of all 16 IC agencies, articulate the mission and commitment of all IC analytic elements to meet the highest standards of integrity and rigorous thinking. To conform with IC Analytic Standards, analysis must be: objective; independent of political considerations; timely; based on all available sources of intelligence; and exhibit proper standards of analytic tradecraft.[66]

ANALYTIC TRADECRAFT The practiced skill of applying learned techniques and methodologies appropriate to an issue to mitigate, gain insight, and provide persuasive understanding of the issue to members of the U.S. government and its allies.[67] *See* ANALYTIC STANDARDS

ANALYTIC TRANSFORMATION Incorporates near-term efforts already underway and longer-term concepts that are just beginning to be formulated into tangible initiatives. Analytic Transformation initiatives are consolidated into three main areas and include—but are not limited to—the following: Enhancing Quality of Analytic Products; Managing the Mission at a Community Level; Building More Integrated Analytic Operations.[68]

ANALYTIC WRITING Written communication focusing on distilling and summarizing factual information to provide concise and clear reports for managers and other customers.[69]

ANALYTICAL FRAMEWORK FOR INTELLIGENCE (AFI) AFI enhances DHS's (Department of Homeland Security) ability to identify, apprehend, and prosecute individuals who pose a potential law enforcement or security risk, and aids in the enforcement of customs and immigration laws, and other laws enforced by DHS at the border. AFI is used for the purposes of: (1) identifying individuals, associations, or relationships that may pose a potential law enforcement or security risk, targeting cargo that may present a threat, and assisting intelligence product users in the field in preventing the illegal entry of people and goods, or identifying other violations of law; (2) conducting additional research on persons and/or cargo to understand whether there are patterns or trends that could assist in the identification of potential law enforcement or security risks; and (3) sharing finished intelligence products developed in connection with the above purposes with DHS employees who have a need to know in the performance of their official duties and who have appropriate clearances or permissions.[70]

ANALYZE The capability and/or process to convert data to actionable information and recommendations as applicable to increase situational awareness and better understand possible courses of action.[71]

ANOMALY An indication of foreign-power activity or knowledge inconsistent with the expected norm that suggests knowledge of U.S. national security information, processes, capabilities, or activities.[72]

ANTEMORTEM DATA Medical records, samples, and photographs taken prior to death. These include (but are not limited to) fingerprints, dental x-rays, body tissue samples, photographs of tattoos, or other identifying marks. These "pre-death" records would be compared against records completed after death to help establish a positive identification of human remains.[73]

ANTITERRORISM (AT) Defensive measures used to reduce the vulnerability of individuals and property to terrorist acts, to include rapid containment by local military and civilian forces.[74]

ANTI-TERRORISM, CRIME AND SECURITY ACT 2001 To amend the Terrorism Act 2000; to make further provision about terrorism and security; to provide for the freezing of assets; to make provision about immigration and asylum; to amend or extend the criminal law and powers for preventing crime and enforcing that law; to make provision about the control of pathogens and toxins; to provide for the retention of communications data.[75]

ANTI-TERRORISM ADVISORY COUNCIL PROGRAM On September 17, 2001, in the wake of the 9/11 terrorist attacks, the Anti-Terrorism Advisory Council (ATAC) Program (previously called the Anti-Terrorism Task Force) was initiated by then Attorney General John Ashcroft. Each United States Attorney's Office (USAO) designated at least one experienced Assistant United States Attorney (AUSA) as the district's ATAC Coordinator. Each USAO formed an ATAC which is comprised of federal, state, and local law enforcement agencies and often pertinent public health and safety officials and security officials from private industry. The numerous responsibilities of the ATAC Coordinator include: convening the ATAC to coordinate counterterrorism efforts in their communities; coordinating specific anti-terrorism initiatives; supporting the investigative efforts of the FBI's Joint Terrorism Task Forces (JTTFs), which have operational responsibility over terrorism cases and matters; initiating training programs; and facilitating information sharing among the ATAC membership and between field and headquarters components of the Department of Justice.[76]

ANTI-TERRORISM INFORMATION EXCHANGE (ATIX) In April 2003, the Regional Information Sharing System (RISS) expanded services and implemented ATIX to provide users with access to homeland security, disaster, and terrorist threat information. Any RISS member agency, as well as executives and officials from other first-responder agencies and crucial infrastructure entities, can access the system. It is designed for use by officials from government and nongovernment organizations who are responsible for planning and implementing prevention, response, mitigation, and recovery.[77]

APPLICATION In the intelligence context, the direct extraction and tailoring of information from an existing foundation of intelligence and near real-time reporting.[78]

APPRECIATION OF THE SITUATION First used as a term from the battlefield. Commanders would use a logical process of reasoning to consider all the factors on a specific environment that would affect a unit's military situation; they would then arrive at a decision as to the course of action to take to accomplish the mission. Later on, it has been used figuratively at the strategic intelligence level.[79]

ARCHIVING The maintenance of records in remote storage after a case has been closed or disposed of, as a matter of contingency, should the records be needed for later reference.[80]

AREA OF CONCERN Specific issue or incident within a warning problem that requires identifiable attention by the analyst, commander, or policy-maker.[81]

AREA OF INTELLIGENCE RESPONSIBILITY An area allocated to a commander in which he or she is responsible for the provision of intelligence.[82]

ARGUMENT A type of discourse or text (a product)—the distillate of the practice of argumentation (the process)—in which the arguer seeks to persuade the other of the truth of a proposition (hypothesis) by advancing the reasons, grounds, and evidence that support it.

A-SPACE (ANALYTIC SPACE) An ODNI project to develop a common collaboration workspace for all Intelligence Community analysts that is accessible from current workstations and provides unprecedented access to interagency databases, a capability to search classified sources and the Internet simultaneously, web-based email, and collaboration tools accredited to the HUMINT Control System and Gamma Information Handling (HCS/G) level.[83] *See* I-SPACE

ASSESSED FACILITY A facility believed to exist based on intelligence reporting, although the specific location has not been confirmed. Assessed facilities are those believed to exist based on evaluation of the number of facilities a given functional program should require and the scope of the country's known underground program.[84]

ASSESSMENT The process of combining all intelligence data into a unified, specific judgment; the result of analysis formed within the context of the intelligence environment. In some intelligence products, these results are found under the "Key Judgment(s)" section of the document.[85] *See* ANALYSIS; CONCLUSION; OPINION

ASSET Any person, facility, equipment, or information that has value and is controlled by a government. An asset also may have value to an adversary, although the nature and magnitude of this value may differ. This term is used interchangeably with the term "agent."[86] *See* AGENT

ASSOCIATED (ENHANCED) MARKINGS Markings, other than those which designate classification level, that are required to be placed on classified documents. These include the "classified by" line, downgrading and declassification instructions, special control notices, and Special Access Program (SAP) caveats, etc.[87]

ASSOCIATED INFORMATION Non-biometric information about a person. For example, a person's name, personal habits, age, current and past addresses, current and past employers, telephone number, email address, place of birth, family names, nationality, education level, group affiliations, and history, including such characteristics as nationality, educational achievements, employer, security clearances, financial and credit history.[88]

ASSOCIATION ANALYSIS/NETWORK ANALYSIS Collection and analysis of information that shows relationships among varied individuals suspected of being involved in criminal activity that may provide insight into the criminal operation and which investigative strategies might work best.[89]

ASSURE A range of actions taken both at home and abroad to solidify resolve and demonstrate commitment.[90]

ASYLUM SEEKER Someone who says he or she is a refugee, but whose claim has not yet been definitively evaluated.[91]

ASYMMETRIC THREAT A broad and unpredictable spectrum of risks, actions, and operations conducted by state and non-state actors that can potentially undermine national and global security.[92]

ASYMMETRY Dissimilarities in organization, equipment, doctrine, [information] and values between other armed forces (formally organized or not) and U.S. forces. Engagements are symmetric if forces, technologies, and weapons are similar; they are asymmetric if forces, technologies, and weapons are different, or if a resort to terrorism and rejection of more conventional rules of engagement are the norm.[93]

A-TEAM/B-TEAM CONCEPT (BLUE TEAM/RED TEAM CONCEPT) An experimental method developed within the intelligence community in the mid-1970s to improve the quality of a National Intelligence Estimate (NIE)

on important warning problems through competitive and alternative analysis. The "A-team" usually included U.S. intelligence analysts, while the "B-team" consisted of members outside of the intelligence community. Both teams would look at the identical warning problem and take different sides of an issue.[94] *See* DEVIL'S ADVOCATE

ATTACHE/ATTACHÉ An official assigned to a diplomatic mission or embassy. Usually, this person has advanced expertise in a specific field, such as agriculture, commerce, or the military.[95]

ATTACK SIGNATURE A specific sequence of events indicative of an unauthorized access attempt.

ATTORNEY GENERAL'S GUIDELINES Officially known as *The Attorney General's Guidelines for Domestic FBI Operations* (AGG-DOM), it applies to investigative and intelligence collection activities conducted by the FBI within the U.S. territories, or outside the territories of all countries. They do not apply to investigative and intelligence collection activities of the FBI in foreign countries, which are governed by the Extraterritorial Guidelines.[96]

ATTRIBUTES OF INTELLIGENCE QUALITY Seven qualitative objectives used to support joint operations and standards against which intelligence activities and products are evaluated. A failure to achieve any one of these may contribute to a failure of operations. These seven objectives include timeliness (available and accessible in time to effectively be of use), objectivity (unbiased and free from any influence or constraint), usability (suitable for application upon receipt with additional analysis), readiness (anticipates and is ready to respond to existing and contingent intelligence requirements), completeness (meets responsibilities to accomplish a mission), accuracy (is factually correct), and relevance (contributes to an understanding of the situation).[97]

A-TYPE DECEPTION Purposeful intent to increase ambiguity by surrounding a target with irrelevant information; confusion based on a lack of certainty. Its aim is to keep the adversary unsure of one's true intentions, especially an adversary who has initially guessed right. A number of alternatives are developed for the target's consumption, built on misinformation that is both plausible and sufficiently significant to cause the target to expend resources to cover them.[98] *See* ACTIVE DECEPTION; DECEPTION; DENIAL AND DECEPTION; M-TYPE DECEPTION; PASSIVE DECEPTION

AUSTRALIA GROUP (AG) Founded in 1984 in the aftermath of the massive use of chemical weapons during the Iran–Iraq war. During the 1980s, evidence surfaced that several countries, including Iraq, were producing chemical weapons using supplies from the international trade in chemicals and related equipment. Thirty countries participate in the AG: Australia, Argentina, Austria, Belgium, Canada, the Czech Republic, Denmark, Finland, France, Germany, Greece, Hungary, Iceland, Ireland, Italy, Japan, Luxembourg, the Netherlands, New Zealand, Norway, Poland, Portugal, Romania, Slovakia, South Korea, Spain, Sweden, Switzerland, UK, and the United States. The AG has no charter or constitution and operates by consensus. The group meets annually in Paris.[99]

AUTHENTIC DOCUMENT A document bearing a signature or seal attesting that it is genuine and official. If it is an enemy document, it may have been prepared for purposes of deception; therefore, the accuracy of such a document, even though authenticated, must be confirmed by other information (e.g., conditions of capture).[100]

AUTHENTICATE To confirm the identity of an entity when that identity is presented.

AUTHENTICATION 1. A security measure designed to protect a communications system against acceptance of a fraudulent transmission or simulation by establishing the validity of a transmission, message, or originator. 2. A means of identifying individuals and verifying their eligibility to receive specific categories of information. 3. Evidence by proper signature or seal that a document is genuine and official. 4. In personnel recovery missions, the process whereby the identity of an isolated person is confirmed.[101]

AUTHENTICATOR Evidence by proper signature or seal that a document is genuine and official; a security measure designed to protect a communication system against fraudulent transmissions.[102]

AUTHENTICITY An attribute of the credibility of tangible evidence, such as a document, message, or object that indicates whether the tangible item is actually what it is represented to be. *See* CREDIBILITY

AUTHORITATIVE ANALYTIC PRODUCTS Any analytic product shared or disseminated outside of the producing organization that contains the sanctioned or official analytic judgment, opinion, or view of that organization.[103]

AUTHORITATIVE SOURCE The primary DoD-approved repository of biometric information on a biometric subject. The authoritative source provides a strategic capability for access to standardized, comprehensive, and current biometric files within the DoD and for the sharing of biometric files with Joint, Interagency, and designated Multinational partners. The DoD may designate authoritative sources for various populations consistent with applicable law, policy and directives.[104]

AUTHORIZED CLASSIFICATION AND CONTROL MARKINGS REGISTER The official list of authorized security control markings and abbreviated forms of such markings for use by all elements of the Intelligence Community (IC) for classified and unclassified information. Also known as the Controlled Access Program Coordination Office (CAPCO) Register.[105] *See* CONTROLLED ACCESS PROGRAM COORDINATION OFFICE

AUTHORIZED FOR RELEASE TO This marking, followed by the name of a country or international organization, is used to identify intelligence information that an originator has predetermined to be releasable or has released, through established foreign disclosure procedures and channels, to the foreign/international organization indicated. This marking may be abbreviated "REL" followed by an abbreviated name.[106]

AUTHORIZED IC PERSONNEL A U.S. person employed by, assigned to, or acting on behalf of an IC element who, through the course of their duties and employment, has a mission need and an appropriate security clearance. Authorized IC personnel shall be identified by their IC element head and shall have discovery rights to information collected and analysis produced by all elements of the IC. The term may include contractor personnel.[107]

AUTHORIZED PERSON A person who has a favorable determination of eligibility for access to classified information, has signed an SF 312, and has a need to know for the specific classified information in the performance of official duties.[108]

AUTOMATED BIOMETRIC IDENTIFICATION SYSTEM (ABIS) The Automated Biometric Identification System (IDENT) is the central DHS-wide system for storage and processing of biometric and associated biographic information for national security; law enforcement; immigration and border management; intelligence; background investigations for national security positions and certain positions of public trust; and associated testing, training, management reporting, planning and analysis, or other administrative uses.[109]

AUTOMATED IDENTIFICATION MANAGEMENT SYSTEM (AIMS)
A system that acts as a central web-based informational portal between U.S. Central Command (USCENTCOM), National Ground Intelligence Center (NGIC), and the Defense Forensics and Biometrics Agency (DFBA) that is designed to fuse intelligence analysis and value-added comments from field users of matched biometric and biographic data.[110]

AUTOMATED LICENSE PLATE RECOGNITION (ALPR) ALPR systems generally consist of a high-speed camera with an infrared ("IR") filter or two cameras—one high-resolution digital camera and one IR camera—to capture images of license plates; a processor and application capable of performing sophisticated optical character recognition (OCR) to transform the image of the plate into alphanumeric characters; application software to compare the transformed license plate characters to databases of license plates of interest to law enforcement; and a user interface to display the images captured, the results of the OCR transformation, and an alert capability to notify operators when a plate matching an agency's "hot list" is observed. The precise configuration of ALPR systems varies depending on the manufacturer of the equipment and the specific operational deployment. ALPR systems are able to capture up to 1,800 plates per minute at speeds up to 120–160 miles per hour.[111]

AUTOMATED LOW-LEVEL ANALYSIS AND DESCRIPTION OF DIVERSE INTELLIGENCE VIDEO (ALADDIN) The Aladdin Video Program seeks to combine the state-of-the art in video extraction, audio extraction, knowledge representation, and search technologies in a revolutionary way to create fast, accurate, robust, and extensible technology that supports the multimedia analytic needs of the future.[112]

AUTOMATED TRUSTED INFORMATION EXCHANGE (ATIX) Operated by the Regional Information Sharing Systems®, ATIX is a secure means to disseminate national security or terrorist threat information to law enforcement and other first responders via the ATIX electronic bulletin board, secure website, and secure e-mail.[113]

AUTOMATIC DECLASSIFICATION Section 3.3(a) of E.O. 13526, mandates the automatic declassification of records of permanent historical value under Title 44, *United States Code*, that are more than 25 years old. However, section 3.3(b) allows an agency head to exempt from automatic declassification specific information, which if released would be expected to damage the national security of the United States for any of the nine reasons provided for in the section.[114]

AVAILABLE PUBLICLY Information that has been published or broadcast for general public consumption, is available on request to a member of the general public, could lawfully be seen or heard by any casual observer, or is made available at a meeting open to the general public. In this context, "general public" also means general availability to persons in a military community even though the military community is not open to the civilian general public.[115]

AWARENESS OF NATIONAL SECURITY ISSUES AND RESPONSE The FBI's ANSIR Program's awareness message is principally aimed at U.S. corporations, although other government agencies and law enforcement also benefit from it. The principal method of disseminating FBI awareness information is through ANSIR Email . . . the ease of replicating email communication accounts for the global nature of the dissemination. American interests abroad receive ANSIR awareness communications primarily from their headquarters in the United States, which relays ANSIR Email to them, though on occasion the awareness message is delivered directly to those overseas. In addition to making potential targets of intelligence and terrorist activities less vulnerable through awareness, the FBI also has a unique capability to respond when these activities are identified in the United States. This response capability is a key part of the awareness message. The FBI does more than simply identify problems; it does something about them.[116]

NOTES

1. Seifert, Jeffrey W. "Data Mining and Homeland Security: An Overview." *CRS Report for Congress*, April 3, 2008 (18–19). Accessed January 4, 2015. https://www.fas.org/sgp/crs/homesec/RL31798.pdf; also see Department of Defense, *Office of the Inspector General. Report of Investigation.* September 18, 2006. Accessed January 4, 2015. http://www.dodig.mil/foia/ERR/r_H05L97905217-PWH.pdf and Able Danger Blog. Accessed January 4, 2015. http://www.abledangerblog.com/AbleDangerTimeline.html.

2. U.S. Department of Homeland Security. Office of Intelligence and Analysis. *Domestic Extremism Lexicon.* March 26, 2009. Accessed July 15, 2015. http://www.fas.org/irp/eprint/lexicon.pdf.

3. Jan Goldman, *Intelligence Warning Terminology*, Joint Military Intelligence, October 2001, accessed July 3, 2015. https://archive.org/details/JMICInteligencel-warnterminology.

4. U.S. Department of Defense. Center for Development of Security Excellence. *Glossary of Security Terms and Definitions*. November 2012. Accessed July 6, 2015. http://www.cdse.edu/documents/cdse/Glossary_Handbook.pdf.

5. U.S. Department of Defense. *Department of Defense Dictionary of Military and Associated Terms.* JP 1-02, 08 November 2010, as Amended through 15 January 2016. Accessed January 26, 2016. http://www.dtic.mil/doctrine/new_pubs/jp1_02.pdf.

6. Kissel, Richard (ed.). *Glossary of Key Information Security Terms, Department of Commerce.* NIST IR 7298 (Revision 2), May 2013. Accessed July 7, 2015. http://nvlpubs.nist.gov/nistpubs/ir/2013/NIST.IR.7298r2.pdf.

7. U.S. Department of Defense. Center for Development of Security Excellence. *Glossary of Security Terms and Definitions*. November 2012. Accessed February 16, 2015. http://www.cdse.edu/documents/cdse/Glossary_Handbook.pdf.

8. U.S. Department of Defense. *Dictionary of Military and Associated Terms.* JP 1-02, 08 November 2010, as Amended through 15 June 2015. Accessed July 6, 2015.

9. Department of Homeland Security, Risk Steering Committee. *DHS Risk Lexicon.* September 2010. Accessed February 14, 2015. http://www.dhs.gov/dhs-risk-lexicon.

10. U.S. Department of Defense. Center for Development of Security Excellence. *Glossary of Security Terms and Definitions.* November 2012. Accessed February 16, 2015. http://www.cdse.edu/documents/cdse/Glossary_Handbook.pdf.

11. Office of the Director of National Intelligence. *Accountability Reviews.* Intelligence Community Directive 111, August 4, 2011. Accessed January 24, 2015. http://www.dni.gov/files/documents/ICD/ICD 111.pdf.

12. U.S. Department of Defense. Center for Development of Security Excellence. *Glossary of Security Terms and Definitions.* November 2012. Accessed February 16, 2015. http://www.cdse.edu/documents/cdse/Glossary_Handbook.pdf.

13. U.S. Department of Defense. Center for Development of Security Excellence. *Glossary of Security Terms and Definitions*. November 2012. Accessed February 16, 2015. http://www.cdse.edu/documents/cdse/Glossary_Handbook.pdf.

14. North Atlantic Treaty Organization. *NATO Glossary of Terms and Definitions*. NATO Standardization Agency, 2008, Accessed July 2, 2015. https://fas.org/irp/doddir/other/nato2008.pdf.

15. U.S. Department of Defense. *Special Access Program (SAP) Policy*. DoD Directive Number 5205.7, July 1, 2010. Accessed January 4, 2015. http://www.dtic.mil/whs/directives/corres/pdf/520507p.pdf.

16. U.S. Department of Defense. Center for Development of Security Excellence. *Glossary of Security Terms and Definitions.* November 2012. Accessed February 16, 2015. http://www.cdse.edu/documents/cdse/Glossary_Handbook.pdf.

17. Office of the Director of National Intelligence. *National Intelligence: A Consumer's Guide.* 2011. Accessed January 25, 2015. http://www.dni.gov/files/documents/IC_Consumers_Guide_2011.pdf.

18. U.S. Department of Defense. *Department of Defense Dictionary of Military and Associated Terms.* JP 1-02, 08 November 2010, as Amended through 15 January 2016. Accessed January 26, 2016. http://www.dtic.mil/doctrine/new_pubs/jp1_02. pdf.

19. CNN. *Bush: Memo had no 'actionable intelligence.'* April 12, 2004. Accessed July 6, 2015. http://www.cnn.com/2004/ALLPOLITICS/04/11/911.investigation/.

20. EPI Medical News and Expose, "U.S. Army Delays, Alters Medical Studies Under a Little-known Scientific Censorship Program." *AAAS Professional Ethics* Report XI, no.4 (2008): 4–5. Accessed July 7, 2015. http://www.aaas.org/sites/default/ files/migrate/uploads/per55.pdf.

21. Thomson, Aimee. "Cellular Dragnet: Active Cell Site Simulators and the Fourth Amendment." January 2015, SSRN-id2546052. Accessed March 13, 2015. http://papers.ssrn.com/sol3/papers.cfm?abstract_id=2546052.

22. Devlin, Barrett. "CIA Aided Program to Spy on U.S. Cellphones; Marshals Service uses Airborne Devices that Mimic Cell Towers to Scan Data on Thousands of Cellphones." *The Wall Street Journal,* March 10, 2015. Also see Muckrock, *US Marshals Service Conceals Key Details of Millions Spent on StingRays.* Accessed March 15, 2015. https://www.muckrock.com/news/archives/2015/mar/03/us-marshals-service-conceal-key-details-millions-s/.

23. Department of State, "Definitions of Diplomatic Security Terms." *Foreign Affairs Manual.* 12FAM090. November 12, 2014. Accessed February 27, 2015. http:// www.state.gov/documents/organization/88330.pdf. Department of State, "Definitions of Diplomatic Security Terms." *Foreign Affairs Manual.* 12FAM090. November 12, 2014. Accessed February 27, 2015. http://www.state.gov/documents/organization/88330.pdf.

24. Jan Goldman, *Intelligence Warning Terminology,* Joint Military Intelligence College, October 2001, accessed July 3, 2015. https://archive.org/details/JMICInteligencelwarnterminology.

25. Department of Homeland Security. *Active Shooter: How to Respond.* Accessed February 24, 2015. http://www.dhs.gov/xlibrary/assets/active_shooter_booklet.pdf.

26. National Geospatial-Intelligence Agency. *Remarks as Prepared Letitia A. Long Director, National Geospatial-Intelligence Agency SPIE 2013 Defense Security + Sensing Symposium.* May 1, 2013. Accessed March 24, 2015. https://www.nga.mil/ MediaRoom/SpeechesRemarks/Pages/SPIEDSSSymposium.aspx.

27. Long, Letitia A. "Activity Based Intelligence: Understanding the Unknown." *The Intelligencer: Journal of U.S. Intelligence Studies* 20 no.2 (2013): 7–16. Accessed March 24, 2015. http://www.afio.com/publications/LONG_Tish_in_AFIO_ INTEL_FALLWINTER2013_Vol20_No2.pdf.

28. Department of Homeland Security, Risk Steering Committee. *DHS Risk Lexicon.* September 2010. Accessed February 14, 2015. http://www.dhs.gov/dhs-risk-lexicon.

29. Office of Management and Budget. *Security of Federal Automated Information Resources.* Circular A-130 Revised (Transmittal Memorandum No. 4), Appendix 3. Accessed July 7, 2015. https://www.whitehouse.gov/omb/circulars_a130_a130appendix_iii.

30. U.S. Department of Defense. Center for Development of Security Excellence. *Glossary of Security Terms and Definitions.* November 2012. Accessed February 16, 2015. http://www.cdse.edu/documents/cdse/Glossary_Handbook.pdf.

31. Department of Homeland Security, Risk Steering Committee. *DHS Risk Lexicon.* September 2010. Accessed February 14, 2015. http://www.dhs.gov/dhs-risk-lexicon.

32. U.S. Department of Defense. Center for Development of Security Excellence. *Glossary of Security Terms and Definitions.* November 2012. Accessed February 16, 2015. http://www.cdse.edu/documents/cdse/Glossary_Handbook.pdf.

33. U.S. Department of Defense. Center for Development of Security Excellence. *Glossary of Security Terms and Definitions.* November 2012. Accessed February 16, 2015. http://www.cdse.edu/documents/cdse/Glossary_Handbook.pdf.

34. U.S. Department of Defense. *National Industrial Security Program Operating Manual (NISPOM).* DoD 5220.22-M. February 28, 2006. Accessed January 5, 2015. http://www.dss.mil/documents/odaa/nispom2006-5220.pdf.

35. U.S. Department of Homeland Security. *DHS Privacy Office Review of the Analysis, Dissemination, Visualization, Insight and Semantic Enhancement (AD-VISE) Program.* July 11, 2007. Accessed January 5, 2015. http://www.dhs.gov/xlibrary/assets/privacy/privacy_rpt_advise.pdf.

36. U.S. Department of State, Office of the Historian. *Authority and Responsibilities.* Accessed January 5, 2015. http://history.state.gov/about/hac/intro.

37. U.S. Department of Defense. Center for Development of Security Excellence. *Glossary of Security Terms and Definitions.* November 2012. Accessed February 16, 2015. http://www.cdse.edu/documents/cdse/Glossary_Handbook.pdf.

38. U.S. Department of Defense. *Department of Defense Dictionary of Military and Associated Terms.* JP 1-02, 08 November 2010, as Amended through 15 January 2016. Accessed January 26, 2016, http://www.dtic.mil/doctrine/new_pubs/jp1_02.pdf.

39. U.S. Department of Defense. *Department of Defense Dictionary of Military and Associated Terms.* JP 1-02, 08 November 2010, as Amended through 15 January 2016. Accessed January 26, 2016, http://www.dtic.mil/doctrine/new_pubs/jp1_02.pdf.

40. North Atlantic Treaty Organization. *NATO Glossary of Terms and Definitions.* NATO Standardization Agency, 2008. Accessed July 2, 2015. https://fas.org/irp/doddir/other/nato2008.pdf.

41. Olsen, James. *Fair Play: The Moral Dilemmas of Spying.* Washington, DC: Potomac Books, 2006, 229.

42. 50 U.S. Code § 1801(k)—"Definitions." (Current through Pub. L. 113–234). Accessed February 10, 2015. http://www.law.cornell.edu/uscode/text/50/1801.

43. Proctor, Robert N. "Agnotology: A Missing Term," *Agnotology: The Making and Unmasking of Ignorance.* Robert N. Proctor and Londa Schiebinger, eds. Stanford Press: 2008. 27.

44. Air Force Office of Special Investigations, Function and Mission, accessed February 3, 2016, http://www.osi.af.mil/main/welcome.asp.

45. North Atlantic Treaty Organization. *NATO Glossary of Terms and Definitions*. NATO Standardization Agency, 2008. Accessed July 2, 2015. https://fas.org/irp/dod-dir/other/nato2008.pdf.

46. North Atlantic Treaty Organization. *NATO Glossary of Terms and Definitions*. NATO Standardization Agency, 2008. Accessed July 2, 2015. https://fas.org/irp/dod-dir/other/nato2008.pdf.

47. North Atlantic Treaty Organization. *NATO Glossary of Terms and Definitions*. NATO Standardization Agency, 2008. Accessed July 2, 2015. https://fas.org/irp/dod-dir/other/nato2008.pdf.

48. U.S. Department of Defense. *Department of Defense Dictionary of Military and Associated Terms.* JP 1-02, 08 November 2010, as Amended through 15 January 2016. Accessed January 26, 2016, http://www.dtic.mil/doctrine/new_pubs/jp1_02.pdf.

49. North Atlantic Treaty Organization. *NATO Glossary of Terms and Definitions*. NATO Standardization Agency, 2014, AAP-06, accessed July 27, 2015, http://nso.nato.int/nso/zPublic/ap/aap6/AAP-6.pdf.

50. Jan Goldman, *Intelligence Warning Terminology*, Joint Military Intelligence College, October 2001, accessed July 3, 2015. https://archive.org/details/JMICInteli-gencelwarnterminology.

51. Ewig, Mark G. "Surprise from Zion: The 1982 Israeli Invasion of Lebanon." *Airpower Journal* 35, no. 6 (1984): 48–57.

52. Jan Goldman, *Intelligence Warning Terminology*, Joint Military Intelligence College, October 2001, accessed July 3, 2015. https://archive.org/details/JMICInteli-gencelwarnterminology.

53. *Presidential Policy Directive/PPD-21 Critical Infrastructure Security and Resilience.* February 12, 2013. Accessed February 15, 2015. http://www.whitehouse.gov/the-press-office/2013/02/12/presidential-policy-directive-critical-infrastructure-security-and-resil.

54. National Initiative for Cybersecurity Education. *A Glossary of Common Cybersecurity Terminology.* n.d. Accessed March 5, 2015. http://niccs.us-cert.gov/glossary.

55. Intelligence and National Security Alliance and the Office of the Director of National Intelligence. *Analytic Transformation: Moving Forward Together*. September 2007. Accessed January 26, 2015. http://wayback.archive.org/web/20080530054342/http://analytic.insaonline.org/atprogram.pdf.

56. U.S. Department of Defense. Center for Development of Security Excellence. *Glossary of Security Terms and Definitions.* November 2012. Accessed February 16, 2015. http://www.cdse.edu/documents/cdse/Glossary_Handbook.pdf.

57. Department of Homeland Security. *Domestic Extremism Lexicon Reference Aid.* March 26, 2009. Accessed January 5, 2015. https://info.publicintelligence.net/-hsra-domestic-extremism-lexicon_165213935473.pdf.

58. Secretary of Defense Robert M. Gates, speech to the American Enterprise Institute, May 24, 2011. Accessed January 5, 2015. http://www.defense.gov/speeches/speech.aspx?speechid=1570.

59. Jan Goldman, *Intelligence Warning Terminology*, Joint Military Intelligence College, October 2001, accessed July 3, 2015. https://archive.org/details/JMICIntelligencelwarnterminology.

60. U.S. Department of Defense. Center for Development of Security Excellence. *Glossary of Security Terms and Definitions.* November 2012. Accessed February 16, 2015. http://www.cdse.edu/documents/cdse/Glossary_Handbook.pdf.

61. Heuer, Richard. *The Psychology of Intelligence Analysis.* Center of the Study of Intelligence, 1999. Accessed July 5, 2015. https://www.cia.gov/library/center-for-the-study-of-intelligence/csi-publications/books-and-monographs/psychology-of-intelligence-analysis/PsychofIntelNew.pdf.

62. Office of the Director of National Intelligence. *Discovery and Dissemination or Retrieval of Information within the Intelligence Community.* Intelligence Community Directive 501, January 21, 2009. Accessed March 2, 2015. http://www.dni.gov/files/documents/ICD/ICD_501.pdf.

63. Office of the Director of National Intelligence. *National Intelligence Program FY 2009 Congressional Budget Justification Book.* Vol. XII, February 2008. Accessed January 17, 2015. http://www.fas.org/irp/dni/cbjb-2009.pdf.

64. Intelligence and National Security Alliance and the Office of the Director of National Intelligence. *Analytic Transformation: Moving Forward Together.* September 2007. Accessed June 9, 2015. http://wayback.archive.org/web/20080530054342/http://analytic.insaonline.org/atprogram.pdf.

65. Office of the Director of National Intelligence. *National Intelligence Program FY 2009 Congressional Budget Justification Book.* Vol. XII, February 2008. Accessed January 17, 2015. http://www.fas.org/irp/dni/cbjb-2009.pdf.

66. Intelligence and National Security Alliance and the Office of the Director of National Intelligence. *Analytic Transformation: Moving Forward Together.* September 2007. Accessed January 26, 2015. http://wayback.archive.org/web/20080530054342/http://analytic.insaonline.org/atprogram.pdf; also see Office of the Director of National Intelligence. *Analytic Standards.* Intelligence Community Directive 203, January 2, 2015. Accessed January 26, 2015. http://www.dni.gov/files/documents/ICD/ICD%20203%20Analytic%20Standards.pdf.

67. Defense Intelligence Agency, Office of Counterintelligence. *CI Glossary—Terms & Definitions of Interest for DoD CI Professionals.* July 2014. Accessed January 17, 2015. https://www.hsdl.org/?view&did=699056.

68. Intelligence and National Security Alliance and the Office of the Director of National Intelligence. *Analytic Transformation: Moving Forward Together.* September 2007. Accessed January 12, 2015. http://wayback.archive.org/web/20080530054342/http://analytic.insaonline.org/atprogram.pdf.

69. United States Department of Justice. *Law Enforcement Analytic Standard.* Global Justice Information Sharing Initiative and International Association of Law Enforcement Intelligence Analysts, Inc., 2nd ed. April 2012, accessed February 1, 2016, https://it.ojp.gov/documents/d/Law%20Enforcement%20Analytic%20Standards%2004202_combined_compliant.pdf.

70. Department of Homeland Security. *Privacy Impact Assessment for the Analytical Framework for Intelligence (AFI).* June 1, 2012. Accessed December 15,

2014. https://www.dhs.gov/publication/analytical-framework-intelligence-afi; also see *EPIC v. CBP* (Analytical Framework for Intelligence), https://epic.org/foia/dhs/cbp/afi/.

71. Defense Forensics and Biometrics Agency. *DoD Biometrics Enterprise Architecture (Integrated) v2.0 Common Biometric Vocabulary.* April 2013. Accessed January 15, 2015. http://www.biometrics.dod.mil/Files/Documents/References/common%20biometric%20vocabulary.pdf.

72. Defense Intelligence Agency, Office of Counterintelligence. *CI Glossary—Terms & Definitions of Interest for DoD CI Professionals.* July 2014. Accessed January 17, 2015. https://www.hsdl.org/?view&did=699056.

73. U.S. Department of Defense. *Department of Defense Dictionary of Military and Associated Terms.* JP 1-02, 08 November 2010, as Amended through 15 January 2016. Accessed January 26, 2016, http://www.dtic.mil/doctrine/new_pubs/jp1_02.pdf.

74. Chairman of the Joint Chiefs of Staff. *National Military Strategic Plan for the War on Terrorism.* February 1, 2006. Accessed February 26, 2015. http://archive.defense.gov/pubs/pdfs/2006-01-25-Strategic-Plan.pdf.

75. *Anti-terrorism, Crime and Security Act 2001.* Accessed March 5, 2015. http://www.legislation.gov.uk/ukpga/2001/24/contents; also see "Anti-terrorism, Crime and Security Act 2001." *The Guardian*, January 19, 2009. Accessed March 5, 2015. http://www.theguardian.com/commentisfree/libertycentral/2009/jan/13/anti-terrorism-act.

76. U.S. Department of Justice. *Anti-Terrorism Advisory Council Program.* Accessed February 15, 2015. http://www.justice.gov/usao/priority-areas/national-security/anti-terrorism-advisory-council-program.

77. DeFede, Jim. "Mining the Matrix." *Mother Jones* October 1, 2004. Accessed January 12, 2016. http://www.motherjones.com/politics/2004/09/mining-matrix.

78. U.S. Department of Defense. *Dictionary of Military and Associated Terms.* JP 1-02, 08 November 2010, as Amended through 15 June 2015. Accessed July 6, 2015. https://web.archive.org/web/20150815204834/http://www.dtic.mil/doctrine/new_pubs/jp1_02.pdf.

79. Department of Defense, *Intelligence Preparation of the Battlefield*, FM-34-130. July 1994. Accessed January 12, 2016. https://fas.org/irp/doddir/army/fm34-130.pdf.

80. U.S. Department of Justice, Global Justice Information Sharing Initiative, *Criminal Intelligence Glossary of Terms, Minimum Criminal Intelligence Training Standards*, Appendix. October 2007. Accessed January 5, 2015. http://www.it.ojp.gov/documents/min_crim_intel_stand.pdf.

81. Jan Goldman, *Intelligence Warning Terminology*. Joint Military Intelligence College, October 2001, accessed July 3, 2015. https://archive.org/details/JMICIntelligencelwarnterminology.

82. North Atlantic Treaty Organization. *NATO Glossary of Terms and Definitions.* NATO Standardization Agency, 2008. Accessed July 2, 2015. https://fas.org/irp/doddir/other/nato2008.pdf.

83. Intelligence and National Security Alliance and the Office of the Director of National Intelligence. *Analytic Transformation: Moving Forward Together*. September

2007. Accessed January 12, 2015. http://wayback.archive.org/web/20080530054342/ http://analytic.insaonline.org/atprogram.pdf; also see Hoover, J. Nicholas. "U.S. Spy Agencies Go Web 2.0 in Effort To Better Share Information." *Information Week*, August 23, 2007. Accessed January 12, 2015. http://www.informationweek.com/us-spy-agencies-go-web-20-in-effort-to-better-share-information/d/d-id/1058453?.

84. Defense Intelligence Agency. *Defense Intelligence Report: Lexicon of Hardened Structure Definitions and Terms*. Washington, DC: 2000.

85. Jan Goldman, *Intelligence Warning Terminology*. Joint Military Intelligence College, October, 2001, accessed July 3, 2015. https://archive.org/details/JMICIntelligencelwarnterminology.

86. Also see Defense Intelligence Agency, Office of Counterintelligence. *CI Glossary—Terms & Definitions of Interest for DoD CI Professionals*. July 2014. Accessed January 17, 2015. https://www.hsdl.org/?view&did=699056.

87. U.S. Department of Defense. Center for Development of Security Excellence. *Glossary of Security Terms and Definitions*. November 2012. Accessed February 16, 2015. http://www.cdse.edu/documents/cdse/Glossary_Handbook.pdf.

88. Defense Forensics and Biometrics Agency. *DoD Biometrics Enterprise Architecture (Integrated) v2.0 Common Biometric Vocabulary*. April 2013. Accessed January 15, 2015. http://www.biometrics.dod.mil/Files/Documents/References/common%20biometric%20vocabulary.pdf.

89. United States Department of Justice. *Law Enforcement Analytic Standards*. Global Justice Information Sharing Initiative. April 2012. Accessed July 3, 2015. https://it.ojp.gov/documents/d/Law%20Enforcement%20Analytic%20Standards%20 04202_combined_compliant.pdf.

90. Chairman of the Joint Chiefs of Staff. *National Military Strategic Plan for the War on Terrorism*. February 1, 2006. Accessed February 26, 2015. http://archive. defense.gov/pubs/pdfs/2006-01-25-Strategic-Plan.pdf.

91. United Nations High Commissioner for Refugees. *Asylum-Seekers*. Accessed July 7, 2015. http://www.unhcr.org/pages/49c3646c137.html.

92. CACI International Inc., U.S. Naval Institute, and Center for Security Policy. *Cyber Threats to National Security: Symposium Five: Keeping the Nation's Industrial Base Safe From Cyber Threats*. March 1, 2011. Accessed February 26, 2015. http://asymmetricthreat.net/docs/asymmetric_threat_5_paper.pdf.

93. Department of the Army. *Operations*. FM 3-0. June 2001. Accessed January 5, 2015. http://www.bits.de/NRANEU/others/amd-us-archive/fm3-0%2801%29.pdf.

94. This concept is discussed in more detail in the Senate Select Committee on Intelligence, Subcommittee on Collection, Production, and Quality's *The National Intelligence Estimates A-B team Episode Concerning Soviet Strategic Capability and Objectives: Report of the Senate Select Committee on Intelligence, Subcommittee on Collection, Production, and Quality, United States Senate, together with separate views*. 95-2, February 16, 1978. Washington, DC: Government Printing Office.

95. U.S. Department of State. *Diplomatic Dictionary*. Accessed March 6, 2015. http://diplomacy.state.gov/discoverdiplomacy/references/169792.htm.

96. Federal Bureau of Investigation. *Domestic Investigations and Operations Guide*. October 15, 2011. Accessed February 25, 2015. http://vault.fbi.gov/. U.S.

Department of Justice. *The Attorney General's Guidelines for Domestic FBI Operations.* 2008. Accessed February 25, 2015. http://www.justice.gov/sites/default/files/ag/legacy/2008/10/03/guidelines.pdf.

97. DoD, Joint Publication 2-0, *Joint Doctrine for Intelligence Support to Operations*, October 2013. Accessed on July 22, 2015, http://www.dtic.mil/doctrine/new_pubs/jp2_0.pdf.

98. Used throughout by Michael Dewar, *The Art of Deception in Warfare* (Newton Abbot, U.K.: David and Charles, 1989). Also see Donald C. Daniel and Katherine L. Herbig (eds.), *Strategic Military Deception* (New York: Pergamon, 1982); Betty Glad (ed.), *Psychological Dimensions of War* (Newbury Park, CA: Sage, 1990); Klaus Knorr and Patric Morgan (eds.), *Strategic Military Surprise: Incentives and Opportunities* (New Brunswick, NJ: National Strategy Information Center, 1983); Stuart Sutherland, *Irrationality: Why We Don't Think Straight* (New Brunswick, NJ: Rutgers University Press, 1992); Ola Svenson and A. John Maule (eds.), *Time Pressure and Stress in Human Judgment and Decision Making* (New York: Plenum, 1993).

99. Chairman of the Joint Chiefs of Staff. *National Military Strategic Plan for the War on Terrorism.* February 1, 2006. Accessed February 26, 2015. http://archive.defense.gov/pubs/pdfs/2006-01-25-Strategic-Plan.pdf.

100. North Atlantic Treaty Organization. *NATO Glossary of Terms and Definitions.* NATO Standardization Agency, 2008. Accessed July 2, 2015. https://fas.org/irp/doddir/other/nato2008.pdf.

101. U.S. Department of Defense. *Personnel Recovery.* JP 3-50, January 2007. Accessed January 5, 2015. http://www.bits.de/NRANEU/others/jp-doctrine/jp3_50(91).pdf.

102. North Atlantic Treaty Organization. *NATO Glossary of Terms and Definitions.* NATO Standardization Agency, 2008. Accessed July 2, 2015. https://fas.org/irp/doddir/other/nato2008.pdf.

103. Office of the Director of National Intelligence. *Sourcing Requirements for Disseminated Analytic Products.* Intelligence Community Directive 206, October 17, 2007. Accessed February 27, 2015. https://fas.org/irp/dni/icd/icd-206.pdf.

104. Defense Forensics and Biometrics Agency. *DoD Biometrics Enterprise Architecture (Integrated) v2.0 Common Biometric Vocabulary.* April 2013. Accessed January 15, 2015. http://www.biometrics.dod.mil/Files/Documents/References/common%20biometric%20vocabulary.pdf.

105. U.S. Department of Defense. Center for Development of Security Excellence. *Glossary of Security Terms and Definitions.* November 2012. Accessed February 16, 2015. http://www.cdse.edu/documents/cdse/Glossary_Handbook.pdf.

106. U.S. Department of Defense. *National Industrial Security Program Operating Manual (NISPOM).* DoD 5220.22-M. February 28, 2006. Accessed January 5, 2015. http://www.dss.mil/documents/odaa/nispom2006-5220.pdf.

107. Office of the Director of National Intelligence. *Discovery and Dissemination or Retrieval of Information within the Intelligence Community.* Intelligence Community Directive 501, January 21, 2009. Accessed March 2, 2015. http://www.dni.gov/files/documents/ICD/ICD_501.pdf.

108. U.S. Department of Defense. *DoD Information Security Program: Protection of Classified Information.* 5200.01, Volume 3, February 24, 2012, March 19, 2013. Accessed January 15, 2015. http://www.dtic.mil/whs/directives/corres/pdf/520001_vol3.pdf.

109. Department of Homeland Security, *DHS/NPPD/Privacy Impact Assessment-002 Automated Biometric Identification System (IDENT)*, December 7, 2012, accessed February 2, 2016, http://www.dhs.gov/publication/dhsnppdpia-002-automated-biometric-identification-system-ident.

110. Defense Forensics and Biometrics Agency. *DoD Biometrics Enterprise Architecture (Integrated) v2.0 Common Biometric Vocabulary.* April 2013. Accessed January 15, 2015. http://www.biometrics.dod.mil/Files/Documents/References/common%20biometric%20vocabulary.pdf.

111. Roberts, David J. and Casanova, Meghann. *Automated License Plate Recognition Systems: Policy and Operational Guidance for Law Enforcement.* September 2012, 9. International Association of Chiefs of Police (IACP), Grant No. 2007-MU-MU-K004, National Institute of Justice. Accessed February 8, 2015. https://www.ncjrs.gov/pdffiles1/nij/grants/239604.pdf; also see Stein, Bennett and Stanley, Jay. *FOIA Documents Reveal Massive DEA Program to Record American's Whereabouts with License Plate Readers.* ACLU, January 26, 2015. Accessed February 8, 2015. https://www.aclu.org/blog/technology-and-liberty-criminal-law-reform/foia-documents-reveal-massive-dea-program-record-ame.

112. Office of the Director of National Intelligence, Intelligence Advanced Research Projects Activity (IARPA). *Aladdin Video BAA.* Accessed January 14, 2015. http://www.iarpa.gov/index.php/research-programs/aladdin-video/baa?highlight=WyJhbGFkZGluIiwidmlkZW8iLCJhbGFkZGluIHZpZGVvvIl0=; also see Office of the Director of National Intelligence. *2012 Data Mining Report for the Period January 1, 2012 through December 31, 2012.* Accessed January 14, 2015. http://www.dni.gov/files/documents/CLPO/Jan%202012%20to%20Dec.%202012%20Data%20Mining%20Report.pdf.

113. U.S. Department of Justice, Global Justice Information Sharing Initiative, *Criminal Intelligence Glossary of Terms, Minimum Criminal Intelligence Training Standards*, Appendix. October 2007. Accessed January 5, 2015. http://www.it.ojp.gov/documents/min_crim_intel_stand.pdf.

114. Executive Order 13526, *Classified National Security Information*, December 29, 2009. Accessed January 5, 2015. http://www.archives.gov/declassification/iscap/auto-declass-exemptions.html; also see U.S. Department of Justice, *Declassification Frequently Asked Questions*, December 5, 2014. Accessed January 5, 2015. http://www.justice.gov/open/declassification/declassification-faq.

115. U.S. Department of Defense. Under Secretary of Defense for Policy. DoD 5240.1-R. *Procedures Governing the Activities of DoD Intelligence Components That Affect United States Persons.* December 1982. Accessed January 5, 2015. http://www.fas.org/irp/doddir/dod/d5240_1_r.pdf.

116. Waguespack, Michael J. *Testimony before the House Committee on Government Reform, Subcommittee on National Security, Veterans Affairs, and International Relations.* Washington, DC, April 3, 2001. Accessed July 7, 2015. https://www.fbi.gov/news/testimony/fbis-ansir-program/.

B

BACKCHANNEL A line of diplomatic communication which bypasses the usual diplomatic channels. The usual reason for this is to maximize secrecy and avoid opposition to a new line of policy. This does not necessarily entail sidelining all professional diplomats, just most of them.[1]

BACKDOOR Generally circumvents security programs and provides access to a program, an online service, or an entire computer system. It can be authorized or unauthorized, documented or undocumented.[2]

BACKGROUND INVESTIGATION An official inquiry into the activities of a person, designed to develop information from a review of records, interviews of the subject, and interviews of people having knowledge of the subject.

BACKSTOPPING 1. Taking steps and arranging information to provide a false impression about a person. This can include placing records and documents at a business, public office, or at a school, and elsewhere, that would verify a false story if anyone decided to check on the story's validity; providing false evidence to support an agent's cover story. 2. CIA term for providing appropriate verification and support of cover arrangements for an agent or asset in anticipation of inquiries or other actions which might test the credibility of his or its cover.[3]

BACK-TELL The transfer of information from a higher to a lower echelon of command.[4] *See* TRACK TELLING

BANK SECRECY ACT Also known as the Currency and Foreign Transactions Reporting Act (P.L. 91-508, 84 Stat. 1118), the Bank Secrecy Act (BSA) of 1970 was enacted to reduce the amount of secrecy in the banking system by requiring financial institutions to help identify activities that may amount to money laundering.[5] *See* FINANCIAL CRIMES ENFORCEMENT NETWORK

BASELINE RISK Current level of risk that takes into account existing risk mitigation measures. Often, the word "risk" is used to imply "baseline risk" with the unstated understanding that the reference is the current circumstances. It should not be confused with risk as a measurement, which can change with the substitution of different variables.[6]

BASIC INTELLIGENCE 1. Intelligence, on any subject, which may be used as reference material for planning and in evaluating subsequent information.[7] 2. The compilation of all available data and information on several subjects of broad interest to policymakers and other members of the intelligence community; fundamental, comprehensive, encyclopedic, and general reference material relating to political, economic, geographic, and military structure, resources, capabilities, and vulnerabilities of foreign nations.[8] 3. Factual, fundamental, and relatively permanent information about all aspects of a nation—physical, social, economic, political, biographical, and cultural—which is used as a base for intelligence products in the support of planning, policymaking, and military operations.[9] 4. Factual, fundamental, and relatively permanent information about all aspects of a nation—physical, social, economic, political, biographical, and cultural—which is used as a base for intelligence products in the support of planning, policymaking, and military operations.[10]

BASIC MEASURES OF MILITARY PREPAREDNESS Minimal precautionary efforts, likely considered routine actions, against a potential future attack.[11] *See* EMERGENCY MEASURES OF MILITARY PREPAREDNESS; POST-SURPRISE MEASURES

BATTLE LAB Interrogations and other procedures that were to some degree experimental and their lessons would benefit DoD in other places.[12]

BAYESIAN (DECISION) ANALYSIS A technique developed by Thomas Bayes in 1763, in which he advanced the proposition that subjective probabilities should be combined with frequency probabilities via what has come to be called Bayes's theorem, a simple formula using conditional probabilities. According to the formula, the prior probability $P(H)$ of proposition H is revised to posterior probability $P(H/D)$ when the datum D is observed and $P(D/H)$ and $P(D)$ are known, as follows: $P(H/D) = P(D/H) \times P(H)/P(D)$. In this formula, $P(D/H)$ is the likelihood of the same information D given that proposition H is true. Even in this simple form, Bayes's theorem has apparent applications in international relations forecasting.[13]

BEAN-COUNTING ASSESSMENT Mostly used as a pejorative term for estimates and forecasting based on quantitative or empirical analysis.[14] For example, General Wesley Clark, Supreme Allied Commander, Europe, in a briefing to the press on NATO's ability to stop Serb aggression, said, "From the very beginning, we said we didn't believe in battle bean-counting as a way of measuring the effects of air power, although many continuously sought to go back to the old body count, bean-counting approach. Meanwhile, some accused of us of flying too high, of not wanting to risk our pilots while others chose to believe that we would strike only decoys or perhaps would hit nothing at all. The short answer of what we struck is clear. How much did we strike, and how much did we destroy? We destroyed and struck enough."[15] *See* PALM-READING ASSESSMENT

BEHAVIORAL ADVERTISING Matches advertisements to a consumer's interests as determined over time. If a consumer visits several different travel sites before viewing a news site, the consumer might see a behaviorally targeted travel advertisement displayed on the news page, even though the news page contains no travel content. A traditional behavioral ad network assembles profiles of individual consumers by tracking users' activities on publisher sites within their network. When the consumer visits a site where the ad network has purchased ad space, the ad network collects data about that visit while serving an advertisement based on the consumer's profile. While only a small portion of online ads are currently targeted this way, behavioral advertising is a growing segment of the online advertising industry. There is also a risk that profiles for behavioral advertising may be used for purposes other than advertising. Behavioral profiles, particularly those that can be tied to an individual, may be a tempting source of information in making decisions about credit, insurance, and employment. The lack of transparency surrounding behavioral advertising makes it difficult, if not impossible, to know whether behavioral profiles are being used for other purposes, and the lack of enforceable rules governing data collection and permissible uses leaves the door wide open for a myriad of secondary uses.[16]

BEHAVIORAL DETECTION ANALYSIS PROGRAM (BDA) Administered by the Transportation Safety Administration, it has taken several positive steps to validate the scientific basis and strengthen program management of BDA and the SPOT program, which has been in place for over 6 years at a total cost of approximately $900 million since 2007. Nevertheless, TSA has not demonstrated that BDOs (behavior detection officers) can consistently interpret the SPOT behavioral indicators, a fact that may contribute to varying passenger referral rates for additional screening. The subjectivity of the SPOT behavioral indicators and variation in BDO referral rates raise questions about the continued use of behavior indicators for detecting passengers who might pose a risk to aviation security. Furthermore, decades of peer-reviewed, published research on the complexities associated with detecting deception through human observation also draw into question the scientific underpinnings of TSA's behavior detection activities (18).[17] *See* SCREENING OF PASSENGERS BY OBSERVATION TECHNIQUES (SPOT)

BEHAVIORAL INSIGHTS TEAM A term used by the British government for a unit dedicated to the application of behavioral sciences. Considered a world-leading "social purpose company" whose mission is to help organizations in the UK and overseas to apply behavioral insights in support of social purpose goals. According to British officials, "We coined the term 'behavioral insights' in 2010 to help bring together ideas from a range of inter-related academic disciplines (behavioral economics, psychology, and social anthropology). These fields seek to understand how individuals take decisions in practice and how they are likely to respond to options. Their insights enable us to design policies or interventions that can encourage, support and enable people to make better choices for themselves and society."[18]

BELLIGERENCY A state of armed conflict; belligerents are direct participants in the conflict.[19]

BIG DATA There are many definitions of "big data," which may differ depending on whether you are a computer scientist, a financial analyst, or an entrepreneur pitching an idea to a venture capitalist. Most definitions reflect the growing technological ability to capture, aggregate, and process an ever-greater volume, velocity, and variety of data. In other words, "data is now available faster, has greater coverage and scope, and includes new types of observations and measurements that previously were not available." More precisely, big datasets are "large, diverse, complex, longitudinal, and/or distributed datasets generated from instruments, sensors, Internet transactions, email, video, click streams, and/or all other digital sources available today and in the future (2–3)."[20]

BIG DATA RESEARCH AND DEVELOPMENT INITIATIVE On March 29, 2012, the Obama administration announced the "Big Data Research and Development Initiative." By improving our ability to extract knowledge and insights from large and complex collections of digital data, the initiative promises to help accelerate the pace of discovery in science and engineering, strengthen our national security, and transform teaching and learning. To launch the initiative, six federal departments and agencies will announce more than $200 million in new commitments that, together, promise to greatly improve the tools and techniques needed to access, organize, and glean discoveries from huge volumes of digital data.[21]

BIGOT LIST 1. A narrow, select group of people with access to the reports from a particularly sensitive agent or espionage operation.[22] 2. A select group of key people who have access to intelligence reports from or about a particularly sensitive operation or project.

BINNING The process of parsing or classifying data in order to accelerate and/or improve biometric matching.[23]

BIODEFENSE KNOWLEDGE CENTER (BKC) This center supports National Biodefense Analysis and Countermeasures Center (NBACC) facility component centers and has its own functions and missions. One is to provide scientific assessments and information to the Homeland Security Operations Center regarding potential bioterrorism events. Another is to be a repository of biodefense information, including genomic sequences for pathogens of concern, the existence and location of vaccines, bio-forensics information, and information about individuals, groups, or organizations that might be developing these pathogens. Finally, the BKC aids in assessing potential bioterrorism agents as "material threats" for the purpose of the Project Bioshield countermeasure procurement process.[24]

BIOGRAPHIC DATA Data that describes physical and non-physical attributes of a biometric subject from whom biometric sample data has been collected. For example, full name, age, height, weight, address, employers, telephone number, email address, birthplace, nationality, education level, group affiliations, also data such as employer and security clearances and financial and credit history.[25]

BIOINFORMATION Biological material that contains information about an individual which may assist in their identification.[26]

BIOMETRIC ANALYSIS PACKET (BAP) A Biometrics Enabled Intelligence (BEI) product that provides identities of personnel who are biometrically enrolled or watch listed for a specified location. The BAP also provides a brief background summary of the personalities associated with the individual.[27]

BIOMETRIC CENTER OF EXCELLENCE (BCOE) The Science and Technology Branch (STB) created the Biometric Center of Excellence (BCOE) in 2007 to support its overall biometrics mission and fully coordinate its various biometric programs and activities. The BCOE is the central program for advancing biometric capabilities for integration into operations. The BCOE is strengthening criminal investigations and enhancing national security, while ensuring compliance with privacy laws, policies, and regulations. The BCOE is a collaborative initiative of the FBI's Criminal Justice Information Services (CJIS) Division, the Laboratory Division, and the Operational Technology Division. By centralizing biometrics and having them serve as a one-stop shop for biometric collaboration and expertise, the FBI's ability to combat crime and terrorism is strengthened as biometric tools and technologies move more quickly from the laboratory to the workplace and into the hands of stakeholders and those protecting us.[28]

BIOMETRIC IDENTITY A biometric identity is established when a biometric sample(s) is used instead of a name to identify a Person of Interest (POI). The biometric identity may consist of the results of one or more biometric encounters for the same individual.[29]

BIOMETRIC IDENTITY INTELLIGENCE RESOURCE (BI2R) Automated database that stores biometric and associated intelligence data from DoD collection devices. Analysts use the BI2R toolset to conduct analysis and develop intelligence reports supporting DoD and national missions. The system is designed to provide the DoD, Intelligence Community (IC), and coalition communities with authoritative, high pedigree, biometrically baselined identities, and advanced tools and technologies necessary to analyze, collaborate, produce, disseminate, and share biometric identity intelligence.[30]

BIOMETRIC INTELLIGENCE ANALYSIS REPORT (BIAR) First phase analytic products that provide current intelligence assessments on individuals who have been biometrically identified at least once and who may pose a threat to U.S. interests. BIARs provide a summary and background on a person's biometric encounters, all-source intelligence analysis, assessments of the subject's threat and intelligence value, summary of actions taken by the analytical element, and recommended actions for operators.[31]

BIOMETRICALLY ENABLED WATCHLIST (BEWL) Any list of person of interests (POI), with individuals identified by biometric sample instead of by name and the desired/recommended disposition instructions for each individual.[32]

BIOMETRICS A general term used alternatively to describe a characteristic or a process. As a characteristic: The measure of a biological (anatomical and physiological) and/or behavioral biometric characteristic that can be used for automated recognition. As a process: Automated methods of recognizing an individual based on the measure of biological (anatomical and physiological) and/or behavioral biometric characteristics.[33]

BIOMETRICS-ENABLED INTELLIGENCE The information associated with and/or derived from biometric signatures and the associated contextual information that positively identifies a specific person and/or matches an unknown identity to a place, activity, device, component, or weapon.[34]

BIOTERRORISM RISK ASSESSMENT (BTRA) A Science and Technology Directorate (S&T) program aimed at providing a comprehensive, quantitative assessment of bioterrorism risk to the homeland to inform investments; to aid in identifying threats, vulnerabilities, and knowledge gaps; and to support strategic risk management planning.[35]

BLACK In the information processing context, denotes data, text, equipment, processes, systems, or installations associated with unencrypted information that requires no emanations security protection. For example, electronic signals are "black" if bearing unclassified information.[36]

BLACK FORCES A term used by NATO forces during the Cold War in reporting of intelligence on Warsaw Pact exercises, to denote those units represent Warsaw Pact forces during such exercises.

BLACK LIST An official counterintelligence listing of actual or potential hostile collaborators, sympathizers, intelligence suspects, or other persons viewed as threatening to the security of friendly military forces.[37]

BLACK PRODUCTS Products that purport to emanate from a source other than the true one are known as black products. Black products are best used to support strategic plans. Gray and black products are always covert because secrecy is key to their success. Credibility is key to successful products because the use and discovery of untruthful information irrevocably damages or destroys their and their originator's credibility.[38]

BLACK SITE 1. Classified, secret facilities where defense and/or intelligence activities are conducted; reporter Seymour M. Hersh wrote in 2005, "All the so-called 'black' programs had one element in common: the Secretary of Defense, or his deputy, had to conclude that the normal military classification restraints did not provide enough security."[39] 2. A "hidden global internment network is a central element in the CIA's unconventional war on terrorism. It depends on the cooperation of foreign intelligence services, and on keeping even basic information about the system secret from the public, foreign officials and nearly all members of Congress charged with overseeing the CIA's covert actions. The existence and locations of the facilities—referred to as 'black sites' in classified White House, CIA, Justice Department and congressional documents—are known to only a handful of officials in the United States and, usually, only to the president and a few top intelligence officers in each host country."[40] 3. "In some cases, we determined that individuals we have captured pose a significant threat or may have intelligence that we and our allies need to have to prevent new attacks. Many are Al Qaeda operatives or Taliban fighters trying to conceal their identities. And they withhold information that could save American lives. In these cases, it has been necessary to move these individuals to an environment where they can be held secretly, questioned by experts and, when appropriate, prosecuted for terrorist acts."[41] 4. The Chicago Police Department operates an off-the-books interrogation compound, rendering Americans unable to be found by family or attorneys while locked inside what lawyers say is the domestic equivalent of a CIA black site. Alleged police practices at Homan Square, according to those familiar with the facility who spoke out to the *Guardian* after its investigation into Chicago police abuse, include: keeping arrestees out of official booking databases; beating by police, resulting in head wounds; shackling for prolonged periods; denying attorneys access to the "secure" facility; holding people without legal counsel for between 12 and 24 hours, including people as young as 15 years old.[42]

BLACK WIDOW To sift through it all, the agency has the world's largest collection of data-eating supercomputers. Its newest, code-named "Black Widow," is a colossal $17.5 million Cray computer made up of sixteen tall cabinets crammed with thousands of processors. It is able to achieve speeds of hundreds of teraflops—hundreds of trillions of operations a second—and the NSA predicts that it will soon break the petaflop barrier, plowing through phone calls, e-mails, and other data at more than a quadrillion operations a second.[43]

BLOW To expose—often unintentionally—personnel, installations, or other elements of a clandestine activity or organization.[44]

BLOWBACK Unintended consequences from an operation that could result in bad publicity if discovered. As an example of blowback, Ralph McGehee

writes that during the "Cultural Revolution in China, the Agency's huge radio transmitters on Taiwan broadcast items as if they were continuations of
mainland programs." McGehee writes that during the "Cultural Revolution
in China, the Agency's huge radio transmitters on Taiwan broadcast items as
if they were continuations of mainland programs. Their broadcasts indicate
the revolution was getting out of hand and was much more serious than it
actually was. These broadcasts were picked up by the Agency's Foreign
Broadcast Information Service (FBIS) and included in its daily booklets of
transcriptions from the mainland. From there the information was picked up
by other offices of the Agency and reported as hard intelligence . . . here was
a dangerous cycle. Agency disinformation, mistaken as fact, seeped into the
files of U.S. government agencies and the CIA itself. It became fixed as fact
in the minds of employees who had no idea where it had originated." One of
the major dangers of disinformation is blowback, in which false information
is believed to be true.[45] *See* DISINFORMATION; HUGGER-MUGGER

BLUE LANTERN A Department of State program administered by the Office of Defense Trade Controls Compliance designed to verify appropriate
end-use, end-users, and final destination of commercial defense exports.[46]

BLUE PAPER On April 11, 1940, FBI director Hoover institutes a special
reporting procedure governing senior FBI officials' written communications
about especially sensitive and administrative matters. Such reports were to be
prepared on colored paper (first blue and then pink) to preclude their serial-
ization in the FBI's central records system. Hoover terminated this reporting
procedure in 1950. Thereafter, FBI officials reported such information in
"informal" memoranda (plain white non-letterhead paper), which were then
maintained in office files until destroyed.[47]

BLUE TEAM/RED TEAM CONCEPT *See* A-TEAM/B-TEAM
CONCEPT

BOLO "BOLO" is for "Be on the Look Out.[48]

BONA FIDES Documents, information, action, codes, or other indications
offered by an unknown or otherwise suspected individual to establish his or
her good faith, identification, dependability, truthfulness, and motivation.

BOOTLEGGING Informal agreements by intelligence officers to share
data outside established, formal channels; seen as a practice between analysts
to share data by bypassing more formal channels of communication.[49] *See*
STOVEPIPE WARNING

BORDER FIELD INTELLIGENCE CENTER (BORFIC) Originally established as the Border Patrol Field Intelligence Center in 2004 in El Paso, Texas, BORFIC conducts all-source intelligence activities to support the border security mission of the BP and other DHS and CBP elements to predict, detect, deter, and interdict terrorists, terrorist weapons, and human traffickers and contraband smugglers entering the United States. In October 2007, the organization was fully integrated into the CBP OIOC and its name changed to the Border Field Intelligence Center. BORFIC is responsible for supporting security efforts on both the northern and southern borders. It exchanges intelligence and law enforcement information with numerous federal, state, local, and tribal organizations agencies and actively participates in several interagency and bilateral groups. These include the El Paso Interagency Intelligence Working Group, which includes EPIC, DoD's Joint Task Force-North, and the FBI; the Bilateral Interdiction Working Group with Mexico, and the Integrated Border Intelligence Teams (IBETS).[50]

BORDER VIOLENCE INTELLIGENCE CELL (BVIC) Established January 2008 to provide intelligence support for ICE weapons-smuggling investigations and government-wide efforts to combat violence along the United States–Mexico border. The BVIC is located at EPIC within the Crime–Terror Nexus Unit and works closely with Intelligence & Analysis' Homeland Intelligence Support Team and other partners at EPIC.[51]

BORN CLASSIFIED Information that is considered a government secret as soon as it comes into existence. Under the information control provisions of the 1946 Atomic Energy Act, practically all information related to nuclear weapons and nuclear energy is "born classified": no governmental act is necessary to classify the information. Moreover, the information, defined as Restricted Data, remains secret until the government affirmatively determines that it may be published. A question latent in the language of the act is whether privately developed or privately generated atomic energy information developed or generated without government funds and without access to classified government documents is Restricted Data, and thus subject to the act.[52]

BOT MASTER The controller of a botnet that, from a remote location, provides direction to the compromised computers in the botnet.[53]

BOTNET A collection of computers compromised by malicious code and controlled across a network.[54]

BOUNDLESS INFORMANT The Boundless Informant documents show the agency collecting almost 3 billion pieces of intelligence from U.S. computer networks over a 30-day period ending in March 2013. One document says it is designed to give NSA officials answers to questions like, "What type of coverage do we have on country X" in "near real-time by asking the SIGINT [signals intelligence] infrastructure." An NSA factsheet about the program, acquired by *The Guardian*, says, "The tool allows users to select a country on a map and view the metadata volume and select details about the collections against that country." Under the heading "Sample use cases," the factsheet also states the tool shows information including: "How many records (and what type) are collected against a particular country."[55]

BREAK EVEN ANALYSIS Variant of cost-benefit analysis that estimates the threshold value at which a policy alternative's costs equal its benefits. Analysts have applied this technique to homeland security by calculating the minimum threat probability required for the risk reduction benefits of a security policy to exceed the costs. If decision makers believe the actual threat is greater than the calculated break-even threat level, then the expected benefits of the policy exceed the costs. The technique also may be applied to other uncertain parameters in the analysis.[56]

BREVITY CODE A code providing no security but which has as its sole purpose the shortening of messages rather than the concealment of their content. Approved brevity codes may be used when preparing military records, publications, correspondence, messages, operation plans, orders, and reports.[57]

BRIEF ENCOUNTER A very short meeting between two people when a short message may be exchanged. Everyone will see the contact, but it will appear to most people as an innocent one, such as asking for directions or two acquaintances saying "haven't seen you in a long time."

BRIEFING The act of giving in advance specific instructions or information, usually in an oral presentation; the preparation of an individual for a specific operation by describing the situation to be encountered, the methods to be employed, and the objective.[58]

BRITISH TEN-YEAR RULE According to Richard Betts, a scholar on strategy, "Those who see the whole interwar period [after World War I] as testimony to Britain's failure to get ready for World War II consider the ten-year rule the perfect symbol of the complacency that led to appeasement.

According to legend, the assumption that no war would occur for at least a decade guided British defense estimates and planning (the rule was renewed annually from 1919 to the early 1930s). In hindsight, the ten-year rule seems arbitrary, and, since it allegedly retarded defense expenditures, foolish."[59]

BROWSING Act of searching through IS (information system) storage to locate or acquire information, without necessarily knowing the existence or format of information being sought.[60]

BRUSH CONTACT A discreet, momentary contact between an intelligence officer and his or her agent, usually prearranged, during which material or oral information is passed.[61]

BUG Small electronic listening, video, or recording device.

BUILDING COMMUNITIES OF TRUST INITIATIVE The Building Communities of Trust (BCOT) initiative focuses on developing trust among law enforcement, fusion centers, and the communities they serve to address the challenges of crime and terrorism prevention. Since initial implementation, the BCOT initiative has been administered primarily by the Nationwide Suspicious Activity Reporting (SAR) Initiative (NSI), a program that provides law enforcement with a capacity for gathering, documenting, processing, analyzing, and sharing suspicious activity reports about behaviors that have a potential nexus to terrorism.[62]

BURDEN The impact on the public of an information collection or record keeping; specifically: burden means the total time, effort, or financial resources expended by persons to generate, maintain, retain, or disclose or provide information to or for a federal agency, including: (i) reviewing instructions; (ii) developing, acquiring, installing, and utilizing technology and systems for the purpose of collecting, validating, and verifying information; (iii) developing, acquiring, installing, and utilizing technology and systems for the purpose of processing and maintaining information; (iv) developing, acquiring, installing, and utilizing technology and systems for the purpose of disclosing and providing information; (v) adjusting the existing ways to comply with any previously applicable instructions and requirements; (vi) training personnel to be able to respond to a collection of information; (vii) searching data sources; (viii) completing and reviewing the collection of information; and (ix) transmitting, or otherwise disclosing the information.[63]

BUREAU OF ENERGY RESOURCES Energy is at the nexus of national security, economic prosperity, and the environment. The Department of

State's work in national security, bilateral and multilateral diplomacy, commercial advocacy, environment, and development are widely affected by energy concerns. The Bureau of Energy Resources (ENR) is working to ensure that all our diplomatic relationships advance our interests in having access to secure, reliable, and ever-cleaner sources of energy. The Bureau of Energy Resources has three core objectives: Energy Diplomacy; Energy Transformation; Energy Transparency and Access.[64]

BUREAU OF INTELLIGENCE AND RESEARCH (INR) The primary mission is to harness intelligence to serve U.S. diplomacy. Drawing on all-source intelligence, INR provides value-added independent analysis of events to U.S. State Department policymakers; ensures that intelligence activities support foreign policy and national security purposes; and serves as the focal point in the State Department for ensuring policy review of sensitive counterintelligence and law enforcement activities around the world. The bureau also analyzes geographical and international boundary issues. The Bureau of Intelligence and Research is a member of the U.S. intelligence community.[65]

BURN BAG The informal name given to a container (usually a paper bag or some other waste receptacle) that holds sensitive or classified documents which are to be destroyed by fire or pulping after a certain period of time. The most common usage of burn bags is by government institutions, in the destruction of materials deemed classified.[66]

BURN NOTICE An official statement by one intelligence agency to other agencies, domestic or foreign, that an individual or group is unreliable for any of a variety of reasons.[67]

BYE Unclassified term that describes sensitive programs and operational data.[68]

NOTES

1. Berridge, G. R. and Lloyd, Lorna (eds.). *Palgrave Macmillan Dictionary of Diplomacy*. 3rd ed. New York: Palgrave Macmillan, 2012.

2. U.S. Department of Justice, Office of Justice Programs. *Investigations Involving the Internet and Computer Networks*. January 2007. Accessed March 7, 2015. https://www.ncjrs.gov/pdffiles1/nij/210798.pdf.

3. United States Senate, Select Committee to Study Governmental Operations with Respect to Intelligence Activities (Church Committee). *Final Report*. Book 1. April 26, 1976. Accessed January 11, 2015. https://archive.org/details/finalreportof-sel01unit.

4. Department of Defense, Under Secretary of Defense for Intelligence. "National Industrial Security Program Operating Manual." February 28, 2006. Accessed September 22, 2015. http://www.dss.mil/documents/odaa/nispom2006-5220.pdf.

5. U.S. Department of Defense. Center for Development of Security Excellence. *Glossary of Security Terms and Definitions.* November 2012. Accessed February 16, 2015. http://www.cdse.edu/documents/cdse/Glossary_Handbook.pdf.

6. Department of Homeland Security, Risk Steering Committee. *DHS Risk Lexicon.* September 2010. Accessed February 14, 2015. http://www.dhs.gov/dhs-risk-lexicon.

7. North Atlantic Treaty Organization. *NATO Glossary of Terms and Definitions.* NATO Standardization Agency, 2008. Accessed July 2, 2015. https://fas.org/irp/doddir/other/nato2008.pdf.

8. Jan Goldman, *Intelligence Warning Terminology*, Joint Military Intelligence College, October 2001, accessed July 3, 2015. https://archive.org/details/JMICIntelligencelwarnterminology.

9. Central Intelligence Agency. *A Consumer's Guide to Intelligence: Gaining Knowledge and Foreknowledge of the World around Us.* Office of Public Affairs. Washington, DC: National Technical Information Service, 1999.

10. Central Intelligence Agency. *A Consumer's Guide to Intelligence: Gaining Knowledge and Foreknowledge of the World Around Us.* Office of Public Affairs. Washington, DC: National Technical Information Service, 1999.

11. Jan Goldman, *Intelligence Warning Terminology*, Joint Military Intelligence College, October 2001, accessed July 3, 2015. https://archive.org/details/JMICIntelligencelwarnterminology.

12. Denbeaux, Mark P., Hafetz, Jonathan and Denbeaux, Joshua. *Guantanamo: America's Battle Lab.* Seton Hall Law Center for Policy and Research, 2014. Accessed January 12, 2015. https://news.vice.com/article/how-guantanamo-became-americas-interrogation-battle-lab.

13. Ashley, Richard. "Bayesian Decision Analysis in International Relations Forecasting: The Analysis of Subjective Processes." In *Forecasting in International Relations: Theory, Methods, Problems, Prospects*, edited by Nazli Choucri and Thomas W. Robinson, 149–71. San Francisco: WH Freeman, 1978.

14. Sinclair, Robert. "A Review of Who the Hell Are We Fighting? The Story of Sam Adams and the Vietnam Intelligence Wars." (Michael Hanover, Steerforth Press, 2006). *Studies in Intelligence* 50, no. 4: 2006. Accessed January 25, 2016. https://www.cia.gov/library/center-for-the-study-of-intelligence/csi-publications/csi-studies/studies/vol50no4/a-review-of-who-the-hell-are-we-fighting-the-story-of-sam-adams-and-the-vietnam-intelligence-wars.html.

15. Clark, Wesley. "NATO Speech: Press Conference SACEUR, NATO HQ, 27 April 1999." September 1, 1999. Accessed September 22, 2015. http://www.nato.int/kosovo/press/p990916a.htm.

16. Center for Democracy & Technology (CDT), *A Primer on Behavioral Advertising*, July 31, 2008. Accessed January 6, 2015. https://cdt.org/insight/a-primer-on-behavioral-advertising.

17. U.S. General Accountability Office. *Aviation Security: TSA Should Limit Future Funding for Behavior Detection Activities.* GAO-14-159, November 2013. Accessed February 15, 2015. http://www.gao.gov/products/GAO-14-159.

18. Behavioral Insights Team. *About Us.* Accessed January 30, 2015. http://www. behaviouralinsights.co.uk/about-us; also see Wintour, Patrick. "Government's Behaviour Insight Team to Become a Mutual and Sell Services." *The Guardian*, February 4, 2014. Accessed January 30, 2015. http://www.theguardian.com/politics/2014/feb/05/government-behaviour-insight-nudge-mutual-nesta-funding.

19. U.S. Department of State. *Diplomatic Dictionary.* Accessed March 6, 2015. http://diplomacy.state.gov/discoverdiplomacy/references/169792.htm.

20. Executive Office of the President. *Big Data: Seizing Opportunities, Preserving Values.* May 2014. Accessed January 11, 2015. http://www.whitehouse.gov/sites/default/files/docs/big_data_privacy_report_may_1_2014.pdf.

21. Office of Science and Technology Policy. *Big Data is a Big Deal.* March 29, 2012. Accessed February 15, 2015. http://www.whitehouse.gov/blog/2012/03/29/big-data-big-deal.

22. Defense Forensics and Biometrics Agency. *DoD Biometrics Enterprise Architecture (Integrated) v2.0 Common Biometric Vocabulary.* April 2013. Accessed January 15, 2015. http://www.biometrics.dod.mil/Files/Documents/References/common%20biometric%20vocabulary.pdf.

23. Defense Forensics and Biometrics Agency. *DoD Biometrics Enterprise Architecture (Integrated) v2.0 Common Biometric Vocabulary.* April 2013. Accessed January 15, 2015. http://www.biometrics.dod.mil/Files/Documents/References/common%20biometric%20vocabulary.pdf.

24. *The Convention on the Prohibition of the Development, Production and Stockpiling of Bacteriological (Biological) and Toxin Weapons and on their Destruction*, referred to as the 1975 *Biological Weapons Convention (BWC)* or *Biological and Toxin Weapons Convention (BTWC)*, stipulates that the signatories must not "develop, produce, stockpile, or otherwise acquire or retain" biological weapons, and does not distinguish between offensive and defensive intentions. Also see Shea, Dana A. "The National Biodefense Analysis and Countermeasures Center: Issues for Congress." *CRS Reports for Congress*, February 15, 2007. Accessed January 6, 2015. http://www.fas.org/sgp/crs/homesec/RL32891.pdf.

25. Defense Forensics and Biometrics Agency. *DoD Biometrics Enterprise Architecture (Integrated) v2.0 Common Biometric Vocabulary.* April 2013. Accessed January 15, 2015. http://www.biometrics.dod.mil/Files/Documents/References/common%20biometric%20vocabulary.pdf.

26. Nuffield Council on Bioethics. *The Forensic Use of Bioinformation: Ethical Issues Report Launch.* November 2007. Accessed February 15, 2015. http://nuffieldbioethics.org/news/2007/the-forensic-use-of-bioinformation-ethical-issues-report/.

27. Defense Forensics and Biometrics Agency. *DoD Biometrics Enterprise Architecture (Integrated) v2.0 Common Biometric Vocabulary.* April 2013. Accessed January 15, 2015. http://www.biometrics.dod.mil/Files/Documents/References/common%20biometric%20vocabulary.pdf.

28. Federal Bureau of Investigation. *About the Biometric Center of Excellence (BCOE)*. Accessed January 16, 2015. https://www.fbi.gov/about-us/cjis/fingerprints_biometrics/biometric-center-of-excellence.

29. Defense Forensics and Biometrics Agency. *DoD Biometrics Enterprise Architecture (Integrated) v2.0 Common Biometric Vocabulary*. April 2013. Accessed January 15, 2015. http://www.biometrics.dod.mil/Files/Documents/References/common%20biometric%20vocabulary.pdf.

30. Defense Forensics and Biometrics Agency. *DoD Biometrics Enterprise Architecture (Integrated) v2.0 Common Biometric Vocabulary*. April 2013. Accessed January 15, 2015. http://www.biometrics.dod.mil/Files/Documents/References/common%20biometric%20vocabulary.pdf.

31. Defense Forensics and Biometrics Agency. *DoD Biometrics Enterprise Architecture (Integrated) v2.0 Common Biometric Vocabulary*. April 2013. Accessed January 15, 2015. http://www.biometrics.dod.mil/Files/Documents/References/common%20biometric%20vocabulary.pdf.

32. Defense Forensics and Biometrics Agency. *DoD Biometrics Enterprise Architecture (Integrated) v2.0 Common Biometric Vocabulary*. April 2013. Accessed January 15, 2015. http://www.biometrics.dod.mil/Files/Documents/References/common%20biometric%20vocabulary.pdf.

33. Defense Forensics and Biometrics Agency. *DoD Biometrics Enterprise Architecture (Integrated) v2.0 Common Biometric Vocabulary*. April 2013. Accessed January 15, 2015. http://www.biometrics.dod.mil/Files/Documents/References/common%20biometric%20vocabulary.pdf.

34. Department of the Army. *ADRP 2.0 Intelligence*. August 2012. Accessed January 11, 2015. http://armypubs.army.mil/doctrine/DR_pubs/dr_a/pdf/adrp2_0.pdf.

35. Department of Homeland Security, Risk Steering Committee. *DHS Risk Lexicon*. September, 2010. Accessed February 14, 2015. http://www.dhs.gov/dhs-risk-lexicon.

36. Department of State, "Definitions of Diplomatic Security Terms." *Foreign Affairs Manual*. 12FAM090. November 12, 2014. Accessed February 27, 2015. http://www.state.gov/documents/organization/88330.pdf.

37. United States Senate, Select Committee to Study Governmental Operations with Respect to Intelligence Activities (Church Committee). *Final Report*. Book 1. April 26, 1976. Accessed January 11, 2015. https://archive.org/details/finalreportof-sel01unit.

38. Department of the Army. *Psychological Operations*. FM 3-05.30, MCRP 3-40.6, April 2005 (A1-A2). Accessed January 10, 2015. http://www.fas.org/irp/doddir/army/fm3-05-30.pdf.

39. Hersh, Seymour M. "The Gray Zone." *The New Yorker* 24, No. 5 (2004). Accessed February 24, 2015. http://www.newyorker.com/magazine/2004/05/24/the-gray-zone.

40. Priest, Dana. "CIA Holds Terror Suspects in Secret Prisons." *The Washington Post* November 2, 2005. Accessed February 24, 2015. http://www.washingtonpost.com/wp-dyn/content/article/2005/11/01/AR2005110101644.html.

41. Bush, George W. *Remarks on the War on Terror.* September 6, 2006. American Presidency Project. Accessed February 24, 2015. https://www.youtube.com/watch?v=qbFs-AxVv6k.

42. Ackerman, Spencer. "The Disappeared: Chicago Police Detain Americans at Abuse-laden 'Black Site.'" *The Guardian,* February 24, 2015. Accessed February 24, 2015. http://www.theguardian.com/us-news/2015/feb/24/chicago-police-detain-americans-black-site.

43. Bamford, James. The *Shadow Factory: The Ultra-secret NSA from 9/11 to the Eavesdropping on America* (New York: Random House, 2009), 3; Hentoff, Nat. "Obama's Black Widow." *Village Voice,* December 24, 2008. Accessed February 14, 2015. http://www.villagevoice.com/2008-12-24/columns/obama-s-black-widow/full/.

44. United States Senate, Select Committee to Study Governmental Operations with Respect to Intelligence Activities (Church Committee). *Final Report.* Book 1. April 26, 1976. Accessed February 7, 2015. https://archive.org/details/finalreportof-sel01unit.

45. McGehee, Ralph W. *Deadly Deceits: My 25 Years in the CIA.* New York: Sheridan Square Publications, 1983. Zakaria, Tabassum. "U.S. Planting False Stories Common Cold War Tactic." *Reuters* February 25, 2002. http://www.fas.org/sgp/news/2002/02/re022502.html.

46. U.S. Department of State. "Political, Economic, and Intelligence Functional Bureaus." *Foreign Affairs Manual.* 1 FAM 400. July 31, 2013. Accessed February 16, 2015. http://www.state.gov/documents/organization/84192.pdf.

47. Theoharis, Athan (ed.). *The FBI: A Comprehensive Reference Guide.* Phoenix: Oryx Press, 1998. 366.

48. Federal Bureau of Investigation. *Protecting America from Terrorist Attacks: Please BOLO For Us.* Accessed January 11, 2015. http://www.fbi.gov/news/stories/2004/may/bolo052604; also see ConsortiumNews. *The Mystery of Ray McGovern's Arrest.* November 8, 2014. Accessed January 11, 2015. https://consortiumnews.com/2014/11/08/the-mystery-of-ray-mcgoverns-arrest/.

49. Jan Goldman, *Intelligence Warning Terminology,* Joint Military Intelligence College, October 2001, accessed July 3, 2015. https://archive.org/details/JMICInteligencelwarnterminology.

50. Mark A. Randol, "The Department of Homeland Security Intelligence Enterprise: Operational Overview and Oversight Challenges for Congress," *CRS Report for Congress* R40602, March 19, 2010, accessed February 3, 2016, https://www.fas.org/sgp/crs/homesec/R40602.pdf.

51. Lake, Jennifer E., Finklea, Kristin M., Eddy, Mark, Franco, Celinda, Haddal, Chad C., Krouse, William J., and Randol, Mark A. "Southwest Border Violence: Issues in Identifying and Measuring Spillover Violence." *CRS Reports for Congress* R41075, February 16, 2010. Accessed January 25, 2016. http://trac.syr.edu/immigration/library/P4351.pdf.

52. Chen, Mary M. "The Progressive Case and the Atomic Energy Act: Waking to the Dangers of Government Information Controls." *George Washington Law Review* 48, no. 2 (1979–1980): 163–311.

53. National Initiative for Cybersecurity Education. *A Glossary of Common Cybersecurity Terminology.* n.d. Accessed March 5, 2015. http://niccs.us-cert.gov/glossary.

54. National Initiative for Cybersecurity Education. *A Glossary of Common Cybersecurity Terminology.* n.d. Accessed March 5, 2015. http://niccs.us-cert.gov/glossary.

55. Greenwald, Glenn and MacAskill, Ewen. "Boundless Informant: The NSA's Secret Tool to Track Global Surveillance Data." *The Guardian*, June 11, 2013. Accessed February 18, 2015. http://www.theguardian.com/world/2013/jun/08/nsa-boundless-informant-global-datamining; also see Greenwald, Glenn. *No Place to Hide.* New York: Henry Holt, 2014.

56. Department of Homeland Security, Risk Steering Committee. *DHS Risk Lexicon.* September 2010. Accessed February 14, 2015. http://www.dhs.gov/dhs-risk-lexicon.

57. Department of the Army, Marine Corps Combat Development Command, Department of the Navy, *Operational Terms and Graphics*, FM 1-02 (FM 101-5), 21 September 2004. http://www.marines.mil/News/Messages/MessagesDisplay/tabid/13286/Article/173332/cancellation-of-mcrp-5-12a-operational-terms-and-graphics.aspx.

58. Office of the Director of National Intelligence. *National Intelligence: A Consumer's Guide.* 2011. Accessed January 25, 2015. http://www.dni.gov/files/documents/IC_Consumers_Guide_2011.pdf.

59. Betts, Richard. *Military Readiness: Concepts, Choices, Consequences.* Washington, DC: Brookings Institute, 1995, 53.

60. Committee for National Security Systems (CNSS). Instruction 4009. *National Information Assurance Glossary.* April 2010. Accessed January 11, 2015. http://www.ncix.gov/publications/policy/docs/CNSSI_4009.pdf.

61. Defense Intelligence Agency, Office of Counterintelligence. *CI Glossary—Terms & Definitions of Interest for DoD CI Professionals.* July 2014. Accessed January 17, 2015. https://www.hsdl.org/?view&did=699056.

62. Nationwide SAR Initiative. *Building Communities of Trust Fact Sheet.* Accessed January 24, 2015. http://nsi.ncirc.gov/documents/BCOT_Fact_Sheet.pdf.

63. Office of Management and Budget. "Controlling Paperwork Burdens on the Public." 5 *CFR* 1320. 3. Accessed January 11, 2015. http://www.gpo.gov/fdsys/pkg/CFR-2014-title5-vol3/pdf/CFR-2014-title5-vol3-chapIII.pdf.

64. U.S. State Department. *Bureau of Energy Resources.* Accessed February 16, 2015. http://www.state.gov/e/enr/; also see U.S. Department of State. "Bureau of Energy Resources." *Foreign Affairs Manual.* 1 FAM 460. October 22, 2012. Accessed February 16, 2015. http://www.state.gov/documents/organization/156858.pdf.

65. U.S. State Department. *Bureau of Intelligence and Research.* Accessed February 15, 2015. http://www.state.gov/s/inr/; also see U.S. Department of State. "Bureau of Intelligence and Research." *Foreign Affairs Manual.* 1 FAM 130. July 28, 2014. Accessed February 16, 2015. http://www.state.gov/documents/organization/205857.pdf.

66. U.S. Department of Defense. Center for Development of Security Excellence. *Glossary of Security Terms and Definitions.* November 2012. Accessed February 16, 2015. http://www.cdse.edu/documents/cdse/Glossary_Handbook.pdf.

67. Defense Intelligence Agency, Office of Counterintelligence. *CI Glossary— Terms & Definitions of Interest for DoD CI Professionals.* July 1, 2014. Accessed January 15, 2015. http://www.fas.org/irp/eprint/ci-glossary.pdf.

68. National Imagery and Mapping Agency, *NIMA Guide to Marking Classified Documents.* October 2001. Accessed January 27. 2016. https://www.fas.org/sgp/othergov/dod/nimaguide.pdf.

C

CADASTRAL DATA For the U.S. Intelligence Community, analysis of heretofore unavailable layers of cadastral data has the potential to identify a group's ideologies and economic pillars. By tying a name to a place, a cadastre can answer the difficult "who" question: Who is behind a given problem? A cadastre can also provide military commanders with detailed knowledge of the human terrain, identification of power brokers on the ground whose support or obstruction may determine mission success. More specifically, this book tells U.S. civil and military planners how cadastral information, where it exists and where it has been maintained, might improve multi-lateral reconstruction and stability (R&S) efforts.[1]

CALL-IDENTIFYING INFORMATION Dialing or signaling information that identifies the origin, direction, destination, or termination of each communication generated or received by a subscriber by means of any equipment, facility, or service of a telecommunications carrier.[2]

CALL SIGN Any combination of characters or pronounceable words that identifies a communication facility, a command, an authority, an activity, or a unit; used primarily for establishing and maintaining communications.[3]

CAMOUFLAGE An act or material that seeks to confuse or mislead. "During the Indian nuclear tests in 1999 that took much of the world by surprise, the Indians knew exactly when the spy cameras would be passing over the testing facility near Pokharan in Rajasthan Desert and, in synchrony with the satellite orbits (every three days), scientists camouflaged their preparations."[4] *See* DECEPTION

CANADIAN SECURITY INTELLIGENCE SERVICE (CSIS) CSIS is at the forefront of Canada's national security establishment, employing some of the country's most intelligent and capable men and women. The Service's role is to investigate threats, analyze information, and produce intelligence. It then reports to, and advises, the government of Canada to protect the country and its citizens. Key threats include terrorism, the proliferation of weapons of mass destruction, espionage, foreign interference, and cyber-tampering affecting critical infrastructure. CSIS programs are proactive and preemptive.[5]

CAPITOL NETWORK (CAPNET) Formerly known as Intelink-P; provides congressional intelligence consumers with connectivity to Intelink-TS.

CAPSTONE PUBLICATION The top joint doctrine publication in the hierarchy of joint publications that links joint doctrine to national strategy and the contributions of other government departments and agencies and multinational partners, and reinforces policy for command and control.[6]

CAPSTONE REQUIREMENTS DOCUMENT A document that contains performance-based requirements to facilitate development of individual operational requirements documents by providing a common framework and operational concept to guide their development.[7]

CAPTURED PERSONS Captured persons (CPERS) is the generic term given to all individuals who are captured and held by UK Armed Forces on operations overseas, whether they are prisoners of war, internees, or detainees.[8]

CARNIVORE A device provides the FBI with a "surgical" ability to intercept and collect the communications which are the subject of the lawful order while ignoring those communications which they are not authorized to intercept. This type of tool is necessary to meet the stringent requirements of the federal wiretapping statutes. The Carnivore device works much like commercial "sniffers" and other network diagnostic tools used by ISPs every day, except that it provides the FBI with a unique ability to distinguish between communications which may be lawfully intercepted and those which may not.[9]

CARVE-OUT A provision approved by the Secretary or Deputy Secretary of Defense that relieves DSS of its National Industrial Security Program obligation to perform industrial security oversight functions for a DoD SAP.[10] *See* NATIONAL INDUSTRIAL SECURITY PROGRAM

CARVER (CRITICALITY, ACCESSIBILITY, RECUPERABILITY, VULNERABILITY, EFFECT, AND RECOGNIZABILITY) A mnemonic composed of the above terms that, when applied to security risk management, are used to characterize assets.[11]

CASE OFFICER A professional employee of an intelligence or counter-intelligence organization who is responsible for providing directions for an agent operation and/or handling intelligence assets.[12] *See* AGENT

CASING Reconnaissance of an operating area, whether for surveillance or for personal or impersonal communications.

CASSANDRA In a warning context, the term refers to anyone who, like Chicken Little, announces that "the sky is falling" when in fact, only very ambiguous indications of a disastrous event actually exist. Concept and name derive from the daughter of King Priam of Troy, a prophetess of evil. A major figure in Greek mythology, one version of the Cassandra myth reports the God Apollo bestowed the gift of prophecy on Cassandra. When Cassandra denied Apollo's advances, a curse was placed on her so no one would believe her predictions, including the destruction of Troy.[13] *See* POLLYANNA

CATALYST A program to compare and link multi-INT data from multiple organizations before providing them to analysts throughout the Intelligence Community (IC). The first phase entails policy, technical, and business-process initiatives that set uniform IC standards for summarizing intelligence data. The resultant "metadata" will be submitted to automated systems that connect some of the "dots" that matter to analysts and collectors engaged in discovery and warning.[14] *See* LIBRARY OF NATIONAL INTELLIGENCE

CATASTROPHIC EVENT Means any incident, regardless of location, that results in extraordinary levels of mass casualties, damage, or disruption severely affecting the U.S. population, infrastructure, environment, economy, or government functions.[15] *See* CONTINUITY OF GOVERNMENT

CATEGORY Restrictive label applied to classified or unclassified information to limit access.[16]

CAUSAL ANALYSIS A method for analyzing the possible causal associations among a set of variables. *See* CAUSAL ASSOCIATION; CAUSAL RELATIONSHIP; CONGRUENCE ANALYSIS

CAUSAL ASSOCIATION A relationship between two variables in which a change in one brings about a change in the other. *See* CAUSAL ANALYSIS; CAUSAL RELATIONSHIP; CONGRUENCE ANALYSIS

CAUSAL RELATIONSHIP The relationship of cause and effect; the cause is the necessary act or event that produces the effect. *See* CAUSAL ANALYSIS; CAUSAL ASSOCIATION; CONGRUENCE ANALYSIS

CAVEAT, CAVEATED INFORMATION 1. Information subject to one of the authorized control markings under Section 9 of DCID 1/7, *Security Controls on the Dissemination of Intelligence Information.*[17] 2. A designator used with a classification to further limit the dissemination of restricted information.[18] *See* CLASSIFICATION MARKINGS

CAVERN A naturally occurring underground opening or a large human-made underground opening.[19]

CENTER FOR THE STUDY OF INTELLIGENCE (CSI) A division of the CIA that publishes *Studies in Intelligence*, the journal of the American Intelligence Professional; hosts independent research and publish books and monographs on intelligence topics; publishes key documentary collections from the Cold War; conducts oral history projects; produces monographs on CIA history and the history of intelligence; supports State Department's *Foreign Relations of the United States* (FRUS) series.[20]

CENTER OF GRAVITY The source of power that provides moral or physical strength, freedom of action, or will to act.[21]

CENTRAL UNITED STATES REGISTRY FOR NORTH ATLANTIC TREATY ORGANIZATION (NATO) The North Atlantic Treaty Organization (NATO) controls its classified records through a registry system in which individual documents are numbered and listed in inventories. The Central United States Registry is located in Arlington, Virginia, and oversees more than 125 sub-registries domestically and abroad.[22]

CHAIN OF CUSTODY Safeguarding, and analysis lifecycle by documenting each person who handled the evidence, the date/time it was collected or transferred, and the purpose for the transfer.[23]

CHAIN OF EVIDENCE A process and record that shows who obtained the evidence; where and when the evidence was obtained; who secured the evidence; and who had control or possession of the evidence. The "sequencing" of the chain of evidence follows this order: collection and identification; analysis; storage; preservation; presentation in court; return to owner.[24]

CHAOS THEORY A means of explaining the dynamics of sensitive systems that seeks to find the underlying order in apparently random data or apparently random systems; used especially to understand the functioning of dysfunctional organizations.

CHARACTER INVESTIGATION (CI) An inquiry into the activities of an individual, designed to develop pertinent information pertaining to trustworthiness and suitability for a position of trust as related to character and reliability.[25]

CHARGÉ D'AFFAIRES Formerly, a chargé d'affaires was the title of a chief of mission, inferior in rank to an ambassador or a minister. It is still used as the title of the head of a U.S. mission where the United States and other nations do not have full diplomatic relations. Today, with the a.i. (ad interim) added, it designates the senior officer taking charge for the interval when a chief of mission is absent from his/her post or the position is vacant.[26]

CHATHAM HOUSE RULES The Chatham House Rule reads as follows: When a meeting, or part thereof, is held under the Chatham House Rule, participants are free to use the information received, but neither the identity nor the affiliation of the speaker(s), nor that of any other participant, may be revealed.[27]

CHECKLIST APPROACH The principal instrument for practical evaluation of associating observation with a predetermined record or list.

CHEMICAL TERRORISM RISK ASSESSMENT (CTRA) A scientific and technical program aimed at providing a comprehensive, quantitative assessment of chemical terrorism risk to the homeland to inform investments; to aid in identifying threats, vulnerabilities, and knowledge gaps; and to support strategic risk management planning.[28]

CHEMICAL WEAPONS CONVENTION (CWC) The 1997 Convention aims to eliminate an entire category of weapons of mass destruction by prohibiting the development, production, acquisition, stockpiling, retention, transfer, or use of chemical weapons by States Parties. States Parties, in turn, must take the steps necessary to enforce that prohibition in respect of persons (natural or legal) within their jurisdiction. All States Parties have agreed to chemically disarm by destroying any stockpiles of chemical weapons they may hold and any facilities which produced them, as well as any chemical weapons they abandoned on the territory of other States Parties in the past. States Parties have also agreed to create a verification regime for certain toxic chemicals and their precursors.[29]

CHILLING EFFECT The very essence of a chilling effect is an act of deterrence. While one would normally say that people are deterred, it seems proper to speak of an activity as being chilled. The two concepts go hand in hand, of course, in that an activity is chilled if people are deterred from participating in that activity. Although an individual's decision not to engage in certain behavior may be influenced by a wide range of stimuli, in law the acknowledged basis of deterrence is the fear of punishment—be it by fine, imprisonment, imposition of civil liability, or deprivation of governmental benefit. Thus, it is apparent that an individual may be deterred or an activity chilled by the threatened operation of virtually any penal statute or by the potential application of any civil sanction. Indeed, these regulating rules are designed to have this precise effect.[30]

CI INFORMATION Knowledge or intelligence regarding CI activities. This includes knowledge or intelligence regarding CI programs, budgets, trends, and other items related to CI.[31]

CIA RECORDS SEARCH TOOL (CREST) Since 2000, CIA has installed and maintained an electronic full-text searchable system, which it has named CREST (the CIA Records Search Tool), at NARA II in College Park, Maryland. The CREST system is the publically accessible repository of the subset of CIA records reviewed under the 25-year program in electronic format (manually reviewed and released records are accessioned directly into the National Archives in their original format). Over 11 million pages have been released in electronic format and reside on the CREST database, from which researchers have printed about 1.1 million pages.[32]

CIPHER Any cryptographic system in which arbitrary symbols (or groups of symbols) represent units of plain text of regular length, usually single letters; units of plain text are rearranged; or both, in accordance with certain predetermined rules.[33]

CIPHER BLOCK CHAINING MESSAGE AUTHENTICATION CODE (CBC-MAC) A secret-key block-cipher algorithm used to encrypt data and to generate a message authentication code (MAC) to provide assurance that the payload and the associated data are authentic.

CIPHER KEY Secret, cryptographic key that is used by the key expansion routine to generate a set of round keys; can be pictured as a rectangular array of bytes, having four rows and columns.

CIPHER TEXT Enciphered information.[34]

CIRCULAR INTELLIGENCE Information that is reported as an unconfirmed fact or assessment that is subsequently repeated in another agency or analyst's assessment as a true report. The first agency or analyst sees it in someone else's report and seizes on it as independent proof that his or her own information has been confirmed by another source. For example, prior to the Yom Kippur War in 1973 between Israel and Egypt, circular intelligence was a contributing factor to lull Israeli intelligence into a false sense of security. For example, "When the Israelis saw that the U.S. was not worried by the buildup, they confirmed their earlier judgments. If Washington was unruffled, concluded Mrs. Meir [Prime Minister Golda Meir of Israel] and her inner policy group on 5 October, then why should they be? It was a classic and vicious example of 'circular intelligence.' (Washington was not worried about Egypt's military buildup because they received intelligence from the Israelis that there was nothing to worry about.)" Egypt attacked the next day.[35] *See* HUGGER-MUGGER

CITIZENSHIP AND IMMIGRAITON SERVICES (USCIS) The agency that oversees lawful immigration to the United States. USCIS establishes immigration services, policies, and priorities to preserve America's legacy as a nation of immigrants while ensuring that no one is admitted who is a threat to public safety. USCIS is neither a law enforcement agency nor a member of the intelligence community, and the vast majority of its funding is derived from fees collected from immigration benefit applicants and petitioners. Thus its activities are limited to adjudication of immigration benefits, which includes conducting background checks on the individuals and organizations who submit applications and petitions, as well as the intended beneficiaries. As part of that process, USCIS collects biometrics, in the form of digital photographs and fingerprints.[36]

CIVIL AUTHORITIES Those elected and appointed officers and employees who constitute the government of the United States, the governments of the 50 states, the District of Columbia, the Commonwealth of Puerto Rico, U.S. territories, and political subdivisions thereof.[37]

CIVIL EMERGENCY Any occasion or instance for which, in the determination of the president, federal assistance is needed to supplement state and local efforts and capabilities to save lives and to protect property and public health and safety, or to lessen or avert the threat of a catastrophe in any part of the United States.[38]

CIVILIAN INTELLIGENCE COMMUNITY The intelligence community (IC) comprises 17 different organizations, or IC elements, across the federal government. Of these, eight are civilian IC elements—the Central Intelligence Agency (CIA), Department of Homeland Security's Office of Intelligence and Analysis (DHS I&A), Department of Energy's Office of Intelligence and Counterintelligence (DOE IN), Department of State's Bureau of Intelligence and Research (State INR), Department of the Treasury's Office of Intelligence and Analysis (Treasury OIA), Drug Enforcement Administration's Office of National Security Intelligence (DEA NN), Federal Bureau of Investigation (FBI), and the Office of the Director of National Intelligence (ODNI). Like other federal agencies, these civilian IC elements rely on contractors to meet a variety of mission needs.[39] *See* INTELLIGENCE-INDUSTRIAL COMPLEX

CLANDESTINE Any activity that is designed not to be detected by a local security service; a concealed, hidden, secret, or surreptitious operation conducted without the knowledge of anyone but the organization conducting the operation or investigation.

CLANDESTINE INTELLIGENCE Intelligence information collected by clandestine sources.[40]

CLANDESTINE OPERATION A secret intelligence collection activity or covert political, economic, propaganda, or paramilitary action conducted to ensure the secrecy of the operation.[41]

CLASSIFICATION 1. The act or process by which information is determined to be classified information; the process of determining and identifying the information that should be protected in the interests of national security—the information that should be concealed from the enemies and potential enemies of the United States.[42] 2. A category or level to which national security information and materials are assigned to denote the degree of damage that unauthorized disclosure would cause to national defense or foreign relations and to denote the degree of protection required.[43] *See* CAVEAT; CLASSIFICATION LEVELS

CLASSIFICATION AND CONTROL MARKING SYSTEM Classification and control markings shall be applied explicitly and uniformly when creating, disseminating, and using classified and unclassified information to maximize information sharing while protecting sources, methods, and activities from unauthorized or unintentional disclosure. The classification and control markings system established by this Directive is implemented through the Controlled Access Program Coordination Office's (CAPCO) Authorized Classification and Control Markings Register (hereinafter referred to as the CAPCO Register) and the accompanying *Intelligence Community Classification and Control Markings Implementation Manual* (hereinafter referred to as the Implementation Manual). Together these documents define and describe the IC's classification and control markings system.[44] *See* CLASSIFICATION MARKINGS, CONTROLLED ACCESS PROGRAM COORDINATION OFFICE, CUI REGISTRY

CLASSIFICATION BLOCK Consists of the following: (1) The identity, by name or personal identifier and position of the OCA (Official Classification Authority), (2) The agency and office of origin, (3) Declassification instructions, (4) Reason for classification.[45]

CLASSIFICATION BY ASSOCIATION (CLASIFICATION BY COMPILATION) A situation where the mere fact that two or more items of information are related is in itself classified; can be associated with masking, which is the act of classifying one piece of information solely to protect a separate item of information.[46]

CLASSIFICATION BY COMPILATION Two or more items of unclassified information, when put together create some additional factor which warrants classification. This is termed "classification by compilation."[47]

CLASSIFICATION CATEGORIES Information shall not be considered for classification unless its unauthorized disclosure could reasonably be expected to cause identifiable or describable damage to the national security in accordance with section 1.2 of this order, and it pertains to one or more of the following: (a) military plans, weapons systems, or operations; (b) foreign government information; (c) intelligence activities (including covert action), intelligence sources or methods, or cryptology; (d) foreign relations or foreign activities of the United States, including confidential sources; (e) scientific, technological, or economic matters relating to the national security; (f) U.S. government programs for safeguarding nuclear materials or facilities; (g) vulnerabilities or capabilities of systems, installations, infrastructures, projects, plans, or protection services relating to the national security; or (h) the development, production, or use of weapons of mass destruction.[48]

CLASSIFICATION GUIDES A documentary form of classification guidance issued by an Original Classification Authority (OCA) that identifies the elements of information regarding a specific subject that must be classified and establishes the level and duration of classification for each such element. A classification guide is created for any system, program, policy, or project under the cognizance of the OCA.[49]

CLASSIFICATION LEVELS A system of designations assigned to specific elements of information based on the potential damage to national security if disclosed to unauthorized persons. A classification level is assigned to information owned by, produced by or for, or controlled by the U.S. government. The three levels, in descending order of potential damage, are Top Secret, Secret, and Confidential:[50]

Top Secret: The highest classification level applied to information; unauthorized disclosure reasonably could be expected to cause exceptionally grave damage to national security. Top Secret access authorizations or clearances are based on background investigations conducted by OPM or another government agency, which conducts personnel security investigations.

Secret: The second highest level; unauthorized disclosure reasonably could be expected to cause serious damage to national security that the original classification authority is able to identify or describe.

Confidential: The third highest level; unauthorized disclosure reasonably could be expected to cause some form of damage to national security.

CLASSIFICATION MARKINGS (CONTROL MARKINGS, DISSEMINATION CONTROL MARKINGS) The physical act of indicating on classified material the assigned classification or change therein, together with such additional information as may be required to show authority for the classification or change and any special limitation on such material.[51] There are several types of markings, including portion, banner, and declassify on markings.[52] Marking has six purposes: Alert the holder that the item requires protection; Advise the holder of the level of protection; Show what is classified and what is not; Show how long the information requires protection; Give the information about the origin of the classification; Provide warnings about any special security requirements.[53] *See* CLASSIFICATION AND CONTROL MARKING SYSTEM; CUI REGISTRY

CLASSIFICATION PRIESTHOOD National classification elite is a kind of secret society, closed to the uninitiated. It is a sect marked by a rigorous internal discipline, highly developed rituals, a strict hierarchy, and a consistent philosophy. Central to this philosophy is the principle of compartmentalization, which holds that the best way to control information is to break it into little pieces, and never to allow too much to be assembled in one place. The classification priesthood has developed an elaborate system to protect its secrets. The priesthood makes a distinction between classifying documents and classifying the information contained within them.[54]

CLASSIFIED AT BIRTH Based on the "born secret" interpretation of the Atomic Energy Act of 1954 wherein a "writer or researcher working from unclassified sources could combine information in such a way as to produce concepts that are 'classified at birth.'" DeVolpi et al. (12) state that the inclusion of privately generated information under classification authority derived from Carter EO 12065 or the Atomic Energy Act is "far from clear." DOE asserts that all information which falls under Restricted Data "comes into existence as classified."[55]

CLASSIFIED CONTRACT Any contract that requires access to classified information, by a contractor or his or her employees. A contract may be a classified contract even though the contract document is not classified. The requirements for a classified contract also are applicable to all phases of pre-contract activity, including solicitations (bids, quotations, and proposals), pre-contract negotiations, post-contract activity, or other Government Contracting Agency (GCA) programs or projects which require access to classified information by a contractor.[56]

CLASSIFIED INFORMATION Any information that has been determined pursuant to Executive Order 13292 or any predecessor order to require protection against unauthorized disclosure and is marked to indicate its classified status when in documentary form.[57]

CLASSIFED INFORMATION IN THE PUBLIC DOMAIN 1. DoD employees and contractors shall not, while accessing the web on unclassified government systems, access or download documents that are known or suspected to contain classified information. This requirement applies to accessing or downloading that occurs when using government computers or employees' or contractors' personally owned computers that access unclassified government systems, either through remote Outlook access or other remote access capabilities that enable connection to government systematized employees or contractors who inadvertently discover potentially classified information in the public domain shall report its existence immediately to their Security Manager.[58] 2. Commenting on classified information in the public domain can cause risk of greater damage to national security by confirming its location, classified nature, or technical accuracy.[59] 3. Several courts have had occasion to consider whether agencies have a duty to disclose classified information that purportedly has found its way into the public domain. This issue most commonly arises when a plaintiff argues that an agency has waived its ability to invoke Exemption 1 as a result of prior disclosure of similar or related information. In this regard, courts have held that, in making an argument of waiver through some prior public disclosure, a FOIA plaintiff bears "the initial burden of pointing to specific information in the public domain that appears to duplicate that being withheld."[60]

CLASSIFIED INFORMATION PROCEDURES ACT (P.L. 96-456, OCTOBER 5, 1980) The tool with which the proper protection of classified information may be ensured in indicted cases. After a criminal indictment becomes public, the prosecutor remains responsible for taking reasonable precautions against the unauthorized disclosure of classified information during the case. This responsibility applies both when the government intends to use classified information in its case-in-chief as well as when the defendant seeks to use classified information in his or her defense.[61]

CLASSIFIED INFORMATION SPILLAGE When classified data is processed or received on an information system with a lower level of classification.[62]

CLASSIFIED MATTER Official information or matter in any form or of any nature that requires protection in the interests of national security. *See* UNCLASSIFIED MATTER

CLASSIFIED MILITARY INFORMATION (CMI) Information originated by or for the Department of Defense (DoD) or its agencies, or is under their jurisdiction or control, and that requires protection in the interests of national security. It is designated TOP SECRET, SECRET, or CONFIDENTIAL. Classified Military Information (CMI) may be conveyed via oral, visual, or material form.[63]

CLASSIFIED NATIONAL SECURITY INFORMATION "Classified national security information" or "classified information" means information that has been determined pursuant to this order or any predecessor order to require protection against unauthorized disclosure and is marked to indicate its classified status when in documentary form.[64]

CLASSIFIER An individual who makes a classification determination and applies a security classification to information or material. A classifier may either be a classification authority or assign a security classification based on a properly classified source or a classification guide.[65]

CLIENTITIS Overly sympathetic analysis of events in the target state; an unrealistic attempt to understand the motivations and values of the target country's leaders or major groupings from the perspective of the target. For example, Warren Christopher said at his Senate confirmation hearing to be secretary of state, "More than ever before, the State Department cannot afford to have clientitis, a malady characterized by undue deference to the potential reactions of other countries. I have long thought the [U.S.] State Department needs an 'America Desk.' This administration will have one—and I'll be sitting behind it."[66] *See* DOUBLE BLIND; PRIDE OF PREVIOUS POSITION

CLOSED MATERIAL PROCEDURE Hearings in private 82.6: (1) If the court considers it necessary for any party and that party's legal representative to be excluded from any hearing or part of a hearing in order to secure that information is not disclosed where disclosure would be damaging to the interests of national security, it must—(a) direct accordingly; and (b) conduct the hearing, or that part of it from which that party and that party's legal representative are excluded, in private but attended by a special advocate to represent the interests of the excluded party. (2) The court may conduct a hearing or part of a hearing in private for any other good reason.[67] *See* IN CAMERA

CLOUD COMPUTING A model for enabling ubiquitous, convenient, on-demand network access to a shared pool of configurable computing resources (e.g., networks, servers, storage, applications, and services) that can be rapidly provisioned and released with minimal management effort or service provider interaction. This cloud model is composed of five essential characteristics (e.g., on demand, resource pooling), three service models (e.g., software as a service), and four deployment models (e.g., private, community).[68] *See* FEDERAL RISK AND AUTHORIZATION MANAGEMENT PROGRAM

CNN EFFECT Media coverage of a real or perceived crisis that sustains public awareness and urges policymakers to take action. CNN stands for Cable News Network, one of the first networks offering 24-hour news coverage. The "CNN effect" now refers to all forms of mass media that focus on and magnify an action, event, or decision by publicizing it worldwide. "Resisting the CNN effect may be one of the most important requirements of U.S. policy-making in the coming period."[69] Televised images of suffering often spur public demands for action and define humanitarian problems, but usually without covering the underlying complexities or leading to accurate problem identification.[70] See AGENDA-SETTING THEORY

COAST GUARD COUNTERINTELLIGENCE SERVICE (CGCIS) CGCIS preserves the operational integrity of the Coast Guard by shielding its operations, personnel, systems, facilities and information from Foreign Intelligence and Security Services (FISS), and the intelligence efforts of terrorist organizations, drug trafficking elements and other organized crime groups, adversaries, and insider threats.[71]

COAST GUARD CRYPTOLOGIC GROUP (CGCG) CGCG provides a unique maritime cryptologic perspective within the SIGINT community, helping to satisfy validated national SIGINT requirements, which also support Coast Guard and DHS missions. CGCG brings cryptologic capabilities and full interoperability with U.S. Navy and U.S. Cryptologic assets to enhance Maritime Domain Awareness for operational commanders as they plan and execute Coast Guard missions.[72]

COAST GUARD INTELLIGENCE AND CRIMINAL INVESTIGATIONS Investigations by the USCG, a military, multi-mission, maritime service that is the principal federal agency responsible for safety, security, and stewardship within the maritime domain. These missions are performed in any maritime region where those interests may be at risk, including international waters and America's coasts, ports, and inland waterways. In March 2003, pursuant to the Homeland Security Act, the USCG was transferred from the Department of Transportation to DHS. The USCG has several diverse missions—national defense, homeland security, maritime safety, and environmental and natural resources stewardship. It is both an armed service and the nation's primary maritime law enforcement agency.[73]

COAST GUARD INTELLIGENCE COORDINATION CENTER (CGICC) The national-level coordinator for collection, analysis, production, and dissemination of Coast Guard intelligence. It is the focal point of interaction with the intelligence components of other government entities such as the Department of Defense and federal law enforcement agencies. The CGICC is co-located with the U.S. Navy's Office of Naval Intelligence at the National Maritime Intelligence Center in Suitland, Maryland, and supports all Coast Guard missions. The CGICC conducts the following activities.[74]

CODE NAME, CODENAME 1. British and U.S. jargon, aka code name. It has been used interchangeably with *codeword* in the past. Both codenames and nicknames were and are used in conjunction with operations and projects, whereas codewords and cryptonyms are used standing alone with a digraph prefix (Central Intelligence Agency (CIA) usage). Code names and nicknames are always the second part of an operation, plan or project title. Code names can be in military usage, either strategic or tactical. The former can be viable for years, unless compromised, while the latter are ephemeral. Additionally, it should be noted that codenames are used in conjunction with military operations, operational or contingency plans, or concepts, whereas military projects are usually nonoperational intelligence, and counterintelligence usage may differ from military practice.[75] 2. There are three types of code names: nicknames, code words, and exercise terms.[76]

CODE WORDS, CODEWORDS 1. A word that has been assigned a classification and a classified meaning to safeguard intentions and information regarding a classified plan or operation.[77] 2. A cryptonym used to identify sensitive intelligence data. Codewords can stand alone, and when used in codeword intelligence, they may or may not designate intelligence operations but are otherwise used for access to the product of such operations.[78]

CODEWORD COMPARTMENT Security device designed to provide special protection, beyond that provided by the federal classification system, to a specific category of sensitive information. Its charter is Section 9 of Executive Order 11652. The codeword compartment is only one form of supplementary protection for sensitive materials, although perhaps the predominant one. Although no exact accounting is possible, it appears that the use of codeword-protected materials may be involved in up to one-half of total (*sic*, Central) Agency man-hours.[79]

COGNITIVE DISSONANCE The rejection of factual information or reality because it does not conform to previously held beliefs. In spite of the overwhelming weight of confirmatory evidence accumulated over eight years, the findings continue to be challenged and contested, sometimes with offerings of bizarre scientific counter explanations that defy common sense. The extreme reluctance to accept the evidence at face value cannot be attributed simply to the fact that intelligence could never meet the rigorous laboratory standards for evidence. Rather, it must surely lie in the unpleasantness of the implications insofar as they raise doubts about the viability of arms control agreements.[80]

COGNIZANT SECURITY AGENCY, COGNIZANT SECURITY AUTHORITY 1. The term Cognizant Security Agency (CSA) denotes the Department of Defense (DoD), the Department of Energy (DoE), the NRC, and the Central Intelligence Agency (CIA). The Secretary of Defense, the Secretary of Energy, the director of the CIA and the chairman, NRC, may delegate any aspect of security administration regarding classified activities and contracts under their purview within the CSA or to another CSA. Responsibility for security administration may be further delegated by a CSA to one or more Cognizant Security Offices (CSO). It is the obligation of each CSA to inform industry of the applicable CSO.[81] 2. Cognizant Security Authority (CSA) is the individual designated by a Senior Official of the Intelligence Community (SOIC) to serve as the responsible official for all aspects of security program management with respect to protection of intelligence sources and methods under SOIC responsibility. The CSA for DHS is the Chief Security Office.[82]

COLD SITE A backup facility that has the necessary electrical and physical components of a computer facility but does not have the computer equipment in place. The site is ready to receive the necessary replacement computer equipment in the event that the user has to move from the main computing location to an alternate site.

COLLABORATIVE INTELLIGENCE A working relationship between the consumer of intelligence and the analyst in developing the requirements for collection and developing the response to what has been collected.

COLLATERAL EFFECT Unintentional or incidental effects including, but not limited to, injury or damage to persons or objects that would not be lawful military targets under the circumstances ruling at the time. Includes effects on civilian or dual-use computers, networks, information, or infrastructure. Such effects are not unlawful as long as they are not excessive in light of the overall military advantage anticipated from the activity. In cyberspace operations, collateral effects are categorized as High, Medium, Low, and No.[83]

COLLATERAL INFORMATION National security information (including intelligence information) classified Top Secret, Secret, or Confidential that is not in the Sensitive Compartmented Information or other Special Access Program category.[84]

COLLATION The process whereby information is assembled together and compared critically.[85]

COLLECT The capability and/or process to capture biometric sample(s) and related contextual data from a scene and/or a biometric subject, with or without his or her knowledge.[86]

COLLECTED Any information, both in its final form and in the form when initially gathered, acquired, held, or obtained by an IC element that is potentially relevant to a mission need of any IC element. This includes information as it is obtained directly from its source, regardless of whether the information has been reviewed or processed.[87]

COLLECTING An activity of information management: the continuous acquisition of relevant information by any means, including direct observation, other organic resources, or other official, unofficial, or public sources from the information environment.[88]

COLLECTION 1. The exploitation of sources by collection agencies, and the delivery of the information obtained to the appropriate processing unit for use in the production of intelligence. 2. The obtaining of information or intelligence information in any manner, including direct observations, liaison with official agencies, or solicitation from official, unofficial, or public sources, or quantitative data from the test or operation of foreign systems.[89]

COLLECTION AGENCY An individual, organization, or unit that has access to sources of information, and the capability of collecting information from them.[90]

COLLECTION ASSET A collection system, platform, or capability that is supporting, assigned, or attached to a particular commander.[91]

COLLECTION CAPABILITIES MANAGEMENT The authority to access collection capabilities strengths and weaknesses in meeting customer requirements and collection strategies; develop and use appropriate collection technologies, techniques, and procedures to meet collection strategies; adapt tools and methods or new methodological approaches required for substantive discipline, domain, or area of work; and identify and recommend usage or realignment in use of management tools to meet requirements and specifications.

COLLECTION CYCLE The interaction between the management of collection needs and the management of assets in gathering data and information to meet those collection needs. Essentially, the collection cycle has Collections Requirements Management (CRM) validating and prioritizing what is needed to be done, while Collection Operations Management (COM) addresses how the collection gets done.

COLLECTION DISCIPLINE Intelligence disciplines with a recognized capability to plan, allocate, and manage specific collection assets and processes in meeting intelligence requirements.

COLLECTION MANAGEMENT (CM) 1. The process of converting intelligence requirements into collection requirements, establishing priorities, tasking or coordinating with appropriate collection sources or agencies, monitoring results, and re-tasking as required. 2. A methodology to verify assumptions and fill in intelligence gaps that occur every day during the planning and employment of military operations.

COLLECTION MANAGEMENT AUTHORITY (CMA) Within the Department of Defense, collection management authority constitutes the authority to establish, prioritize, and validate theater collection requirements, establish sensor tasking guidance, and develop theater-wide collection policies.[92]

COLLECTION MANAGEMENT STRATEGIST (COLLECTION STRATEGIST) An individual who specializes in the art and science of developing and executing multi-discipline intelligence, surveillance, and reconnaissance (ISR) collection strategies, plans, and assessments that answer priority intelligence requirements of national and DoD customers, optimize the allocation and application of ISR resources and capabilities, and support the adaptive planning process. The strategist (1) understands how to apply the classic principles of strategy, the "strategy-to-task" framework, and project management principles to develop collection strategies and plans; (2) is fully proficient in the use of tools, techniques, and procedures required to create collection plans that satisfy intelligence information needs; and (3) is able to develop and implement integrated multi-INT collection operations strategies that enable dynamic tasking across ISR domains and disciplines, achieve persistent ISR, and drive efficiencies in ISR employment, net-centric and effects-based operations and assessment.

COLLECTION MANAGER (CM) An individual with responsibility for the timely and efficient tasking of organic collection resources and the development of requirements for theater and national assets that could satisfy specific information needs in support of the mission.[93]

COLLECTION OF INFORMATION (A) The obtaining, causing to be obtained, soliciting, or requiring the disclosure to third parties or the public, of facts or opinions by or for an agency, regardless of form or format, calling for either (i) answers to identical questions posed to, or identical reporting or record-keeping requirements imposed on, 10 or more persons, other than agencies, instrumentalities, or employees of the United States; or (ii) answers to questions posed to agencies, instrumentalities, or employees of the United States which are to be used for general statistical purposes; and (B) shall not include a collection of information described under section 3518(c) (1) of title 44, *United States Code*.[94]

COLLECTION OPERATIONS In the NICE (National Initiative for Cybersecurity Education) Workforce Framework, the area that develops and demonstrates operational knowledge of capabilities of the collection disciplines, the strengths and weaknesses of specific technical sensors platforms, and human sources in the area of responsibility. Collection is executed using appropriate collection strategies and within the priorities established through the collection management process.[95]

COLLECTION OPERATIONS MANAGEMENT (COM) The authoritative direction, scheduling, and control of specific collection operations and associated processing, exploitation, and reporting resources.[96]

COLLECTION PLAN A plan directing the collection of data on a particular topic with a specific objective, a list of potential sources of that data, and an estimated time frame.[97]

COLLECTION PLANNING A continuous process that coordinates and integrates the efforts of all collection units and agencies.[98]

COLLECTION REQUIREMENT 1. An intelligence need considered in the allocation of intelligence resources to fulfill the essential elements of information and other intelligence needs of a commander. 2. An established intelligence need, validated against the appropriate allocation of intelligence resources (as a requirement) to fulfill the essential elements of information and other intelligence needs of an intelligence consumer.[99]

COLLECTION REQUIREMENTS MANAGEMENT (CRM) The development and control of collection, processing, exploitation, and/or reporting requirements that normally result in either the direct tasking of assets over which the collection manager has authority, or the generation of tasking requests to collection management authorities at a higher, lower, or lateral echelon to accomplish the collection mission. CRM focuses on what gets done in the collection cycle.[100]

COLLECTION RESOURCES A collection system, platform, or capability that is not assigned or attached to a specific unit or echelon, which must be requested and coordinated through the chain of command.[101]

COLLECTION RESOURCES MANAGEMENT The process of receiving and analyzing customer requirements, determining resource availability and capability, prioritizing and developing collection strategies, identifying task collection resources, evaluating performance and/or reporting, and updating collection plans.[102]

COMBAT INFORMATION Unevaluated data gathered by or provided directly to a tactical unit, which, due to its highly perishable nature or the criticality of the situation, cannot be processed into tactical intelligence in time to satisfy the customer's tactical intelligence requirements.

COMBAT INTELLIGENCE Usually refers to the weather, enemy, and geographical features required by a military unit in the planning and conduct of combat operations. *See* TACTICAL INTELLIGENCE

COMBAT MISSION Unevaluated data gathered by or provided directly to a tactical unit, which, due to its highly perishable nature or the criticality of the situation, cannot be processed into tactical intelligence in time to satisfy the customer's tactical intelligence requirements.

COMBAT READINESS Synonymous with operational readiness; usually relates to the missions or functions that will be required to perform in combat. *See* OPERATIONAL READINESS

COMBATING TERRORISM Actions, including antiterrorism (defensive measures taken to reduce vulnerability to terrorist acts) and counterterrorism (offensive measures taken to prevent, deter, and respond to terrorism), taken to oppose terrorism throughout the entire threat spectrum.[103]

COMBINED DNA INDEX SYSTEM (CODIS) The generic term used to describe the FBI's program of support for criminal justice DNA databases as well as the software used to run these databases. The National DNA Index System or NDIS is considered one part of CODIS, the national level, containing the DNA profiles contributed by federal, state, and local participating forensic laboratories. CODIS was designed to compare a target DNA record against the DNA records contained in the database. Once a match is identified by the CODIS software, the laboratories involved in the match exchange information to verify the match and establish coordination between their two agencies. The match of the forensic DNA record against the DNA record in the database may be used to establish probable cause to obtain an evidentiary DNA sample from the suspect.[104]

COMBINED INTELLIGENCE WATCH CENTER (CIWC)/COMBINED INTELLIGENCE CENTER (CIC) The indications and warning center for worldwide threats from space, missile, and strategic air activity, as well as geopolitical unrest that could affect North America and U.S. forces/interests abroad. The center's personnel gather intelligence information to assist all the Cheyenne Mountain work centers in correlating and analyzing events to support North American Air Defense and U.S. Space Command decision makers.

COMMAND INFORMATION Communication by a military organization directed to the internal audience that creates an awareness of the organization's goals, informs them of significant developments affecting them and the organization, increases their effectiveness as ambassadors of the organization, and keeps them informed about what is going on in the organization.[105]

COMMERICAL COVER When a person is given a job with a business or other organization to hide his or her real work as an intelligence operative. In such cases, this person does not have the benefit of diplomatic immunity.

COMMITTEE ON FOREIGN INVESTMENT IN THE U.S. (CFIUS) Twelve-agency committee chaired by the Department of the Treasury, originally established by Executive Order in 1975 to monitor and evaluate the impact of foreign investments in the United States. The National Intelligence Council's CFIUS Support Group under the NIO for Military Issues is the intelligence community interlocutor with CFIUS.[106]

COMMON TERRORISM INFORMATION SHARING STANDARDS (CTISS) The CTISS program integrates information exchange standards, based on common ISE business processes and developed through the DOJ and DHS NIEM program management office, into new ISE-wide functional standards. NIEM epitomizes a successful federal, state, local, tribal, and private sector initiative and provides a foundation for nationwide information exchanges leveraging data exchange standards efforts successfully implemented by the Global Justice Information Sharing Initiative. NIEM is also being strongly embraced by the private sector technology community.[107]

COMMUNICATE To use any means or method to convey information of any kind from one person or place to another.[108]

COMMUNICATIONS ANALYSIS The review of records reflecting communications (telephone, email, pager, text messaging, etc.) among entities for indicators of criminal associations or activity. Results may recommend steps to take to continue or expand the investigation or study.[109]

COMMUNICATIONS COVER Concealing or altering of characteristic communications patterns to hide information that could be of value to an adversary.[110]

COMMUNICATIONS INTELLIGENCE (COMINT) Technical information and intelligence derived from foreign communications by other than the intended recipients; it does not include the monitoring of foreign public media or the intercept of communications obtained during the course of counterintelligence investigations within the United States. COMINT is produced by the collection and processing of foreign communications passed by electromagnetic means, and by the processing of foreign encrypted communications however transmitted. Collection comprises search, intercept, and direction finding. Processing comprises range estimation, transmitter/operator analysis, traffic analysis, cryptanalysts, decryption, study of plain text, the fusion of these processes, and the reporting of results. COMINT includes the fields of traffic analysis, cryptanalysis, and direction finding, and it is a part of Signals Intelligence (SIGINT).[111] *See* SOURCES OF INTELLIGENCE

COMMUNICATIONS INTELLIGENCE DATABASE The aggregate of technical information and intelligence derived from the interception and analysis of foreign communications (excluding press, propaganda, and public broadcast) used in the direction and redirection of communications intelligence intercept, analysis, and reporting activities.[112]

COMMUNICATIONS SECURITY (COMSEC) Measures designed to deny unauthorized persons information of value that might be derived from the possession and study of telecommunications, or to mislead unauthorized persons in their interpretation of the results of such possession and study. This includes crypto-security transmission security, emission security, and physical security of communication security materials and information.[113]

COMMUNITY ACQUISITION RISK CENTER (CARC) CARC is charged with developing and deploying a common risk assessment methodology across the IC to ensure, to the maximum extent feasible, that NIP acquisitions are shielded from foreign exploitation.[114]

COMMUNITY OF INTEREST (COI) Distributed, collaborative and inclusive groupings working to discover, synthesize and exchange knowledge through the sharing of information in order to: take better decisions; implement change; and create effects.[115]

COMMUNITY ON-LINE INTELLIGENCE SYSTEM FOR END USERS AND MANAGERS (COLISEUM) 1. The management system for production requirements and requests for information, CI production (DoDI 5240.18, CI Analysis & Production, 17 Nov 2009 with change 1 dated 15 Oct 2013). 2. Also, an analysis requirements management tool used throughout the DIE for tasking and managing requirements for finished intelligence production (DoDI 3020.51, Intelligence Support to DCIP, 23 Jun 2011). 3. Also, the primary production requirements management system for the Defense Intelligence Analysis Program (DIAP). It supports the DIAP mission to consolidate and gain synergism of DoD intelligence production resources by automating the basic production requirement process defined in the DIAP and its key operational concepts (DIA DIAP). 4. Also, an analysis requirement management tool used throughout the Defense Intelligence Community to register and track requests for information/analytical requirements, search for existing intelligence, and manage/account for analytical resources. It is a web-based application available through Intelink.[116]

COMPARTMENTALIZATION 1. A formal system of restricted access to intelligence activities to protect the sensitive aspects of sources, methods, and analytical procedures of foreign intelligence programs. 2. A nonhierarchical grouping of sensitive information used to control access to data more finely than with hierarchical security classification alone.[117]

COMPARTMENTATION 1. The principle of controlling access to sensitive information so that it is available only to those individuals or organizational components with an official "need-to-know" and only to the extent required for the performance of assigned responsibilities (National HUMINT Glossary). 2. Also, establishment and management of an organization so that information about the personnel, internal organization, or activities of one component is made available to any other component only to the extent required for the performance of assigned duties. 3. Also, management of an intelligence service so that information about personnel, organization, or activities of one component is made available to any other component only to the extent required for the performance of assigned duties (FBI FCI Terms). 4. Also, the practice of establishing special channels for handling sensitive intelligence information. The channels are limited to individuals with a specific need for such information and who are therefore given special security clearances in order to have access to it (Senate Report 94–755, Book I—Glossary, 26 Apr 1976). 5. Also, the process of strictly limiting the number of people who are aware of a given intelligence operation. . . . Only personnel with an absolute "need to know" should be admitted into the compartment.[118] *See* BIGOT LIST

COMPARTMENTATION OF INTELLIGENCE Establishment and management of an organization so that information about the personnel, internal organization, or activities of one component is made available to any other component only to the extent required for the performance of assigned duties.

COMPARTMENTED INTELLIGENCE National intelligence placed in an approved control system to ensure handling by specifically identified and access-approved individuals. These programs include:

- Sensitive Compartmented Information (SCI): compartments that protect national intelligence concerning or derived from intelligence sources, methods, or analytical processes.
- Special Access Programs (SAPS): pertaining to intelligence activities (including special activities, but excluding military operational, strategic, and tactical programs) and intelligence sources and methods.
- restricted collateral information: affects areas other than SCI or SAPs; imposes controls governing access to national intelligence or control procedures beyond those normally provided for access to CONFIDENTIAL, SECRET, or TOP SECRET information and for which funding is specifically identified.[119]

COMPARTMENTED MODE Mode of operation wherein each user with direct or indirect access to a system, its peripherals, remote terminals, or remote hosts has all of the following: (a) valid security clearance for the most restricted information processed in the system; (b) formal access approval and signed nondisclosure agreements for that information which a user is to have access; and (c) valid need-to-know for information which a user is to have access.[120]

COMPETENCY DIRECTORY Listing of those IC-wide, departmental, independent agency and component-specific competencies, including established labels and definitions, typically defined for mission categories and major occupational groups.[121]

COMPETING HYPOTHESES *See* ANALYSIS OF COMPETING HYPOTHESES

COMPILATION A diagram giving details of the source material from which the map or chart has been compiled; does not necessarily include reliability information.[122]

COMPLEX EMERGENCY A natural or human-made disaster with economic, social, and political dimensions; a humanitarian crisis in a country, region, or society where there is a total or considerable breakdown of authority resulting from internal or external conflict, and which requires an international response that goes beyond the mandate or capacity of any single agency and the ongoing United Nations country program.[123]

COMPROMISE The disclosure of information to unauthorized persons; a violation of the security policy of a system in which unauthorized intentional or unintentional disclosure, modification, destruction, or loss of an object may have occurred.[124]

COMPROMISED A term applied to classified matter, knowledge of which has, in whole or in part, passed to an unauthorized person or persons, or which has been subject to risk of such passing.[125]

COMPUTER-BASED ASSESSMENT TOOL (CBAT) A tactical tool that creates an interactive visual guide of a location by integrating data to generate a 360-degree geospherical video and geospatial panoramic imagery of facilities, surrounding areas, routes, and other areas of interest. The visual guide incorporates a wide variety of data including vulnerability assessments, evacuation plans, standard operating procedures, and schematic/floor plans.[126]

COMPUTER FORENSICS We define computer forensics as the discipline that combines elements of law and computer science to collect and analyze data from computer systems, networks, wireless communications, and storage devices in a way that is admissible as evidence in a court of law.[127]

COMPUTER NETWORK ATTACK A category of "fires" employed for offensive purposes in which actions are taken through the use of computer networks to disrupt, deny, degrade, manipulate, or destroy information resident in the target information system or computer networks, or the systems and networks themselves. The ultimate intended effect is not necessarily on the target system itself, but may support a larger effort, such as information operations or counterterrorism (e.g., altering or spoofing specific communications or gaining or denying access to adversary communications or logistics channels).[128]

COMPUTER NETWORK DEFENSE 1. Computer network defense is defined as actions taken to protect, monitor, analyze, detect, and respond to unauthorized activity within DoD information systems and computer networks.[129] 2. Efforts to defend against Computer Network Operations (CNO) of others, especially that directed against U.S. and allied computers.[130] 3. In the NICE (National Initiative for Cybersecurity Education) Workforce Framework, cybersecurity work where a person: Uses defensive measures and information collected from a variety of sources to identify, analyze, and report events that occur or might occur within the network in order to protect information, information systems, and networks from threats.[131]

COMPUTER NETWORK EXPLOITATION (CNE) Enabling operations and intelligence collection capabilities conducted through the use of computer networks to gather data about target or adversary automated information systems or networks.[132]

COMPUTER SECURITY INCIDENT A violation or imminent threat of violation of computer security policies, acceptable use policies, or standard computer security practices.

COMPUTER SECURITY TOOLBOX A set of tools (e.g., BUSTER, FLUSH, and Secure Copy) designed specifically to assist Information Assurance Officers (IAOs) and System Administrators (SAs) in performing their duties. The functions within the Toolbox can erase appended data within files; eliminate appended data in free or unallocated space; search for specific words or sets of words for verifying classification; and locate unapproved share programs. It also includes a program which allows you to clear laser toner cartridges and drums.[133]

COMPUTER VIRUS A computer program that contains hidden code and usually performs some unwanted function as a side effect. The main difference between a virus and a Trojan horse is that the hidden code in a computer virus can only replicate by attaching a copy of itself to other programs and may also include an additional "payload" that triggers when specific conditions are met.

CONCEALMENT The protection from observation or surveillance; the provision of protection from observation only.[134]

CONCENTRATED WARNING The responsibility of warning held by a singular body of analysts, focusing on threat management, whose sole duty and purpose is to communicate and forecast a possible threat. See DISTRIBUTIVE WARNING

CONCEPT OF INTELLIGENCE OPERATIONS A verbal or graphic statement, in broad outline, of an intelligence directorate's assumptions or intent in regard to intelligence support of an operation or series of operations. The concept of intelligence operations, which supports the commander's concept of operations, is contained in the intelligence annex of operation plans. The concept of intelligence operations is designed to give an overall picture of intelligence support for joint operations. It is included primarily for additional clarity of purpose.[135]

CONCEPT OF OPERATIONS A clear and concise statement of the line of action chosen in order to accomplish a particular mission.

CONCLUSION A well-supported explanation of the final inference in the intelligence analysis thought process. *See* ASSESSMENT; DEDUCTIVE LOGIC; HYPOTHESIS; INDUCTIVE LOGIC; INFERENCE

CONDITIONAL PROBABLITY The probability of some event A, given the occurrence of some other event B, written as $P(A|B)$. An example is the conditional probability of a person dying (event A), given that they contract the pandemic flu (event B).[136]

CONDITIONING AND COVER Routine or repetitive acts used to cloak intentions; for example, holding routine military maneuvers as cover for aggressive action.

CONE OF SILENCE 1. An inverted cone-shaped space directly over the aerial towers of some forms of radio beacons in which signals are unheard or greatly reduced in volume.[137] 2. The term was used in the popular 1960s television comedy spy show *Get Smart* for a dome that allowed two individuals to talk without anyone else hearing their discussion.

CONFIDENCE AND SECURITY BUILDING MEASURES (CSBMs) Measures requiring effective and concrete actions concerning the military activities and force structure of the states concerned and aimed at reducing tension and strengthening confidence and security among those states.[138]

CONFIDENCE-LEVEL SCALE A verbal and/or numerical value used in a uniform and consistent manner that an assessment will be correct; usually based on the analyst's experience, judgment, and intuition. Typically, such a scale will include "confirmed," indicating a 95 percent or greater chance that the information or assessment is correct; "probable," for a 75 percent or greater chance; "likely," for a 50 percent or greater chance; "possible," for at least a 5 percent or greater chance; and "doubtful," for less than a 5 percent chance that the information or assessment is correct.

CONFIDENTIAL COMMERCIAL INFORMATION Records provided by a submitter that may contain material exempt from release under the FOIA because disclosure could reasonably be expected to cause the submitter substantial competitive harm.

CONFIDENTIAL INFORMATION Confidential personal information (such as medical records or spiritual counseling), confidential journalistic material, confidential discussions between Members of Parliament and their constituents, or matters subject to legal privilege.[139]

CONFIDENTIAL SOURCE Any individual or organization that has provided, or that may reasonably be expected to provide, information to the United States on matters pertaining to national security with the expectation that the information or relationship, or both, will be held in confidence.[140]

CONFIDENTIALITY 1. A property that information is not disclosed to users, processes, or devices unless they have been authorized to access the information. Extended Definition: Preserving authorized restrictions on information access and disclosure, including means for protecting personal privacy and proprietary information.[141] 2. Assurance that information is not disclosed to unauthorized individuals, processes, or devices.[142]

CONFIRMATION OF INFORMATION (CONFIRMATION OF INTELLIGENCE) Support for the credibility of previously received information or intelligence. An information item is said to be confirmed when it is reported for the second time, preferably by another independent source whose reliability is considered when confirming information.[143]

CONFLICT PREVENTION Those measures that can be implemented before a difference or dispute escalates into violence, designed to counter the spread of conflict into other geographical areas; those measures that prevent violence from flaring up again after the signing of a peace agreement or a cease-fire.[144]

CONFUSION AGENT An individual dispatched by his sponsor to confound the intelligence or counterintelligence apparatus of another country rather than to collect and transmit information.[145]

CONGRUENCE ANALYSIS The verification of data by using more than one instrument or source of data for assessing a threat on the same criterion. *See* CAUSAL ANALYSIS; CAUSAL ASSOCIATION; CAUSAL RELATIONSHIP

CONSENSUAL MONITORING Monitoring of communications for which a court order or warrant is not legally required because of the consent of a party to the communication.[146]

CONSENT The agreement by a person or organization to permit DoD intelligence components to take particular actions that affect the person or organization. Consent may be oral or written unless a specific form of consent is required by a particular procedure. Consent may be implied if adequate notice is provided that a particular action (such as entering a building) carries with it the presumption of consent to an accompanying action (such as search of briefcases).[147]

CONSEQUENCE 1. Effect of an event, incident, or occurrence Sample Usage: One consequence of the explosion was the loss of over 50 lives. Consequence is commonly measured in four ways: human, economic, mission, and psychological, but may also include other factors such as impact on the environment.[148] 2. The effect of an event, incident, or occurrence. Extended Definition: In cybersecurity, the effect of a loss of confidentiality, integrity or availability of information or an information system on an organization's operations, its assets, on individuals, other organizations, or on national interests.[149]

CONSEQUENCE ANALYSIS Forecasting the implications of an event or result of an action rather than predicting when the event or action will occur. *See* CONSEQUENCE MANAGEMENT

CONSEQUENCE ASSESSMENT Product or process of identifying or evaluating the potential or actual effects of an event, incident, or occurrence.[150]

CONSEQUENCE MANAGEMENT Sometimes confused with crisis management. "Historical analysis of patterns of behavior of CBW terrorists, such as the choice of agent and delivery system, can also help improve the effectiveness of medical countermeasures and other consequence management activities."[151] *See* CONSEQUENCE ANALYSIS; CRISIS MANAGEMENT

CONSOLIDATED TERRORIST SCREENING DATABASE (CTSDB) The Terrorist Screening Center receives international and domestic terrorist identity records and maintains them in the TSDB. *See* TERRORIST SCREENING CENTER

CONSPIRACY THEORIES Conspiracy theories are similar to urban legends, but center around the idea that powerful, evil hidden forces are secretly manipulating the course of world events and history and that nothing is as it seems. The *book 9/11: The Big Lie* by French author Thierry Meyssan (published as *L'Effroyable Imposture* [The Horrifying Fraud] in French) is an example of conspiracy thinking. Meyssan suggests that no plane hit the Pentagon on September 11 and that, instead, a cabal of conspirators within the U.S. government attacked the Pentagon with a cruise missile with a depleted uranium warhead in order to manufacture an excuse for greater defense spending and war against the Taliban. Meyysan did not interview or credit the eyewitnesses to the September 11 events, who reported seeing a plane strike the Pentagon, and he offers no explanation for what happened to American Airlines flight #77 and its 64 passengers and crew, but inconvenient facts such as these are regularly ignored or dismissed by conspiracy theories in favor of extraordinarily complex and convoluted conspiracies, for which there is no evidence, merely uninformed speculation. Nevertheless, by blaming powerful alleged villains, conspiracy theories find a wide audience for whom suspicions are much more powerful in forming beliefs than logic, reason, or facts.[152]

CONSTANT SURVEILLANCE SERVICE A transportation protective service provided by a commercial carrier qualified by Surface Deployment and Distribution Command.[153]

CONSTRAINT In the context of joint operation, a requirement placed on the command by a higher command that dictates an action, thus restricting freedom of action.[154]

CONSTRUCTION SURVEILLANCE TECHNICAN A citizen of the United States, who is at least 18 years of age, cleared at the TOP SECRET level, experienced in construction and trained in accordance with the Construction Surveillance Technician (CST) Field Guidebook to ensure the security integrity of a site.[155]

CONSUMER A person or agency that uses information or intelligence produced by either its own staff or other agencies.[156]

CONTACT PRINT A print made from a negative or a dispositive (a positive image on a transparent substance) in direct contact with sensitized material.

CONTAIN Efforts taken to limit freedom of action, minimize the effects of terrorist activities, preclude the regeneration of lost capabilities, and/or limit terrorist influence.[157]

CONTENT VALIDITY An evaluation scale generally represented from 1 to 5 or 1 to 4, which reflects the level of accuracy of the content of a raw data report. The scale ranges from "known to be true" to "truthfulness unknown."[158]

CONTEXTUAL DATA Contextual Data Elements of biographic data and situational information (who, what, when, where, how, why, etc.) associated with a collection event and permanently recorded as an integral component of the biometric file.[159]

CONTINENTAL UNITED STATES (CONUS) A military term which refers to U.S. territory, including adjacent territorial waters, located within the North American continent between Canada and Mexico.[160]

CONTINGENCY PLAN Management policy and procedures designed to maintain or restore business operations, including computer operations, possibly at an alternate location, in the event of emergencies, system failures, or disaster.

CONTINGENCY PLANNING PROCESS (CRISIS ACTION PLANNING PROCESS) The development of a course of action to mitigate chance or uncertain, unforeseen, or accidental events. Typically, contingency planning involves 6 phases, as indicated in figure C.1.[161]

CONTINUING SIGNIFICANT THREAT A threat to the national security of the United States that cannot be sufficiently mitigated through feasible and appropriate security measures associated with a transfer of the detainee.[162]

Phase I	Phase II	Phase III	Phase IV	Phase V	Phase VI
situation development	crisis assessment	course of action development	course of action selection	execution planning	execution
event perception	increased reporting	warning order issued	refine/present course of action	plan and/or alert order	execute order
problem recognition	evaluation	development of Task Force	course of action are decided upon	operations order developed	operations order are given
assessment		develop courses of action		force participation	
		evaluate courses of action			

Figure C.1. Contingency Planning Process (Courtesy of Integrated C4 I Architecture Division, *C4ISR Handbook for Integrated Planning* [Washington, DC: Defense Intelligence Agency Publications Division])

CONTINUITY OF GOVERNMENT (COG) 1. A coordinated effort within the federal government's executive branch to ensure that National Essential Functions continue to be performed during a Catastrophic Emergency.[163] 2. Also, a coordinated effort within the Executive Branch that ensures the continuation of minimum essential functions in any emergency situation, including catastrophic emergencies that impair or threaten day-to-day operations of departments/agencies within the branch. COG activities involve ensuring the continuity of minimum essential functions utilizing infrastructures outside the Washington Metropolitan Area (WMA) and must be capable of implementation with and without warning.[164]

CONTINUITY OF OPERATIONS (COOP) An effort within individual executive departments and agencies to ensure that Primary Mission-Essential Functions continue to be performed during a wide range of emergencies, including localized acts of nature, accidents, and technological or attack-related emergencies.[165]

CONTINUITY OF OPERATIONS PLAN A document that sets forth procedures for the continued performance of core capabilities and critical operations during any disruption or potential disruption.[166]

CONTRACT CHAIN, CALL CHAIN A form of network analysis used by the National Security Agency to establish relationships among individuals, groups, and communication.[167]

CONTRACTOR For the purposes of this Directive, the term "contractor" refers to either an independent contractor or an industrial contractor.[168]

CONTRACTOR ACCESS RESTRICTED INFORMATION Unclassified information that involves functions reserved to the federal government as vested by the Constitution as inherent power or as implied power as necessary for the proper performance of its duties. In many instances, CARI prevents contractors from making decisions that would affect current or future contracts and procurement procedures, primarily during pre-award activities.[169]

CONTRACTOR WIDE AREA NETWORK (CWAN) The National Reconnaissance Office's top-secret computer network for contractors.

CONTROL 1. Authority of the agency that originates information, or its successor in function, to regulate access to the information. 2. A department's legal authority over a record, taking into account the ability of the department to use and dispose of the record as it sees fit, to legally determine the disposition of a record, the intent of the record's creator to retain or relinquish control over the record, the extent to which department personnel have read or relied upon the record, and the degree to which the record has been integrated into the department's record-keeping system or files.[170]

CONTROLLED ACCESS AREA Specifically designated areas within a building where classified information may be handled, stored, discussed, or processed.[171]

CONTROLLED ACCESS PROGRAM (CAP) Director of National Intelligence (DNI)–approved programs that protect national intelligence. These include: 1. Sensitive Compartmented Information (SCI): Compartments that protect national intelligence concerning or derived from intelligence sources, methods, or analytical processes; 2. Special Access Programs (SAPs): Pertaining to intelligence activities (including special activities, but excluding military, operational, strategic, and tactical programs) and intelligence sources and methods; 3. Restricted Collateral Information: Other than Sensitive Compartmented Information (SCI) and Special Access Programs (SAPs) that impose controls governing access to national intelligence or control procedures beyond those normally provided for access to CONFIDENTIAL,

SECRET, or TOP SECRET information, and for which funding is specifically identified.[172]

CONTROLLED ACCESS PROGRAM COORDINATION OFFICE (CAPCO)

The Controlled Access Program Coordination Office (CAPCO) is established within the Office of the DCI. The Director of the CAPCO shall be appointed by the DCI. The CAPCO shall conduct the following activities: a. develop risk assessment criteria and procedures for the review and evaluation of controlled access programs; b. provide guidance to Intelligence Community agencies concerning submissions to the CAPOC (Controlled Access Program Oversight Committee); c. coordinate with other controlled access program oversight to meet the review requirements of the CAPOC; d. coordinate the CAPOC agenda and monitor directed taskings; e. review and evaluate agency submissions and make recommendations to the CAPOC; provide secretariat services for the CAPOC; and g. maintain a register of all controlled access programs in the NFIP.[173] *See* AUTHORIZED CLASSIFICATION AND CONTROL MARKINGS REGISTER

CONTROLLED DOSSIER A file of a particularly sensitive nature, due to substantive content or method of collection that is physically segregated from the body of ordinary materials.[174]

CONTROLLED INFORMATION 1. Information conveyed to an adversary in a deception operation. 2. Information and indicators deliberately conveyed or denied to foreign targets to evoke invalid official estimates that result in foreign official actions advantageous to U.S. interests and objectives.[175]

CONTROLLED SOURCE A person in the employment or under the control of the intelligence activity and responding to intelligence tasking.[176]

CONTROLLED UNCLASSIFIED INFORMATION At present, executive departments and agencies (agencies) employ ad hoc, agency-specific policies, procedures, and markings to safeguard and control this information, such as information that involves privacy, security, proprietary business interests, and law enforcement investigations. This inefficient, confusing patchwork has resulted in inconsistent marking and safeguarding of documents, led to unclear or unnecessarily restrictive dissemination policies, and created impediments to authorized information sharing. The fact that these agency-specific policies are often hidden from public view has only aggravated these issues. To address these problems, this order establishes a program for managing this information, hereinafter described as Controlled Unclassified Information, that emphasizes the openness and uniformity of government-wide practice.[177]

CONTROLLED UNCLASSIFIED INFORMATION OFFICE Executive Order 13556 "Controlled Unclassified Information" (the Order), establishes a program for managing CUI across the Executive branch and designates the National Archives and Records Administration (NARA) as Executive Agent to implement the Order and oversee agency actions to ensure compliance.[178]

CONVENTIONAL WEAPON A weapon that is neither nuclear, biological, nor chemical.

CONVERGED ANALYSIS Converged mobile devices offering advanced capabilities, often with PC-like functionality. No set industry standard definition. The gradual "blurring" of telecommunications, computers, and the Internet. Examples of convergence in SIGINT: Blackberry, iPhone data, smartphones, VOIP, Wireless Local Loop, GPRS—General Packet Radio Service.[179]

CONVERGENT EVIDENCE The association of two or more items of evidence that favor the same conclusion. *See* DIVERGENT EVIDENCE; REDUNDANT EVIDENCE

COOPERATIVE DETAINEE A detainee who has established a pattern of answering all questions truthfully and unconditionally and, in fact, answers all questions truthfully and unconditionally. A detainee is not cooperative if the detainee refuses to answer, avoids answering, or falsely answers questions, or if the detainee is intentionally deceptive. A detainee who fluctuates between cooperation and resistance is not cooperative.[180]

COORDINATOR FOR COUNTERTERRORISM The Coordinator for Counterterrorism (CT) or other appropriate senior appointee serves as the principal advisor to the Secretary of State, other Department principals, and policy bureaus on international counterterrorism strategy, policy, and operations, and directs the Department's counterterrorism programs. For the purposes of counterterrorism strategy, threats, and operations, the Coordinator reports to the Secretary of State. For matters relating to counterterrorism programs and other routine activities of the Bureau, the Coordinator reports to the Under Secretary for Civilian Security, Democracy and Human Rights.

CORE Competencies that apply universally to all Intelligence Community employees regardless of agency or element, mission category, occupational group, or work category. Clusters of competencies provide the foundation for the performance elements as established in Intelligence Community Directives 651 and 656.[181]

CORE CONTRACT PERSONNEL For the purposes of this Directive (ICD 612), core contract personnel are those independent contractors or individuals employed by industrial contractors who augment USG civilian and military personnel by providing direct technical, managerial, or administrative support to IC elements. Core contract personnel typically work alongside and are integrated with USG civilian and military personnel and perform staff-like work.[182]

CORRELATES OF WAR THEORY According to this approach, national capabilities typically consist of demographic, industrial, and military characteristics, which are then measured by comparative percentages with other characteristics such as a nation's population, the number of cities with populations of 20,000 or more, energy consumption, iron and steel production, and military expenditures.[183]

CORRELATION ANALYSIS Deciphering whether a relationship exists between two seemingly independent parameters or events. Time-based correlations are of fundamental importance when building a threat scenario.

CORROBORATE To strengthen, confirm, or make certain the substance of a statement through the use of an independent but not necessarily authoritative source. For example, the date and place of birth recorded in an official personnel file could be used to corroborate the date and place of birth claimed on a standard form. *See* VERIFY

COST-BENEFIT ANALYSIS (CBA) Analytic technique used to compare alternatives according to the relative costs incurred and the relative benefits gained. Extended Definition: typically measured in monetary terms.[184]

COST-EFFECTIVENESS ANALYSIS (CEA) Analytic technique that compares the cost of two or more alternatives with the same outcome. Alternatively: analytic technique that evaluates an alternative by how much it delivers per unit cost, or how much has to be spent per unit benefit.[185]

COUNTERESPIONAGE 1. Action designed to detect and counteract espionage. 2. Actions undertaken to investigate specific allegations or circumstances and to acquire information concerning a person or persons involved in the violation of espionage laws. *See* COUNTERINTELLIGENCE

COUNTERINFORMATION Actions dedicated to controlling the information realm.[186]

COUNTERING VIOLENT EXTREMISM (CVE) Encompasses programs and policies intended both to prevent individuals and groups from radicalizing and mobilizing to commit violence and to disengage individuals and groups who are planning to commit, or who have already engaged in, extremist violence.[187]

COUNTERING WEAPONS OF MASS DESTRUCTION (CWMD) Efforts against actors of concern to curtail the conceptualization, development, possession, proliferation, use, and effects of weapons of mass destruction, related expertise, materials, technologies, and means of delivery.[188]

COUNTERINTELLIGENCE (CI) Information gathered and activities conducted to protect against espionage, other intelligence activities, sabotage, or assassinations conducted by or on behalf of foreign governments or elements thereof, foreign organizations, or foreign persons, or international terrorist activities.[189] Within the Marine Corps, for example, counterintelligence constitutes active and passive measures intended to deny a threat force valuable information about the friendly situation, to detect and neutralize hostile intelligence collection, and to deceive the enemy as to friendly capabilities and intentions.[190] *See* COUNTERESPIONAGE; COUNTERSUBVERSION; SECURITY INTELLIGENCE; SOURCES OF INTELLIGENCE.

COUNTERINTELLIGENCE ACTIVITIES Information gathered and activities conducted to identify, deceive, exploit, disrupt, or protect against espionage, other intelligence activities, sabotage, or assassinations conducted for or on behalf of foreign powers, organizations or persons or their agents, or international terrorist organizations or activities.[191]

COUNTERINTELLIGENCE ASSESSMENT A Department of Defense (DoD) component's comprehensive analysis or study of a relevant Counterintelligence (CI) topic, event, situation, issue, or development. CI assessments require exhaustive amounts of research, and the production timeline can range from days to months. When conducted in support of a Research, Development, and Acquisition (RDA) program with Critical Program Information (CPI), the assessment describes the threat a foreign entity (person, representative, corporation, government, military, commercial, etc.) represents to the

CPI or system assessed. The assessment is multi-disciplinary, as it includes an analysis of the diverse foreign collection modalities available, the relative effectiveness of each, and capability of the foreign entity to collect information about research efforts, the technology, and/or system under development. The assessment may include the impact to the DoD if the technology is compromised and be complimentary to, integrated with, or independent of the Technology-Targeting Risk Assessment (TTRA) provided by the Defense Intelligence Community (DIC).[192]

COUNTERINTELLIGENCE COLLECTION The systematic acquisition of information concerning espionage, sabotage, terrorism, other intelligence activities or assassinations conducted by or on behalf of terrorists, foreign powers, and other entities.[193]

COUNTERINTELLIGENCE OPERATIONS Proactive activities designed to identify, exploit, neutralize, or deter foreign intelligence collection and terrorist activities directed against the United States.[194]

COUNTERMEASURES 1. Devices and/or techniques employed with the objective of impairing the operational effectiveness of an adversary. 2. Actions, devices, procedures, techniques, or other measures that reduce the vulnerability of an information system. Synonymous with security controls and safeguards.[195]

COUNTERPROLIFERATION Those actions taken to reduce the risks posed by extant weapons of mass destruction to the United States, allies, and partners.[196]

COUNTERSIGN A secret challenge and its reply. *See* PASSWORD

COUNTERSUBVERSION Action designed to detect and counteract subversion. *See* COUNTERINTELLIGENCE

COUNTERSURVEILLANCE All measures, active or passive, taken to counteract hostile surveillance. Countersurveillance may include: (1) techniques designed to protect an intelligence operation from surveillance personnel; (2) attempts to detect surveillance of particular targets by personnel other than the target; (3) employing additional assets specifically to determine if surveillance is being employed against an individual or specific area; (4) an act designed to discover any surveillance present, which may involve a self-analysis of a surveillance detection route/run or the stationing of other persons along a given route to analyze possible coverage. *See* SURVEILLANCE

COUNTERTERRORISM CENTER (CTC) A 24-hour CIA operation that has existed since 1986; working there are counterterrorism analysts who work at the CIA and are not on loan to other entities. Various types of research and strategic documents are disseminated, and warning intelligence is primarily disseminated to other agencies working with the CTC; personnel size is classified. *See* INFORMATION ANALYSIS AND INFRASTRUCTURE PROTECTION DIRECTORATE; JOINT TERRORISM TASK FORCE; TERRORIST THREAT INTEGRATION CENTER

COUNTRY REPORTS ON TERRORISM U.S. law requires the Secretary of State to provide Congress, by April 30 of each year, a full and complete report on terrorism with regard to those countries and groups meeting criteria set forth in the legislation. This annual report is titled *Country Reports on Terrorism*. Beginning with the report for 2004, it replaced the previously published *Patterns of Global Terrorism*.[197]

COVER 1. A protective guise used by an individual, organization, or installation to prevent identification with intelligence activities.[198] 2. To hide, conceal, obscure, or otherwise protect the exact identity of an individual, unit, or activity. A cover may be supported with or without documentation and backstopping, depending on the sensitivity and scope of the operation. Cover can be anything that masks the true nature of an activity.

COVER FOR ACTION A logical reason for doing a specific action.[199]

COVER FOR STATUS A logical and backstopped reason for being in an area or possessing a particular item at a particular time.[200]

COVER WITHIN COVER A credible confession to an act that is less serious than espionage and will explain all actions under suspicion by foreign intelligence services.

COVERED COMMUNICATION Any nonpublic telephone or electronic communication acquired without the consent of a person who is a party to the communication, including communications in electronic storage.[201]

COVERT ACTIONS 1. Activities conducted in a concealed manner, making it difficult or impossible to attribute them to the intelligence service involved or the government that sponsors the intelligence service. 2. Secret or hidden operations or investigations intended to be conducted outside the view of the target and the general population. The exact nature of surveillance would be immediately exposed and compromised by a simple discovery.[202]

COVERT COLLECTION Collection of biometrics without the knowledge of an individual. An instance in which biometric samples are being collected at a place and/or time that is not known to the subjects. An example of a covert environment might involve an airport checkpoint where facial images of passengers are captured and compared to a watchlist without their knowledge.[203]

COVERT HUMAN INTELLIGENCE SOURCE (CHIS) 1. Under the 2000 Act (*sic, Regulation of Investigatory Powers Act*), a person is a CHIS if: a) he establishes or maintains a personal or other relationship with a person for the covert purpose of facilitating the doing of anything falling within paragraph b) or c); b) he covertly uses such a relationship to obtain information or to provide access to any information to another person; or c) he covertly discloses information obtained by the use of such a relationship or as a consequence of the existence of such a relationship. 2. A relationship is established or maintained for a covert purpose if and only if it is conducted in a manner that is calculated to ensure that one of the parties to the relationship is unaware of the purpose. 3. A relationship is used covertly, and information obtained is disclosed covertly, if and only if the relationship is used or the information is disclosed in a manner that is calculated to ensure that one of the parties to the relationship is unaware of the use or disclosure in question.[204]

COVERT OPERATION 1. Military or political activities undertaken in a manner that disguises the identity of the perpetrators. They are employed in situations where openly operating against a target would jeopardize the operation's success. 2. Operations that are so planned and executed as to conceal the identity of or permit plausible denial by the sponsor. This differs from clandestine operations in that emphasis is placed on concealment of identity or sponsor rather than concealment of the operation.[205] *See* CLANDESTINE OPERATION

COVERT PRODUCTS Covert products require exceptional coordination, integration, and oversight. The operations are planned and conducted in such a manner that the responsible agency or government is not evident, and if uncovered, the sponsor can plausibly disclaim any involvement. Gray and black products are employed in covert operations.[206]

CREATE TERRORISM MODELING SYSTEM (CTMS) The Homeland Security Center for Risk and Economic Analysis of Terrorism Events (CREATE) methodology and software system for assessing risks of terrorism within the framework of economic analysis and structured decision making.[207]

CREDIBILITY The extent to which something is believable; commonly used with reference to sources of evidence, to evidence itself, and to hypotheses based on evidence. Credibility is sometimes confused with "reliability," but there are differences: reliability is just one attribute of the credibility of certain forms of evidence, while credibility (of sources of evidence) is both context and time dependent. For example, a person or sensor may be more credible regarding certain events and at certain times but not so credible regarding other events or at other times. *See* ACCURACY; AUTHENTICITY; EVIDENCE

CREEPING NORMALCY 1. The methodical increment of a country's military capability so that its more capable posture is unnoticeable and accepted over time by outside observers. For example, the North Korean army has been accused of using a strategy of creeping normalcy to build up its forces near the demilitarized zone next to South Korea.[208] 2. The way a major change can be accepted as normality if it happens slowly, in unnoticed increments, although it would be regarded as objectionable if it took place all at once or within a short time period. The "boiling frog" story is used to explain this concept; if a frog is placed in boiling water, it will jump out, but if it is placed in cold water that is slowly heated, it will never jump out. The lesson to be learned is that people should make themselves aware of gradual change lest they suffer a catastrophic loss. *See* MISSION CREEP; PRECISION ATTACK/ENGAGEMENT; SALAMI TACTICS

CRIME PATTERN ANALYSIS A process that looks for links between crimes and other incidents to reveal similarities and differences that can be used to help predict and prevent future criminal activity.[209]

CRIMES REPORTS Official notifications that are sent by U.S. intelligence agencies to the Department of Justice when an unauthorized disclosure of classified information (or another potential federal crime) is believed to have occurred. Crimes reporting is required by statute, by executive order, and by interagency agreement between the Attorney General and the heads of intelligence agencies.[210]

CRIMINAL ANALYSIS The application of analytical methods and products to raw data that produces intelligence within the criminal justice field.[211]

CRIMINAL BUSINESS PROFILE A product that details how criminal operations or techniques work, including how victims are chosen, how they are victimized, how proceeds of crime are used, and the strengths and weaknesses in the criminal system.[212]

CRIMINAL INTELLIGENCE Information relevant to the identification of, and criminal activity engaged in by, an individual or organization reasonably suspected of involvement in criminal activity. Certain criminal activities, including but not limited to loan sharking, drug trafficking, trafficking in stolen property, gambling, extortion, smuggling, bribery, and corruption of public officials often involve some degree of regular coordination and permanent organization involving a large number of participants over a broad geographical area.[213]

CRIMINAL INTELLIGENCE SYSTEM Arrangements, equipment, facilities, and procedures used for the receipt, storage, interagency exchange or dissemination, and analysis of criminal intelligence information.[214]

CRISIS 1. The convergence of rapidly unfolding events in an outcome that is detrimental to national security. The outcome is to some degree indeterminate, which could create elements of both threat and opportunity. Crisis response typically requires critical timing and decision making under extreme personal and organizational stress. 2. An incident or situation involving a threat to the United States, its territories, citizens, military forces, possessions, or vital interests that develops rapidly and creates a condition of such diplomatic, economic, political, or military importance that commitment of U.S. military forces and resources is contemplated to achieve national objectives.[215]

CRISIS ACTION PLANNING PROCESS. *See* CONTINGENCY PLANNING PROCESS

CRISIS MANAGEMENT An organization's ability to prepare for perceived catastrophic events—such as terrorism—and its capacity to employ appropriate force and specialized capabilities to minimize damage to U.S. interests. Domestically, crisis management also employs every resource at the disposal of federal, state, and local governments. *See* CONSEQUENCE MANAGEMENT; CRITICAL INDICATOR

CRITERIA FOR SUCCESS Information requirements developed during the operations process that measure the degree of success in accomplishing the unit's mission. They are normally expressed as an explicit evaluation of the present situation or as a forecast of the degree of mission accomplishment.[216]

CRITICAL AND SENSITIVE INFORMATION LIST A list containing the most important aspects of a program or technology, whether classified or unclassified, requiring protection from adversary exploitation.[217]

CRITICAL INDICATOR (KEY INDICATOR) An action or decision that will immediately and directly affect a threat scenario. Critical indicators constitute a small portion of the overall number of indicators which can easily be monitored. "Detection of excessive ammunition production and export would be a critical indicator of impending armed conflict, since no military operation can succeed without adequate ammunition supplies, despite adequate numbers of weapons."[218] *See* CRISIS MANAGEMENT

CRITICAL INFORMATION 1. Specific facts about friendly intentions, capabilities, and activities needed by adversaries for them to plan and act effectively so as to guarantee failure or unacceptable consequences for friendly mission accomplishment.[219] 2. Critical information (CRITIC) is information concerning possible threats to U.S. national security that are so significant that they require the immediate attention of the president and the National Security Council. Critical information includes the decisions, intentions, or actions of foreign governments, organizations, or individuals that could imminently and materially jeopardize vital U.S. policy, economic, information system, critical infrastructure, cyberspace, or military interests. Critical information may originate with any U.S. government official in the IC. CRITIC reporting may be based on either classified or unclassified information. CRITIC reporting should be based solely on unclassified information only if that information is unlikely to be readily available to the president and the National Security Council.[220]

CRITICAL INFRASTRUCTURE Provided in section 1016(e) of the USA Patriot Act of 2001 (42 U.S.C. 5195c(e))—namely, systems and assets, whether physical or virtual, so vital to the United States that the incapacity or destruction of such systems and assets would have a debilitating impact on security, national economic security, national public health or safety, or any combination of those matters.[221] *See* NATIONAL INFRASTRUCTURE PROTECTION PLAN

CRITICAL INFRASTRUCTURE AND KEY RESOURCES (CIKR) Critical infrastructure are the assets, systems, and networks, whether physical or virtual, so vital to the United States that their incapacitation or destruction would have a debilitating effect on security, national economic security, public health or safety, or any combination thereof. Key resources are publicly or privately controlled resources essential to the minimal operations of the economy and government.[222] *See* ENHANCED CRITICAL INFRASTRUCTURE PROTECTION ASSESSMENT

CRITICAL INFRASTRUCTURE COMMUNITY Critical infrastructure owners and operators, both public and private; federal departments and agencies; regional entities; SLTT governments; and other organizations from the private and nonprofit sectors with a role in securing and strengthening the resilience of the nation's critical infrastructure and/or promoting practices and ideas for doing so.[223]

CRITICAL INFRASTRUCTURE INFORMATION (CII) Information that is not customarily in the public domain and is related to the security of critical infrastructure or protected systems. CII consists of records and information concerning any of the following: actual, potential, or threatened interference with, attack on, compromise of, or incapacitation of critical infrastructure or protected systems by either physical or computer-based attack or other similar conduct (including the misuse of or unauthorized access to all types of communications and data transmission systems) that violates federal, state, or local law; harms the interstate commerce of the United States; or threatens public health or safety. The ability of any critical infrastructure or protected system to resist such interference, compromise, or incapacitation, including any planned or past assessment, projection, or estimate of the vulnerability of critical infrastructure or a protected system, including security testing, risk evaluation, risk management planning, or risk audit. Any planned or past operational problem or solution regarding critical infrastructure or protected systems, including repair, recovery, insurance, or continuity, to the extent that it is related to such interference, compromise, or incapacitation.[224]

CRITICAL INFRASTRUCTURE PARTNER Those federal and governmental entities, public and private sector owners and operators and representative organizations, regional organizations and coalitions, academic and professional entities, and certain not-for-profit and private volunteer organizations that share responsibility for securing and strengthening the resilience of the nation's critical infrastructure.[225]

CRITICAL INFRASTRUCTURE PROTECTION (CIP) Actions taken to prevent, remediate, or mitigate the risks resulting from vulnerabilities of critical infrastructure assets.[226]

CRITICAL INFRASTRUCTURE RISK MANAGEMENT FRAMEWORK A planning and decision-making framework that outlines the process for setting goals and objectives, identifying infrastructure, assessing risks, implementing risk management activities, and measuring effectiveness to inform continuous improvement in critical infrastructure security and resilience.[227]

CRITICAL INFRASTRUCTURE SECTORS *Presidential Policy Directive-21* identifies 16 critical infrastructure sectors and designates associated federal SSAs (sector-specfic agency). In some cases co-SSAs are designated where those departments share the roles and responsibilities of the SSA. The Secretary of Homeland Security shall periodically evaluate the need for and approve changes to critical infrastructure sectors and shall consult with the Assistant to the President for Homeland Security and Counterterrorism before changing a critical infrastructure sector or a designated SSA for that sector. The sectors and SSAs are as follows: Chemical, Commercial Facilities, Communications, Critical Manufacturing, Dams, Defense Industrial Base, Emergency Services, Energy, Financial Services, Food and Agriculture, Government Facilities, Healthcare and Public Health, Information Technology, Nuclear Reactors, Materials, and Waste, Transportation Systems, Water and Wastewater Systems.[228] *See* SECTOR-SPECIFIC AGENCY

CRITICAL INTELLIGENCE 1. Intelligence that requires immediate attention by a commander or policymaker and which may enhance or refute previously held beliefs about hostilities or actions, leading to a change of policy. 2. Information of such urgent importance to the security of the United States that it is directly transmitted at the highest priority to the president and other national decision-making officials before passing through regular evaluative channels.[229] In the military, it is intelligence that requires the immediate attention of the commander. It includes but is not limited to strong indications of the immediate outbreak of hostilities of any type (warning of attack); aggression of any nature against a friendly country; indications or use of nuclear/biological chemical weapons (targets); significant events within potential enemy countries that may lead to modifications of nuclear strike plans.[230] 3. A handling symbol and precedence for specially formatted cables conveying national security information that must be routed to NSA and then delivered to the highest levels of the U.S. government as fast as possible.[231]

CRITICAL INTELLIGENCE MESSAGE Information about a situation that so critically affects the security interests of a country or its allies that it may require the immediate attention of the government's highest official.

CRITICAL NATIONAL ASSETS (CNA) Critical National Assets are any information, policies, plans, technologies, or capabilities that, if acquired (stolen), modified, or manipulated by an adversary, would seriously threaten U.S. national or economic security.[232]

CRITICAL NUCLEAR WEAPONS DESIGN INFORMATION (CNWDI) Information classified "TOP SECRET Restricted Data (RD)" or

"SECRET Restricted Data (RD)" revealing the theory of operation or design of the components of a thermonuclear or implosion-type fission bomb, warhead, demolition munitions, or test device. The sensitivity of Critical Nuclear Weapons Design Information (CNWDI) is such that it is in the national interest to assure that access is granted to the absolute minimum number of employees who require it for the accomplishment of assigned responsibilities on the strictest need-to-know basis.[233]

CRITICAL PROGRAM INFORMATION (CPI) Critical Program Information, or CPI, is defined as that "key" information about the program, technologies, and/or systems that if compromised would degrade combat effectiveness or shorten the expected life of the system. CPI may also provide insight into program vulnerabilities, countermeasures, and limitations. Unauthorized access to this information or systems could allow someone to kill, counter and clone, negate, or degrade the system before or near the scheduled deployment, forcing a major design change to maintain the same level of effectiveness and capability. CPI may be classified or unclassified information. Given the potentially grave consequences that can result from the compromise of CPI, everyone who uses this sensitive information must ensure it is adequately identified and protected.[234]

CRITICAL THINKING The objective, open, and critical cognitive process applied to information to achieve a greater understanding of data, often through developing and answering questions about the data.[235]

CRITICALITY Importance to a mission or function, or continuity of operations.[236]

CRITICALITY ASSESSMENT Product or process of systematically identifying, evaluating, and prioritizing based on the importance of an impact to mission(s), function(s), or continuity of operations.[237]

CROSS DOMAIN SOLUTION (CDs) The federal portion of the ISE will encompass policies, business processes, and technologies to ensure that terrorism information can be freely and transparently shared across three broad security domains—SCI, Secret, and SBU information.[238]

CRYPTANALYSIS The operations performed in defeating or circumventing cryptographic protection of information by applying mathematical techniques and without an initial knowledge of the key employed in providing the protection. Extended Definition: The study of mathematical techniques for attempting to defeat or circumvent cryptographic techniques and/or information systems security.[239]

CRYPTO A marking or designator identifying COMSEC keying material used to secure or authenticate telecommunications carrying classified or sensitive U.S. government or U.S. government-derived information.[240]

CRYPTOCURRENCY A digital or virtual currency that uses cryptography for security. A cryptocurrency is difficult to counterfeit because of this security feature. A defining feature of a cryptocurrency is that it is not issued by any central authority, rendering it theoretically immune to government interference or manipulation. The anonymous nature of cryptocurrency transactions makes them well suited for a host of nefarious activities such as money laundering and tax evasion. The first cryptocurrency to capture the public imagination was Bitcoin, which was launched in 2009. Bitcoin's success has spawned a number of competing cryptocurrencies such as Litecoin, Namecoin and PPCoin.[241]

CRYPTOGRAPHY 1. The art or science concerning the principles, means, and methods for rendering plain information unintelligible and for restoring encrypted information to intelligible form.[242] 2. The art or science concerning the principles, means, and methods for converting plaintext into ciphertext and for restoring encrypted ciphertext to plaintext.[243]

CRYPTOMATERIAL All material, including documents, devices, or equipment, that contains crypto information and is essential to the encryption, decrypting, or authentication of telecommunications.[244]

CRYPTONYMS Code names; sometimes called "crypts" for short.

CRYPTOPART A division of a message, as prescribed for security reasons. The operating instructions for certain cryptosystems prescribe the number of groups that may be encrypted in the systems, using a single message indicator. Cryptoparts are identified in plain language. They are not to be confused with message parts.[245]

CRY-WOLF SYNDROME (CRYING WOLF) The desensitization of observers after previous warnings has been issued without threatening consequences. For example, "In 1968, CIA analyst Hovey's bull's-eye analysis of North Vietnam's ability to strike at U.S. troops had made the rounds among the CIA's top brass and it was even dispatched to the White House, where

President Johnson read it 15 days before the attack. However, a note from George Carver, a top CIA official, shot down Hovey's warning. Carver said Hovey was crying wolf."[246] *See* ALERT FATIGUE

CUBAN MISSILE CRISIS The tense Cold War standoff that developed in October 1962 when a routine reconnaissance mission by a U.S. U-2 spy plane indicated the Soviet Union was building a missile base in Cuba. The base would enable launching short- and intermediate-range ballistic missiles that could quickly carry nuclear warheads to American soil. Ultimately, through direct contacts between President John F. Kennedy and Soviet leader Nikita Khrushchev, the missiles were removed from Cuba.

CUI REGISTRY CUI markings will be developed and scheduled for implementation following publication of additional guidance. Safeguarding: For each CUI category and subcategory, federal agencies shall comply with information security requirements defined by the National Institute of Standards and Technology (NIST). Dissemination: CUI shall be disseminated only to individuals who require the information for an authorized mission purpose. Decontrol: Information shall be decontrolled as soon as possible when it no longer requires safeguarding measures and dissemination controls pursuant to its associated authorities. CUI that has been publicly released via authorized agency procedures shall be considered decontrolled.[247] See CLASSIFICATION AND CONTROL MARKING SYSTEM; CLASSIFICATION MARKINGS; CUI REGISTRY

CULTIVATION A deliberate and calculated association with a person for the purpose or recruitment, obtaining information, or gaining control for these or other purposes.

CULTURAL INTELLIGENCE Knowledge resulting from all-source analysis of cultural factors, which assists in anticipating the actions of people or groups of people.[248]

CURRENT INDICATIONS Activities relating to information, in varying degrees of evaluation, which bear on the intention of a potentially hostile force to adopt or reject a course of action or which bear on an impending crisis.

CURRENT INTELLIGENCE Information gathered on a day-to-day basis; information of all types and forms concerning events of immediate interest, characteristically focusing on descriptive snapshots of generally static conditions; highly perishable information covering events that is disseminated without delay and lacks complete evaluation, interpretation, analysis, or integration. The fall of the shah in Iran is a case that revealed current intelligence weaknesses. CIA and State Department daily reports, the primary vehicles for political intelligence, consistently failed to draw Washington's attention to Iran in the early spring and summer of 1978, following the worst rioting in a decade. Early identification of factors such as the shah's vulnerability and mounting dissidence could have prevented the crisis that evolved between the two countries.[249] *See* CURRENT OPERATIONAL INTELLIGENCE; COMBAT INTELLIGENCE; ESTIMATIVE INTELLIGENCE; NEAR-REAL TIME; WARNING INTELLIGENCE; RESEARCH INTELLIGENCE; SCIENTIFIC AND TECHNICAL INTELLIGENCE

CURRENT OPERATIONAL INTELLIGENCE Required for final planning and execution of all operations; especially important to military commanders in executing a tactical operation.

CUSTODIAN An individual who has possession of classified information or is charged with the responsibility of safeguarding and accounting for classified information.

CUSTOMER A person or entity that requires intelligence and information, consistent with applicable laws, EO, and Attorney General procedures promulgated in accordance with EO 12333, as amended. A customer external to the IC does not have the same rights to access, search, discover, and retrieve information and intelligence data in the form initially gathered as do IC personnel.[250]

CUSTOMERS Consumers of intelligence products, who may be within the agency of the analyst or in other agencies or organizations.[251]

CUSTOMS AND BORDER PROTECTION (CBP) INTELLIGENCE ELEMENT CBP is the agency responsible for securing the nation's borders at and between ports of entry (POE). It was established in 2003 as a result of the Homeland Security Act of 2002, consolidating the inspection and patrol functions of the legacy U.S. Customs Service, the Immigration and Naturalization Service (INS), the U.S. Border Patrol (BP), and the Animal and Plant Health Inspection Service (APHIS). CBP's primary mission is to prevent the entry of terrorists and the instruments of terrorism into the United States. It also has responsibility to prevent illegal immigration, regulate and facilitate international trade, collect import duties, enforce U.S. trade and drug laws, and protect Americans and U.S. agricultural and economic interests by preventing the importation of harmful pests, diseases, and contaminated, diseased, infested, or adulterated agricultural and food products.[252]

CYBER ACTION TEAM (CAT) Established by the FBI's Cyber Division in 2006 to provide rapid incident response on major computer intrusions and cyber-related emergencies, the team has approximately 50 members located in field offices around the country. They are either special agents or computer scientists, and all possess advanced training in computer languages, forensic investigations, and malware analysis.[253]

CYBER ARMAGEDDON Rather than a "Cyber Armageddon" scenario that debilitates the entire U.S. infrastructure, we envision something different. We foresee an ongoing series of low-to-moderate-level cyber attacks from a variety of sources over time, which will impose cumulative costs on U.S. economic competitiveness and national security.[254]

CYBER ATTACK A hostile act using computer or related networks or systems intended to disrupt and/or destroy an adversary's critical cyber systems, assets, or functions. The intended effects of a cyber attack are not necessarily limited to the targeted computer systems or data themselves—for instance, attacks on computer systems which are intended to degrade or destroy the infrastructure of Command and Control (C2) capability. A cyber attack may use intermediate delivery vehicles including peripheral devices, electronic transmitters, embedded code, or human operators. The activation or effect of a cyber attack may be widely separated temporally and geographically from the delivery.[255]

CYBER COUNTERINTELLIGENCE Measures to identify, penetrate, or neutralize foreign operations that use cyber means as the primary tradecraft methodology, as well as foreign intelligence service collection efforts that use traditional methods to gauge cyber capabilities and intentions.[256]

CYBER CRIME The U.S. government does not appear to have an official definition of cybercrime that distinguishes it from crimes committed in what many consider the real world. Similarly, there is not a definition of cybercrime that distinguishes it from other forms of cyber threats, and the term is often used interchangeably with other Internet or technology-based malicious acts such as cyber warfare, cyber attack, and cyber terrorism. Rather, government officials, law enforcement, and policymakers have often described cybercrime in terms of a number of computer, Internet, or advanced technology-related offenses. It has been an umbrella term, encompassing a range of crimes and malicious activities that may differ depending upon who is asked. Federal law enforcement agencies often define cybercrime based on their jurisdiction and the crimes they are charged with investigating. And, just as there is no overarching definition for cybercrime, there is no single agency that has been designated as the lead investigative agency for combating "cybercrime."[257]

CYBER CRIMINALS Individuals or groups whose criminal conduct is primarily through or are dependent on operating through cyberspace/cyber domain.[258]

CYBER ECOSYSTEM The interconnected information infrastructure of interactions among persons, processes, data, and information and communications technologies, along with the environment and conditions that influence those interactions.[259]

CYBER EXERCISE A planned event during which an organization simulates a cyber disruption to develop or test capabilities such as preventing, detecting, mitigating, responding to or recovering from the disruption.[260]

CYBER INFRASTRUCTURE An electronic information and communications systems and services and the information contained therein. Extended Definition: The information and communications systems and services composed of all hardware and software that process, store, and communicate information, or any combination of all of these elements: processing includes the creation, access, modification, and destruction of information; storage includes paper, magnetic, electronic, and all other media types; communications include sharing and distribution of information.[261]

CYBER MANIPULATION A cyber attack involving an information operation resulting in a compromise of the operation or product delivered through a supply chain. For example, products are delivered to the wrong place, at the wrong time, or not at all, or there is a quality or type problem.[262]

CYBER OPERATIONS In the NICE (National Initiative for Cybersecurity Education) Workforce Framework, cybersecurity work where a person: performs activities to gather evidence on criminal or foreign intelligence entities in order to mitigate possible or real-time threats, protect against espionage or insider threats, foreign sabotage, international terrorist activities, or to support other intelligence activities.[263]

CYBER OPERATIONS PLANNING In the NICE (National Initiative for Cybersecurity Education) Workforce Framework, cybersecurity work where a person: performs in-depth joint targeting and cyber planning process. Gathers information and develops detailed Operational Plans and Orders supporting requirements. Conducts strategic and operational-level planning across the full range of operations for integrated information and cyberspace operations.[264]

CYBER SHOCKWAVE A simulated cyber attack on the United States that examined how the government would respond to a large-scale cyber crisis. The simulation was hosted by the Bipartisan Policy Center (BPC) on February 16, 2010, in Washington, D.C., and was created by former CIA director General Michael Hayden and the BPC. The simulation envisioned an attack that disables 20 million smartphones through a malware program planted through a popular smartphone application. The attack escalates, shutting down an electronic energy trading platform and crippling the power grid on the Eastern seaboard.[265]

CYBER SYSTEM Any combination of facilities, equipment, personnel, procedures, and communications integrated to provide cyber services; examples include business systems, control systems, and access control systems.[266]

CYBER THREAT INDICATOR Means information that is necessary to describe or identify—(A) malicious reconnaissance, including anomalous patterns of communications that appear to be transmitted for the purpose of gathering technical information related to a cybersecurity threat or security vulnerability; (B) a method of defeating a security control or exploitation of a security vulnerability; (C) a security vulnerability, including anomalous activity that appears to indicate the existence of a security vulnerability; (D) a method of causing a user with legitimate access to an information system or information that is stored on, processed by, or transiting an information system to unwittingly enable the defeat of a security control or exploitation of a security vulnerability; (E) malicious cyber command and control; (F) the actual or potential harm caused by an incident, including a description of the information exfiltrated as a result of a particular cybersecurity threat; (G) any other attribute of a cybersecurity threat, if disclosure of such attribute is not otherwise prohibited by law; or (H) any combination thereof.[267]

CYBER THREAT INTELLIGENCE INTEGRATION CENTER (CTIIC) The CTIIC will be a national intelligence center focused on "connecting the dots" regarding malicious foreign cyber threats to the nation and cyber incidents affecting U.S. national interests, and on providing all-source analysis of threats to U.S. policymakers. The CTIIC will also assist relevant departments and agencies in their efforts to identify, investigate, and mitigate those threats. The CTIIC will provide integrated all-source intelligence analysis related to foreign cyber threats and cyber incidents affecting U.S. national interests; support the U.S. government centers responsible for cybersecurity and network defense; and facilitate and support efforts by the government to counter foreign cyber threats. Once established, the CTIIC will join the National Cybersecurity and Communications Integration Center (NCCIC), the National Cyber Investigative Joint Task Force (NCIJTF), and U.S. Cyber Command as integral parts of the United States government's capability to protect our citizens, our companies, and our nation from cyber threats.[268]

CYBER THREAT INVESTIGATION Any actions taken within the United States, consistent with applicable law and presidential guidance, to determine the identity, location, intent, motivation, capabilities, alliances, funding, or methodologies of one or more cyber threat groups or individuals.[269]

CYBERACTIVISTS Individuals who perform cyberattacks for pleasure, philosophical, political, or other nonmonetary reasons. Examples include someone who attacks a technology system as a personal challenge (who might be termed a "classic" hacker), and a "hacktivist," such as a member of the cyber-group Anonymous, who undertakes an attack for political reasons. The activities of these groups can range from nuisance-related denial of service attacks and website defacement to disrupting government and private corporation business processes.[270]

CYBERSECURITY 1. Prevention of damage to, protection of, and restoration of computers, electronic communications systems, electronic communication services, wire communication, and electronic communication, including information contained therein, to ensure its availability, integrity, authentication, confidentiality, and non-repudiation.[271] 2. The activity or process, ability or capability, or state whereby information and communications systems and the information contained therein are protected from and/or defended against damage, unauthorized use or modification, or exploitation. Extended Definition: Strategy, policy, and standards regarding the security of and operations in cyberspace, and encompass[ing] the full range of threat reduction, vulnerability reduction, deterrence, international engagement, incident response, resiliency, and recovery policies and activities, including computer network operations, information assurance, law enforcement, diplomacy, military, and intelligence missions as they relate to the security and stability of the global information and communications infrastructure.[272]

CYBERSECURITY RISK Threats to and vulnerabilities of information or information systems and any related consequences caused by or resulting from unauthorized access, use, disclosure, degradation, disruption, modification, or destruction of information or information systems, including such related consequences caused by an act of terrorism.[273]

CYBERSECURITY THREAT An action, not protected by the First Amendment to the Constitution of the United States, on or through an information system that may result in an unauthorized effort to adversely impact the security, availability, confidentiality, or integrity of an information system or information that is stored on, processed by, or transiting an information system.[274]

CYBERSPACE 1. A global domain within the information environment consisting of the independent networks of information technology infrastructures and resident data, including the Internet, telecommunications networks, computer systems, and embedded processors and controllers.[275] 2. "Cyberspace" means the interdependent network of information technology infrastructures, and includes the Internet, telecommunications networks, computer systems, and embedded processors and controllers in critical industries.[276] 3. The interdependent network of information technology infrastructures, that includes the Internet, telecommunications networks, computer systems, and embedded processors and controllers.[277]

CYBERSPACE OPERATIONS A global domain within the information environment consisting of the interdependent networks of information technology infrastructures and resident data, including the Internet, telecommunications networks, computer systems, and embedded processors and controllers.[278]

CYBERSPACE SUPERIORITY The degree of dominance in cyberspace by one force that permits the secure, reliable conduct of operations by that force, and its related land, air, maritime, and space forces at a given time and place without prohibitive interference by an adversary.[279]

CYBERSPIES Cyberspies are individuals who steal classified or proprietary information used by governments or private corporations to gain a competitive strategic, security, financial, or political advantage. These individuals often work at the behest of, and take direction from, foreign government entities. Targets include government networks, cleared defense contractors, and private companies.[280]

CYBERTERRORISM 1. A criminal act perpetrated by the use of computers and telecommunications capabilities, resulting in violence, destruction and/or disruption of services, where the intended purpose is to create fear by causing confusion and uncertainty within a given population, with the goal of influencing a government or population to conform to a particular political, social or ideological agenda.[281] 2. Also, cyberterrorism: the unlawful attacks and threats of attack against computers, networks, and the information stored therein when done to intimidate or coerce a government or its people to further political or social objectives. Actors who engage in these kinds of activities are commonly referred to as cyber terrorists.[282]

CYBERTERRORISTS Cyberterrorists are state-sponsored and non-state actors who engage in cyberattacks to pursue their objectives. Transnational terrorist organizations, insurgents, and jihadists have used the Internet as a tool for planning attacks, radicalization and recruitment, a method of propaganda distribution, and a means of communication, and for disruptive purposes.[283]

CYBERTHIEVES Cyberthieves are individuals who engage in illegal cyberattacks for monetary gain. Examples include an organization or individual who illegally accesses a technology system to steal and use or sell credit card numbers and someone who deceives a victim into providing access to a financial account.[284]

CYBERVETTING Cybervetting is an assessment of a person's suitability to hold a position using information found on the Internet to help make that determination. Cybervetting occurs even though there are no generally accepted guidelines and procedures for fair, complete, and efficient Internet searches for this purpose. Job applicants, employees, and employers are often uncertain whether cybervetting is legal, where privacy rights begin and end, and what cyber behaviors and postings should be subject to cybervetting.[285]

CYBERWARRIORS Cyberwarriors are agents or quasi-agents of nation-states who develop capabilities and undertake cyberattacks in support of a country's strategic objectives. These entities may or may not be acting on behalf of the government with respect to target selection, timing of the attack, and type(s) of cyberattack and are often blamed by the host country when accusations are levied by the nation that has been attacked. Often, when a foreign government is provided evidence that a cyberattack is emanating from its country, the nation that has been attacked is informed that the perpetrators acted of their own volition and not at the behest of the government.[286]

CYCLE OF INTELLIGENCE (INTELLIGENCE CYCLE) The continuous process of work done within the intelligence community. The phases are: (1) planning and direction, what intelligence needs to be developed based on existing gaps of knowledge; (2) collection, obtaining the information; (3) processing, converting the raw information into products such as transcriptions, translations, or imagery interpretations; (4) analysis and assessment, turning the information into a finished intelligence product by evaluating and integrating the information; (5) distribution of the product to those who have a "need to know."

NOTES

1. Douglas E. Batson, *Registering the Human Domain: A Valuation of Cadastre*, National Defense Intelligence College, 3 (2008), http://ni-u.edu/ni_press/pdf/Registering_the_Human_Terrains.pdf (accessed October 28, 2015).

2. Federal Bureau of Investigation, L. No. 103-414, *Ask CALEA, Section 102.* Section 102(2) of CALEA [Communications Assistance for Law Enforcement Act, Pub, http://askcalea.fbi.gov/calea/102.html (accessed October 28, 2015).

3. U.S. Department of Defense. *Department of Defense Dictionary of Military and Associated Terms.* JP 1-02, 08 November 2010, as Amended through 15 January 2016. Accessed January 26, 2016, http://www.dtic.mil/doctrine/new_pubs/jp1_02.pdf.

4. John Hughes-Wilson, *Military Intelligence Blunders* (Boston: Da Capo Press, 2004), 251.

5. Canadian Security Intelligence Service, *The Role of the CSIS*, accessed February 3, 2016, https://www.csis-scrs.gc.ca/bts/role-en.php.

6. U.S. Department of Defense, Center for Development of Security Excellence, *Glossary of Security Terms and Definitions*, November 2012, accessed February 3, 2016, http://www.cdse.edu/documents/cdse/Glossary_Handbook.pdf.

7. U.S. Department of Defense, *Department of Defense Dictionary of Military and Associated Terms*, JP 1-02, 08 November 2010, as Amended through 15 January 2015, accessed February 2, 2016, https://web.archive.org/web/20150326010957/http://www.dtic.mil/doctrine/new_pubs/jp1_02.pdf.

8. Ministry of Defense. *Captured Persons (CPERS).* Joint Doctrine Publication 1–10, 3rd edition, January 2015. https://www.gov.uk/government/uploads/system/uploads/attachment_data/file/455589/20150820-JDP_1_10_Ed_3_Ch_1_Secured.pdf (accessed January 26, 2016).

9. Federal Bureau of Investigation, *Carnivore Diagnostic Tool* (2000), accessed October 28, 2015, http://wayback.archive.org/web/20001207023100/http://www.fbi.gov/programs/carnivore/carnivore2.htm; also see Federal Bureau of Investigation, *Carnivore/DCS 1000 Report to Congress*, December 18, 2003, accessed October 28, 2015, http://www.epic.org/privacy/carnivore/2003_report.pdf.

10. U.S. Department of Defense, *Special Access Program (SAP) Policy*, DoD Directive Number 5205.07, July 1, 2010, accessed February 1, 2016, http://www.dtic.mil/whs/directives/corres/pdf/520507p.pdf.

11. Department of Homeland Security, Risk Steering Committee, *DHS Risk Lexicon*, September 2010, accessed February 2, 2016, http://www.dhs.gov/dhs-risk-lexicon.

12. U.S. Department of Defense. *Department of Defense Dictionary of Military and Associated Terms.* JP 1-02, 08 November 2010, as Amended through 15 January 2016. Accessed January 26, 2016, http://www.dtic.mil/doctrine/new_pubs/jp1_02.pdf.

13. Jan Goldman, *Intelligence Warning Terminology*, Joint Military Intelligence College, October 2001, accessed July 3, 2015. https://archive.org/details/JMICInteligencelwarnterminology.

14. Intelligence and National Security Alliance and the Office of the Director of National Intelligence, *Analytic Transformation: Moving Forward Together*, September 2007, accessed January 26, 2015. http://wayback.archive.org/web/20080530054342/http://analytic.insaonline.org/atprogram.pdf.

15. National Security and Homeland Security Presidential Directive/NSPD-51/HSPD 20. *National Continuity Policy.* May 9, 2007, accessed February 27, 2015. http://fas.org/irp/offdocs/nspd/nspd-51.htm; also see U.S. Department of Defense. *Defense Support of Civil Authorities.* JP 3-28, July 31, 2013, accessed January 26, 2015. http://www.dtic.mil/doctrine/new_pubs/jp3_28.pdf.

16. Committee for National Security Systems (CNSS), *National Information Assurance Glossary*, Instruction 4009, April 2010, accessed February 3, 2016, http://www.ncix.gov/publications/policy/docs/CNSSI_4009.pdf.

17. Director of Central Intelligence, *Security Controls on the Dissemination of Intelligence Information*, Directive 1/7, June 30, 1998, accessed June 2, 2015, https://fas.org/irp/offdocs/dcid17.htm.

18. U.S. Department of Defense. *Dictionary of Military and Associated Terms*, JP 1-02, 08 November 2010, as Amended through 15 January 2015, accessed January 12, 2015. https://web.archive.org/web/20150326010957/http://www.dtic.mil/doctrine/new_pubs/jp1_02.pdf.

19. U.S. Department of Defense, *Department of Defense Dictionary of Military and Associated Terms*, JP 1-02, 08 November 2010, as Amended through 15 January 2015, https://web.archive.org/web/20150326010957/http://www.dtic.mil/doctrine/new_pubs/jp1_02.pdf (accessed October 28, 2015).

20. Central Intelligence Agency. *About CSI*, accessed January 26, 2016. https://www.cia.gov/library/center-for-the-study-of-intelligence/about-csi.html.

21. U.S. Department of Defense, *Dictionary of Military and Associated Terms*, JP 1-02, 08 November 2010, as Amended through 15 January 2015, accessed January 26, 2015, https://web.archive.org/web/20150326010957/http://www.dtic.mil/doctrine/new_pubs/jp1_02.pdf.

22. U.S. Department of Defense, Center for Development of Security Excellence, *Glossary of Security Terms and Definitions*, November 2012, accessed February 2, 2016, http://www.cdse.edu/documents/cdse/Glossary_Handbook.pdf.

23. Committee for National Security Systems (CNSS), *National Information Assurance Glossary*, Instruction 4009, April 2010, accessed October 28, 2015, http://www.ncix.gov/publications/policy/docs/CNSSI_4009.pdf.

24. Committee for National Security Systems (CNSS), *National Information Assurance Glossary*, Instruction 4009, April 2010, accessed October 28, 2015, http://www.ncix.gov/publications/policy/docs/CNSSI_4009.pdf.

25. U.S. Department of Defense, Center for Development of Security Excellence, *Glossary of Security Terms and Definitions*, November 2012, accessed February 2, 2016, http://www.cdse.edu/documents/cdse/Glossary_Handbook.pdf.

26. U.S. Department of State. *Diplomatic Dictionary*, accessed March 6, 2015, http://diplomacy.state.gov/discoverdiplomacy/references/169792.htm.

27. Chatham House, the Royal Institute of International Affairs, *Chatham House Rule*, accessed January 26, 2016, http://www.chathamhouse.org/about/chatham-house-rule.

28. Department of Homeland Security, Risk Steering Committee, *DHS Risk Lexicon*, September 2010, accessed October 28, 2015, http://www.dhs.gov/dhs-risk-lexicon.

29. Organisation for the Prohibition of Chemical Weapons, *Chemical Weapons*, accessed February 20, 2015, http://www.opcw.org/chemical-weapons-convention/.

30. Frederick Schauer, "Fear, Risk and the First Amendment: Unraveling the Chilling Effect," *Boston University Law Review* 58 (1978): 685–732.

31. U.S. Department of Defense, *Counterintelligence*, DoD Directive Number 5240.02, March 17, 2015, accessed October 28, 2015, https://fas.org/irp/doddir/dod/d5240_02.pdf.

32. Central Intelligence Agency, *CREST: 25 Year Program Archive*, accessed October 28, 2015, http://www.foia.cia.gov/collection/crest-25-year-program-archive.

33. Defense Intelligence Agency, Office of Counterintelligence. *CI Glossary—Terms & Definitions of Interest for DoD CI Professionals.* July 2014. Accessed January 17, 2015. https://www.hsdl.org/?view&did=699056.

34. Committee for National Security Systems (CNSS), *National Information Assurance Glossary*, Instruction 4009, April 2010, accessed October 28, 2015, http://www.ncix.gov/publications/policy/docs/CNSSI_4009.pdf.

35. Jan Goldman, *Intelligence Warning Terminology*, Joint Military Intelligence College, October 2001, accessed July 3, 2015. https://archive.org/details/JMICInteligencelwarnterminology.

36. U.S. Citizenship and Immigration Services. *About Us*, accessed January 26, 2016, http://www.uscis.gov/aboutus; also see two reports by Ruth Ellen Wasem, "Toward More Effective Immigration Policies: Selected Organizational Issues," *CRS Report for Congress* RL33319, March 17, 2006, http://www.hlswatch.com/sitedocs/RL33319.pdf, and "U.S. Immigration Policy on Permanent Admission," *CRS Report for Congress* RL32235, March 13, 2012, accessed February 1, 2016, https://www.fas.org/sgp/crs/homesec/RL32235.pdf.

37. U.S. Department of Defense, *Defense Support of Civil Authorities*, JP 3-28, July 31, 2013, accessed October 28, 2015, http://www.dtic.mil/doctrine/new_pubs/jp3_28.pdf.

38. U.S. Department of Defense, *Defense Support of Civil Authorities*, JP 3-28, July 31, 2013, accessed October 28, 2015, http://www.dtic.mil/doctrine/new_pubs/jp3_28.pdf.

39. Government Accountability Office, *Civilian Intelligence Community: Additional Actions Needed to Improve Reporting on and Planning for the Use of Contract Personnel*, GAO-14-204, January 2014, http://www.gao.gov/products/GAO-14-204 (accessed October 28, 2015); also see Tim Shorrock's "The Corporate Intelligence Community: A Photo Exclusive," accessed January 25, 2015, http://timshorrock.com/?p=710 and U.S. Department of State, Office of Inspector General, Office of Evaluations and Special Projects, *Review of the Use of Confidentiality Agreements by Department of State Contractors*, ESP-15-03, March 2015, accessed January 25, 2015, https://oig.state.gov/system/files/esp-15-03.pdf.

40. United States Senate, Select Committee to Study Governmental Operations with Respect to Intelligence Activities (Church Committee), *Final Report*, Book 1, Washington, DC, April 26, 1976, accessed October 28, 2015, https://archive.org/details/finalreportofsel01unit.

41. Central Intelligence Agency, Office of Public Affairs, *A Consumer's Guide to Intelligence: Gaining Knowledge and Foreknowledge of the World Around Us*, Washington, DC: National Technical Information Service, 1999.

42. U.S. Department of Energy, *Understanding Classification* (Washington, DC: DOE, Office of Classification, 1987).

43. U.S. Department of Defense, *Department of Defense Dictionary of Military and Associated Terms*, JP 1-02, 08 November 2010, as Amended through 15 January 2015, accessed October 28, 2015, https://web.archive.org/web/20150326010957/http://www.dtic.mil/doctrine/new_pubs/jp1_02.pdf.

44. Office of the Director of National Intelligence. *Classification and Control Markings Systems*. Intelligence Community Directive 710, September 11, 2009, accessed January 14, 2015. http://www.ncix.gov/publications/policy/docs/ICD_710-Classification_and_Control_Markings_System.pdf; for a compilation of markings, see the Controlled Access Program Coordination Office (ODNI), *Authorized Classification and Control Markings Register*, March 30, 2012 (volume 5, edition 1), accessed January 13, 2015. http://fas.org/sgp/othergov/intel/capco_reg_v5-1.pdf, and the Information Security Oversight Office, *Marking Classified National Security Information.* Revision 2, December 2014, accessed January 14, 2015. http://www.archives.gov/isoo/training/marking-booklet.pdf.

45. National Imagery and Mapping Agency. *Guide to Marking Documents*. October 4, 2001, accessed January 12, 2015. https://www.fas.org/sgp/othergov/dod/nimaguide.pdf.

46. National Imagery and Mapping Agency. *Guide to Marking Documents*. October 4, 2001, accessed January 12, 2015. https://www.fas.org/sgp/othergov/dod/nimaguide.pdf.

47. National Imagery and Mapping Agency. *Guide to Marking Documents*. October 4, 2001, accessed January 12, 2015. https://www.fas.org/sgp/othergov/dod/nimaguide.pdf, and also see K-25 Site Classification and Information Control Office, Central Safeguards and Security Organization, *Classification of Compilations of*

Information, by Arvin S. Quist (Oak Ridge, Tennessee, June 1991), accessed January 25, 2015, http://www.fas.org/sgp/library/compilations.pdf.

48. National Archives, *Classified National Security Information*, Executive Order 13526, December 29, 2009, accessed January 25, 2015 http://www.archives.gov/isoo/policy-documents/cnsi-eo.html.

49. U.S. Department of Defense, *Department of Defense Dictionary of Military and Associated Terms*, JP 1-02, 08 November 2010, as Amended through 15 January 2015, https://web.archive.org/web/20150326010957/http://www.dtic.mil/doctrine/new_pubs/jp1_02.pdf (accessed October 28, 2015).

50. EO 12356 *National Security Information*, http://www.archives.gov/federal-register/executive-orders/1982.html (accessed October 28, 2015); *Further Amendment to Executive Order 12958, as Amended, Classified National Security Information, EO 13292*, http://www.archives.gov/federal-register/executive-orders/2003.html (accessed October 28, 2015); *Classified National Security Information* (Amended), EO 12958, http://www.archives.gov/isoo/policy-documents/eo-12958-amendment.html.

51. Relyea, Harold. "Security Classified and Controlled Information: History, Status, and Emerging Management Issues." *CRS Report for Congress*, June 26, 2006, accessed February 1, 2016, http://www.fas.org/sgp/crs/secrecy/RL33494.pdf.

52. Center for Development of Security Excellence. *Marking Classified Information*. December 18, 2014, accessed January 13, 2015. http://www.cdse.edu/documents/cdse/Marking_Classified_Information.pdf.

53. National Imagery and Mapping Agency. *Guide to Marking Documents*. October 4, 2001, accessed January 12, 2015. https://www.fas.org/sgp/othergov/dod/nima-guide.pdf, and Susan Maret, *On Their Own Terms: A Lexicon with an Emphasis on Information-Related Terms Produced by the U.S. Federal Government*, 6th edition, 2016, accessed February 1, 2016, http://www.fas.org/sgp/library/maret.pdf.

54. Stephen Hilgartner, Richard C. Bell, and Rory O'Connor, *Nukespeak* (New York: Penguin Books, 1982), 58–59.

55. Atomic Energy Act of 1954 (P.L. 83-703); Alexander DeVolpi, et al, *Born Secret: the H-bomb, the Progressive Case and National Security* (New York: Pergamon Press, 1981); Howard Morland, "The Holocaust Bomb: a Question of Time," February 8, 2007, accessed October 28, 2015, http://www.fas.org/sgp/eprint/morland.html.

56. U.S. Department of Defense, Center for Development of Security Excellence, *Glossary of Security Terms and Definitions*, November 2012, accessed February 1, 2016, http://www.cdse.edu/documents/cdse/Glossary_Handbook.pdf.

57. *Further Amendment to Executive Order 12958, as Amended, Classified National Security Information*, EO 13292, accessed February 1, 2016, http://www.archives.gov/federal-register/executive-orders/2003.html.

58. Office of the Undersecretary for Defense. *Memorandum for DOD Security Directors*, June 7, 2013, accessed February 8, 2015. http://fas.org/sgp/othergov/dod/notice.pdf.

59. U.S. Department of Energy. *No Comment Policy on Classified Information in the Public Domain*. August 31, 2011, accessed February 8, 2015. http://energy.gov/sites/prod/files/2013/06/f1/GEN-16_Revision_2011.pdf.

60. U.S. Department of Justice. *FOIA Exemption 1*. April 17, 2009, accessed February 8, 2015. http://www.justice.gov/sites/default/files/oip/legacy/2014/07/23/exemption1_1.pdf.

61. U.S. Attorneys' Manual. Classified Information Procedures Act, P.L. 96-456, *Synopsis of CIPA*, accessed January 13, 2015. http://www.justice.gov/usao/eousa/foia_reading_room/usam/title9/crm02054.htm; also see *U.S.C.* Title 18, accessed January 13, 2015. http://www.law.cornell.edu/uscode/html/uscode18a/usc_sup_05_18_10_sq3.html.

62. U.S. Department of State, "Definitions of Diplomatic Security Terms," *Foreign Affairs Manual*, 12FAM090, November 12, 2014, accessed January 13, 2015, http://www.state.gov/documents/organization/88330.pdf.

63. U.S. Department of Defense, Center for Development of Security Excellence, *Glossary of Security Terms and Definitions*, November 2012, accessed February 8, 2015. http://www.cdse.edu/documents/cdse/Glossary_Handbook.pdf.

64. Executive Order 13526, *Classified National Security Information*, December 29, 2009, accessed February 8, 2015, http://www.archives.gov/isoo/policy-documents/cnsi-eo.html.

65. U.S. Department of State, "Definitions of Diplomatic Security Terms," *Foreign Affairs Manual*, 12FAM090, November 12, 2014, accessed February 8, 2015. http://www.state.gov/documents/organization/88330.pdf.

66. Statement of Warren Christopher, in Jan Goldman, *Intelligence Warning Terminology*, Joint Military Intelligence College, October 2001, accessed July 3, 2015. https://archive.org/details/JMICInteligencelwarnterminology.

67. Ministry of Justice, *Rules and Practice Directions, Part 82, Closed Material Procedure*, accessed February 8, 2015, http://www.justice.gov.uk/courts/procedure-rules/civil/rules/part-82-closed-material-procedure-II.

68. National Institute of Standards and Technology, *NIST Definition of Cloud Computing*, Special Publication 800-14, accessed February 8, 2015, http://www.nist.gov/itl/csd/cloud-102511.cfm.

69. U.S. Commission on National Security 21st Century. *Commission on National Security 21st Century, Seeking a National Strategy: A Concept for Preserving Security and Promoting Freedom*, Phase II Report. April 2000, accessed February 8, 2015, http://www.au.af.mil/au/awc/awcgate/nssg/.

70. John A. Gentry, "Complex Civil-Military Operations: A U.S. Military-Centric Perspective," *Naval War College Review* 53, no. 4 (2000): 60.

71. U.S. Coast Guard, *Intelligence*, Coast Guard Publication 2-0, May 2010, https://www.uscg.mil/doctrine/CGPub/CG_Pub_2_0.pdf.

72. U.S. Coast Guard, *Intelligence*, Coast Guard Publication 2-0, May 2010, https://www.uscg.mil/doctrine/CGPub/CG_Pub_2_0.pdf.

73. The White House, *National Strategy for Maritime Security* (September 2005), http://georgewbush-whitehouse.archives.gov/homeland/maritime-security.html; Randol, Mark A. "The Department of Homeland Security Intelligence Enterprise: Operational Overviewand Oversight Challenges for Congress." *CRS Report for Congress* R40602, March 19, 2010. https://www.fas.org/sgp/crs/homesec/R40602.pdf (accessed January 26, 2016).

74. Randol, Mark A. "The Department of Homeland Security Intelligence Enterprise: Operational Overview and Oversight Challenges for Congress." *CRS Report for Congress* R40602, March 19, 2010. https://www.fas.org/sgp/crs/homesec/R40602. pdf (accessed January 26, 2016).

75. Leo D. Carl, *International Dictionary of Intelligence* (McLean, VA: International Defense Consultant Services, Inc., 1990).

76. William M. Arkin, *Code Names: Deciphering US Military Plans, Programs, and Operations in the 9/11 World* (Hanover, NH: Steerforth Press, 2005).

77. U.S. Department of Defense, *Dictionary of Military and Associated Terms*, JP 1-02, 08 November 2010, as Amended through 15 January 2015, https://web.archive. org/web/20150326010957/http://www.dtic.mil/doctrine/new_pubs/jp1_02.pdf (accessed November 2, 2015).

78. Leo D. Carl, *International Dictionary of Intelligence* (McLean, VA: International Defense Consultant Services, Inc., 1990).

79. Central Intelligence Agency, Center for the Study of Intelligence, *Critique of the Codeword Compartment of the CIA*, March 1977, accessed July 2, 2015, http:// www.fas.org/sgp/othergov/codeword.html.

80. Harold Ford, *Estimative Intelligence: The Purposes and Problems of National Intelligence Estimating* (Lanham, MD: University Press of America, 1993), 330.

81. U.S. Department of Defense, *National Industrial Security Manual (NISPOM)*, DoD 5220.22-M (February 28, 2006), accessed January 14, 2015. http://www.dss. mil/documents/odaa/nispom2006-5220.pdf; also see 32 *CFR* 148.12, http://www. gpo.gov/fdsys/browse.

82. Department of Homeland Security, *Sensitive Compartmented Information Program Management*, Management Directives System Number 11043, September 17, 2004, accessed February 1, 2016, https://www.dhs.gov/xlibrary/assets/foia/ mgmt_directive_11043_sensitive_compartmented_information_program_management.pdf.

83. U.S. Department of Defense, Center for Development of Security Excellence, Glossary of Security Terms and Definitions, November 2012, accessed February 1, 2016, http://www.cdse.edu/documents/cdse/Glossary_Handbook.pdf.

84. National Imagery and Mapping Agency, *Guide to Marking Documents*, October 4, 2001, accessed February 1, 2016, https://www.fas.org/sgp/othergov/dod/ nimaguide.pdf.

85. United States Senate, Select Committee to Study Governmental Operations with Respect to Intelligence Activities (Church Committee), *Final Report*, Book 1, Washington, DC, April 26, 1976, accessed June 2, 2015, https://archive.org/details/ finalreportofsel01unit.

86. Defense Forensics and Biometrics Agency, *DoD Biometrics Enterprise Architecture (Integrated) v2.0 Common Biometric Vocabulary*, April 2013, accessed June 2, 2015, http://www.biometrics.dod.mil/Files/Documents/References/common biometric vocabulary.pdf.

87. Office of the Director of National Intelligence, *Discovery and Dissemination or Retrieval of Information within the Intelligence Community*, Intelligence Community Directive 501, January 21, 2009, accessed February 2, 2015, http://www.dni.gov/ files/documents/ICD/ICD_501.pdf.

88. Department of the Army. Marine Corps Combat Development Command. Department of the Navy. *Operational Terms and Graphics*. FM 1-02 (FM 101-5). September 21, 2004, accessed July 3, 2015. http://www.udel.edu/armyrotc/current_cadets/cadet_resources/manuals_regulations_files/FM%201-02%20-%20Operational%20Terms%20&%20Graphics.pdf.

89. Central Intelligence Agency, Office of Public Affairs, *A Consumer's Guide to Intelligence: Gaining Knowledge and Foreknowledge of the World Around Us* (Washington, DC: National Technical Information Service, 1999).

90. U.S. Department of Defense. *Joint and National Intelligence Support to Military Operations*. JP 2-01. January 5, 2012, accessed February 26, 2015. http://www.dtic.mil/doctrine/new_pubs/jp2_01.pdf.

91. U.S. Department of Defense. *Joint and National Intelligence Support to Military Operations*. JP 2-01. January 5, 2012. Accessed February 26, 2015. http://www.dtic.mil/doctrine/new_pubs/jp2_01.pdf.

92. U.S. Department of Defense. *Dictionary of Military and Associated Terms.* JP 1-02, 08 November 2010, as Amended through 15 June 2015, accessed July 6, 2015, https://web.archive.org/web/20150815204834/http://www.dtic.mil/doctrine/new_pubs/jp1_02.pdf.

93. U.S. Department of Defense. *Department of Defense Dictionary of Military and Associated Terms.* JP 1-02, 08 November 2010, as Amended through 15 January 2016, accessed January 26, 2016, http://www.dtic.mil/doctrine/new_pubs/jp1_02.pdf.

94. "5 U.S.C. 601-Definitions" (Current through Pub. L. 113-234), accessed November 2, 2015, http://www.law.cornell.edu/uscode/text/5/601.

95. Office of the Director of National Intelligence, *Competency Directories for the Intelligence Community Workforce*, Intelligence Community Directive 610, October 4, 2010, accessed February 1, 2016, http://www.dni.gov/files/documents/ICD/ICD_610.pdf.

96. U.S. Department of Defense. *Joint and National Intelligence Support to Military Operations*. JP 2-01. January 5, 2012, accessed February 26, 2015. http://www.dtic.mil/doctrine/new_pubs/jp2_01.pdf.

97. United States Department of Justice. *Law Enforcement Analytic Standard.* Global Justice Information Sharing Initiative and International Association of Law Enforcement Intelligence Analysts, Inc. 2nd ed. April 2012, accessed February 1, 2016, https://it.ojp.gov/documents/d/Law%20Enforcement%20Analytic%20Standards%2004202_combined_compliant.pdf.

98. U.S. Department of Defense. *Joint and National Intelligence Support to Military Operations*. JP 2-01. January 5, 2012, accessed February 26, 2015. http://www.dtic.mil/doctrine/new_pubs/jp2_01.pdf.

99. U.S. Department of Defense. *Joint and National Intelligence Support to Military Operations*. JP 2-01. January 5, 2012, accessed February 26, 2015. http://www.dtic.mil/doctrine/new_pubs/jp2_01.pdf.

100. U.S. Department of Defense. *Joint and National Intelligence Support to Military Operations*. JP 2-01. January 5, 2012, accessed February 26, 2015. http://www.dtic.mil/doctrine/new_pubs/jp2_01.pdf.

101. U.S. Department of Defense. *Joint and National Intelligence Support to Military Operations*. JP 2-01. January 5, 2012, accessed February 26, 2015. http://www.dtic.mil/doctrine/new_pubs/jp2_01.pdf.

102. Office of the Director of National Intelligence, *Competency Directories for the Intelligence Community Workforce*, Intelligence Community Directive 610, October 4, 2010, accessed January 26, 2016, http://www.dni.gov/files/documents/ICD/ICD_610.pdf.

103. Chairman of the Joint Chiefs of Staff, *National Military Strategic Plan for the War on Terrorism*, February 1, 2006, accessed February 24, 2015, http://www.bits.de/NRANEU/others/strategy/National-Strategic-Plan-War_on_Terrorism-06.pdf; also see U.S. Department of Defense, *Counterrorism*, JP 3-26 (October 24, 2014), accessed February 24, 2015, http://www.dtic.mil/doctrine/new_pubs/jp3_26.pdf.

104. Federal Bureau of Investigation, *Frequently Asked Questions (FAQs) on the CODIS Program and the National DNA Index System*, accessed February 24, 2015, http://www.fbi.gov/about-us/lab/biometric-analysis/codis/codis-and-ndis-fact-sheet.

105. United States Air Force, *Public Affairs Operations*, Air Force Doctrine Document 3-6, 24 June 2005 Certified Current 20 August 2013, accessed February 24, 2015, Incorporating Changes 1, 23 December 2010, http://static.e-publishing.af.mil/production/1/af_cv/publication/afdd3-61/afdd3-61.pdf.

106. Office of the Director of National Intelligence, *National Intelligence Program FY 2009 Congressional Budget Justification Book*, Vol. XII (Washington, DC, February 2008), accessed January 26, 2016, http://www.fas.org/irp/dni/cbjb-2009.pdf.

107. Information Sharing Environment, *Annual Report to Congress on the Information Sharing Environment*, June 30, 2008, accessed February 24, 2015, http://www.fas.org/irp/agency/ise/2008report.pdf.

108. U.S. Department of Defense, *Dictionary of Military and Associated Terms*, JP 1-02, 08 November 2010, as Amended through 15 January 2015, accessed January 24, 2016, https://web.archive.org/web/20150326010957/http://www.dtic.mil/doctrine/new_pubs/jp1_02.pdf.

109. United States Department of Justice. *Law Enforcement Analytic Standard*. Global Justice Information Sharing Initiative and International Association of Law Enforcement Intelligence Analysts, Inc. 2nd ed. April 2012, accessed February 1, 2016, https://it.ojp.gov/documents/d/Law%20Enforcement%20Analytic%20Standards%2004202_combined_compliant.pdf.

110. Committee for National Security Systems (CNSS), *National Information Assurance Glossary*, Instruction 4009, April 2010, accessed January 26, 2016, http://jitc.fhu.disa.mil/pki/documents/committee_on_national_security_systems_instructions_4009_june_2006.pdf.

111. Central Intelligence Agency, *A Consumer's Guide to Intelligence: Gaining Knowledge and Foreknowledge of the World Around Us*, Office of Public Affairs (Washington, DC: National Technical Information Service, 1999).

112. U.S. Department of Defense, *Dictionary of Military and Associated Terms*, 12 April 2001, as Amended through 22 March 2007, accessed February 1, 2016, http://www.bits.de/NRANEU/others/doctrine.htm.

113. Office of the Director of National Intelligence. *Protection of National Intelligence*. Intelligence Community Directive 700, June 7, 2012, accessed January 26, 2016, http://www.dni.gov/files/documents/ICD/ICD_700.pdf.

114. Office of the Director of National Intelligence, *National Intelligence Program FY 2009 Congressional Budget Justification Book*, Vol. XII, February 2008, accessed February 1, 2016, http://fas.org/irp/dni/cbjb-2009.pdf.

115. U.S. Central Command Assessment Team, *Command and Control Knowledge Management*, February 2009, accessed February 1, 2016, http://cryptome.org/dodi/centcom-c2km.pdf.

116. Defense Intelligence Agency, Office of Counterintelligence. *CI Glossary—Terms & Definitions of Interest for DoD CI Professionals.* July 2014, accessed January 17, 2015. https://www.hsdl.org/?view&did=699056.

117. Committee for National Security Systems (CNSS), *National Information Assurance Glossary*, Instruction 4009, April 2010, accessed January 17, 2015, https://www.ecs.csus.edu/csc/iac/cnssi_4009.pdf.

118. Defense Intelligence Agency, Office of Counterintelligence. *CI Glossary—Terms & Definitions of Interest for DoD CI Professionals.* July 2014, accessed January 17, 2015. https://www.hsdl.org/?view&did=699056.

119. Office of the Director of National Intelligence. *Protection of National Intelligence*. Intelligence Community Directive 700, June 7, 2012, accessed January 26, 2016, http://www.dni.gov/files/documents/ICD/ICD_700.pdf.ODNI.

120. Committee for National Security Systems (CNSS), *National Information Assurance Glossary*, Instruction 4009, April 2010, accessed January 26, 2016, https://www.ecs.csus.edu/csc/iac/cnssi_4009.pdf.

121. Office of the Director of National Intelligence, *Competency Directories for the Intelligence Community Workforce*, Intelligence Community Directive 610, October 4, 2010, accessed January 26, 2016, http://www.dni.gov/files/documents/ICD/ICD_610.pdf.

122. North Atlantic Treaty Organization, *Glossary of Terms and Definitions*, NATO Standardization Agency, 2008, accessed January 26, 2016, https://fas.org/irp/doddir/other/nato2008.pdf.

123. United States Agency for International Development, *Conflict Early Warning Systems: Terms and Concepts* (New Orleans: Tulane Institute for International Development, May 1999), under the term "complex emergency."

124. United States Senate, Select Committee to Study Governmental Operations with Respect to Intelligence Activities (Church Committee), *Final Report*, Book 1 (Washington, DC, April 26, 1976), accessed January 26, 2016, https://archive.org/details/finalreportofsel01unit.

125. U.S. Department of Defense, *Dictionary of Military and Associated Terms*, JP 1-02, 08 November 2010, as Amended through 15 January 2015, accessed January 26, 2016, https://web.archive.org/web/20150326010957/http://www.dtic.mil/doctrine/new_pubs/jp1_02.pdf.

126. Department of Homeland Security, Risk Steering Committee, *DHS Risk Lexicon*, September 2010, accessed January 26, 2016, http://www.dhs.gov/dhs-risk-lexicon.

127. U.S. Computer Readiness Team, *Computer Forensics*, 2008. Accessed January 26, 2016, https://www.us-cert.gov/sites/default/files/publications/forensics.pdf.

128. U.S. Department of Defense, Center for Development of Security Excellence, *Glossary of Security Terms and Definitions*, November 2012, accessed January 26, 2016, http://www.cdse.edu/documents/cdse/Glossary_Handbook.pdf.

129. U.S. General Accountability Office, *Defense Department Cyber Efforts: Definitions, Focal Point, and Methodology Needed for DOD to Develop Full-Spectrum Cyberspace Budget Estimates*, GAO-11-695R, July 29, 2011, accessed January 26, 2016, http://www.gao.gov/products/GAO-11-695R.

130. Office of the Director of National Intelligence, *National Intelligence Program FY 2009 Congressional Budget Justification Book*, Vol. XII (Washington, DC, February 2008), accessed January 26, 2016, http://www.fas.org/irp/dni/cbjb-2009.pdf.

131. National Initiative for Cybersecurity Education, *A Glossary of Common Cybersecurity Terminology*, accessed January 26, 2016, http://niccs.us-cert.gov/glossary.

132. U.S. Department of Defense, Center for Development of Security Excellence, *Glossary of Security Terms and Definitions*, November 2012, accessed January 26, 2016, http://www.cdse.edu/documents/cdse/Glossary_Handbook.pdf.

133. U.S. Department of Defense, Center for Development of Security Excellence, *Glossary of Security Terms and Definitions*, November 2012, accessed January 26, 2016, http://www.cdse.edu/documents/cdse/Glossary_Handbook.pdf.

134. United States Senate, Select Committee to Study Governmental Operations with Respect to Intelligence Activities (Church Committee), *Final Report*, Book 1 (Washington, DC, April 26, 1976), accessed January 26, 2016, https://archive.org/details/finalreportofsel01unit.

135. U.S. Department of Defense, Center for Development of Security Excellence, *Glossary of Security Terms and Definitions*, November 2012, accessed January 26, 2016, http://www.cdse.edu/documents/cdse/Glossary_Handbook.pdf.

136. Department of Homeland Security, Risk Steering Committee, *DHS Risk Lexicon*, September 2010, accessed February 14, 2015, http://www.dhs.gov/dhs-risk-lexicon.

137. North Atlantic Treaty Organization, *NATO Glossary of Terms and Definitions*, NATO Standardization Agency, 2008, accessed January 26, 2016, https://fas.org/irp/doddir/other/nato2008.pdf.

138. U.S. Department of State, "Bureau of Arms Control, Verification, and Compliance (AVC)," *Foreign Affairs Manual*, 1 FAM 440, May 9, 2013, accessed January 26, 2016, http://www.state.gov/documents/organization/156858.pdf.

139. Home Office, *Covert Surveillance and Property Interference: Revised Code of Practice Pursuant to Section 71 of the Regulation of Investigatory Powers Act*, The Stationary Office, 2010, accessed January 26, 2016, https://www.gov.uk/government/uploads/system/uploads/attachment_data/file/97960/code-of-practice-covert.pdf.

140. EO 132 92, *Further Amendment to Executive Order 12958, as Amended, Classified National Security Information*, accessed January 26, 2016, http://www.archives.gov/federal-register/executive-orders/2003.html.

141. National Initiative for Cybersecurity Education, *A Glossary of Common Cybersecurity Terminology*, accessed January 26, 2016, http://niccs.us-cert.gov/glossary.

142. Committee for National Security Systems (CNSS), *National Information Assurance Glossary*, Instruction 4009, April 2010, accessed January 26, 2016, http://www.ncsc.gov/nittf/docs/CNSSI-4009_National_Information_Assurance.pdf.

143. U.S. Department of Defense. *Dictionary of Military and Associated Terms.* JP 1-02, 08 November 2010, as Amended through 15 June 2015, accessed July 6, 2015, https://web.archive.org/web/20150815204834/http://www.dtic.mil/doctrine/new_pubs/jp1_02.pdf.

144. Stockholm International Peace Research Institute. *Preventing Violent Conflict: The Search for Political Will, Strategies and Effective Tools*, Report of the Krusenberg Seminar, organized by the Swedish Ministry for Foreign Affairs, the Stockholm International Peace Research Institute and the Swedish Institute of International Affairs, June 19–20, 2000. Stockholm: SIPRI.

145. United States Senate, Select Committee to Study Governmental Operations with Respect to Intelligence Activities (Church Committee), *Final Report*, Book 1, April 26, 1976, accessed February 1, 2016, https://archive.org/details/finalreportofsel01unit.

146. U.S. Department of Justice, *The Attorney General's Guidelines for Domestic FBI Operations*, 2008, accessed November 4, 2015, http://www.justice.gov/sites/default/files/ag/legacy/2008/10/03/guidelines.pdf.

147. U.S. Department of Defense, Under Secretary of Defense for Policy, *Procedures Governing the Activities of DoD Intelligence Components That Affect United States Persons*, DoD 5240.1-R, December 1982, accessed November 4, 2015, http://www.fas.org/irp/doddir/dod/d5240_1_r.pdf.

148. Department of Homeland Security, Risk Steering Committee, *DHS Risk Lexicon*, September 2010, accessed February 1, 2016, http://www.dhs.gov/dhs-risk-lexicon.

149. National Initiative for Cybersecurity Education, *A Glossary of Common Cybersecurity Terminology*, accessed November 4, 2015, http://niccs.us-cert.gov/glossary.

150. Department of Homeland Security, Risk Steering Committee, *DHS Risk Lexicon*, September 2010, accessed February 1, 2016, http://www.dhs.gov/dhs-risk-lexicon.

151. Jonathan B. Tucker and Amy Sands, "An Unlikely Threat," *Bulletin of the Atomic Scientists* 55, no. 4 (1999): 46–52.

152. U.S. Department of State, Bureau of International Information Programs, "Definitions," Wayback Machine, January 14, 2005, accessed February 1, 2016, http://wayback.archive.org/web/20080213085231/http://usinfo.state.gov/media/Archive/2005/Jan/26-288268.html.

153. U.S. Department of Defense, Center for Development of Security Excellence, *Glossary of Security Terms and Definitions*, November 2012, http://www.cdse.edu/documents/cdse/Glossary_Handbook.pdf.

154. Defense Intelligence Agency, Office of Counterintelligence, *CI Glossary— Terms & Definitions of Interest for DoD CI Professionals*, July 2014, accessed February 1, 2016, https://www.hsdl.org/?view&did=699056.

155. U.S. Department of Defense, Center for Development of Security Excellence, *Glossary of Security Terms and Definitions*, November 2012, accessed February 1, 2016, http://www.cdse.edu/documents/cdse/Glossary_Handbook.pdf.

156. United States Senate, Select Committee to Study Governmental Operations with Respect to Intelligence Activities (Church Committee), *Final Report*, Book 1, April 26, 1976, accessed February 1, 2016, https://archive.org/details/finalreportof-sel01unit.

157. Chairman of the Joint Chiefs of Staff, *National Military Strategic Plan for the War on Terrorism*, February 1, 2006, accessed February 1, 2016, https://www.hsaj.org/articles/170.

158. United States Department of Justice. *Law Enforcement Analytic Standard*. Global Justice Information Sharing Initiative and International Association of Law Enforcement Intelligence Analysts, Inc. 2nd ed. April 2012, accessed February 1, 2016, https://it.ojp.gov/documents/d/Law%20Enforcement%20Analytic%20Standards%2004202_combined_compliant.pdf.

159. Defense Forensics and Biometrics Agency, *DoD Biometrics Enterprise Architecture (Integrated) v2.0 Common Biometric Vocabulary*, April 2013, accessed February 1, 2016, http://www.biometrics.dod.mil/Files/Documents/References/common biometric vocabulary.pdf.

160. United States Senate, Select Committee to Study Governmental Operations with Respect to Intelligence Activities (Church Committee), *Final Report*, Book 1, April 26, 1976, https://archive.org/details/finalreportofsel01unit.

161. Integrated C4 I Architecture Division, *C4ISR Handbook for Integrated Planning* (Washington, DC: Defense Intelligence Agency Publications Division).

162. Deputy Secretary of Defense. *Directive-Type Memorandum (DTM) 12-005, Implementing Guidelines for Periodic Review of Detainees Held at Guantanamo Bay per Executive Order 13567.* May 9, 2012 (November 4, 2012), accessed January 22, 2015. http://fas.org/irp/doddir/dod/dtm-12-005.pdf.

163. National Security and Homeland Security Presidential Directive/NSPD-51/ HSPD 20. *National Continuity Policy.* May 9, 2007, accessed February 27, 2015, http://fas.org/irp/offdocs/nspd/nspd-51.htm.

164. Office of the Director of National Intelligence, *National Intelligence Program FY 2009 Congressional Budget Justification Book*, Vol. XII, February 2008, http://www.fas.org/irp/dni/cbjb-2009.pdf.

165. National Security and Homeland Security Presidential Directive/NSPD-51/ HSPD 20. *National Continuity Policy.* May 9, 2007, accessed February 27, 2015, http://fas.org/irp/offdocs/nspd/nspd-51.htm.

166. National Initiative for Cybersecurity Education, *A Glossary of Common Cybersecurity Terminology*, accessed January 26, 2016, http://niccs.us-cert.gov/glossary.

167. "Documents on N.S.A. Efforts to Diagram Social Networks of U.S. Citizens." *The New York Times*, September 28, 2013, accessed January 13, 2015, http://www.

nytimes.com/interactive/2013/09/29/us/documents-on-nsa-efforts-to-diagram-social-networks-of-us-citizens.html and National Security Agency, *Module 4: Access, Sharing, Dissemination, and Retention Under the BR and PR/TT FISC Orders*, October 17, 2011, accessed February 2, 2016, http://www.dni.gov/files/documents/1118/CLEANEDOVSC1205_L4_storyboard_v28_Final.pdf.

168. Office of the Director of National Intelligence, *Intelligence Community Core Contract Personnel*, Intelligence Community Directive 612, March 2, 2015, accessed February 2, 2016, http://www.dni.gov/files/documents/ICD/ICD_612.pdf.

169. EO 13292, *Further Amendment to Executive Order 12958, as Amended, Classified National Security Information*, accessed January 26, 2016, http://www.archives.gov/federal-register/executive-orders/2003.html.

170. Centers for Disease Control. *Manual Guide—Information Security CDC-02*. Office of Security and Emergency Preparedness. "Sensitive But Unclassified Information." Part B. 07/22/2005, accessed February 1, 2016, http://www.fas.org/sgp/othergov/cDC-sbu.pdf.

171. U.S. Department of State, "Bureau of Arms Control, Verification, and Compliance (AVC),"Foreign Affairs Manual, 1 FAM 440, May 9, 2013, accessed February 1, 2016, http://www.state.gov/documents/organization/156858.pdf.

172. U.S. Department of Defense, Center for Development of Security Excellence, *Glossary of Security Terms and Definitions*, November 2012, accessed February 2, 2016, http://www.cdse.edu/documents/cdse/Glossary_Handbook.pdf.

173. Central Intelligence Agency, *Controlled Access Program Oversight Committee: Director of Central Intelligence Directive 3/29*, June 2, 1995, accessed February 2, 2016, http://fas.org/irp/offdocs/dcid3-29.pdf; also see Office of the Director of National Intelligence, *Classification and Control Markings*, Intelligence Community Directive 710, June 21, 2013, accessed February 2, 2016, http://www.dni.gov/files/documents/ICD/ICD_710.pdf.

174. Department of the Army. *Investigative Records Repository*. AR381-45, accessed July 2, 2015. http://armypubs.army.mil/epubs/pdf/r381_45.pdf.

175. U.S. Department of Defense. *Dictionary of Military and Associated Terms*. JP 1-02, 08 November 2010, as Amended through 15 June 2015. Accessed July 6, 2015, https://web.archive.org/web/20150815204834/http://www.dtic.mil/doctrine/new_pubs/jp1_02.pdf.

176. U.S. Department of Defense, *DoD Counterintelligence Collection Reporting*, 5240.17, October 26, 2005, accessed February 2, 2016, https://www.fas.org/irp/doddir/dod/i5240_17.pdf.

177. EO 13556 *Controlled Unclassified Information*, November 4, 2010, accessed https://www.gpo.gov/fdsys/pkg/FR-2010-11-09/pdf/2010-28360.pdf, and Steven Aftergood, "Controlled Unclassified Information is Coming," *Secrecy News Blog*, May 11, 2015, accessed February 1, 2016, https://fas.org/blogs/secrecy/2015/05/cui-is-coming/.

178. National Archives and Records Administration, *About Controlled Unclassified Information*, accessed February 2, 2016, http://www.archives.gov/cui/about/index.html.

179. National Security Agency, *Converged Analysis of Smartphone Devices Identification/Processing/Tasking—All in a Day's Work*, accessed February 2, 2016, http://cryptome.org/2014/01/nsa-smartphones-analysis.pdf.

180. U.S. Department of Defense, *DoD Intelligence Interrogations, Detainee Debriefings, and Tactical Questioning*, Directive Number 3115.09, October 11, 2012 Incorporating Change 1, Effective November 15, 2013, accessed February 2, 2016, http://www.dtic.mil/whs/directives/corres/pdf/311509p.pdf.

181. Office of the Director of National Intelligence, *Competency Directories for the Intelligence Community Workforce*, Intelligence Community Directive 610, October 4, 2010, accessed February 2, 2016, http://www.dni.gov/files/documents/ICD/ICD_610.pdf.

182. Office of the Director of National Intelligence, *Intelligence Community Core Contract Personnel*, Intelligence Community Directive 612, October 30, 2009, accessed February 2, 2016, http://www.dni.gov/files/documents/ICD/ICD_612.pdf.

183. J. David Singer and Paul F. Diehl, *Measuring the Correlates of War* (Ann Arbor: University of Michigan Press, 1990), 11.

184. Department of Homeland Security, Risk Steering Committee, *DHS Risk Lexicon*, September 2010, accessed February 2, 2016, http://www.dhs.gov/dhs-risk-lexicon.

185. Department of Homeland Security, Risk Steering Committee, *DHS Risk Lexicon*, September 2010, accessed February 2, 2016, http://www.dhs.gov/dhs-risk-lexicon.

186. Department of the Air Force, *Cornerstones of Information Warfare*. 1995, accessed January 26, 2016, http://www.dtic.mil/get-tr-doc/pdf?AD=ADA307436.

187. National Counterterrorism Center, *Countering Violent Extremism: A Guide for Practitioners and Analysts*, May 2014, accessed February 2, 2016, https://www.documentcloud.org/documents/1657824-cve-guide.html.

188. United States Department of Defense, *Countering Weapons of Mass Destruction*, JP 3-40, October 31, 2014, accessed February 2, 2016, http://www.dtic.mil/doctrine/new_pubs/jp3_40.pdf.

189. National Security Act of 1947, as amended, 50 U.S.C., chap. 15, 401(a), http://www.law.cornell.edu/uscode/ and EO 12333 *United States Intelligence Activities*, December 4, 1981, accessed January 26, 2016, http://www.archives.gov/federal-register/codification/executive-order/12333.html.

190. Department of the Army. Marine Corps Combat Development Command. Department of the Navy. *Operational Terms and Graphics*. FM 1-02 (FM 101-5). September 21, 2004, accessed July 3, 2015. http://www.udel.edu/armyrotc/current_cadets/cadet_resources/manuals_regulations_files/FM%201-02%20-%20Operational%20Terms%20&%20Graphics.pdf.

191. U.S. Department of Defense, *Department of Defense Dictionary of Military and Associated Terms*, JP 1-02, 08 November 2010, as Amended through 15 January 2015, accessed February 2, 2016, https://web.archive.org/web/20150326010957/http://www.dtic.mil/doctrine/new_pubs/jp1_02.pdf.

192. U.S. Department of Defense, Center for Development of Security Excellence, *Glossary of Security Terms and Definitions*, November 2012, accessed February 2, 2016, http://www.cdse.edu/documents/cdse/Glossary_Handbook.pdf.

193. U.S. Department of Defense, *DoD Counterintelligence Collection Report*, January 14, 2015, accessed February 2, 2016, http://www.fas.org/irp/doddir/dod/i5240_17.pdf.

194. Defense Intelligence Agency, Office of Counterintelligence. *CI Glossary—Terms & Definitions of Interest for DoD CI Professionals.* July 2014. Accessed January 17, 2015. https://www.hsdl.org/?view&did=699056.

195. Committee for National Security Systems (CNSS), Instruction 4009, *National Information Assurance Glossary*, April 2010, accessed February 1, 2016, http://jitc.fhu.disa.mil/pki/documents/committee_on_national_security_systems_instructions_4009_june_2006.pdf.

196. United States Department of Defense, *Countering Weapons of Mass Destruction*, JP 3-40, October 31, 2014, accessed February 2, 2016, http://www.dtic.mil/doctrine/new_pubs/jp3_40.pdf.

197. U.S. Department of State, *Country Reports on Terrorism*, accessed February 2, 2016, http://www.state.gov/j/ct/rls/crt/.

198. Defense Intelligence Agency, Office of Counterintelligence. *CI Glossary—Terms & Definitions of Interest for DoD CI Professionals.* July 2014. Accessed January 17, 2015. https://www.hsdl.org/?view&did=699056.

199. Defense Intelligence Agency, Office of Counterintelligence. *CI Glossary—Terms & Definitions of Interest for DoD CI Professionals.* July 2014. Accessed January 17, 2015. https://www.hsdl.org/?view&did=699056.

200. Defense Intelligence Agency, Office of Counterintelligence. *CI Glossary—Terms & Definitions of Interest for DoD CI Professionals.* July 2014. Accessed January 17, 2015. https://www.hsdl.org/?view&did=699056.

201. *Intelligence Authorization Act for Fiscal Year 2015*, 113-2nd session, H.R.468, accessed February 2, 2016, https://www.congress.gov/113/bills/hr4681/BILLS-113hr4681enr.pdf.

202. Defense Intelligence Agency, Office of Counterintelligence. *CI Glossary—Terms & Definitions of Interest for DoD CI Professionals.* July 2014. Accessed January 17, 2015. https://www.hsdl.org/?view&did=699056.

203. Defense Forensics and Biometrics Agency, *DoD Biometrics Enterprise Architecture (Integrated) v2.0.*, accessed January 15, 2015, http://www.biometrics.dod.mil/Files/Documents/References/common biometric vocabulary.pdf.

204. (UK) Home Office, *Covert Human Intelligence Sources: Code of Practice, Pursuant to Section 71 of the Regulation of Investigatory Powers Act 2000*, The Stationary Office, 2010, accessed February 2, 2016, https://www.gov.uk/government/uploads/system/uploads/attachment_data/file/97958/code-practice-human-intel.pdf.

205. Defense Intelligence Agency, Office of Counterintelligence. *CI Glossary—Terms & Definitions of Interest for DoD CI Professionals.* July 2014. Accessed January 17, 2015. https://www.hsdl.org/?view&did=699056.

206. U.S. Department of Defense, *Psychological Operations*, FM 3-05.30, MCRP 3-40.6, April 2005, accessed February 2, 2016, http://www.fas.org/irp/doddir/army/fm3-05-30.pdf.

207. Department of Homeland Security, Risk Steering Committee, *DHS Risk Lexicon*, September 2010, accessed February 2, 2016, http://www.dhs.gov/dhs-risk-lexicon.

208. Global Security, *Korean People's Army*, accessed January 25, 2016. http://www.globalsecurity.org/military/world/dprk/army.htm.

209. United States Department of Justice. *Law Enforcement Analytic Standards.* Global Justice Information Sharing Initiative. April 2012, accessed July 3, 2015. https://it.ojp.gov/documents/d/Law%20Enforcement%20Analytic%20Standards%2004202_combined_compliant.pdf.

210. Steven Aftergood, "Crimes Reports and the Leak Referral Process," *Secrecy News*, December 12, 2012, accessed January 14, 2015, http://fas.org/blogs/secrecy/2012/12/crimes_reports/; also see U.S. Department of Justice reply to Sen. Patrick Leahy, *Questions and Answers from FBI Director Mueller*, April 8, 2010, accessed February 16, 2015, http://fas.org/irp/agency/doj/intel-leak.pdf.

211. United States Department of Justice. *Law Enforcement Analytic Standards.* Global Justice Information Sharing Initiative. April 2012, accessed July 3, 2015. https://it.ojp.gov/documents/d/Law%20Enforcement%20Analytic%20Standards%2004202_combined_compliant.pdf.

212. United States Department of Justice. *Law Enforcement Analytic Standards.* Global Justice Information Sharing Initiative. April 2012, accessed July 3, 2015. https://it.ojp.gov/documents/d/Law%20Enforcement%20Analytic%20Standards%2004202_combined_compliant.pdf.

213. Department of Justice, *Judicial Administration*, 28 CFR 23, https://www.gpo.gov/fdsys/browse/collectionCfr.action?collectionCode=CFR.

214. Department of Justice, *Criminal Intelligence Information Operating Systems*, 28 CFR 23.3(b)(1), accessed February 1, 2016, https://www.gpo.gov/fdsys/browse/collectionCfr.action?collectionCode=CFR.

215. U.S. Department of Defense. *Dictionary of Military and Associated Terms.* JP 1-02, 08 November 2010, as Amended through 15 June 2015, accessed July 6, 2015, https://web.archive.org/web/20150815204834/http://www.dtic.mil/doctrine/new_pubs/jp1_02.pdf.

216. Department of the Army. Marine Corps Combat Development Command. Department of the Navy. *Operational Terms and Graphics*. FM 1-02 (FM 101-5). September 21, 2004, accessed July 3, 2015. http://www.udel.edu/armyrotc/current_cadets/cadet_resources/manuals_regulations_files/FM%201-02%20-%20Operational%20Terms%20&%20Graphics.pdf.

217. Department of Energy, Office of Safeguards and Security, *Safeguards and Security Glossary of Terms*, December 18, 1995, accessed January 26, 2016), http://www.directives.doe.gov/references/.

218. Laurence, Edward J. *Light Weapons and Intrastate Conflict Early Warning Factors and Preventative Action.* Carnegie Commission on Preventing Deadly Conflict Report, July 1998, accessed July 8, 2015, http://www.dtic.mil/cgi-bin/GetTRDoc?AD=ADA372359.

219. U.S. Department of Defense, *Joint Intelligence*, JP 2-0, October 22, 2013, accessed February 16, 2015, http://www.dtic.mil/doctrine/new_pubs/jp2_0.pdf.

220. Office of the Director of National Intelligence, *Critical Information*, Intelligence Community Directive 190, February 3, 2015, accessed December 1, 2015, http://www.fas.org/irp/dni/icd/icd-190.pdf.

221. Presidential Policy Directive/PPD-21, *Critical Infrastructure Security and Resilience*, February 12, 2013, accessed February 2, 2016, http://www.whitehouse. gov/the-press-office/2013/02/12/presidential-policy-directive-critical-infrastructure-security-and-resil; also see Homeland Security Act of 2002 (6 U.S.C. 101), P.L.107-296, accessed February 2, 2016, http://www.dhs.gov/homeland-security-act-2002.

222. Department of Homeland Security, Risk Steering Committee, *DHS Risk Lexicon*, September 2010, accessed December 1, 2015, http://www.dhs.gov/dhs-risk-lexicon.

223. Department of Homeland Security, *NIPP 2013: Partnering for Critical Infrastructure Security and Resilience*, accessed December 1, 2015, http://www.dhs. gov/sites/default/files/publications/NIPP 2013_Partnering for Critical Infrastructure Security and Resilience_508_0.pdf.

224. "6 U.S.C. § 131- Definitions" (Current through Pub. L. 113-234), Legal Information Institute, accessed November 5, 2015, http://www.law.cornell.edu/uscode/text/6/131.

225. Department of Homeland Security, *NIPP 2013: Partnering for Critical Infrastructure Security and Resilience*, accessed October 28, 2015, http://www.dhs. gov/sites/default/files/publications/NIPP 2013_Partnering for Critical Infrastructure Security and Resilience_508_0.pdf.

226. U.S. Department of Defense, *Defense Support of Civil Authorities*, JP 3-28, July 31, 2013, accessed October 28, 2015, http://www.dtic.mil/doctrine/new_pubs/jp3_28.pdf.

227. Department of Homeland Security, *National Infrastructure Protection Plan: Partnering to Enhance Protection and Resiliency*, 2009, accessed October 28, 2015, http://www.dhs.gov/xlibrary/assets/NIPP_Plan.pdf.

228. Presidential Policy Directive/PPD-21, *Critical Infrastructure Security and Resilience*, February 12, 2013, accessed February 2, 2016, http://www.whitehouse. gov/the-press-office/2013/02/12/presidential-policy-directive-critical-infrastructure-security-and-resil.

229. United States Senate, Select Committee to Study Governmental Operations with Respect to Intelligence Activities (Church Committee), *Final Report*, Book 1, April 26, 1976, accessed February 1, 2016, https://archive.org/details/finalreportof-sel01unit.

230. Central Intelligence Agency, *A Consumer's Guide to Intelligence: Gaining Knowledge and Foreknowledge of the World Around Us*, Office of Public Affairs (Washington, DC: National Technical Information Service, 1999).

231. U.S. Department of State, "State Messaging and Archive Retrieval Toolset," *Foreign Affairs Manual*, 5 FAM 1200, March 5, 2012, accessed December 1, 2015, http://www.state.gov/documents/organization/187326.pdf.

232. Office of the Director of National Intelligence, *National Intelligence Program FY 2009 Congressional Budget Justification Book*, Vol. XII, February 2008, accessed December 1, 2015, http://www.fas.org/irp/dni/cbjb-2009.pdf.

233. U.S. Department of Defense, Center for Development of Security Excellence, *Glossary of Security Terms and Definitions*, November 2012, accessed December 1, 2015, http://www.cdse.edu/documents/cdse/Glossary_Handbook.pdf.

234. Department of Defense, Air Force Classification Guide for the Global Broadcast System, *Security Classification/Declassification Guide*, April 29, 2007, accessed December 1, 2015, http://www.fas.org/sgp/othergov/dod/gbs.pdf.

235. United States Department of Justice. *Law Enforcement Analytic Standard.* Global Justice Information Sharing Initiative and International Association of Law Enforcement Intelligence Analysts, Inc. 2nd ed. April 2012, accessed February 1, 2016, https://it.ojp.gov/documents/d/Law%20Enforcement%20Analytic%20Standards%2004202_combined_compliant.pdf.

236. Department of Homeland Security, Risk Steering Committee, *DHS Risk Lexicon*, September 2010, accessed December 1, 2015, http://www.dhs.gov/dhs-risk-lexicon.

237. Department of Homeland Security, Risk Steering Committee, *DHS Risk Lexicon*, September 2010, accessed December 1, 2015, http://www.dhs.gov/dhs-risk-lexicon.

238. Office of the Director of National Intelligence, *National Intelligence Program FY 2009 Congressional Budget Justification Book*, Vol. XII, February 2008, accessed December 1, 2015, http://www.fas.org/irp/dni/cbjb-2009.pdf.

239. National Initiative for Cybersecurity Education, *A Glossary of Common Cybersecurity Terminology*, accessed December 1, 2015, http://niccs.us-cert.gov/glossary.

240. North Atlantic Treaty Organization, *NATO Glossary of Terms and Definitions*, NATO Standardization Agency, 2008, accessed December 1, 2015, https://fas.org/irp/doddir/other/nato2008.pdf.

241. Investopedia, *Cryptocurrency*, accessed December 1, 2015, http://www.investopedia.com/terms/c/cryptocurrency.asp.

242. Committee for National Security Systems (CNSS), *National Information Assurance Glossary*, Instruction 4009, April 2010, accessed December 1, 2015, http://www.ncix.gov/publications/policy/docs/CNSSI_4009.pdf.

243. National Initiative for Cybersecurity Education, *A Glossary of Common Cybersecurity Terminology*, accessed December 1, 2015, http://niccs.us-cert.gov/glossary.

244. North Atlantic Treaty Organization, *NATO Glossary of Terms and Definitions*, NATO Standardization Agency (2008), accessed July 2, 2015, https://fas.org/irp/doddir/other/nato2008.pdf.

245. North Atlantic Treaty Organization, *NATO Glossary of Terms and Definitions*, NATO Standardization Agency (2008), accessed July 2, 2015, https://fas.org/irp/doddir/other/nato2008.pdf.

246. Department of State, "Definitions of Diplomatic Security Terms," *Foreign Affairs Manual*, 12FAM090 (November 12, 2014), accessed February 27, 2015, http://www.state.gov/documents/organization/88330.pdf.

247. National Archives and Records Administration, *CUI Registry*, http://www.archives.gov/cui/registry/category-list.html.

248. Office of the Director of National Intelligence, *National Intelligence: A Consumer's Guide*, 2009, accessed February 1, 2016, http://www.dni.gov/files/documents/IC_Consumers_Guide_2009.pdf.

249. Jan Goldman, *Intelligence Warning Terminology*, Joint Military Intelligence College, October 2001, accessed July 3, 2015. https://archive.org/details/JMICInteligencelwarnterminology.

250. Office of the Director of National Intelligence, *Writing for Maximum Utility*, Intelligence Community Directive 208, December 17, 2008, accessed February 2, 2016, http://www.dni.gov/files/documents/ICD/icd_208.pdf.

251. United States Department of Justice. *Law Enforcement Analytic Standard*. Global Justice Information Sharing Initiative and International Association of Law Enforcement Intelligence Analysts, Inc. 2nd ed. April 2012, accessed February 1, 2016, https://it.ojp.gov/documents/d/Law%20Enforcement%20Analytic%20Standards%2004202_combined_compliant.pdf.

252. Customs and Border Protection. *Ports of Entry and User Fee Airports.* Accessed January 26, 2016, http://www.cbp.gov/trade/trade-community/programs-outreach/ports.

253. Federal Bureau of Investigation, *The Cyber Action Team Rapidly Responding to Major Computer Intrusions*, March 4, 2015, accessed February 2, 2016, http://www.fbi.gov/news/stories/2015/march/the-cyber-action-team/the-cyber-action-team.

254. Clapper, James R. Opening Statement to the Worldwide Threat Assessment Hearing Senate Armed Services Committee, February 26, 2015, accessed January 26, 2016, http://www.dni.gov/index.php/newsroom/testimonies/209-congressional-testimonies-2015/1175-dni-clapper-opening-statement-on-the-worldwide-threat-assessment-before-the-senate-armed-services-committee.

255. U.S. Department of Defense, Center for Development of Security Excellence, *Glossary of Security Terms and Definitions*, November 2012, accessed February 2, 2016, http://www.cdse.edu/documents/cdse/Glossary_Handbook.pdf.

256. U.S. Department of Defense, *Dictionary of Military and Associated Terms*, JP 1-02, 08 November 2010, as Amended through 15 January 2015, accessed January 26, 2016, https://web.archive.org/web/20150326010957 and http://www.dtic.mil/doctrine/new_pubs/jp1_02.pdf.

257. Finklea, Kristin and Theohary, Catherine A. "Cybercrime: Conceptual Issues for Congress and U.S. Law Enforcement." *CRS Report for Congress* R42547, January 15, 2015. Accessed March 21, 2015. http://fas.org/sgp/crs/misc/R42547.pdf.

258. CACI International Inc., U.S. Naval Institute, and Center for Security Policy, *Cyber Threats to National Security: Symposium Five: Keeping the Nation's Industrial Base Safe From Cyber Threats*, March 1, 2011, accessed December 1, 2015, http://asymmetricthreat.net/docs/asymmetric_threat_5_paper.pdf.

259. National Initiative for Cybersecurity Education, *A Glossary of Common Cybersecurity Terminology*, accessed January 26, 2016, http://niccs.us-cert.gov/glossary.

260. National Initiative for Cybersecurity Education, *A Glossary of Common Cybersecurity Terminology*, accessed January 26, 2016, http://niccs.us-cert.gov/glossary.

261. National Initiative for Cybersecurity Education, *A Glossary of Common Cybersecurity Terminology*, accessed January 26, 2016, http://niccs.us-cert.gov/glossary.

262. CACI International Inc., U.S. Naval Institute, and Center for Security Policy, *Cyber Threats to National Security: Symposium Five: Keeping the Nation's Industrial Base Safe From Cyber Threats*, March 1, 2011, accessed December 1, 2015, http://asymmetricthreat.net/docs/asymmetric_threat_5_paper.pdf.

263. National Initiative for Cybersecurity Education, *A Glossary of Common Cybersecurity Terminology*, accessed January 26, 2016, http://niccs.us-cert.gov/glossary.

264. National Initiative for Cybersecurity Education, *A Glossary of Common Cybersecurity Terminology*, accessed January 26, 2016, http://niccs.us-cert.gov/glossary.

265. CACI International Inc., U.S. Naval Institute, and Center for Security Policy, *Cyber Threats to National Security: Symposium Five: Keeping the Nation's Industrial Base Safe From Cyber Threats*, March 1, 2011, accessed July 2, 2015, http://asymmetricthreat.net/docs/asymmetric_threat_5_paper.pdf.

266. Department of Homeland Security, *National Infrastructure Protection Plan: Partnering to Enhance Protection and Resiliency*, 2009, accessed June 2, 2015, http://www.dhs.gov/xlibrary/assets/NIPP_Plan.pdf.

267. *Cybersecurity Act of 2015* (Omnibus Appropriations Act), December 15, 2015. Riles Committee Print, 114–39, accessed January 26, 2016, http://docs.house.gov/billsthisweek/20151214/CPRT-114-HPRT-RU00-SAHR2029-AMNT1final.pdf.

268. The White House, Office of the Press Secretary, *Fact Sheet: Cyber Threat Intelligence Integration Center*, February 25, 2015, accessed July 15, 2015, https://www.whitehouse.gov/the-press-office/2015/02/25/fact-sheet-cyber-threat-intelligence-integration-center.

269. National Security Presidential Directive-54/Homeland Security Presidential Directive-23, *Cybersecurity Policy*, January 9, 2008, accessed February 2, 2016, http://www.fas.org/irp/offdocs/nspd/nspd-54.pdf.

270. Theohary, Catherine A. and Rollins, John A. "Cyberwarfare and Cyberterrorism: In Brief," *CRS Report for Congress* R43955, March 27, 2015. Accessed January 25, 2016. http://fas.org/sgp/crs/natsec/R43955.pdf.

271. National Security Presidential Directive-54/Homeland Security Presidential Directive-23, *Cybersecurity Policy*, January 9, 2008, accessed February 2, 2016, http://www.fas.org/irp/offdocs/nspd/nspd-54.pdf.

272. National Initiative for Cybersecurity Education, *A Glossary of Common Cybersecurity Terminology*, accessed January 26, 2016, http://niccs.us-cert.gov/glossary.

273. *National Cybersecurity and Communications Integration Center Act of 2014*, S. 2519, accessed February 2, 2016, https://www.congress.gov/congressional-report/113th-congress/senate-report/240/1.

274. *Cybersecurity Act of 2015* (Omnibus Appropriations Act), December 15, 2015. Riles Committee Print, 114–39, accessed June 2, 2015, http://docs.house.gov/billsthisweek/20151214/CPRT-114-HPRT-RU00-SAHR2029-AMNT1final.pdf.

275. United States Department of Defense, *Cyberspace Operations*, JP 3-12, February 5, 2013, accessed February 3, 2016, http://www.dtic.mil/doctrine/new_pubs/jp3_12R.pdf.

276. National Security Presidential Directive-54/Homeland Security Presidential Directive-23, *Cybersecurity Policy*, January 9, 2008, accessed February 3, 2016, http://www.fas.org/irp/offdocs/nspd/nspd-54.pdf.

277. National Initiative for Cybersecurity Education, *A Glossary of Common Cybersecurity Terminology*, accessed January 26, 2016, http://niccs.us-cert.gov/glossary.

278. U.S. General Accountability Office, *Defense Department Cyber Efforts: Definitions, Focal Point, and Methodology Needed for DOD to Develop Full-Spectrum Cyberspace Budget Estimates*, GAO-11-695R, July 29, 2011, accessed February 2, 2016, http://www.gao.gov/products/GAO-11-695R.

279. United States Department of Defense, *Cyberspace Operations*, JP 3-12, February 5, 2013, accessed February 2, 2016, http://www.dtic.mil/doctrine/new_pubs/jp3_12R.pdf.

280. Theohary, Catherine A. and Rollins, John A. "Cyberwarfare and Cyberterrorism: In Brief," *CRS Report for Congress* R43955, March 27, 2015, accessed January 25, 2016, http://fas.org/sgp/crs/natsec/R43955.pdf.

281. Testimony of Keith Lourdeau, Deputy Assistant Director, Cyber Division, FBI Before the Senate Judiciary Subcommittee on Terrorism, Technology, and Homeland Security, February 24, 2004, Accessed February15, 2015, http://www2.fbi.gov/congress/congress04/lourdeau022404.htm.

282. CACI International Inc., U.S. Naval Institute, and Center for Security Policy, *Cyber Threats to National Security: Symposium Five: Keeping the Nation's Industrial Base Safe From Cyber Threats*, March 1, 2011, accessed December 1, 2015, http://asymmetricthreat.net/docs/asymmetric_threat_5_paper.pdf.

283. Theohary, Catherine A. and Rollins, John A. "Cyberwarfare and Cyberterrorism: In Brief," *CRS Report for Congress* R43955, March 27, 2015, accessed January 25, 2016, http://fas.org/sgp/crs/natsec/R43955.pdf.

284. Theohary, Catherine A. and Rollins, John A. "Cyberwarfare and Cyberterrorism: In Brief," *CRS Report for Congress* R43955, March 27, 2015, accessed January 25, 2016, http://fas.org/sgp/crs/natsec/R43955.pdf.

285. Rose, Andree, Timm, Howard, Pogson, Corrie, Gonzalez, Jose, Appel, Edward, and Kolb, Nancy. *Developing a Cybervetting Strategy for Law Enforcement.* Defense Personnel Security Research Center, U.S. Department of Defense, December 2010, accessed January 26, 2016, http://www.dhra.mil/perserec/reports/pp11-02.pdf.

286. Theohary, Catherine A. and Rollins, John A. "Cyberwarfare and Cyberterrorism: In Brief," CRS Report for Congress R43955, March 27, 2015, accessed January 25, 2016, http://fas.org/sgp/crs/natsec/R43955.pdf.

D

DAILY INTELLIGENCE SUMMARY (DINSUM) A report that has daily analysis of possible crisis situations and a summary of relevant intelligence information that was disseminated within the past 24 hours.[1]

DAMAGE ASSESSMENT The determination of the effect of attacks on targets;[2] or the determination of the effect of compromised classified information on national security.[3]

DAMAGE CAUSED BY UNAUTHORIZED DISCLOSURE An element of the classification process in which the classifier assesses the harm that would be caused by unauthorized disclosure of the information. The decision requires the application of "reasoned judgment" on the part of the classifier in determining "that the unauthorized disclosure of the information could reasonably be expected to cause damage to the national security of the United States, and that the damage can be identified or described. It is not necessary for the original classifier to produce a written description of the damage at the time of the classification, but the classifier must be prepared to do so if the information becomes the subject of a classification challenge, a request for mandatory review for declassification, or a request under the Freedom of Information Act."[4]

DAMAGE THREAT A determination of the harm that would result from a particular situation, such as the probability that a target ship passing through a mined area will explode one or more mines and sustain a certain amount of damage.[5]

DAMAGE TO THE NATIONAL SECURITY Harm to the national defense or foreign relations of the United States from the unauthorized disclosure of information, taking into consideration such aspects of the information as the sensitivity, value, utility, and provenance of that information.[6]

DANGEROUS ASSUMPTION A conceptual framework that makes sense of complex and disparate data by providing intellectual shortcuts and an anchor for interpretation, to the detriment of security considerations. For example, "This reality adds to the risks associated with President Clinton's nuclear testing bridge-leap insofar as he makes the dangerous assumption that he will be able to 'direct the Department of Energy to prepare to conduct additional tests while seeking approval to do so from Congress' in the event another nation conducts a nuclear test before the end of September 1994.[7] The human talents and diagnostic skills necessary to prepare and conduct such tests are no more immutable to change over time than are the weapons themselves."[8]

DANGLE A person controlled by one intelligence service who is made to appear as a lucrative and exploitable target to an opposing intelligence service.[9]

DA-NOTICE SYSTEM In Great Britain, the Defense Advisory Notice System provides a set of guidelines, agreed by representatives of the government directly concerned with national security and of all elements from the British Media. It informs editors, broadcasters, authors, publishers and others about what types of information need to be protected, and provides the basis for prior negotiation when there is disagreement about what should be disclosed to the general public. It also provides a negotiator (the DA-Notice Secretary) who is available to both sides 365 days a year; negotiation normally provides a solution acceptable to both sides—that is, the story goes out with only a few genuinely secret details removed. According to the government, it is much quicker, cheaper and more satisfactory than legal recourse, which also tends to block a whole story or source rather than just a few details. This system is voluntary, and even when they do use the system, they do not have to accept the advice of the DA-Notice Secretary nor accede to his requests. The final decision as to whether to publish or broadcast something is that of the editor.[10]

DARK NET Used to refer to websites whose operators can conceal their identity with sophisticated anonymity systems.[11]

DARK WEB The other content is that of the Deep Web, content that has not been indexed by traditional search engines such as Google. The furthest corners of the Deep Web, segments known as the Dark Web, contain content that has been intentionally concealed. The Dark Web may be used for legitimate purposes as well as to conceal criminal or otherwise malicious activities. It is the exploitation of the Dark Web for illegal practices that has garnered the interest of officials and policymakers. Individuals can access the Dark Web by using special software such as Tor (short for The Onion Router).[12]

DATA The lowest class of information on the cognitive hierarchy. Data are raw signals communicated by any nodes in an information system, or sensing from the environment detected by a collector of any kind (human, mechanical, or electronic).[13]

DATA AGGREGATION 1. The process of gathering and combining data from different sources, so that the combined data reveals new information. 2. New information is more sensitive than the individual data elements themselves, and the person who aggregates the data was not granted access to the totality of the information.[14] 3. Compilation of unclassified individual data systems and data elements that could result in the totality of the information being classified or of beneficial use to an adversary.[15]

DATA BASE (DATABASE) A set of data, consisting of at least one data file, that is sufficient for a given purpose.[16]

DATA BREACH The unauthorized movement or disclosure of sensitive information to a party, usually outside the organization, that is not authorized to have or see the information.[17]

DATA-IN-MOTION Data that transverses a network either internally or externally, and is not in a state of storage, such as DAR. This includes active communications via telephone (both cellular and conventional), radio, and pager, as well as computer traffic that is transmitted between any network nodes.[18]

DATA INTEGRITY The property that data is complete, intact, and trusted and has not been modified or destroyed in an unauthorized or accidental manner.[19]

DATA LOSS PREVENTION A set of procedures and mechanisms to stop sensitive data from leaving a security boundary.[20]

DATA MINING 1. The process or techniques used to analyze large sets of existing information to discover previously unrevealed patterns or correlations.[21] 2. Extracting useful information from large data sets or databases. 3. The application of database technology and techniques (such as statistical analysis and modeling) to uncover hidden patterns and subtle relationships in data and to infer rules that allow for the prediction of future results.[22]

DATA SOURCE A specific device, part of the computer or data asset (e.g., data set, file, website, database, etc.) where data is stored electronically and from which data can be obtained.[23]

DATAVEILLANCE (DATA SURVEILLANCE) The systematic use of personal data systems in the investigation or monitoring of the actions or communications of one or more persons. Dataveillance is significantly less expensive than physical and electronic surveillance, because it can be automated. As a result, the economic constraints on surveillance are diminished, and more individuals, and larger populations, are capable of being monitored. Like surveillance more generally, dataveillance is of two kinds: 1. Personal Dataveillance is the systematic use of personal data systems in the investigation or monitoring of the actions or communications of an identified person. In general, a specific reason exists for the investigation or monitoring of an identified individual. It may also, however, be applied as a means of deterrence against particular actions by the person, or repression of the person's behavior. 2. Mass Dataveillance is the systematic use of personal data systems in the investigation or monitoring of the actions or communications of groups of people. In general, the reason for investigation or monitoring is to identify individuals who belong to some particular class of interest to the surveillance organization. It may also, however, be used for its deterrent effects. Dataveillance comprises a wide range of techniques. These include: *Front-End Verification.* This is the cross-checking of data in an application form, against data from other personal data systems, in order to facilitate the processing of a transaction. *Computer Matching.* This is the expropriation of data maintained by two or more personal data systems, in order to merge previously separate data about large numbers of individuals. *Profiling.* This is a technique whereby a set of characteristics of a particular class of person is inferred from past experience, and data-holdings are then searched for individuals with a close fit to that set of characteristics.[24]

DEAD DROP A place unattended by individuals at which communications, materials, equipment, or a package can be left by one individual to be picked up later by another individual without the two meeting or seeing each other. The package is disguised to conceal its contents.[25]

DEBRIEFING The process of acquiring information from an individual that might have possible worthwhile intelligence information. This process can range from conducting an interview with business people who have traveled overseas to interrogating defectors or capturing spies.[26]

DEBUG The finding and eliminating of a secret recording device.

DECAPITATION STRIKE A planned attack on key government buildings and installations with the purpose of rendering useless the command and control functions of enemy forces. This type of strike intensifies the element of surprise by enhancing the notion of a "leaderless victim," or separating the head from the body. "A clandestine nuclear detonation in the city [Washington, D.C.] would likely doom the U.S. president, the vice president, Cabinet members, the Joint Chiefs of Staff, and members of Congress who were there at the time. The chaos that such an attack would cause would be difficult to overstate. One of the more difficult questions to answer in the hours after such a [nuclear, biological, or chemical terrorist] decapitation attack would be 'who is in charge here?' This chaos would be compounded if the headquarters housing the U.S. regional CINC [commander in chief] and his staff also were to suffer a similar decapitation strike at the same time. It is possible that the national leadership and the regional military forces of the United States would be plunged into chaos for some time."[27]

DECEPTION 1. Those measures designed to mislead a foreign power, organization, or person by manipulation, distortion, or falsification of evidence to induce a reaction prejudicial to the target's interests. 2. The practice of employing various ruses to disguise real intentions and true capabilities. There are three main reasons to conduct deception. One type of deception attempts to misdirect the enemy's attention, causing a concentration of forces in the wrong place. The deceiver thus makes the adversary violate the principle of concentration of forces. An example would be the Allied deception plans that diverted German attention from the beaches of Normandy to Norway and Pas de Calais as possible landing sites for an Allied invasion. A second type of deception makes the adversary violate the principle of economy of force, which causes the opponent to waste resources. An example of this would be any artificial radar signal that draws enemy firepower and attention, as when during World War II the British led the Germans to attack nonexistent airfields and factories by setting up phony targets and interfering with German electronic navigation aids. A third type of deception is designed to surprise an opponent by creating a situation that will later catch the enemy off guard and unprepared for action. An example is Hitler's policy toward Russia until the eve of his attack (Operation Barbarossa) in June 1941. This third type of deception is also related to the other two types.[28] *See* A-TYPE DECEPTION; ACTIVE DECEPTION; CAMOUFLAGE; DENIAL; MANIPULATION; PASSIVE DECEPTION

DECEPTION MEANS Methods, resources, and techniques that can be used to convey information to the deception target. There are three categories of deception means:[29]

- Administrative means: Resources, methods, and techniques to convey or deny oral, pictorial, documentary, or other physical evidence to a foreign power.
- Physical means: Activities and resources used to convey or deny selected information to a foreign power (e.g., military operations, including exercises, reconnaissance, training activities, and movement of forces; the use of dummy equipment and devices; tactics; bases, logistic actions, stockpiles, and repair activity; test and evaluation activities).
- Technical means: Military materiel resources and their associated operating techniques used to convey or deny selected information to a foreign power through the deliberate radiation, re-radiation, alteration, absorption, or reflection of energy; the emission or suppression of chemical or biological odors and the emission or suppression of nuclear particles.

DECIDE/ACT Take action based on a biometric file's match results and analysis of associated information.[30]

DECISION ANALYSIS Techniques, body of knowledge, and professional practice used to provide analytical support for making decisions through a formalized structure. Decision analysis can be used in the context of risk analysis to evaluate complex risk management decisions. Decision analysis can be applied to strategic, operational, and tactical decisions.[31]

DECLASSIFICATION 1. The authorized change in the status of information from classified to unclassified. 2. The determination that classified information no longer requires, in the interests of national security, any degree of protection against unauthorized disclosure, coupled with a removal or cancellation of the classification designation. 3. The process of reviewing and disclosing previously designated (classified) national security and nuclear-related information classified by U.S. government branches, departments, and agencies. 4. Defined by the Obama administration's Executive Order 13526 (2009), *Classified National Security Information*, as "the authorized change in the status of information from classified information to unclassified information." Classification levels are Top Secret, Secret, and Confidential; declassification "downgrades" these levels in portions of a record/document or the entire material.[32]

DECLASSIFICATION GUIDE Written instructions issued by a declassification authority that describes the elements of information regarding a specific subject that may be declassified and the elements that must remain classified. Also a guide providing classification and declassification instructions specifically for information that is 25 years old or older and of permanent historical value. A declassification guide is the most commonly used vehicle for obtaining ISCAP approval of 25-year exemptions from the automatic declassification provisions of Reference (d).[33]

DECONFLICTION The process of sharing information regarding collection between multiple agencies to eliminate potential duplication of effort, multiple unintended use of the same source, or circular reporting.[34]

DECOY An imitation in any sense of a person, object, or phenomenon that is intended to deceive enemy surveillance devices or mislead enemy evaluation.[35]

DECRYPTION The process of changing ciphertext into plain text using a cryptographic algorithm and key or using just a cryptographic algorithm. *See* ENCRYPTION

DEDUCTIVE LOGIC 1. Reasoning from the general to the specific. 2. Applying the rules of a logical system to manipulate statements of belief (premises) to form new logically consistent statements of belief (conclusions). If the premises are true, the conclusion must necessarily be true. 3. Inferences made in which the conclusion about particulars follows necessarily from general or universal premises (key facts). Key facts are included in the premises. The most famous logical sequence, called the syllogism, was developed by the Greek philosopher Aristotle. His most famous syllogism is: Premise 1: All men are mortal. Premise 2: Socrates is a man. Conclusion: Therefore, Socrates is mortal. In this sequence, premise 2 is tested against premise 1 to reach the logical conclusion. Within this system, if both premises are considered valid, there is no other logical conclusion than determining that Socrates is a mortal.[36] *See* CONCLUSION; HYPOTHESIS; INDUCTIVE LOGIC; INFERENCE

DEEP WEB Content that is not part of the traditional WWW. This content is estimated to be more than twice the content saved and accessible on the traditional WWW. The content and information contained on the Deep Web is designed around Web-based databases. Unlike the WWW, the Deep Web is not indexed. Nonstatic websites and databases located on the Deep Web cannot be accessed or indexed by traditional search engines. The Deep Web offers a tremendous amount of resources. Deep Web resources could fall into one or more of the following: Dynamic content. Web pages that are returned in response to a submitted query; Unlinked content. Web pages that are not linked to other Web pages that prevent standard Web crawling programs from accessing the content; Private Web content. Web pages without backlinks or inlinks; Limited access content. Websites that limit access to information; Nonhypertext markup language content. Textual content encoded in multimedia files that are not handled by search engines.[37]

DEFEAT ASSESSMENT Application of intelligence and targeting processes to assess denial, disruption, or destruction of a function/facility both before and after an attack.[38] *See* ASSESSMENT; FUNCTIONAL DEFEAT; PHYSICAL DEFEAT

DEFECTOR A person who has abandoned loyalty to his or her country and who possesses intelligence information of value to another country or countries; a person who repudiates his or her country and leaves its jurisdiction or control.[39]

DEFECTOR IN PLACE A government official who agrees to work for a foreign intelligence service while remaining in position in his own government.

DEFEND Actions taken to deter, preempt, or prevent attacks against the homeland. Can include conducting preemptive attacks to protect U.S. interests.[40]

DEFENSE AUTOMATED WARNING SYSTEM (DAWS) A sophisticated intelligence data-handling system which provides the I&W community analysts with a highly effective applications suite to expedite analysis of all-source intelligence. All Unified and Specified (U&S) commands make daily decisions on the appropriate posture of their forces, based upon the current threat. The force posture options include changes in alert status to improve response times, relocation of assets to increase warning time, and launch under positive control. These decisions are based upon the best assessment of enemy capabilities and demand sophisticated and timely intelligence.[41]

DEFENSE CENTRAL INDEX OF INVESTIGATIONS (DCII) An automated Department of Defense (DoD) repository that identifies investigations conducted by DoD investigative agencies and personnel security determinations made by DoD adjudicative authorities.[42]

DEFENSE CENTRAL SECURITY INDEX An automated sub-system of the Defense Central Index of Investigations (DCII) designed to record the issuance, denial or revocation of security clearances, access to classified information, or assignment to a sensitive position by all Department of Defense (DOD) Components for military, civilian, and contractor personnel. The Defense Central Security Index will serve as the central DoD repository of security-related actions in order to assist DoD security officials in making sound clearance and access determinations and provide accurate and reliable statistical data for senior DoD officials, congressional committees, the General Accounting Office (GAO), and other authorized federal requesters.[43]

DEFENSE CONDITION (DEFCON) Progressive alert postures, primarily for use between the Joint Chiefs of Staff and the commanders of unified commands. Levels progress to match situations of varying military severity and reflect phased increases in combat readiness.

DEFCON 5: Normal peacetime readiness.
DEFCON 4: Normal, increased intelligence and strengthened security measures.
DEFCON 3: An increase in force readiness above normal readiness.
DEFCON 2: A further increase in force readiness, but less than maximum readiness.
DEFCON 1: Maximum force readiness.

An example of changes in DEFCON occurred during the Cuban Missile Crisis in 1962, the U.S. Strategic Air Command (SAC) was placed on DEFCON 2 for the first time in history, while the rest of U.S. military commands (with the exception of the U.S. Air Forces in Europe) went on DEFCON 3. On 22 October 1962, SAC established DEFCON 3 and ordered B-52s on airborne alert. Tension grew, and the next day SAC declared DEFCON 2, a heightened state of alert, ready to strike targets within the Soviet Union. Another example occurred on 6 October 1973, when Egyptian and Syrian forces launched a surprise attack on Israel. On 25 October, U.S. forces went on DEFCON 3 alert status, as possible intervention by the Soviet Union was feared. On 26 October, SAC and Continental Air Defense Command reverted to normal DEFCON status. On 31 October, U.S. European Command except for the Sixth Fleet went off DEFCON 3 status. The Sixth Fleet resumed its normal DEFCON status on 17 November 1973.[44] *See* THREAT CONDITION; WATCH CONDITION

DEFENSE FORENSICS AND BIOMETRICS AGENCY (DFBA) The Department of the Army General Order (DAGO) 2013-08, signed by the

Secretary of the Army, re-designated BIMA (Biometrics Identity Management Agency) as DFBA on 18 June 2013, retroactive to 1 June 2013. The agency is responsible for applying biometrics and forensics capabilities through various tactics, techniques and processes. Biometrics and forensics are critical to identifying known and unknown individuals by matching them with automated records (such as for access control) or with anonymous samples (such as crime scene investigations).[45]

DEFENSE HUMAN INTELLIGENCE EXECUTOR (DHE) The senior Department of Defense intelligence official as designated by the head of each of the Department of Defense components who are authorized to conduct human intelligence and related intelligence activities.[46]

DEFENSE IN DEPTH Information security strategy integrating people, technology, and operations capabilities to establish variable barriers across multiple layers and missions of the organization.[47]

DEFENSE INFORMATION SYSTEMS NETWORK (DISN) A sub-element of the Defense Information Infrastructure (DII), the Defense Information Systems Network (DISN) is the Department of Defense's (DoD) consolidated worldwide, enterprise-level telecommunications infrastructure that provides the end-to-end information transfer network for supporting military operations. The DISN, transparent to users, facilitates the management of information resources and is responsive to national security and defense needs under all conditions in the most efficient manner. The DISN is an information transfer network with value-added services for supporting national defense Command, Control, Communication, and Intelligence (C3I) decision support requirements and Classified Military Information (CMI) functional business areas.[48]

DEFENSE INTELLIGENCE AGENCY The agency that issues periodic and special warning reports designed to give guidance on threats to the U.S. commands around the world. The Weekly Intelligence Forecast and the Weekly Warning Forecast Report include assessments from the various commands. The Quarterly Warning Forecast reviews a broad range of potential developments that could have an impact on U.S. security interests. In addition, DIA and the Unified Commands, as members of the Defense I&W system, publish two ad hoc products as issues arise: the Warning Report is an assessment of a specific warning issue; the Watch Condition Change is a notification of a change, either up or down, in the threat level presented by a specific warning problem. The Warning Report is the vehicle by which the

Department of Defense's I&W system communicates warning intelligence that is worthy of the immediate, specific attention of senior U.S. officials within the Washington area.[49]

DEFENSE INTELLIGENCE COMPONENTS Refers to all DoD organizations that perform National Intelligence, Defense Intelligence, and intelligence-related functions, including: the Defense Intelligence Agency; the National Geospatial-Intelligence Agency; the National Reconnaissance Office; the National Security Agency/Central Security Service; and the intelligence elements of the Active and Reserve Components of the Military Department (Reference (c)); DoD Directive 5143.01, "Under Secretary of Defense for Intelligence (USD(I))," November 23, 2005).[50]

DEFENSE SECURITY SERVICE (DSS) An agency of the Department of Defense (DoD) located in Quantico, Virginia, with field offices throughout the United States. The Under Secretary of Defense for Intelligence provides authority, direction and control over DSS. DSS provides the military services, Defense Agencies, 27 federal agencies and approximately 13,500 cleared contractor facilities with security support services. DSS contributes to national security by serving as an interface between the government and cleared industry. DSS administers and implements the defense portion of the National Industrial Security Program pursuant to Executive Order 12829.[51]

DEFENSE SWITCHED NETWORK (DSN) A primary information transfer network for the Defense Information System Network (DISN). The DSN provides the worldwide nonsecure voice, secure voice, data, facsimile, and video teleconferencing services for DoD Command and Control (C2) elements, their supporting activities engaged in logistics, personnel, engineering, and intelligence, as well as other federal agencies.[52]

DEFENSIVE COUNTER-CYBER (DCC) All defensive countermeasures designed to detect, identify, intercept, and destroy or negate harmful activities attempting to penetrate or attack through cyberspace.[53]

DEGRADE To use nonlethal or temporary means to reduce the effectiveness or efficiency of an adversary's command and control systems and the adversary's information collection efforts or means.[54]

DELIBERATE COMPROMISE OF CLASSIFIED INFORMATION 1. Any intentional act done with the object of conveying classified information to any person not officially authorized to receive the information.[55] 2. The act, attempt, or reported contemplation of intentionally conveying classified documents, information, or material to any unauthorized person, including unauthorized public disclosure.[56] The U.S. Code describes such disclosure as follows:[57]

> Whoever knowingly and willfully communicates, furnishes, transmits, or otherwise makes available to an unauthorized person, or publishes, or uses in any manner prejudicial to the safety or interest of the United States or for the benefit of any foreign government to the detriment of the United States any classified information—(1) concerning the nature, preparation, or use of any code, cipher, or cryptographic system of the United States or any foreign government; or (2) concerning the design, construction, use, maintenance, or repair of any device, apparatus, or appliance used or prepared or planned for use by the United States or any foreign government for cryptographic or communication intelligence purposes; or (3) concerning the communication intelligence activities of the United States or any foreign government; or (4) obtained by the processes of communication intelligence from the communications of any foreign government, knowing the same to have been obtained by such processes.

DELPHI METHOD An approach in which the opinions of experts are pooled; as many as 50 experts may be consulted, depending on the complexity of the problem. A questionnaire (or interview) is prepared asking for the probability of occurrences of certain events (such as technological breakthroughs by a certain date, or alternatively, for the date by which the occurrence is judged to have a given probability, or even for an entire probability distribution over time).

ROUND 1: A first set of estimated answers is solicited. Sometimes the respondents are asked to select only the questions about which they consider themselves especially competent. Alternatively, answers to all questions may be requested, accompanied by a self-rating of relative competence for each question.

ROUND 2: The participants are then provided with the Round 1 response distribution, which is usually presented in terms of the median and the first and third quartiles. And new, possibly revised, responses are solicited.

ROUND 3: The resulting response distribution is fed back, together with a summary of the argument, defending relatively deviant responses. Again, the participants are asked for re-estimates.

ROUND 4: Again, the new response distribution and a summary of the counterarguments are fed back, and a final set of answers is issued based on due considerations of all arguments and counterarguments that were presented.

The medians of the responses of this final round are then accepted as the group's position, representing the nearest thing to a consensus that is attainable. A report on the outcome usually also includes an indication of the residual spread of opinions, as well as of minority arguments in defense of deviant opinions, particularly in cases where sizeable dissent remains.[58]

DEMARCHE An official protest delivered through diplomatic channels from one government to another.

DEMOGRAPHIC/SOCIAL TREND ANALYSIS An examination of the nature of demographic changes and their impact on criminality, the community, and law enforcement.[59]

DEMONSTRATION 1. Activity to divert a victim's strength and attention from the real or primary operation; to fix the enemy's local forces by actual combat, hopefully drawing forces into irrelevant battle. 2. An attack or show of force on a front where a decision is not sought, made with the aim of deceiving the enemy.[60] *See* DIVERSION; FABRICATION; FEINT

DENIAL Measures taken to impede or preclude collection of information or access to a location or activity. *See* DECEPTION

DENIAL AND DECEPTION (D&D) Denial is the ability to prevent or impair the collection of intelligence by the enemy; deception is the ability to mislead intelligence gathering by providing a distortion of reality. "Precise forecasts of the growth in ballistic missile capabilities over the next two decades—tests by year, production rates, weapons deployed by year, weapon characteristics by system type and circular error probable (CEP)—cannot be provided with confidence. Deception and denial efforts are intense and often successful, and U.S. collection and analysis assets are limited. Together they create a high risk of continued surprise. The question is not simply whether we will have warning of an emerging capability, but whether the nature and magnitude of a particular threat will be perceived with sufficient clarity in time to take appropriate action. Concealment denial and deception efforts by key target countries are intended to delay the discovery of strategically significant activities until well after they had been carried out successfully. The fact that some of these secret activities are discovered over time is to the credit of the U.S. Intelligence Community. However, the fact that there are delays in discovery of those activities provides a sharp warning that a great deal of activity goes undetected."[61] *See* A-TYPE DECEPTION; ACTIVE DECEPTION

DENIAL MEASURE An action to hinder or deny the enemy the use of space, personnel, or facilities. It may include destruction, removal, contamination, or erection of obstructions.[62]

DENIAL OF SERVICE ATTACK (DOS) An attack that attempts to prevent or impair the intended functionality of computer networks, systems, or applications. Depending on the type of system targeted, the attack can employ a variety of mechanisms and means.[63]

DENY In information operations, to withhold information about armed force capabilities and intentions that adversaries need for effective and timely decision making.[64]

DEPARTMENT OF DEFENSE (DOD) DIRECTIVE A Department of Defense (DoD) issuance that transmits information required by law, the president, or the Secretary of Defense that applies to all branches of DoD on the way they initiate, govern, or regulate actions. DoD Directives establish or describe policy, programs, and organizations; define missions; provide authority; and assign responsibilities. DoD Directives do not prescribe one-time tasks or deadline assignments.[65]

DEPARTMENT OF DEFENSE (DOD) INSTRUCTION A DoD issuance that implements policies and tells the user how to carry out a policy, operate a program or activity, and assign responsibilities.[66]

DEPARTMENT OF DEFENSE DICTIONARY OF MILITARY AND ASSOCIATED TERMS Joint Publication 1-02, *Department of Defense Dictionary of Military and Associated Terms* sets forth standard U.S. military and associated terminology to encompass the joint activity of the Armed Forces of the United States. These military and associated terms, together with their definitions, constitute approved Department of Defense (DoD) terminology for general use by all DoD components. This publication supplements standard English-language dictionaries and standardizes military and associated terminology to improve communication and mutual understanding within DoD, with other federal agencies, and among the United States and its allies. This publication applies to the Office of the Secretary of Defense, the Services, the Joint Staff, combatant commands, DoD agencies, and all other DoD components. It is the primary terminology source when preparing correspondence, to include policy, strategy, doctrine, and planning documents.[67]

DEPARTMENT OF DEFENSE INTELLIGENCE INFORMATION SYSTEM (DODIS) The DoD personnel, procedures, equipment, computer programs, and supporting communications that support the timely and comprehensive preparation and presentation of intelligence and information to military commanders and national-level decision makers.[68]

DEPARTMENT OF DEFENSE METADATA REGISTRY Managed by the Defense Information Systems Agency (DISA), it provides data services and other data-related infrastructures that promote interoperability and software reuse in the secure, reliable, and networked environment planned for the Global Information Grid (GIG).[69] *See* GLOBAL INFORMATION GRID

DEPARTMENT OF HOMELAND SECURITY (DHS) 1. With the passage of the Homeland Security Act by Congress in November 2002 (P.L.107-296), the Department of Homeland Security formally came into being as a stand-alone, cabinet-level department to further coordinate and unify national homeland security efforts, opening its doors on March 1, 2003. DHS was created through the integration of all or part of 22 different federal departments and agencies into a unified, integrated Department.[70] 2. When George W. Bush proposed the creation of the Department of Homeland Security (DHS) on June 8, 2002, he called it "the most extensive reorganization of the federal government since the 1940s." Indeed, at its inception on March 1, 2003, the DHS brought together twenty-two federal agencies and more than 170,000 employees—the largest restructuring since the creation of the Department of Defense (DOD) in 1947.[71]

DEPARTMENT OF STATE SENSITIVE BUT UNCLASSIFIED Information that originated within the State Department that warrants a degree of protection or administrative control and meets the criteria for exemption from mandatory public disclosure under FOIA. Prior to January 26, 1995, this information was designated and marked LOU [Limited Use Only]. The LOU designation is no longer used.[72]

DEPUTY COORDINATOR FOR HOMELAND SECURITY AND MULTILATERAL AFFAIRS (CT/HSMA) Coordinates the Department's participation in international counterterrorism activities as they affect homeland security, and collaborates closely with the U.S. Department of Homeland Security and other U.S. departments and agencies with respect to international CT activities.[73]

DERADICALIZATION Encourages an individual to renounce extremist ideas. This term is sometimes used to describe the entire process of changing a violent extremist's attitudes and behaviors and reintegrating him or her into society.[74]

DERIVATIVE CLASSIFICATION 1. While working with classified information, individuals sometimes generate or create new documents and materials based upon that classified information. These individuals who reproduce, extract, or summarize classified information, or who apply classification markings derived from source material or as directed by a security classification guide, need not possess original classification authority. The newly created documents must be classified based upon the classification level of the information from which the new document was developed. This is defined as "derivative classification."[75] 2. A determination that a document or material contains or reveals information already classified. 3. A determination that information is in substance the same as information currently classified.

DERIVED INFORMATION A parameter (such as angle, range, position, velocity, etc.) is said to be derived in the first receiver or other sensor in which that parameter exists or is capable of existing without references to further information.[76]

DEROGATORY INFORMATION Unfavorable information regarding an individual which brings into question the individual's eligibility or continued eligibility for access authorization or suitability for federal employment.[77]

DESCRIPTIVE ANALYSIS Provides no evaluation or interpretation of collected data but instead organizes and structures the information so that it can subsequently be used for interpretation. Typical tasks associated with this type of analysis are compiling, organizing, structuring, indexing, and cross-checking. Descriptive analytic materials would include maps and public records such as phone books and birth records. *See* INFERENTIAL ANALYSIS

DESIGNATED INTELLIGENCE DISCLOSURE OFFICIAL (DIDO) The heads of Intelligence Community (IC) organizations or those United States (U.S.) Government Officials who have been designated by the Director of National Intelligence (DNI), in writing, as having the authority to approve or deny disclosure or release of uncaveated intelligence information to foreign governments in accordance with applicable disclosure policies and procedures.[78]

DESIGNATED STATE AND/OR MAJOR URBAN AREA FUSION CENTER The fusion center in each state designated as the primary or lead fusion center for the information sharing environment.[79]

DESIGNATION OF DAYS AND HOURS Day and hour designations in common use include:

> D-DAY: The day on which an operation commences or is due to commence. This may be the commencement of hostilities or any other operation.
> E-DAY: The day on which a convoy system is introduced or is due to be introduced on any particular convoy lane.
> K-DAY: The day on which a convoy system is introduced or is due to be introduced on any particular convoy lane.
> M-DAY: The day on which mobilization commences or is due to commence.
> H-HOUR: The specific time at which an operation or exercise commences or is due to commence.

DESTROYING The process of physically damaging the media to the level that the media is not usable, and that there is no known method of retrieving the data.[80]

DETAINEE Any person captured, detained, or otherwise under the control of Department of Defense personnel.[81]

DETAINEE OPERATIONS A broad term that encompasses the capture, initial detention and screening, transportation, treatment and protection, housing, transfer, and release of the wide range of persons who could be categorized as detainees.[82]

DETAINEE REPORTING SYSTEM (DRS) A system designed to support the processing of prisoner of war (POWs) and detainees.[83]

DETECT, PREVENT, DISRUPT AND DETER 1. Among our most important missions in denying entry to terrorists, their weapons, and other implements of terror is to detect, disrupt, and interdict the movement of WMD-related materials into the Homeland. This is one objective in our comprehensive strategy to prevent WMD terrorism, which is fully discussed in the *National Strategy for Combating Terrorism* (2006). 2. In December 2004, Congress passed and the president signed the Intelligence Reform and Terrorism Prevention Act of 2004 (IRTPA). IRTPA calls for, among other things, the creation of the Information Sharing Environment (ISE)—a trusted partnership among all levels of government, the private sector, and our foreign partners to detect, prevent, disrupt, preempt, and mitigate the effects of terrorism against the territory, people, and interests of the United States through the appropriate exchange of terrorism information.[84]

DETENTION The National Defense Authorization Act for FY2012 (2012 NDAA; P.L. 112-81) arguably constituted the most significant legislation informing wartime detention policy since the 2001 Authorization for the Use of Military Force (AUMF; P.L. 107-40), which serves as the primary legal authority for U.S. operations against Al Qaeda and associated forces. Much of the debate surrounding passage of the 2012 NDAA centered on what appeared to be an effort to confirm or, as some observers view it, expand the detention authority that Congress implicitly granted the president via the AUMF in the aftermath of the terrorist attacks of September 11, 2001.[85]

DETERMINATION AUTHORITY A designee of a Senior Official of the Intelligence Community (SOIC) with responsibility for decisions rendered with respect to Sensitive Compartmented Information (SCI) access eligibility or ineligibility.[86]

DETERRENT Measure that discourages, complicates, or delays an adversary's action or occurrence by instilling fear, doubt, or anxiety.[87]

DEVIL'S ADVOCATE, DEVIL'S ADVOCACY 1. A person that challenges a strongly held view or consensus by developing the possible case for an alternative explanation. Devil's advocacy is considered most effective when challenging key assumptions that are critically important to the analytic process of developing an assessment. 2. Challenging a single, strongly held view or consensus by building the best possible case for an alternative explanation.[88] *See* A-TEAM/B-TEAM CONCEPT

DHS DAILY OPEN SOURCE INFRASTRUCTURE REPORT The DHS Daily Open Source Infrastructure Report is collected each business day as a summary of open-source published information concerning significant critical infrastructure issues. Each Daily Report is divided by the critical infrastructure sectors and key assets defined in the National Infrastructure Protection Plan.[89]

DIGITAL ASSASSINATION A willful act by someone who wishes to do harm through the Internet. It unfolds as a deliberate campaign to spread harmful lies that the assassin has concocted about you or as an attempt to take a fact about you grossly out of context or embellish it, making an ordinary shortcoming seem ghastly. Words are then forged into swords to be thrust into the gut. Digital assassination is most effective when others—as knowing conspirators or unknowing parrots—are incited by social media to thrust swords of their own. The result is multiple slices and stabs, leaving a permanent, searchable Internet record that continues to harm your brand, fan base, business, or reputation among friends, customers, investors or other media on a 24/7 basis.[90]

DIGITAL FORENSICS The processes and specialized techniques for gathering, retaining, and analyzing system-related data (digital evidence) for investigative purposes. Extended Definition: In the NICE Workforce Framework, cybersecurity work where a person: collects, processes, preserves, analyzes, and presents computer-related evidence in support of network vulnerability, mitigation, and/or criminal, fraud, counterintelligence or law enforcement investigations.[91]

DIGITAL RIGHTS MANAGEMENT (DRM) 1. A form of access control technology to protect and manage use of digital content or devices in accordance with the content or device provider's intentions.[92] 2. DRM restricts entirely different activities than copyright does, and serves an entirely separate function. While copyright restricts who can distribute media, DRM restricts how users can access their media. Copyright already provides leverage against illegal distribution, meaning that the largest distribution platforms must already adhere to the demands of large publishers, studios, music labels, and software companies. DRM provides antifeatures (features that exist only to worsen the service for users) and charges for their removal. This gives major media and technology companies much broader control over the use of media than is enabled by copyright law, while copyright allows them to force all legal media distribution services to use DRM.[93]

DIGITAL SIGNATURE The result of a cryptographic transformation of data that, when properly implemented, provides a mechanism for verifying origin authentication, data integrity and signatory non-repudiation.[94]

DIMEFIL The acronym for Diplomatic, Information, Military, Economic, Financial, Intelligence, and Law Enforcement instruments of national power articulated in the *National Strategy for Combating Terrorism* (2003).[95]

DIPLOMAT A foreign official who has presented credentials to the U.S. secretary of state and has been officially sanctioned as a diplomatic representative of his or her country by the U.S. government.

DIPLOMATIC ESTABLISHMENT A mission, consulate, embassy, residential compound, or other premises owned or leased and used by a government for official purposes.

DIPLOMATIC IMMUNITY Diplomatic immunity is a status granted to diplomatic personnel that exempts them from the laws of a foreign jurisdiction. The Vienna Convention of Diplomatic Relations (1961), which most states have ratified, offers diplomats acting as officials of state almost total protection from subjection to criminal, administrative, and civil laws belonging to the country in which the diplomatic mission is located. Diplomats assigned to missions located in foreign countries remain subject to the laws of their home countries. The diplomat's country of origin has prerogative over whether or not a host country may prosecute a diplomat under its (i.e., "foreign") laws.[96]

DIRECT CONSEQUENCE Effect that is an immediate result of an event, incident, or occurrence. 1) Direct consequences can include injuries, loss of life, on-site business interruption, immediate remediation costs, and damage to property and infrastructure as well as to the environment. 2) The distinction between direct and indirect consequences is not always clear, but what matters in risk analysis is a) capturing the likely effects—be they designated as direct or indirect—that should be part of the analysis, b) clearly defining what is contained as part of direct consequences and what is part of indirect consequences, and c) being consistent across the entire analysis.[97]

DIRECT INFORMATION WARFARE Changing the adversary's information without involving the intervening perceptive and analytical functions.[98]

DIRECTED SURVEILLANCE Surveillance is defined as being directed if all of the following criteria are met: it is covert, but not intrusive surveillance; it is conducted for the purposes of a specific investigation or operation; it is likely to result in the obtaining of private information about a person (whether or not one specifically identified for the purposes of the investigation or operation); it is conducted otherwise than by way of an immediate response to events or in circumstances the nature of which is such that it would not be reasonably practicable for an authorization under Part II of the Regulation of Investigatory Powers Act 2000 to be sought.[99]

DIRECTOR OF NATIONAL INTELLIGENCE (DNI) One of the recommendations of the National Commission on the Terrorist Attacks upon the

United States ("9/11 Commission") was to replace the position of the director of central intelligence (DCI) with a national intelligence director who would oversee and coordinate national intelligence agencies and programs. The DNI coordinates the 15 agencies that comprise the intelligence community (IC), is the principal intelligence adviser to the president, and is the statutory intelligence adviser to the National Security Council.[100]

DISASTER A serious disruption of the functioning of a community or a society involving widespread human, material, economic or environmental losses and impacts, which exceeds the ability of the affected community or society to cope using its own resources.[101]

DISASTER RISK MANAGEMENT The systematic process of using administrative directives, organizations, and operational skills and capacities to implement strategies, policies and improved coping capacities in order to lessen the adverse impacts of hazards and the possibility of disaster.[102]

DISCLOSURE A transfer by any means of a record, a copy of a record, or the information contained in a record to a recipient other than the subject individual, or the review of a record by someone other than the subject individual.[103]

DISCLOSURE OF INTELLIGENCE Showing, revealing, communicating, or transferring intelligence information by any means of communication (such as oral, written, electronic, mechanical, or actual review) to any person, private entity, U.S. government agency or foreign entity, other than the subject of the record, the subject's designated agent, or the subject's legal guardian.[104]

DISCOVERY 1. The process in which evidence is collected and hypotheses are generated and linked through arguments. Discovery involves asking questions about evidence in order to establish its relevance, credibility, and inferential force on the postulated conclusions. The process may be marked by hypotheses in search of evidence at the same time evidence is in search of hypotheses (inductive and deductive reasoning). Discovery is aided by imaginative reasoning—marshaling existing evidence to stimulate new insights (adductive reasoning).[105] 2. The act of obtaining knowledge of the existence, but not necessarily the content, of information collected or analysis produced by any IC element. Discovery, as it is applicable under this directive, is not defined or intended to be interpreted as discovery under the Federal Rules of Civil Procedure, Federal Rules of Criminal Procedure or other individual state discovery rules regarding non-privileged matter that is relevant to any party's claim or defense.[106]

DISCRETIONARY ACCESS CONTROL An access control policy that is enforced over all subjects and objects in an information system where the policy specifies that a subject that has been granted access to information can do one or more of the following: (i) pass the information to other subjects or objects; (ii) grant its privileges to other subjects; (iii) change security attributes on subjects, objects, information systems, or system components; (iv) choose the security attributes to be associated with newly created or revised objects; or (v) change the rules governing access control. Mandatory access controls restrict this capability.[107]

DISINFORMATION 1. False information prepared by an intelligence service for the purpose of misleading, deluding, disrupting, or undermining confidence in individuals, organizations, or governments. 2. Information disseminated primarily by intelligence organizations or other covert agencies designed to distort information or deceive or influence decision makers, armed forces, coalition allies, key actors, or individuals via indirect or unconventional means.[108] 3. False and irrelevant information made available to deceive. For example, according to one report, Iraq's disinformation charges usually originate in their media and have been widely and often uncritically repeated by sympathetic media in Yemen, Algeria, Tunisia, Jordan, and, to a lesser extent, media in Pakistan, Morocco, Mauritania, Bangladesh, and other countries. Iraqi disinformation is often picked up and disseminated by otherwise responsible news media that fail to verify a story's source or facts. Iraqi ambassadors and embassy spokesmen have also made blatant disinformation claims in media appearances worldwide. Disinformation is a cheap, crude, and often very effective way to inflame public opinion and affect attitudes. It involves the deliberate production and dissemination of falsehoods by a government for a political purpose. Disinformation differs fundamentally from misinformation—unintentional errors which occur when facts are unclear and deadline pressures are urgent—in its clearly misleading and propagandistic purposes. Iraq's disinformation strategy is predictable. Its leaders have tried to make it appear that: Iraq is strong and the multinational coalition is weak; Israel is part of the multinational coalition; Allied Forces are committing crimes against Islam and atrocities in general; the United States is at odds with various countries in the coalition.[109]

DISLOCATED CIVILIAN A broad term primarily used by the Department of Defense that includes a displaced person, an evacuee, an internally displaced person, a migrant, a refugee, or a stateless person.[110]

DISPLACED PERSON A broad term used to refer to internally and externally displaced persons collectively.[111]

DISRUPT Actions taken to interrupt, temporarily prevent, or desynchronize a terrorist network's capability to conduct operations.[112]

DISRUPTIVE POWERS It is not always possible to prosecute or deport terrorists and other individuals who threaten our national security. For example, where there is not enough evidence to advance a prosecution, or where there are concerns about an individual's treatment were they to be deported back to their home country. It is therefore vital that the government has the tools it needs to ensure the activities of individuals who pose a threat to our national security can be effectively disrupted. There are a number of "disruptive powers" that range from powers of search and seizure, port and border controls, terrorist asset-freezing, and Terrorism Prevention and Investigation Measures (TPIMs), to the Royal Prerogative, where persons may be refused a British passport or may have their existing passport withdrawn on a number of grounds, including that the grant to them, or their continued enjoyment, of passport facilities is contrary to the public interest.[113]

DISRUPTIVE TECHNOLOGY OFFICE Incorporated into IARPA (Intelligence Advanced Research Projects Activity), is a project that provides funds to agencies for R&D activities that benefit the whole IC or do not fit into other existing agencies.[114]

DISSEMINATE An information management activity: to communicate relevant information of any kind from one person or place to another in a usable form by any means to improve understanding or to initiate or govern action.[115]

DISSEMINATED ANALYTIC PRODUCTS Products containing intelligence analysis intended to convey authoritative agency, bureau, office, center, department, or IC analytic judgments and officially distributed to consumers outside the producing IC element.[116]

DISSEMINATION 1. The act of a steward providing information collected or analysis produced by an IC element to authorized IC personnel, either through the ordinary course of business or in response to a request following discovery—(information "pushed" to authorized IC personnel).[117] 2. The release of information, usually under certain protocols.[118]

DISSEMINATION AND EXTRACTION OF INFORMATION CONTROLLED BY ORIGINATOR (ORCON) The marking used with a security classification to enable the originator to supervise the use of information. This marking may be used only on intelligence information that clearly identifies or would reasonably permit ready identification of an intelligence source or method that is particularly susceptible to countermeasures that would nullify or measurably reduce its effectiveness.[119]

DISSEMINATION PLAN A plan that shows how an intelligence product is to be disseminated, at what security level, and to whom.

DISSENT CHANNEL The State Department has a strong interest in facilitating open, creative, and uncensored dialogue on substantive foreign policy issues within the professional foreign affairs community, and a responsibility to foster an atmosphere supportive of such dialogue, including the opportunity to offer alternative or dissenting opinions without fear of penalty. The Dissent Channel was created to allow its users the opportunity to bring dissenting or alternative views on substantive foreign policy issues, when such views cannot be communicated in a full and timely manner through regular operating channels or procedures, to the attention of the Secretary of State and other senior State Department officials in a manner which protects the author from any penalty, reprisal, or recrimination.[120]

DISSUADE The focused application of all elements of national power to convince or persuade an organization, state, or non-state entity.[121]

DISTANT EARLY WARNING (DEW LINE) A radar network that was constructed by the United States and Canada to ensure a four-hour warning of a Soviet air attack. Specifically, it was a passive detection system intended to give advance notice to both the military and civil defense authorities regarding the deployment of air bombers. The DEW line's radar stations could chart aircraft heading toward the North American continent. Of primary concern was the first strike capability of the Soviet Union. First considered as far back as 1946, it went through several abortive attempts to bring it to fruition before its completion in 1957. Its 22 radar stations spanned 5,944 kilometers. It took more than 25,000 people to build. The usefulness of the system declined for several reasons: the system's inability to detect deployment of nuclear-armed submarines or intercontinental ballistic missiles (ICBMs); the rapid growth and superior results obtained from satellites; more advanced warning stations constructed in Alaska and Greenland. Development of the cruise missile finally sounded the death knell for the DEW line. Today most of the stations are abandoned ruins, victims of both technology and diplomacy.[122]

DISTRIBUTIVE WARNING A warning emanating from several analysts or agencies whose focus may overlap and whose duties may have other purposes than to communicate and forecast a possible threat.[123] *See* CONCENTRATED WARNING

DIVERGENT EVIDENCE Two or more items of evidence that support different conclusions. *See* CONVERGENT EVIDENCE; REDUNDANT EVIDENCE

DIVERSION 1. An act perpetrated for the purpose of turning attention or interest from a given area. Two modes of diversion are feints and demonstrations. 2. A change made in a prescribed route for operational or tactical reasons; except in the case of aircraft, a diversion order will not constitute a change of destination.[124] *See* DEMONSTRATION; FABRICATION; FEINT

DO NOT FILE FBI director J. Edgar Hoover necessitated the creation of written records, which might need to be produced in response to a congressional subpoena or court-ordered discovery motion. Hoover minimized this risk through a Do Not File procedure. Documents captioned "Do Not File" were not to be indexed in the FBI's central records system but instead were to be routed to the office files of senior FBI officials at the FBI's Washington, DC, headquarters for review and approval (and were then to be regularly destroyed). The head of an FBI field office, in turn, created an "informal" memorandum (that is, a nonofficial record) of each authorization and filed it in the office safe "until the next inspection by Bureau Inspectors, at which time it [the informal memo] is destroyed." The Do Not File procedure refined another special records procedure that Hoover had devised in 1940 to safeguard sensitive communications among senior FBI officials. To distinguish these more sensitive informal memoranda from official memoranda that were to be serialized and indexed in the FBI's central records system, an informal memorandum was to be written on pink paper (official memoranda were written on white paper) and to contain the notation that the memorandum was "to be destroyed after action is taken and not sent to files." Dating from their inception as a special record-keeping method, informal and Do Not File memoranda were to be destroyed "after action is taken." FBI assistant directors retained these memoranda in their office files and decided when to destroy them. In March 1953, Hoover ended this discretionary arrangement and ordered FBI assistant directors to "destroy them as promptly as possible but in no case shall they be retained in excess of six months."[125]

DOCTRINE 1. Fundamental principles by which the military forces or elements thereof guide their actions in support of national objectives. It is authoritative but requires judgment in application.[126] 2. Every profession develops a unique body of knowledge. For the army profession, this body of professional knowledge is doctrine. United States (U.S.) Army doctrine is about the conduct of operations by army forces in the field (and to a limited extent the guidelines for training for operations). Doctrine is the body of professional knowledge that guides how soldiers perform tasks related to the army's role: the employment of landpower in a distinctly American context. Doctrine establishes the language of the profession. Just as physicians must remain proficient and current regarding the body of medical knowledge, army professionals must remain proficient and current in doctrine. The lives of the men and women who make up the army—not to mention the security of the state—rely on all soldiers and leaders to be proficient in the army's body of professional knowledge: doctrine. Doctrine fits into a larger body of army knowledge. Each organization develops specific ways to do things—policies about the conduct of its tasks. Large, complex organizations often require more than one body of knowledge to address the variety of tasks they perform. The army is such an organization. Some policies are prescriptive and include penalties for failure to follow a procedure while others are simply accepted, descriptive ways to do things. Some organizations call these operating procedures, rule books, or some other term for organizational guidelines. For the army, this larger body of knowledge includes, but is not limited, to the following: army regulations and pamphlets, which address the administration of the army; doctrine, which addresses the conduct of operations; training publications, which address specific training tasks and procedures; technical manuals, which address specific equipment-related topics.[127]

DOCTRINE 2015 This doctrine creates a top-to-bottom hierarchy of publications, beginning with the top-level, easy-to-read doctrinal principles called Army Doctrine Publications (ADPs). They are 10–15 pages long and easily accessible to soldiers through technology. The lower-level publications, called Army Techniques Publications, or ATPs, will likely change the fastest. The army can update these more rapidly without having to change the whole body of information on a specific subject. A 2009 doctrine conference recognized the army had too many field manuals—about 550—and it was time to look at how to best develop, update and deliver doctrine. U.S. Army Training and Doctrine Command created a task force focused on making fewer doctrine publications that would be shorter, more collaborative and more accessible.[128]

DOCUMENT Any recorded information, regardless of the nature of the medium or the method or circumstances of recording.[129]

DOCUMENT AND MEDIA EXPLOITATION (DOMEX) 1. The processing, translation, analysis, and dissemination of collected hard copy documents and electronic media, which are under the U.S. government's physical control and are not publicly available; excludes: handling of documents and media during collection, initial review, and inventory process; and documents and media withheld from the IC DOMEX dissemination system in accordance with DNI-sanctioned agreements and policies to protect sources and methods.[130] 2. Also, the processing, translation, analysis, and dissemination of collected hard-copy documents and electronic media that are under U.S. government physical control and are not publicly available. In the Department of Defense this includes the handling of documents and media during their collection, initial review, inventory, and input to a database.[131] *See* NATIONAL MEDIA EXPLOTATION CENTER

DOCUMENT EXPLOITATION (DOCEX) The systematic extraction of information from documents either produced by the threat, having been in the possession of the threat, or that are directly related to the current or future threat situation for the purpose of producing intelligence or answering information requirements. This may be conducted in conjunction with human intelligence (HUMINT) collection activities or may be a separate activity.[132]

DOCUMENTARY INFORMATION Any information, which is recorded on paper, film, transparency, electronic medium, or any other medium. This includes, but is not limited to, printed publications, reports, correspondence, maps, audiotapes, email, spreadsheets, databases and graphical slides, technical drawings, software code, and information embodied in hardware.[133]

DOD AUTOMATED BIOMETRIC IDENTIFICATION SYSTEM (DoD ABIS) The central, authoritative, multi-modal biometric data repository. The system operates and enhances associated search and retrieval services and interfaces with existing DoD and interagency biometrics systems. The repository interfaces with collection systems, intelligence systems and other deployed biometric repositories across the federal government.[134]

DOMAIN AWARENESS SYSTEM The NYPD and Microsoft worked together to develop the Domain Awareness System, a sophisticated law enforcement technology solution that aggregates and analyzes existing public safety data streams in real time, providing NYPD investigators and analysts with a comprehensive view of potential threats and criminal activity. For example, analysts are quickly notified of suspicious packages and vehicles, and NYPD personnel can actively search for suspects using advanced technologies such as smart cameras and license plate readers. The NYPD and Microsoft jointly developed the system by bringing together Microsoft's technical expertise and technologies with the day-to-day experience and knowledge of NYPD officers.[135]

DOMESTIC EMERGENCIES Civil defense emergencies, civil disturbances, major disasters, or natural disasters affecting the public welfare and occurring within the United States and its territories.[136]

DOMESTIC INTELLIGENCE Activities or conditions within the United States which threaten internal security (in general or to a governmental department, agency, or official) and which might require the employment of troops.[137]

DOMESTIC TERRORISM 1. Terrorism perpetrated by the citizens of one country against persons in that country. This includes acts against citizens of a second country when they are in the host country, and not the principal or intended target.[138] 2. Besides the statutory definitions regarding the crime of domestic terrorism, the FBI has historically emphasized particular qualities inherent to the *actors* who engage in domestic terrorism. According to the Bureau, domestic *terrorists* do not simply operate in the homeland, but they also *lack foreign direction*. In fact, the Bureau's practical, shorthand definition of domestic terrorism is "Americans attacking Americans based on U.S.-based extremist ideologies." The Department of Homeland Security (DHS) follows this construction (4).[139]

DOSSIER An official file of investigative, intelligence, or CI materials collected by or on behalf of the army. It may consist of documents, film, magnetic tape, photographs, digital images, or a combination thereof. Synonymous in this publication with "file" or "record." May be "personal" referring to an individual, or "impersonal" referring to a thing, event, or organization.[140]

DOUBLE AGENT A person who is in contact with the intelligence service of one government on behalf and under control of the counterintelligence and security service of another government.[141]

DOUBLE BLIND A situation in which an analyst purposely skews information or intelligence to support an already held contention or perspective, to further advance a theory or scenario.[142] *See* CLIENTITIS; PRIDE OF PREVIOUS POSITION

DOWNGRADE (DOWNGRADING) 1. To change a security classification from a higher to a lower level. 2. A determination made by a declassification authority that information classified and safeguarded at a specified level shall be classified and safeguarded at a lower level.[143] *See* DECLASSIFICATION

DOWNING STREET MEMO What is termed "The Downing Street Memo" are secret British documents leaked to the press that implicate the Bush administration "fixed" intelligence about Iraq and that actions at the United Nations were designed to give legal cover to British prime minister Tony Blair before an invasion to oust Saddam Hussein. Michael Smith, a reporter for the *Sunday Times of London*, led the coverage, starting with his report on May 1, 2005.[144]

DOX, DOXING Dox generally has a negative connotation—not only because it's seen to violate someone's privacy, but also because it's often used as a kind of retaliation mechanism in online discussions.[145]

DRIVERS (KEY VARIABLES) Over the past 15 months, the National Intelligence Council (NIC), in close collaboration with U.S. government specialists and a wide range of experts outside the government, has worked to identify major drivers and trends that will shape the world of 2015. The key drivers identified are: demographics; natural resources and environment; science and technology; the global economy and globalization; national and international governance; future conflict; and the role of the United States. In examining these drivers, several points should be kept in mind:

- No single driver or trend will dominate the global future in 2015.
- Each driver will have varying impacts in different regions and countries.
- The drivers are not necessarily mutually reinforcing; in some cases, they will work at cross purposes.

Taken together, these drivers and trends intersect to create an integrated picture of the world of 2015, about which we can make projections with varying degrees of confidence and identify some troubling uncertainties of strategic importance to the United States.[146]

DROP *See* DEAD DROP

DRUG ENFORCEMENT ADMINISTRATION SENSITIVE INFOR-MATION Unclassified information originated by the DEA that requires protection against unauthorized disclosure to protect sources and methods of investigative activity, evidence, and the integrity of pretrial investigative reports. The DoD has agreed to implement protective measures for DEA sensitive information in its possession. Types of information to be protected include: (1) information and material that is investigative in nature; (2) information and material to which access is restricted by law; (3) information and material that is critical to the operation and mission of the DEA; (4) information and material the disclosure of which would violate a privileged relationship. Access to DEA sensitive information is granted only to persons who have a valid need to know. A security clearance is not required. DEA sensitive information in the possession of the DoD may not be released outside the department without authorization by the DEA.[147]

DRY CLEANING Any technique used to elude surveillance. A usual precaution used by intelligence personnel when actively engaged in an operation.[148]

DUMPING Sending information or messages in short electronic bursts.

DUTY TO WARN A requirement to warn U.S. and non-U.S. persons of impending threats of intentional killing, serious bodily injury, or kidnapping.[149]

NOTES

1. Committee for National Security Systems (CNSS). Instruction 4009. *National Information Assurance Glossary.* April 2010. Accessed January 11, 2015. http://www.ncix.gov/publications/policy/docs/CNSSI_4009.pdf.

2. North Atlantic Treaty Organization. *NATO Glossary of Terms and Definitions.* NATO Standardization Agency, 2008. Accessed July 2, 2015. https://fas.org/irp/doddir/other/nato2008.pdf.

3. Office of the Director of National Intelligence. *Damage Assessments.* Intelligence Community Directive 732, June 27, 2014. Accessed September 29, 2015. http://www.dni.gov/files/documents/ICD/ICD%20732.pdf.

4. North Atlantic Treaty Organization. *NATO Glossary of Terms and Definitions.* NATO Standardization Agency, 2008. Accessed July 2, 2015. https://fas.org/irp/doddir/other/nato2008.pdf.

5. North Atlantic Treaty Organization. *NATO Glossary of Terms and Definitions.* NATO Standardization Agency, 2008. Accessed July 2, 2015. https://fas.org/irp/doddir/other/nato2008.pdf.

6. Office of Inspector General of the Intelligence Community. *Evaluation of the Office of the Director of National Intelligence Under the Reducing Over-Classification Act.* Report Number INS-2014-002. 30 December 2014. Accessed January 14, 2015. http://fas.org/sgp/othergov/intel/icig-roca.pdf.

7. Gaffney, Frank. *New Democrat Watch #8: Clinton Bungee Jumping on Nuclear Testing Endangers National Security.* Decision Brief No. 93-D58. Center for Secu-

rity Policy, July 1993. Accessed July 2, 2015. http://www.centerforsecuritypolicy. org/1993/07/06/new-democrat-watch-8-clinton-bungee-jumping-on-nuclear-testing-endangers-national-security-2/.

8. Department of the Army. Marine Corps Combat Development Command. Department of the Navy. *Operational Terms and Graphics.* FM 1-02 (FM 101-5). September 21, 2004. Accessed July 3, 2015. http://www.udel.edu/armyrotc/current_cadets/cadet_resources/manuals_regulations_files/FM%201-02%20-%20Operational%20Terms%20&%20Graphics.pdf.

9. Defense Intelligence Agency, Office of Counterintelligence. *CI Glossary—Terms & Definitions of Interest for DoD CI Professionals.* July 2014. Accessed January 17, 2015. https://www.hsdl.org/?view&did=699056.

10. Defense Advisory (DA) Notice System. *Frequently Asked Questions.* Accessed September 29, 2015. http://www.dnotice.org.uk/faqs/index.htm.

11. Houses of Parliament. *The Darknet and Online Anonymity.* PostNote Number 488, March 2015. Accessed April 4, 2015. http://www.parliament.uk/business/publications/research/briefing-papers/POST-PN-488/the-darknet-and-online-anonymity.

12. Finklea, Kristin. "Dark Web." *CRS Report to Congress* R44101, July 7, 2015. http://www.fas.org/sgp/crs/misc/R44101.pdf (accessed January 26, 2016).

13. Committee for National Security Systems (CNSS). Instruction 4009. *National Information Assurance Glossary.* April 2010. Accessed January 11, 2015. http://www.ncix.gov/publications/policy/docs/CNSSI_4009.pdf.

14. National Initiative for Cybersecurity Education. A Glossary of Common Cybersecurity Terminology. n.d. Accessed September 29, 2015. https://niccs.us-cert.gov/glossary.

15. National Initiative for Cybersecurity Education. *A Glossary of Common Cybersecurity Terminology.* n.d. Accessed September 29, 2015. https://niccs.us-cert.gov/glossary.

16. Siefert, Jeffrey W. "Data Mining: An Overview." *CRS Report for Congress*, RL31798. December 16, 2004. Accessed July 2, 2015. http://fas.org/irp/crs/RL31798.pdf; also see Government Accountability Office. *Data Mining: Federal Efforts Cover a Wide Range of Uses.* GAO-04-548, May 27, 2004. Accessed July 2, 2015. http://www.gao.gov/products/GAO-04-548.

17. National Initiative for Cybersecurity Education. *A Glossary of Common Cybersecurity Terminology.* n.d. Accessed September 29, 2015. https://niccs.us-cert.gov/glossary.

18. Department of the Army. *Communications Security Monitoring.* Army Regulation 380–53, December 2011. Accessed January 14, 2015. http://www.apd.army.mil/jw2/xmldemo/r380_53/main.asp.

19. National Initiative for Cybersecurity Education. *A Glossary of Common Cybersecurity Terminology.* n.d. Accessed March 5, 2015. https://niccs.us-cert.gov/glossary.

20. National Initiative for Cybersecurity Education. *A Glossary of Common Cybersecurity Terminology.* n.d. Accessed March 5, 2015. https://niccs.us-cert.gov/glossary.

21. National Initiative for Cybersecurity Education. *A Glossary of Common Cybersecurity Terminology.* n.d. Accessed March 5, 2015. https://niccs.us-cert.gov/glossary.

22. Schneider, Barry R. "Principles of War for the Battlefield of the Future." In *Battlefield of the Future: 21st Century Warfare Issues,* edited by Barry R. Schneider and Lawrence E. Grinter, 5–42. Studies in National Security, 3. Air War College, Maxwell AFB, September 1998. Accessed July 2, 2015. http://www.dtic.mil/dtic/tr/fulltext/u2/a358618.pdf.

23. Clarke, Roger. *Introduction to Dataveillance and Information Privacy, and Definitions of Terms.* October 2013. Accessed February 15, 2015. http://www.rogerclarke.com/DV/Intro.html.

24. Defense Forensics and Biometrics Agency. *DoD Biometrics Enterprise Architecture (Integrated) v2.0 Common Biometric Vocabulary.* April 2013. Accessed January 15, 2015. http://www.biometrics.dod.mil/Files/Documents/References/common%20biometric%20vocabulary.pdf.

25. Defense Intelligence Agency, Office of Counterintelligence. *CI Glossary— Terms & Definitions of Interest for DoD CI Professionals.* July 2014. Accessed January 17, 2015. https://www.hsdl.org/?view&did=699056.

26. Also see Defense Intelligence Agency, Office of Counterintelligence. *CI Glossary—Terms & Definitions of Interest for DoD CI Professionals.* July 2014. Accessed January 17, 2015. https://www.hsdl.org/?view&did=699056.

27. Handel, Michael. "Intelligence and Deception." In *Military Deception and Strategic Surprise,* edited by John Gooch and Amos Perlmutter, 124–25. London: Frank Cass, 1982.

28. Department of the Army. Marine Corps Combat Development Command. Department of the Navy. *Operational Terms and Graphics.* FM 1-02 (FM 101-5). September 21, 2004. Accessed July 3, 2015. http://www.udel.edu/armyrotc/current_cadets/cadet_resources/manuals_regulations_files/FM%201-02%20-%20Operational%20Terms%20&%20Graphics.pdf.

29. Department of the Army. Marine Corps Combat Development Command. Department of the Navy. *Operational Terms and Graphics.* FM 1-02 (FM 101-5). September 21, 2004. Accessed July 3, 2015. http://www.udel.edu/armyrotc/current_cadets/cadet_resources/manuals_regulations_files/FM%201-02%20-%20Operational%20Terms%20&%20Graphics.pdf.

30. Defense Forensics and Biometrics Agency. *DoD Biometrics Enterprise Architecture (Integrated) v2.0 Common Biometric Vocabulary.* April 2013. Accessed January 15, 2015. http://www.biometrics.dod.mil/Files/Documents/References/common%20biometric%20vocabulary.pdf.

31. Department of Homeland Security, Risk Steering Committee. *DHS Risk Lexicon.* September 2010. Accessed February 14, 2015. http://www.dhs.gov/dhs-risk-lexicon.

32. EO 13526, *Classified National Security Information.* December 29, 2009. Accessed July 2, 2015. https://www.whitehouse.gov/the-press-office/executive-order-classified-national-security-information.

33. U.S. Department of Defense. *DoD Information Security Program: Protection of Classified Information.* 5200.01, Volume 3, February 24, 2012, March 19, 2013. Accessed January 15, 2015. http://www.dtic.mil/whs/directives/corres/pdf/520001_vol3.pdf.

34. Defense Intelligence Agency, Office of Counterintelligence. *CI Glossary—Terms & Definitions of Interest for DoD CI Professionals.* July 2014. Accessed January 17, 2015. https://www.hsdl.org/?view&did=699056.

35. U.S. Department of Defense. *Department of Defense Dictionary of Military and Associated Terms.* JP 1-02, 08 November 2010, as Amended through 15 January 2016. Accessed January 26, 2016. http://www.dtic.mil/doctrine/new_pubs/jp1_02.pdf.

36. Purdue Online Writing Lab, *Logic in Argumentative Writing.* Accessed February 3, 2016. https://owl.english.purdue.edu/owl/resource/659/01/.

37. Department of the Army. *Open-Source Intelligence.* Army Techniques Publication (ATP) 2-22.9, July 2012. Accessed January 16, 2015. http://fas.org/irp/doddir/army/atp2-22-9.pdf.

38. Defense Intelligence Agency. *Defense Intelligence Report: Lexicon of Hardened Structure Definitions and Terms.* Washington, DC: 2000.

39. North Atlantic Treaty Organization. *NATO Glossary of Terms and Definitions.* NATO Standardization Agency, 2008. Accessed July 2, 2015. https://fas.org/irp/doddir/other/nato2008.pdf.

40. Chairman of the Joint Chiefs of Staff. *National Military Strategic Plan for the War on Terrorism.* February 1, 2006. Accessed September 29, 2015. http://archive.defense.gov/pubs/pdfs/2006-01-25-Strategic-Plan.pdf.

41. Federation of American Scientists. *Defense Automated Warning System.* Accessed July 2, 2015. http://fas.org/irp/program/process/daws.htm.

42. U.S. Department of Defense. Center for Development of Security Excellence. *Glossary of Security Terms and Definitions.* November 2012. Accessed February 16, 2015. http://www.cdse.edu/documents/cdse/Glossary_Handbook.pdf.

43. U.S. Department of Defense. Center for Development of Security Excellence. *Glossary of Security Terms and Definitions.* November 2012. Accessed February 16, 2015. http://www.cdse.edu/documents/cdse/Glossary_Handbook.pdf.

44. FAS. *DEFCON DEFense CONdition.* April 29, 1998. Accessed February 3, 2016. https://fas.org/nuke/guide/usa/c3i/defcon.htm.

45. Defense Forensics and Biometrics Agency. *Overview.* Accessed January 11, 2015. http://www.biometrics.dod.mil/.

46. U.S. Department of Defense. *Department of Defense Dictionary of Military and Associated Terms.* JP 1-02, 08 November 2010, as Amended through 15 January 2016. Accessed January 26, 2016. http://www.dtic.mil/doctrine/new_pubs/jp1_02.pdf.

47. Joint Task Force Transformation Initiative. *Security and Privacy Controls for Federal Information Systems and Organizations.* NIST Special Publication 800-53, Revision 4, April 2013. Accessed September 29, 2015. http://nvlpubs.nist.gov/nistpubs/SpecialPublications/NIST.SP.800-53r4.pdf.

48. U.S. Department of Defense. Center for Development of Security Excellence. *Glossary of Security Terms and Definitions.* November 2012. Accessed February 16, 2015. http://www.cdse.edu/documents/cdse/Glossary_Handbook.pdf.

49. Pike, John. *Defense Intelligence Agency Products.* Accessed July 2, 2015. http://fas.org/irp/dia/product/.

50. U.S. Department of Defense. *DoD Human Intelligence (HUMINT) Training.* DoD Instruction Number 3305.15, February 25, 2008. Certified Current through February 25, 2015, Incorporating Change 1, Effective October 15, 2013. Accessed February 28, 2015. http://www.dtic.mil/whs/directives/corres/pdf/330515p.pdf.

51. U.S. Department of Defense. *About Us: Defense Security Service.* Accessed February 19, 2015. http://www.dss.mil/about_dss/index.html.

52. Defense Information Systems Agency. *DSN History.* Accessed July 3, 2015. http://www.disa.mil/network-services/Voice/SBU-Voice/History.

53. U.S. Department of Defense. Center for Development of Security Excellence. *Glossary of Security Terms and Definitions.* November 2012. Accessed February 16, 2015. http://www.cdse.edu/documents/cdse/Glossary_Handbook.pdf.

54. Department of the Army. Marine Corps Combat Development Command. Department of the Navy. *Operational Terms and Graphics.* FM 1-02 (FM 101-5). September 21, 2004. Accessed July 3, 2015. http://www.combatindex.com/store/field_man/Sample/FM_1-02.pdf.

55. U.S. Department of Defense. Center for Development of Security Excellence. *Glossary of Security Terms and Definitions.* November 2012. Accessed February 16, 2015. http://www.cdse.edu/documents/cdse/Glossary_Handbook.pdf.

56. U.S. Department of Defense. *Threat Awareness and Reporting Program*, AR 381-12. October 4, 2010. Accessed on July 15, 2015. http://www.apd.army.mil/pdf-files/r381_12.pdf.

57. 18 U.S.C. 798. "Disclosure of Classified Information." Accessed on September 1, 2015. https://www.law.cornell.edu/uscode/text/18.

58. This explanation comes from one of the designers of this method, Olaf Helmer, "The Use of Expert Opinion in International Relations Forecasting." In *Forecasting in International Relations: Theory, Methods, Problems, Prospects*, edited by Nazli Choucri and Thomas W. Robinson (San Francisco: WH Freeman, 1978), 116–23.

59. United States Department of Justice. *Law Enforcement Analytic Standards.* Global Justice Information Sharing Initiative. April 2012. Accessed July 3, 2015. https://it.ojp.gov/documents/d/Law%20Enforcement%20Analytic%20Standards%2004202_combined_compliant.pdf.

60. North Atlantic Treaty Organization. *NATO Glossary of Terms and Definitions.* NATO Standardization Agency, 2008. Accessed July 2, 2015. https://fas.org/irp/dod-dir/other/nato2008.pdf.

61. Commission to Assess the Ballistic Missile Threat to the United States. *Report of the U.S. Congressional Commission to Assess the Ballistic Missile Threat to the United States.* 1998. Accessed July 3, 2015. http://fas.org/irp/threat/missile/rumsfeld/toc.htm.

62. U.S. Department of Defense. *Department of Defense Dictionary of Military and Associated Terms.* JP 1-02, 08 November 2010, as Amended through 15 January

2016. Accessed January 26, 2016. http://www.dtic.mil/doctrine/new_pubs/jp1_02. pdf.

63. U.S. Department of Homeland Security. Office of Intelligence and Analysis. *Domestic Extremism Lexicon.* March 26, 2009. Accessed January 15, 2015. http:// www.fas.org/irp/eprint/lexicon.pdf.

64. Department of the Army. Marine Corps Combat Development Command. Department of the Navy. *Operational Terms and Graphics.* FM 1-02 (FM 101-5). September 21, 2004. Accessed July 3, 2015. http://www.udel.edu/armyrotc/current_cadets/cadet_resources/manuals_regulations_files/FM%201-02%20-%20Operational%20Terms%20&%20Graphics.pdf.

65. U.S. Department of Defense. Center for Development of Security Excellence. *Glossary of Security Terms and Definitions.* November 2012. Accessed February 16, 2015. http://www.cdse.edu/documents/cdse/Glossary_Handbook.pdf.

66. U.S. Department of Defense. Center for Development of Security Excellence. *Glossary of Security Terms and Definitions.* November 2012. Accessed February 16, 2015. http://www.cdse.edu/documents/cdse/Glossary_Handbook.pdf.

67. U.S. Department of Defense. *Department of Defense Dictionary of Military and Associated Terms.* JP 1-02, 08 November 2010, as Amended through 15 January 2015. Accessed January 26, 2016. https://web.archive.org/web/20150329113844/http://www.dtic.mil/doctrine/new_pubs/jp1_02.pdf.

68. Federation of American Scientists. Department of Defense Intelligence Information System. Intelligence Resource Program, 1997. Accessed July 3, 2015. http:// fas.org/irp/program/core/dodiis.htm.

69. Defense Acquisition University. *Glossary: Defense Acquisition Acronyms and Terms.* 13th ed., November 2009. Accessed February 24, 2015. http://www.dau.mil/pubscats/pubscats/13th_edition_glossary.pdf.

70. U.S. Department of Homeland Security. *Creation of the U.S. Department of Homeland Security.* Accessed January 27, 2015. http://www.dhs.gov/creation-department-homeland-security.

71. Kettl, Donald F. (ed.). *The Department of Homeland Security's First Year: A Report Card.* Century Foundation Report, 2004. Accessed January 26, 2015. http:// wayback.archive.org/web/20081129141445/http://www.tcf.org/Publications/HomelandSecurity/overview.pdf.

72. Department of State, Department of State Classification Guide (DSCG 05-01), January 2005, Edition 1. Accessed August 3, 2015. https://www.fas.org/sgp/other-gov/dos-class.pdf.

73. U.S. Department of State. "Bureau of Counterrorism." *Foreign Affairs Manual.* 1 FAM 480. March 5, 2013. Accessed February 16, 2015. http://www.state.gov/documents/organization/205857.pdf.

74. National Counterterrorism Center. *Countering Violent Extremism: A Guide for Practitioners and Analysts.* May 2014. Accessed February 9, 2015. https://www.documentcloud.org/documents/1657824-cve-guide.html.

75. U.S. Department of Defense. Center for Development of Security Excellence. *Derivative Classification Training.* Accessed February 3, 2015. http://www.cdse.edu/documents/cdse/DerivativeClassification.pdf.

76. North Atlantic Treaty Organization. *NATO Glossary of Terms and Definitions*. NATO Standardization Agency, 2008. Accessed July 3, 2015. https://fas.org/irp/doddir/other/nato2008.pdf.

77. Types of derogatory information are listed in "General Criteria and Procedures for Determining Eligibility for Access to Classified Matter or Special Nuclear Material." 10 CFR 710. Accessed July 3, 2015. http://www.ecfr.gov/cgi-bin/text-idx?tpl=/ecfrbrowse/Title10/10cfr710_main_02.tpl and Executive Order 10450. *Security Requirements for Government Employment*. April 27, 1953. Accessed July 3, 2015. http://www.archives.gov/federal-register/codification/executive-order/10450.html.

78. U.S. Department of Defense. Center for Development of Security Excellence. *Derivative Classification Training*. Accessed February 3, 2015. http://www.cdse.edu/documents/cdse/DerivativeClassification.pdf.

79. Federal Bureau of Investigation. *Minimum Criminal Intelligence Training Standards for Law Enforcement and Other Criminal Justice Agencies in the United States*. October 2007. Accessed January 22, 2015. https://it.ojp.gov/gist/108/Minimum-Criminal-Intelligence-Training-Standards.

80. U.S. Department of Defense. Center for Development of Security Excellence. *Derivative Classification Training*. Accessed February 3, 2015. http://www.cdse.edu/documents/cdse/DerivativeClassification.pdf.

81. U.S. Department of Defense. *Detainee Operations*. Joint Publication 3-63. November 13, 2014. Accessed February 26, 2015. http://www.dtic.mil/doctrine/new_pubs/jp3_63.pdf.

82. U.S. Department of Defense. *Detainee Operations*. Joint Publication 3-63. November 13, 2014. Accessed February 26, 2015. http://www.dtic.mil/doctrine/new_pubs/jp3_63.pdf.

83. U.S. Department of Defense. *Detainee Operations*. Joint Publication 3-63. November 13, 2014. Accessed February 26, 2015. http://www.dtic.mil/doctrine/new_pubs/jp3_63.pdf.

84. Defense Forensics and Biometrics Agency. *DoD Biometrics Enterprise Architecture (Integrated) v2.0 Common Biometric Vocabulary*. April 2013. Accessed January 15, 2015. http://www.biometrics.dod.mil/Files/Documents/References/common%20biometric%20vocabulary.pdf.

85. Elsea, Jennifer K. and Garcia, Michael John. "Wartime Detention Provisions in Recent Defense Authorization Legislation." *CRS Report for Congress* R42143. May 28, 2015. Accessed January 26, 2016. https://www.fas.org/sgp/crs/natsec/R42143.pdf.

86. U.S. Department of Defense. Center for Development of Security Excellence. *Derivative Classification Training*. Accessed February 3, 2015. http://www.cdse.edu/documents/cdse/DerivativeClassification.pdf.

87. U.S. Department of Defense. Center for Development of Security Excellence. *Derivative Classification Training*. Accessed February 3, 2015. http://www.cdse.edu/documents/cdse/DerivativeClassification.pdf.

88. Central Intelligence Agency, *Tradecraft Primer: Structured Analytical Techniques for Improving Intelligence Analysis*, March 2009, accessed February 3, 2015,

https://www.cia.gov/library/center-for-the-study-of-intelligence/csi-publications/books-and-monographs/Tradecraft%20Primer-apr09.pdf.

89. Department of Homeland Security. *DHS Daily Open Source Infrastructure Report.* Accessed January 27, 2015. http://www.dhs.gov/dhs-daily-open-source-infrastructure-report; for an archive, see https://archive.org/details/DHSDailyReports.

90. Torrenzano, Richard and Mark Davis. *Digital Assassination: Protecting Your Reputation, Brand, or Business against Online Attacks.* New York: St. Martin's Press, 2011, 9.

91. National Initiative for Cybersecurity Education. *A Glossary of Common Cybersecurity Terminology.* n.d. Accessed March 5, 2015. http://niccs.us-cert.gov/glossary.

92. National Initiative for Cybersecurity Education. *A Glossary of Common Cybersecurity Terminology.* n.d. Accessed March 5, 2015. http://niccs.us-cert.gov/glossary.

93. Free Software Foundation. *Defective by Design: DRM Frequently Asked Questions.* 2014. Accessed March 7, 2015.

94. National Institute of Standards. *Digital Signature Standard (DSS).* FIPS PUB 186-4, July 2013. Accessed February 15, 2015. http://nvlpubs.nist.gov/nistpubs/FIPS/NIST.FIPS.186-4.pdf.

95. Chairman of the Joint Chiefs of Staff. *National Military Strategic Plan for the War on Terrorism.* February 1, 2006. Accessed February 26, 2015. http://www.defense.gov/qdr/docs/2006-02-08-Strategic-Plan.pdf. Executive Office of the President. *National Strategy for Combatting Terrorism.* 2003. Accessed February 26, 2015. https://www.cia.gov/news-information/cia-the-war-on-terrorism/Counter_Terrorism_Strategy.pdf.

96. Legal Information Institute. *Diplomatic Immunity.* Accessed February 3, 2016. https://www.law.cornell.edu/wex/diplomatic_immunity.

97. Department of Homeland Security, Risk Steering Committee. *DHS Risk Lexicon.* September 2010. Accessed November 4, 2015. http://www.dhs.gov/dhs-risk-lexicon.

98. Henning, Paul. Department of the Air Force. *Air Force Information Warfare Doctrine: Valuable or Valueless.* Air Command Staff College, AU/ACSC/97-0604C/97-0, 1997. Accessed on July 1, 2015. http://www.au.af.mil/au/awc/awcgate/acsc/97-0604c.pdf.

99. Waller, Mark. *Report of the Intelligence Services Commissioner for 2014.* Stationary Office, 2015. Accessed January 26, 2016. http://intelligencecommissioner.com/content.asp?id=19.

100. Office of the Director of National Intelligence. *History.* Accessed February 3, 2016. http://www.dni.gov/index.php/about/history.

101. United Nations International Strategy for Disaster Reduction. *2009 UNISDR Terminology Disaster Risk Reduction.* Geneva. Accessed July 3, 2015. http://www.unisdr.org/we/inform/terminology.

102. United Nations International Strategy for Disaster Reduction. *2009 UNISDR Terminology Disaster Risk Reduction.* Geneva. Accessed July 3, 2015. http://www.unisdr.org/we/inform/terminology.

103. National Archives and Records Administration. 36 CFR 1202.4. Accessed February 3, 2016. http://www.gpoaccess.gov/CFR/index.html.

104. U.S. Department of Defense. *DoD Intelligence Interrogations, Detainee Debriefings, and Tactical Questioning.* Directive Number 3115.09, October 11, 2012 Incorporating Change 1, Effective November 15, 2013. Accessed February 15, 2015. http://www.dtic.mil/whs/directives/corres/pdf/311509p.pdf.

105. Hughes, Francis J. and Schum, David. *The Art and Science of the Process of Intelligence Analysis.* Unpublished manuscript, Washington, DC: Joint Military Intelligence College.

106. Office of the Director of National Intelligence. *Writing for Maximum Utility.* Intelligence Community Directive 208, December 17, 2008. Accessed January 24, 2015. http://www.dni.gov/files/documents/ICD/icd_208.pdf.

107. Joint Task Force Transformation Initiative. *Security and Privacy Controls for Federal Information Systems and Organizations.* NIST Special Publication 800-53, Revision 4, April 2013. Accessed September 29, 2015. http://nvlpubs.nist.gov/nistpubs/SpecialPublications/NIST.SP.800-53r4.pdf.

108. Department of the Army. Marine Corps Combat Development Command. Department of the Navy. *Operational Terms and Graphics.* FM 1-02 (FM 101-5). September 21, 2004. Accessed July 3, 2015. http://www.udel.edu/armyrotc/current_cadets/cadet_resources/manuals_regulations_files/FM%201-02%20-%20Operational%20Terms%20&%20Graphics.pdf.

109. Leventhal, Todd. *Disinformation Integral Part of Iraqi Strategy.* Backgrounder from USIA, February 4, 1991. Accessed July 3, 2015. http://fas.org/news/iraq/1991/910204-171055.htm.

110. United States Department of Defense. *Foreign Humanitarian Assistance.* JP 3-29, January 3, 2014. Accessed March 7, 2015. http://www.dtic.mil/doctrine/new_pubs/jp3_29.pdf.

111. United States Department of Defense. *Foreign Humanitarian Assistance.* JP 3-29, January 3, 2014. Accessed March 7, 2015. http://www.dtic.mil/doctrine/new_pubs/jp3_29.pdf.

112. United States Department of Defense. *Foreign Humanitarian Assistance.* JP 3-29, January 3, 2014. Accessed March 7, 2015. http://www.dtic.mil/doctrine/new_pubs/jp3_29.pdf.

113. Secretary of State for the Home Office. *HM Government Transparency Report on the Use of Disruptive and Investigatory Powers.* Stationery Office, 2015. https://www.gov.uk/government/publications/hm-government-transparency-report-on-the-use-of-disruptive-and-investigatory-powers (accessed January 26, 2016).

114. Joint Task Force Transformation Initiative. *Security and Privacy Controls for Federal Information Systems and Organizations.* NIST Special Publication 800-53, Revision 4, April 2013. Accessed September 29, 2015. http://nvlpubs.nist.gov/nistpubs/SpecialPublications/NIST.SP.800-53r4.pdf.

115. Department of the Army. Marine Corps Combat Development Command. Department of the Navy. *Operational Terms and Graphics.* FM 1-02 (FM 101-5). September 21, 2004. Accessed July 3, 2015. http://www.udel.edu/armyrotc/cur-

rent_cadets/cadet_resources/manuals_regulations_files/FM%201-02%20-%20Operational%20Terms%20&%20Graphics.pdf.

116. Office of the Director of National Intelligence. *Sourcing Requirements for Disseminated Analytic Products.* Intelligence Community Directive 206, October 17, 2007. Accessed February 27, 2015. https://fas.org/irp/dni/icd/icd-206.pdf.

117. Office of the Director of National Intelligence. *Discovery and Dissemination or Retrieval of Information within the Intelligence Community.* Intelligence Community Directive 501, January 21, 2009. Accessed March 2, 2015. http://www.dni.gov/files/documents/ICD/ICD_501.pdf.

118. United States Department of Justice. *Law Enforcement Analytic Standards.* Global Justice Information Sharing Initiative. April 2012. Accessed July 3, 2015. https://it.ojp.gov/documents/d/Law%20Enforcement%20Analytic%20Standards%2004202_combined_compliant.pdf.

119. Department of State, Department of State Classification Guide (DSCG 05-01), January 2005, Edition 1. Accessed August 3, 2015. https://www.fas.org/sgp/othergov/dos-class.pdf.

120. U.S. Department of State. "Dissent Channel." *Foreign Affairs Manual.* 2 FAM 070. September 28, 2011. Accessed February 16, 2015. http://www.state.gov/documents/organization/84374.pdf.

121. Chairman of the Joint Chiefs of Staff. *National Military Strategic Plan for the War on Terrorism.* February 1, 2006. Accessed September 29, 2015. http://archive.defense.gov/pubs/pdfs/2006-01-25-Strategic-Plan.pdf.

122. AT&T. *Distant Early Warning Radar: The DEW Line Story.* Parts 1 and 2, 1958. Accessed July 2, 2015. https://www.youtube.com/watch?v=UTIbqZL2Sas.

123. Jan Goldman, *Intelligence Warning Terminology*, Joint Military Intelligence College, October 2001, accessed July 3, 2015. https://archive.org/details/JMICIntelligencelwarnterminology.

124. U.S. Department of Defense. *Department of Defense Dictionary of Military and Associated Terms.* JP 1-02, 08 November 2010, as Amended through 15 January 2016. Accessed January 26, 2016. http://www.dtic.mil/doctrine/new_pubs/jp1_02.pdf.

125. Theoharis, Athan (ed.). *The FBI: A Comprehensive Reference Guide* (Phoenix: Oryx Press, 1998).

126. U.S. Department of Defense. *Department of Defense Dictionary of Military and Associated Terms.* JP 1-02, 08 November 2010, as Amended through 15 June 2015. Accessed January 26, 2016. https://web.archive.org/web/20150714135402/http://www.dtic.mil/doctrine/new_pubs/jp1_02.pdf.

127. Department of the Army. *Doctrine Primer.* September 2014. ADP 1-0. Accessed July 3, 2015. http://armypubs.army.mil/doctrine/DR_pubs/dr_a/pdf/adp1_01.pdf.

128. Department of the Army. "Doctrine 2015." *Stand-To!* Accessed July 2, 2015. http://www.army.mil/standto/archive/issue.php?issue=2012-11-28.

129. Office of Inspector General of the Intelligence Community. *Evaluation of the Office of the Director of National Intelligence Under the Reducing Over-Classifica-*

tion Act. Report Number INS-2014-002. December 30, 2014. Accessed January 14, 2015. http://fas.org/sgp/othergov/intel/icig-roca.pdf.

130. Office of the Director of National Intelligence. *Document and Media Exploitation.* Intelligence Community Directive 302, July 6, 2007. Accessed February 24, 2015. http://www.dtic.mil/whs/directives/corres/pdf/330003p.pdf.

131. U.S. Department of Defense. *DoD Document and Media Exploitation (DO-MEX).* DoD Directive Number 3300.03, January 11, 2011. Accessed January 29, 2015. http://www.dtic.mil/whs/directives/corres/pdf/330003p.pdf.

132. Department of the Army. Marine Corps Combat Development Command. Department of the Navy. *Operational Terms and Graphics.* FM 1-02 (FM 101-5). September 21, 2004. Accessed July 3, 2015. http://www.udel.edu/armyrotc/current_cadets/cadet_resources/manuals_regulations_files/FM%201-02%20-%20Operational%20Terms%20&%20Graphics.pdf.

133. U.S. Department of Defense. Center for Development of Security Excellence. *Glossary of Security Terms and Definitions.* November 2012. Accessed February 16, 2015. http://www.cdse.edu/documents/cdse/Glossary_Handbook.pdf.

134. Defense Forensics and Biometrics Agency. *DoD Biometrics Enterprise Architecture (Integrated) v2.0 Common Biometric Vocabulary.* April 2013. Accessed January 15, 2015. http://www.biometrics.dod.mil/Files/Documents/References/common%20biometric%20vocabulary.pdf.

135. *Mayor Bloomberg, Police Commissioner Kelly and Microsoft Unveil New State-of-the-Art Law Enforcement Technology.* Press release, PR-291-12. August 8, 2012. Accessed January 26, 2016. http://www.nyc.gov/portal/site/nycgov/menuitem.c0935b9a57bb4ef3daf2f1c701c789a0/index.jsp?pageID=mayor_press_release&catID=1194&doc_name=http%3A%2F%2Fwww.nyc.gov%2Fhtml%2Fom%2Fhtml%2F2012b%2Fpr291-12.html&cc=unused1978&rc=1194&ndi=1; also see Horise, Mariko. "Documents Uncover NYPD's Vast License Plate Reader Database." *The Huffington Post*, January 25, 2016. Accessed January 26, 2016. http://www.huffingtonpost.com/mariko-hirose-/documents-uncover-nypds-v_b_9070270.html.

136. U.S Department of Defense. *Homeland Defense.* JP 3-27. July 29, 2013. Accessed February 26, 2015. http://www.dtic.mil/doctrine/new_pubs/jp3_27.pdf.

137. United States Senate, Select Committee to Study Governmental Operations with Respect to Intelligence Activities (Church Committee). *Final Report.* Book 1. April 26, 1976. Accessed September 29, 2015. https://archive.org/details/finalreportofsel01unit.

138. United States Department of Defense. *DoD Antiterrorism (AT) Program.* DoD Instruction Number 2000.12, DoD Antiterrorism Program, 1 Mar 2012 with change 1 dated 9 Sep 2013. Accessed January 17, 2015. http://www.dtic.mil/whs/directives/corres/pdf/200012p.pdf.

139. Bjelopera, Jerome P. *The Domestic Terrorist Threat: Background and Issues for Congress. CRS Report for Congress* R42536, January 17, 2013. Accessed January 17, 2015. http://fas.org/sgp/crs/terror/R42536.pdf.

140. Department of the Army. *Investigative Records Repository.* AR381-45. Accessed July 2, 2015. http://armypubs.army.mil/epubs/pdf/r381_45.pdf.

141. Also see Defense Intelligence Agency, Office of Counterintelligence. *CI Glossary—Terms & Definitions of Interest for DoD CI Professionals.* July 2014. Accessed January 17, 2015. https://www.hsdl.org/?view&did=699056.

142. Jan Goldman, *Intelligence Warning Terminology*, Joint Military Intelligence College, October 2001, accessed July 3, 2015. https://archive.org/details/JMICInteligencelwarnterminology.

143. Executive Order 13526 (2009). *Classified National Security Information.* December 29. Accessed July 2, 2015. https://www.whitehouse.gov/the-press-office/executive-order-classified-national-security-information.

144. Smith, Michael. "The Downing Stree Memo:Transcript." *The Washington Post*, June 16, 2005. Accessed January 26, 2016. http://www.washingtonpost.com/wp-dyn/content/discussion/2005/06/14/DI2005061401261.html. David Manning, *The Secret Downing Street Memo.* Accessed January 26, 2016. http://nsarchive.gwu.edu/NSAEBB/NSAEBB328/II-Doc14.pdf.

145. Garber, Megan. "Doxing: An Etymology." *The Atlantic*, March 6, 2014. http://www.theatlantic.com/technology/archive/2014/03/doxing-an-etymology/284283/ (accessed January 26, 2016).

146. U.S. National Intelligence Council. *Global Trends 2015: A Dialogue about the Future with Nongovernment Experts.* Director of Central Intelligence. NIC 2000-02, December 2000. Accessed July 2, 2015. http://fas.org:8080/irp/cia/product/globaltrends2015/.

147. Assistant Secretary of Defense for Command, Control, Communications, and Intelligence. *Information Security Program.* Appendix C, Controlled Unclassified information. Accessed July 3, 2015. http://fas.org/irp/doddir/dod/5200-1r/appendix_c.htm.

148. Defense Intelligence Agency, Office of Counterintelligence. *CI Glossary—Terms & Definitions of Interest for DoD CI Professionals.* July 1, 2014. Accessed January 15, 2015. http://www.fas.org/irp/eprint/ci-glossary.pdf.

149. Office of the Director of National Intelligence. *Duty to Warn.* Intelligence Community Directive 191, July 21, 2015. Accessed January 26, 2016. http://www.dni.gov/index.php/intelligence-community/ic-policies-reports/intelligence-community-directives.

E

EARLY REPORT A document of 7 to 9 pages based on reporting of editorial commentary from major posts commenting on the issues of the day. It is electronically transmitted to high-level officials at the White House, State Department, Pentagon, and other senior decision makers by 8:00 am Monday through Friday.[1]

EARLY WARNING SYSTEM The set of capacities needed to generate and disseminate timely and meaningful warning information to enable individuals, communities and organizations threatened by a hazard to prepare and to act appropriately and in sufficient time to reduce the possibility of harm or loss.[2] Established early warning systems include:

- COUNTRY INDICATORS FOR FOREIGN POLICY (CIFP): A geopolitical database developed by the Canadian Department of National Defense in 1991 and now operated under guidance of principal investigator at Carleton University. The database includes statistical data in the form of over 100 performance indicators for 196 countries. (www.carleton.ca/cifp)
- GLOBAL INFORMATION AND EARLY WARNING SYSTEM (GIEWS): Operated under the UN Food and Agriculture Organization, the system reviews the world food supply and demand for food, issues reports on the world food situation, and provides early warnings of impending food crises in individual countries. (www.fao.org)
- INTERNATIONAL CRISIS GROUP (ICG): An independent, nonprofit NGO with over 110 staff members on five continents, working through field-based analysis and high-level advocacy to prevent and resolve deadly conflict. (www.crisisgroup.org)
- INTERNATIONAL STRATEGY FOR DISASTER REDUCTION (ISDR): A UN system to promote disaster-resilient communities by promoting increased awareness of the importance of disaster reduction as a component of sustainable development, with the goal of reducing human, social, economic, and environmental losses due to natural hazards and related technological and environmental disasters. (www.unisdr.org)

- NATIONAL OCEANIC AND ATMOSPHERIC ADMINISTRATION (NOAA): The U.S. agency that provides information about weather-related warnings and watches. (http://weather.gov)

ECHELON Associated with a global network of computers that automatically search through millions of intercepted messages for pre-programmed keywords or fax, telex and e-mail addresses. Every word of every message in the frequencies and channels selected at a station is automatically searched. The processors in the network are known as the ECHELON Dictionaries. ECHELON connects all these computers and allows the individual stations to function as distributed elements in an integrated system. An ECHELON station's dictionary contains not only its parent agency's chosen keywords but also lists for each of the other four agencies in the UK-USA system (NSA, GCHQ, DSD, GCSB and CSE).[3]

eCHIRP A U.S. intelligence community secure, internal network patterned after Twitter to allow its analysts to weigh in on breaking news from across several agencies.[4]

ECONOMIC INTELLIGENCE Intelligence regarding foreign economic resources, activities, and policies.[5]

EDUCING INFORMATION (EI) From a technical perspective, EI encompasses "elicitation" (engaging with a source in such a manner that he or she reveals information without being aware of giving away anything of value), "strategic debriefing" (systematically covering topics and areas with a voluntary source who consents to a formal interview), and "interrogation" (interaction and conversation with a source who appears initially unwilling to provide information). EI implies a "system" of gathering information about and from a source and a spectrum of approaches, tools, activities, and techniques. This may involve investigative efforts, development of scenarios, and involvement of others (teams of interviewers and analysts, willing sources, and collaborators). Effective practice of EI usually extends beyond one-to-one interactions with a source.[6]

EFFECTS-BASED Actions, such as operations, targeting, or strategy, that are designed to produce distinctive and desired effects while avoiding unintended or undesired effects.[7]

E-GOVERNMENT ACT OF 2002 SECTION 208 A statutory provision that requires sufficient protections for the privacy of personally identifiable information (PII) by requiring agencies to assess the privacy impact of all substantially revised or new information technology (IT) systems as agencies implement citizen-centered electronic government.[8]

eGUARDIAN In 2007, eGuardian was developed to help meet the challenges of collecting and sharing terrorism-related activities among law enforcement agencies across various jurisdictions. The eGuardian system is a sensitive but unclassified (SBU) information-sharing platform hosted by the FBI's Criminal Justice Information Services (CJIS) Division as a service on the Law Enforcement Enterprise Portal (LEEP). The eGuardian system allows law enforcement agencies to combine new suspicious activity reports (SARs) with existing (legacy) SAR reporting systems to form a single information repository accessible to thousands of law enforcement personnel and analysts directly supporting law enforcement. The information captured in eGuardian is also migrated to the FBI's internal Guardian system, where it is assigned to the appropriate Joint Terrorism Task Force (JTTF) for any further investigative action. eGuardian is designed to be used by federal, state, local, tribal, and territorial law enforcement agencies and local and state fusion centers. eGuardian is also used by Department of Defense as their sole SAR reporting mechanism, which provides a global base for SAR reporting.[9]

EINSTEIN PROGRAM An automated process for collecting, correlating, analyzing, and sharing computer security information across the federal civilian government. By collecting information from participating federal government agencies, the US-CERT builds and enhances our nation's cyber-related situational awareness. Awareness will facilitate identifying and responding to cyber threats and attacks, improve network security, increase the resiliency of critical, electronically delivered government services, and enhance the survivability of the Internet.[10]

EL PASO INTELLIGENCE CENTER (EPIC) A cooperative intelligence center serving as a clearinghouse and intelligence resource for local, state, and federal law enforcement agencies. Its primary concern is drug trafficking; however, intelligence on other crimes is also managed by EPIC.[11]

ELECTRO-EXPLOSIVE DEVICE An electrically initiated device having an explosive or pyrotechnic output, or having a mechanical output resulting from an explosive or pyrotechnic action.[12]

ELECTRONIC COUNTER-COUNTERMEASURES A division of electronic warfare involving actions taken to ensure friendly effective use of the electronic magnetic spectrum despite the enemy's use of electronic warfare.

ELECTRONIC COUNTERMEASURES A division of electronic warfare involving actions taken to prevent or reduce an enemy's effective use of the electromagnetic spectrum.

ELECTRONIC DECEPTION Activity designed to mislead enemies in the interpretation or use of information received by their electronic systems.

ELECTRONIC GOVERNMENT The use by the government of web-based Internet applications and other information technologies, combined with processes that implement these technologies, to (A) enhance the access to and delivery of government information and services to the public, other agencies, and other government entities; or (B) bring about improvements in government operations that may include effectiveness, efficiency, service quality, or transformation. E-Government Act.[13]

ELECTRONIC INTELLIGENCE (ELINT) Technical and geolocation intelligence derived from foreign noncommunications electromagnetic radiations emanating from other than nuclear detonations or radioactive sources.[14] *See* SOURCES OF INTELLIGENCE

ELECTRONIC JAMMING The deliberate radiation, reradiation, or reflection of electromagnetic energy for the purpose of preventing or reducing an enemy's effective use of the electromagnetic spectrum, and with the intent of degrading or neutralizing the enemy's combat capability.[15] *See* JAMMING

ELECTRONIC MANIPULATIVE DECEPTION The alteration of friendly electronic magnetic emission characteristics, patterns, or procedures to eliminate revealing or to convey misleading, tell-tale indicators that may be used by hostile forces.[16]

ELECTRONIC SIGNATURE Any mark in electronic form associated with an electronic document, applied with the intent to sign the document.[17]

ELECTRONIC SIMULATIVE DECEPTION The creation of electromagnetic emissions to represent friendly notional or actual capabilities to mislead hostile forces.[18]

ELECTRONIC STORAGE (A) any temporary, intermediate storage of a wire or electronic communication incidental to the electronic transmission thereof; and (B) any storage of such communication by an electronic communication service for purposes of backup protection of such communication.[19]

ELECTRONIC SURVEILLANCE 1. Acquisition of a non-public communication by electronic means without the consent of a person who is a party to an electronic communication or, in the case of a person who is visibly present at the place of communication, but not including the use of radio direction-finding equipment solely to determine the location of the transmitter. Electronic Surveillance (ES) may involve consensual interception of electronics. A more precise statutory definition may be found in Title 50, Foreign Intelligence Surveillance Act (FISA).[20] 2. Electronic Surveillance means: the acquisition by an electronic, mechanical, or other surveillance device of the contents of any wire or radio communication sent by or intended to be received by a particular, known U.S. person who is in the United States, if the contents are acquired by intentionally targeting that U.S. person, under circumstances in which a person has a reasonable expectation of privacy and a warrant would be required for law enforcement purposes; the acquisition by an electronic, mechanical, or other surveillance device of the contents of any wire communication to or from a person in the United States, without the consent of any party thereto, if such acquisition occurs in the United States, but does not include the acquisition of those communications of computer trespassers that would be permissible under section 2511 (2)(i) of title 18; the intentional acquisition by an electronic, mechanical, or other surveillance device of the contents of any radio communication, under circumstances in which a person has a reasonable expectation of privacy and a warrant would be required for law enforcement purposes, and if both the sender and all intended recipients are located within the United States; or the installation or use of an electronic, mechanical, or other surveillance device in the United States for monitoring to acquire information, other than from a wire or radio communication, under circumstances in which a person has a reasonable expectation of privacy and a warrant would be required for law enforcement purposes.[21]

ELECTRO-OPTICAL INTELLIGENCE *See* SOURCES OF INTELLIGENCE

ELEMENTS OF NATIONAL POWER All the means available for employment in the pursuit of national objectives as determined by available indicators.[22]

ELICITATION Acquisition of information from a person or group in a manner that does not disclose the intent of the interview or conversation. A technique of human source intelligence collection, generally overt, unless the collector is other than he or she purports to be.[23] *See* SOURCES OF INTELLIGENCE

ELIGIBILITY FOR ACCESS TO CLASSFIED INFORMATION The result of the determination whether an employee (a) is eligible for access to classified information in accordance with Executive Order 12968 (relating to access to classified information), or any successor thereto, and Executive Order 10865 of February 20, 1960, as amended (relating to safeguarding classified information with industry), or any successor thereto; and (b) possesses a need to know under such orders.[24]

EMERGENCY An extraordinary situation in which people are unable to meet their basic survival needs, or there are serious and immediate threats to human life and well-being. An emergency situation may arise as a result of a disaster, a cumulative process of neglect or environmental degradation, or when a disaster threatens and emergency measures have to be taken to prevent or at least limit the effects of the eventual impact.[25]

EMERGENCY ACTION PLAN (EAP) A plan developed to prevent loss of national intelligence; protect personnel, facilities, and communications; and recover operations damaged by terrorist attack, natural disaster, or similar events.[26]

EMERGENCY MEASURES OF MILITARY PREPAREDNESS Additional efforts undertaken to buttress the basic measures of readiness, usually in response to strategic warning, to counter a massive attack.[27] *See* BASIC MEASURES OF MILITARY PREPAREDNESS; POST-SURPRISE MEASURES

EMERGENCY RESPONSE The action taken immediately following a disaster warning or alert to minimize or contain the eventual negative effects, and those actions taken to save and preserve lives and provide basic services in the immediate aftermath of a disaster, and for as long as an emergency situation prevails.[28]

EMIGRÉ A person who departs from his or her country for any lawful reason with the intention of living in another country.

ENCRYPTION 1. Conversion of data or text into a form, called a ciphertext, which cannot be easily understood by unauthorized people. 2. Conversion of plain text to ciphertext through the use of a cryptographic algorithm. *See* ENIGMA

ENTERPRISE • 199

ENDURING CONSTITUTIONAL GOVERNMENT (ECG) A cooperative effort among the executive, legislative, and judicial branches of the federal government, coordinated by the president, as a matter of comity with respect to the legislative and judicial branches and with proper respect for the constitutional separation of powers among all branches, to preserve the constitutional framework under which the nation is governed and the capability of all three branches of government to execute constitutional responsibilities, and provide for orderly succession, appropriate transition of leadership, and interoperability and support of the National Essential Functions during a catastrophic emergency.[29]

ENHANCED CRITICAL INFRASTRUCTURE PROTECTION ASSESSMENT (ECIP) A security survey conducted in collaboration with federal, state, local, and private sector stakeholders to assess the overall security posture for CIKR.[30] *See* CRITICAL INFRASTRUCTURE

ENHANCED INTERROGATION TECHNIQUES Mock burials, mock executions, waterboarding, "walling, attention grasps, slapping, facial hold, stress positions, cramped confinement, white noise and sleep deprivation" utilized by Central Intelligence Agency (CIA) interrogators as a means of "obtaining accurate information or gaining detainee cooperation" of detainees. Throughout the program, multiple CIA detainees who were subjected to the CIA's enhanced interrogation techniques and extended isolation exhibited psychological and behavioral issues, including hallucinations, paranoia, insomnia, and attempts at self-harm and self-mutilation. Multiple psychologists identified the lack of human contact experienced by detainees as a cause of psychiatric problems.[31] *See* EXTRAORDINARY RENDITION

ENIGMA Mechanical encryption device used by the Germans in World War II.[32] *See* ENCRYPTION

ENIGMA FACILITY A located facility that cannot be categorized satisfactorily by function.[33]

ENTERPRISE A large-scale undertaking characterized by the range of operations, breadth of interorganizational coordination and integration, and level of impact on stakeholders. At the department level, a designated officer reporting to a DoD delegated authority with specified responsibilities to include advising on the management of resources, policies and procedures, technology tools and architectures, personnel development and usage, and other issues as determined by that delegated authority.[34]

ENTERPRISE RISK MANAGEMENT 1. Comprehensive approach to risk management that engages organizational systems and processes together to improve the quality of decision making for managing risks that may hinder an organization's ability to achieve its objectives.[35] 2. A comprehensive approach to risk management that engages people, processes, and systems across an organization to improve the quality of decision making for managing risks that may hinder an organization's ability to achieve its objectives. An extended definition of this term involves identifying mission dependencies on enterprise capabilities, identifying and prioritizing risks due to defined threats, implementing countermeasures to provide both a static risk posture and an effective dynamic response to active threats; and assessing enterprise performance against threats and adjusts countermeasures as necessary.[36]

ENTROPY A measure of the amount of uncertainty that an attacker faces to determine the value of a secret.

EPIDEMIC INTELLIGENCE SERVICE (EIS) A part of the Centers for Disease Control established in 1951 following the start of the Korean War as an early warning system against biological warfare. The EIS is composed of medical doctors, researchers, and scientists who serve two-year assignments, and it has expanded into a surveillance and response unit for all types of epidemics, including chronic disease and injuries.[37]

EQUITY Information that was originated, classified by, or concerns the activities of another government agency or organization, and only they can declassify it. Records that contain other agency "equities" must be referred to those agencies for declassification review.[38]

ESOTERIC COMMUNICATIONS Public statements whose surface meaning (manifest content) does not reveal the real purpose, meaning, or significance (latent content) of the author.[39]

ESPIONAGE 1. Intelligence activity directed toward the acquisition of information through clandestine means and proscribed by the laws of the country against which it is committed. 2. The act of obtaining, delivering, transmitting, communicating, or receiving information in respect to the national defense with an intent or reason to believe that the information may be used to the injury of the United States or to the advantage of any foreign nation.[40]

ESSENTIAL ELEMENTS OF FRIENDLY INFORMATION (EEFI) Key questions likely to be asked by adversary officials and intelligence systems about specific friendly intentions, capabilities, and activities, so they can obtain answers critical to their operational effectiveness.[41]

ESSENTIAL ELEMENTS OF INFORMATION (EEI) Crucial items of information regarding the enemy and the environment needed by the commander by a particular time to relate with other available information and intelligence in order to assist in reaching a logical decision.[42]

ESTIMATE Analysis of a situation, development, or trend that identifies its major elements, interprets its significance, and appraises the possibilities and the potential results of the various actions that might be taken; an appraisal of a nation's capabilities, vulnerabilities, and potential courses of action.[43] *See* FORECAST; PREDICTION

ESTIMATE OF THE SITUATION *See* APPRECIATION OF THE SITUATION

ESTIMATING An effort to appraise and analyze the future possibilities or courses of action in a situation under study and the various results or consequences of foreign or U.S. actions relating to that situation. This analysis of such a foreign situation would consider its development and trends to identify its major elements, interpret the significance of the situation, and evaluate the future possibilities and prospective results of various actions which might be taken, including clandestine operations.[44]

ESTIMATIVE INTELLIGENCE 1. A category of intelligence analysis in which judgments are made despite incomplete information. There are two basic types: What is going on? And what will happen?[45] 2. A type of intelligence that projects or forecasts potential foreign courses of action and developments; implications or predictive judgment on a possible course of action by a potential enemy; an appraisal of the capabilities, vulnerabilities, and potential courses of action of a foreign nation or combination of nations.[46] *See* CURRENT INTELLIGENCE; CURRENT OPERATIONAL INTELLIGENCE; COMBAT INTELLIGENCE; INTELLIGENCE ASSESSMENT; WARNING INTELLIGENCE; RESEARCH INTELLIGENCE; SCIENTIFIC AND TECHNICAL INTELLIGENCE

ESTIMATIVE LANGUAGE When we use words such as "we judge" or "we assess"—terms we use synonymously—as well as "we estimate," "likely" or "indicate," we are trying to convey an analytical assessment or judgment. These assessments, which are based on incomplete or at times fragmentary information, are not a fact, proof, or knowledge. Some analytical judgments are based directly on collected information; others rest on previous judgments, which serve as building blocks. In either type of judgment, we do not have "evidence" that shows something to be a fact, or that definitively links two items or issues.[47]

ESTIMATIVE PROBABILITY In assessments, an assigned qualitative or quantitative value that an action, event, or decision will occur. Sherman Kent, a major figure in the development of intelligence analysis at the Central Intelligence Agency, sought consistency in interpretation in the following terms:[48]

- Estimative Term: Percentage of Likelihood
- Even chance: 40–60
- Improbable (and equivalent terms such as not likely): 10–40
- Near certainty (and equivalent terms such as highly likely): 90–99
- Near impossibility (and equivalent terms such as highly unlikely): 1–10
- Probable (and equivalent terms such as most likely): 60–90

EVALUATION An assessment of the reliability of the source and accuracy of raw data.[49]

EVASION The actions of a person isolated in hostile or unfriendly territory to elude capture.[50] *See* EXFILTRATION; INFILTRATION

EVASIVE TACTICS Techniques employed to elude or deceive surveillance.

EVENT FLOW ANALYSIS Graphic depictions and descriptions of incidents, behaviors, and people involved in an unlawful event, intended to help understand how an event occurred as a tool to aid in prosecution as well as prevention of future unlawful events.[51]

EVENT TREE Graphical tool used to illustrate the range and probabilities of possible outcomes that arise from an initiating event.[52]

EVIDENCE 1. The many types of information presented to a judge or jury designed to convince them of the truth or falsity of key facts. Evidence typically includes testimony of witnesses, documents, photographs, items of damaged property, government records, videos, and laboratory reports. Strict rules limit what can be properly admitted as evidence, but dozens of exceptions often mean that creative lawyers find a way to introduce such testimony or other items into evidence.[53] 2. An element of data becomes evidence in some analytic problem when its relevance to conjectures (hypotheses) being considered is established. It is always a relative term; it signifies a relation between two facts. Evidence about an event and the event itself are not the same.[54]

EVIDENTIAL VALUE Usefulness of records in documenting the organization, functions, and activities of the agency creating or receiving them; considered in appraising records for permanent retention.

EXCEPTIONAL THEORY Projecting an adversary's behavior based heavily on explanations of the past in specific incidents, where unusual possibilities may turn out to be relevant; assuming deviance of behavior rather than continuity.[55] *See* NORMAL THEORY

EXCEPTIONALLY GRAVE DAMAGE "Exceptionally grave damage" include armed hostilities against the United States or its allies; disruption of foreign relations vitally affecting the national security; the compromise of vital national defense plans or complex cryptologic and communications intelligence systems; the revelation of sensitive intelligence operations; and the disclosure of scientific or technological developments vital to national security. This classification shall be used with the utmost restraint.[56]

EXCULPATORY EVIDENCE Evidence that tends to decrease the likelihood of fault or guilt.

EXECUTION INFORMATION Communicates a decision and directs, initiates, or governs action, conduct, or procedure.

EXECUTIVE INTELLIGENCE SUMMARY (EIS) A daily, web-based compendium on the Joint Worldwide Intelligence Communication System (JWICS) of relevant, high-quality finished analytic products from across the IC and organized by either issue or region developed by the Office of the Director of National Intelligence (ODNI). The EIS is produced each weekday morning by the ODNI and presents articles spanning the "dailies," such as the Central Intelligence Agency's World Intelligence Review (WIRe), the DIA/J2 Executive Highlights, and National Security Agency and National Geospatial-Intelligence Agency daily highlights, to strategic assessments from the various analytic offices throughout the Intelligence Community (IC), including the National Intelligence Council, CIA's Directorate of Intelligence, the State Department's Bureau of Intelligence and Research; and contributions from service agencies such as the National Ground Intelligence Center, military regional commands, as well as newer members of the IC such as the Drug Enforcement Agency.[57]

EXECUTIVE ORDER 1. Official documents, numbered consecutively, through which the president of the United States manages the operations of the federal government. The text of executive orders appears in the daily *Federal Register* as each executive order is signed by the president and received by the Office of the Federal Register. The text of executive orders beginning with Executive Order 7316 of March 13, 1936, also appears in the sequential editions of Title 3 of the *Code of Federal Regulations* (CFR).[58] 2. The president's authority to issue Executive Orders derives from powers enumerated in, implied in, and inferred from the Constitution, as well as from authority delegated to the president by federal statute. In the overwhelming majority of cases, Executive Orders and proclamations are an appropriate public way of guiding the actions of numerous federal agencies and other components of the executive branch. Federal courts have been extremely reluctant to challenge executive authority. When Executive Orders are issued without a constitutional or legal basis, they implicate the separation of powers doctrine that underpins divided government.[59]

EXEMPTED Nomenclature and marking indicating information has been determined to fall within an enumerated exemption from automatic declassification under Executive Order (EO) 13526, "Classified National Security Information," as amended.[60]

EXFILTRATION 1. The unauthorized transfer of information from an information system.[61] 2. The removal of personnel from areas under enemy control.[62] *See* EVASION; INFILTRATION

EXFORMATION Explicitly discarded information: "what we call information in everyday life is really more like exformation: in everyday language if something contains information, it is a result of the production of exformation, it is a summary, an abbreviation suitable for guiding a transaction. Exformation is perpendicular to information. What is rejected before expression; it is about the mental work we do to probe what we want to say."[63]

EXPEDITIONARY INTELLIGENCE Intelligence in support of an armed force organized to accomplish a specific objective in a foreign country.

EXPLICIT KNOWLEDGE Tangible, external, documented knowledge that has been captured and codified into abstract human symbols (such as logical propositions, and structured and natural language) that can be stored, repeated, and passed along to other humans because it is impersonal and universal. Examples are newspapers, reports, and data of any kind. *See* TACIT KNOWLEDGE

EXPLOIT To gain access to adversary command and control systems to collect information or to plant false or misleading information.[64]

EXPLOIT CODE A computer program that allows attackers to automatically break into a system.

EXPLOITABLE RESOURCES Formulae, designs, drawings, research data, computer programs, technical data packages, and the like, which are not considered records within the congressional intent of reference because of development costs, utilization, or value. These items are considered exploitable resources to be utilized in the best interest of all the public and are not preserved for informational value nor as evidence of agency functions. Requests for copies of such material shall be evaluated in accordance with policies expressly directed to the appropriate dissemination or use of these resources. Requests to inspect this material to determine its content for informational purposes shall normally be granted, unless inspection is inconsistent with the obligation to protect the property value of the material, as, for example, may be true for patent information and certain formulae, or is inconsistent with another significant and legitimate governmental purpose.[65]

EXPLOITATION 1. Taking full advantage of success in military operations, following up initial gains, and making permanent the temporary effects already achieved. 2. Taking full advantage of any information that has come to hand for tactical, operational, or strategic purposes. 3. An offensive operation that usually follows a successful attack and is designed to disorganize the enemy in depth.[66]

EXPORT CONTROLLED INFORMATION Information and technology that may only be released to foreign nationals or foreign persons in accordance with Export Administration Regulations (15 CFR parts 730–74) and International Traffic in Arms Regulations (22 CFR parts 120–30), respectively. Export controls regulate the transfer of certain information and potential equipment to foreign nationals, and "therefore constrain who can participate in associated research and educational activities."[67]

EXPULSION The formal deportation of a diplomat, often as a form of protest against the diplomat's home country or as a result of actions by the diplomat, such as espionage.[68]

EXTRADITION The legal process by which an accused or confirmed criminal is transferred from one country to another. Generally, treaties signed between governments determine the precise requirements, rules, and exemptions for transferring suspected criminals from one sovereign legal authority to another.[69]

EXTRAORDINARY RENDITION The terms "irregular rendition" and "extraordinary rendition" have been used to refer to the extrajudicial transfer of a person from one state to another, generally for the purpose of arrest, detention, and/or interrogation by the receiving state (for purposes of this report, the term "rendition" will be used to describe irregular renditions, and not extraditions, unless otherwise specified). Unlike in extradition cases, persons subject to this type of rendition typically have no access to the judicial system of the sending state by which they may challenge their transfer. Sometimes persons are rendered from the territory of the rendering state itself, while other times they are seized by the rendering state in another country and immediately rendered, without ever setting foot in the territory of the rendering state. Sometimes renditions occur with the consent of the state where the fugitive is located; other times, they do not.[70] *See* RENDITION

EXTRAORDINARY SECURITY MEASURE A security measure necessary to adequately protect particularly sensitive information but which imposes a substantial impediment to normal staff management and oversight. Extraordinary security measures include: program access non-disclosure agreements (read-on statements); specific officials authorized to determine Need-to-Know (Access Approval Authority (AAA); nicknames or code words for program identification; special access required markings; program billet structure; access roster; use of cover; use of special mission funds or procedures; use of a Special Access Program (SAP) facility or vault; use of a dedicated SAP Security Manager (SM); any other security measure beyond those required to protect collateral information.[71]

EXTREMELY SENSITIVE INFORMATION Information and material related to the Single Integrated Operational Plan (SIOP) for the conduct of nuclear war–fighting operations.[72]

EXTREMIST Those who (1) oppose—in principle and practice—the right of people to choose how to live and how to organize their societies and (2) support the murder of ordinary people to advance extremist political purposes.[73]

EXTREMIST ACTIVITY As used in this regulation, an activity that involves the use of unlawful violence or the threat of unlawful violence directed against the Army, DoD, or the United States based on political, ideological, or religious tenets, principals, or beliefs.[74]

EXTREMIST VIOLENCE Committed by non-state actors in the name of a political, ethnic, or ideological cause and includes recruiting as well as facilitating violence.[75]

EYEWASH False entries made in files, usually to protect the security of a source, often indicating that a particular target has rejected a pitch, when in fact the offer was accepted.[76]

NOTES

1. U.S. Department of State. "Definitions of Diplomatic Security Terms." *Foreign Affairs Manual.* 12FAM090. November 12, 2014. Accessed February 4, 2015. http://www.state.gov/documents/organization/88330.pdf.

2. United Nations International Strategy for Disaster Reduction. *2009 UNISDR Terminology Disaster Risk Reduction.* Geneva. Accessed July 3, 2015. http://www.unisdr.org/we/inform/terminology.

3. Temporary Committee on the ECHELON Interception System, European Parliament. *On the Existence of a Global System for the Interception of Private and Commercial Communications (ECHELON Interception System).* Part 1 & 2, July 11, 2011. Accessed July 3, 2015. http://www.europarl.europa.eu/sides/getDoc.do?pubRef=-//EP//TEXT+REPORT+A5-2001-0264+0+DOC+XML+V0//EN.

4. Nakamura, David. "For the National Security and Social Media Communities, a Delicate Relationship Persists." *The Washington Post,* November 1, 2013. Accessed January 15, 2015. http://www.washingtonpost.com/politics/for-the-national-security-and-social-media-communities-a-delicate-relationship-persists/2013/11/01/5aacd098-40ba-11e3-a751-f032898f2dbc_story.html.

5. United States Senate, Select Committee to Study Governmental Operations with Respect to Intelligence Activities (Church Committee). *Final Report.* Book 1. April 26, 1976. Accessed February 7, 2015. https://archive.org/details/finalreportofsel01unit.

6. Fein, Robert A. "Intelligence Science Board Study on Educing Information Phase 1 Report." In Intelligence Science Board. *Educing Information—Interrogation:*

Science and Art: Foundations for the Future. Phase 1 Report, National Defense Intelligence College, 2006. Accessed January 16, 2015. http://www1.umn.edu/humanrts/OathBetrayed/Intelligence%20Science%20Board%202006.pdf.

7. United States Air Force. *Public Affairs Operations.* Air Force Doctrine Document 3-6, 24 June 2005 Certified Current 20 August 2013 Incorporating Changes 1, December 23, 2010. Accessed February 4, 2015. http://static.e-publishing.af.mil/production/1/af_cv/publication/afdd3-61/afdd3-61.pdf.

8. U.S. Department of State. "The Privacy Act and Personally Identifiable Information." *Foreign Affairs Manual.* 5 FAM 460. October 1, 2014. Accessed February 14, 2015. http://www.state.gov/documents/organization/85694.pdf.

9. Federal Bureau of Investigation. *eGuardian: Introduction.* Accessed January 16, 2015. http://www.fbi.gov/stats-services/eguardian.

10. Department of Homeland Security. *Privacy Impact Assessment: EINSTEIN Program Collecting, Analyzing, and Sharing Computer Security Information Across the Federal Civilian Government.* September 2004. Accessed July 3, 2015. http://www.dhs.gov/sites/default/files/publications/privacy-pia-nppd-einstein-june2013-3-year-review.pdf; also see Department of Homeland Security. *Privacy Impact Assessment for the Initiative Three Exercise.* March 18, 2010. Accessed July 3, 2015. http://www.dhs.gov/xlibrary/assets/privacy/privacy_pia_nppd_initiative3.pdf. Sternstein, Aliya. "DHS Set to Destroy Governmentwide Network Surveillance Records." *NextGov,* November 13, 2014. Accessed July 3, 2015. http://www.nextgov.com/cybersecurity/2014/11/dhs-set-destroy-governmentwide-network-surveillance-records/99737/.

11. Federal Bureau of Investigation. *Minimum Criminal Intelligence Training Standards for Law Enforcement and Other Criminal Justice Agencies in the United States.* October 2007. Accessed January 22, 2015. https://it.ojp.gov/gist/108/Minimum-Criminal-Intelligence-Training-Standards.

12. North Atlantic Treaty Organization. *NATO Glossary of Terms and Definitions.* NATO Standardization Agency, 2008. Accessed July 2, 2015. https://fas.org/irp/doddir/other/nato2008.pdf.

13. U.S. Department of Defense. *Chief Information Office Desk Reference. Volume 1. Foundation Documents.* August 2006. Accessed February 13, 2015. https://www.csiac.org/sites/default/files/DoD%20CIO%20Desk%20Ref%20Vol%201%20(2006)_0.pdf.

14. U.S. Department of Defense. *Department of Defense Dictionary of Military and Associated Terms.* JP 1-02, 08 November 2010, as Amended through 15 January 2016. Accessed January 26, 2016. http://www.dtic.mil/doctrine/new_pubs/jp1_02.pdf.

15. U.S. Department of Defense. *Department of Defense Dictionary of Military and Associated Terms.* JP 1-02, 08 November 2010, as Amended through 15 January 2016. Accessed January 26, 2016. http://www.dtic.mil/doctrine/new_pubs/jp1_02.pdf.

16. North Atlantic Treaty Organization. *NATO Glossary of Terms and Definitions.* NATO Standardization Agency, 2008. Accessed July 2, 2015. https://fas.org/irp/doddir/other/nato2008.pdf.

17. National Initiative for Cybersecurity Education. *A Glossary of Common Cybersecurity Terminology.* n.d. Accessed March 5, 2015. http://niccs.us-cert.gov/glossary.

18. North Atlantic Treaty Organization. *NATO Glossary of Terms and Definitions.* NATO Standardization Agency, 2008. Accessed July 2, 2015. https://fas.org/irp/dod-dir/other/nato2008.pdf.

19. 18 U.S.C. § 2510(17)—"Definitions" (Current through Pub. L. 113-234). Accessed February 15, 2015. http://www.law.cornell.edu/uscode/text/18/2510; also see Zwillinger, Marc J. and Genetski, Christian S. "Criminal Discovery of the Internet under the Stored Communications Act: It's Not a Level Playing Field." *The Journal of Criminal Law and Criminology* 97 no. 2 (2007): 569–600. http://blog.zwillgen.com/wp-content/uploads/2010/05/Journal_Criminal_Law_Criminology_97_2.pdf.

20. U.S. Department of Defense. Center for Development of Security Excellence. *Glossary of Security Terms and Definitions.* November 2012. Accessed February 16, 2015. http://www.cdse.edu/documents/cdse/Glossary_Handbook.pdf.

21. 50 U.S. Code § 1801(f) "Definitions" (Current through Pub. L. 113-234). Accessed February 16, 2015. http://www.law.cornell.edu/uscode/text/50/1801.

22. David Jablonsky, "National Power," *Parameters* (spring 1997): 34–54, accessed February 3, 2016, http://strategicstudiesinstitute.army.mil/pubs/parameters/Articles/97spring/jablonsk.htm.

23. Department of the Army. Marine Corps Combat Development Command. Department of the Navy. *Operational Terms and Graphics.* FM 1-02 (FM 101-5). September 21, 2004. Accessed July 3, 2015. http://www.udel.edu/armyrotc/current_cadets/cadet_resources/manuals_regulations_files/FM%201-02%20-%20Operational%20Terms%20&%20Graphics.pdf.

24. Presidential Policy Directive/PPD-19. *Protecting Whistleblowers with Access to Classified Information.* October 12, 2012. Accessed February 21, 2015. http://fas.org/irp/offdocs/ppd/ppd-19.pdf.

25. FAO. *The Emergency Sequence: What FAO Does—How FAO Does It.* n.d. Accessed July 3, 2015. http://www.fao.org/3/a-mj548e.pdf.

26. U.S. Department of Defense. Center for Development of Security Excellence. *Glossary of Security Terms and Definitions.* November 2012. Accessed February 16, 2015. http://www.cdse.edu/documents/cdse/Glossary_Handbook.pdf.

27. Jan Goldman, *Intelligence Warning Terminology*, Joint Military Intelligence College, October 2001, accessed July 3, 2015. https://archive.org/details/JMICIntelligencewarnterminology.

28. Jan Goldman, *Intelligence Warning Terminology*, Joint Military Intelligence College, October 2001, accessed July 3, 2015. https://archive.org/details/JMICIntelligencewarnterminology.

29. Office of the Director of National Intelligence. *Intelligence Community Continuity Program.* Intelligence Community Directive 118, November 12, 2013. Accessed January 24, 2015. http://www.dni.gov/files/documents/ICD/ICD 118 IC Continuity Program.pdf; also see National Security and Homeland Security Presidential

Directive/NSPD-51/HSPD 20. *National Continuity Policy.* May 9, 2007. Accessed February 27, 2015. http://fas.org/irp/offdocs/nspd/nspd-51.htm.

30. Department of Homeland Security, Risk Steering Committee. *DHS Risk Lexicon.* September 2010. Accessed February 14, 2015. http://www.dhs.gov/dhs-risk-lexicon.

31. Senate Select Committee on Intelligence. *Committee Study of the Central Intelligence Agency's Detention and Interrogation Program.* Declassification revisions December 3, 2014. Accessed January 16, 2015. http://www.intelligence.senate. gov/study2014.html; also see Miles, Anne Daugherty. "Perspectives on the Senate Select Committee on Intelligence (SSCI) 'Torture Report' and Enhanced Interrogation Techniques: In Brief." *CRS Report for Congress*, February 10, 2015. Accessed February 20, 2015. http://www.fas.org/sgp/crs/intel/R43906.pdf.

32. Bletchley Park. *Breaking Enigma.* Accessed July 3, 2015. http://www.bletchleypark.org.uk/content/hist/worldwartwo/enigma.rhtm.

33. Defense Intelligence Agency. *Defense Intelligence Report: Lexicon of Hardened Structure Definitions and Terms.* Washington, DC: 2000.

34. National Initiative for Cybersecurity Education. *A Glossary of Common Cybersecurity Terminology.* n.d. Accessed March 5, 2015. http://niccs.us-cert.gov/glossary.

35. Department of Homeland Security, Risk Steering Committee. *DHS Risk Lexicon.* September 2010. Accessed February 14, 2015. http://www.dhs.gov/dhs-risk-lexicon.

36. National Initiative for Cybersecurity Education. *A Glossary of Common Cybersecurity Terminology.* n.d. Accessed March 5, 2015. http://niccs.us-cert.gov/glossary.

37. Centers for Disease Control and Prevention. *Epidemic Intelligence Service.* Accessed July 3, 2015. http://www.cdc.gov/eis/.

38. U.S. Department of Justice. *Declassification Frequently Asked Questions.* Accessed January 27, 2015. http://www.justice.gov/open/declassification/declassification-faq.

39. Department of the Army. *Open-Source Intelligence.* ATP 2-22.9. July 2012, Accessed July 3, 2015. http://fas.org/irp/doddir/army/atp2-22-9.pdf.

40. Department of the Army. *Subversion and Espionage Directed against the U.S. Army.* AR 381–12, January 1993. Accessed July 3, 2015. http://fas.org/irp/doddir/army/ar381-12-1993.pdf; also see 18 U.S.C., http://uscode.house.gov/, and *Uniform Code of Military Justice*, Article 106a, http://www.ucmj.us/.

41. U.S. Department of Defense. *Department of Defense Dictionary of Military and Associated Terms.* JP 1-02, 08 November 2010, as Amended through 15 January 2016. Accessed January 26, 2016. http://www.dtic.mil/doctrine/new_pubs/jp1_02.pdf.

42. U.S. Department of Defense. Center for Development of Security Excellence. *Glossary of Security Terms and Definitions.* November 2012. Accessed February 16, 2015. http://www.cdse.edu/documents/cdse/Glossary_Handbook.pdf.

43. Jan Goldman, *Intelligence Warning Terminology*, Joint Military Intelligence College, October 2001, accessed July 3, 2015. https://archive.org/details/JMICIntelligencelwarnterminology.

44. Senate Select Committee on Intelligence. *Committee Study of the Central Intelligence Agency's Detention and Interrogation Program.* Declassification revisions December 3, 2014. Accessed January 16, 2015. http://www.intelligence.senate.gov/study2014.html.

45. Office of the Director of National Intelligence. *National Intelligence: A Consumer's Guide.* 2011. Accessed January 25, 2015. http://www.dni.gov/files/documents/IC_Consumers_Guide_2011.pdf.

46. Jan Goldman, *Intelligence Warning Terminology*, Joint Military Intelligence College, October 2001, accessed July 3, 2015. https://archive.org/details/JMICIntelligencelwarnterminology.

47. Office of the Director of National Intelligence. *Prospects for Iraq's Stability: A Challenging Road Ahead.* January 2007. Accessed January 16, 2015. https://www.fas.org/irp/dni/iraq020207.pdf.

48. Department of the Army. Marine Corps Combat Development Command. Department of the Navy. *Operational Terms and Graphics.* FM 1-02 (FM 101-5). September 21, 2004. Accessed July 3, 2015. http://www.udel.edu/armyrotc/current_cadets/cadet_resources/manuals_regulations_files/FM%201-02%20-%20Operational%20Terms%20&%20Graphics.pdf; also see Sherman Kent, "Words of Estimated Probability," in *Sherman Kent and the Board of National Estimates: Collected Essays*, ed. Donald P. Steury (Washington, DC: Center for the Study of Intelligence, 1994), 132–39.

49. U.S. Department of Defense. *Department of Defense Dictionary of Military and Associated Terms.* JP 1-02, 08 November 2010, as Amended through 15 January 2016. Accessed January 26, 2016. http://www.dtic.mil/doctrine/new_pubs/jp1_02.pdf.

50. U.S. Department of Defense. *Department of Defense Dictionary of Military and Associated Terms.* JP 1-02, 08 November 2010, as Amended through 15 January 2016. Accessed January 26, 2016. http://www.dtic.mil/doctrine/new_pubs/jp1_02.pdf.

51. Federal Bureau of Investigation. *Minimum Criminal Intelligence Training Standards for Law Enforcement and Other Criminal Justice Agencies in the United States.* October 2007. Accessed January 22, 2015. https://it.ojp.gov/gist/108/Minimum-Criminal-Intelligence-Training-Standards.

52. Department of Homeland Security, Risk Steering Committee. DHS Risk Lexicon. September 2010. Accessed February 14, 2015. http://www.dhs.gov/dhs-risk-lexicon.

53. *Nolo's Plain-English Law Dictionary.* n.d. Accessed July 3, 2015. http://www.nolo.com/dictionary.

54. DOE Chief Information Officer. "Records Management Definitions." Accessed November 2, 2015. https://www.archives.gov/records-mgmt/resources/self-assessment-2012.pdf.

55. Betts, Richard. "Warning Dilemmas: Normal Theory vs. Exceptional Theory." *Orbis* 26 (Winter 1983): 828–33.

56. 40 CFR 11.4(f)(1)—"Definitions (Top Secret)." Accessed February 18, 2015. http://www.law.cornell.edu/cfr/text/40/11.4.

57. Intelligence and National Security Alliance and the Office of the Director of National Intelligence. *Analytic Transformation: Moving Forward Together*. September 2007. Accessed January 26, 2015. http://wayback.archive.org/web/20080530054342/http://analytic.insaonline.org/atprogram.pdf.

58. National Archives and Records Administration. *Executive Order FAQ's*. Accessed February 19, 2015. http://www.archives.gov/federal-register/executive-orders/about.html.

59. Schlesinger, Arthur. *The Imperial Presidency*. New York: Atlantic Monthly, 1973.

60. U.S. Department of Defense. Center for Development of Security Excellence. *Glossary of Security Terms and Definitions*. November 2012. Accessed February 16, 2015. http://www.cdse.edu/documents/cdse/Glossary_Handbook.pdf.

61. Joint Task Force Transformation Initiative. *Security and Privacy Controls for Federal Information Systems and Organizations*. NIST Special Publication 800-53, Revision 4, April 2013. Accessed March 7, 2015. http://dx.doi.org/10.6028/NIST.SP.8.

62. U.S. Department of Defense. *Department of Defense Dictionary of Military and Associated Terms*. JP 1-02, 08 November 2010, as Amended through 15 January 2016. Accessed January 26, 2016. http://www.dtic.mil/doctrine/new_pubs/jp1_02.pdf.

63. Nørretranders, Tor. *The User Illusion: Cutting Consciousness Down to Size*, trans. Jonathan Sydenham. New York: Viking Penguin, 1998.

64. Department of the Army. Marine Corps Combat Development Command. Department of the Navy. *Operational Terms and Graphics*. FM 1-02 (FM 101-5). September 21, 2004. Accessed July 3, 2015. http://www.udel.edu/armyrotc/current_cadets/cadet_resources/manuals_regulations_files/FM%201-02%20-%20Operational%20Terms%20&%20Graphics.pdf.

65. Federal Emergency Management Agency (FEMA). "Production or Disclosure of Information." 44 CFR 5.3. Accessed July 3, 2015. http://www.ecfr.gov.

66. U.S. Department of Defense. *Department of Defense Dictionary of Military and Associated Terms*. JP 1-02, 08 November 2010, as Amended through 15 January 2016. Accessed January 26, 2016. http://www.dtic.mil/doctrine/new_pubs/jp1_02.pdf.

67. *Federal Register*, vol. 70, no. 132, July 12, 2005. Accessed July 3, 2015. https://www.federalregister.gov.

68. U.S. Department of State. *Diplomatic Dictionary*. Accessed March 6, 2015. http://diplomacy.state.gov/discoverdiplomacy/references/169792.htm.

69. U.S. Department of State. *Diplomatic Dictionary*. Accessed March 6, 2015. http://diplomacy.state.gov/discoverdiplomacy/references/169792.htm.

70. Garcia, Michael John. "Renditions: Constraints Imposed by Laws on Torture." *CRS Report for Congress* RL32890. September 8, 2009. Accessed February 8, 2015. http://www.fas.org/sgp/crs/natsec/RL32890.pdf.

71. U.S. Department of Defense. Center for Development of Security Excellence. *Glossary of Security Terms and Definitions*. November 2012. Accessed February 16, 2015. http://www.cdse.edu/documents/cdse/Glossary_Handbook.pdf.

72. Department of the Air Force. Safeguarding the Single Integrated Operational Plan (SIOP). Air Force Instruction 10-110, July 15, 2002. Accessed July 3, 2015. https://fas.org/irp/doddir/usaf/afi10-1102.pdf.

73. Chairman of the Joint Chiefs of Staff. *National Military Strategic Plan for the War on Terrorism.* February 1, 2006. Accessed February 26, 2015. http://www.defense.gov/qdr/docs/2006-02-08-Strategic-Plan.pdf.

74. Department of the Army. *Threat Awareness and Reporting Program.* Army Regulation 381–1. October 4, 2010. Accessed February 8, 2015. http://www.apd.army.mil/pdffiles/r381_12.pdf.

75. National Counterrorism Center. *Countering Violent Extremism: A Guide for Practitioners and Analysts.* May 2014. Accessed February 9, 2015. https://www.documentcloud.org/documents/1657824-cve-guide.html.

76. West, Nigel. *Historical Dictionary of Cold War Counterintelligence.* Lanham, MD: Scarecrow Press, 2007.

FABRIC The interconnection between IC computer systems at a given level of security. There is a fabric for the Top Secret, Secret-Collateral, and Unclassified levels.

FABRICATION A deceptive practice that makes an unreal event or situation seem actually to have occurred.[1] *See* DEMONSTRATION; DIVERSION; FEINT

FABRICATOR An individual or group that, without genuine resources, invents information or inflates or embroiders over news for personal gain or for political purposes.

FACT An event or action that has occurred and has been verified by two independent sources.

FALKLAND ISLANDS CRISIS The surprise invasion by Argentina of the British colony. British estimates on March 30, 1982, stated that an invasion was not imminent, but three days later Argentine marines landed and occupied the islands. The 1982 invasion took Margaret Thatcher by surprise. The then-prime minister only saw it was likely after getting "raw intelligence" two days before the Argentines landed.[2] *See* CUBAN MISSILE CRISIS; OPERATION BARBAROSSA, PEARL HARBOR; SINGAPORE INTELLIGENCE FAILURE; TET OFFENSIVE; YOM KIPPUR WAR

FALSE FLAG 1. Development or execution of any imitative or operation under false national sponsorship or credentials (aka "false colors"). The Russian term is foreign flag. 2. Also, the technique for misrepresenting an individual's country of origin is a risky but well-established tactic adopted by all counterintelligence agencies in the absence of other, safer alternatives. Invariably, the strategy is one of last resort when a suspect is known to have engaged in espionage but is thought to be currently inactive. The offer to be reengaged as a spy may be accepted and result in sufficient evidence to secure a conviction, or may prompt an incriminating action. 3. Also, approach by a hostile intelligence officer who misrepresents himself or herself as a citizen of a friendly country or organization. The person who is approached may give up sensitive information believing that it is going to an ally, not a hostile power.[3]

FALSE-FLAG RECRUITMENT A situation in which an individual believes he or she is cooperating with an intelligence service of a specific country but has been deceived and is cooperating with an intelligence service of another country. Forecasts may refer either to events or to trends, and these changes must be verifiable if forecasts are to be operationally meaningful. According to experts, "This puts a special strain on forecasts in social science areas as opposed to, say, technological forecasts, because the terminology we tend to use ('risking dissatisfaction,' 'détente,' 'nationalism') does not always have the crispness necessary to allow unambiguously verifiable assertions. As a consequence, forecasts, in order to be meaningful, sometimes have to be formulated in terms of certain indicators. If possible, these are social or political indicators whose values are objectively measurable."[4] In an article that appeared in South Korea media, "Seoul-based banks demand that the government honor the payment guarantee at the earliest date possible, as they have failed to receive the loans from Russia. But analysts forecast that the government payment is unlikely within the year. And the banks may even fail to get the payment by next year, given the protracted negotiations regarding the state budget toward that end."[5] *See* ESTIMATE; PREDICTION

FALSE POSITIVE An alert that incorrectly indicates malicious activity is occurring.

FAMILY JEWELS Slang term for a 692-page internal CIA report drawn up by order of Director of Central Intelligence James Schlesinger in 1974 so he would not face unpleasant surprises. The report contained details of all CIA operations since 1947 that were or might have been considered illegal, embarrassing, or unwise. It leaked to reporter Seymour Hersh, and his sensational December 1974 articles on CIA misdeeds led to passage of the Hughes-Ryan Amendment plus Senate and House investigations.[6]

FAST LIGHTWEIGHT AUTONOMY (FLA) The goal of the FLA program is to explore non-traditional perception and autonomy methods that could enable a new class of algorithms for minimalistic high-speed navigation in cluttered environments. Through this exploration, the program aims to develop and demonstrate the capability for small (i.e., able to fit through windows) autonomous UAVs to fly at speeds up to 20 m/s with no communication to the operator and without GPS waypoints. The FLA program will demonstrate a sequence of capabilities, beginning with lower-clutter, fly-by missions and progressing to higher-clutter, fly-through missions.[7]

FATIDIC Relating to predicting fates; prophetic. From Latin *fatidicus*, from *fatum* (fate) and *dicere* (to say). *See* ONEIROMANCY

FAULT TREE Graphical tool used to illustrate the range, probability, and interaction of causal occurrences that lead to a final outcome.[8]

FBI ELECTRONIC BIOMETRIC TRANSMISSION SPECIFICATION (EBTS) The FBI EBTS specifies the file and record content, format, and data codes necessary for the exchange of fingerprint, palm print, photo, facial, iris and other contextual (biographic and/or situational) information between federal, state, and local users and the FBI/CJIS. It provides a description of all requests and responses associated with electronic fingerprint identification service and other services. As FBI/CJIS moves to NGI, this specification is being re-organized into User Services that include the following: Identification Service; Verification Service; Information Service; Investigation Service; Notification Service; Data Management Service.[9]

FBI NETWORK (FBINET) The FBI's secret-level primary computer operations network. It does not connect directly to SIPRNet but can connect remotely.[10]

FEDERAL ADVISORY COMMITTEE ACT (FACA) 1. The Federal Advisory Committee Act was enacted in 1972 to ensure that advice by the various advisory committees formed over the years is objective and accessible to the public. The Act formalized a process for establishing, operating, overseeing, and terminating these advisory bodies and created the Committee Management Secretariat to monitor compliance with the Act. In 1976, Executive Order 12024 delegated to the administrator of GSA all responsibilities of the president for implementing the Federal Advisory Committee Act (FACA). Secretariat operations are directed at reporting to the president and Congress on the activities of at least 1000 federal advisory committees.[11] 2. Notice that in 1998, the Highlands "Group" became a "Forum." According to O'Neill, this was to avoid subjecting Highlands Forums meetings to "bureaucratic restrictions." What he was alluding to was the Federal Advisory Committee Act (FACA), which regulates the way the U.S. government can formally solicit the advice of special interests. Known as the "open government" law, FACA requires that U.S. government officials cannot hold closed-door or secret consultations with people outside government to develop policy. All such consultations should take place via federal advisory committees that permit public scrutiny. FACA requires that meetings be held in public, announced via the *Federal Register*, that advisory groups are registered with an office at the General Services Administration, among other requirements intended to maintain accountability to the public interest. But *Government Executive* reported that "O'Neill and others believed" such regulatory issues "would quell the free flow of ideas and no-holds-barred discussions they sought." Pentagon lawyers had warned that the word "group" might necessitate certain obligations and advised running the whole thing privately.[11]

FEDERAL AGENCY DATA MINING REPORTING ACT OF 2007 (Pub. L. No. 110-53, 121 Stat. 266). The Data Mining Reporting Act of 2007 require all federal agencies using or developing data mining programs to report annually to Congress on "pattern-based queries" of databases used to identify "predictive patterns or anomalies that indicate terrorist or criminal activity." The Central Intelligence Agency does not compile annual reports.[12, 13]

FEDERAL INTELLIGENCE COORDINATOR OFFICE (FICO) Offices within an individual executive branch department or agency that coordinate with the IC to support policymakers and other intelligence customers within their organization.[14]

FEDERAL PIV A physical artifact issued by the federal government to an individual that contains a photograph, cryptographic keys, and a digitized fingerprint representation so that the claimed identity of the card holder can be verified by another person (human readable and verifiable) or a computer system (readable and verifiable).[15]

FEDERAL RECORD Includes all books, papers, maps, photographs, machine-readable materials, or other documentary materials, regardless of physical form or characteristics, made or received by an Agency of the United States (U.S.) government under federal law or in connection with the transaction of public business and preserved or appropriate for preservation by that agency or its legitimate successor as evidence of the organization, functions, policies, decisions, procedures, operations, or other activities of the government or because of the informational value of data in them.[16]

FEDERAL RISK AND AUTHORIZATION MANAGEMENT PROGRAM (FedRAMP) The result of close collaboration with cybersecurity and cloud experts from GSA, NIST, DHS, DOD, NSA, OMB, the Federal

CIO Council and its working groups, as well as private industry. The Fe-dRAMP assessment process is initiated by agencies or cloud service provider (CSPs) beginning a security authorization using the FedRAMP requirements which are FISMA compliant and based on the NIST 800-53 rev3 and initiating work with the FedRAMP PMO.[17] *See* CLOUD COMPUTING

FEDERAL SENIOR INTELLIGENCE COORDINATOR (FSIC) The senior position within an individual executive branch department or agency that has been designated by the head of that organization upon request of the DNI to serve as the primary liaison between the respective department or agency and the IC.[18]

FEEDBACK In information operations, information that reveals how the deception target is responding to the deception story and if the military deception plan is working.[19]

FEINT An act intended to divert a victim's attention from the main target of an attack by contriving a mock attack where actual combat is not intended; simulating a buildup for an imminent attack. During World War II, a feint codenamed Fortitude was used to distract German attention from the real landing area in Normandy. "A very busy signals staff contrived, by sending out the right sort of dummy wireless traffic, to assemble a fictitious 4th Army in Scotland. The 'wireless training' of this army contained some purposeful indiscretions. By these furtive, impressionistic and devious indiscretions, Fortitude sought to let the Germans convince themselves of what they had always wanted to believe anyway—that the invaders would pour across the Channel at the narrowest point, from Dover to the Pas de Calais; the buildup in Scotland itself suggested a preliminary feint-like assault on southern Norway. In fact, so conclusive did the evidence seem to be that more than a month after the invasion in Normandy, Hitler declared that 'the enemy will probably attempt a second landing in the 15th Army sector'—the zone of the Pas de Calais."[20] *See* DECEPTION; DEMONSTRATION; DIVERSION; FABRICATION

FFU HYPOTHESIS The Communications Security Establishment, or CSE, Canada's equivalent of the NSA, hypothesis that extremists use free file upload (FFU) sites "differently than the general public."[21]

FIE (FOREIGN INTELLIGENCE ENTITY) Any known or suspected foreign organization, person, or group (public, private, or governmental) that conducts intelligence activities to acquire U.S. information, block or impair

U.S. intelligence collection, influence U.S. policy, or disrupts U.S. systems and programs. The term includes foreign intelligence and security services and international terrorists.[22]

FIELD INTELLIGENCE AGENTS FBI intelligence analysts, special agents, language analysts, and surveillance specialists assigned to a Field Intelligence Group (FIG), at one of the 56 FBI Field Offices in the United States. "They take raw information from local cases and make big-picture sense of it . . . fill gaps in national cases with local information . . . and share their findings, assessments, and reports with fellow FIGs across the country and with our partners in law enforcement and intelligence to, say, shut down that money laundering scheme or keep a bomb from going off. Intelligence analysts (IAs) are key to the effort. Some are dedicated to the big picture—others are actually 'embedded' in squads to work with street agents on specific counterterrorism, counterintelligence, and criminal cases."[23]

FIG LEAF An event or activity of seemingly minor consequence used for the justification of a larger or more important and significant action; often used as an excuse. "He [Secretary of State Dean Rusk] said he felt we might be confronted by serious uprisings all over Latin America if U.S. forces were to go in, not to mention the temptation that the commitment of such forces in Cuba would provide elsewhere in the world. In this connection he again mentioned the possibility of a physical base on the Isle of Pines for a provisional government that we could recognize. This he thought would be a powerful step forward. What we needed was a fig leaf. A Cuban provisional government on the Isle of Pines, for example, could sink Soviet ships carrying supplies to Castro with less danger than would be the case with direct involvement of U.S. forces."[24]

FILE An arrangement of records; papers, photographs, photographic copies, maps, machine-readable information, or other recorded information regardless of physical form or characteristics, accumulated or maintained in filing equipment, boxes, or machine-readable media, or on shelves, and occupying office or storage space.[25]

FILE SERIES File units or documents arranged according to a filing system or kept together because they relate to a particular subject or function, result from the same activity, document a specific kind of transaction, take a particular physical form, or have some other relationship arising out of their creation, receipt, or use, such as restrictions on access or use.[26]

FINANCIAL ANALYSIS A review and analysis of financial data to ascertain the presence of criminal activity. It can include bank record analysis, net worth analysis, financial profiles, source and application of funds, financial statement analysis, and/or bank secrecy record analysis. It can also show destinations of proceeds of crime and support prosecutions.

FINANCIAL CRIMES ENFORCEMENT NETWORK (FINCEN) FinCEN's mission is to safeguard the financial system from illicit use and combat money laundering and promote national security through the collection, analysis, and dissemination of financial intelligence and strategic use of financial authorities. Financial data that FinCEN collects from financial institutions under the Bank Secrecy Act (BSA) has proven to be of considerable value in investigations of financial crime. When combined with other data collected by law enforcement, FinCEN data assists investigators in connecting the dots by allowing for a more complete identification of subjects with previously unknown information.[27]

FINDING A written directive in which the president of the United States states that he finds a certain covert action is important for national security; intelligence determined from collected sources.

FINISHED INTELLIGENCE (FI) Raw information analyzed and corroborated. It should be produced in a consistent format to enhance utility and regularly disseminated to a defined audience.[28] *See* RAW INTELLIGENCE

FITNESS Level of character and conduct determined necessary for the basis of physical access control decisions.[29]

FLOW ANALYSIS The review of raw data to determine the sequence of events or interactions that may reflect criminal activity. It can include timelines, event-flow analysis, commodity-flow analysis, and activity-flow analysis. It may show missing actions or events that need further investigation.[30]

FOR OFFICIAL USE ONLY (FOUO) A designation used for unclassified information that may be shared only with individuals who have a "need to know." FOUO is used by the Department of Defense and a number of other federal agencies to identify information or material which, although unclassified, may not be appropriate for public release. In the DHS, employees and contractors are required to sign a special Non-Disclosure Agreement before receiving access to this information. Within the DHS, the FOUO designation is used "to identify unclassified information of a sensitive nature, not otherwise categorized by statute or regulation, the unauthorized disclosure of which could adversely impact a person's privacy and welfare, the conduct of a federal program, or other programs or operations essential to the national interest." Within DHS, the caveat "For Official Use Only" will be used to identify Sensitive but Unclassified (SBU) information within the DHS community that is not otherwise governed by state or regulation. At this point, the designation applies only to DHS advisories and bulletins.[31]

FORCE MANAGEMENT RISK (DOD) ability to recruit, retain, train, educate, and equip the All-Volunteer Force, and to sustain its readiness and morale. This requires the Department to examine its ability to provide trained and ready personnel in the near term, midterm, and long term.[32]

FORCED ENTRY Unauthorized individual that leaves evidence of the act.

FORECAST A look at what has happened or what may happen, based on what is known and verifiable, suspected and not verifiable, and unknown. Likelihoods or probabilities of future activity are usually included, with suggested steps to protect against criminal activity. This term should not be confused with prediction. Whereas predictions assert the occurrence of some event with certainty ("insurgents will capture the city next year"), a forecast is a probabilistic statement ("there is a 3 to 1 chance that the insurgents will capture the city next year"). A prediction may be viewed as a limiting case of a forecast, where the assigned probability reaches the level of certainty; however, forecasts very rarely take the form of predictions.[33]

FOREGROUND INFORMATION All information and material jointly generated and funded pertaining to the cooperative program. This information is available for use by all participating governments in accordance with the terms of a Memorandum of Agreement (MOA).[34]

FOREIGN AFFAIRS The relations among states within the international system, including the roles of states and international organizations; can also include the roles of non-governmental organizations and multinational corporations.[35]

FOREIGN AGENTS REGISTRATION ACT OF 1938 The Foreign Agents Registration Act (FARA) was enacted in 1938. FARA is a disclosure statute that requires persons acting as agents of foreign principals in a political or quasi-political capacity to make periodic public disclosure of their relationship with the foreign principal, as well as activities, receipts and disbursements in support of those activities. Disclosure of the required information facilitates evaluation by the government and the American people of the statements and activities of such persons in light of their function as foreign agents. The FARA Registration Unit of the Counterintelligence and Export Control Section (CES) in the National Security Division (NSD) is responsible for the administration and enforcement of the Act.[36]

FOREIGN CIVIL INTELLIGENCE Derived from all sources regarding the social, political, and economic aspects of governments and civil populations, their demographics, structures, capabilities, organizations, people, and events.[37]

FOREIGN COUNTERINTELLIGENCE Actions taken to detect, counteract, or prevent intelligence gathering, espionage, sabotage, and other activities conducted on behalf of another country.

FOREIGN DENIAL AND DECEPTION COMMITTEE (FDDC) Chaired by the National Intelligence Officer for Science and Technology, advises and assists the DNI on foreign activities that thwart U.S. intelligence through denial and deception (D&D), promotes the effective use of IC resources to counter foreign D&D, and serves as one of four DNI Production Committees.[38]

FOREIGN DISCLOSURE The disclosure of Classified Military Information (CMI) or Controlled Unclassified Information (CUI) to an authorized representative of a foreign government or international organization. NOTE: The transfer or disclosure of CMI or CUI to a foreign national who is an authorized employee of the United States (U.S.) government or a U.S. contractor technically is not a "foreign disclosure," since the disclosure is not made to the person's government.[39]

FOREIGN GOVERNMENT INFORMATION (FGI) 1. Information provided to the U.S. government by a foreign government, an international organization of governments, or any element thereof, with the expectation that the information, the sources of the information, or both are to be held in confidence. 2. Information produced by the United States pursuant to or as a result of a joint arrangement with a foreign government or international organization of governments or any element thereof, requiring that the information, the arrangement, or both are to be held in confidence. 3. Information received and treated as "foreign government information" under the terms of EO 12958.[40] Bush EO 13292 makes FGI classified information.[41] *See* NATIONAL INTELLIGENCE

FOREIGN INSTRUMENTAL SIGNALS INTELLIGENCE (FISINT)
Intelligence information derived from electromagnetic emissions associated
with the testing and operational deployment of foreign aerospace, surface,
and subsurface systems. Technical information and intelligence information
derived from the intercept of foreign instrumentation signals by other than
the intended recipients. Foreign instrumentation signals include, but are not
limited to, signals from telemetry, beaconry, electronic interrogators, tracking, fusing, arming, or firing command systems, and video data links.[42] *See*
SOURCES OF INTELLIGENCE

FOREIGN INTELLIGENCE (FI) Information relating to capabilities, intentions, and activities of foreign governments or elements thereof, foreign
organizations, or foreign persons, or international terrorist activities.[43]

FOREIGN INTELLIGENCE COLLECTION THREAT The potential of
a foreign power, organization, or person to overtly or covertly collect information about United States (U.S.) acquisition program technologies, capabilities, and methods of employment that could be used to develop a similar
weapon system or countermeasures to the U.S. system or related operations.[44]

FOREIGN INTELLIGENCE ENTITY (FIE) Any known or suspected
foreign organization, person, or group (public, private, or governmental) that
conducts intelligence activities to acquire U.S. information, block or impair
U.S. intelligence collection, influence U.S. policy, or disrupt U.S. systems
and programs. This term includes a foreign intelligence and security service
and international terrorist organizations.[45]

FOREIGN INTELLIGENCE INFORMATION Relating to the capabilities, intentions, or activities of foreign governments or elements thereof, foreign organizations, or foreign persons. The U.S. government allows the sharing of foreign intelligence information between agencies, and gives license
to intelligence officers who conduct electronic surveillance to "coordinate
efforts" with law enforcement to coordinate investigations.[46]

FOREIGN INTELLIGENCE OFFICER A member of a foreign intelligence service.

FOREIGN INTELLIGENCE SERVICE An organization of a foreign
country capable of executing all or part of the intelligence cycle.

FOREIGN INTELLIGENCE SURVEILLANCE ACT (FISA) Enacted in
1978, the legal authority authorizing and regulating electronic surveillance

within the United States for foreign intelligence or counterintelligence purposes and physical searches within the United States for foreign intelligence purposes. The Foreign Intelligence Surveillance Act (FISA) P.L. 95-511, 92 STAT 1783, provides a statutory framework by which government agencies may, when gathering foreign intelligence investigation, obtain authorization to conduct electronic surveillance or physical searches, utilize pen registers and trap and trace devices, or access specified business records and other tangible things. Authorization for such activities is typically obtained via a court order from the Foreign Intelligence Surveillance Court (FISC), a specialized court created to act as a neutral judicial decision maker in the context of FISA. Since 1978, FISA has been amended by Sections 206 (roving wiretaps) and 215 of the USA PATRIOT Act (P.L. 107-56, 115 STAT 272), which broadens the types of records and other tangible things that can be made accessible to the government under FISA; and Section 6001(a) of the Intelligence Reform and Terrorism Prevention Act (IRTPA), P.L. 108-458, 118 STAT 3638, also known as the "lone wolf" provision, which simplifies the evidentiary showing needed to obtain a FISA court order to target non-U.S. persons who engage in international terrorism. These amendments had been scheduled to expire on May 27, 2011. However, on the day before they were set to expire, the three provisions were extended for approximately four years, until June 1, 2015. On July 10, 2008, P.L.110-261, the FISA Amendments Act of 2008, was signed into law. Although many of the changes enacted by the FISA Amendments Act were controversial, one particularly contentious issue was whether to grant retroactive immunity to telecommunications providers that may have facilitated warrantless surveillance by the federal government under a Terrorist Surveillance Program between 2001 and 2007.[47]

FOREIGN LANGUAGE PROGRAM (FLP) In the National DNI University that focuses on long-term investment to enhance and sustain foreign language capabilities within the IC.[48]

FOREIGN MILITARY INTELLIGENCE COLLECTION ACTIVITIES (FORMICA) Entails the overt debriefing, by trained human intelligence personnel, of all U.S. persons employed by the Department of Defense who have access to information of potential national security value.[49]

FOREIGN MILITARY SALES That part of security assistance authorized by the Arms Export Control Act (AECA) and conducted using formal contracts or agreements between the United States (U.S.) government and an authorized foreign purchaser. These contracts, called Letters of Offer and Acceptance (LOAs), are signed by both the U.S. government and the purchasing government or international organization and provide for the sale of defense articles and/or defense services (to include training) from Department of Defense (DoD) stocks or through purchase under DoD-managed contracts.[50]

FOREIGN NATIONAL Any person who is not a citizen of the United States.

FOREIGN OWNERSHIP, CONTROL, OR INFLUENCE (FOCI) Whenever a foreign interest has the power, direct or indirect, whether or not exercised, and whether or not exercisable, to direct or decide matters affecting the management or operations of a company in a manner which may result in unauthorized access to classified information or may adversely affect the performance of classified contracts.[51]

FOREIGN POLICY In the United States, the plan or strategy that the president and senior policymakers define and establish to achieve national objectives and interests.[52]

FOREIGN POWER 1. A foreign government or any component thereof, whether or not recognized by the United States; 2. A faction of a foreign nation or nations, not substantially composed of U.S. persons; 3. An entity that is openly acknowledged by a foreign government or governments to be directed and controlled by such foreign government or governments; 4. A group engaged in international terrorism or activities in preparation therefor; 5. A foreign-based political organization, not substantially composed of U.S. persons; or 6. An entity that is directed or controlled by a foreign government or government.[53]

FOREIGN SOVEREIGN IMMUNITIES ACT (FSIA) Applies to all foreign states and their "agents and instrumentalities." Immunity for sovereign nations against suits in U.S. courts has a long history and is based on the principle that conflicts with foreign nations are more effectively addressed through diplomatic efforts than through judicial proceedings. Congress passed the FSIA to codify these long-standing principles and to clarify limitations on the scope of immunity that had emerged in international practice. The FSIA contains both a general, presumptive rule against litigation in U.S. courts and a number of exceptions permitting suits. As a general rule, foreign states, together with their agents and instrumentalities, are "immune from the jurisdiction of the courts of the United States and from the states." However, the FSIA authorizes jurisdiction over foreign nations in several exceptions. Namely, a foreign state is not immune from U.S. courts' jurisdiction where (1) the foreign state has waived its immunity; (2) the claim is a specific type of admiralty claim; (3) the claim involves commercial activities; (4) the claim implicates property rights connected with the United States; (5) the claim arises from tortious conduct that occurred in the United States; the claim is made pursuant to an arbitration agreement; or the claim seeks money damages against a designated state sponsor of terrorism for injuries arising from a terrorist act.[54]

FOREIGN TERRORIST ORGANIZATIONS (FTOs) Designated by the Secretary of State in accordance with section 219 of the Immigration and Nationality Act (INA). FTO designations play a critical role in the fight against terrorism and are an effective means of curtailing support for terrorist activities. Legal Criteria for Designation under Section 219 of the INA as amended: 1. It must be a foreign organization. 2. The organization must engage in terrorist activity, as defined in section 212 (a)(3)(B) of the INA (8 U.S.C. § 1182(a)(3)(B)), or terrorism, as defined in section 140(d)(2) of the Foreign Relations Authorization Act, Fiscal Years 1988 and 1989 (22 U.S.C. § 2656f(d)(2)), or retain the capability and intent to engage in terrorist activity or terrorism. 3. The organization's terrorist activity or terrorism must threaten the security of U.S. nationals or the national security (national defense, foreign relations, or the economic interests) of the United States.[55]

FOREIGN TERRORIST TRACKING TASK FORCE (FTTTF) Created October 29, 2001, to (1) deny entry into the United States of aliens associated with, suspected of being engaged in, or supporting terrorist activity; and (2) locate, detain, prosecute, or deport any such aliens already present in the United States. The task force is staffed by personnel from the Department of State, INS, FBI, Secret Service, Customs Service, intelligence community, military support components, and personnel of other federal agencies.[56]

FORENSIC SPECIALIST A professional who locates, identifies, collects, examines, and analyzes data while preserving the integrity and maintaining a strict chain of custody of information discovered.

FORENSIC-ENABLED INTELLIGENCE The intelligence resulting from the integration of scientifically examined materials and other information to establish full characterization, attribution, and the linkage of events, locations, items, signatures, nefarious intent, and persons of interest.[57]

FORMAL ACCESS APPROVAL Process for authorizing access to classified or sensitive information with specified access requirements, such as Sensitive Compartmented Information (SCI), or Privacy Data, based on the specified access requirements and a determination of the individual's security eligibility and need-to-know.[58]

FORMERLY RESTRICTED DATA (FRD) Formerly Restricted Data (FRD) is a separate category of information (defined under 10 CFR 1045) concerning the military utilization of atomic weapons as jointly determined by DoE and the Department of Defense (DoD). FRD includes broad categories related to military utilization, including storage locations, military planning information, stockpile numbers, negotiations with foreign nations concerning nuclear weapons, and testing information. Unlike information classified by Executive Order 13526, "Classified National Security Information," (the Order) or its predecessor orders, RD and FRD information remains classified indefinitely with no distinction between sensitive, current information and innocuous, historical information.[59]

FORWARD OBSERVER 1. An observer in a position to call for and adjust supporting fire and pass battlefield information. 2. Any person responsible for monitoring an area for future activity.

FOUND SHIPMENT 1. Freight received but not listed or manifested. 2. Any discovery of material or people that was not originally intended to be found.

FREE FLOW OF INFORMATION A means in which open government allows the press, interested individuals, and others to see and hear what is going on in government and take the initiative to publicize, comment on, and influence governmental activities.[60]

FREE ROCKET Any ballistic missile not subject to guidance or control in flight.

FREEDOM OF INFORMATION ACT (FOIA) Legislation enacted in 1966 (with subsequent amendments) that requires federal government agencies to release information requested by a person who submits a formal request. However, some categories of information are exempt from disclosure. One impetus for such legislation occurred in 1953, when Congressman John Moss requested information from the Civil Service Commission to verify its claim that 2,800 federal employees had been fired due to "security reasons." The Civil Service Commission refused to comply, and Moss learned he had no legal recourse to force the commission to disclose the information. Moss convened the Special Government Information Subcommittee in 1955, "tasked with monitoring executive secrecy." The committee's investigations led to greater understanding of security classification in the executive branch, how secrecy impairs not only the political participation of Congress but also damages citizen participation. In seeking a model for FOIA, Moss looked for guidance on information rights from the U.S. Constitution, English common law, statutory law, and federal case law.[61] *See* FREEDOM OF INFORMATION EXEMPTIONS

FREEDOM OF INFORMATION ACT (FOIA) ADVISORY COMMITTEE One flagship initiative (of the second Open Government National Action Plan or NAP on December 5, 2013) includes various efforts to modernize the Freedom of Information Act (FOIA), including creating a FOIA Federal Advisory Committee to be "comprised of government and non-governmental members of the FOIA community, to foster dialog between the Administration and the requester community, solicit public comments, and develop consensus recommendations for improving FOIA administration and proactive disclosures." The Committee is established in accordance with the NAP and the directive in the Freedom of Information Act, 5 U.S.C. § 552(h)(1)(C), that the Office of Government Information Services (OGIS) "recommend policy changes . . . to improve" the Freedom of Information Act (FOIA) administration. The Committee is governed by the provisions of the Federal Advisory Committee Act, as amended, 5 U.S.C. App.[62]

FREEDOM OF INFORMATION EXEMPTIONS The Freedom of Information Act lists nine categories of information that are exempt from disclosure: documents classified for national security reasons, internal personnel rules and practices, documents exempted by statute, trade secrets, inter- and intra-agency materials (executive privilege), personnel and medical records, records compiled for law enforcement purposes, information used in regulating financial institutions (bank examination reports), and geological information about oil wells and water resources.[63]

FREQUENCY Number of occurrences of an event per defined period of time or number of trials.[64]

FREQUENTIST PROBABILITY Interpretation or estimate of probability as the long-run frequency of the occurrence of an event as estimated by historical observation or experimental trials.[65]

FRIEND In relation to national security, a country, individual, or organization with which one is allied in a struggle or cause.

FRONT An organization that serves to provide a disguised identification for an intelligence operation or project. *See* COMMERCIAL COVER

FULL SPECTRUM CYBER OPERATIONS The employment of the full range of cyberspace operations to support combatant command operational requirements and the defense of DoD information networks. This includes efforts such as computer network defense, computer network attack, and computer network exploitation.[66]

FUNCTIONAL DAMAGE ASSESSMENT The estimate of the effect of force to degrade or destroy the functional or operational capability of equipment, infrastructures, and associated Information Systems (IS), and/or supporting applications to perform its intended mission and on the level of success in achieving operational objectives.[67]

FUNCTIONAL DEFEAT Denial, disruption, or destruction of a facility's ability to accomplish its intended mission for a desired period. *See* DEFEAT ASSESSMENT; PHYSICAL DEFEAT

FUNCTIONAL MANAGEMENT 1. An organizational designation indicating the responsibility to develop and implement guidance and policies, set tradecraft and procedural standards, and oversee coordination of activities related to a specific intelligence discipline or set of intelligence activities.[68] 2. A management approach in which an organization, usually a defense agency, oversees and coordinates defense-wide activities in an assigned intelligence area or discipline.[69]

FUNCTIONAL MANAGER A designated officer reporting to the director of national intelligence with the responsibility of developing and implementing strategic guidance, policies, and procedures for activities related to a specific intelligence discipline or set of intelligence activities; setting training and tradecraft standards; and ensuring coordination within and across intelligence disciplines and intelligence community elements and with related non-intelligence activities. Functional managers may also advise the director on: the management of resources; policies and procedures; collection capabilities and gaps; processing and dissemination of intelligence; technical architectures; and other issues or activities determined by the director. Designated functional managers are the director of the National Security Agency (NSA), for signal intelligence; the director of the Central Intelligence Agency (CIA), for human intelligence; and the director of the National Geospatial-Intelligence Agency (NGA), for geospatial intelligence.[70]

FUNDAMENTALISM A movement or point of view characterized by adherence to fundamental or basic principles. Radical Islamic movements are frequently referred to in the West as fundamentalist, but in fact the use of this term is an intellectual error. In a purely scriptural sense all Muslims are fundamentalists, since all believing Muslims, whether Sunni or Shi'a, hold that the Qur'an is the literally revealed word of God. Therefore, the word *fundamentalist* does not represent a useful distinction in discussing Islam.[71]

FUSION In intelligence usage, the process of managing information to conduct all-source analysis and derive a complete assessment of activity.[72]

FUSION CENTERS Considered an effective and efficient mechanism to exchange information and intelligence, maximize resources, streamline operations, and improve the ability to fight crime and terrorism by merging data from a variety of sources. In addition, fusion centers are a conduit for implementing portions of the National Criminal Intelligence Sharing Plan (NCISP).[73] *See* NATIONAL CRIMINAL INTELLIGENCE SHARING PLAN (NCISP)

FUTURE CHALLENGES RISK The Department's (DOD) capacity to execute future missions successfully, and to hedge against shocks. Here most consideration is given to the Department's ability to field superior capabilities and sufficient capacity to deter/defeat emerging threats in the midterm and long term.[74]

NOTES

1. Jan Goldman, *Intelligence Warning Terminology*, Joint Military Intelligence College, October 2001, accessed July 3, 2015. https://archive.org/details/JMICInteligencelwarnterminology.

2. Peter Biles, "Falklands invasion 'surprised' Thatcher," *BBC News*, December 28, 2012, accessed February 3, 2016, http://www.bbc.com/news/uk-20800447.

3. Defense Intelligence Agency, Office of Counterintelligence. *CI Glossary—Terms & Definitions of Interest for DoD CI Professionals.* July 2014. Accessed July 3, 2015. https://www.hsdl.org/?view&did=699056; also see Daniele Ganser's *Secret Warfare: Operation Gladio and NATO's Stay-Behind Armies* (Hoboken, NJ: Routledge, 2004); the infamous *Justification for U.S. Military Intervention in Cuba* (OPERATION Northwoods, March 13, 1962). Accessed July 3, 2015. http://nsarchive. gwu.edu/news/20010430/; Geraint Hughes, *The Military's Role in Counterterrorism: Examples and Implications for Liberal Democracies.* Strategic Studies Institute, 2011. Accessed July 3, 2015. http://www.strategicstudiesinstitute.army.mil/pdffiles/ PUB1066.pdf.

4. Helmer, Olaf. *Systematic Use of Expert Opinions.* RAND, November 1967. Accessed July 3, 2015. http://www.rand.org/content/dam/rand/pubs/papers/2006/P3721.pdf.

5. Jae-yun, Shim. "Seoul Banks Ask Gov't to Repay Russian Debts." *Korea Times*, December 20, 2000, B1.

6. National Security Archive. *Family Jewels: Then and Now.* October 25, 2013. Accessed July 3, 2015. https://nsarchive.wordpress.com/2013/10/25/the-family-jewels-then-and-now/.

7. DARPA. *Fast Lightweight Autonomy (FLA).* Defense Science Office. Accessed February 11, 2015. http://www.defenseinnovationmarketplace.mil/resources/OTI_TechnicalAssessment-AutonomyPublicRelease_vF.pdf.

8. Department of Homeland Security, Risk Steering Committee. *DHS Risk Lexicon.* September 2010. Accessed February 14, 2015. http://www.dhs.gov/dhs-risk-lexicon.

9. Defense Forensics and Biometrics Agency. *DoD Biometrics Enterprise Architecture (Integrated) v2.0 Common Biometric Vocabulary.* April 2013. Accessed February 25, 2015. http://www.biometrics.dod.mil/Files/Documents/References/common%20biometric%20vocabulary.pdf.

10. Office of the Director of National Intelligence. *National Intelligence: A Consumer's Guide.* 2009. Accessed July 3, 2015. http://www.dni.gov/files/documents/IC_Consumers_Guide_2009.pdf.

11. U.S. General Services Administration. *Federal Advisory Committee Act (FACA) Management Overview: Background.* Accessed February 11, 2015. http://www.gsa.gov/portal/category/21242.

12. Ahmed, Nafeez. *How the CIA Made Google: Inside the Secret Network Behind Mass Surveillance, Endless War, and Skynet, Part 1.* Accessed February 11, 2015. https://medium.com/@NafeezAhmed/how-the-cia-made-google-e836451a959e; also see Highlands Group. *Overview.* Accessed February 11, 2015. http://www.highlandsgroup.net/about.php?ID=1.

13. 42 *U.S.C.* § 2000ee–3, "Federal Agency Data Mining Reporting" (Current through Pub. L. 113-234). Accessed January 15, 2015. http://www.law.cornell.edu/uscode/text/42/2000ee-3. Also see Sledge, Matt. "CIA Does Not Submit Congressionally Mandated Data Mining Report." *The Huffington Post*, April 8, 2013. Accessed January 15, 2015. http://www.huffingtonpost.com/2013/04/08/cia-data-mining_n_3039461.html.

14. U.S. Department of Defense. Center for Development of Security Excellence. *Glossary of Security Terms and Definitions.* November 2012. Accessed February 16, 2015. http://www.cdse.edu/documents/cdse/Glossary_Handbook.pdf.

15. Undersecretary of Defense. 2015. *Directive-type Memorandum (DTM) 14-005—DoD Identity Management Capability Enterprise Services Application (IMESA) Access to FBI National Crime Information Center (NCIC) Files.* May 13. Accessed January 26, 2016, http://www.dtic.mil/whs/directives/corres/pdf/DTM14005_2014.pdf.

16. U.S. General Services Administration. *About FedRAMP.* Accessed February 15, 2015. http://www.gsa.gov/portal/category/102375.

17. Office of the Director of National Intelligence. *Executive Branch Intelligence Customer.* Intelligence Community Directive 404, July 22, 2013. Accessed February 27, 2015. http://www.dni.gov/files/documents/ICD/ICD%20404%20-%20Executive%20Branch%20Intelligence%20Customers.pdf.

18. Office of the Director of National Intelligence. *Executive Branch Intelligence Customer.* Intelligence Community Directive 404, July 22, 2013. Accessed February 27, 2015. http://www.dni.gov/files/documents/ICD/ICD%20404%20-%20Executive%20Branch%20Intelligence%20Customers.pdf.

19. Department of the Army. Marine Corps Combat Development Command. Department of the Navy. *Operational Terms and Graphics.* FM 1-02 (FM 101-5). September 21, 2004. Accessed July 3, 2015. http://www.udel.edu/armyrotc/current_cadets/cadet_resources/manuals_regulations_files/FM%201-02%20-%20Operational%20Terms%20&%20Graphics.pdf.

20. Kahn, David. *The Code-Breakers: The Comprehensive History of Secret Communications from Ancient Times to the Internet.* New York: Scribner, 1996, 508–9.

21. Gallagher, Ryan and Greenwald, Glenn. "Canada Casts Global Surveillance Dragnet Over File Downloads" (CSE "LEVITATION and the FFU Hypothesis" memo). *The//INTERCEPT*, January 28, 2015. Accessed February 9, 2015. https://firstlook.org/theintercept/2015/01/28/canada-cse-levitation-mass-surveillance/.

22. U.S. Department of Defense. *Counterintelligence.* DoD Directive Number 5240.02, March 17, 2015. Accessed April 4, 20105. http://www.dtic.mil/whs/directives/corres/pdf/524002p.pdf.

23. Federal Bureau of Investigation. *Focus on FIGS.* Accessed January 27, 2015. http://www.fbi.gov/news/stories/2005/april/figs_042705.

24. Department of State, Memorandum Prepared in the Central Intelligence Agency, January 19, 1961 (planning an invasion of Cuba). *Foreign Relations of the United States*, 1961–1963, vol. 10, Cuba, 1961–1962. Accessed July 3, 2015. https://history.state.gov/historicaldocuments/kennedy.

25. "Federal Records, General," 36 CFR 1220. Accessed July 3, 2015. http://www.ecfr.gov.

26. Executive Order 12958 *Classified National Security Information, Amended*, and Executive Order 13292, *Further Amendment to Executive Order 12958, as Amended, Classified National Security Information.* Accessed July 3, 2015. http://www.archives.gov/federal-register/executive-orders/disposition.html.

27. U.S. Department of the Treasury. *FINCEN.* Accessed February 15, 2015. http://www.fincen.gov/.

28. Carter, David L. *Law Enforcement Intelligence: A Guide for State, Local, and Tribal Law Enforcement Agencies.* U.S. Dept. of Justice, Office of Community Oriented Policing Services, 2004.

29. Undersecretary of Defense. 2015. *Directive-type Memorandum (DTM) 14-005—DoD Identity Management Capability Enterprise Services Application (IMESA) Access to FBI National Crime Information Center (NCIC) Files.* May 13. Accessed June 6, 2015. Accessed January 26, 2016, http://www.dtic.mil/whs/directives/corres/pdf/DTM14005_2014.pdf.

30. Defense Intelligence Agency. *Defense Intelligence Report: Lexicon of Hardened Structure Definitions and Terms.* Washington, DC: 2000.

31. Carter, David L. *Law Enforcement Intelligence: A Guide for State, Local, and Tribal Law Enforcement Agencies.* U.S. Dept. of Justice, Office of Community Oriented Policing Services, 2004; Department of Homeland Security. *Safeguarding Sensitive but Unclassified (For Official Use Only) Information.* Management Directive 11042, May 11, 2004. Accessed July 3, 2015. http://www.fas.org/sgp/othergov/dhs-sbu.html.

32. U.S. Department of Defense. *Quadrennial Defense Review Report.* February 2010. Accessed February 11, 2015. http://www.defense.gov/qdr/qdr%20as%20of%2029jan10%201600.pdf.

33. Joint Military Intelligence College. *Intelligence Warning Terminology.* October 2001. Accessed July 3, 2015. https://archive.org/details/JMICInteligencelwarnterminology.

34. U.S. Department of Defense. Center for Development of Security Excellence. *Glossary of Security Terms and Definitions.* November 2012. Accessed February 16, 2015. http://www.cdse.edu/documents/cdse/Glossary_Handbook.pdf.

35. U.S. Department of State. *Diplomatic Dictionary.* Accessed March 6, 2015. http://diplomacy.state.gov/discoverdiplomacy/references/169792.htm.

36. U.S. Department of Justice, *Foreign Agents Registration Act*, accessed February 3, 2016, http://www.fara.gov/.

37. Air Force Research Laboratory. *Urban Sunrise.* AFRL-IF-RS-TR-2004-2, February 2004. Accessed July 3, 2015. http://fas.org/man/eprint/urban.pdf.

38. Office of the Director of National Intelligence. *National Intelligence Program FY 2009 Congressional Budget Justification Book.* Vol. XII, February 2008. Accessed January 17, 2015. http://www.fas.org/irp/dni/cbjb-2009.pdf.

39. U.S. Department of Defense. Center for Development of Security Excellence. *Glossary of Security Terms and Definitions.* November 2012. Accessed February 17, 2015. http://www.cdse.edu/documents/cdse/Glossary_Handbook.pdf.

40. Office of the Director of National Intelligence. *Glossary of Security Terms, Definitions, and Acronyms.* Intelligence Community Standard (ICS) 700-1. April 4, 2008. Accessed June 5, 2015. https://fas.org/irp/dni/icd/ics-700-1.pdf.

41. Office of the Press Secretary. *White House Conference Call Briefing: Executive Order 12958.* March 23, 2003. http://www.fas.org/sgp/news/2003/03/wh032503.html.

42. U.S. Department of Defense. Center for Development of Security Excellence. *Glossary of Security Terms and Definitions.* November 2012. Accessed February 17, 2015. http://www.cdse.edu/documents/cdse/Glossary_Handbook.pdf.

43. U.S. Department of Defense. *Department of Defense Dictionary of Military and Associated Terms.* JP 1-02, 08 November 2010, as Amended through 15 January 2016. Accessed January 26, 2016, http://www.dtic.mil/doctrine/new_pubs/jp1_02.pdf.

44. U.S. Department of Defense. *Counterintelligence Awareness and Reporting (CIAR).* Directive (DoDD) 5240.06. May 17, 2011. Accessed February 17, 2015. http://www.dtic.mil/whs/directives/corres/pdf/524006p.pdf.

45. U.S. Department of Defense. *Counterintelligence Awareness and Reporting (CIAR).* Directive (DoDD) 5240.06. May 17, 2011. Accessed February 17, 2015. http://www.dtic.mil/whs/directives/corres/pdf/524006p.pdf.

46. National Security Act of 1947, as amended, 50 U.S.C. chap. 15, 401(a), Accessed July 3, 2015. http://uscode.house.gov/; Executive Order 12333 *United States Intelligence Activities.* Accessed July 3, 2015, and USA PATRIOT Act, P.L.107-56. Accessed July 3, 2015. http://www.gpo.gov/fdsys/pkg/PLAW-107publ56/content-detail.html.

47. Liu, Edward C. "Amendments to the Foreign Intelligence Surveillance Act (FISA) Extended Until June 1, 2015." *CRS Report for Congress* R40138. June 16, 2011. Accessed February 18, 2015. https://www.fas.org/sgp/crs/intel/R40138.pdf; Liu, Edward C. "Retroactive Immunity Provided by the FISA Amendments Act of 2008." *CRS Report for Congress* RL34600. July 25, 2008. Accessed February 18, 2015. https://www.fas.org/sgp/crs/intel/RL34600.pdf.

48. Office of the Director of National Intelligence. *National Intelligence Program FY 2009 Congressional Budget Justification Book.* Vol. XII, February 2008. Accessed January 17, 2015. http://www.fas.org/irp/dni/cbjb-2009.pdf.

49. U.S. Department of Defense. *Department of Defense Dictionary of Military and Associated Terms.* JP 1-02, 08 November 2010, as Amended through 15 January 2016. Accessed January 26, 2016, http://www.dtic.mil/doctrine/new_pubs/jp1_02.pdf.

50. U.S. Department of Defense. Center for Development of Security Excellence. *Glossary of Security Terms and Definitions.* November 2012. Accessed February 16, 2015. http://www.cdse.edu/documents/cdse/Glossary_Handbook.pdf.

51. U.S. Department of Defense. Center for Development of Security Excellence. *Glossary of Security Terms and Definitions.* November 2012. Accessed February 16, 2015. http://www.cdse.edu/documents/cdse/Glossary_Handbook.pdf.

52. Office of Government Information Services. *FOIA Advisory Committee.* Accessed February 8, 2015. https://ogis.archives.gov/foia-advisory-committee.htm.

53. U.S. Department of State. *Diplomatic Dictionary.* Accessed March 6, 2015. http://diplomacy.state.gov/discoverdiplomacy/references/169792.htm.

54. U.S. Department of Justice. *The Attorney General's Guidelines for Domestic FBI Operations.* 2008. Accessed February 25, 2015. http://www.justice.gov/sites/default/files/ag/legacy/2008/10/03/guidelines.pdf.

55. U.S. State Department. Foreign Terrorist Organizations. Office of the Coordinator for Counterterrorism. *Foreign Terrorist Organizations.* Country Reports on Terrorism, 2012. May 2013. Accessed February 9, 2015. http://www.state.gov/j/ct/rls/crt/2012/209989.htm.

56. Elsea, Jennifer K. "In Re Terrorist Attacks on September 11, 2001: Claims against Saudi Defendants Under the Foreign Sovereign Immunities Act (FSIA)." *CRS Report for Congress* R42547, January 22, 2015. Accessed March 21, 2015. http://fas.org/sgp/crs/misc/RL34726.pdf. Also see the Foreign Sovereign Immunities Act of 1976, P.L. 94-583, 28 U.S.C. §1602 et seq.

57. U.S. Department of Defense. *Joint Intelligence.* JP 2-0. October 22, 2013. Accessed February 15, 2015. http://www.dtic.mil/doctrine/new_pubs/jp2_0.pdf.

58. Committee for National Security Systems (CNSS). Instruction 4009. *National Information Assurance Glossary.* April 2010. Accessed July 3, 2015. http://jitc.fhu.disa.mil/pki/documents/committee_on_national_security_systems_instructions_4009_june_2006.pdf.

59. Public Interest Declassification Board. *A Half Life for Historical Formerly Restricted Data (FRD).* April 19, 2011. Accessed July 3, 2015. http://transforming-classification.blogs.archives.gov/2011/04/19/a-half-life-for-historical-formerly-restricted-data-frd/.

60. Advisory Commission on Intergovernmental Relations. *Citizen Participation in the American Federal System.* Washington, DC: Advisory Commission on Intergovernmental Relations, 1979. Accessed July 3, 2015. http://www.library.unt.edu/gpo/acir/Reports/brief/B-3.pdf.

61. Senate Committee on Governmental Affairs, *Report of the Commission on Protecting and Reducing Government Secrecy.* Hearing before the Committee on Governmental Affairs, 105-1st, May 7, 1997. July 3, 2015. https://www.fas.org/sgp/library/moynihan/; Paul E. Kostyu, "Nothing More, Nothing Less: Case Law Leading to the Freedom of Information Act," *American Journalism* 12, no. 4 (1995): 464–76; Herbert N. Foerstel, *Freedom of Information and the Right to Know: The Origins and Applications of the Freedom of Information Act* (Westport, CT: Greenwood, 1999) and the John Moss Foundation. Accessed July 3, 2015. http://www.johnemossfoundation.org.

62. Office of Government Information Services. *FOIA Advisory Committee.* Accessed February 8, 2015. https://ogis.archives.gov/foia-advisory-committee.htm.

63. U.S. Department of Justice. *The United States Department of Justice Guide to the Freedom of Information Act.* 2009 Accessed July 3, 2015. http://www.justice.gov/oip/doj-guide-freedom-information-act.

64. Department of Homeland Security, Risk Steering Committee. *DHS Risk Lexicon.* September 2010. Accessed February 14, 2015. http://www.dhs.gov/dhs-risk-lexicon.

65. Department of Homeland Security, Risk Steering Committee. *DHS Risk Lexicon.* September 2010. Accessed February 14, 2015. http://www.dhs.gov/dhs-risk-lexicon.

66. U.S. General Accountability Office. *Defense Department Cyber Efforts: Definitions, Focal Point, and Methodology Needed for DOD to Develop Full-Spectrum Cyberspace Budget Estimates.* GAO-11-695R. July 29, 2011. January 15, 2015. http://www.gao.gov/products/GAO-11-695R.

67. U.S. Department of Defense. Center for Development of Security Excellence. *Glossary of Security Terms and Definitions.* November 2012. Accessed February 16, 2015. http://www.cdse.edu/documents/cdse/Glossary_Handbook.pdf.

68. White House, United States Intelligence Activities, December 4, 1981, National Archives. Accessed on July 5, 2015, http://www.archives.gov/federal-register/codification/executive-order/12333.html.

69. Elkins, Dan. *Managing Intelligence Resources.* 2nd ed. Alexandria, VA: DWE Press, 2006.

70. White House, United States Intelligence Activities, December 4, 1981, National Archives. Accessed on July 5, 2015, at http://www.archives.gov/federal-register/codification/executive-order/12333.html.

71. Chairman of the Joint Chiefs of Staff. *National Military Strategic Plan for the War on Terrorism.* February 1, 2006. Accessed February 26, 2015. http://www.bits.de/NRANEU/others/strategy/National-Strategic-Plan-War_on_Terrorism-06.pdf

72. U.S. Department of Defense, *Joint Intelligence*, JP2-0, October 22, 2013, accessed February 2, 2016, http://www.dtic.mil/doctrine/new_pubs/jp2_0.pdf.

73. U.S. Department of Justice. *Fusion Centers and Intelligence Sharing.* Accessed January 16, 2015. https://it.ojp.gov/default.aspx?area=nationalInitiatives&page=1181.

74. U.S. Department of Defense. *Quadrennial Defense Review Report.* February, 2010. Accessed February 11, 2015. http://www.defense.gov/qdr/qdr%20as%20of%2029jan10%201600.pdf.

G

GAME-CHANGING TECHNOLOGY Technology or a collection of technologies applied to a relevant problem in a manner that radically alters the symmetry of military power between competitors. The use of this technology immediately outdates the policies, doctrines and organizations of all actors. This definition is notable for two main reasons. First, it reinforces the point that game-changing technology is disruptive, representing a discontinuous shift from the prevailing paradigm. Second, it stresses that technology itself is merely one, albeit vital, component of a game-changing technology. A scientific breakthrough or a new manufacturing method, power source, weapons system or platform provides potential; a variety of other factors determine that technology's game-changing value.[1]

GAME THEORY Branch of applied mathematics that models interactions among agents where an agent's choice and subsequent success depend on the choices of other agents that are simultaneously acting to maximize their own results or minimize their losses.[2]

GAMMA (G) Unclassified term used to describe a type of sensitive compartmentalized information (SCI).[3]

GANG OF FOUR Intelligence notifications generally are oral briefings of certain particularly sensitive non-covert action intelligence activities, including principally, but not exclusively, intelligence collection programs, that the intelligence community typically limits to the chairmen and ranking members of the two congressional intelligence committees. Gang of Four notifications are not based in statute but have constituted a practice generally accepted by the leadership of the intelligence committees and that is employed when the intelligence community believes a particular intelligence activity to be of such sensitivity that a restricted notification is warranted in order to reduce the risk of disclosure, inadvertent or otherwise. Intelligence activities viewed as being less sensitive typically are briefed to the full membership of each committee.[4]

GANG OF EIGHT Under current statute, the president generally is required keep the congressional intelligence committees fully and currently informed of all covert actions (National Security Act as amended, §503 [50 U.S.C. 413b] (b) and (c).) and that any covert action "finding" shall be reported to the committees as soon as possible after such approval and before the initiation of the covert action authorized by the finding. If, however, the president determines that it is essential to limit access to a covert action finding in order to "meet extraordinary circumstances affecting vital interests of the United States," then, rather than providing advanced notification to the full congressional intelligence committees, as is generally required, the president may limit such notification to the "Gang of Eight" (National Security Act of 1947 as amended, §503 [50 U.S.C. 413b] (c) (2)) and any other congressional leaders he may choose to inform. The statute defines the "Gang of Eight" as being comprised of the chairmen and ranking members of the two congressional intelligence committees and the House and Senate majority and minority leadership.[5]

GAP ANALYSIS An evaluation of differences between an organization's situation or position and its desired future using specific strategies and allocation of capabilities to close the gap.

GENERAL DEFENSE INTELLIGENCE PROGRAM (GDIP) An integrated capability, and the director, DIA, serves as the program manager. The GDIP is part of the NIP, as defined in E.O. 12333. The GDIP is an integrated Defense Intelligence capability that includes DIA, the service technical production centers, and special collection activities. The GDIP integrates and produces National Intelligence for Defense and national consumers. It represents the national Defense Intelligence priorities for operational customers, national and Defense-wide collection management, All-Source Analysis, HUMINT, MASINT, IT, and Special Activities. The GDIP may include other NIP activities as agreed between the Secretary of Defense and the DNI.[6]

GENERAL MILITARY INTELLIGENCE (GMI) Intelligence concerning the military capabilities of foreign countries or organizations, or topics affecting potential U.S. or multinational military operations.[7]

GENERIC INDICATOR DIRECTORY (GID) Any source document that contains a listing of a general set of indicators from which to choose in developing a specific indicator list for a given warning problem or concern.[8]

GEOGRAPHIC ANALYSIS A look at the locations of criminal activity or criminals to determine whether future criminal activity can be deterred or interdicted through forecasting activity based on historical raw data.

GEOSPATIAL INFORMATION AND SERVICES The collection, information extraction, storage, dissemination, and exploitation of geodetic, geomagnetic, imagery, gravimetric, aeronautical, topographic, hydrographic, littoral, cultural, and toponymic data accurately referenced to a precise location on the Earth's surface.[9]

GEOSPATIAL INTELLIGENCE (GEOINT) The exploitation and analysis of imagery and geospatial information to describe, assess, and visually depict physical features and geographically referenced activities on the Earth. Geospatial intelligence consists of imagery, imagery intelligence, and geospatial information.[10]

GHOST DETAINEES The various detention facilities operated by the 800th MP Brigade have routinely held persons brought to them by Other Government Agencies (OGAs) without accounting for them, knowing their identities, or even the reason for their detention. The Joint Interrogation and Debriefing Center (JIDC) at Abu Ghraib called these detainees "ghost detainees." On at least one occasion, the 320th MP Battalion at Abu Ghraib held a handful of "ghost detainees" (6–8) for OGAs that they moved around within the facility to hide them from a visiting International Committee of the Red Cross (ICRC) survey team. This maneuver was deceptive, contrary to army doctrine, and in violation of international law.[11]

GHOST PLANE CIA planes (e.g., Gulfstream V and Boeing Business Jet operating from North Carolina) used in rendering.[12] *See* EXTRAORDINARY RENDITION; RENDITION

GHOSTSEC Our mission is to eliminate the online presence of Islamic extremist groups such as Islamic State (IS), Al-Qaeda, Al-Nusra, Boko Haram and Al-Shabaab in an effort to stymie their recruitment and limit their ability to organize international terrorist efforts. This site provides a means for people to report known Islamic extremist content including websites, blogs, videos and social media accounts. Once verified by our Intel team, our operations teams set to work on removing the content. Removing content involves both official channels, reporting the content to the site hosts and requesting it be removed, and the employment of digital weapons to forcibly remove content where official channels fail.[13]

GIG SECTOR (GLOBAL INFORMATION GRID DEFENSE) The globally interconnected, end-to-end set of information capabilities, associated processes, and personnel for collecting, processing, storing, disseminating, and managing information on demand to warfighters, policymakers, and support personnel. It includes all owned and leased communications (commercial telecommunication infrastructure) and computing systems and services, software (including applications), data, security services and other associated services necessary to achieve information superiority. It also includes National Security Systems as defined in section 11103 of title 40, U.S.C.[14]

GLOBAL COMMONS Areas of air, sea, space and cyberspace that belong to no one state. Access to the global commons is vital to U.S. national interests, both as an end in itself and as a means to projecting military force into hostile territory.[15]

GLOBAL INFORMATION AND EARLY WARNING SYSTEM ON FOOD AND AGRICULTURE To keep the world food supply/demand situation under continuous review, we issue reports on the world food situation and provide early warnings of impending food crises in individual countries. For countries facing a serious food emergency, FAO/GIEWS and the World Food Programme also carry out joint Crop and Food Security Assessment Missions (CFSAMs). Their purpose is to provide timely and reliable information so that appropriate actions can be taken by the governments, the international community, and other parties.[16]

GLOBAL INFORMATION ENVIRONMENT All individuals, organizations, or systems, most of which are outside the control of the military or national command authorities, that collect, process, and disseminate information to national and international audiences.[17]

GLOBAL INFORMATION GRID The globally interconnected, end-to-end set of information capabilities, associated processes for collecting, processing, storing, disseminating, and managing information on demand to warfighters, policymakers, and support personnel. The Global Information Grid includes owned and leased communications and computing systems and services, software (including applications), data, security services, other associated services and National Security Systems.[18] *See* DEPARTMENT OF DEFENSE METADATA REGISTRY

GLOBAL INFORMATION INFRASTRUCTURE (GII) Worldwide interconnections of the information systems of all countries, international and multinational organizations, and international commercial communications.[19]

GLOBAL INITIATIVE TO COMBAT NUCLEAR TERRORISM (GICNT) Participants in the Global Initiative to Combat Nuclear Terrorism are committed to the following Statement of Principles to develop partnership capacity to combat nuclear terrorism on a determined and systematic basis, consistent with national legal authorities and obligations they have under relevant international legal frameworks, notably the Convention for the Suppression of Acts of Nuclear Terrorism, the Convention on the Physical Protection of Nuclear Material and its 2005 Amendment, United Nations Security Council Resolutions 1373 and 1540.[20]

GLOBAL JUSTICE INFORMATION SHARING INITIATIVE The Global Justice Information Sharing Initiative (Global) serves as a Federal Advisory Committee (FAC) and advises the U.S. Attorney General on justice information sharing and integration initiatives. Global was created to support the broad-scale exchange of pertinent justice and public safety information. It promotes standards-based electronic information exchange to provide the justice community with timely, accurate, complete, and accessible information in a secure and trusted environment. To help steer and facilitate Global efforts, the U.S. Attorney General reached out to key personnel from local, state, tribal, federal, and international justice entities to form the Global Advisory Committee (GAC). GAC's efforts have direct impact on the work of 4 million justice and public safety professionals and positions Global to impact citizens of the United States, Canada, and beyond.[21] *See* NATIONAL INFORMATION EXCHANGE MODEL

GLOBAL NAME RECOGNITION The ability to look for variations in multicultural name spellings to determine matches.[22]

GLOBAL STRUGGLE AGAINST VIOLENT EXTREMISM In recent speeches and news conferences, Defense Secretary Donald H. Rumsfeld and the nation's senior military officer have spoken of "a global struggle against violent extremism" rather than "the global war on terror," which had been the catchphrase of choice. Administration officials say that phrase may have outlived its usefulness, because it focused attention solely, and incorrectly, on the military campaign. Gen. Richard B. Myers, chairman of the Joint Chiefs of Staff, told the National Press Club on Monday that he had "objected to the use of the term 'war on terrorism' before, because if you call it a war, then you think of people in uniform as being the solution." He said the threat instead should be defined as violent extremists, with the recognition that "terror is the method they use."[23]

GLOBAL TERRORISM DATABASE An open-source database including information on terrorist events around the world from 1970 through 2013

(with additional annual updates planned for the future). Unlike many other event databases, the GTD includes systematic data on domestic as well as transnational and international terrorist incidents that have occurred during this time period and now includes more than 125,000 cases. For each GTD incident, information is available on the date and location of the incident, the weapons used and nature of the target, the number of casualties, and—when identifiable—the group or individual responsible. The National Consortium for the Study of Terrorism and Responses to Terrorism (START) makes the GTD available via this online interface in an effort to increase understanding of terrorist violence so that it can be more readily studied and defeated.[24]

GLOBALIZATION A complex process involving the worldwide diffusion of cultural products, the streamlining of international manufacturing and trade, the standardization of global financial markets, and the prevalence of new media technology capable of simultaneous real-time transmission of content everywhere in the world. Often described in terms of a "shrinking" of the planet, the reality is in fact the opposite: globalization is the result of the massive expansion of processes and enterprises that were once national or at most regional in scale and scope. Globalization is a highly contested term. First of all, there is no agreement that it actually exists; second, where there is agreement that it exists, there is considerable argument about when it began; third, where there is agreement about both its existence and its origin, there is disagreement about whether this constitutes anything new. Complicating matters is the fact that globalization is not "owned" by any single discipline and could even be said to have been simultaneously invented by several disciplines at once.[25]

GLORIFICATION OF TERRORISM At a press conference on August 5, the prime minister (*sic* Blair) outlined a series of further measures the government intended to take in response to the threat from terrorism. These included creating an offence of glorifying terrorism, in the UK or abroad; examining calls for police to be able to hold terror suspects for longer prior to charging; the proposed offence of "glorification of terrorism," which would have been punishable by up to five years' imprisonment and a fine, would have been committed by a person who published a statement or caused another to publish a statement on his behalf if the statement glorified, exalted or celebrated the commission, preparation or instigation (whether in the past, in the future or generally) of acts of terrorism and the circumstances and manner of the statement's publication (taken together with its contents) were such that it would be reasonable for members of the public to whom it was published to assume that the statement expressed the views of that person or had his endorsement. The offence of glorifying terrorism would have applied only in respect of anything occurring within 20 years of the publication of the statement to which the offence related, unless the Secretary of State had made an order specifying conduct or events which occurred outside this period.[26]

GOVERNANCE The state's ability to serve the citizens through the rules, processes, and behavior by which interests are articulated, resources are managed, and power is exercised in a society, including the representative participatory decision-making processes typically guaranteed under inclusive, constitutional authority.[27]

GOVERNMENT COMMUNICATIONS HEADQUARTERS (GCHQ) One of the three UK Intelligence and Security Agencies, along with MI5 and the Secret Intelligence Service (MI6). In February 6, 2015, judgment in response to a complaint submitted by the National Council of Civil Liberties, Privacy International, Amnesty International, and other claimants, the United Kingdom's (UK) Investigatory Powers Tribunal (IPT), which investigates infractions of the right to privacy, ruled that intelligence sharing between the United States and the UK was unlawful prior to December 2014, because the rules and policies governing the UK's participation in the NSA's PRISM and UPSTREAM programs were secret and "contravened Articles 8 or 10 ECHR" (*European Convention on Human Rights*, right to respect for private and family life, freedom of expression, respectively). The IPT relied on documents disclosed by NSA whistleblower Edward Snowden.[28]

GOVERNMENT COORDINATING COUNCIL (GCC) The government counterpart to the Sector Coordinating Council for each sector, established to enable interagency and intergovernmental coordination; comprises representatives across various levels of government (federal and SLTT) as appropriate to the risk and operational landscape of each sector.[29]

GOVERNMENT EMERGENCY TELECOMMUNICATIONS SERVICE (GETS) A national phone network that is designed to provide voice communications in an emergency or disaster. It uses standard long-distance, local, and federally leased telephone networks.

GOVERNMENT FUNCTIONS Means the collective functions of the heads of executive departments and agencies as defined by statute, regulation, presidential direction, or other legal authority, and the functions of the legislative and judicial branches.[30]

GOVERNMENT INFORMATION Information that is owned by, produced by or for, or under the control of the U.S. government.[31]

GOVERNMENT PUBLICATION The term "government publication" means information which is published as an individual document at government expense, or as required by law.[32]

GOVERNMENT TO GOVERNMENT TRANSFER (G2G) The principle that classified information and material will be transferred by government officials through official government channels (e.g., military postal service, diplomatic courier) or through other channels expressly agreed upon in writing by the governments involved. In either case, the information or material may be transferred only to a person specifically designated in writing by the foreign government as its designated government representative for that purpose.[33]

GOVERNMENT WIDE AREA NETWORK (GWAN) Also known as the National Reconnaissance Office (NRO) Management Information System (NMIS), the NRO's classified computer network.

GRADUATED SECURITY A security system that provides several levels (e.g., low, moderate, high) of protection based on threats, risks, available technology, support services, time, human concerns, and economics.[34]

GRANULARITY Considers the specific details and pieces of information, including nuances and situational inferences, that constitute the elements on which intelligence is developed through analysis.[35]

GRAY LITERATURE (GREY LITERATURE) A non-doctrinal term used by various professions. Gray literature refers to a subset of open source information usually produced by research establishments that is neither published commercially nor universally accessible. Regardless of media, gray literature can include data or primary source information, academic reports and institutional data, informal personal or draft papers, unofficial or government exchanges.[36]

GRAYMAIL (GREYMAIL) The threat by defendants and their counsel to press for the release or disclosure of sensitive (national security), classified information, or state secrets during a trial.[37]

GREEN DOOR Slang term for the metaphorical locked door behind which intelligence personnel are said to hide their codeword secrets and important information not shared with consumers who need and should get it.

GROUPTHINK A decision-making flaw that occurs when a group does not consider alternatives and desires unanimity at the expense of quality decisions. Groupthink can lead to seeking out few alternative solutions because there is an illusion of group invulnerability ("we all can't be wrong"). Some symptoms of groupthink are the absence of critical discussion of information, a sharing of stereotypes to guide decisions, a strong moral climate, and the suppression of true feelings among the participants in the group.[38]

GSA SENSITIVE BUT UNCLASSIFIED BUILDING INFORMATION (GSA-SBU-BI) Information concerning General Services Administration (GSA) Public Building Services controlled space, including owned, leased, or delegated federal facilities. GSA-SBU-BI includes building designs, such as floor plans, construction plans and specifications, renovation/alteration plans, equipment plans and locations, building operating plans, information used for building services contracts or contract guard services, or any other information considered a security risk.[39]

NOTES

1. Brimley, Shawn, FitzGerald, Ben, and Sayler, Kelley. *Game Changers: Disruptive Technology and U.S. Defense Strategy.* Disruptive Defense Papers, September 2013. Center for a New American Security. Accessed April 2, 2015. http://www.cnas.org/files/documents/publications/CNAS_Gamechangers_BrimleyFitzGeraldSayler.pdf; also see Kadtke, James and Wells II, Linton. *DTP 106: Policy Challenges of Accelerating Technological Change: Security Policy and Strategy Implications of Parallel Scientific Revolutions.* Center for Technology and National Security Policy. September 2014. Accessed April 2, 2015. http://ctnsp.dodlive.mil/2014/09/12/dtp-106-policy-challenges-of-accelerating-technological-change-security-policy-and-strategy-implications-of-parallel-scientific-revolutions/.

2. Department of Homeland Security, Risk Steering Committee. *DHS Risk Lexicon.* September 2010. Accessed February 14, 2015. http://www.dhs.gov/dhs-risk-lexicon.

3. National Imagery and Mapping Agency. *NIMA Guide to Marking Classified Documents.* October 4, 2001. Accessed January 26, 2016. http://www.fas.org/sgp/othergov/DoD/nimaguide.pdf.

4. Erwin, Marshall Curtis. "'Gang of Four' Congressional Intelligence Notifications." *CRS Report for Congress* R40698, April 16, 2013. Accessed January 17, 2015. https://www.fas.org/sgp/crs/intel/R40698.pdf.

5. Erwin, Marshall Curtis. "Sensitive Covert Action Notifications: Oversight Options for Congress." *CRS Report for Congress* R4069, April 10, 2013. Accessed January 17, 2015. http://www.fas.org/sgp/crs/intel/R40691.pdf.

6. U.S. Department of Defense. *Defense Intelligence Agency (DIA).* Directive Number 5105.21, March 18, 2008. Accessed January 15, 2015. http://www.dtic.mil/whs/directives/corres/pdf/510521p.pdf.

7. U.S. Department of Defense. *Joint Intelligence.* JP 2-0. October 22, 2013. Accessed February 15, 2015. http://www.dtic.mil/doctrine/new_pubs/jp2_0.pdf.

8. Jan Goldman, *Intelligence Warning Terminology,* Joint Military Intelligence College, October 2001, accessed July 3, 2015. https://archive.org/details/JMICIntelligencewarnterminology.

9. U.S. Department of Defense. *Department of Defense Dictionary of Military and Associated Terms.* JP 1-02, 08 November 2010, as Amended through 15 January 2016. Accessed January 26, 2016. http://www.dtic.mil/doctrine/new_pubs/jp1_02.pdf.

10. U.S. Department of Defense. Department of Defense Dictionary of Military and Associated Terms. JP 1-02, 08 November 2010, as Amended through 15 January 2015. Accessed January 26, 2016. https://web.archive.org/web/20150329113844/http://www.dtic.mil/doctrine/new_pubs/jp1_02.pdf.

11. *AR 15-6 Investigation of the 800th Military Police Brigade* (The "Taguba Report" on Treatment of Abu Ghraib Prisoners in Iraq). May 27, 2004. Accessed February 19, 2015. https://www.aclu.org/sites/default/files/torturefoia/released/TR3.pdf; also see Annex 53. Accessed February 19, 2015. https://fas.org/irp/agency/dod/taguba.pdf.

12. Grey, Stephen. *Ghost Plane: The True Story of the CIA Torture Program* (New York: St. Martin's Press, 2006).

13. GhostSec. *About.* Accessed January 26, 2016. http://www.ghostsec.org/.

14. U.S. Department of Defense. *DOD Policy and Responsibilities for Critical Infrastructure.* January 14, 2010. Accessed January 26, 2016. https://fas.org/irp/doddir/dod/d3020_40.pdf.

15. U.S. Department of Defense. *Joint Operational Access Concept (JOAC).* January 17, 2012. Version 1.0. Accessed February 19, 2015. http://www.defense.gov/Portals/1/Documents/pubs/JOAC_Jan%202012_Signed.pdf.

16. Food and Agriculture Organization of the United Nations. *About GIEWS.* Accessed January 26, 2016. http://www.fao.org/GIEWS/english/about.htm.

17. Department of the Army. *Information Operations.* FM-100-6, 1996. Accessed January 26, 2016. http://www.bits.de/NRANEU/others/amd-us-archive/fm100-6%2896%29.pdf.

18. U.S. Department of Defense. *Joint Communications System.* JP 6-0. June 10, 2010. Accessed February 14, 2015. http://www.dtic.mil/doctrine/new_pubs/jp6_0.pdf.

19. Committee for National Security Systems (CNSS). Instruction 4009. National Information Assurance Glossary, June 2006. Accessed February 3, 2016. http://www.cnss.gov/Assets/pdf/cnssi_4009.pdf.

20. U.S. Department of State. *Global Initiative to Combat Nuclear Terrorism: Principles.* Accessed February 20, 2015. http://www.state.gov/t/isn/rls/other/126995.htm.

21. U.S. Department of Justice. Office of Justice Programs. *Global Justice Information Sharing Initiative (Global).* Accessed January 22, 2015. https://it.ojp.gov/global.

22. Undersecretary of Defense. 2015. *Directive-type Memorandum (DTM) 14-005—DoD Identity Management Capability Enterprise Services Application (IMESA) Access to FBI National Crime Information Center (NCIC) Files.* May 13. Accessed June 6, 2015. http://www.dtic.mil/whs/directives/corres/pdf/DTM14005_2014.pdf.

23. Schmitt, Eric and Shanker, Thom. "U.S. Officials Retool Slogan for Terror War." *The New York Times,* July 26, 2005. Accessed March 11, 2015. http://www.nytimes.com/2005/07/26/politics/26strategy.html.

24. National Consortium for the Study of Terrorism and Responses to Terrorism. *Overview of GTD.* Accessed March 6, 2015. http://www.start.umd.edu/gtd/about.

25. Buchanan, Ian. *Dictionary of Critical Theory.* New York: Oxford University Press, 2010.

26. House of Commons Library. *The Terrorism Bill 2005-06, Bill 55 of 2005-06.* Research Paper 05/66, October 20, 2005. Accessed March 6, 2015. http://www.parliament.uk/briefing-papers/RP05-66.pdf; also see Jeffrey, Simon. "Q & A: The Glorification of Terrorism." *The Guardian,* February 15, 2006. Accessed March 6, 2015. http://www.theguardian.com/world/2006/feb/15/qanda.terrorism.

27. United States Department of Defense. *Counterinsurgency.* JP 3-24, November 22, 2013. Accessed March 7, 2015. http://www.dtic.mil/doctrine/new_pubs/jp3_24.pdf.

28. Investigatory Powers Tribunal. *Liberty & Others vs. the Security Service, SIS, GCHQ.* February 6, 2015. IPT/13/77/H. Accessed February 9, 2015. http://www.ipt-uk.com/section.aspx?pageid=8.

29. Department of Homeland Security. *National Infrastructure Protection Plan: Partnering to Enhance Protection and Resiliency.* 2009. Accessed February 15, 2015. http://www.dhs.gov/xlibrary/assets/NIPP_Plan.pdf.

30. National Security and Homeland Security Presidential Directive/NSPD-51/HSPD 20. *National Continuity Policy.* May 9, 2007. Accessed February 27, 2015. http://fas.org/irp/offdocs/nspd/nspd-51.htm.

31. 10 CFR 1045. "Energy." Accessed February 3, 2016. http://www.gpoaccess.gov/CFR/index.html.

32. U.S. Department of Defense, Center for Development of Security Excellence. *Glossary of Security Terms and Definitions.* November 2012. Accessed March 1, 2015. http://www.cdse.edu/documents/cdse/Glossary_Handbook.pdf.

33. 44 U.S. Code § 1901—"Definition of Government Publication." Accessed February 9, 2015. http://www.law.cornell.edu/uscode/text/44/1901.

34. Committee for National Security Systems (CNSS). Instruction 4009. *National Information Assurance Glossary.* April 2010. Accessed January 11, 2015. http://www.ncix.gov/publications/policy/docs/CNSSI_4009.pdf.

35. Federal Bureau of Investigation. *Minimum Criminal Intelligence Training Standards for Law Enforcement and Other Criminal Justice Agencies in the United States.* October 2007. Accessed January 22, 2015. https://it.ojp.gov/gist/108/Minimum-Criminal-Intelligence-Training-Standards.

36. U.S. Department of Defense. *Joint Intelligence*, JP2-0, October 22, 2013. Accessed February 2, 2016. http://www.dtic.mil/doctrine/new_pubs/jp2_0.pdf.

37. Louis Fisher, *In the Name of National Security: Unchecked Presidential Power and the Reynolds Case* (Lawrence: University Press of Kansas, 2006), and Larry M. Eig, "The Classified Procedures Information Act: An Overview," *CRS Report to Congress* 89-172A, March 2, 1989, accessed February 3, 2016, http://www.fas.org/sgp/crs/secrecy/89-172.pdf.

38. Janis Irving, *Victims of Groupthink* (Boston: Houghton Mifflin, 1972); Janis Irving, *Groupthink: Psychological Studies of Policy Decisions and Fiascos*, 2nd ed. (Boston: Houghton Mifflin, 1982).

39. Centers for Disease Control. *Manual Guide—Information Security CDC-02.* Office of Security and Emergency Preparedness. "Sensitive But Unclassified Information." Part B. 07/22/2005. http://www.fas.org/sgp/othergov/cDC-sbu.pdf.

H

HACKER Unauthorized user who attempts to or gains access to an information system.[1]

HANDLE VIA SPECIAL ACCESS CONTROL CHANNELS ONLY A protective marking used within Special Access Program (SAP) control channels. It is used to identify unclassified information which requires protection in Special Access channels. When Handle Via Special Access Channels Only is used to help identify classified SAP information, the material will be protected in accordance with the security requirements of the individual SAP or the highest standard where more than one SAP is included.[2]

HANDLER (CASE OFFICER) An intelligence officer or co-opted worker directly responsible for the operational activities of an agent.

HARD INDICATOR Any generalized, theoretical action, usually focusing on capabilities, that can be linked without a doubt to intentions of an aggressor. For example, the forward deployment of tanks or the sudden expansion of medical facilities or beds in a hospital would be a hard indicator that a target country is planning, without a doubt, aggressive action.[3]

HARDCOPY DOCUMENT Any document that is initially published and distributed by the originating component in paper form and that is not stored or transmitted by electrical means.

HAZARD Natural or man-made source or cause of harm or difficulty.[4]

HAZARD IDENTIFICATION AND RISK ASSESSMENT (HIRA) A DHS process to identify hazards and associated risk to persons, property, and structures.[5]

HEALTH ALERT NETWORK (HAN) Provides rapid and timely access to emergent health information and evidence-based practices and procedures for effective public health preparedness, response, and service on a 24/7 basis; provides health information and the infrastructure to support the dissemination of that information at the state and local levels covering 90 percent of the population. The HAN Messaging System directly and indirectly transmits health alerts, advisories, and updates to over 1 million recipients.

HEALTH SURVEILLANCE The regular or repeated collection, analysis, and interpretation of health-related data and the dissemination of information to monitor the health of a population and to identify potential health risks, thereby enabling timely interventions to prevent, treat, reduce, or control disease and injury, which includes occupational and environmental health surveillance and medical surveillance subcomponents.[6]

HIGH 2 INFORMATION Substantial internal matters, the disclosure of which would risk circumvention of a legal requirement; records that "are related solely to the internal personnel rules and practices of an agency."[7]

HIGH-CONTAINMENT LABORATORIES The number of biosafety level (BSL)-3 and BSL-4 laboratories (high-containment laboratories) began to rise in the late 1990s, accelerating after the anthrax attacks throughout the United States. The laboratories expanded across federal, state, academic, and private sectors. Information about their number, location, activities, and ownership is available for high-containment laboratories registered with CDC's Division of Select Agent and Toxins (DSAT) or the U.S. Department of Agriculture's (USDA) Animal and Plant Health Inspection Service (APHIS) as part of the Federal Select Agent Program. These entities register laboratories that work with select agents that have specific potential human, animal, or plant health risks. Other high-containment laboratories work with other pathogens that may also be dangerous but are not identified as "select agents" and therefore these laboratories are not required to register with DSAT or APHIS (2). No federal entity is responsible for strategic planning and oversight of high-containment laboratories; no one agency is responsible for determining the aggregate or cumulative risks associated with the continued expansion of high-containment laboratories; according to experts and federal officials GAO interviewed for prior work, the oversight of these laboratories is fragmented and largely self-policing (Summary).[8] *See* PROJECT BIOSHIELD

HIGH-IMPACT/LOW-PROBABILITY ANALYSIS An analysis of a seemingly unlikely event that would have major policy consequences if it happened. The exercise seeks to sensitize analysts to the potential impact of seemingly low-probability events that would have major repercussions.[9]

HIGH-VALUE DETAINEE INTERROGRATION GROUP (HIG) Chartered by the National Security Council, the mission of the HIG is to deploy the nation's best available interrogation resources against detainees identified as having information regarding terrorist attacks against the United States and its allies. In order to accomplish its mission, the HIG is tasked "to study and evaluate whether the interrogation practices and techniques in Army Field Manual 2-22.3, when employed by departments and agencies outside the military, provide an appropriate means of acquiring the intelligence necessary to protect the nation and, if warranted, to recommend any additional or different guidance for other departments or agencies" (Executive Order 13491). In order to support this requirement, the HIG will conduct research in intelligence interviewing and interrogations.[10]

HOLY GRAIL An unattainable object, such as a specific indication that clearly delineates the exact time and location of an adversary's attack, or a singular piece of data that fully validates all previous existing intelligence analysis or assessments. For example, although the United States had intercepted Japanese message traffic prior to the attack on Pearl Harbor, not one of the messages was the holy grail that stated the day, time, and avenues of approach of the attack.[11] *See* ACTIONABLE INTELLIGENCE

HOMEGROWN JIHADIST TERRORISTS "Homegrown" is the term that describes terrorist activity or plots perpetrated within the United States or abroad by American citizens, legal permanent residents, or visitors radicalized largely within the United States. The term "jihadist" describes radicalized individuals using Islam as an ideological and/or religious justification for their belief in the establishment of a global caliphate, or jurisdiction governed by a Muslim civil and religious leader known as a caliph. The Congressional Research Service (CRS) estimates that there have been 63 homegrown violent jihadist plots or attacks in the United States since September 11, 2001 (9/11). As part of a much discussed apparent expansion of terrorist activity in the United States, from May 2009 through December 2012, arrests were made for 42 "homegrown," jihadist-inspired terrorist plots by American citizens or legal permanent residents of the United States. Two of these resulted in attacks. Most of the 2009–2012 homegrown plots likely reflect a trend in jihadist terrorist activity away from schemes directed by core members of significant terrorist groups such as Al Qaeda.[12]

HOMELAND The physical region that includes the continental United States, Alaska, Hawaii, U.S. territories, and surrounding territorial waters and airspace.[13]

HOMELAND DEFENSE (HD) 1. The protection of U.S. territory, sovereignty, domestic population and critical infrastructure against external threats and aggression.[14] 2. The protection of U.S. sovereignty, territory, domestic population, and critical infrastructure against external threats and aggression or other threats as directed by the president.[15]

HOMELAND INFRASTRUCTURE THREAT AND RISK ANALYSIS CENTER (HITRAC) HITRAC is the Department's infrastructure-intelligence fusion center. It is not a formal part of I&A, but is jointly resourced and managed by I&A and the Office of Infrastructure Protection, an office within the DHS National Protection and Programs Directorate. HITRAC's mission is to produce and disseminate timely and meaningful threat- and risk-informed analytic products that can effectively influence the development of infrastructure protection strategies. HITRAC is organized into two divisions responsible for the Center's principal functions. The Risk Analysis Division performs infrastructure risk analysis and prioritization to support decision making. The division manages congressionally mandated and priority initiatives, including the Tier 1 and Tier 2 Program 87 and the Critical Foreign Dependencies Initiative (CFDI).[16]

HOMELAND SECURITY 1. From the *2007 National Strategy for Homeland Security* (White House): A concerted national effort to prevent terrorist attacks within the United States, reduce America's vulnerability to terrorism, and minimize the damage and recover from attacks that do occur. 2. From the *2008 U.S. Department of Homeland Security Strategic Plan, Fiscal Years 2008–2013* (DHS): A unified national effort to prevent and deter terrorist attacks, protect and respond to hazards, and to secure the national borders. 3. *2010 National Security Strategy* (White House): A seamless coordination among federal, state, and local governments to prevent, protect against and respond to threats and natural disasters. 4. From the *2010 Quadrennial Homeland Security Review* (DHS): A concerted national effort to ensure a homeland that is safe, secure, and resilient against terrorism and other hazards where American interests, aspirations, and ways of life can thrive. 5. From the *2010 Bottom-Up Review* (DHS): Preventing terrorism, responding to and recovering from natural disasters, customs enforcement and collection of customs revenue, administration of legal immigration services, safety and stewardship of the nation's waterways and marine transportation system, as well as other legacy missions of the various components of DHS. 6. From the *2011 National Strategy for Counterterrorism* (White House): Defensive efforts to counter terrorist threats. 7. From the 2012 Strategic Plan (DHS): Efforts to ensure a homeland that is safe, secure, and resilient against terrorism and other hazards. 8. A concerted national effort to prevent terrorist attacks within the United States; reduce America's vulnerability to terrorism, major disasters, and other emergencies; and minimize the damage and recover from attacks, major disasters, and other emergencies that occur.[17] 9. There is no statutory definition of homeland security that reflects the breadth of the enterprise as currently understood. Although there is a federal Department of Homeland Security, it is neither solely dedicated to homeland security missions, nor is it the only part of the federal government with significant responsibilities in this arena (1). Prior to 9/11, the United States addressed threats to our homeland through the separate prisms of national defense, law enforcement, and emergency management. Policy discussions about how the government should confront emerging threats were made more urgent by the 9/11 attacks. Despite the reorganization put in motion after the attacks, including the Homeland Security Act of 2002, and concurrent evolution of homeland security policy, over 30 federal departments, agencies, and entities have homeland security responsibilities and receive annual appropriations to execute homeland security missions (2).[18]

HOMELAND SECURITY ADVISORY COUNCIL (HSAC) The Homeland Security Advisory Council (HSAC) leverages the experience, expertise, and national and global connections of the HSAC membership to provide the Secretary real-time, real-world, sensing and independent advice to support decision making across the spectrum of homeland security operations. The Homeland Security Advisory Council: provides organizationally independent advice and recommendations to the Secretary, including the creation and implementation of critical and actionable policies for the security of the homeland; conducts research and provides policy analysis and recommendations on a variety of security issues; and evaluates the impact of security-related public and private policies in an attempt to formulate prospective security policies.[19]

HOMELAND SECURITY ADVISORY SYSTEM (HSAS) A system to provide information regarding the risk of terrorist acts to federal, state, and local authorities and to the American people. The HSAS is designed to guide protective measures when specific information to a particular sector or geographic region is received. It combines threat information with vulnerability assessments and provides communications to public safety officials and the public. The system's Homeland Security Threat Advisories contain actionable information about an incident involving, or a threat targeting, crucial national networks or infrastructures or key assets. Homeland Security Information Bulletins communicate information of interest to the nation's crucial infrastructures that do not meet the timeliness, specificity, or significance thresholds of warning messages. A color-coded Threat Level System is used to communicate with public safety officials and the public so that protective measures can be implemented to reduce the likelihood or impact of an attack. The levels and their associated protective measures are as follows:[20]

- LOW (GREEN): A low risk of terrorist attacks.
- GUARDED (BLUE): A general risk of terrorist attacks.
- ELEVATED (YELLOW): A significant risk of terrorist attacks.
- HIGH (ORANGE): A high risk of terrorist attacks.
- SEVERE (RED): A severe risk of terrorist attacks.

HOMELAND SECURITY DATA NETWORK (HSDN) The Homeland Secure Data Network (HSDN) enables classified information to reach federal agencies that are involved in homeland security missions. HSDN is a classified wide-area network utilized by DHS, DHS Components and other partners, providing effective interconnections to the intelligence community and federal law enforcement resources.[21]

HOMELAND SECURITY DIGITAL LIBRARY The Homeland Security Digital Library (HSDL) is the nation's premier collection of documents related to homeland security policy, strategy, and organizational management. The HSDL is sponsored by the U.S. Department of Homeland Security's National Preparedness Directorate, FEMA and the Naval Postgraduate School Center for Homeland Defense and Security.[22]

HOMELAND SECURITY INFORMATION Any information possessed by a federal, state, or local agency that relates to the threat of terrorist activity; relates to the ability to prevent, interdict, or disrupt terrorist activity; would improve the identification or investigation of a suspected terrorist or terrorist organization; or would improve the response to a terrorist act.[23]

HOMELAND SECURITY INFORMATION NETWORK (HSIN) The Homeland Security Information Network (HSIN) is the trusted network for homeland security mission operations to share Sensitive But Unclassified information. Federal, state, local, territorial, tribal, international and private sector homeland security partners use HSIN to manage operations, analyze data, send alerts and notices, and in general, share the information they need to do their jobs.[24]

HOMELAND SECURITY INTELLIGENCE COUNCIL (HSIC) In the aftermath of the 9/11 attacks, President George W. Bush established the

Homeland Security Council (HSC) on October 8, 2001, through the issuance of Executive Order 13228. The organization and operation of the HSC was further specified by the president in Homeland Security Presidential Directive-1, which was issued on October 29, 2001. The establishment of the HSC was subsequently codified in Title IX of the Homeland Security Act of 2002 (Pub. L. 107-296; 116 Stat. 2135; 6 U.S.C 491 et seq.). The HSC's purpose is to ensure coordination of all homeland security–related activities among executive departments and agencies, and to promote the effective development and implementation of all homeland security policies. The HSC meets at the president's direction, and the president presides at HSC meetings.[25]

HOMELAND SECURITY OPERATIONS MORNING BRIEF Comprises mostly suspicious activity reports minus any information on U.S. persons contained within criminal intelligence protected by privacy laws. The brief is shared on a Sensitive but Unclassified (SBU) level with about 1,500 federal, state, and local intelligence and law enforcement agencies and subscribers.[26]

HOMELAND SECURITY PRESIDENTIAL DIRECTIVES (HSPDs) In the aftermath of the September 11, 2001, terrorist attacks on the World Trade Center in New York City and the Pentagon in suburban Washington, DC, President George W. Bush established, with E.O. 13228 of October 8, 2001, the Office of Homeland Security and the Homeland Security Council within the Executive Office of the President to assist with the planning and coordination of federal efforts to combat terrorism and maintain the domestic security of the United States. On October 29, 2001, the president issued the first instrument in a new series denominated Homeland Security Presidential Directives (HSPDs) "that shall record and communicate presidential decisions about the homeland security policies of the United States." HSPDs are not published in the *Federal Register*, but are available from the White House website upon issuance and are subsequently published in the Weekly Compilation of Presidential Documents. The initial directive concerned the organization and operation of the Homeland Security Council.[27]

HORIZON SCANNING Process of identifying future trends, drivers, and/ or conditions that may have an effect on future events, incidents, or occurrences.[28]

HORIZONTAL INTEGRATION Refers to the desired end-state where intelligence of all kinds flows rapidly and seamlessly to the warfighter, and enables information dominance warfare.[29]

HOSTILE ACT Force or other means used directly to attack the United States (U.S.), U.S. forces, or other designated persons or property, to include critical cyber assets, systems, or functions. The term also includes force or other means to preclude or impede the mission and/or duties of U.S. forces, including the recovery of U.S. personnel or vital U.S. government property.[30]

HOT SITE A fully operational data-processing facility equipped with hardware and system software to be used in the event of a disaster.

HOUSE PERMANENT SELECT COMMITTEE ON INTELLIGENCE (HPSCI) The U.S. House Permanent Select Committee on Intelligence (HPSCI) is a committee of the U.S. House of Representatives, currently chaired by U.S. Congressman Devin Nunes (California). The HPSCI is charged with the oversight of the U.S. Intelligence Community, which includes the intelligence and intelligence-related activities of 17 elements of the U.S. government, and the Military Intelligence Program.[31]

HUGGER-MUGGER 1. A manipulation of information that produces false signals which are believed to be true indications, as in "hugger-mugger occurred among watch officers in the 1970s when the CIA generated stories detrimental to Chilean president Salvador Allende, creating so much activity that U.S. watch centers began picking up false information that the CIA itself had planted, and reported it back to Washington." 2. A stealthy, confused, or disorderly thought process that reinforces preconceived notions. "Most reporting from Kosovo still tilts toward the Albanians and against the Serbs even though, for many months, the real story has been about NATO's failure to prevent the ethnic cleansing of Serbs. Why should this be? One reason is that many of the reporters in Kosovo are old Balkan hands that first reported Serbian atrocities in Bosnia and then Serbian excesses in Kosovo. They are hugger-mugger with Albanian intellectuals . . . their mindset is such that they find it very difficult to see the Serbs as victims."[32] *See* CIRCULAR INTELLIGENCE

HUMAN CONSEQUENCE Effect of an incident, event, or occurrence that results in injury, illness, or loss of life. When measuring human consequence in the context of homeland security risk, consequence is assessed as negative and can include loss of life or limb, or other short-term or long-term bodily harm or illness.[33]

HUMAN RIGHTS Human rights are rights inherent to all human beings, whatever our nationality, place of residence, sex, national or ethnic origin, color, religion, language, or any other status. We are all equally entitled to our human rights without discrimination. These rights are all interrelated, interdependent and indivisible. Universal human rights are often expressed and guaranteed by law, in the forms of treaties, customary international law, general principles and other sources of international law. International human rights law lays down obligations of governments to act in certain ways or to refrain from certain acts, in order to promote and protect human rights and fundamental freedoms of individuals or groups. The principle of universality of human rights is the cornerstone of international human rights law. This principle, as first emphasized in the *Universal Declaration on Human Rights* in 1948, has been reiterated in numerous international human rights conventions, declarations, and resolutions. The 1993 Vienna World Conference on Human Rights, for example, noted that it is the duty of states to promote and protect all human rights and fundamental freedoms, regardless of their political, economic and cultural systems.[34]

HUMAN SOURCE A Confidential Human Source as defined in the Attorney General's Guidelines Regarding the Use of FBI Confidential Human Sources.[35]

HUMAN SOURCE INTELLIGENCE (HUMINT) 1. A category of intelligence derived from information collected and provided by human sources. In U.S. Army and Marine Corps usage, human intelligence operations cover a wide range of activities encompassing reconnaissance patrols, aircrew reports and debriefs, debriefing of refugees, interrogations of prisoners of war, and the conduct of counterintelligence force protection source operations.[36] 2. The collection by a trained HUMINT collector of foreign information from people and multimedia to identify elements, intentions, composition, strength, dispositions, tactics, equipment, and capabilities.[37]

HUMANE TREATMENT The treatment standards and principles in Enclosure 4 of DoDD 2310.01E (Reference (ap)), Article 3 of Reference (z) during non-international armed conflict, and the principles set forth in Article 75 of Protocol Additional to the Geneva Conventions of August 12, 1949, and relating to the Protection of Victims of International Armed Conflicts (Protocol I), June 8, 1977 (Reference (aq)), during international armed conflict, as construed and supported under U.S. policy and law.[38]

HUMANITARIAN AND CIVIC ASSISTANCE Assistance to the local populace, specifically authorized by Title 10, United States Code, Section 401, and funded under separate authorities, provided by predominantly U.S. forces in conjunction with military operations.[39]

HUMINT ENABLING An operational support function in which non-HUMINT intelligence collection operations are facilitated by HUMINT collection sources/operations.

HUMINT OPERATIONAL COMMUNICATIONS NETWORK (HOC-NET) Computer system that provides information technology, communications, and desktop services for DoD HUMINT needs.[40]

HUMINT TRAINING Instruction and applied exercises for acquiring and retaining skills and knowledge required in the acquisition of foreign intelligence derived from the collection discipline that uses human beings as both sources and collector.[41]

HYPOTHESIS 1. Something assumed for the purpose of argument; a theory to be later proven or disproven. 2. A general proposition put forward as a possible explanation for known facts from which additional investigations can be planned to generate evidential data that will tend to strengthen or weaken the basis for accepting the proposition as the best or strongest explanation of the available information. 3. A tentative assumption that is to be proven or disproved by further investigation and analysis. *See* ASSESSMENT; CONCLUSION; DEDUCTIVE LOGIC; HYPOTHESIS TESTING; INDUCTIVE LOGIC; INFERENCE

HYPOTHESIS TESTING The process of asking questions and seeking and analyzing evidence that can prove or disprove a proposition. *See* CONCLUSION; DEDUCTIVE LOGIC; HYPOTHESIS; INDUCTIVE LOGIC; INFERENCE

NOTES

1. Committee for National Security Systems (CNSS). Instruction 4009. *National Information Assurance Glossary.* April 2010. Accessed January 15, 2015. http://www.ncsc.gov/nittf/docs/CNSSI-4009_National_Information_Assurance.pdf.

2. U.S. Department of Defense. Center for Development of Security Excellence. *Glossary of Security Terms and Definitions.* November 2012. Accessed February 17, 2015. http://www.cdse.edu/documents/cdse/Glossary_Handbook.pdf.

3. Joint Military Intelligence College. *Intelligence Warning Terminology.* October 2001. Accessed July 3, 2015. https://archive.org/details/JMICInteligencelwarnterminology.

4. Department of Homeland Security, Risk Steering Committee. *DHS Risk Lexicon.* September 2010. Accessed February 14, 2015. http://www.dhs.gov/dhs-risk-lexicon.

5. Department of Homeland Security, Risk Steering Committee. *DHS Risk Lexicon.* September 2010. Accessed February 14, 2015. http://www.dhs.gov/dhs-risk-lexicon.

6. U.S. Department of Defense. *Department of Defense Dictionary of Military and Associated Terms.* JP 1-02, 08 November 2010, as Amended through 15 January 2016. Accessed January 26, 2016, http://www.dtic.mil/doctrine/new_pubs/jp1_02. pdf.

7. U.S. Department of Justice, *Department of Justice Guide to the Freedom of Information Act*, n.d. Accessed January 26, 2016, http://www.justice.gov/sites/default/ files/oip/legacy/2014/07/23/exemption2_0.pdf.

8. U.S. General Accountability Office. *High-Containment Laboratories: Recent Incidents of Biosafety Lapses.* Statement of Nancy Kingsbury, Testimony before the Subcommittee on Oversight and Investigations, Committee on Energy and Commerce, House of Representatives. GAO-14-785T, July 16, 2014. Accessed April 5, 2015. http://www.gao.gov/products/GAO-14-785T.

9. Central Intelligence Agency, *Tradecraft Primer: Structured Analytical Techniques for Improving Intelligence Analysis*, March 2009, accessed February 3, 2015, https://www.cia.gov/library/center-for-the-study-of-intelligence/csi-publications/ books-and-monographs/Tradecraft%20Primer-apr09.pdf.

10. Federal Bureau of Investigation. The *High Value Detainee Interrogation Group: Intelligence Interviewing and Interrogation Research.* Broad Agency Announcement BAA-202200. Accessed January 22, 2015. http://fas.org/irp/news/2012/04/hig-baa. pdf; also see Ackerman, Spencer. "New U.S. Interrogation Tool: Science." *Wired*, April 16, 2012. Accessed January 22, 2015. http://www.wired.com/2012/04/interrogation-science/.

11. Jan Goldman, *Intelligence Warning Terminology*, Joint Military Intelligence College, October 2001, accessed July 3, 2015. https://archive.org/details/JMICInteligencelwarnterminology.

12. Bjelopera, Jerome P. "American Jihadist Terrorism: Combating a Complex Threat." *CRS Report for Congress* R41416. January 23, 2013. Accessed January 26, 2015. http://www.fas.org/sgp/crs/terror/R41416.pdf.

13. U.S. Department of Defense. *Defense Support of Civil Authorities.* JP 3-28, July 31, 2013. Accessed January 26, 2015. http://www.dtic.mil/doctrine/new_pubs/ jp3_28.pdf.

14. Chairman of the Joint Chiefs of Staff. *National Military Strategic Plan for the War on Terrorism.* February 1, 2006. Accessed February 26, 2015. http://archive. defense.gov/pubs/pdfs/2006-01-25-Strategic-Plan.pdf.

15. U.S Department of Defense. *Homeland Defense.* JP 3-27. July 29, 2013. Accessed February 26, 2015. http://www.dtic.mil/doctrine/new_pubs/jp3_27.pdf.

16. Mark A. Randol, "The Department of Homeland Security Intelligence Enterprise: Operational Overview and Oversight Challenges for Congress," CRS Report for Congress R40602, March 19, 2010, accessed January 26, 2016, https://fas.org/ sgp/crs/homesec/R40602.pdf.

17. Reese, Shawn. "Defining Homeland Security: Analysis and Congressional Considerations." *CRS Report for Congress* R42462, January 8, 2013. Accessed

January 17, 2015. http://www.fas.org/sgp/crs/homesec/R42462.pdf; U.S Department of Defense. *Homeland Defense*. JP 3-27. July 29, 2013. Accessed February 26, 2015. http://www.dtic.mil/doctrine/new_pubs/jp3_27.pdf.

18. Painter, William L. Selected Issues in Homeland Security Policy for the 114th Congress. *CRS Report to Congress* R44041, May 19, 2015, accessed January 26, 2016, http://www.fas.org/sgp/crs/homesec/R44041.pdf.

19. Department of Homeland Security, *Homeland Security Advisory Council*, January 7, 2016, accessed January 26, 2016, http://www.dhs.gov/homeland-security-advisory-council.

20. Department of Homeland Security, *Chronology of Changes to the Homeland Security Advisory System*, September 22, 2015, accessed January 26, 2016, http://www.dhs.gov/homeland-security-advisory-system.

21. Department of Homeland Security, *Homeland Secure Data Network*, n.d., accessed February 2, 2016, https://www.dhs.gov/xlibrary/assets/mgmt/itpa-dhs-hsdn2012.pdf.

22. Department of Homeland Security's National Preparedness Directorate, FEMA and the Naval Postgraduate School Center for Homeland Defense and Security. *About the Homeland Security Digital Library*. Accessed February 10, 2015. https://www.hsdl.org/?about.

23. Alice R. Buchalter, John Gibbs, and Marieke Lewis, *Laws and Regulation Governing the Protection of Sensitive but Unclassified Information*, Federal Research Division, Library of Congress, September 2004, accessed January 26, 2016, http://www.loc.gov/rr/frd/pdf-files/sbu.pdf.

24. Department of Homeland Security, *Homeland Security Information Network*, accessed February 3, 2016, http://www.dhs.gov/what-hsin.

25. The White House. *Homeland Security Intelligence Council*. Bush administration legacy site. Accessed January 26, 2016, http://georgewbush-whitehouse.archives.gov/hsc/.

26. Matthew E. Broderick, Director of Homeland Security Operations Center, Statement before the House Committee on Homeland Security, Intelligence, Information Sharing, and Terrorism Risk Assessment Subcommittee, 20 July 2005.

27. Relyea, Harold C. "Presidential Directives: Background and Overview." *CRS Report for Congress* Updated November 26, 2008. 8–9. Accessed February 25, 2015. http://fas.org/sgp/crs/misc/98-611.pdf.

28. Department of Homeland Security, Risk Steering Committee. *DHS Risk Lexicon*. September 2010. Accessed February 14, 2015. http://www.dhs.gov/dhs-risk-lexicon.

29. Jason Program Office, Mitre Corporation, Horizontal Integration: Broader Access Models for Realizing Information Dominance, JSR-04-132, December 2004, accessed February 3, 2016, http://www.fas.org/irp/agency/DoD/jason/classpol.pdf.

30. U.S. Department of Defense. *Defense Support of Civil Authorities*. JP 3-28, July 31, 2013. Accessed January 26, 2015. http://www.dtic.mil/doctrine/new_pubs/jp3_28.pdf.

31. United States House Permanent Select Committee on Intelligence, *History and Jurisdiction*, accessed February 1, 2016, https://intelligence.house.gov/about/history-jurisdiction.

32. Stephen Glover, "The Serbs Are Still Being Presented as the Bad Guys," *Spectator*, March 4, 2000, 28.

33. Department of Homeland Security, Risk Steering Committee, *DHS Risk Lexicon*, September 2010, accessed November 4, 2015, http://www.dhs.gov/dhs-risk-lexicon.

34. Office of the High Commissioner for Human Rights. *What are Human Rights?* United Nations. Accessed January 27, 2015. http://www.ohchr.org/EN/Issues/Pages/WhatareHumanRights.aspx.

35. U.S. Department of Justice. *The Attorney General's Guidelines for Domestic FBI Operations*. 2008. Accessed February 25, 2015. http://www.justice.gov/sites/default/files/ag/legacy/2008/10/03/guidelines.pdf.

36. Department of the Army. Marine Corps Combat Development Command. Department of the Navy. *Operational Terms and Graphics*. FM 1-02 (FM 101-5). September 21, 2004. Accessed July 3, 2015. http://www.udel.edu/armyrotc/current_cadets/cadet_resources/manuals_regulations_files/FM%201-02%20-%20Operational%20Terms%20&%20Graphics.pdf.

37. Department of the Army. *Human Intelligence Collector Operations*. FM 2-22.3 (FM 34-52). September 2006. Accessed February 26, 2015. https://www.fas.org/irp/doddir/army/fm2-22-3.pdf.

38. U.S. Department of Defense. *DoD Intelligence Interrogations, Detainee Debriefings, and Tactical Questioning*. Directive Number 3115.09, October 11, 2012 Incorporating Change 1, Effective November 15, 2013. Accessed February 15, 2015. http://www.dtic.mil/whs/directives/corres/pdf/311509p.pdf.

39. United States Department of Defense. *Foreign Humanitarian Assistance*. JP 3-29, January 3, 2014. Accessed March 7, 2015. http://www.dtic.mil/doctrine/new_pubs/jp3_29.pdf.

40. John Pike, *HUMINT Operational Communications Network*, June 21, 1997, accessed February 2, 2016, https://fas.org/irp/program/disseminate/hocnet.htm.

41. U.S. Department of Defense. *DoD Human Intelligence (HUMINT) Training*. DoD Instruction Number 3305.15, February 25, 2008. Certified Current through February 25, 2015, Incorporating Change 1, Effective October 15, 2013. Accessed February 28, 2015. http://www.dtic.mil/whs/directives/corres/pdf/330515p.pdf.

I

IC CIVILIAN JOINT DUTY QUALIFYING EXPERIENCE IC Civilian Joint Duty Qualifying Experience provides substantive professional, technical, or leadership experience that includes policy, program, managerial, analytical, or operational responsibility for intelligence resources, programs, policies, analysis, or operations in conjunction with one or more other IC elements, or relevant organizations external to the IC. A joint duty qualifying experience provides a wider understanding of the missions and functions of the IC, or the IC's relationships with relevant organizations outside the IC; develops a broader knowledge of the operations and management of the IC; and helps to build collaborative networks.[1]

IC CIVILIAN JOINT DUTY ROTATION IC Civilian Joint Duty Rotation means (a) the detail of IC civilian personnel to a position in another IC element or other relevant organization that provides an IC civilian joint duty qualifying experience, or (b) the assignment of IC civilian personnel to an approved internal position at the individual's employing element that provides an IC civilian joint duty qualifying experience.[2]

IC COMMUNITY CAPABILITIES CATALOG (IC3) A subset of the IC Human Capital Repository (ICHCR), containing an inventory of IC employees according to their competencies and experience.[3]

IC E-MAIL E-mail between organizations over the JWICS network; also referred to as ICE-MAIL or JWICS (Joint Worldwide Intelligence Communications System) email.

IC SENIOR PROGRAM EXECUTIVE (SPE) Senior ODNI or IC official vested by the DNI with IC-wide policy and/or program responsibility for a particular professional community (e.g., intelligence analysis or science and technology), professional discipline (e.g., financial management or acquisition), or mission function (e.g., counterterrorism or clandestine operations).[4]

IC3 (INTERNET CRIME COMPLAINT CENTER) The IC3 was established as a partnership between the Federal Bureau of Investigation (FBI) and the National White Collar Crime Center (NW3C) to receive Internet-related criminal complaints and to further research, develop, and refer the criminal complaints to federal, state, local, or international law enforcement and/or regulatory agencies for any investigation they deem to be appropriate. The IC3 was intended, and continues to emphasize, serving the broader law enforcement community to include federal, as well as state, local, and international agencies, which are combating Internet crime and, in many cases, participating in Cyber Crime Task Forces. Since its inception, the IC3 has received complaints crossing the spectrum of cyber crime matters, to include online fraud in its many forms including intellectual property rights (IPR) matters, computer intrusions (hacking), economic espionage (theft of trade secrets), online extortion, international money laundering, identity theft, and a growing list of Internet facilitated crimes.[5]

ICARS (INTEGRATED COLLECTION AND ANALYSIS REQUIRE-MENTS SYSTEM) A web-based collection requirements management environment that provides a common, secure, single point of entry for analysts to drive collection. It will connect all Intelligence Community (IC) collection requirements management systems and make it easier for analysts to submit their collection needs or describe intelligence gaps. Furthermore, analysts will be able to search and view existing requirements complementary to their own. ICARS will foster collaboration across organizational boundaries as analysts subscribe to each other's requests and work together with collectors to formulate optimal collection strategies.[6]

ICONS Categories of "information that are reflexively classified, without serious evaluation of any national security threat their release might pose. These icons are rarely or never declassified, no matter what the law, or the U.S. Constitution might say."[7]

IDENTITY ECOSYSTEM Online environment where individuals and organizations will be able to trust each other because they follow agreed-upon standards to obtain and authenticate their digital identities—and the digital identities of devices. The Identity Ecosystem is designed to securely support transactions that range from anonymous to fully authenticated and from low to high value. The Identity Ecosystem, as envisioned here, will increase the following: privacy protections for individuals, who will be able to trust that their personal data is handled fairly and transparently; convenience for individuals, who may choose to manage fewer passwords or accounts than they do today; efficiency for organizations, which will benefit from a reduction in paper-based and account management processes; ease-of-use, by automating identity solutions whenever possible and basing them on technology that is simple to operate; security, by making it more difficult for criminals to compromise online transactions; confidence that digital identities are adequately protected, thereby promoting the use of online services; innovation, by lowering the risk associated with sensitive services and by enabling service providers to develop or expand their online presence; choice, as service providers offer individuals different—yet interoperable—identity credentials and media.[8]

IDENTITY HISTORY SUMMARY Often referred to as a criminal history record or a "rap sheet," a listing of certain information taken from fingerprint submissions retained by the FBI in connection with arrests and, in some instances, federal employment, naturalization, or military service. If the fingerprints are related to an arrest, the Identity History Summary includes name of the agency that submitted the fingerprints to the FBI, the date of the arrest, the arrest charge, and the disposition of the arrest, if known to the FBI. All arrest data included in an Identity History Summary is obtained from fingerprint submissions, disposition reports, and other information submitted by agencies having criminal justice responsibilities. The U.S. Department of Justice Order 556-73 establishes rules and regulations for the subject of an Identity History Summary to obtain a copy of his or her own record for review. The FBI's Criminal Justice Information Services (CJIS) Division processes these requests.[9]

IDENTITY INTELLIGENCE (I2 OR I²) The intelligence resulting from the processing of identity attributes concerning individuals, groups, networks, or populations of interest.[10]

IDENTITY PROOFING The process of providing or reviewing federally authorized acceptable documentation for authenticity.[11]

IDENTITY THEFT A catch-all term for crimes involving illegal use of another individual's identity.[12]

IF YOU SEE SOMETHING, SAY SOMETHING "If You See Something, Say Something™" is a national campaign that raises public awareness of the indicators of terrorism and terrorism-related crime, as well as the importance of reporting suspicious activity to state and local law enforcement. Informed, alert communities play a critical role in keeping our nation safe. The U.S. Department of Homeland Security (DHS) is committed to strengthening hometown security by creating partnerships with state, local, tribal, and territorial (SLTT) governments and the private sector, as well as the communities they serve.[13]

ILLEGAL RESIDENCY An intelligence apparatus established in a foreign country and composed of one or more intelligence officers, which has no apparent connection with the sponsoring intelligence organization or with the government of the country operating the intelligence organization.[14]

IMAGERY A likeness or presentation of any natural or man-made feature or related object or activity, and the positional data acquired at the same time the likeness or representation was acquired, including: products produced by space-based national intelligence reconnaissance systems; and likeness and presentations produced by satellites, airborne platforms, unmanned aerial vehicles, or other similar means (except that such term does not include hand-held or clandestine photography taken by or on behalf of human intelligence collection organizations).[15]

IMAGERY CORRELATION The mutual relationship among the different signatures on imagery from different types of sensors in terms of position and the physical characteristics signified.

IMAGERY EXPLOITATION The cycle of processing, using, interpreting, mensuration and/or manipulating imagery, and any assembly or consolidation of the results for dissemination.[16]

IMAGERY INTELLIGENCE (IMINT) Intelligence derived from the exploitation of collection by visual photography, infrared sensors, lasers, electro-optics, and radar sensors such as synthetic aperture radar wherein images of objects are reproduced optically or electronically on film, electronic display devices, or other media.[17] *See* SOURCES OF INTELLIGENCE

IMAGERY INTERPRETATION KEY Any diagram, chart, table, list, set of examples, or similar aid that helps imagery interpreters in the rapid identification of objects visible on imagery.

IMAGERY PACK An assembly of the records from different imagery sensors covering a common target area.

IMAGERY SORTIES One flight by one aircraft for the purpose of recording air imagery.

IMMEDIATE MESSAGE A precedence category reserved for messages relating to situations that gravely affect the security of national or allied forces or people and requires immediate delivery to the addressees.

IMMEDIATE RESPONSE Any form of immediate action taken in the United States and territories to save lives, prevent human suffering, or mitigate great property damage in response to a request for assistance from a civil authority, under imminently serious conditions when time does not permit approval from a higher authority.[18]

IMMIGRANT ALIEN Any alien lawfully admitted into the United States under an immigration visa for permanent residence.[19]

IMMIGRATION AND CUSTOMS ENFORCEMENT (ICE), OFFICE OF INTELLIGENCE (OI) The largest investigative organization within DHS. It was established in 2003 and incorporated into DHS by consolidating the investigative elements of the former U.S. Customs Service and Immigration and Naturalization Service (INS) and by transferring the Federal Protective Service from the General Services Administration (GSA). ICE's mission is to enforce trade and immigration laws through the investigation of activities, persons, and events that may pose a threat to the safety or security of the United States and its people. It also investigates illegal trafficking in weapons (including weapons of mass destruction), smuggling of narcotics and other contraband, human smuggling and trafficking, money laundering and other financial crimes, fraudulent trade practices, identity and benefit fraud, child pornography, child sex tourism, and health and public safety dangers. It has four operational divisions. ICE special agents are the largest non-FBI component of the Joint Terrorism Task Force (JTTF). ICE's intelligence activities are coordinated and managed within the Office of Intelligence. The OI is responsible for collecting, analyzing, and disseminating strategic and tactical intelligence for use by the operational elements of ICE and DHS. Although ICE is not a member of the intelligence community (IC), the OI participates in all aspects of the intelligence cycle.[20]

IMPLANT Electronic device or electronic equipment modification designed to gain unauthorized interception of information-bearing emanations.[21]

IN CAMERA In private, especially in a judge's chambers ("the judge reviewed the sensitive material in camera").[22]

INADVERTENT DISCLOSURE A set of circumstances or a security incident in which a person has had involuntary access to classified information that he or she was or is not normally authorized.[23]

INCIDENT 1. Occurrence, caused by either human action or natural phenomena, that may cause harm and that may require action. Homeland security incidents can include major disasters, emergencies, terrorist attacks, terrorist threats, wildland and urban fires, floods, hazardous materials spills, nuclear accidents, aircraft accidents, earthquakes, hurricanes, tornadoes, tropical storms, war-related disasters, public health and medical emergencies, law enforcement encounters and other occurrences requiring a mitigating response. Harm can include human casualties, destruction of property, adverse economic impact, and/or damage to natural resources.[24] 2. An occurrence, caused by either human action or natural phenomena, that requires action to prevent or minimize loss of life, or damage, loss of, or other risks to property, information, and/or natural resources.[25]

INCIDENT AWARENESS AND ASSESSMENT The Secretary of Defense–approved use of Department of Defense intelligence, surveillance, reconnaissance, and other intelligence capabilities for domestic non-intelligence support for defense support of civil authorities.[26]

INCIDENT MANAGEMENT A national comprehensive approach to preventing, preparing for, responding to, and recovering from terrorist attacks, major disasters, and other emergencies.[27]

INCIDENT OF SECURITY CONCERN An event that, at the time of occurrence, cannot be determined to be an actual violation of law but is of such significance as to warrant preliminary inquiry and subsequent reporting.[28]

INCIDENT REPORT An official account of a specific security-related occurrence.

INCIDENT RESPONSE CENTER (IRC) The IC-IRC manages and monitors the IC's networks, including conducting network threat analysis and correlation. It provides 24 × 7 collection and sharing of cyber event information among the IC.[29]

INCULPATORY EVIDENCE Evidence that tends to increase the likelihood of fault or guilt.[30]

INDEPENDENT CONTRACTOR A self-employed individual with whom an IC element enters into a contract to provide specific services.[31]

INDEPENDENT RESEARCH AND DEVELOPMENT (IR&D) A contractor-funded research and development effort that is not sponsored by, or required in performance of, a contract or grant that consists of projects falling within the areas of basic research, applied research, development, systems, and/or other concept formulation studies.[32]

INDICATION In intelligence usage, information in various degrees of evaluation, all of which bear on the intention of a potential enemy to adopt or reject a course of action.[33] *See* INDICATOR; INTENTION; SIGNPOSTS

INDICATIONS In intelligence usage, information in various degrees of evaluation, all of which bear on the intention of a potential enemy to adopt or reject a course of action.[34]

INDICATIONS ANALYSIS A deductive process for evaluating the significance of observed intelligence against an established list of indicators to signify an increase in the hostile policy/attitudes of an aggressor. These factors are logical or plausible moves or acts, based on Western reasoning or observed during past conflicts or crises, or based on the results of intelligence assessments of enemy strategic offensive military doctrine and strategic standard operating procedures.[35] *See* INDICATOR LIST

INDICATIONS AND WARNING (I&W) A generic term usually associated with intelligence activities needed to detect and report time-sensitive knowledge on foreign events that could threaten a country's allies, its citizens abroad, or the country's military, economic, or political interests.[36]

INDICATIONS AND WARNING INTELLIGENCE Information that alerts or warns of an impending course of action by a foreign power that is detrimental to the interests of a country. This information is the product of recognition and correlation of threat indications and the synthesis of a threat posture.[37]

INDICATIONS AND WARNING SYSTEMS A network of intelligence production facilities with analytical resources capable of contributing to or developing indications and warning intelligence, and disseminating this product within their own command and to other facilities, organizations, or commands.[38]

INDICATIONS CENTER An intelligence situation room distinguished by around-the-clock operations, comprehensive communications, concentration on all aspects of possible enemy attack or other situations which might require action by the military, and adherence to procedures established for operation within an indications and warning system. Sometimes it may be the focal point for performing the operational intelligence functions for a command.[39] *See* ALERT CENTER; WARNING CENTER; WATCH CENTER

INDICATIONS WATCH OFFICER An intelligence watch officer or duty officer who serves in an indications center and is trained to identify indications of hostilities and cope with other intelligence matters requiring immediate action.[40]

INDICATOR 1. A future event, action, or decision that could occur as it relates to a particular threat scenario. 2. A generalized, theoretical statement of a course of action or decision that is expected to be taken in preparation for an aggressive act and that can be used to guide intelligence collection resources. Commonly, indicators are developed from enemy doctrine, or from previous military operations or exercises, and an analyst's ability to apply logic and common sense. "The progress that the Government of Lebanon is making in counter narcotics through the steps being taken toward acceding to the 1988 Convention on Narcotics and the drafting of laws addressing money laundering schemes, constitute grounds for cautious optimism. The willingness of the Government of Lebanon to pursue the prosecution of a member of Parliament is another indicator of its increased seriousness in its counter narcotics efforts."[41] *See* INDICATION

INDICATOR ANALYSIS A review of past criminal activity to determine whether certain actions or postures taken can reflect future criminal activity. It can result in the development of behavioral profiles or early warning systems in computerized environments.[42]

INDICATOR ELEMENT A term used mostly in communications and signals intelligence analysis to distinguish message traffic; not considered a strategic indications and warning term.

INDICATOR LIST A list of the factors or acts (military, political, economic, diplomatic, and internal) that would be present if a foreign power intended to initiate hostilities. The list is based on moves or acts observed during past conflicts and crises and on intelligence assessments of enemy strategic offensive military doctrine and strategic-level standard operating procedures.[43]

INDICATOR ORGANIZATION A counterintelligence term for a model group or organization that represents several other groups or organizations seeking the same political or ideological goals. In instances where counterintelligence and security assets are limited, the prototype would be targeted for extensive surveillance, and the results would be considered applicable to the other organizations in the set.[44]

INDIRECT ACCESS Descriptor used for sources who do not have firsthand access to the information provided and who have come upon it through one or more sub-sources.[45]

INDIRECT CONSEQUENCE Effect that is not a direct consequence of an event, incident, or occurrence, but is caused by a direct consequence, subsequent cascading effects, and/or related decisions. Indirect consequences are also sometimes referred to as ripple, multiplier, general equilibrium, macroeconomic, secondary, and tertiary effects.[46]

INDOCTRINATION An initial indoctrination and/or instruction provided to each individual approved to a Special Access Program (SAP) prior to exposure concerning the unique nature of program information and the policies, procedures, and practices for its handling.[47]

INDUCTIVE LOGIC 1. Reasoning from the specifics to the general. 2. A method of inference by which a more general belief is developed by observing a limited set of observations or instances. 3. Inferences are made in generalized conclusions from particular instances. They go beyond what is known in the key facts or premises. For example,

- Premise 1: Socrates is a man.
- Premise 2: Socrates is strong.
- Inference: Therefore, all men are strong.

See CONCLUSION; DEDUCTIVE LOGIC; HYPOTHESIS; INFERENCE

INDUSTRIAL CONTRACTOR A commercial business entity (other than an independent contractor or sole proprietorship), which enters into contracts with the IC to provide goods or services.[48]

INDUSTRIAL ESPIONAGE The act of seeking a competitive, commercial advantage by obtaining a competitor's trade secrets and/or logistics. The acquisition of industrial information through clandestine operations.[49]

INDUSTRIAL SECURITY The portion of information security that is concerned with the protection of classified information in the custody of United States (U.S.) industry.[50]

INFERENCE 1. A conclusion derived from facts or from other inferences such as forecasts, predictions, extrapolations, and estimates; a conclusion that is logically drawn after reviewing certain facts or premises; a deduction.[51] 2. The reasoning process that creates, modifies, and maintains belief and in which we reason from evidence toward conclusions. See ARGUMENT; CONCLUSION; DEDUCTIVE LOGIC; HYPOTHESIS; INDUCTIVE LOGIC; INFERENCE NETWORK

INFERENCE NEWORK Directed acyclic graphs whose nodes indicate propositions and whose arcs represent probabilistic linkages among those nodes. See ARGUMENT; CONCLUSION; DEDUCTIVE LOGIC; HYPOTHESIS; INDUCTIVE LOGIC; INFERENCE

INFERENTIAL ANALYSIS The use of collected relevant data sets (evidence) to infer and synthesize explanations that describe the meaning of the underlying data.[52] See DESCRIPTIVE ANALYSIS

INFILTRATION A technique and process in which a force moves as individuals or small groups over, through, or around enemy positions without detection.[53]

INFLUENCE OPERATION Influence operations are focused on affecting the perceptions and behaviors of leaders, groups, or entire populations. Influence operations employ capabilities to affect behaviors, protect operations, communicate commander's intent, and project accurate information to achieve desired effects across the cognitive domain. These effects should result in differing behavior or a change in the adversary's decision cycle, which aligns with the commander's objectives. The military capabilities of influence operations are psychological operations (PSYOP), military deception (MILDEC), operations security (OPSEC), counterintelligence (CI) operations, counterpropaganda operations and public affairs (PA) operations. Public affairs, while a component of influence operations, is predicated on its ability to project truthful information to a variety of audiences. These activities of influence operations allow the commander to prepare and shape the operational battlespace by conveying selected information and indicators to target audiences, shaping the perceptions of decision makers, securing critical-friendly information, defending against sabotage, protecting against espionage, gathering intelligence, and communicating selected information about military activities to the global audience.[54]

INFORMATION 1. Unevaluated material, at all levels of reliability and from any source, which may contain intelligence information. To distinguish between information and intelligence, information is data that have been collected but not further developed through analysis, interpretation, or correlation with other data and intelligence. The application of analysis transforms information into intelligence. Both information and intelligence are important, and both may exist together in some form. They are not, however, the same thing, and thus they have different connotations, applicability, and credibility.[55] 2. Any knowledge that can be communicated or documentary material, regardless of its physical form or characteristics, which is owned by, produced by or for, or is under the control of the U.S. government. 3. Facts, data, or knowledge that has not been subjected to analysis. Often referred to as "knowledge in raw form."[56] 4. Knowledge that can be communicated by any means.[57] *See* INFORMATION LIFE CYCLE; INTELLIGENCE; INTELLIGENCE DATA

INFORMATION ANALYSIS AND INFRASTRUCTURE PROTECTION DIRECTORATE (IA&IP) The Information Analysis and Infrastructure Protection (IAIP) directorate was created to support a key strategic mission of the Department of Homeland Security (DHS). IAIP analyzes and integrates terrorist threat information, mapping those threats against both physical and cyber vulnerabilities to critical infrastructure and key assets, and implementing actions that protect the lives of Americans, ensures the delivery of essential government services, and protects infrastructure assets owned by U.S. industry. IAIP is unique in that no other federal organization has the statutory mandate to carry out these responsibilities under one organizational framework (1). IAIP was vested with responsibility to analyze and integrate terrorist threat information, map threats against both physical and cyber vulnerabilities to critical infrastructure and key assets, and implement actions that protect the lives of Americans, ensure the delivery of essential government services, and protect infrastructure assets owned by U.S. industry. IAIP carries out its mission through the Administrative and Outreach, Intelligence and Warning, and the Protecting Critical Infrastructure and Key Assets programs, as well as the Homeland Security Operations Center (3).[58]

INFORMATION ARMY 35,000 individuals have reportedly signed up to join Ukraine's "information army"—the new project drafted by the country's Ministry of Information Policy which seeks to combat the "Russian occupation on the information front." The new initiative, which seeks to mobilize Ukrainian bloggers to post their accounts of the war online, was made live earlier this month in a bid to counter Russian propaganda coverage of the conflict.[59]

INFORMATION ASSURANCE (IA) Actions that protect and defend information systems by ensuring availability, integrity, authentication, confidentiality, and nonrepudiation.[60]

INFORMATION ASSURANCE (IA)–ENABLED INFORMATION TECHNOLOGY (IT) PRODUCT Product or technology whose primary role is not security, but provides security services as an associated feature of its intended operating capabilities. Examples include such products as security-enabled web browsers, screening routers, trusted operating systems, and security-enabled messaging systems.[61]

INFORMATION ASSURANCE OFFICER (IAO) The individual responsible to the Information Assurance Manager (IAM) for ensuring that Operations Security (OPSEC) is maintained for a specific Information System (IS). The Information Assurance Officer (IAO) may have the responsibility for more than one system. NOTES: The IAO may be referred to as a Network Security Officer (NSO) or a Terminal Area or Information System Security Custodian.[62]

INFORMATION ASSURANCE PRODUCT Product or technology whose primary purpose is to provide security services (e.g., confidentiality, authentication, integrity, access control, nonrepudiation of data); correct known vulnerabilities; and/or provide layered defense against various categories of non-authorized or malicious penetrations of information systems or networks. Examples include such products as data/network encryptors, firewalls, and intrusion detection devices.[63]

INFORMATION ATTACK An action that directly corrupts information without visibly changing the physical entity within which it resides.[64]

INFORMATION BOX A space on an annotated overlay, mosaic, map, or other item that is used for identification, reference, and scale information.

INFORMATION CAPTURE Information capture is an implicit requirement of knowledge exchange. It is also a part of a continuous process enabling people of differing interests to exchange their information, thereby creating the transparencies necessary to create knowledge for exchange. In

Afghanistan, for example, while internal-national learning has been well applied by U.S. forces at the operational and tactical level (based upon "lessons learned," pre-deployment training, exercises, application and post-deployment debriefing), this does not necessarily apply to Allies or even between coalition partners (e.g., between RC(E) and RC(S)). The situation is often even more pronounced with international organizations and NGOs, whose people often stay longer, but frequently in less well-structured and supported environments. Put together as a whole, it is clear that individual units and commands are learning, but the capture and knowledge exchange of this learning may not be evaluated against national or regional plans, sub-goals, and objectives.[65] *See* KNOWLEDGE MANAGEMENT

INFORMATION DISSEMINATION PRODUCT The term "information dissemination product" means any book, paper, map, machine-readable material, audiovisual production, or other documentary material, regardless of physical form or characteristic, disseminated by an agency to the public.[66]

INFORMATION DOMINANCE The degree of information superiority that allows the possessor to use information systems and capabilities to achieve an operational advantage in a conflict or to control the situation in operations other than war while denying those capabilities to the adversary.[67]

INFORMATION DOMINANCE CENTER This project involved the renovation of standard office space into a highly classified, ultra-modern operations center. The Center's primary function is to enable 24-hour worldwide visualization, planning, and execution of coordinated information operations for the U.S. Army and other federal agencies. The futuristic, yet distinctly military, setting is further reinforced by the Commander's console, which gives the illusion that one has boarded a star ship. The prominently positioned chair provides the commanding officer an uninterrupted field of vision to a 22'0" wide projection screen.[68]

INFORMATION ENVIRONMENT The aggregate of individuals, organizations, or systems that collect, process, or disseminate information, also included is the information itself.[69]

INFORMATION FORAGING Information foraging theory is an approach to understanding how strategies and technologies for information seeking, gathering, and consumption are adapted to the flux of information in the environment. The theory assumes that people, when possible, will modify their strategies or the structure of the environment to maximize their rate of gaining valuable information. The theory is developed by (a) adaptation (rational) analysis of information foraging problems and (b) a detailed process model (adaptive control of thought in information foraging [ACT-IF]). The adaptation analysis develops (a) information patch models, which deal with time allocation and information filtering and enrichment activities in environments in which information is encountered in clusters; (b) information scent models, which address the identification of information value from proximal cues; and (c) information diet models, which address decisions about the selection and pursuit of information items.[70]

INFORMATION FRATRICIDE The results of employing information operations elements in a way that causes effects in the information environment that impede the conduct of friendly operations or cause adverse effects on friendly forces.[71]

INFORMATION FUNCTION Any activity involving the acquisition, transmission, storage, or transformation of information.[72]

INFORMATION INTEGRATION CELL A small, physically separated unit composed of officers from multiple agencies who have the authority to access all terrorist-related data of their agencies; explore alternative sources of information; and develop new techniques, processes, and tools to detect indicators and patterns of terrorist organizations and their operations. Although the objective is to develop new capabilities, a critical component of this effort is the inclusion of privacy and legal advisors to ensure compliance with current statutes and policies and develop recommendations for possible changes in the future to detect terrorists while also protecting the rights of U.S. persons.[73]

INFORMATION INTEGRITY The state that exists when information is unchanged from its source and has not been accidentally or intentionally modified, altered, or destroyed.[74]

INFORMATION LIFE CYCLE The stages through which information passes, typically characterized as creation or collection, processing, dissemination, use, storage, and disposition.[75] Thirteen distinct steps have been identified: 1. created and produced (by authors in all agencies, in all branches, at all levels, and in many different formats and mediums); 2. cataloged and indexed (metadata tools applied); 3. temporary and permanent availability and entitlement established (ownership and disclosure rights of creators, publishers, disseminators, licensees, franchisees); 4. published in the public domain or withheld from disclosure pursuant to a wide variety of statutes, internal agency policies, foreign agreements, and so forth; 5. put into files, databases, collections, holdings, and other storage repositories; 6. communicated, disseminated, and distributed; 7. searched for and retrieved (full text, abstracts, key words); 8. used for decision making and problem solving; 9. archived; 10. re-used over and over again by government officials, journalists, archivists, researchers, citizens, and others (information recycled); 11. disposed of (temporarily or permanently); 12. expunged or destroyed if permanent retention period exceeded; 13. need for new information to replace old information established.[76]

INFORMATION MANAGEMENT Provision of relevant information to the right person at the right time in a usable form to facilitate situational understanding and decision making. It uses procedures and information systems to collect, process, store, display, and disseminate information.[77]

INFORMATION OPERATIONS (IO) 1. Any actions involving the acquisition, transmission, storage, or transformation of information that enhance the employment of military forces. 2. Employment of the core capabilities of electronic warfare, computer network operations, psychological operations, military deception, and operations security, in concert with specified supporting and related capabilities, to affect and defend information and information systems and to influence decision making.[78] 3. The integrated employment, during military operations, of information-related capabilities in concert with other lines of operation to influence, disrupt, corrupt, or usurp the decision making of adversaries and potential adversaries while protecting our own. Also called IO.[79]

INFORMATION OPERATIONS INTELLIGENCE INTEGRATION (IOII) The integration of intelligence disciplines and analytic methods to characterize and forecast, identify vulnerabilities, determine effects, and assess the information environment.[80]

INFORMATION OPERATIONS ROADMAP Information intended for foreign audiences, including public diplomacy and PSYOP, increasingly is consumed by our domestic audience, and vice versa, but argues that "the distinction between foreign and domestic audiences becomes more a question of USG [U.S. government] intent rather than information dissemination practices."[81]

INFORMATION OPERATIONS TASK FORCE Created shortly after the September 11, 2001, terrorist attacks, to focus on "developing, coordinating, deconflicting, and monitoring the delivery of timely, relevant, and effective messages to targeted international audiences."[82]

INFORMATION OWNER An official with statutory or operational authority for specified information and responsibility for establishing the controls for its generation, collection, processing, dissemination, and disposal.[83]

INFORMATION PEACEKEEPING 1. Information peacekeeping is the active exploitation of information and information technology in order to modify peacefully the balance of power between specific individual and groups so as to achieve national policy objectives. The three elements of information peacekeeping, in order of priority, are: open-source intelligence (providing useful actionable unclassified information); information technology (providing "tools for truth" that afford the recipient access to international information and the ability to communicate with others); and electronic security and counter-intelligence (a strictly defensive aspect of information operations). Although information peacekeeping is not to be confused with clandestine or covert methods, there are gray areas. Information peacekeeping may require the clandestine delivery of classified or open source intelligence, or the covert delivery of "tools for truth" such as the traditional radio broadcast equipment, or the more recently popular cellular telephones and facsimile machines. Information peacekeeping may also require covert assistance in establishing and practicing electronic security and counterintelligence in the face of host country censorship or interference.[84] 2. A neglected aspect of information operations. Consists of three aspects: open source intelligence, information technology, electronic security and counterintelligence.[85]

INFORMATION POLLUTION Using commercial messages as a source for an editorial; when ads are formatted to resemble news stories.[86]

INFORMATION PROTECTION Security of information and command, control, communications, and computer (C4) systems involves the procedural and technical protection of information and C4 systems' major components (terminal devices, transmission media, switches, and control and management), and is an integral component of the joint force commander's command and control protection effort.[87]

INFORMATION REPORT Report used to forward raw information collected to fulfill intelligence requirements.[88]

INFORMATION REQUIREMENTS (IR) Those items of information regarding the enemy and his environment which need to be collected and processed in order to meet the intelligence requirements of a commander. All information elements the commander and staff require to successfully conduct operations—that is, all elements necessary to address the factors of METT-TC.[89]

INFORMATION RESOURCES Information and related resources, such as personnel, equipment, funds, and information technology.[90]

INFORMATION RESOURCES MANAGEMENT (IRM) The planning, budgeting, organizing, directing, training, controlling, and management activities associated with the burden, collection, creation, use, and dissemination of information by agencies. The term includes the management of information and related resources, such as federal information processing resources. Information resources management planning is an integral part of overall mission planning. Agencies need to plan from the outset for the steps in the information life cycle. When creating or collecting information, agencies must plan how they will process and transmit the information, how they will use it, how they will protect its integrity, what provisions they will make for access to it, whether and how they will disseminate it, how they will store and retrieve it, and finally, how the information will ultimately be disposed of.[91]

INFORMATION SECURITY 1. Protection of unauthorized access to or modification of information, whether in storage, processing, or transit, and against the denial of service to authorized users or the provision of service to unauthorized users, including those measures necessary to detect, document, and counter such threats.[92] 2. Protecting information and information systems from unauthorized access, use, disclosure, disruption, modification, or destruction in order to provide—(A) integrity, which means guarding against improper information modification or destruction, and includes ensuring information nonrepudiation and authenticity; (B) confidentiality, which means preserving authorized restrictions on access and disclosure, including means for protecting personal privacy and proprietary information; (C) availability, which means ensuring timely and reliable access to and use of information; and (D) authentication, which means utilizing digital credentials to assure the identity of users and validate their access.[93] 3. The protection and defense of information and information systems against unauthorized access or modification of information, whether in storage, processing, or transit, and against the denial of service to authorized users. Information security includes those measures necessary to detect, document, and counter such threats. Information security is composed of computer security and communications security.[94]

INFORMATION SECURITY INCIDENT A "computer security incident" within federal government systems (as described in National Institute of Standards and Technology Special Publication 800-61 "Computer Security Incident Handling Guide") or critical infrastructure systems that is a violation or imminent threat of violation of computer security policies, acceptable use policies, or standard computer security practices.[95]

INFORMATION SECURITY OVERSIGHT OFFICE (ISOO) ISOO develops, coordinates and issues implementing directives and instructions regarding Executive Order 13526, Order 12829 that are binding on executive branch agencies. ISOO also reviews and approves the implementing regulations issued by the agencies. ISOO's analysts maintain continuous liaison with their agency counterparts on all matters relating to the government-wide security classification program and the National Industrial Security Program. ISOO also conducts on-site inspections and special classified document reviews to monitor agency compliance with the Order.[96]

INFORMATION SHARING Exchanging information between collectors, analysts, and end users. In the intelligence community, information sharing has become a priority: "The need to share information became an imperative to protect our nation in the aftermath of the 9/11 attacks on our homeland. The intelligence community's "need-to-know" culture, a necessity during the Cold War, is now a handicap that threatens our ability to uncover, respond, and protect against terrorism and other asymmetric threats. Each intelligence agency has its own networks and data repositories that make it very difficult to piece together facts and suppositions that, in the aggregate, could provide warning of the intentions of our adversaries."[97] According to the 2005 report of the Commission on the Intelligence Capabilities of the United States Regarding Weapons of Mass Destruction, "The term information 'sharing' suggests that the federal government entity that collects the information 'owns' it and can decide whether or not to 'share' it with others—a concept deeply embedded in the Intelligence Community's culture. This concept should be rejected. Information collected by the Intelligence Community—or for that matter, any government agency—belongs to the U.S. government. Officials are fiduciaries who hold the information in trust for the nation. They do not have authority to withhold or distribute it except as such authority is delegated by the President or provided by law." The commission suggested replacing the term "information sharing" with "information integration" or "information access."[98]

INFORMATION SHARING AND ACCESS INTERAGENCY POLICY COMMITTEE (ISA IPC) The ISA IPC was established by the White House in 2009 and subsumed the role of a predecessor body, the Information Sharing Council, which was established by Executive Order 13356: Strengthening the Sharing of Terrorism Information to Protect Americans in 2004.[99]

INFORMATION SHARING AND ANALYSIS CENTERS Information Sharing and Analysis Centers (ISAC) are trusted private sector entities established by Critical Infrastructure Key Resource (CI/KR) owners and operators to provide comprehensive sector analysis, which is shared ISAC members and government. The goal of the ISAC program is to provide members with accurate, actionable, and relevant information for risk mitigation, incident response, alert and information sharing.[100]

INFORMATION SHARING AND ANALYSIS ORGANIZATION (ISAO) America's cyber adversaries move with speed and stealth. To keep pace, all types of organizations, including those beyond traditional critical infrastructure sectors, need to be able to share and respond to cyber risk in as close to real time as possible. Organizations engaged in information sharing related to cybersecurity risks and incidents play an invaluable role in the collective cybersecurity of the United States. However, many companies have found it challenging to develop effective information sharing organizations—or Information Sharing and Analysis Organizations (ISAOs). In response, President Obama has issued an Executive Order directing the Department of Homeland Security (DHS) to encourage the development of ISAOs. Executive Order 13691 *Promoting Private Sector Cybersecurity Information Sharing* directs DHS to:

- Develop a more efficient means for granting clearances to private sector individuals who are members of an ISAO via a designated critical infrastructure protection program.
- Engage in continuous, collaborative, and inclusive coordination with ISAOs via the DHS National Cybersecurity and Communications Integration Center (NCCIC), which coordinates cybersecurity information sharing and analysis among the federal government and private sector partners.
- Select, through an open and competitive process, a non-governmental organization to serve as the ISAO Standards Organization. This ISAO Standards Organization will identify a set of voluntary standards or guidelines for the creation and functioning of ISAOs.[101]

INFORMATION SHARING ENVIRONMENT A trusted partnership among all levels of government, the private sector, and foreign partners to detect, prevent, preempt, and mitigate the effects of terrorism against territory, people, and interests of the United States of America. This partnership enables the trusted, secure, and appropriate exchange of terrorism information, in the first instance, across the five federal communities; to and from state, local, and tribal governments, foreign allies, and the private sector; and at all levels of security classifications.[102] The Information Sharing Environment (ISE) was established by the United States Intelligence Reform and Terrorism Prevention Act of 2004 P.L. 108-458.[103]

INFORMATION SHARING SYSTEM An integrated and secure methodology, whether computerized or manual, designed to efficiently and effectively distribute critical information about offenders, crimes, and/or events in order to enhance prevention and apprehension activities by law enforcement.[104]

INFORMATION SILO AFFECT 1. Information "silo affect," by which agencies across the federal and state levels fail to share information with each other. The 9/11 Commission cited silo effect as a contributing factor to the failure of U.S. intelligence and law enforcement agencies to track down the terrorists involved in the 9/11 attacks.[105] 2. Ten years ago, our law enforcement and intelligence communities were driven by a Cold War "need to know" culture that stovepiped information and stymied cooperation. As demonstrated by the ten lost "operational opportunities" to derail the September 11 attacks that the 9/11 Commission identified, both the CIA and the FBI failed to disseminate information in the run-up to the attacks. This was, in part, because of the so-called "wall" between law enforcement and intelligence. What information they did share often lacked the full context that might have shed light on its big-picture significance. The culture that led to this failure is vividly illustrated by a CIA analyst who told the 9/11 Commission that he did not volunteer information he knew about a suspected terrorist when the FBI showed him surveillance pictures of the individual because he "was not authorized to answer FBI questions regarding CIA information."[106]

INFORMATION SUPERIORITY 1. Capability to collect, process, and disseminate an uninterrupted flow of information while exploiting or denying an adversary's ability to do the same.[107] 2. That degree of dominance in the information domain which permits the conduct of operations without effective opposition. The operational advantage derived from the ability to collect, process, and disseminate an uninterrupted flow of information while exploiting or denying an adversary's ability to do the same.[108]

INFORMATION SYSTEM (IS, INFOSYS) "Information system" means a discrete set of information resources organized for the collection, processing, maintenance, use, sharing, dissemination, or disposition of information.[109]

INFORMATION SYSTEM SECURITY (INFOSEC) Information Systems Security (INFOSEC) is the protection afforded to Information Systems (IS) in order to preserve the availability, integrity, and confidentiality of the systems and the information contained with the system. INFOSEC encompasses the protection of information systems against unauthorized access to, or modification of, information, whether in storage, processing, or transit, and against the denial of service to authorized users, including those measures necessary to detect, document, and counter such threats. Such protection is the integrated application of Communications Security (COMSEC), Transient Electromagnetic Pulse Emanation Standard (TEMPEST), and Information Assurance (IA) executed in unison with personnel security, operations security, industrial security, resources protection, and physical security.[110]

INFORMATION TECHNOLOGY INCIDENT An occurrence that actually or potentially jeopardizes the confidentiality, integrity, or availability of an information system or the information the system processes, stores, or transmits or that constitutes a violation or imminent threat of violation of security policies, security procedures, or acceptable use policies.[111]

INFORMATION TERRORISM Information terrorism is the nexus between criminal information system fraud or abuse, and the physical violence of terrorism. However, particularly in a legal sense, information terrorism can be the intentional abuse of a digital information system, network, or component toward an end that supports or facilitates a terrorist campaign or action. In this case, the system abuse would not necessarily result in direct violence against humans, although it may still incite fear. The U.S. government faces this same paradox as it confronts information terrorism. Military, civilian and commercial databases, computer systems, and information infrastructures all are potential targets of information terrorists. Whether through digital or physical means, the information terrorists can destroy, disrupt, degrade, deny or delay vital information that the military relies upon, and thus become a threat in peacetime, as well as in time of war.[112]

INFORMATION WARFARE (IW) 1. Actions taken to achieve information superiority by affecting adversary information, information-based processes, and information systems, while defending one's own. 2. The use of information to achieve objectives. 3. Any action to deny, exploit, corrupt, or destroy the enemy's information and its functions while protecting one's own against those actions; exploiting one's own military information functions.[113]

INFORMATION WARRIOR A member of the military trained in information warfare, information interoperability, and "the design, protection, and denial of systems that seek sufficient knowledge to dominate the battlespace."[114]

INFORMATION WORK The favored euphemism for propaganda during and for many years after the Second World War. Separate information services were created under new ministries or agencies; information officers (attachés d'information in the French diplomatic service), formerly known as "press attachés," were sent to embassies to staff their new information sections (sometimes called information and cultural relations sections), which were later known in the U.S. Foreign Service as "public affairs sections."[115]

INFORMED CONSENT The basic elements of informed consent include: a statement that the study involves research, an explanation of the purposes of the research and the expected duration of the subject's participation, a description of the procedures to be followed, identification of any procedures which are experimental, and a description of any reasonably foreseeable risks or discomforts to the subject. Most codes of research establish specific items for disclosure intended to assure that subjects are given sufficient information. These items generally include: the research procedures, their purposes, risks and anticipated benefits, alternative procedures (where therapy is involved), and a statement offering the subject the opportunity to ask questions and to withdraw at any time from the research.[116]

INFOSPHERE Cyberspace relating to "global systems of internetted computers, communications infrastructure, online conferencing entities, databases and information utilities generally known as the Net." Space control of the infosphere is the ability to use the infosphere for the furtherance of strategic objectives and to deter the enemy from doing the same.[117]

INFRACTION Any knowing, willful, or negligent action contrary to the requirements of this order or its implementing directives that does not constitute a violation.[118]

INFRAGARD 1. InfraGard is a partnership between the FBI and the private sector. It is an association of persons who represent businesses, academic institutions, state and local law enforcement agencies, and other participants dedicated to sharing information and intelligence to prevent hostile acts against the U.S.[119] 2. InfraGard is a public-private volunteer organization that serves as the critical link that forms a tightly knit working relationship across all levels. Each InfraGard chapter is geographically linked with an FBI Field Office, providing all stakeholders immediate access to experts from law enforcement, industry, academic institutions and other federal, state and local government agencies. By utilizing the talents and expertise of the InfraGard network, information is shared to mitigate threats to our nation's critical infrastructures and key resources. Collaboration and communication are the keys to protection. Providing timely and accurate information to those responsible for safeguarding our critical infrastructures, even at a local level, is paramount in the fight to protect the United States and its resources. InfraGard members have access to the organization's secure internal website, powered by CyberCop.[120]

INFRARED INTELLIGENCE (IRINT) *See* SOURCES OF INTELLIGENCE

INFRASTRUCTURE The framework of interdependent networks and systems comprising identifiable industries, institutions (including people and procedures), and distribution capabilities that provide a reliable flow of products and services essential to the defense and economic security of the United States, the smooth functioning of government at all levels and society as a whole; consistent with the definition in the Homeland Security Act, infrastructure includes physical, cyber, and/or human elements.[121]

INFRASTRUCTURE ATTACK An attack designed to significantly compromise the function of a whole infrastructure rather than individual components. "Attacks against infrastructure are relatively new and are of interest in the study of information warfare. In considering infrastructure vulnerabilities, threats to both individual systems and the infrastructure itself must be evaluated when considering criminal activity. Both share similar enablers as a pre-requisite to compromise; however, infrastructure attacks require a more concerted and coordinated effort and provide better data points for indicator and warning analysis."[122]

INFRASTRUCTURE RISK ASSESSMENT PARTNERSHIP PROGRAM (IRAPP) A framework for working with state authorities to develop, evaluate and support the implementation of CIKR risk assessment and risk-management decision support processes in a state/local environment.[123] *See* CRITICAL INFRASTRUCTURE AND KEY RESOURCES

INHERENTLY GOVERNMENTAL FUNCTION Two primary definitions of inherently governmental function currently exist in federal law and policy. One is a statutory definition, enacted as part of the Federal Activities Inventory Reform (FAIR) Act of 1998. This definition states that an inherently governmental function is "a function so intimately related to the public interest as to require performance by Federal Government employees." The other is a policy-oriented definition contained in Office of Management and Budget (OMB) Circular A-76. This definition states that an inherently governmental activity is "an activity that is so intimately related to the public interest as to mandate performance by government personnel."[124]

IN-Q-TEL Launched in 1999 as an independent, not-for-profit organization, In-Q-Tel (IQT) was created to bridge the gap between the technology needs of the U.S. Intelligence Community (IC) and emerging commercial innovation. We identify and invest in venture-backed startups developing technologies that will provide "ready-soon innovation" (within 36 months) vital to the IC mission. These technology startups are traditionally outside the reach of the IC; in fact, more than 70 percent of the companies that IQT invests in have never before done business with the government.[125]

INSIDER Anyone who has authorized access to Department of Defense (DoD) resources by virtue of employment, volunteer activities, or contractual relationship with DoD.[126]

INSIDER THREAT 1. A person with placement and access who intentionally causes loss or degradation of resources or capabilities or compromises the ability of an organization to accomplish its mission through espionage, providing support to international terrorism, or the unauthorized release or disclosure of information about the plans and intentions of U.S. military forces (AR 381–20).[127] 2. An insider threat arises when a person with authorized access to U.S. government resources, to include personnel, facilities, information, equipment, networks, and systems, uses that access to harm the security of the United States. Malicious insiders can inflict incalculable damage. They enable the enemy to plant boots behind our lines and can compromise our nation's most important endeavors.[128] 3. A person or group of persons within an organization who pose a potential risk through violating security policies. Extended Definition: One or more individuals with the access and/or inside knowledge of a company, organization, or enterprise that would allow them to exploit the vulnerabilities of that entity's security, systems, services, products, or facilities with the intent to cause harm.[129]

INSPECTABLE SPACE (IS) A determination of the three-dimensional space surrounding equipment that processes classified and/or sensitive information within which Transient Electromagnetic Pulse Emanation Standard (TEMPEST) exploitation is not considered practical, or where legal authority to identify and remove a potential TEMPEST exploitation exists.[130]

INSTABILITY INDICATOR (I2) A specific issue or factor that may represent a potential threat to mission force operations and protection.[131] *See* INDICATOR

INSTITUTIONAL RISK The capacity of management and business practices to plan for, enable, and support the execution of DoD missions. It encompasses the ability to develop effective and efficient organizations and processes over the near term, midterm, and long term.[132]

INSTRUMENTS OF NATIONAL POWER All of the means available to the government in its pursuit of national objectives. They are expressed as diplomatic, economic, informational, and military.[133]

INSURGENCY The organized use of subversion and violence to seize, nullify, or challenge political control of a region. Insurgency can also refer to the group itself.[134]

INSURGENT Member of an organized movement who rebels against established leadership.[135]

INTEGRAL FILE BLOCK A distinct component of a file series that should be maintained as a separate unit in order to ensure the integrity of the records. An integral file block may consist of a set of records covering either a specific topic or a range of time, such as a presidential administration or a 5-year retirement schedule within a specific file series that is retired from active use as a group.[136]

INTEGRATED CHEMICAL, BIOLOGICAL, RADIOLOGICAL, NUCLEAR TERRORISM RISK ASSESSMENT (ITRA) An S&T program aimed at providing an integrated quantitative assessment of the relative risks associated with chemical, biological, radiological and nuclear (CBRN) terrorism to the homeland. Applications of the ITRA include informing strategic resource allocation investments and risk management planning and identifying the relative threats, vulnerabilities and knowledge gaps associated with CBRN terrorism.[137]

INTEGRATED CONCEPTS DEVELOPMENT OFFICE (ICDO) The Integrated Concepts Development Office, under the auspices of the ADNI/C, brings together collectors and analysts to study regional or issue areas of concern, study collection problems, and develop new tools and methods to help understand and assess prospective collection processes.[138]

INTEGRATED RISK MANAGEMENT Structured approach that enables the distribution and employment of shared risk information and analysis and the synchronization of independent yet complementary risk management strategies to unify efforts across the enterprise.[139]

INTEGRITY OF INFORMATION 1. The accuracy of information—keeping it from being modified or corrupted. 2. The security of information—protection of the information from unauthorized access or revision, to ensure that the information is not compromised through corruption or falsification. 3. The state that exists when information is unchanged from its source and has not been accidentally or intentionally modified, altered, or destroyed.[140]

INTELINK 1. Created in 1994 for the Intelligence Community, pioneered the culture shift from "need to know" to a "need to share." Was the first in government to use "world wide web" and pioneered "community shared space." "Supports a broad range of intelligence providers and consumers sharing a common mission purpose: Intelligence Community, Homeland Security, National Defense, Law Enforcement, and Diplomatic/Foreign Relations." The system supports instant messaging, eChirp, a microblogging application, Intellipedia, documents platform, iVideo, and shared bookmarks.[141] 2. Woolsey also approved Intelink, a CMS initiative aimed at unifying the Intelligence Community electronically. This web-based classified communications system became the main electronic information system tying the disparate members of the community together. He placed a senior DoD officer in charge of establishing the system, and DoD elements in the community adopted it, ensuring its widespread impact. The CIA was concerned about the security of the system but participated in it at ordinary levels of classification.[142]

INTELINK-S INTELINK-S is similar to INTELINK except that it is accessed through the Secret Internet Protocol Router Network (SIPRNet). It is a 24-hour-a-day network designed to meet the requirements for secure multimedia intelligence communications worldwide at the Secret level and below.[143]

INTELLIGENCE 1. A body of information and the conclusions drawn therefrom that is acquired and furnished in response to the known or perceived requirements of customers; it is often derived from information that may be concealed or not intended to be available for use by the acquirer; it is the product of a cyclical process. 2. The functions, activities, and organizations involved in the process of planning, gathering, and analyzing information of potential value to decision makers. 3. The product resulting from the collection, collation, evaluation, analysis, integration, and interpretation of all collected information.[144] 4. Simply defined, intelligence is information that has been analyzed and refined so that it is useful to policymakers in making decisions—specifically, decisions about potential threats to our national security. The FBI and the other organizations that make up the U.S. Intelligence Community use the term "intelligence" in three different ways: intelligence is a product that consists of information that has been refined to meet the needs of policymakers; intelligence is also a process through which that information is identified, collected, and analyzed; and intelligence refers to both the individual organizations that shape raw data into a finished intelligence product for the benefit of decision makers and the larger community of these organizations.[145] See BASIC INTELLIGENCE; CURRENT INTELLIGENCE; MILITARY INTELLIGENCE; STRATEGIC INTELLIGENCE; TACTICAL INTELLIGENCE; TECHNICAL INTELLIGENCE

INTELLIGENCE ACTIVITIES All activities that agencies within the intelligence community are authorized to conduct pursuant to Executive Order 12333.[146]

INTELLIGENCE ADVANCED RESEARCH PROJECTS ACTIVITY (IARPA) IARPA does not have an operational mission and does not deploy technologies directly to the field. Instead, IARPA facilitates the transition of research results to our IC customers for operational application. IARPA is led by a distinguished group of accomplished scientists and researchers. There are four research thrusts within IARPA: anticipating surprise; incisive analysis; safe and secure operations and smart collection.[147]

INTELLIGENCE AGENCIES The following are known major national (global) intelligence organizations:

ABIN: Brazilian National Intelligence Agency (domestic intelligence)
aSio: Australian Security Intelligence Organization (domestic intelligence)
aSiS: Australian Secret Intelligence Service (external intelligence)
BN: German Federal Office for the Protection of the Constitution (domestic intelligence)

BND: German Federal Intelligence Service (external intelligence)

BOEICHO JOHOBU/DIH: Japanese Defense Intelligence Headquarters (military intelligence)

BSIS/MI6: British Secret Intelligence Service (external intelligence)

BSS/Mi5: British Security Service (domestic intelligence)

BVD: Dutch National Intelligence Service (domestic intelligence)

CESID: Spanish High Center for Defense Intelligence (external/military intelligence)

CIA: U.S. Central Intelligence Agency (external intelligence)

CIO: Zimbabwean Central Intelligence Organization (domestic/external intelligence)

CISEN: Mexican Center for Investigation and National Security (domestic intelligence)

CNI: Spanish National Intelligence Center (external/military intelligence) (successor to CESID)

CSE: Canadian Communications Security Establishment (SIGINT)

CSIS: Canadian Security Intelligence Service (domestic intelligence)

DEA: U.S. Drug Enforcement Administration

DGI: Cuban General Intelligence Directorate (external intelligence)

DGSE: French General Directorate for Exterior Security (external intelligence) (successor to SDECE)

DIA: U.S. Defense Intelligence Agency (military intelligence)

DSD: Australian Defense Signals Directorate (SIGINT)

DST: French Directorate for Security of the Territory (domestic intelligence)

FAPSI: Russian Federal Agency for Government Communications and Information (SIGINT)

FBI: U.S. Federal Bureau of Investigation (domestic intelligence service)

FSB: Russian Federal Security Service (domestic intelligence) (successor to Soviet KGB)

GCHO: British Government Communications Headquarters (SIGINT)

GCSB: New Zealand Government Communications Security Bureau

GRU: Russian Chief Intelligence Directorate of the General Staff (military intelligence)

GUOANBU: Chinese Ministry of State Security (domestic/external intelligence)

ISI: Pakistani Inter-Service Intelligence Organization (military/external intelligence)

MIT: Turkish National Intelligence Organization (domestic/external intelligence)

MOSSAD: Israeli Institute for Intelligence and Special Tasks (external intelligence)

NIA: South Korean National Intelligence Agency (external intelligence)

NSA: U.S. National Security Agency (SIGINT)

NSB: Taiwan National Security Bureau (external/domestic intelligence)

NZSIS: New Zealand Security Intelligence Service (external intelligence)

RAW: Indian Research and Analysis Wing (external/SIGINT intelligence)

SAN LA: South African National Intelligence Agency (domestic intelligence)

SASS: South African Secret Service (external intelligence)

SHIN BETISHABAK: Israeli General Security Service (domestic intelligence)

SIS: Secret Intelligence Service (MI6)

SISDE: Italian Intelligence and Democratic Security Service (domestic intelligence)

SISMI: Italian Service for Information and Military Security (foreign and military intelligence)

SVR: Russian Foreign Intelligence Service (successor to Soviet KGB)

VEVAK/MOIS: Iranian Military of Intelligence and Security

INTELLIGENCE ANALYSIS A process by which intelligence is produced and that reflects allegiance to the methods of rigor and precision, science, and logical techniques in order to illuminate and interpret (value-adding) the nature and implication of concepts and information. *See* INFORMATION; INTELLIGENCE AS A PRODUCT; INTELLIGENCE DATA

INTELLIGENCE ANALYST A professional position in which the incumbent is responsible for taking the varied facts, documentation of circumstances, evidence, interviews, and any other material related to a crime and organizing them into a logical and related framework for the purposes of developing a criminal case, explaining a criminal phenomenon, describing crime and crime trends and/or preparing materials for court and prosecution, or arriving at an assessment of a crime problem or crime group.[148]

INTELLIGENCE AND NATIONAL SECURITY ALLIANCE (INSA)
The Intelligence and National Security Alliance was established as the Security Affairs Support Association (SASA) in 1979 to bring together professionals in the intelligence field, primarily employees of the National Security Agency, and to help members keep abreast of intelligence and national security community issues. SASA's main office was in Annapolis Junction, Maryland. In November 2005, the Intelligence and National Security Alliance (INSA) was established to facilitate cooperation, information sharing, and innovation within the IC. With this new mission, INSA began to broaden its membership base, becoming more inclusive of the private and academic sectors. Now serving as a unique venue for collaboration, networking, and

dialogue, INSA became an invaluable asset for members of the Intelligence Community seeking answers to the day's most inscrutable technological and policy issues.[149]

INTELLIGENCE AS A PRODUCT 1. That which results from the collection, processing, integration, analysis, evaluation, and interpretation of available information. 2. Timely, accurate, and actionable (value-added) information about what other nations or groups, especially potential adversaries, are doing that helps policymakers, decision makers, and military leaders carry out their mission of formulating and implementing national security policy. *See* INFORMATION; INTELLIGENCE ANALYSIS; INTELLIGENCE DATA

INTELLIGENCE ASSESSMENT Analytical studies dealing with subjects of policy significance. Intelligence assessment is thorough in its treatment of subject matter, but unlike estimative intelligence, an assessment may not attempt to project future developments and their implications. Assessment is usually coordinated within the producing organization but may not be coordinated with other intelligence agencies.[150] *See* ESTIMATIVE INTELLIGENCE

INTELLIGENCE COLLECTION The act of gathering information from all available sources to meet an intelligence requirement.

INTELLIGENCE COLLECTION PLAN A plan for gathering information from all available sources to meet an intelligence requirement. Specifically, a logical plan for transforming specific requests for information (possible indicators) into orders to collection sources within a required time limit.[151] *See* INDICATOR; SCENARIO

INTELLIGENCE COMMITTEES By virtue of his constitutional role as commander-in-chief and head of the executive branch, the president has access to all national intelligence collected, analyzed and produced by the Intelligence Community. Due to the intelligence agencies being part of the executive branch, the president's position affords him the authority—which, at certain times, has been asserted—to restrict the flow of intelligence information to Congress and its two intelligence committees, which are charged with providing legislative oversight of the Intelligence Community. The Senate established its intelligence oversight committee, the Senate Select Committee on Intelligence (SSCI), in May 1976. The House of Representatives followed suit in July 1977, creating the House Permanent Select Committee on Intelligence (HPSCI).[152]

INTELLIGENCE COMMUNITY (IC) The intelligence community is a federation of executive branch agencies and organizations that work separately and together to conduct intelligence activities necessary for the conduct of foreign relations and the protection of the national security of the United States. These activities include: collection of information needed by the president, the National Security Council, the Secretaries of State and Defense, and other executive branch officials for the performance of their duties and responsibilities; production and dissemination of intelligence; collection of information concerning, and the conduct of activities to protect against, intelligence activities directed against the United States, international terrorist and international narcotics activities, and other hostile activities directed against the United States by foreign powers, organizations, persons, and their agents; special activities; administrative and support activities within the United States and abroad necessary for the performance of authorized activities; and such other intelligence activities as the president may direct from time to time. Members of the IC include the Central Intelligence Agency (CIA), National Security Agency (NSA), National Reconnaissance Office (NRO), National Geospatial-Intelligence Agency (NGA), Defense Intelligence Agency (DIA), State Department Bureau of Intelligence and Research (INR), Federal Bureau of Investigation (FBI), intelligence organizations of the four military services (Air Force, Army, Navy, and Marines), Department of Homeland Security (DHS), Energy Department, and Department of the Treasury.[153]

INTELLIGENCE COMMUNITY DIRECTIVES AND POLICY GUIDANCE As defined in ICD 10, Intelligence Community Policy System, ICDs (Intelligence Community Directives) and ICPGs (Intelligence Community Directives and Policy Guidance), hereafter referred to as policies, are policy instruments of the IC Policy System. ICDs and ICPGs establish policy and guidance, and provide formal and definitive direction to the IC for the purposes of achieving a unified, integrated and effective IC.[154]

INTELLIGENCE COMMUNITY POLICY SYSTEM The IC Policy System shall establish policies applicable to the IC using the following instruments: a. Intelligence Community Directive (ICD); b. Intelligence Community Policy Guidance (ICPG); c. Intelligence Community Standard (ICS); d. DNI Executive Correspondence (EC). The IC Policy System includes the following bodies, which serve an integral role in the process of developing and coordinating IC policy: a. Intelligence Community Policy Review Board (IC-PRB) and b. Intelligence Policy Advisory Group (IPAG).[155]

INTELLIGENCE CYCLE 1. The five-step process of tasking, collecting, processing, analyzing, and disseminating intelligence. The intelligence cycle drives the day-to-day activities of the intelligence community (IC). It starts with the needs intelligence "consumers"—that is, policymakers, military officials, and other decision makers who need intelligence information in conducting their duties and responsibilities. These needs—also referred to as intelligence requirements—are sorted and prioritized within the IC and drive the collection activities of the members of the IC. Once information has been collected, it is processed, initially evaluated, and reported to both consumers and "all-source" intelligence analysts at agencies like the CIA, DIA, and State Department Bureau of Intelligence and Research. All-source analysts are responsible for performing a more thorough evaluation and assessment of the collected information by integrating the data obtained from a variety of collection agencies and sources, both classified and unclassified. This assessment leads to a finished intelligence report being disseminated to the consumer. The "feedback" part of the cycle assesses the degree to which the finished intelligence addresses the needs of the intelligence consumer and will determine if further collection and analysis is required.[156] 2. The FBI uses a six-step intelligence cycle. The FBI intelligence cycle includes requirements (identified information needs), planning and direction (management of the entire effort, from identifying the need for information to delivering an intelligence product to a consumer), collection (the gathering of raw information based on requirements), and processing and exploitation (converting the vast amount of information collected into a form usable by analysts). This is done through a variety of methods including decryption, language translations, and data reduction. Analysis and production is the conversion of raw information into intelligence. It includes integrating, evaluating, and analyzing available data, and preparing intelligence products. Dissemination, the last step, is the distribution of raw or finished intelligence to the consumers whose needs initiated the intelligence requirements. The FBI disseminates information in three standard formats: Intelligence Information Reports (IIRs), FBI Intelligence Bulletins, and FBI Intelligence Assessments.[157] *See* AGENCY

INTELLIGENCE DATA Information extracted from a variety of sensing devices, objects, emanations, documents, and records. *See* INFORMATION; INTELLIGENCE ANALYSIS; INTELLIGENCE AS A PRODUCT

INTELLIGENCE DATABASE The sum of holdings of intelligence data and finished intelligence products at a given organization.[158]

INTELLIGENCE DAY (I-DAY) The day on which the intelligence community determines that, within a potential crisis situation, a development occurs that may signal a heightened threat, although the scope and direction of the threat may be ambiguous. The intelligence community responds by focusing collection and other resources to monitor and report on the situation as it evolves.[159]

INTELLIGENCE DISCIPLINE A well-defined area of intelligence collection, processing, exploitation, and reporting using a specific category of technical or human resources. There are seven major disciplines: human intelligence, imagery intelligence, measurement and signature intelligence, signals intelligence, open-source intelligence, technical intelligence, and counterintelligence.[160] *See* PROFESSIONAL TRADECRAFT

INTELLIGENCE ENTERPRISE EXERCISE PROGRAM The Intelligence Enterprise Exercise Program enables the DNI to prepare the IC for transformation into an Intelligence Enterprise through the use of U.S. government (USG), departmental, and IC exercises. This ICD identifies the roles and responsibilities of the IC Exercise Coordinator under the Deputy Director of National Intelligence for Policy, Plans, and requirements (DDNI/PPR), of the Exercise Forum, and of all IC elements to ensure existing exercise programs are effectively leveraged to support attainment of DNO objectives.[161]

INTELLIGENCE ESTIMATE An appraisal of elements of intelligence relating to a specific situation or condition in order to determine a target's courses of action, as well as their probable order of adoption; a prediction of future events, developments or courses of action and their implications and consequences.[162] *See* NATIONAL INTELLIGENCE ESTIMATE

INTELLIGENCE FAILURE Any misunderstanding of a situation that leads a government or its military forces to take actions that are inappropriate and counterproductive to its own interests.[163] "Despite our best intentions, the system is sufficiently dysfunctional that intelligence failure is guaranteed. Though the form is less important than the fact, the variations are endless. Failure may be of the traditional variety: we fail to predict the fall of a friendly government; we do not provide sufficient warning of a surprise attack against one of our allies or interests; we are completely surprised by a state-sponsored terrorist attack; or we fail to detect an unexpected country acquiring a weapon of mass destruction. Or it may take a more nontraditional form: we overstate numerous threats leading to tens of billions of dollars of unnecessary expenditures; database errors lead to a politically unaccept-able number of casualties in a peace-enforcement operation; or an operation does not go well because the IC is not able to provide the incredibly specific data necessary to support a new generation of weapons."[164] *See* WARNING FAILURE

INTELLIGENCE FEDERATION A formal agreement in which a combat-ant command joint intelligence center receives preplanned intelligence sup-port from other joint intelligence centers, service intelligence organizations, reserve organizations, and national agencies during crisis or contingency operations.[165]

INTELLIGENCE FINDING Order by the president of the United States to the CIA to perform a covert action. *See* FINDING

INTELLIGENCE GAIN/LOSS CALCULUS Tensions between a web-site's purported intelligence value and operational threat level can deter-mine the particular capabilities used to thwart the site. For example, a "honey pot" jihadist website reportedly was designed by the CIA and Saudi Arabian government to attract and monitor terrorist activities. The informa-tion collected from the site was used by intelligence analysts to track the operational plans of jihadists, leading to arrests before the planned attacks could be executed. However, the website also was reportedly being used to transmit operational plans for jihadists entering Iraq to conduct attacks on U.S. troops. Debates between representatives of the NSA, CIA, DOD, DNI, and NSC led to a determination that the threat to troops in theater was greater than the intelligence value gained from monitoring the website, and a computer network team from the JTF-GNO ultimately dismantled it. This case raised questions of whether computer network attacks on a website are a covert operation or a traditional military activity, and under what author-ity they are conducted. It also illustrated the risk of collateral damage that an interconnected, networked world represents, as the operation to target and dismantle the honey pot inadvertently disrupted servers in Saudi Ara-bia, Germany, and Texas.[166]

INTELLIGENCE GAP A topic requiring additional information collection and analysis.[167]

INTELLIGENCE GATHERING Collection of intelligence on other units or forces by one's own units or forces.

INTELLIGENCE-INDUSTRIAL COMPLEX Around Washington, from Reston and Tyson's Corner, Virginia, to Columbia and Fort Meade, Maryland, the intelligence industrial complex generates billions of dollars a year in government contracts that go to a handful of big contractors and scores of smaller high tech firms. The biggest ones, which build and service the NRO's satellites and the NSA's listening posts, can be counted on one's fingers: Lockheed Martin, TRW, Rockwell, Hughes, Boeing, ESystems, and General Dynamics. The companies and their lobbyists provide a grateful flow of campaign funds to congressional treasuries. At the same time, they dangle offers of lucrative private sector jobs for congressional staff and intelligence officials seeking higher pay. The result is a revolving door that allows contractors to cultivate networks of influence.[168] See CIVILIAN INTELLIGENCE COMMUNITY

INTELLIGENCE INFORMATION 1. Information and knowledge about an adversary obtained through observation, investigation, analysis, or understanding. 2. Information that is under the jurisdiction and control of the director of central intelligence or a member of the intelligence community (IC); information on IC protective security programs (e.g., personnel, physical, technical, and information security). 3. Information describing U.S. foreign intelligence and counterintelligence activities, sources, methods, equipment, or methodology used for the acquisition, processing, or exploitation of such intelligence; foreign military hardware obtained for exploitation; and photography or recordings resulting from U.S. intelligence collection efforts.

INTELLIGENCE INFORMATION NEED A need, expressed by users of intelligence, for information necessary to support their mission (Intellipedia).[169]

INTELLIGENCE INFORMATION REPORT (IIR) The IIR is the primary vehicle to provide human intelligence information to the consumer. It uses a message format structure which supports automated data entry into Intelligence Community databases.[170]

INTELLIGENCE INTERROGATION The systematic process of using approved interrogation approaches to question a captured or detained person to obtain reliable information to satisfy intelligence requirements, consistent with applicable law.[171]

INTELLIGENCE-LED POLICING 1. The collection and analysis of information to produce an intelligence end product, designed to inform police decision making at both the tactical and strategic levels.[172] 2. A business model and managerial philosophy in which data analysis and crime intelligence are pivotal to an objective, decision-making framework that facilitates crime and problem reduction, disruption, and prevention through both strategic management and effective enforcement strategies that target prolific and serious offenders.[173]

INTELLIGENCE LIAISON Activity which includes official contacts between a component of the U.S. intelligence community and a foreign intelligence or security service which are directly related to espionage or counterintelligence, or other intelligence activities.[174]

INTELLIGENCE LIFE Length of time in which information has value.

INTELLIGENCE METHOD The method used to provide support to an intelligence source or operation, and which, if disclosed, is vulnerable to counteraction that could nullify or significantly reduce its effectiveness in supporting the foreign intelligence or foreign counterintelligence activities of the United States, or which would, if disclosed, reasonably lead to the disclosure of an intelligence source or operation.

INTELLIGENCE MISSION The role that the intelligence function of an agency fulfills in support of the overall mission of the agency; the intelligence mission specifies in general language what the intelligence function is intended to accomplish.[175]

INTELLIGENCE OFFICER A professionally trained member of an intelligence service. He or she may be serving in the home country or abroad as a member of a legal or illegal residency.[176]

INTELLIGENCE OPERATIONS The variety of intelligence and counterintelligence tasks that are carried out by various intelligence organizations and activities within the intelligence process. Intelligence operations include planning and direction, collection, processing and exploitation, analysis and production, dissemination and integration, and evaluation and feedback.[177]

INTELLIGENCE OVERSIGHT The process of independently ensuring all DoD intelligence, counterintelligence, and intelligence-related activities are conducted in accordance with applicable U.S. law, EOs, presidential directives, and DoD issuances designed to balance the requirement for acquisition of essential information by the IC, and the protection of constitutional and statutory rights of U.S. persons. Intelligence Oversight also includes the identification, investigation, and reporting of questionable intelligence activities and S/HS matters involving intelligence activities.[178]

INTELLIGENCE OVERSIGHT BOARD 1. Established by Executive Order 11905 (1976), the Oversight Board shall have three members who shall be appointed by the president and who shall be from outside the government and be qualified on the basis of ability, knowledge, diversity of background and experience. The members of the Oversight Board may also serve on the president's Foreign Intelligence Advisory Board (Executive Order No. 11460 of March 20, 1969). No member of the Oversight Board shall have any personal contractual relationship with any agency or department of the Intelligence Community. The Oversight Board shall: (i) Receive and consider reports by Inspectors General and General Counsels of the Intelligence Community concerning activities that raise questions of legality or propriety; (ii) Review periodically the practices and procedures of the Inspectors General and General Counsels of the Intelligence Community designed to discover and report to the Oversight Board activities that raise questions of legality or propriety; (iii) Review periodically with each member of the Intelligence Community their internal guidelines to ensure their adequacy; (iv) Report periodically, at least quarterly, to the attorney general and the president on its findings.[179] 2. Amended by Executive Order 12863 (1993) as a standing committee of the PFIAB (President's Foreign Intelligence Advisory Board). The IOB shall consist of no more than four members appointed from among the membership of the PFIAB by the chairman of the PFIAB. The IOB (Sec. 2.2.) (a) prepare for the president reports of intelligence activities that the IOB believes may be unlawful or contrary to executive order or presidential directive; (b) forward to the Attorney General reports received concerning intelligence activities that the IOB believes may be unlawful or contrary to executive order or presidential directive; (c) review the internal guidelines of each agency within the Intelligence Community that concern the lawfulness of intelligence activities; (d) review the practices and procedures of the Inspectors General and General Counsel of the Intelligence Community for discovering and reporting intelligence activities that may be unlawful or contrary to executive order or presidential directive. The IOB shall, when required by this order, report to the president through the Chairman of the PFIAB. The IOB shall consider and take appropriate action with respect to matters identified by the director of Central Intelligence, the Central Intelligence Agency or other agencies of the Intelligence Community (Sec. 2.3.).[180] *See* PRESIDENT'S FOREIGN INTELLIGENCE ADVISORY BOARD

INTELLIGENCE POINT OF CONTACT (IPOC) Personnel within individual executive branch departments and agencies who have been designated by their organization to act as a liaison with the IC.[181]

INTELLIGENCE PROCESS 1. The process by which information is converted into intelligence and made available to users. 2. Conversion of collected information and/or intelligence information into a form more suitable for the production of intelligence. 3. The process consists of six interrelated intelligence operations: planning and direction, collection, processing and exploitation, analysis and production, dissemination and integration, and evaluation and feedback.[182]

INTELLIGENCE PRODUCTION Conversion of material into finished intelligence through the integration, analysis, evaluation, and/or interpretation of all available data and the preparation of intelligence products in support of known or anticipated customer requirements.[183]

INTELLIGENCE READINESS A state of optimal organizational and procedural conditions to manage security threats, achieved through information management for timely, expert analysis, tailored synthesis, and provision of support to consumers.[184]

INTELLIGENCE RECORDS (FILES) Stored information on the activities and associations of individuals, organizations, businesses, and groups who are suspected (reasonable suspicion) of being involved in the actual or attempted planning, organizing, financing, or commissioning of criminal acts or are suspected of being or having been involved in criminal activities with known or suspected crime figures.[185]

INTELLIGENCE REFORM AND TERRORISM PREVENTION ACT OF 2004 (IRTPA) IRTPA, PL 108-458 (December 17, 2004), "an act to reform the intelligence community and the intelligence and intelligence-related activities of the United States Government, and for other purposes" among other actions, revised the definition of national intelligence, established the Director of National Intelligence (DNI), National Counterterrorism Center (NCTC), the National Counter Proliferation Center and the Privacy and Civil Liberties Oversight Board.[186]

INTELLIGENCE-RELATED ACTIVITIES Those activities outside the consolidated defense intelligence program that: respond to operational commanders' tasking for time-sensitive information on foreign entities; respond to nation's intelligence community tasking of systems whose primary mission is support to operating forces; train personnel for intelligence duties; provide an intelligence reserve; or are devoted to research and development of intelligence or related capabilities. Specifically excluded are programs that are so closely integrated with a weapon system that their primary function is to provide immediate-use targeting data.[187]

INTELLIGENCE REPORT (INTREP) 1. A specific report of information, usually on a single item, made at any level of command in tactical operations and disseminated as rapidly as possible in keeping with the timeliness of the information.[188] 2. An official account of a specific intelligence-related occurrence.

INTELLIGENCE REPORTING The preparation and conveyance of information by any means. More commonly, the term is restricted to reports as they are prepared by the collector and as they are transmitted by the collector to the latter's headquarters and by this component of the intelligence structure to one or more intelligence-producing components. Thus, even in this limited sense, reporting embraces both collection and dissemination. The term is applied to normal and specialist intelligence reports.[189]

INTELLIGENCE REQUIREMENT 1. Any subject, general or specific, upon which there is a need for the collection of information or the production of intelligence. 2. A requirement for intelligence to fill a gap in the commands' knowledge or undemanding of the battlespace or threat forces.[190]

INTELLIGENCE SAP A SAP established primarily to protect the planning and execution of especially sensitive intelligence or CI operations or collection activities.[191]

INTELLIGENCE SCIENCE BOARD The Intelligence Science Board (ISB), an advisory panel established to ensure independent scientific advice to the U.S. Director of National Intelligence (DNI), is being abolished (2010) . . . the abolition appears to be part of an efficiency sweep by newly appointed DNI James Clapper, who was sworn in August. The philosophy behind the sweep is inspired by the findings of the 9/11 Commission, which concluded that the terrorist attacks of September 11, 2001, were not prevented in part because the U.S. intelligence community was divided into multiple, competing agencies that ought to be better integrated.[192]

INTELLIGENCE SENSEMAKING Encompasses the processes by which specialized knowledge about ambiguous, complex, and uncertain issues is created. This knowledge is generated by professionals who in this context become known as Intelligence Sensemakers.[193]

INTELLIGENCE SOURCE The means or system that can be used to observe and record information relating to the condition, situation, or activities of a targeted location, organization, or individual.[194]

INTELLIGENCE SOURCES AND METHODS *Sources*: Persons, images, signals, documents, databases, and communications media capable of providing intelligence information through collection and analysis programs (e.g., Human Intelligence (HUMINT), Imagery Intelligence (IMINT), Signals Intelligence (SIGINT), Geospatial Intelligence (GEOINT), and Measurement and Signature Intelligence (MASINT)). *Methods*: Information collection and analysis strategies, tactics, operations, and technologies employed to produce intelligence products. If intelligence sources or methods are disclosed without authorization, their effectiveness may be substantially negated or impaired. NOTE: The term "intelligence sources and methods" is used in legislation and executive orders to denote specific protection responsibilities of the Director of National Intelligence (DNI).[195]

INTELLIGENCE-SPECIFIC (INT-SPECIFIC) A term referring to the use of a designated, single intelligence discipline to address and answer an issue or request for information. See SINGLE-DISCIPLINE; SINGLE-INTELLIGENCE

INTELLIGENCE, SURVEILLANCE, AND RECONNAISSANCE (ISR) The capability to graphically display the current and future locations of intelligence, surveillance, and reconnaissance sensors, their projected platform tracks, vulnerability to threat capabilities and meteorological and oceanographic phenomena, fields of regard, tasked collection targets, and products to provide a basis for dynamic retasking and time-sensitive decision making. An activity that synchronizes and integrates the planning and operation of sensors, assets, and processing, exploitation, and dissemination systems in direct support of current and future operations. This is an integrated intelligence and operations function.[196]

INTELLIGENCE SYSTEM Any system (formal or informal) which is used to manage data by gathering, obtaining, processing, interpreting, and providing analytically sound opinions to decision makers so that they may make informed decisions with regard to various courses of action. The term is not limited to intelligence organizations or services, but includes any system, in all its parts, that accomplishes the listed tasks.[197]

INTELLIGENCE THREAT ASSESSMENT AND COORDINATION GROUP (ITACG) The September 11, 2001, attacks spurred the United States to reexamine its defense, intelligence, and law enforcement priorities and structure. In its report issued July 2004, the Commission on Terrorist Attacks Upon the United States ("9/11 Commission") highlighted the threat of international terrorist groups and identified gaps in information sharing capabilities as a contributing factor in the government's failure to prevent the attack. The president established the Interagency Threat Assessment and Coordination Group (ITACG) to address some of these gaps, and Congress subsequently codified the group's existence, creating an ITACG Detail and an ITACG Advisory Council. Both the Detail and the Council are led by senior federal law enforcement and intelligence personnel but consist primarily of representatives from state and local government. By statute, the Detail's purpose is to improve the sharing of intelligence between the Intelligence Community (IC) and state, local, and tribal ("state and local") governments; the Council's purpose is to oversee the Detail.[198]

INTELLIPEDIA (IPED) Intellipedia is the Intelligence Community's version of the famous encyclopedia. It is used by analysts, working groups, and engineers throughout the IC. Since its unveiling in 2006, Intellipedia has grown exponentially—with more than 1.5 million edits on the top secret network alone. The catalyst for applying this revolutionary approach to collaboration in the Intelligence Community was a 2004 award-winning paper by CIA employee Calvin Andrus titled "The Wiki and the Blog: Toward a Complex Adaptive Intelligence Community." The paper detailed the need for the IC to adapt to the increased pace of the world.[199]

INTENSITY FACTOR A multiplying factor used in planning activities to evaluate the foreseeable intensity or the specific nature of an operation in a given area for a given period of time. It is applied to the standard day of supply in order to calculate the combat day of supply.[200]

INTENTION An adversary's purpose, plan, commitment, or design for action as possibly exhibited by a leader, decision maker, nation, or a nation's foreign policy.[201] *See* INDICATION; INDICATOR

INTENTIONAL HAZARD Source of harm, duress, or difficulty created by a deliberate action or a planned course of action.[202]

INTERAGENCY BORDER INSPECTION SYSTEM (IBIS) IBIS assists the majority of the traveling public with the expeditious clearance at ports of entry while allowing the border enforcement agencies to focus their limited resources on those potential non-compliant travelers. IBIS provides the law enforcement community with access to computer-based enforcement files of common interest. It also provides access to the FBI's National Crime Information Center (NCIC), and allows its users to interface with all fifty states via the National Law Enforcement Telecommunications Systems (NLETS). IBIS keeps track of information on suspect individuals, businesses, vehicles, aircraft, and vessels. IBIS terminals can also be used to access NCIC records on wanted persons, stolen vehicles, vessels or firearms, license information, and criminal histories. The information is used to assist law enforcement and regulatory personnel.[203]

INTERAGENCY SECURITY CLASSIFICATION APPEALS PANEL (ISCAP) The Interagency Security Classification Appeals Panel, or "IS-CAP," was created under Executive Order 12958, "Classified National Security Information," when it was signed on April 17, 1995. Today the ISCAP receives its guidelines from Executive Order 13526. The ISCAP held its first meeting in May of 1996 and has met regularly since that time. Section 5.3 of E.O. 13526 directs the ISCAP to perform four critical functions: 1. Classification Challenges: deciding on appeals by authorized persons who have filed classification challenges under Section 1.8 of E.O. 13526; 2. Exemptions from Automatic Declassification: approving, denying or amending agency exemptions from automatic declassification, as provided in Section 3.3 of E.O. 13526; and File Series Exemptions: deciding on agency requests to exempt a designated file series from automatic declassification at 25 years; 3. Mandatory Declassification Review Appeals: deciding on mandatory declassification review appeals by parties whose requests for declassification under Section 3.5 of E.O. 13526 have been denied at the agency level; 4. Inform Decisions: appropriately inform senior agency officials and the public of final Panel decisions on appeals under Sections 1.8 and 3.5 of E.O. 13526.[204]

THE INTERCEPT *The Intercept* is a publication of First Look Media. Launched in 2013 by eBay founder and philanthropist Pierre Omidyar, First Look Media is a multi-platform media company devoted to supporting independent voices, from fearless investigative journalism and documentary filmmaking to arts, culture, media and entertainment. First Look Media produces and distributes content in a wide range of forms including feature films, short-form video, podcasts, interactive media and long-form journalism, for its own digital properties and with partners. *The Intercept*, launched in 2014 by Glenn Greenwald, Laura Poitras and Jeremy Scahill, is dedicated to producing fearless, adversarial journalism. We believe journalism should bring transparency and accountability to powerful governmental and corporate institutions, and our journalists have the editorial freedom and legal support to pursue this mission.[205]

INTERDEPARTMENTAL INTELLIGENCE The synthesis of departmental intelligence which is required by departments and agencies of the U.S. government for performance of their missions; such intelligence is viewed as transcending the exclusive production competence of a single department or agency.[206]

INTERDEPENDENCY Mutually reliant relationship between entities (objects, individuals, or groups); the degree of interdependency does not need to be equal in both directions.[207]

INTERGRATED SPACE *See* I-SPACE

INTERIM SECURITY CLEARANCE A security clearance based on the completion of minimum investigative requirements, which is granted on a temporary basis, pending the completion of the full investigative requirements.[208]

INTERNALLY DISPLACED PERSON (IDP) Any person who has been forced or obliged to flee or to leave their home or places of habitual residence, in particular as a result of or in order to avoid the effects of armed conflict, situations of generalized violence, violations of human rights or natural or human-made disasters, and who have not crossed an internationally recognized state border.[209]

INTERNATIONAL COURT OF JUSTICE The International Court of Justice (ICJ) is the principal judicial organ of the United Nations (UN). It was established in June 1945 by the Charter of the United Nations and began work in April 1946. The seat of the Court is at the Peace Palace in The Hague (Netherlands). Of the six principal organs of the United Nations, it is the only one not located in New York (United States of America). The Court's role is to settle, in accordance with international law, legal disputes submitted to it by States and to give advisory opinions on legal questions referred to it by authorized United Nations organs and specialized agencies. The Court is composed of 15 judges, who are elected for terms of office of nine years by the United Nations General Assembly and the Security Council. It is assisted by a Registry, its administrative organ. Its official languages are English and French.[210]

INTERNATIONAL CRIMINAL COURT The International Criminal Court (ICC), governed by the Rome Statute, is the first permanent, treaty-based, international criminal court established to help end impunity for the perpetrators of the most serious crimes of concern to the international community. The ICC is an independent international organization and is not part of the United Nations system. Its seat is at The Hague in the Netherlands. Although the Court's expenses are funded primarily by States Parties, it also receives voluntary contributions from governments, international organizations, individuals, corporations and other entities.[211]

INTERNATIONAL CRIMINAL POLICE ORGANIZATION (INTERPOL) INTERPOL is a worldwide law enforcement organization established for mutual assistance in the prevention, detection, and deterrence of international crimes. It houses international police databases, provides secure international communications between member countries for the exchange of routine criminal investigative information, and is an information clearinghouse on international criminals/fugitives and stolen properties. The idea of INTERPOL was born in 1914 at the first International Criminal Police Congress, held in Monaco. Officially created in 1923 as the International Criminal Police Commission, the organization became known as INTERPOL in 1956. INTERPOL is the world's largest international police organization, with 190 member countries.[212]

INTERNATIONAL CRIMINAL POLICE ORGANIZATION (INTERPOL) NOTICES Color-coded notices, with each color representing a different type of action from the recipient agencies.

- Red: Used to seek the arrest with a view to extradition of subjects wanted and based upon an arrest warrant.[213]
- Blue: Used to collect additional information about a person's identity or illegal activities related to a criminal matter. This notice is primarily used for tracing and locating offenders when the decision to extradite has not yet been made, and for locating witnesses to crimes.
- Green: Used to provide warnings and criminal intelligence about persons who have committed criminal offences and are likely to repeat these crimes in other countries.
- Yellow: Used to help locate missing persons, especially minors, or to help identify persons who are not able to identify themselves, such as a person suffering from amnesia.
- Black: Used to seek the true identity of unidentified bodies.

INTERNATIONAL ORGANIZATION An entity established by recognized governments under an international agreement which, by charter or otherwise, is able to acquire and transfer property, make contracts and agreements, obligate its members, and pursue legal remedies.[214]

INTERNATIONAL TERRORISM Activities that involve violent acts or acts dangerous to human life that violate federal, state, local, or tribal criminal law, or would violate such law if committed within the United States or a state, local, or tribal jurisdiction; appear to be intended to intimidate or coerce a civilian population, to influence the policy of a government by intimidation or coercion, or to affect the conduct of a government by assassination or kidnapping; and occur totally outside the United States, or transcend national borders in terms of the means by which they are accomplished, the persons they appear to be intended to coerce or intimidate, or the locale in which their perpetrators operate or seek asylum.[215]

INTERNEE A civilian who is interned for imperative reasons of security.[216]

INTERPRETABILITY Suitability of imagery for interpretation with respect to answering adequately requirements on a given type of target in terms of quality and scale.[217]

- Poor: Imagery is unsuitable for interpretation to answer adequately requirements on a given type of target.
- Fair: Imagery is suitable for interpretation to answer requirements on a given type of target but with only average detail.
- Good: Imagery is suitable for interpretation to answer requirements on a given type of target in considerable detail.
- Excellent: Imagery is suitable for interpretation to answer requirements on a given type of target in complete detail.

INTERSTATE PHOTO SYSTEM FACIAL RECOGNITION PILOT (IPSFRP) The NGI Interstate Photo System Facial Recognition Pilot (IPSFRP) Project is a collaborative effort between the FBI and pilot agencies to identify user needs and develop a useful investigative tool for the law enforcement community. The Interstate Photo System will provide a search of a limited population of criminal mug shots using a submitted probe image. The candidates resulting from the facial recognition search will be processed automatically and the system will return the results in a ranked candidate list.[218] *See* NEXT GENERATION IDENTIFICATION

INTRUSION "Intrusion" means unauthorized access to a federal government or critical infrastructure network, information system, or application.[219]

INTRUSIVE SURVEILLANCE Intrusive surveillance is covert surveillance that is carried out in relation to anything taking place on residential premises or in any private vehicle, and involving the presence of an individual on the premises or in the vehicle, or the deployment of a surveillance device. The definition of surveillance as intrusive relates to the location of the surveillance, as it is likely to reveal private information.[220]

INTUITIVE DECISIONMAKING (Army-Marine Corps) The act of reaching a conclusion which emphasizes pattern recognition based on knowledge, judgment, experience, education, intelligence, boldness, perception, and character. This approach focuses on assessment of the situation by comparison of multiple options.[221]

INVALIDATION An administrative action that renders a contractor ineligible to receive additional classified information, except that information necessary for completion of essential contracts, as determined by the appropriate Government Contracting Agencies (GCAs).[222]

IRAN A major failure of the U.S. intelligence community was its inability to foresee the fall of the shah of Iran in 1978 and the rise of an anti-American government. According to one analyst, this failure "was the result of certain mind-sets, shared widely throughout the government, which tended to (1) take the Shah for granted; (2) overestimate Iran's stability; (3) place domestic trends within Iran down the list of U.S. intelligence priorities there; (4) underestimate the disruptive effects of forced modernization in Iran, the growing revolutionary pressures, the increasing grievances against the West, and the embodying of these disruptive forces in a then-exile in Paris, the aged Ayatollah Khomeini; and (5) fail to consider what the enormous consequences for U.S. interests would be in the event America's ally, the Shah, did fall from power."[223] *See* CUBAN MISSILE CRISIS

ISOLATED PERSON An official U.S. citizen, and/or eligible family member, or in some cases as identified by post, a private U.S. citizen, national and/ or lawful permanent resident, who is isolated from support and who, if not recovered or assisted, is at risk for serious harm.[224]

I-SPACE (i-SPACE, INTEGRATED SPACE) A U.S. Intelligence Community (IC) social networking and collaboration service hosted on JWICS; intended to foster and facilitate collaboration between IC members. Previously known as "A-Space," the transformation to i-Space broadens membership from analyst only to virtually any intelligence professional with access and a mission need (Intellipedia, accessed November 1, 2013).[225] *See* A-SPACE (ANALYTIC SPACE); LIBRARY OF NATIONAL INTELLIGENCE

NOTES

1. Office of the Director of National Intelligence. *IC Civilian Joint Duty Program.* Intelligence Community Directive 660, February 11, 2013. Accessed March 2, 2015. http://www.dni.gov/files/documents/ICD/ICD%20660.pdf.

2. Office of the Director of National Intelligence. *IC Civilian Joint Duty Program.* Intelligence Community Directive 660, February 11, 2013. Accessed March 2, 2015. http://www.dni.gov/files/documents/ICD/ICD%20660.pdf.

3. Office of the Director of National Intelligence. *Competency Directories for the Intelligence Community Workforce.* Intelligence Community Directive 610, October 4, 2010. Accessed March 2, 2015. http://www.dni.gov/files/documents/ICD/ICD_610.pdf.

4. Office of the Director of National Intelligence. *Competency Directories for the Intelligence Community Workforce.* Intelligence Community Directive 610, October 4, 2010. Accessed March 2, 2015. http://www.dni.gov/files/documents/ICD/ICD_610.pdf.

5. Federal Bureau of Investigation and National White Collar Crime Center. *About the IC3.* Accessed January 26, 2015. https://www.ic3.gov/about/default.aspx.

6. Intelligence and National Security Alliance and the Office of the Director of National Intelligence. *Analytic Transformation: Moving Forward Together.* September 2007. Accessed January 26, 2015. http://wayback.archive.org/web/20080530054342/http://analytic.insaonline.org/atprogram.pdf.

7. Aftergood, Steve. "Release of National Intelligence Daily Sought." *Secrecy News*, April 23, 2001. Accessed January 23, 2015. http://www.fas.org/sgp/news/secrecy/2001/04/042301.html.

8. Executive Office of the President. *National Strategy for Trusted Identities in Cyberspace: Enhancing Online Choice, Efficiency, Security, and Privacy.* April 2011. Accessed February 14, 2015. http://www.whitehouse.gov/sites/default/files/rss_viewer/NSTICstrategy_041511.pdf.

9. Federal Bureau of Investigation. *Identity History Summary.* Accessed January 26, 2015. http://www.fbi.gov/about-us/cjis/identity-history-summary-checks.

10. U.S. Department of Defense. *Joint Intelligence.* JP 2-0. October 22, 2013. Accessed February 15, 2015. http://www.dtic.mil/doctrine/new_pubs/jp2_0.pdf.

11. Undersecretary of Defense. 2015. *Directive-type Memorandum (DTM) 14-005—DoD Identity Management Capability Enterprise Services Application (IMESA) Access to FBI National Crime Information Center (NCIC) Files.* May 13. Accessed June 6, 2015. http://www.dtic.mil/whs/directives/corres/pdf/DTM14005_2014.pdf.

12. Rose, Andrée, Timm, Howard, Pogson, Corrie, Gonzalez, Jose, Appel, Edward, and Kolb, Nancy. *Developing a Cybervetting Strategy for Law Enforcement.* Defense Personnel Security Research Center, U.S. Department of Defense, December 2010. Accessed January 17, 2015. http://www.dhra.mil/perserec/reports/pp11-02.pdf.

13. Department of Homeland Security. *About the Campaign.* Accessed February 15, 2015. http://www.dhs.gov/see-something-say-something/about-campaign.

14. Defense Intelligence Agency, Office of Counterintelligence. *CI Glossary— Terms & Definitions of Interest for DoD CI Professionals.* July 2014. Accessed January 17, 2015. https://www.hsdl.org/?view&did=699056.

15. U.S. Department of Defense. *Department of Defense Dictionary of Military and Associated Terms.* JP 1-02, 08 November 2010, as Amended through 15 January 2016. Accessed January 26, 2016. http://www.dtic.mil/doctrine/new_pubs/jp1_02.pdf.

16. U.S. Department of Defense. *Department of Defense Dictionary of Military and Associated Terms.* JP 1-02, 08 November 2010, as Amended through 15 January 2016. Accessed January 26, 2016. http://www.dtic.mil/doctrine/new_pubs/jp1_02.pdf.

17. Department of the Army. Marine Corps Combat Development Command. Department of the Navy. *Operational Terms and Graphics.* FM 1-02 (FM 101-5). September 21, 2004. Accessed July 8, 2015. http://www.udel.edu/armyrotc/current_cadets/cadet_resources/manuals_regulations_files/FM%201-02%20-%20Operational%20Terms%20&%20Graphics.pdf.

18. U.S. Department of Defense. *Defense Support of Civil Authorities.* JP 3-28, July 31, 2013. Accessed January 26, 2015. http://www.dtic.mil/doctrine/new_pubs/jp3_28.pdf.

19. U.S. Department of Defense. Center for Development of Security Excellence. *Glossary of Security Terms and Definitions.* November 2012. Accessed February 17, 2015. http://www.cdse.edu/documents/cdse/Glossary_Handbook.pdf.

20. U.S. Immigration and Customs Enforcement. *Homeland Security Investigations: Office of Intelligence.* Accessed January 26, 2016. https://www.ice.gov/intelligence.

21. Committee for National Security Systems (CNSS). Instruction 4009. *National Information Assurance Glossary.* April 2010. Accessed January 11, 2015. http://www.ncix.gov/publications/policy/docs/CNSSI_4009.pdf.

22. Findlaw Dictionary. *In Camera.* Accessed March 5, 2015. http://dictionary.findlaw.com/definition/in-camera.html.

23. U.S. Department of Defense. Center for Development of Security Excellence. *Glossary of Security Terms and Definitions.* November 2012. Accessed February 17, 2015. http://www.cdse.edu/documents/cdse/Glossary_Handbook.pdf.

24. Department of Homeland Security, Risk Steering Committee. *DHS Risk Lexicon.* September 2010. Accessed February 14, 2015. http://www.dhs.gov/dhs-risk-lexicon.

25. U.S. Department of Defense. *Department of Defense Dictionary of Military and Associated Terms.* JP 1-02, 08 November 2010, as Amended through 15 January 2016. Accessed January 26, 2016. http://www.dtic.mil/doctrine/new_pubs/jp1_02.pdf.

26. U.S. Department of Defense. *Defense Support of Civil Authorities.* JP 3-28, July 31, 2013. Accessed January 26, 2015. http://www.dtic.mil/doctrine/new_pubs/jp3_28.pdf.

27. U.S. Department of Defense. *Defense Support of Civil Authorities.* JP 3-28, July 31, 2013. Accessed January 26, 2015. http://www.dtic.mil/doctrine/new_pubs/jp3_28.pdf.

28. Office of the Director of National Intelligence. *Glossary of Security Terms, Definitions, and Acronyms.* Intelligence Community Standard (ICS) 700-1. April 4, 2008. Accessed June 5, 2015. https://fas.org/irp/dni/icd/ics-700-1.pdf.

29. Department of Homeland Security. *National Cyber Incident Response Plan.* Interim version December 2010. Accessed February 20, 2015. http://www.federal-newsradio.com/pdfs/NCIRP_Interim_Version_September_2010.pdf.

30. Richard Kissel (ed.), *Glossary of Key Information Security Terms*, NISTIR 7298, Revision 2, accessed February 1, 2016, http://nvlpubs.nist.gov/nistpubs/ir/2013/NIST.IR.7298r2.pdf.

31. Office of the Director of National Intelligence. *Intelligence Community Core Contract Personnel.* Intelligence Community Directive 612, October 30, 2009. Accessed March 2, 2015. http://www.dni.gov/files/documents/ICD/ICD_612.pdf.

32. U.S. Department of Defense. Center for Development of Security Excellence. *Glossary of Security Terms and Definitions.* November 2012. Accessed February 17, 2015. http://www.cdse.edu/documents/cdse/Glossary_Handbook.pdf.

33. U.S. Department of Defense. *Department of Defense Dictionary of Military and Associated Terms.* JP 1-02, 08 November 2010, as Amended through 15 January 2016. Accessed January 26, 2016. http://www.dtic.mil/doctrine/new_pubs/jp1_02.pdf.

34. U.S. Department of Defense. *Department of Defense Dictionary of Military and Associated Terms.* JP 1-02, 08 November 2010, as Amended through 15 January 2016. Accessed January 26, 2016. http://www.dtic.mil/doctrine/new_pubs/jp1_02.pdf.

35. Joint Military Intelligence College. *Intelligence Warning Terminology.* October 2001. Accessed July 3, 2015. https://archive.org/details/JMICInteligencelwarn-terminology.

36. Bruce Watson, Susan Watson, and Gerald Hopple, *United States Intelligence: An Encyclopedia* (New York: Garland, 1990), 594.

37. Bruce Watson, Susan Watson, and Gerald Hopple, *United States Intelligence: An Encyclopedia* (New York: Garland, 1990), 286.

38. Jan Goldman, *Intelligence Warning Terminology*, Joint Military Intelligence College, October 2001, accessed July 3, 2015, https://archive.org/details/JMICInteli-gencelwarnterminology.

39. Jan Goldman, *Intelligence Warning Terminology*, Joint Military Intelligence College, October 2001, accessed July 3, 2015, https://archive.org/details/JMICInteli-gencelwarnterminology.

40. Bruce Watson, Susan Watson, and Gerald Hopple, *United States Intelligence: An Encyclopedia* (New York: Garland, 1990), 287.

41. Jan Goldman, *Intelligence Warning Terminology*, Joint Military Intelligence College, October 2001, accessed July 3, 2015, https://archive.org/details/JMICInteli-gencelwarnterminology.

42. United States Department of Justice. *Law Enforcement Analytic Standards.* Global Justice Information Sharing Initiative. April 2012. Accessed July 3, 2015. https://it.ojp.gov/documents/d/Law%20Enforcement%20Analytic%20Standards%20 04202_combined_compliant.pdf.

43. Jan Goldman, *Intelligence Warning Terminology*, Joint Military Intelligence College, October 2001, accessed July 3, 2015, https://archive.org/details/JMICInteligencelwarnterminology.

44. Jan Goldman, *Intelligence Warning Terminology*, Joint Military Intelligence College, October 2001, accessed July 3, 2015, https://archive.org/details/JMICInteligencelwarnterminology.

45. U.S. Department of Defense. *Defense Human Intelligence (HUMINT) and Related Intelligence Activities.* Instruction, Number S-5200.42, December 8, 2009. Accessed February 26, 2015. http://www.dod.mil/pubs/foi/homeland_defense/ intelligence/10_F_0682_DoD_Instruction_S_5200_42_Defense_Human_Intell.pdf.

46. Department of Homeland Security, Risk Steering Committee. *DHS Risk Lexicon.* September 2010. Accessed November 4, 2015. http://www.dhs.gov/dhs-risk-lexicon.

47. U.S. Department of Defense. Center for Development of Security Excellence. *Glossary of Security Terms and Definitions.* November 2012. Accessed February 17, 2015. http://www.cdse.edu/documents/cdse/Glossary_Handbook.pdf.

48. Office of the Director of National Intelligence. *Intelligence Community Core Contract Personnel.* Intelligence Community Directive 612, October 30, 2009. Accessed March 2, 2015. http://www.dni.gov/files/documents/ICD/ICD_612.pdf.

49. U.S. Department of Defense. Center for Development of Security Excellence. *Glossary of Security Terms and Definitions.* November 2012. Accessed February 17, 2015. http://www.cdse.edu/documents/cdse/Glossary_Handbook.pdf.

50. U.S. Department of Defense. Center for Development of Security Excellence. *Glossary of Security Terms and Definitions.* November 2012. Accessed February 17, 2015. http://www.cdse.edu/documents/cdse/Glossary_Handbook.pdf.

51. Joint Military Intelligence College. *Intelligence Warning Terminology.* October 2001. Accessed July 3, 2015. https://archive.org/details/JMICInteligencelwarnterminology.

52. Edward Waltz, *Knowledge Management: In the Intelligence Enterprise* (Norwood, MA: Artech House, 2003), 11–12. Waltz refers to four different types of inferential analyses: those that explain past events, the structure of an organization, current behaviors, and foreknowledge that forecast future attributes.

53. North Atlantic Treaty Organization. *NATO Glossary of Terms and Definitions.* NATO Standardization Agency, 2008. Accessed July 2, 2015. https://fas.org/irp/doddir/other/nato2008.pdf.

54. U.S. Air Force. *Information Operations.* AFDD3, Air Force Doctrine Document 3-1311, January 2005 Incorporating Change 1, July 28, 2011. Accessed January 25, 2015. https://www.fas.org/irp/doddir/usaf/afdd3-13.pdf.

55. U.S. Department of Defense. *Dictionary of Military and Associated Terms.* JP 1-02, 08 November 2010, as Amended through 15 June 2015. Accessed June 24, 2015. http://www.dtic.mil/doctrine/dod_dictionary/.

56. United States Department of Justice. *Law Enforcement Analytic Standard.* Global Justice Information Sharing Initiative and International Association of Law Enforcement Intelligence Analysts, Inc. 2nd ed. April 2012. Accessed February 1, 2016. https://it.ojp.gov/documents/d/Law%20Enforcement%20Analytic%20Standards%2004202_combined_compliant.pdf.

57. Office of Management and Budget. *Management of Federal Information Resources.* Circular No. A-130, February 8, 1996. Accessed July 8, 2015. https://www.whitehouse.gov/omb/circulars_a130#6.

58. Office of Inspector General. *Survey of the Information Analysis and Infrastructure Protection Directorate,* Department of Homeland Security, Office of Inspections, Evaluations, & Special Reviews, OIG-04-13, February 2004, accessed January 26, 2016, https://www.oig.dhs.gov/assets/Mgmt/OIG_SurveyIAIP_0204.pdf.

59. Sharkov, Damien. "35,000 Volunteers Sign Up for Ukraine's 'Information Army' on First Day." *Newsweek,* February 27, 2015. Accessed March 4, 2015. http://europe.newsweek.com/35000-volunteers-sign-ukraines-information-army-first-day-310121?rx=us; also see Ukraine Information Army. *Welcome to the Headquarters of the Information Army.* Accessed March 4, 2015. http://i-army.org/index_en.php.

60. U.S. Department of Defense. *Dictionary of Military and Associated Terms.* JP 1-02, 08 November 2010, as Amended through 15 June 2015. Accessed July 4, 2015. http://www.dtic.mil/doctrine/dod_dictionary/.

61. U.S. Department of Defense. Center for Development of Security Excellence. *Glossary of Security Terms and Definitions.* November 2012. Accessed February 17, 2015. http://www.cdse.edu/documents/cdse/Glossary_Handbook.pdf.

62. U.S. Department of Defense. Center for Development of Security Excellence. *Glossary of Security Terms and Definitions.* November 2012. Accessed February 17, 2015. http://www.cdse.edu/documents/cdse/Glossary_Handbook.pdf.

63. U.S. Department of Defense. Center for Development of Security Excellence. *Glossary of Security Terms and Definitions.* November 2012. Accessed February 17, 2015. http://www.cdse.edu/documents/cdse/Glossary_Handbook.pdf.

64. Department of the Air Force. *Cornerstones of Information Warfare.* 1995. Accessed January 26, 2016. http://www.dtic.mil/get-tr-doc/pdf?AD=ADA307436.

65. U.S. Central Command Assessment Team. *Annex I Command and Control Knowledge Management.* February 2009. Accessed January 25, 2015. http://cryptome.org/dodi/centcom-c2km.pdf.

66. Office of Management and Budget. *Management of Federal Information Resources.* Circular A-130, Revised. November 28, 2000. Accessed February 10, 2015. http://www.whitehouse.gov/omb/circulars_a130_a130trans4.

67. Department of the Army. *Information Operations.* U.S. Army Field Manual 100-6, August 1996. Accessed July 8, 2015. http://www.fas.org/irp/doddir/army/fm100-6/.

68. Klein, Jennifer. *Information Dominance Center.* DBI Architects. Accessed January 25, 2015. http://cryptome.org/2013/09/info-dominance.pdf; also see Greenwald, Glenn. "Inside the Mind of NSA Chief Gen Keith Alexander." September 15, 2013. Accessed January 25, 2015. http://www.theguardian.com/commentisfree/2013/sep/15/nsa-mind-keith-alexander-star-trek.

69. U.S. Department of Defense. *Dictionary of Military and Associated Terms.* JP 1-02, 08 November 2010, as Amended through 15 June 2015. Accessed July 6, 2015. https://web.archive.org/web/20150815204834/http://www.dtic.mil/doctrine/new_pubs/jp1_02.pdf.

70. Pirolli, Peter and Card, Stuart. "Information Foraging." *Psychological Review* 106, no. 4 (1999): 643–75; also see Pirolli, Peter. *Assisting People to Become Independent Learners in the Analysis of Intelligence.* Office of Naval Research, 2006. ADA444562. Accessed January 25, 2015. http://www.dtic.mil/dtic/tr/fulltext/u2/a444562.pdf.

71. Department of the Army. Marine Corps Combat Development Command. Department of the Navy. *Operational Terms and Graphics.* FM 1-02 (FM 101-5). September 21, 2004. Accessed July 8, 2015. http://www.udel.edu/armyrotc/current_cadets/cadet_resources/manuals_regulations_files/FM%201-02%20-%20Operational%20Terms%20&%20Graphics.pdf.

72. Department of the Air Force. *Cornerstones of Information Warfare.* 1995. Accessed January 26, 2016. http://www.dtic.mil/get-tr-doc/pdf?AD=ADA307436.

73. Office of the Director of National Intelligence. *National Intelligence Program FY 2009 Congressional Budget Justification Book.* Vol. XII, February 2008. Accessed January 17, 2015. http://www.fas.org/irp/dni/cbjb-2009.pdf.

74. U.S. Department of Defense. Center for Development of Security Excellence. *Glossary of Security Terms and Definitions.* November 2012. Accessed February 16, 2015. http://www.cdse.edu/documents/cdse/Glossary_Handbook.pdf.

75. Office of Management and Budget. *Management of Federal Information Resources.* Circular No. A-130 Revised, November 28, 2000. Accessed July 8, 2015. https://www.whitehouse.gov/omb/circulars_a130_a130trans4/.

76. Horton, F. Woody. "Government Information Life Cycle Management." *Comprehensive Assessment of Public Information Dissemination, Appendix 16.* National Commission on Libraries and Information Science, June 2000–March 2001. Washington, DC: The Commission.

77. U.S. Department of Defense. Center for Development of Security Excellence. *Glossary of Security Terms and Definitions.* November 2012. Accessed February 16, 2015. http://www.cdse.edu/documents/cdse/Glossary_Handbook.pdf.

78. Department of the Army. Marine Corps Combat Development Command. Department of the Navy. *Operational Terms and Graphics.* FM 1-02 (FM 101-5). September 21, 2004. Accessed July 3, 2015. http://www.udel.edu/armyrotc/current_cadets/cadet_resources/manuals_regulations_files/FM%201-02%20-%20Operational%20Terms%20&%20Graphics.pdf. Department of the Air Force. *Cornerstones of Information Warfare.* 1995. Accessed January 26, 2016. http://www.dtic.mil/get-tr-doc/pdf?AD=ADA307436. Defense Acquisition University, *Glossary: Defense Acquisition Acronyms and Terms*, 13th ed., November 2009. Accessed February 27, 2015. http://www.dau.mil/pubscats/pubscats/13th_edition_glossary.pdf.

79. U.S. Department of Defense. *Information Operations.* Joint Publication 3-1327. November 2012 Incorporating Change 1 20 November 2014. Accessed February 12, 2015. http://www.dtic.mil/doctrine/new_pubs/jp3_13.pdf.

80. U.S. Department of Defense. *Information Operations*. Joint Publication 3-1327. November 2012 Incorporating Change 1 20 November 2014. Accessed February 12, 2015. http://www.dtic.mil/doctrine/new_pubs/jp3_13.pdf.

81. Adair, Kristin and Blanton, Thomas. *Rumsfeld's Roadmap to Propaganda: Information Operations Roadmap*. National Security Archive, January 26, 2006. Accessed July 8, 2015. http://www.gwu.edu/~nsarchiv/NSAEBB/NSAEBB177/ and U.S. Department of Defense. *Information Operations Roadmap*. 2003. Accessed July 8, 2015. http://www.gwu.edu/~nsarchiv/NSAEBB/NSAEBB177/info_ops_roadmap.pdf.

82. Schulman, Daniel. "Mind Games: CJR on the Military's Media Manipulation." *Columbia Journalism Review* 45, no. 1 (2006): 38.

83. CNSS, Instruction 4009, National Information Assurance Glossary. www.archives.gov/isoo/reports/2004-annual-report.html.

84. Steele, Robert D. *Information Peacekeeping: The Purest Form of War*. 1998. Accessed July 8, 2015. http://www.fas.org/irp/eprint/cyberwar-chapter.htm.

85. Steele, Robert D. *On Intelligence: Spies and Secrecy in an Open World*. Fairfax, VA: AFCEA 2000.

86. Cameron, C. T. and Curtin, Patricia. "Tracing Sources of Information Pollution: A Survey and Experimental Test of Print Media's Labeling Policy for Feature Advertising." *Journalism and Mass Communication Quarterly* 71, no. 1 (1995): 178–89.

87. Joint Chiefs of Staff. *Joint Doctrine Encyclopedia*. July 16, 1997. http://www.fas.org/man/dod-101/dod/.

88. U.S. Department of Defense. *Joint and National Intelligence Support to Military Operations*. JP 2-01. January 5, 2012. Accessed February 26, 2015. http://www.dtic.mil/doctrine/new_pubs/jp2_01.pdf.

89. Department of the Army. Marine Corps Combat Development Command. Department of the Navy. *Operational Terms and Graphics*. FM 1-02 (FM 101-5). September 21, 2004. Accessed July 3, 2015. http://www.udel.edu/armyrotc/current_cadets/cadet_resources/manuals_regulations_files/FM%201-02%20-%20Operational%20Terms%20&%20Graphics.pdf.

90. 44 U.S.C. 3502 (6), "Public Printing and Documents." http://www.gpoaccess.gov/uscode/browse.html.

91. Office of Management and Budget. Management of Federal Information Resources. Circular A-130. February 1996. Accessed July 8, 2015. http://www.whitehouse.gov/omb/circulars/a130/a130.html.

92. Department of the Army. *Information Operations*. U.S.Army Field Manual 100-6, August 1996. Accessed July 8, 2015.http://www.fas.org/irp/doddir/army/fm100-6/.

93. 44 U.S.C. 35 Subchapter II § 3532, "Public Printing and Documents." http://www.gpoaccess.gov/U.S.C.ode/.

94. Department of the Army. Marine Corps Combat Development Command. Department of the Navy. *Operational Terms and Graphics*. FM 1-02 (FM 101-5). September 21, 2004. Accessed July 3, 2015. http://www.udel.edu/armyrotc/cur

rent_cadets/cadet_resources/manuals_regulations_files/FM%201-02%20-%20Op-erational%20Terms%20&%20Graphics.pdf.

95. National Security Presidential Directive-54 / Homeland Security Presidential Directive-23. *Cybersecurity Policy*. January 9, 2008. Accessed February 14, 2015. http://www.fas.org/irp/offdocs/nspd/nspd-54.pdf.

96. Information Security Oversight Office. *ISOO's Mission, Vision, Values, Functions, and Goals*. Accessed July 8, 2015. http://www.archives.gov/isoo/about/.

97. Office of the Director of National Intelligence. *U.S. Intelligence Community Information Sharing Strategy*. February 22, 2008. Accessed July 8, 2015. https://fas.org/irp/dni/iss.pdf.

98. Commission on the Intelligence Capabilities of the United States Regarding Weapons of Mass Destruction. *Report to the President* (Silberman-Robb Commission). March 31, 2005. Accessed July 8, 2015. http://www.gpo.gov/fdsys/pkg/GPO-WMD/content-detail.html.

99. Information Sharing Environment. *ISE Governance*. Accessed January 22, 2015. http://ise.gov/ise-governancehttp://www.isaccouncil.org/aboutus.html.

100. National Council of ISACs. *About Us*. Accessed January 24, 2015. https://www.isaccouncil.org/; also see *Presidential Decision Directive/ NSC-63: Policy on Critical Infrastructure Protection*. May 22, 1998. Accessed February 15, 2015. http://www.fas.org/irp/offdocs/pdd/pdd-63.pdf.

101. U.S. Department of Homeland Security. *Information Sharing and Analysis Organizations*. Accessed July 9, 2015. https://www.whitehouse.gov/the-press-office/2015/02/13/executive-order-promoting-private-sector-cybersecurity-informa-tion-shari.

102. Federal Bureau of Investigation. *Minimum Criminal Intelligence Training Standards for Law Enforcement and Other Criminal Justice Agencies in the United States*. October 2007. Accessed January 22, 2015. https://it.ojp.gov/gist/108/Minimum-Criminal-Intelligence-Training-Standards; also see Information Sharing Environment. *Mission and Vision*. Accessed January 22, 2015. http://www.ise.gov/mission-and-vision.

103. *Intelligence Reform and Terrorism Prevention Act of 2004*, P.L.108–458, December 17, 2004. Accessed January 24, 2015. http://www.gpo.gov/fdsys/pkg/STATUTE-118/pdf/STATUTE-118-Pg3638.pdf.

104. Federal Bureau of Investigation. *Minimum Criminal Intelligence Training Standards for Law Enforcement and Other Criminal Justice Agencies in the United States*. October 2007. Accessed January 22, 2015. https://it.ojp.gov/gist/108/Minimum-Criminal-Intelligence-Training-Standards.

105. National Commission on Terrorist Attacks Upon the United States. *9/11 Commission Report*. 2004. Accessed July 8, 2015. http://govinfo.library.unt.edu/911/report/index.htm.

106. Statement of Zoe Baird Budinger and Jeffrey H. Smith. Senate Committee on Homeland Security & Governmental Affairs, October 12, 2011. *Ten Years After 9/11: A Status Report on Information Sharing*. Accessed July 8, 2015. https://fas.org/irp/congress/2011_hr/101211smith.pdf.

107. Defense Acquisition University. *Glossary: Defense Acquisition Acronyms and Terms.* 11th ed., 2003, Wayback Machine. http://wayback.archive. org/web/20041016024744/http://www.dau.mil/pubs/glossary/11th%20Glossary%20 2003.pdf.

108. Department of the Army. Marine Corps Combat Development Command. Department of the Navy. *Operational Terms and Graphics.* FM 1-02 (FM 101-5). September 21, 2004. Accessed July 3, 2015. http://www.udel.edu/armyrotc/current_cadets/cadet_resources/manuals_regulations_files/FM%201-02%20-%20Operational%20Terms%20&%20Graphics.pdf.

109. National Security Presidential Directive-54 / Homeland Security Presidential Directive-23. *Cybersecurity Policy.* January 9, 2008. Accessed February 14, 2015. http://www.fas.org/irp/offdocs/nspd/nspd-54.pdf.

110. U.S. Department of Defense. Center for Development of Security Excellence. *Glossary of Security Terms and Definitions.* November 2012. Accessed February 16, 2015. http://www.cdse.edu/documents/cdse/Glossary_Handbook.pdf.

111. National Institute of Standards and Technology. *Minimum Security Requirements for Federal Information and Information Systems.* FIPS Pub 200, March 2006. Accessed July 8, 2015. http://csrc.nist.gov/publications/fips/fips200/FIPS-200-final-march.pdf.

112. Devost, Matthew G., Houghton, Brian K., and Pollard, Neal A. *Information Terrorism: Can You Trust Your Toaster?* Terrorism Research Center, September 1998, 10, 12. Accessed January 24, 2015. https://www.devost.net/papers/suntzu.pdf.

113. Defense Acquisition University. *Glossary: Defense Acquisition Acronyms and Terms.* 13th ed., November 2009. Accessed February 27, 2015. http://www.dau.mil/pubscats/pubscats/13th_edition_glossary.pdf. Department of the Air Force. *Cornerstones of Information Warfare.* 1995. Accessed January 26, 2016. http://www.dtic.mil/get-tr-doc/pdf?AD=ADA307436. Also see Porche III, Isaac R., Paul, Christopher, York, Michael, et al. *Redefining Information Warfare Boundaries for an Army in a Wireless World.* RAND MG1113, 2013. Accessed January 25, 2015. http://www.rand.org/pubs/monographs/MG1113.html.

114. Martin Libicki, "The Mesh and the Net: Speculations on Armed Conflict in an Age of Free Silicon," National Defense University, March 1994, http://digitalndulibrary.ndu.edu/cdm/ref/collection/ndupress/id/6106; and "What Is Information Warfare?" National Defense University ACIS Paper 3, August 1995.

115. Berridge, G.R. and Lloyd, Lorna (eds.) *Palgrave Macmillan Dictionary of Diplomacy.* 3rd ed. New York: Palgrave Macmillan, 2012.

116. "Protection of Human Subjects," 21 CFR 50; National Commission for the Protection of Human Subjects of Biomedical and Behavioral Research, Ethical Principles and Guidelines for the Protection of Human Subjects of Research (Belmont Report), 18 April 1979.

117. John Arquilla and David Ronfeldt, *The Emergence of Noopolitik: Toward an American Information Strategy* (Santa Monica, CA: Rand, 1999).

118. U.S. Department of Defense. Center for Development of Security Excellence. *Glossary of Security Terms and Definitions.* November 2012. Accessed February 16, 2015. http://www.cdse.edu/documents/cdse/Glossary_Handbook.pdf.

119. InfraGard. *About InfraGard.* Accessed January 22, 2015. https://www.infra-gard.org/.

120. InfraGard Members Alliance. *What is InfraGard? Collaboration for National Infrastructure Protection.* Accessed January 22, 2015. http://www.infragardmembers.org/about-infragard.html.

121. Department of Homeland Security, Risk Steering Committee. *DHS Risk Lexicon.* September 2010. Accessed February 14, 2015. http://www.dhs.gov/dhs-risk-lexicon.

122. Anderson, Kent. *Intelligence-Based Threat Assessments for Information Networks and Infrastructures: A White Paper.* Portland, OR: Global Technology Research, 1998, 4.

123. Department of Homeland Security, Risk Steering Committee. *DHS Risk Lexicon.* September 2010. Accessed February 14, 2015. http://www.dhs.gov/dhs-risk-lexicon.

124. Manuel, Kate M. "Definitions of 'Inherently Governmental Function' in Federal Procurement Law and Guidance." *CRS Report for Congress* R442325. December 23, 2014. Accessed January 25, 2015. http://www.fas.org/sgp/crs/misc/R42325.pdf (for a discussion of multiple definitions).

125. In-Q-Tel. *About In-Q-Tel.* Accessed January 22, 2015. https://www.iqt.org/about-iqt/; also see Mahle, Melissa Boyle. *Denial and Deception: An Insider's View of the CIA from Iran-Contra to 9/11.* New York: Nation Books. 267–68.

126. U.S. Department of Defense. Center for Development of Security Excellence. *Glossary of Security Terms and Definitions.* November 2012. Accessed February 16, 2015. http://www.cdse.edu/documents/cdse/Glossary_Handbook.pdf.

127. Department of the Army. Threat *Awareness and Reporting Program.* Army Regulation 381–1. October 4, 2010. Accessed February 8, 2015. http://www.apd.army.mil/pdffiles/r381_12.pdf.

128. National Counterintelligence and Security Center. *Insider Threat.* Accessed February 14, 2015. http://www.ncix.gov/issues/ithreat/index.php; also see National Counterintelligence and Security Center. *National Insider Threat Task Force Mission Fact Sheet.* February 14, 2015. http://www.ncix.gov/nittf/docs/National_Insider_Threat_Task_Force_Fact_Sheet.pdf.

129. National Initiative for Cybersecurity Education. *A Glossary of Common Cybersecurity Terminology.* n.d. Accessed March 5, 2015. http://niccs.us-cert.gov/glossary.

130. U.S. Department of Defense. Center for Development of Security Excellence. *Glossary of Security Terms and Definitions.* November 2012. Accessed February 16, 2015. http://www.cdse.edu/documents/cdse/Glossary_Handbook.pdf.

131. Joint Military Intelligence College. *Intelligence Warning Terminology.* October 2001. Accessed July 3, 2015. https://archive.org/details/JMICInteligencelwarn-terminology.

132. U.S. Department of Defense. *Quadrennial Defense Review Report.* February 2010. Accessed February 11, 2015. http://www.defense.gov/qdr/qdr%20as%20of%2029jan10%201600.pdf.

133. U.S. Department of Defense. Center for Development of Security Excellence. *Glossary of Security Terms and Definitions.* November 2012. Accessed February 16, 2015. http://www.cdse.edu/documents/cdse/Glossary_Handbook.pdf.

134. U.S. Department of Defense. *Department of Defense Dictionary of Military and Associated Terms.* JP 1-02, 08 November 2010, as Amended through 15 January 2016. Accessed January 26, 2016. http://www.dtic.mil/doctrine/new_pubs/jp1_02.pdf.

135. Department of the Army. *Army Special Operations Forces Unconventional Warfare.* FM 3-05.130, September 2008. Accessed February 9, 2015. http://fas.org/irp/doddir/army/fm3-05-130.pdf.

136. U.S. Department of Defense. Center for Development of Security Excellence. *Glossary of Security Terms and Definitions.* November 2012. Accessed February 16, 2015. http://www.cdse.edu/documents/cdse/Glossary_Handbook.pdf.

137. Department of Homeland Security, Risk Steering Committee. *DHS Risk Lexicon.* September 2010. Accessed February 14, 2015. http://www.dhs.gov/dhs-risk-lexicon.

138. Office of the Director of National Intelligence. National *Intelligence Program FY 2009 Congressional Budget Justification Book.* Vol. XII, February 2008. Accessed January 17, 2015. http://www.fas.org/irp/dni/cbjb-2009.pdf.

139. Department of Homeland Security, Risk Steering Committee. *DHS Risk Lexicon.* September 2010. Accessed February 14, 2015. http://www.dhs.gov/dhs-risk-lexicon.

140. Office of Management and Budget. *Guidelines for Ensuring and Maximizing the Quality, Objectivity, Utility, and Integrity of Information Disseminated by Federal Agencies.* October 1, 2001. Accessed January 26, 2016. https://www.whitehouse.gov/omb/fedreg_final_information_quality_guidelines/.

141. Chief Information Officer, Intelligence Community. *Intelink 15th Anniversary.* August 2010. Accessed July 8, 2015. https://www.ndia.org/Divisions/Divisions/C4ISR/Documents/Breakfast%20Presentations/2010%20Presentations/Intelink%20Basic%20presentation.pdf.

142. Garthoff, Douglas F. *Directors of Central Intelligence 1946–2005.* Chapter 12. Center for the Study of Intelligence, CIA. Accessed July 8, 2015. https://www.cia.gov/library/center-for-the-study-of-intelligence/csi-publications/books-and-monographs/directors-of-central-intelligence-as-leaders-of-the-u-s-intelligence-community/dci_leaders.pdf.

143. Defense Intelligence Agency, Office of Counterintelligence. *CI Glossary— Terms & Definitions of Interest for DoD CI Professionals.* July 2014. Accessed January 25, 2015. https://www.hsdl.org/?view&did=699056.

144. U.S. Department of Defense. *Department of Defense Dictionary of Military and Associated Terms.* JP 1-02, 08 November 2010, as Amended through 15 January 2016. Accessed January 26, 2016. http://www.dtic.mil/doctrine/new_pubs/jp1_02.pdf.

145. Federal Bureau of Investigation. *Intelligence Defined.* Accessed July 7, 2015. http://www.fbi.gov/about-us/intelligence/defined.

146. Department of State, 22 CFR 9, Appendix A. https://www.law.cornell.edu/cfr/text/22/part-9.

147. Intelligence Advanced Research Projects Activity. *About IARPA.* Accessed January 17, 2015. http://www.iarpa.gov/index.php/about-iarpa.

148. Federal Bureau of Investigation. *Minimum Criminal Intelligence Training Standards for Law Enforcement and Other Criminal Justice Agencies in the United States.* October 2007. Accessed January 22, 2015. https://it.ojp.gov/gist/108/Minimum-Criminal-Intelligence-Training-Standards.

149. Intelligence and National Security Alliance. *History.* Accessed March 1, 2015. www.insaonline.org/i/a/ih/i/a/INSA_history.aspx.

150. Joint Military Intelligence College. *Intelligence Warning Terminology.* October 2001. Accessed July 3, 2015. https://archive.org/details/JMICInteligencelwarnterminology.

151. Joint Military Intelligence College. *Intelligence Warning Terminology.* October 2001. Accessed July 3, 2015. https://archive.org/details/JMICInteligencelwarnterminology.

152. Cumming, Alfred. "Congress as a Consumer of Intelligence Information." *CRS Report for Congress* RL32525. January 15, 2009. Accessed January 22, 2015. http://www.fas.org/sgp/crs/intel/RL32525.pdf.

153. Office of the Director of National Intelligence. *National Intelligence: A Consumer's Guide.* 2011. Accessed January 25, 2015. http://www.dni.gov/files/documents/IC_Consumers_Guide_2011.pdf. Commission on the Intelligence Capabilities of the United States Regarding Weapons of Mass Destruction. *Report to the President* (Silberman-Robb Commission). March 31, 2005. Accessed July 8, 2015. http://www.gpo.gov/fdsys/pkg/GPO-WMD/content-detail.html.

154. Office of the Director of National Intelligence. *Intelligence Community Policy Guidance.* Number 101.1. January 16, 2009. Accessed January 22, 2015. http://www.dni.gov/files/documents/ICPG/icpg_101_1.pdf.

155. Office of the Director of National Intelligence. *Intelligence Community Policy System.* Intelligence Community Directive 101, Effective January 16, 2009, Amended June 12, 2009. Accessed January 22, 2015. http://www.dni.gov/files/documents/ICD/ICD_101.pdf. Also see Office of the Director of National Intelligence. *Intelligence Community Policy Memorandum Number 2006-100-1: The Intelligence Community Policy Process.* April 25, 2006. Accessed February 4, 2015.

156. Central Intelligence Agency, Office of Public Affairs, *A Consumer's Guide to Intelligence: Gaining Knowledge and Foreknowledge of the World Around Us* (Washington, DC: National Technical Information Service, 1999); *Report of the Commission on the Intelligence Capabilities of the United States Regarding Weapons of Mass Destruction* (Silberman-Robb Commission), March 2005, accessed January 26, 2016, http://govinfo.library.unt.edu/wmd/about.html; and Defense Intelligence Agency, Office of Counterintelligence. *CI Glossary—Terms & Definitions of Interest for DoD CI Professionals.* July 2014. Accessed January 17, 2015. https://www.hsdl.org/?view&did=699056.

157. Federal Bureau of Investigation. *Intelligence Cycle.* Accessed January 26, 2016. https://www.fbi.gov/about-us/intelligence/intelligence-cycle.

158. U.S. Department of Defense. *Joint and National Intelligence Support to Military Operations*. JP 2-01. January 5, 2012. Accessed February 26, 2015. http://www.dtic.mil/doctrine/new_pubs/jp2_01.pdf.

159. Jan Goldman, *Intelligence Warning Terminology*, Joint Military Intelligence College, October 2001, accessed July 3, 2015. https://archive.org/details/JMICIntelligencelwarnterminology.

160. U.S. Department of Defense. *Joint Intelligence*. JP 2-0. October 22, 2013. Accessed February 15, 2015. http://www.dtic.mil/doctrine/new_pubs/jp2_0.pdf.

161. Office of the Director of National Intelligence. *Intelligence Enterprise Exercise Program*. Intelligence Community Directive 103, July 14, 2008. Accessed January 24, 2015. http://www.dni.gov/files/documents/ICD/ICD_103.pdf.

162. Jan Goldman, *Intelligence Warning Terminology*, Joint Military Intelligence College, October 2001, accessed July 3, 2015. https://archive.org/details/JMICIntelligencelwarnterminology.

163. Schulsky Abram N. and Schmitt, Gary J. *Silent Warfare: Understanding the World of Intelligence*. 3rd ed. Washington, DC: Brassey's, 2002.

164. Travers, Russ. "The Coming Intelligence Failure." *Studies in Intelligence* 1, no. 1 (1997): 35–43. Accessed July 8, 2015. https://www.cia.gov/library/center-for-the-study-of-intelligence/kent-csi/vol40no5/pdf/v40i5a05p.pdf.

165. Department of Defense. *Dictionary of Military and Associated Terms*. JP 1-02, 08 November 2010, as Amended through 15 January 2015. Accessed January 24, 2015. http://www.dtic.mil/doctrine/dod_dictionary/.

166. Theohary, Catherine A. and Rollins, John. "Terrorist Use of the Internet: Information Operations in Cyberspace."*CRS Report for Congress* R41674, March 8, 2011. Accessed March 20, 2015. http://fas.org/sgp/crs/terror/R41674.pdf.

167. United States Department of Justice. *Law Enforcement Analytic Standard*. Global Justice Information Sharing Initiative and International Association of Law Enforcement Intelligence Analysts, Inc. 2nd ed. April 2012, accessed February 1, 2016, https://it.ojp.gov/documents/d/Law%20Enforcement%20Analytic%20Standards%2004202_combined_compliant.pdf.

168. Dreyfuss, Robert. "TECHINT: The NSA, the NRO, and NIMA." In *National Insecurity: US Intelligence after the Cold War*, edited by Craig Eisendrath, 149–71. Temple University Press, 2000; also see Shorrock, Tim. *Spies for Hire: The Secret World of Intelligence Outsourcing* (New York: Simon & Schuster, 2008).

169. Defense Intelligence Agency, Office of Counterintelligence. *CI Glossary—Terms & Definitions of Interest for DoD CI Professionals*. July 2014. Accessed January 25, 2015. https://www.hsdl.org/?view&did=699056.

170. U.S. Department of Defense. *DoD Counterintelligence Collection Reporting*. 5240.17. October 26, 2005. Accessed January 14, 2015. https://www.fas.org/irp/doddir/dod/i5240_17.pdf.

171. U.S. Department of Defense. *Dictionary of Military and Associated Terms*. JP 1-02, 08 November 2010, as Amended through 15 January 2015. Accessed January 24, 2015. http://www.dtic.mil/doctrine/dod_dictionary/.

172. United States Department of Justice. *Law Enforcement Analytic Standards*. Global Justice Information Sharing Initiative. April 2012. Accessed July 9, 2015.

https://it.ojp.gov/documents/d/Law%20Enforcement%20Analytic%20Standards%20 04202_combined_compliant.pdf.

173. Ratcliffe, J. H. *Intelligence-Led Policing.* Cullompton, UK: Willan, 2008.

174. Defense Intelligence Agency, Office of Counterintelligence. *CI Glossary— Terms & Definitions of Interest for DoD CI Professionals.* July 2014. Accessed January 17, 2015. https://www.hsdl.org/?view&did=699056.

175. Office of the Director of National Intelligence. *National Intelligence: A Consumer's Guide.* 2011. Accessed January 25, 2015. http://www.dni.gov/files/documents/IC_Consumers_Guide_2011.pdf.

176. Defense Intelligence Agency, Office of Counterintelligence. *CI Glossary— Terms & Definitions of Interest for DoD CI Professionals.* July 2014. Accessed January 17, 2015. https://www.hsdl.org/?view&did=699056.

177. U.S. Department of Defense. *Joint Intelligence.* JP 2-0. October 22, 2013. Accessed February 15, 2015. http://www.dtic.mil/doctrine/new_pubs/jp2_0.pdf.

178. U.S. Department of Defense. *Assistant to the Secretary of Defense for Intelligence Oversight.* Directive Number 5148.11, April 24, 2013. Accessed January 25, 2015. http://www.dtic.mil/whs/directives/corres/pdf/514811p.pdf. Also see Office of the Director of National Intelligence. *National Intelligence: A Consumer's Guide.* 2011. Accessed January 25, 2015. http://www.dni.gov/files/documents/IC_Consumers_Guide_2011.pdf.

179. Federal Bureau of Investigation. *Minimum Criminal Intelligence Training Standards for Law Enforcement and Other Criminal Justice Agencies in the United States.* October 2007. Accessed January 25, 2015. https://it.ojp.gov/gist/108/Minimum-Criminal-Intelligence-Training-Standards.

180. *Intelligence Reform and Terrorism Prevention Act* P.L.108–458, 118 STAT. 3638. December 17, 2004. Accessed February 15, 2015. http://www.gpo.gov/fdsys/pkg/PLAW-108publ458/pdf/PLAW-108publ458.pdf.

181. Office of the Director of National Intelligence. *Executive Branch Intelligence Customer.* Intelligence Community Directive 404, July 22, 2013. Accessed February 27, 2015. https://fas.org/irp/dni/icd/icd-404.pdf.

182. U.S. Department of Defense. *Joint Intelligence.* JP 2-0. October 22, 2013. Accessed February 15, 2015. http://www.dtic.mil/doctrine/new_pubs/jp2_0.pdf.

183. U.S. Department of Defense. *Department of Defense Dictionary of Military and Associated Terms.* JP 1-02, 08 November 2010, as Amended through 15 January 2016. Accessed January 26, 2016. http://www.dtic.mil/doctrine/new_pubs/jp1_02.pdf.

184. Jan Goldman, *Intelligence Warning Terminology*, Joint Military Intelligence College, October 2001, accessed July 3, 2015. https://archive.org/details/JMICInteligencelwarnterminology.

185. EO11905 *United States Foreign Intelligence Activities*, February 8, 1976. Accessed February 8, 2015. http://www.presidency.ucsb.edu/ws/?pid=59348.

186. EO 12863 *President's Foreign Intelligence Advisory Board*, September 13, 1993. Accessed February 8, 2015. http://www.presidency.ucsb.edu/ws/index.php?pid=59355; also see Electronic Privacy Information Center. *Intelligence Oversight Board: FOIA Documents.*

187. U.S. Department of Defense. *Joint Intelligence.* JP 2-0. October 22, 2013. Accessed February 15, 2015. http://www.dtic.mil/doctrine/new_pubs/jp2_0.pdf.

188. U.S. Department of Defense. *Dictionary of Military and Associated Terms.* JP 1-02, 08 November 2010, as Amended through 15 June 2015. Accessed July 4, 2015. http://www.dtic.mil/doctrine/dod_dictionary/.

189. U.S. Department of Defense. *Department of Defense Dictionary of Military and Associated Terms.* JP 1-02, 08 November 2010, as Amended through 15 January 2016. Accessed January 26, 2016. http://www.dtic.mil/doctrine/new_pubs/jp1_02.pdf.

190. U.S. Department of Defense. *Joint Intelligence.* JP 2-0. October 22, 2013. Accessed February 15, 2015. http://www.dtic.mil/doctrine/new_pubs/jp2_0.pdf.

191. U.S. Department of Defense. *Special Access Program (SAP) Policy.* DoD Directive Number 5205.07, July 1, 2010. Accessed January 25, 2015. http://www.dtic.mil/whs/directives/corres/pdf/520507p.pdf.

192. Reich, Eugenie Samuel. "Intelligence Science Board Disbanded." *Nature Newsblog,* October 15, 2010. Accessed January 25, 2015. http://blogs.nature.com/news/2010/10/intelligence_science_board_dis_1.html; also see John Young's 2014 FOIA requests, http://cryptome.org/2014/11/isb-interrogation.pdf.

193. Moore, David T. *Sensemaking: A Structure for an Intelligence Revolution.* Accessed January 25, 2015. http://ni-u.edu/ni_press/pdf/Sensemaking.pdf. Also see Dervin, Brenda. "Sense-Making's Journey from Metatheory to Methodology to Method: An Example Using Information Seeking and Use as Research Focus." In *Sense-making Methodology Reader: Selected Writings of Brenda Dervin,* edited by Brenda Dervin, Lois Foreman-Wernet, and Eric Lauterbach (Cresskill, NJ: Hampton Press, 2003), 133–16.

194. U.S. Department of Defense. *Joint Intelligence.* JP 2-0. October 22, 2013. Accessed February 15, 2015. http://www.dtic.mil/doctrine/new_pubs/jp2_0.pdf.

195. U.S. Department of Defense. Center for Development of Security Excellence. *Glossary of Security Terms and Definitions.* November 2012. Accessed February 16, 2015. http://www.cdse.edu/documents/cdse/Glossary_Handbook.pdf.

196. U.S. Department of Defense. *Joint Intelligence.* JP 2-0. October 22, 2013. Accessed February 15, 2015. http://www.dtic.mil/doctrine/new_pubs/jp2_0.pdf.

197. U.S. Department of Defense. Center for Development of Security Excellence. *Glossary of Security Terms and Definitions.* November 2012. Accessed February 16, 2015. http://www.cdse.edu/documents/cdse/Glossary_Handbook.pdf.

198. Margo Schlanger, Alexander W. Joel, Nancy C. Libin (reviewing officials), *Civil Liberties Impact Assessment for the Interagency Threat Assessment and Coordination Group (ITACG),* September 29, 2010, accessed January 26, 2016, http://www.dhs.gov/xlibrary/assets/crcl-itacg.pdf.

199. Central Intelligence Agency. *Intellepedia Marks Second Anniversary.* March 20, 2008. https://www.cia.gov/news-information/featured-story-archive/2008-featured-story-archive/intellipedia-marks-second-anniversary.html.

200. North Atlantic Treaty Organization. *NATO Glossary of Terms and Definitions.* NATO Standardization Agency, 2008. Accessed July 2, 2015. https://fas.org/irp/doddir/other/nato2008.pdf.

201. Jan Goldman, *Intelligence Warning Terminology*, Joint Military Intelligence College, October 2001, accessed July 3, 2015. https://archive.org/details/JMICInteligencelwarnterminology.

202. Department of Homeland Security, Risk Steering Committee. *DHS Risk Lexicon.* September 2010. Accessed February 14, 2015. http://www.dhs.gov/dhs-risk-lexicon.

203. U.S. Customs and Border Protection. *What Is IBIS?* Accessed February 25, 2015. https://help.cbp.gov/.

204. Interagency Security Classification Appeals Panel. *Establishment and Function.* Accessed February 9, 2015. http://www.archives.gov/declassification/iscap/.

205. The Intercept. *About.* Accessed January 26, 2016. https://theintercept.com/staff/#about-flm.

206. United States Senate, Select Committee to Study Governmental Operations with Respect to Intelligence Activities (Church Committee). *Final Report.* Book 1. April 26, 1976. Accessed February 7, 2015. https://archive.org/details/finalreportof-sel01unit.

207. Department of Homeland Security, Risk Steering Committee. *DHS Risk Lexicon.* September 2010. Accessed February 14, 2015. http://www.dhs.gov/dhs-risk-lexicon.

208. U.S. Department of Defense. Center for Development of Security Excellence. *Glossary of Security Terms and Definitions.* November 2012. Accessed February 16, 2015. http://www.cdse.edu/documents/cdse/Glossary_Handbook.pdf.

209. United States Department of Defense. *Foreign Humanitarian Assistance.* JP 3-29, January 3, 2014. Accessed March 7, 2015. http://www.dtic.mil/doctrine/new_pubs/jp3_29.pdf.

210. International Court of Justice. *The Court.* Accessed March 6, 2015. http://www.icj-cij.org/court/index.php?p1=1.

211. International Criminal Court. *About the Court.* Accessed March 6, 2015. http://www.icc-cpi.int/en_menus/icc/about%20the%20court/Pages/about%20the%20court.aspx.

212. Federal Bureau of Investigation. *Minimum Criminal Intelligence Training Standards for Law Enforcement and Other Criminal Justice Agencies in the United States.* October 2007. Accessed January 25, 2015. https://it.ojp.gov/gist/108/Minimum-Criminal-Intelligence-Training-Standards; INTERPOL. *Overview.* Accessed January 25, 2015. http://www.interpol.int/About-INTERPOL/Overview.

213. For an example of Red Notices, see INTERPOL, accessed January 26, 2016, http://www.interpol.int/notice/search/wanted.

214. U.S. Department of Defense. Center for Development of Security Excellence. *Glossary of Security Terms and Definitions.* November 2012. Accessed February 16, 2015. http://www.cdse.edu/documents/cdse/Glossary_Handbook.pdf.

215. U.S. Department of Justice. *The Attorney General's Guidelines for Domestic FBI Operations.* 2008. Accessed February 25, 2015. http://www.justice.gov/sites/default/files/ag/legacy/2008/10/03/guidelines.pdf.

216. Ministry of Defense. Captured Persons (CPERS). Joint Doctrine Publication 1-10, 3rd edition, January 2015. https://www.gov.uk/government/uploads/system/uploads/attachment_data/file/455589/20150820-JDP_1_10_Ed_3_Ch_1_Secured.pdf.

217. North Atlantic Treaty Organization. *NATO Glossary of Terms and Definitions*. NATO Standardization Agency, 2008. Accessed July 2, 2015. https://fas.org/irp/doddir/other/nato2008.pdf.

218. Federal Bureau of Investigation. *Next Generation Identification (NGI): Identification and Investigative Services*. Accessed February 11, 2015. http://www.fbi.gov/about-us/cjis/fingerprints_biometrics/ngi.

219. National Security Presidential Directive-54/Homeland Security Presidential Directive-23. *Cybersecurity Policy*. January 9, 2008. Accessed February 14, 2015. http://www.fas.org/irp/offdocs/nspd/nspd-54.pdf.

220. Waller, Mark. *Report of the Intelligence Services Commissioner for 2014*. Stationary Office, 2015. Accessed January 26, 2016. http://intelligencecommissioner.com/content.asp?id=19.

221. Department of the Army. *Counterinsurgency*. FM 3-24, MCWP 3-33.5. December 2006. Accessed January 14, 2015. http://usacac.army.mil/cac2/Repository/Materials/COIN-FM3-24.pdf.

222. U.S. Department of Defense. Center for Development of Security Excellence. *Glossary of Security Terms and Definitions*. November 2012. Accessed February 16, 2015. http://www.cdse.edu/documents/cdse/Glossary_Handbook.pdf.

223. Grabo, Cynthia M. *Warning Intelligence*. Intelligence Profession Series, no.4. McLean, VA: Association of Former Intelligence Officers, 1987.

224. U.S. Department of State. "Definitions of Diplomatic Security Terms." *Foreign Affairs Manual*. 12FAM090. November 12, 2014. Accessed January 13, 2015. http://www.state.gov/documents/organization/88330.pdf.

225. Defense Intelligence Agency, Office of Counterintelligence. *CI Glossary—Terms & Definitions of Interest for DoD CI Professionals*. July 2014. Accessed January 25, 2015. https://www.hsdl.org/?view&did=699056.

J

JAMMING The overwhelming interference of electronic signals so that the intended receiver of those signals is unable to distinguish the true signal from other signals; also known as "noise." *See* ELECTRONIC JAMMING

JIHAD The Arabic word *jihad* is derived from a verb that means "to struggle, strive, or exert oneself." It appears in the Quran in the context of calls to strive for the advancement of Islam and to make a personal commitment to struggle "in the cause of God." At its most general level, jihad denotes taking action on behalf of Islam and fellow Muslims, and thereby improving one's standing as a pious member of the religious community. The concept has been understood by Muslims in various ways over time to include fighting (qital) against those who oppose the advancement of Islam or who harm Muslims, fundraising for Islamic causes, proselytizing, doing charitable work, and struggling against personal desires. Historically, key Sunni and Shi'a religious texts such as collections of sayings and deeds of the prophet Mohammed (hadith) most often referred to jihad in terms of religiously approved fighting on behalf of Islam and Muslims. Some Muslims have emphasized nonviolent social and personal means of jihad or have sought to shape the modern meaning of the term to refer to fighting only under defensive circumstances.[1]

JOINT Connotes activities, operations, organizations, and more, in which elements of two or more military departments participate.[2]

JOINT ADVERTISING AND MARKET RESEARCH STUDIES (JAMRS) RECRUITING DATABASE 1. JAMRS is an official Department of Defense program responsible for joint marketing communications and market research and studies. One of JAMRS's objectives is to explore the perceptions, beliefs, and attitudes of American youth as they relate to joining the military. Understanding these factors is critical to the success of sustaining an All-Volunteer Force and helps ensure recruiting efforts are directed in the most efficient and beneficial manner.[3] 2. In 2005, the Pentagon announced in the *Federal Register* the existence of the JAMRS Database—a massive registry of 30 million Americans between the ages of 16 and 25 for military recruitment purposes. First authorized in 2002, the JAMRS program collects information on young people from a variety of sources, including the Selective Service, Departments of Motor Vehicles, and commercial data brokers. The Defense Act of 1982 gave the Department of Defense permission to gather information for recruitment purposes but set limits on what type of information could be maintained. For example, the Defense Act limited the database to only include students over 17 years old or in the eleventh grade or higher, only contain "directory information" (i.e., name, school, contact info), and only allowed the Pentagon to keep the information for a maximum of three years. In practice, the JAMRS database violated the Defense Act in a number of troubling ways. The JAMRS database included much more than directory information: the Department of Defense was collecting phone numbers, mailing addresses, e-mail addresses, social security numbers, racial and ethnic data, grade point averages, college intentions, and height and weight information. Also, the database included all sixteen-year-olds, and the Department of Defense was keeping information for five years.[4]

JOINT COLLECTION MANAGEMENT BOARD (JCMB) Combatant command commanders management board for coordinating the interactions of their analytical and collection functions as a comprehensive collaborative effort.[5]

JOINT DEPLOYABLE INTELLIGENCE SUPPORT SYSTEM (JDISS)
1. A transportable workstation and communications suite that electronically extends a joint intelligence center to a joint task force or other tactical user.[6]
2. A software suite that can be hooked up to several government computer networks at the classified and unclassified level to include JWICS, SIPRNet, or NIPRnet.

JOINT DOCTRINE Joint doctrine presents fundamental principles that guide the employment of U.S. military forces in coordinated and integrated action toward a common objective. It promotes a common perspective from which to plan, train, and conduct military operations. It represents what is taught, believed, and advocated as what is right (i.e., what works best). It provides distilled insights and wisdom gained from employing the military instrument of national power in operations to achieve national objectives.[7]

JOINT DOCTRINE DEVELOPMENT COMMUNITY The Chairman of the Joint Chiefs of Staff, the Services, the combatant commands, the Joint Staff, the combat support agencies, and the doctrine development agencies of the Services and the joint community.[8]

JOINT DOCUMENT EXPLOITATION CENTER (JDEC) An element, normally subordinate to the intelligence directorate of a joint staff, responsible for deriving intelligence information from captured adversary documents including all forms of electronic data and other forms of stored textual and graphic information.[9]

JOINT INFORMATION ENVIRONMENT A secure joint information environment, comprised of shared information technology (IT) infrastructure, enterprise services achieve full-spectrum superiority, improve mission effectiveness, increase security and realize IT efficiencies. JIE is operated and managed per Unified Command Plan (UCP) using enforceable standards, specifications, and common tactics, techniques, and procedures, and a single security architecture to TTPs.[10]

JOINT INTELLIGENCE Intelligence produced by elements of more than one military service.[11]

JOINT INTERROGRATION OPERATIONS (JIO) 1. Activities conducted by a joint or interagency organization to extract information for intelligence purposes from enemy prisoners of war, dislocated civilians, enemy combatants, or other uncategorized detainees. 2. Activities conducted in support of law enforcement efforts to adjudicate enemy combatants who are believed to have committed crimes against U.S. persons or property.[12]

JOINT PROBABILITY The probability of two events occurring in conjunction—that is, the probability that event A and event B both occur, written as P(AB) and pronounced A intersect B. The probability of someone dying from the pandemic flu is equal to the joint probability of someone contracting the flu (event A) and the flu killing them (event B). Joint probabilities are regularly used in Probabilistic Risk Assessments and Event Trees.[13]

JOINT REGIONAL INFORMATION EXCHANGE SYSTEM (JRIES) A secure collaborative system used by the DHS Homeland Security Operations Center (HSOC) to collect and disseminate information between DHS and federal, state, tribal, and local agencies involved in counterterrorism. Information passed along this system includes analytical tools and capabilities to support distributed collaborative analysis, reporting, and intelligence.[14]

JOINT TERRORISM ANALYSIS CENTRE (JTAC) ATTACK METHODOLOGY TEAM JTAC brings together counter-terrorist expertise from the police and government departments and agencies. JTAC is a self-standing organization comprised of representatives from sixteen government departments and agencies. It forms a key element of the (UK) National Intelligence Machinery.[15]

JOINT TERRORISM TASK FORCE (JTTF) 1. The mission of the JTTF is to organize federal, state, and local law enforcement agencies in a coordinated manner for the purpose of detecting, preventing, and responding to domestic and international terrorist organizations or individuals who may threaten or attack U.S. citizens or interests abroad or conduct criminal activity within the United States, and/or any threat or incident involving weapons of mass destruction (WMD) or the proliferation of same directed against the population or interests of the United States.[16] 2. Developed in New York City in 1980 with 11 members from the New York Police Department and 11 FBI investigators whose goal was to be both responsive and proactive. After September 11, 2001, the FBI expanded the initiative nationwide, significantly increasing the number of JTTFs and, according to the GAO, the number of cities that participated in information-sharing centers.[17] *See* COUNTERTERRORISM CENTER; INFORMATION ANALYSIS AND INFRASTRUCTURE PROTECTION DIRECTORATE; NATIONAL JOINT TERRORISM TASK FORCE; TERRORIST THREAT INTEGRATION CENTER

JOINT THREAT RESEARCH INTELLIGENCE GROUP (JTRIG) A unit of the signals intelligence agency Government Communications Headquarters (GCHQ), is involved in efforts against political groups it considers "extremist," Islamist activity in schools, the drug trade, online fraud and financial scams.[18]

JOINT WORLDWIDE INTELLIGENCE COMMUNICATIONS SYSTEM (JWICS) The sensitive compartmented information portion of the Defense Information Systems Network, which incorporates advanced networking technologies that permit point-to-point or multipoint information exchange involving voice, text, graphics, data, and video teleconferencing.[19] The DIA's top-secret computer network for the intelligence community's TS-SCI global network, JWICS is a communications network that delivers secure information services to national and defense intelligence components around the world. All U.S. government use TS-SCI networks run off of JWICS.

JOURNALIST Full-time or part-time journalists, regardless of nationality (including stringers, who are part-time correspondents covering a local area for a paper published elsewhere, or a freelance journalist who is paid for each piece of broadcast or published work rather than accepting a salary) accredited by a U.S. news service, newspaper, periodical, radio, or television network or station. The term "accredited" means a full- or part-time employee, regardless of nationality, who is formally authorized by contract or by the issuance of press credentials to represent himself or herself either in the United States or abroad, as a correspondent of a U.S. news media organization, or is officially recognized by a foreign government as a representative of a U.S. news media organization.[20]

JUDGMENT 1. A process of inference; the evaluation of one or more possibilities with respect to a specific set of evidence and criteria by which to evaluate the evidence. 2. [As used in intelligence analysis] Judgment is what analysts use to fill gaps in their knowledge. It entails going beyond the available information and is the principal means of coping with uncertainty. It always involves an analytical leap, from the known into the uncertain. Judgment is an integral part of all intelligence analysis.[21] (*Psychology of Analysis* by Richards J. Heuer Jr., 1999) *See* INFERENCE

NOTES

1. Rollins, John. "Al Qaeda and Affiliates: Historical Perspective, Global Presence, and Implications for U.S. Policy." CRS Report for Congress R41070. January 25, 2011. Accessed January 26, 2015. https://www.fas.org/sgp/crs/terror/R41070.pdf; also see Theohary, Catherine A. and Rollins, John. "Terrorist Use of the Internet: Information Operations in Cyberspace." CRS Report for Congress R41674. March 8, 2011. http://www.dtic.mil/dtic/tr/fulltext/u2/a544308.pdf.

2. U.S. Department of Defense. *Doctrine for the Armed Forces of the United States.* JP 1, March 25, 2013. Accessed February 21, 2015. http://www.dtic.mil/doctrine/new_pubs/jp1.pdf.

3. U.S. Department of Defense. *Welcome to Joint Advertising, Market Research & Studies.* Accessed January 26, 2015. http://jamrs.defense.gov/.

4. New York Civil Liberties Union. *Information about the JAMRS Database.* Accessed January 25, 2015. http://www.nyclu.org/milrec/jamrsinfo; also see EPIC. *DOD Recruiting Database*, which includes FOIA requests to the DOD on JAMRS. Accessed January 26, 2015. https://epic.org/privacy/student/doddatabase.html and National Archives and Records Administration. *Request for Records Disposition Authority.* September 3, 2014. Accessed January 26, 2015. http://www.archives.gov/records-mgmt/rcs/schedules/departments/department-of-defense/office-of-the-secretary-of-defense/rg-0330/daa-0330-2014-0009_sf115.pdf.

5. U.S. Department of Defense. *Joint and National Intelligence Support to Military Operations*, Joint Publication 2-01, January 5, 2012. Accessed January 26, 2016. http://www.dtic.mil/doctrine/new_pubs/jp2_01.pdf.

6. U.S. Department of Defense. *Department of Defense Dictionary of Military and Associated Terms.* JP 1-02, 08 November 2010, as Amended through 15 January

2016. Accessed January 26, 2016, http://www.dtic.mil/doctrine/new_pubs/jp1_02.
pdf.

7. U.S. Department of Defense, Joint Electronic Library. *Joint Doctrine.* January 8, 2014. Accessed February 4, 2015. http://www.dtic.mil/doctrine/new_pubs/
jointpub.htm.

8. U.S. Department of Defense. *Department of Defense Dictionary of Military and Associated Terms.* JP 1-02, 08 November 2010, as Amended through 15 January 2015. Accessed February 18, 2015. http://www.dtic.mil/doctrine/dod_dictionary/
data/j/18104.html.

9. U.S. Department of Defense. *Department of Defense Dictionary of Military and Associated Terms.* JP 1-02, 08 November 2010, as Amended through 15 January 2016. Accessed January 26, 2016, http://www.dtic.mil/doctrine/new_pubs/jp1_02.
pdf.

10. Defense Information Systems Agency. *Enabling the Joint Information Environment (JIE).* May 5, 2014. Accessed January 26, 2015. http://www.disa.mil/about/
our-work/~/media/files/disa/about/jie101_000.pdf; also see Joint Chiefs of Staff. *Joint Information Environment White Paper.* January 22, 2013. Accessed January 26, 2015. http://www.jcs.mil/Portals/36/Documents/Publications/environmentalwhitepaper.pdf.

11. United States Senate, Select Committee to Study Governmental Operations with Respect to Intelligence Activities (Church Committee). *Final Report.* Book 1. April 26, 1976. Accessed February 7, 2015. https://archive.org/details/finalreportof-sel01unit.

12. U.S. Department of Defense. *Joint and National Intelligence Support to Military Operations.* JP 2-01. January 5, 2012. Accessed February 26, 2015. http://www.
dtic.mil/doctrine/new_pubs/jp2_01.pdf.

13. Department of Homeland Security, Risk Steering Committee. *DHS Risk Lexicon.* September 2010. Accessed February 14, 2015. http://www.dhs.gov/dhs-
risk-lexicon.

14. Harold C. Relyea and Jeffrey W. Seifert, "Information Sharing for Homeland Security: A Brief Overview." *CRS Report for Congress* RL32597, January 10, 2005, accessed February 1, 2016, https://www.fas.org/sgp/crs/RL32597.pdf.

15. The Intercept, *JTAC Attack Methodology Team,* May 18, 2015, accessed February 1, 2016, https://theintercept.com/document/2015/05/18/jtac-attack-methodology/.

16. Federal Bureau of Investigation, *National Joint Terrorism Task Force,* accessed January 26, 2016, https://www.fbi.gov/about-us/investigate/terrorism/national-joint-terrorism-task-force.

17. U.S. General Accounting Office, *U.S. Attorneys: Performance-Based Initiatives Are Evolving,* May 2004, GAO-04-422. Accessed February 1, 2016, http://
www.gao.gov/assets/250/242667.pdf. *Statement of Robert F. Dacey: Homeland Security: Information Sharing Responsibilities, Challenges, and Key Management Issues,* September 17, 2003, GAO-03-1165T, accessed February 2016, http://www.
gao.gov/new.items/d031165t.pdf.

18. Glenn Greenwald and Andrew Fishman, "Controversial GCHQ Unit Engaged in Domestic Law Enforcement, Online Propaganda, Psychology Research," *The Inter-*

cept, June 22, 2015, accessed February 2, 2016, https://theintercept.com/2015/06/22/controversial-gchq-unit-domestic-law-enforcement-propaganda/.

19. U.S. Department of Defense. *Department of Defense Dictionary of Military and Associated Terms.* JP 1-02, 08 November 2010, as Amended through 15 January 2016. Accessed January 26, 2016, http://www.dtic.mil/doctrine/new_pubs/jp1_02.pdf.

20. U.S. Department of Defense. *Defense Human Intelligence (HUMINT) and Related Intelligence Activities.* Instruction, Number S-5200.42, December 8, 2009. Accessed February 26, 2015. http://nsarchive.gwu.edu/NSAEBB/NSAEBB520-the-Pentagons-Spies/EBB-PS45.pdf.

21. Defense Intelligence Agency, Office of Counterintelligence. *CI Glossary—Terms & Definitions of Interest for DoD CI Professionals.* July 2014. Accessed January 17, 2015. https://www.hsdl.org/?view&did=699056.

K

KENT, SHERMAN A major figure in developing the academic and professional study of intelligence. Kent was a prominent Yale history professor when he joined the Research and Analysis Branch of OSS in World War II. After the war, Kent authored the still-important 1949 book *Strategic Intelligence for American World Policy*. Later, he joined the Central Intelligence Agency, where he served for many years. The Sherman Kent School, located at CIA University, is named after the "father of intelligence."[1]

KEY ASSUMPTION Any hypothesis that analysts accept to be true and forms the basis of an assessment. For example, analysts refused to accept the possible collapse of the Soviet Union because their key assumption was that the Communist Party would never relinquish control of their East European allies.

KEY DRIVERS Variables within a threat scenario that seemingly have a dynamic influence on the environment or the success or failure of the outcome of a particular scenario. For example, as stated in *Global Trends 2015*, over the past 15 months, the National Intelligence Council (NIC), in close collaboration with U.S. government specialists and a wide range of experts outside the government, has worked to identify major drivers and trends that will shape the world of 2015. The key drivers identified are: (1) demographics; (2) natural resources and environment; (3) science and technology; (4) the global economy and globalization; (5) national and international governance; (6) future conflict; (7) the role of the United States. In examining these drivers, several points should be kept in mind: No single driver or trend will dominate the global future in 2015. Each driver will have varying impacts in different regions and countries. The drivers are not necessarily mutually reinforcing; in some cases, they will work at cross-purposes. Taken together, these drivers and trends intersect to create an integrated picture of the world of 2015, about which we can make projections with varying degrees of confidence and identify some troubling uncertainties of strategic importance to the United States.[2]

KEY INDICATOR (CRITICAL INDICATOR) An action or decision that will immediately and directly affect a threat scenario, will constitute a small proportion of the overall indicators, and which can easily be monitored.[3]

KEY INTELLIGENCE QUESTIONS (KZQ) Topics of particular importance to national policymakers, as defined by the DCI.[4]

KEY JUDGMENT Extraction of the overall situation and likely outcome based on an extensive review or research of a given situation; encapsulation of a lengthy estimate, found in the first few pages of an estimate.[5] *See* KEY QUESTIONS

KEY QUESTIONS An element of estimative intelligence. "Basic, 'so-what' kernels of the particular estimative situation that should be fashioned at the very outset of any estimate. Framing such key questions is usually a much more difficult task than the novice might assume, and in practice many [estimates] have been rushed into with no clear picture of what the really essential elements of the situation were in which the policymaker would be most interested."[6] *See* KEY JUDGMENT

KEY SYMBOL In psychological operations, a simple, suggestive, repetitive element (rhythm, sign, color, etc.) that has an immediate impact on a target audience and creates a favorable environment for the acceptance of a psychological theme.

KEY TERRAIN A locality or area the seizure or retention of which affords a marked advantage to a combatant.

KEYLOGGER Software or hardware that tracks keystrokes and keyboard events, usually surreptitiously/secretly, to monitor actions by the user of an information system.[7]

KEYSTONE PUBLICATIONS Joint doctrine publications that establish the doctrinal foundation for a series of joint publications in the hierarchy of joint publications.[8]

KHOBAR TOWERS A terrorist car bombing of the residence of U.S. military personnel at the Khobar Towers complex in Dhahran, Saudi Arabia, June 25, 1996. The bombing killed 19 American military personnel and wounded hundreds more. According to the official congressional report, "It exposed the shortcomings of a U.S. intelligence apparatus that left Americans unprepared for the threat that confronted them." The report raises three points that led to this intelligence failure and operational deficiencies by military leaders and policymakers: (1) intelligence was devoid of specific knowledge of the threat; (2) there were failures in pro-active analysis (which was mostly reactive); (3) assessments did not acknowledge their own limitations and provided a false sense of confidence in the level of the threat.[9]

KNOWLEDGE MANAGEMENT 1. A cross-disciplinary organic enterprise connecting and integrating social, cultural, communication and technical processes—including trust, obligation, commitment, and accountability—to facilitate creative learning and adaptation and leverage information capture and knowledge exchange (ICKE) by connecting communities "who-need to-know" with those "who-need-to-share" with those "who-need-to-use."[10] 2. In the NICE (National Initiative for Cybersecurity Education) Workforce Framework, cybersecurity work where a person manages and administers processes and tools that enable the organization to identify, document, and access intellectual capital and information content.[11]

KNOWN FACILITY A facility that has been detected, confirmed, and categorized by function with some degree of confidence.[12]

KOREAN WAR The Korean War involved a number of intelligence failures and represented a "watershed in U.S. national estimating because intelligence failed to ring alarm bells either in June 1950 when the North Koreans were about to invade South Korea, or in November when the Chinese Communists had infiltrated great numbers of combat troops into North Korea in preparation for launching a massive offensive against U.S.-UN forces. This failure to warn led to the creation of the Office of National Estimates and of a system of more effective national intelligence estimating that has endured essentially unchanged to this day."[13] See OFFICE OF NATIONAL ESTIMATES

NOTES

1. Central Intelligence Agency. *A Look Back . . . Sherman Kent: The Father of Intelligence*, May 6, 2010, accessed February 1, 2016, https://www.cia.gov/news-information/featured-story-archive/2010-featured-story-archive/sherman-kent-the-father-of-intelligence.html.

2. National Intelligence Council, *Global Trends 2015: A Dialogue about the Future with Nongovernmental Experts*, December 2000, accessed February 1, 2016, https://fas.org/irp/cia/product/globaltrends2015/.

3. Jan Goldman, *Intelligence Warning Terminology*, Joint Military Intelligence College, October 2001, accessed July 3, 2015. https://archive.org/details/JMICInteligencelwarnterminology.

4. United States Senate, Select Committee to Study Governmental Operations with Respect to Intelligence Activities (Church Committee). *Final Report.* Book 1. April 26, 1976. Accessed February 7, 2015. https://archive.org/details/finalreportofsel01unit.

5. Jan Goldman, *Intelligence Warning Terminology*, Joint Military Intelligence College, October 2001, accessed July 3, 2015. https://archive.org/details/JMICInteligencelwarnterminology.

6. Ford, Harold P. *Estimative Intelligence: Purposes and Problems of National Intelligence Estimating* (Lanham, MD: University Press of America, 1993), 36.

7. National Initiative for Cybersecurity Education, *A Glossary of Common Cybersecurity Terminology.* n.d. Accessed March 5, 2015. https://niccs.us-cert.gov/glossary#letter_k.

8. U.S. Department of Defense. *Department of Defense Dictionary of Military and Associated Terms.* JP 1-02, 08 November 2010, as Amended through 15 January 2015. Accessed February 18, 2015. http://www.dtic.mil/doctrine/dod_dictionary/?zoom_query=keystone+publications&zoom_sort=0&zoom_per_page=10&zoom_and=1.

9. House Committee on National Security, *The Khobar Towers Bombing Incident: Staff Report*, August 14, 1996, Washington, DC.

10. U.S. Central Command Assessment Team. *Annex I Command and Control Knowledge Management.* February 2009. Accessed January 25, 2015. http://cryptome.org/dodi/centcom-c2km.pdf.

11. National Initiative for Cybersecurity Education. *A Glossary of Common Cybersecurity Terminology.* n.d. Accessed March 5, 2015. https://niccs.us-cert.gov/glossary#letter_k.

12. Defense Intelligence Agency. *Defense Intelligence Report: Lexicon of Hardened Structure Definitions and Terms.* Washington, DC: 2000.

13. Ford, Harold P. *Estimative Intelligence: Purposes and Problems of National Intelligence Estimating* (Lanham, MD University Press of America, 1993), 44.

L

LASER INTELLIGENCE (LASINT) Technical and geo-location intelligence derived from laser systems. *See* SOURCES OF INTELLIGENCE

LATEST TIME INFORMATION IS OF VALUE The time by which an intelligence organization or staff must deliver information to the requester in order to provide decision makers with timely intelligence. This must include the time anticipated for processing and disseminating that information as well as for making the decision.[1]

LAUNDERING 1. A process of hiding sources, transmittal, and people involved in financial matters and transfers of money for intelligence and today more commonly for criminal purposes, primarily associated with terrorist activity and narcotics trafficking. 2. In counterdrug operations, the process of transforming drug money into a more manageable form while concealing its illicit origin. Foreign bank accounts and dummy corporations are used as shelters.[2]

LAW ENFORCEMENT AGENCY Any of a number of agencies (outside the Department of Defense) chartered and empowered to enforce U.S. laws in the United States, a state or territory (or political subdivision) of the United States, a federally recognized Native American tribe or Alaskan Native Village, or within the borders of a host nation.[3]

LAW ENFORCEMENT ARCHIVAL AND REPORTING NETWORK (LEARN) Vigilant Solution's proprietary online portal of license plate data and images. Images are aggregated and analyzed for law enforcement. Vigilant Solutions, founded in 2009, claims to have the nation's largest repository of license-plate images with nearly 2 billion records stored in its National Vehicle Location Service (NVLS).[4] *See* NATIONAL VEHICLE LOCATION SERVICE

LAW ENFORCEMENT INTELLIGENCE The product of an analytic process that provides an integrated perspective to disparate information about

341

crime, crime trends, crime and security threats, and conditions associated with criminality.[5] *See* NATIONAL INTELLIGENCE

LAW ENFORCEMENT INTELLIGENCE UNIT (LEIU) Founded in 1956, LEIU is responsible to gather, record, and exchange confidential information not available through regular law enforcement channels, concerning organized crime and terrorism. There are no employees and no capability as an entity to conduct any investigation or law enforcement activity. Each member agency is bound by, and acts pursuant to, local law and its own agency regulations. The organization is divided geographically into four zones: Eastern, Central, Northwestern, and Southwestern. LEIU membership is limited to law enforcement agencies of general jurisdiction having an intelligence function. Virtually any type of information that may be lawfully retained in law enforcement intelligence records may be exchanged as long as the recipient meets the need-to-know and right-to know standards.[6]

LAW ENFORCEMENT ONLINE (LEO) For more than 17 years, the Law Enforcement Online (LEO) system has been providing free, secure, Web-based communications to the law enforcement community. Over the years, LEO has continuously grown and modified to meet changing law enforcement requirements. In October 2012, LEO access was transformed with a "rehost" project that modernized both hardware and software and migrated LEO capabilities to the LEO Enterprise Portal (LEO-EP). The LEO program continues to work with its partners to add new services and link criminal justice customers to useful tools. Services currently available to authorized users via the LEO-EP include: Regional Information Sharing System (RISS); Intelink; N-DEx; JABS; IC3; National Gang Intelligence Center; and U.S. DOJ IDEA my FX.[7]

LAW ENFORCEMENT SENSITIVE Sensitive But Unclassified information specifically compiled for law enforcement purposes that, if not protected from unauthorized access, could reasonably be expected to 1) interfere with law enforcement proceedings, 2) deprive a person of a right to a fair trial or impartial adjudication, 3) constitute an unwarranted invasion of the personal privacy of others, 4) disclose the identity of a confidential source, 5) disclose investigative techniques and procedures, and/or 6) endanger the life or physical safety of an individual.[8]

LAW OF WAR For the purposes of this manual, the *law of war* is that part of international law that regulates the resort to armed force; the conduct of hostilities and the protection of war victims in both international and non-international armed conflict; belligerent occupation; and the relationships between belligerent, neutral, and non-belligerent States.[9]

LAW OF WAR DETENTION For the purpose of these implementing guidelines, law of war detention means detention authorized by the Congress under Reference (b), as informed by the laws of war.[10]

LAWFUL PERMANENT RESIDENT Any person not a citizen of the United States (U.S.) who is residing in the United States under a legally recognized and lawfully recorded permanent residence as an immigrant. Also known as a "Permanent Resident Alien," "Resident Alien Permit Holder," and "Green Card Holder."[11]

LEAD Single investigative element of a case requiring action. Leads include reference interviews, record checks, subject interviews, Local Agency Checks (LACs), and National Agency Checks (NACs).[12]

LEAD FEDERAL AGENCY The federal agency that leads and coordinates the overall federal response to an emergency. Designation and responsibilities of a lead federal agency vary according to the type of emergency and the agency's statutory authority (JP 1-02 and JP 3-41, CBRNE Consequence Management, 2 October 2006).[13]

LEAK 1. A disclosure of classified information or unauthorized disclosure established under EO 10501.[14] 2. An inadvertent slip in which information is picked up by reporters or any calculated release of information to reporters with the stipulation that the source remains unidentified.[15] 3. According to Stephen Hess, there are six types of leaks: ego leak (giving information primarily to satisfy a sense of self); goodwill leak (information offered to "accumulate credit" as a play for a future favor); policy leak (a straightforward pitch for or against a proposal using some document or insider information as the lure to get more attention than might be otherwise justified. The leak of the Pentagon Papers falls into this category); animus leak (used to settle grudges; information is released in order to cause embarrassment to another person); trial-balloon leak (revealing a proposal that is under consideration in order to assess its assets and liabilities); and the whistleblower leak (usually used by career personnel; going to the press may be the last resort of frustrated civil servants who feel they cannot resolve their dispute through administrative channels).[16]

LEGAL ADVICE AND ADVOCACY In the NICE (National Initiative for Cybersecurity Education) Workforce Framework, cybersecurity work where a person: provides legally sound advice and recommendations to leadership and staff on a variety of relevant topics within the pertinent subject domain; advocates legal and policy changes and makes a case on behalf of client via a wide range of written and oral work products, including legal briefs and proceedings.[17]

LEGEND A cover story made up to provide provable background about an intelligence officer, which can include college attended, home town, family connections, all of which may be fabricated and memorized to become a different person—"a legend in one's own time," so to speak.[18] See COMMERCIAL COVER; COVER

LIBRARY OF NATIONAL INTELLIGENCE (LNI) Agencies will be able to make internal databases accessible to A-Space, and programs such as the Library of National Intelligence and Catalyst will enhance the ability of analysts to sort through this information to identify the most relevant information. The Library of National Intelligence (LNI) is an ODNI project to create a repository of all Intelligence Community–disseminated intelligence, regardless of classification. The Central Intelligence Agency is the executive agent for this project. The Library's electronic card catalog—containing summary information for each report—will be classified at the lowest possible level, permitting analysts to discover everything that has been published by the Intelligence Community (IC) regardless of the original classification of the document. Analysts will be able to request the products in accordance with individual access levels and security guidelines. Services provided by LNI will include the ability to request information directly from producers, qualitative measures of value, and statistics on Community coverage of priorities.[19] See A-SPACE (ANALYTIC SPACE), CATALYST, I-SPACE

LIKELIHOOD Chance of something happening, whether defined, measured or estimated objectively or subjectively, or in terms of general descriptors (such as rare, unlikely, likely, almost certain), frequencies, or probabilities. (1) Qualitative and semi-quantitative risk assessments can use qualitative estimates of likelihood such as high, medium, or low, which may be represented numerically but not mathematically. Quantitative assessments use mathematically derived values to represent likelihood. (2) The likelihood of a successful attack occurring is typically broken into two related, multiplicative quantities: the likelihood that an attack occurs (which is a common mathematical representation of threat), and the likelihood that the attack succeeds, given that it is attempted (which is a common mathematical representation of vulnerability). In the context of natural hazards, likelihood of occurrence is typically informed by the frequency of past incidents or occurrences. (3) The intelligence community typically estimates likelihood in bins or ranges such as "remote," "unlikely," "even chance," "probable/likely," or "almost certain." (4) Probability is a specific type of likelihood. Likelihood can be communicated using numbers (e.g., 0–100, 1–5) or phrases (e.g., low, medium, high), while probabilities must meet more stringent conditions.[20]

LIKELIHOOD (STATISTICAL) Conditional probability of observing a particular event given the hypothesis under consideration is true.[21]

LIMITED ACCESS AUTHORIZATION (LAA) Authorization for access to CONFIDENTIAL or SECRET information granted to non-United States (U.S.) citizens and immigrant aliens, which is limited to only that information necessary to the successful accomplishment of their assigned duties and based on a background investigation scoped for 10 years.[22]

LIMITED BACKGROUND INVESTIGATION (LBI) A Limited Background Investigation (LBI) consists of a Personal Subject Interview; National Agency Check (NAC) plus credit search; personal interviews with employers (3 years), residence and educational sources (3 years); and law enforcement searches (5 years).[23]

LINCHPIN ASSUMPTIONS Premises that hold the argument together and warrant the validity of the conclusion.[24] *See* CRITICAL INDICATOR; KEY DRIVERS

LINK ANALYSIS Subset of network analysis, exploring associations between objects.[25]

LINKABILITY In terms of what the user actually expects, user privacy is more accurately modeled as the level of linkability between subsequent actions on the web—not just the sum of her unique identifiers and authentication tokens. When privacy is expanded to cover all items that enable or substantially contribute to linkability, a lot more components of the browser are now in scope. We will briefly enumerate these three categories of components: First, the obvious properties are found in the state of the browser: cookies, DOM storage, cache, cryptographic tokens and cryptographic state, and location. These identifiers are what technical people tend to think of first when it comes to user identity and private browsing, but they are not the whole story. Next, we have long-term properties of the browser and the computer. These include the User Agent string, the list of installed plugins, rendering capabilities, window decoration size, browser widget size, desktop size, IP address, clock offset and timezone, and installed fonts. Finally, linkability also includes the properties of the multi-origin model of the web that allow tracking due to partnerships and ubiquitous third-party content elements. These include the implicit cookie transmission model, and also explicit click referral and data exchange partners.[26]

LOCAL AGENCY CHECK (LAC) 1. A review of the appropriate criminal history and court records in the jurisdictions over the areas where the subject has resided, attended school, or been employed during a specific period of time. 2. A records or files check of official or publically available information retained by any local office or government agency within the jurisdiction of the CI element conducting the check. Records may include holdings and databases maintained by local and state law enforcement agencies, local courts, local offices of federal agencies, and others, and National Agency Check (NAC): formal requests to federal agencies for searches of their records and supporting databases and files for information of investigative or operational interest. NACs include DoD agencies, as well as other federal agency holdings—for example, FBI, CIA, DHS, ICE, IRS, OPM, State Department, FINCEN, and more.[27]

LOCAL INDICATOR LIST A supplementary collection guide, developed for select activities and specific commands, which can be activated whenever there exists a need to acquire I&W-related information during critical periods; this list specifies local activities that can significantly impact a warning problem.[28]

LOCAL LAW ENFORCEMENT CHECK (LAC) *See* LOCAL AGENCY CHECK

LOCATIONAL PRIVACY When individuals are moving about in public and private spaces, they do not expect to be tracked wherever they go. However, this expectation is being challenged as cell phones and other electronic devices now collect and store location data throughout the day. The expansion of location tracking technologies has significant implications for consumers and for their constitutional privacy rights. Over the last 10 years, law enforcement has stepped up its use of location tracking technologies, such as GPS (Global Positioning System) trackers and cell phones, to monitor the movements of individuals who may or may not be suspected of a crime.

GPS is a geolocation network that consists of satellites and receivers that can calculate the precise location of a GPS device 24 hours a day (subject to environmental constraints). As of March 19, 2013, there are 31 satellites in the GPS constellation. The satellites and ground stations in the GPS network are maintained by the U.S. Air Force Global Positioning Systems Wing.[29]

LOGIC BOMB A logic bomb is a program or code fragment which triggers an unauthorized, malicious act when some predefined condition occurs. The most common type is the "time bomb," which is programmed to trigger an unauthorized or damaging act long after the bomb is "set." For example, a logic bomb may check the system date each day until it encounters the specified trigger date and then executes code that carries out its hidden mission. Due to the built-in delay, a logic bomb virus is particularly dangerous because it can infect numerous generations of backup copies of data and software before its existence is discovered.[30]

LOGISTIC ASSESSMENT An evaluation of the logistic support required to support particular military operations in a theater of operations, country, or area. The actual and/or potential logistics support available for the conduct of military operations either within the theater, country, or area, or located elsewhere.[31]

LONE WOLF Commonly referred to as the "lone wolf" provision, § 6001(a) of IRTPA simplifies the evidentiary standard used to determine whether an individual, other than a citizen or a permanent resident of the United States, who engages in international terrorism, may be the target of a FISA court order. It does not modify other standards used to determine the secondary question of whether the electronic surveillance or a physical search of the subject of a court order is justified in a specific situation.[32]

LOOKOUT Plant stationary position from which a fixed surveillance is conducted and is ostensibly hidden from view or knowledge of the target of the surveillance.

NOTES

1. Department of the Army. Marine Corps Combat Development Command. Department of the Navy. *Operational Terms and Graphics*. FM 1-02 (FM 101-5). September 21, 2004. Accessed July 3, 2015. http://www.udel.edu/armyrotc/current_cadets/cadet_resources/manuals_regulations_files/FM%201-02%20-%20Operational%20Terms%20&%20Graphics.pdf.

2. Defense Intelligence Agency, Office of Counterintelligence. *CI Glossary— Terms & Definitions of Interest for DoD CI Professionals.* July 2014. Accessed January 17, 2015. https://www.hsdl.org/?view&did=699056.

3. U.S. Department of Defense. *Defense Support of Civil Authorities.* JP 3-28, July 31, 2013. Accessed January 26, 2015. http://www.dtic.mil/doctrine/new_pubs/jp3_28.pdf.

4. Kim Zetter, "Cops Must Swear Silence to Access Vehicle Tracking System," *Wired*, May 1, 2014, accessed February 2, 2016, http://www.wired.com/2014/05/license-plate-tracking/.

5. Carter, David L. *Law Enforcement Intelligence*: *A Guide for State, Local, and Tribal Law Enforcement Agencies.* U.S. Dept. of Justice, Office of Community Oriented Policing Services, 2004.

6. Carter, David L. *Law Enforcement Intelligence*: *A Guide for State, Local, and Tribal Law Enforcement Agencies.* U.S. Dept. of Justice, Office of Community Oriented Policing Services, 2004.

7. Federal Bureau of Investigation, *Law Enforcement Online Enterprise Portal Makes Access More Convenient*, accessed February 1, 2016, https://www.fbi.gov/about-us/cjis/cjis-link/december-2012/Law%20Enforcement%20Online%20Enterprise%20Portal%20Makes%20Access%20More%20Convenient.

8. Federal Bureau of Investigation. *Minimum Criminal Intelligence Training Standards for Law Enforcement and Other Criminal Justice Agencies in the United States.* October 2007. Accessed January 25, 2015. https://it.ojp.gov/gist/108/Minimum-Criminal-Intelligence-Training-Standards.

9. U.S. Department of Defense. *Law of War Manual.* Office of General Counsel, June 2015, accessed February 2, 2016, http://www.defense.gov/Portals/1/Documents/pubs/Law-of-War-Manual-June-2015.pdf.

10. Deputy Secretary of Defense. *Directive-Type Memorandum (DTM) 12-005, Implementing Guidelines for Periodic Review of Detainees Held at Guantanamo Bay per Executive Order 13567.* May 9, 2012 (November 4, 2012). Accessed January 22, 2015. http://fas.org/irp/doddir/dod/dtm-12-005.pdf.

11. U.S. Department of Defense. Center for Development of Security Excellence. *Glossary of Security Terms and Definitions.* November 2012. Accessed February 16, 2015. http://www.cdse.edu/documents/cdse/Glossary_Handbook.pdf.

12. U.S. Department of Defense. Center for Development of Security Excellence. *Glossary of Security Terms and Definitions.* November 2012. Accessed February 16, 2015. http://www.cdse.edu/documents/cdse/Glossary_Handbook.pdf.

13. Defense Intelligence Agency, Office of Counterintelligence. *CI Glossary— Terms & Definitions of Interest for DoD CI Professionals.* July 2014. Accessed January 26, 2015. https://www.hsdl.org/?view&did=699056.

14. EO 10501, November 5, 1953, *Safeguarding Official Information in the Interests of the Defense of the United States*, accessed February 1, 2016, https://fas.org/irp/offdocs/eo10501.html; also see Department of Defense Directive 5210.50 *Management of Serious Security Incidents Involving Classified Information*, October 27, 2014, accessed February 2, 2016, http://www.dtic.mil/whs/directives/corres/pdf/521050p.pdf.

15. Richard Kielbowicz, "Leaks to the Press as a Communication within and between Organizations," *Newspaper Research Journal* 1, no. 2 (1979/1980): 53–58.

16. Stephen Hess, *The Government/Press Connection: Press Officers and Their Offices* (Washington, DC: Brookings Institution, 1984), 77–79.

17. National Initiative for Cybersecurity Education. *A Glossary of Common Cybersecurity Terminology.* n.d. Accessed March 5, 2015. https://niccs.us-cert.gov/glossary#letter_l.

18. Defense Intelligence Agency, Office of Counterintelligence. *CI Glossary— Terms & Definitions of Interest for DoD CI Professionals.* July 2014. Accessed February 28, 2015. https://www.hsdl.org/?view&did=699056.

19. Intelligence and National Security Alliance and the Office of the Director of National Intelligence. *Analytic Transformation: Moving Forward Together.* September 2007. Accessed January 26, 2015. http://wayback.archive.org/web/20080530054342/http://analytic.insaonline.org/atprogram.pdf.

20. Department of Homeland Security, Risk Steering Committee. *DHS Risk Lexicon.* September 2010. Accessed February 14, 2015. http://www.dhs.gov/dhs-risk-lexicon.

21. Department of Homeland Security, Risk Steering Committee. *DHS Risk Lexicon.* September 2010. Accessed February 14, 2015. http://www.dhs.gov/dhs-risk-lexicon.

22. U.S. Department of Defense. Center for Development of Security Excellence. *Glossary of Security Terms and Definitions.* November 2012. Accessed February 16, 2015. http://www.cdse.edu/documents/cdse/Glossary_Handbook.pdf.

23. U.S. Department of Defense. Center for Development of Security Excellence. *Glossary of Security Terms and Definitions.* November 2012. Accessed February 16, 2015. http://www.cdse.edu/documents/cdse/Glossary_Handbook.pdf.

24. Jan Goldman, *Intelligence Warning Terminology*, Joint Military Intelligence College, October 2001, accessed July 3, 2015. https://archive.org/details/JMICInteligencelwarnterminology.

25. Defense Intelligence Agency, Office of Counterintelligence. *CI Glossary— Terms & Definitions of Interest for DoD CI Professionals.* July 2014. Accessed January 26, 2015. https://www.hsdl.org/?view&did=699056.

26. Perry, Mike. *Bridging the Disconnect Between Web Privacy and User Perceptions.* 2011. Accessed February 18, 2015. http://www.w3.org/2011/identity-ws/papers/idbrowser2011_submission_38.pdf; also see *CITIZENFOUR.* Directed by Laura Poitras. New York: RADIUS-TWC, 2015.

27. Defense Intelligence Agency, Office of Counterintelligence. *CI Glossary— Terms & Definitions of Interest for DoD CI Professionals.* July 2014. Accessed February 8, 2015. https://www.hsdl.org/?view&did=699056.

28. Jan Goldman, *Intelligence Warning Terminology*, Joint Military Intelligence College, October 2001, accessed July 3, 2015. https://archive.org/details/JMICInteligencelwarnterminology.

29. Electronic Privacy Information Center. *Locational Privacy.* Accessed February 8, 2015. https://epic.org/privacy/location_privacy/#Issues.

30. U.S. Department of Defense. Center for Development of Security Excellence. *Glossary of Security Terms and Definitions.* November 2012. Accessed February 16, 2015. http://www.cdse.edu/documents/cdse/Glossary_Handbook.pdf.

31. North Atlantic Treaty Organization. *NATO Glossary of Terms and Definitions.* NATO Standardization Agency, 2014, AAP-06, accessed July 27, 2015, http://nso.nato.int/nso/zPublic/ap/aap6/AAP-6.pdf.

32. Liu, Edward C. "Amendments to the Foreign Intelligence Surveillance Act (FISA) Extended Until June 1, 2015," *CRS Report to Congress* R40138, June 16, 2011, accessed February 2, 2016, https://fas.org/sgp/crs/intel/R40138.pdf.

M

MADRASSA A building or group of buildings used for teaching Islamic theology and religious law, typically including a mosque.[1]

MAGIC LANTERN 1. A program that is remotely installed on a computer via e-mail containing a virus disguised as a harmless computer file, known as a "Trojan horse" program, or through other common vulnerabilities hackers use to break into computers. Keystrokes recorded by Magic Lantern can be stored to be seized later in a raid or even transmitted back to the FBI over the Internet.[2] 2. Under the "sneak and peek" provision of the USA PATRIOT Act, pushed through Congress by John Ashcroft, the FBI, with a warrant, can break into your home and office when you're not there and, on the first trip, look around. They can examine your hard drive, snatch files, and plant the Magic Lantern on your computer. It's also known as the "sniffer keystroke logger." Once installed, the Magic Lantern creates a record of every time you press a key on the computer. It's all saved in plain text, and during the FBI's next secret visit to your home or office, that information is downloaded as the agents also pick up whatever other records and papers they find of interest.[3]

MAJOR INFORMATION SYSTEM An information system that requires special management attention because of its importance to an agency mission; its high development, operating, or maintenance costs; or its significant role in the administration of agency programs, finances, property, or other resources.[4]

MALICIOUS CODE Software or firmware intended to perform an unauthorized process that will have adverse impact on the confidentiality, integrity, or availability of an information system. A virus, worm, Trojan horse, or other code-based entity that infects a host. Spyware and some forms of adware are also examples of malicious code.[5]

MALICIOUS CYBER ACTIVITY Activities, other than those authorized by or in accordance with U.S. law, that seek to compromise or impair the confidentiality, integrity, or availability of computers, information or communications systems, networks, physical or virtual infrastructure controlled by computers or information systems, or information resident thereon.[6]

MALICIOUS LOGIC Hardware, firmware, or software that is intentionally included or inserted in a system to perform an unauthorized function or process that will have adverse impact on the confidentiality, integrity, or availability of an information system.[7]

MALWARE 1. Software that compromises the operation of a system by performing an unauthorized function or process.[8] 2. A computer program inserted into a system, usually covertly, with the intent of compromising the confidentiality, integrity, or availability of the victim's data, applications, or operating system or of otherwise annoying or disrupting the victim.

MANDATORY DECLASSIFICATION REVIEW (MDR) 1. A mechanism through which the public can request declassification review of classified records, regardless of age or origin, subject to certain limitations set forth in E.O. 13526.[9] 2. The process of filing and following-up on an MDR request is similar in many ways to the FOIA process. First a requester writes to an agency requesting that certain documents be reviewed under the terms of EO 12958. The agency then has one year to determine whether those documents may be released to the public. If the agency does not release the documents, or if the requester is unsatisfied with the results of that review, the requester may appeal to the agency. If the requester is unsatisfied with the results of the second agency review, or if the agency misses certain deadlines in responding to an initial request or an administrative appeal, the requester may appeal to the Interagency Security Classification Appeals Panel (ISCAP). ISCAP is a six-member body, created by EO 12958, which consists of senior-level representatives from the Department of State, Department of Defense, Department of Justice, the Central Intelligence Agency, the National Archives and Records Administration, and the National Security Council. In addition to deciding MDR appeals, ISCAP also hears classification challenges from government officials and approves automatic declassification exemptions.[10]

MANIPULATION A deceptive practice of quoting factual information out of context or reporting only part of a given situation.[11] *See* DECEPTION

MASS EFFECT Any military or terrorist activity seeking to achieve surprise and momentum on such a scale that the application of a small amount of force will have effects far greater than would be expected from such a force;

maximizing the effect of surprise by selecting a point of application of force that will have the most effect on an adversary. *See* WEAPONS OF MASS DESTRUCTION OR EFFECT

MASS SURVEILLANCE Also known as "passive" or "undirected" surveillance. It is not targeted on any particular individual but gathers images and information for possible future use. Closed circuit television (CCTV) and databases are examples of mass surveillance.[12]

MEASUREMENT AND SIGNATURE INTELLIGENCE (MASINT) Technically derived intelligence data other than imagery and signals intelligence that locates, identifies, or describes distinctive characteristics of targets. Several disciplines are involved, including nuclear, optical, radio frequency, acoustic, seismic, and materials sciences. Examples of this might be the distinctive radar signatures of specific aircraft systems or the chemical composition of air and water samples. The Central MASINT Organization, a component of DIA, is responsible for all national and DoD MASINT matters.[13] *See* SOURCES OF INTELLIGENCE

MEDIA SANITIZATION The actions taken to render data written on media unrecoverable by both ordinary and extraordinary means.[14]

MEDIA SOURCE ANALYSIS The systematic comparison of the content, behavior, patterns, and trends of organic media organizations and sources of a country.[15]

MEDICAL INTELLIGENCE (MEDINT) That category of intelligence resulting from collection, evaluation, analysis, and interpretation of foreign medical, bio-scientific, and environmental information that is of interest to strategic planning and military medical planning and operations for the conservation of the fighting strength of friendly forces and the formation of assessments of foreign medical capabilities in both military and civilian sectors.[16]

MEDICAL PATTERN OF LIFE (MEDPOL) Identification of all recurring, and therefore predictable, patterns of behavior that constitute a specific treatment regimen for a target's medical illness.[17]

MEETING ENGAGEMENT A combat action that occurs when a moving force, incompletely deployed for battle, engages an enemy at an unexpected time and place.

MEMORANDUM OF AGREEMENT/UNDERSTANDING (MOA/ MOU) A written agreement among relevant parties that specifies roles, responsibilities, terms, and conditions for each party to reach a common goal. The memorandum establishes a mechanism for cooperation by an agreement that describes, often in minute detail, policies, procedures, and specifics. For example, in relation to the Joint Terrorism Task Forces, MOUs and MOAs are signed by lead federal agencies, and spell out the details of state and local activities.

MESSAGE Any thought or idea expressed briefly in a plain, coded, or secret language, prepared in a form suitable for transmission by any means of communication.

METADATA Structured information that describes, explains, locates, or otherwise makes it easier to retrieve, use, or manage an information resource. Metadata is often called data about data or information about information. The term *metadata* is used differently in different communities. Some use it to refer to machine-understandable information, while others use it only for records that describe electronic resources . . . There are three types of metadata: descriptive metadata, structural metadata, and administrative metadata. Metadata is key to ensuring that resources will survive and continue to be accessible into the future.[18] *See* TELEPHONY METADATA

METADATA TAGGING Uses encoded data that describes characteristics of information entities to enable identification, discovery, assessment, and management of the described entities.[19]

METHODOLOGY TECHNICAL IMPLEMENTATION (MTI) A program within the Infrastructure Information Collection Division that collaborates with the Sector Specific Agencies, Sector Coordinating Councils, and Government Coordinating Councils of each of the CIKR sectors to integrate risk and vulnerability assessment methodologies into automated tools to enable the identification, analysis, and management of sector-specific security risks.[20]

METHODS These are the methodologies (e.g., electronic surveillance or undercover operations) of how critical information is obtained and recorded.[21]

METT-TC A memory aid used in information management for military operations and for mission analysis. The acronym stands for: Mission, Enemy, Terrain and weather, Troops and support available, Time available, Civil considerations.[22] (2) In the context of tactics, the major factors considered during mission analysis.[23]

MI-5 (MI5) The Security Service, often known as MI-5, is the UK's national security intelligence agency. Since 1909 we have been responsible for countering covertly organized threats to national security. We also provide security advice to a range of other organizations, helping them reduce their vulnerability to the threats. The Service is organized into nine branches, each with specific areas of responsibility, who work to counter a range of threats including terrorism, espionage, cyber and the proliferation of weapons of mass destruction.[24] *See* MI-6

MI-6 (MI6) The Secret Intelligence Service (SIS) was established in 1909 as the Foreign Section of the Secret Service Bureau. The Foreign Section's responsibility for overseas intelligence collection has been retained ever since by SIS under a variety of names and acronyms. This responsibility was placed on a statutory basis in the Intelligence Services Act 1994. SIS contributes to the larger inter-departmental national intelligence community, where it works closely with the other two British intelligence and security agencies, Government Communications Headquarters (GCHQ) and the Security Service (MI5). Until 1994 SIS did not have a statutory basis and its existence was not publicly confirmed before it was formally avowed in 1992. The Service was put on a statutory basis with the Intelligence Services Act (ISA) 1994.[25] *See* MI-5

MICRO-INTELLIGENCE Intelligence activities focusing on current problems and crimes for either case development or resource allocation.[26]

MIGRANT A person who (1) belongs to a normally migratory culture who may cross national boundaries, or (2) has fled his or her native country for economic reasons rather than fear of political or ethnic persecution.[27]

MILITARY ASSISTANCE FOR CIVIL DISTURBANCES (MACDIS) A mission set of civil support involving Department of Defense support, normally based on the direction of the president, to suppress insurrections, rebellions, and domestic violence, and provide federal supplemental assistance to the states to maintain law and order.

MILITARY COMMISSIONS On November 13, 2001, President Bush issued a Military Order (M.O.) pertaining to the detention, treatment, and trial of certain non-citizens in the war against terrorism. Military commissions pursuant to the M.O. began in November 2004 against four persons declared eligible for trial, but the Supreme Court in *Hamdan v. Rumsfeld* invalidated the military commissions as improper under the *Uniform Code of Military Justice* (UCMJ). To permit military commissions to go forward, Congress approved the Military Commissions Act of 2006 (MCA), conferring authority to promulgate rules that depart from the strictures of the UCMJ and possibly U.S. international obligations. Military commission proceedings were reinstated and resulted in three convictions under the Bush administration. Upon taking office in 2009, President Obama temporarily halted military commissions to review their procedures as well as the detention program at Guantánamo Bay in general, pledging to close the prison facilities there by January 2010, a deadline that passed unmet. One case was moved to a federal district court. In May 2009, the Obama administration announced that it was considering restarting the military commission system with some changes to the procedural rules. Congress enacted the Military Commissions Act of 2009 (MCA 2009) as part of the Department of Defense Authorization Act (NDAA) for FY2010, P.L. 111-84, to provide some reforms the administration supported and to make other amendments to the Military Commissions.[28] *See* MILITARY TRIBUNALS, UNPRIVILEGED ENEMY BELLIGERENTS

MILITARY INFORMATION SUPPORT OPERATIONS (MISO) Planned operations to convey selected information and indicators to foreign audiences to influence their emotions, motives, objective reasoning, and ultimately the behavior of foreign governments, organizations, groups, and individuals in a manner favorable to the originator's objectives.[29]

MILITARY INTELLIGENCE 1. Information that is analyzed, evaluated, and interpreted and that describes and defines a nation's military capabilities for both offensive and defensive postures. The information is used to estimate the probable use of military strategy, tactics, and doctrine. It provides decision makers, planners, and commanders with data needed to choose courses of action required to counter foreign military threats and to conduct operations if necessary.[30] 2. An agency of the armed forces that obtains and analyzes and uses information of strategic or tactical military value information about the armed forces of another country that is useful in planning and conducting military policy or military operations. *See* INTELLIGENCE

MILITARY NECESSITY The principle whereby a belligerent has the right to apply any measures which are required to bring about the successful conclusion of a military operation and which are not forbidden by the laws of war.[31]

Probability Level		Specific Event
I.	Catastrophic	Death, system loss or severe environmental damage
II.	Critical	Severe injury or occupational illness, major system or environmental damage
III.	Marginal	Minor insurer or occupational illness, minor system or environmental damage
IV.	Negligible	Less than minor injury, occupational illness, or less than minor system or environmental damage

Figure M.1. Probability Levels of Undesired Events (Courtesy of Department of Defense, Standard Practices of System Safety, MIL-STD-882E, 11 May 2012)

Severity	Level Characteristics
Frequent	Likely to occur frequently
Probable	Will occur several times
Occasional	Likely to occur sometime
Remote	Unlikely but possible to occur
Improbable	So unlikely it can be assumed occurrence may not be experienced

Figure M.2. Severity Levels of Undesired Event Consequences (Courtesy of Department of Defense, Standard Practices of System Safety, MIL-STD-882E, 11 May 2012)

MILITARY STANDARD 882 (MIL-STD-882E) A U.S. military document that outlines the probability levels of an undesired event and the severity levels of undesired event consequences as established by the Department of Defense's program for system safety. A risk assessment team also assigns values to key assets.[32] (See figures M.1 and M.2) *See* ESTIMATIVE PROBABILITY

MILITARY SUPPORT TO CIVIL AUTHORITIES (MSCA) A mission of civil support consisting of support for natural or manmade disasters and chemical, biological, radiological, nuclear, or high-yield explosive consequence management, and other support as required.[33]

MILITARY TRIBUNALS On November 13, 2001, President George W. Bush authorized a military tribunal to try whoever provided assistance for the terrorist attacks of September 11 against New York City and Washington, DC. Vice President Dick Cheney supported Bush's initiative by arguing that terrorists, because they are not lawful combatants, "don't deserve to be treated as a prisoner of war." He spoke favorably of the treatment of German saboteurs in 1942, who were "executed in relatively rapid order." The concept of a military tribunal had been developed by William P. Barr, former attorney general in the first Bush administration. Barr's previous position with the Justice Department, as head of the Office of Legal Counsel (OLC), put him in the same space occupied by the 1942 military tribunal. He said that the idea of a tribunal came to him as one way to try the men charged with blowing up the Pan Am jetliner over Lockerbie, Scotland (484).[34] *See* MILITARY COMMISSIONS

MINIMIZATION PROCEDURES With respect to electronic surveillance, means—(1) specific procedures, which shall be adopted by the Attorney General, that are reasonably designed in light of the purpose and technique of the particular surveillance, to minimize the acquisition and retention, and prohibit the dissemination, of non-publicly available information concerning unconsenting U.S. persons consistent with the need of the United States to obtain, produce, and disseminate foreign intelligence information; (2) procedures that require that non-publicly available information, which is not foreign intelligence information, as defined in subsection (e) (1) of this section, shall not be disseminated in a manner that identifies any U.S. person, without such person's consent, unless such person's identity is necessary to understand foreign intelligence information or assess its importance.[35]

MINIMUM BACKGROUND INVESTIGATION (MBI) An investigation includes a National Agency Check Plus Written Inquiries (NACI), a credit record search, a face-to-face personal interview between the investigator and the subject, and telephone inquiries to selected employers. A Minimum Background Investigation is typically reserved for public trust positions and/ or when there is a break in federal service.[36]

MINOR ISSUE INFORMATION Information that meets a threshold of concern set out in "Adjudicative Guidelines for Determining Eligibility for Access to Classified Information," but for which adjudication determines that adequate mitigation, as provided by the existing guidelines, exist.[37]

MIRROR-IMAGING A belief that leaders of a nation will behave in the same manner as leaders of another nation, particularly in a tense and confusing situation. For example, mirror-imaging occurred prior to the bombing of the U.S. naval base in Pearl Harbor in 1941 when U.S. personnel reasoned that the United States had far greater military, economic, and industrial strength than Japan, thus the Japanese would recognize that they could not win a war against the United States. In a sense, U.S. analysts perceived a Japanese attack as irrational based on American perceptions and assumptions.[38]

MISINFORMATION False or misleading information that is spread unintentionally. If one unwittingly spreads false or misleading information, that is misinformation. Of course, many times it is impossible to ascertain intentions, so it may not be clear whether false information represents disinformation or misinformation.[39]

MISSILE GAP American perception during the 1960 presidential campaign, fueled by candidate John F. Kennedy, that a gap existed or would soon exist between the number of U.S. intercontinental ballistic missiles (ICBM) and the operational number of Soviet ICBMs. Reportedly, a U.S. Air Force estimate had 600–800 Soviet missiles, CIA had an estimate of 450 missiles, and the U.S. Navy had an estimate of 200 missiles. Proponents of the missile gap thesis were able to put public pressure to increase defense spending and a greater procurement of newer ICBMs. Over time, the differences in estimates of Soviet ICBMs force levels were attributed to differing methodologies, changes in information collection, and varying strategic perceptions by the agencies involved.[40] *See* CUBAN MISSILE CRISIS

MISSING PERSON An official U.S. citizen, and/or eligible family member of an official U.S. citizen, or in some cases as defined by post, a private U.S. citizen, national, and/or lawful permanent resident, whose whereabouts are unknown, and whose safety cannot be determined.[41]

MISSION CATEGORIES The highest classification in the IC occupational structure comprising broad sets of related occupations representing a particular function. For purposes of job classification, a position is characterized in a particular mission category based on its duties and responsibilities; however, for purposes of financial accountability, the position may be funded by a different National Intelligence Program (NIP) budget category. For example, scientists and engineers funded by the Collection and Operations budget category may be classified under the Research and Technology Mission Category.[42]

MISSION CONSEQUENCE Effect of an incident, event, operation, or occurrence on the ability of an organization or group to meet a strategic objective or perform a function.[43]

MISSION CREEP Any military mission lacking clear goals or objectives that in the continuance of that mission slowly evolves into additional duties and responsibilities. Not to be confused with "creeping normalcy." National-level orders may contain internal inconsistencies that make a mission especially difficult or even impossible. By analyzing their directives, commanders can (though the literature suggests they rarely do) largely predict what the courses of their operations will be if guidance is not modified. Flawed specifications lead, if not to failure, to changes in missions while they are in progress. The United States has a term for such adjustment to intelligence, policy, planning, and operational shortcomings: mission creep.[44] *See* CREEPING NORMALCY

MISSION FACILITY The operational purpose of a given facility.[45] *See* ASSESSED FACILITY; KNOWN FACILITY

MISSION MANAGER A designated officer or employee of the United States who serves as principal substantive adviser on all or specified aspects of intelligence related to designated countries, regions, topics, or functional issues.

MITIGATING INFORMATION As used in this directive, mitigating information is any information that is pertinent to the determination of whether continued law of war detention of the detainee is necessary to protect against a continuing significant threat to the security of the United States and that serves to weigh plausibly against a determination of continuing detention.[46] *See* LAW OF WAR DETENTION

MITIGATION 1. The term "mitigation" refers to those capabilities necessary to reduce loss of life and property by lessening the impact of disasters. Mitigation capabilities include, but are not limited to, community-wide risk reduction projects; efforts to improve the resilience of critical infrastructure and key resource lifelines; risk reduction for specific vulnerabilities from natural hazards or acts of terrorism; and initiatives to reduce future risks after a disaster has occurred.[47] 2. Ongoing and sustained action to reduce the probability of, or lessen the impact of, an adverse incident.[48] The application of one or more measures to reduce the likelihood of an unwanted occurrence and/or lessen its consequences. Extended Definition: Implementing appropriate risk-reduction controls based on risk management priorities and analysis of alternatives.[49]

MOBILIZATION 1. The act of preparing for war or other emergencies through assembling and organizing resources. 2. The process by which the armed forces or part of them are brought to a state of readiness for war or other national emergency. This includes assembling and organizing personnel, supplies, and material for active military service.[50]

MODEL 1. Hypothetical sets of facts or circumstances that are developed to test the likelihood of a hypothesis. 2. Approximation, representation, or idealization of selected aspects of the structure, behavior, operation, or other characteristics of a real-world process, concept, or system.[51]

MODERATE The terms *moderates* or *mainstream* refer to those individuals who do not support the extremists. The term *moderate* does not necessarily mean unobservant, secular, or Westernizing. It applies to people who may differ from each other and from the average American in any number of ways except that they oppose the killing of ordinary people.[52]

MODERNIZED INTEGRATED DATABASE (MIDB) The national level repository for the general military intelligence available to the entire Department of Defense Intelligence Information System community and, through Global Command and Control System–integrated imagery and intelligence, to tactical units.[53]

MOLE A person inside a government agency, usually an intelligence agency, who is obtaining information about that organization's secrets and activities.

MOLEHUNTING *See* COUNTERINTELLIGENCE

MONEY LAUNDERING Money laundering generally refers to financial transactions in which criminals, including terrorist organizations, attempt to disguise the proceeds, sources or nature of their illicit activities. Money laundering facilitates a broad range of serious underlying criminal offenses and ultimately threatens the integrity of the financial system. The U.S. Department of the Treasury is fully dedicated to combating all aspects of money laundering at home and abroad, through the mission of the Office of Terrorism and Financial Intelligence (TFI).[54]

MONITORING 1. The act of listening to, carrying out surveillance on, and/or recording the emissions of one's own or allied forces for the purpose of maintaining and improving procedural standards and security or for reference. 2. The continuous conduct of cyber or Internet searches for any discussions, posts, videos, blogs, online conversations, and other communication, with the purpose of discovering what is being said.[55] *See* SURVEILLANCE

MONSTERMIND Think of it as a digital version of the Star Wars initiative President Reagan proposed in the 1980s, which in theory would have shot down any incoming nuclear missiles. In the same way, MonsterMind could identify a distributed denial of service attack lobbed against U.S.

banking systems or a malicious worm sent to cripple airline and railway systems and stop—that is, defuse or kill— it before it did any harm. More than this, though, Snowden suggests MonsterMind could one day be designed to return fire—automatically, without human intervention—against the attacker. Because an attacker could tweak malicious code to avoid detection, a counterstrike would be more effective in neutralizing future attacks.[56] *See* SKYNET

MOSAIC THEORY Even using the government's theoretical model of a mosaic, it must be acknowledged that the mosaic theory is only as persuasive as the tiles which compose it and the glue which binds them together—just as a brick wall is only as strong as the individual bricks which support it and the cement that keeps the bricks in place. Therefore, if the individual pieces of a mosaic are inherently flawed or do not fit together, then the mosaic will split apart, just as the brick wall will collapse. A final point must be kept in mind. One consequence of using intelligence reports and summaries in lieu of direct evidence is that certain questions simply cannot be answered—for example, there are no witnesses to cross-examine or deposition transcripts to consult. Sizeable gaps may appear in the record and may well remain unfilled; each party will attempt to account for these deficiencies by positing what they think are the most compelling logical inferences to be drawn from the existing evidence. Accordingly, that existing evidence must be weighed and evaluated as to its strength, its reliability, and the degree to which it is corroborated.[57]

MOSSAD The Israeli intelligence agency (Institute for Intelligence and Special Tasks or ha-Mossad le-Modiin ule-Tafkidim Meyuhadim; Mossad is Hebrew for institute) has responsibility for human intelligence collection, covert action, and counterterrorism.[58]

M-TYPE DECEPTION Achieving a reduction of ambiguity, as perceived by the intended target, by building attractiveness of a wrong alternative; may be more difficult than A-type deception because it requires time and carefully orchestrated resources to build a series of misleading false signals. A deception program may start out as an M-type ploy to confirm the adversary's expectations about what is going to happen based on what he expects on the basis of logic and experience. However, since most adversaries are prudent enough to consider other possibilities (of which one may be the real solution), the deceiver also may employ an A-type program to increase the number of alternatives. This, if effective, causes the deception target to spread remaining resources over a number of possibilities.[59] *See* A-TYPE DECEPTION, ACTIVE DECEPTION, DENIAL AND DECEPTION, PASSIVE DECEPTION

MULTI-DISCIPLINARY INTELLIGENCE EXPERIMENTS (MIEs)
Multi-disciplinary Intelligence Experiments serve to identify innovative methods for leveraging cross-agency systems and processes to address difficult, high-priority intelligence problems. The MIE Program is a collaborative effort by the CIA, DIA, NGA, NSA, NRO and FBI to develop, evaluate and analyze new concepts for operating in an integrated and synchronized manner.[60]

MULTI-DISCIPLINE The method by which two or more intelligence collection disciplines are used to cross-queue one another to activate collection activities or operations against a predetermined target or set of targets.

MULTI-INTELLIGENCE (MULTI-INT) Refers to the use of two or more intelligence disciplines to address and answer an intelligence issue or request for information.

MULTI-INTELLIGENCE COLLECTION Two or more intelligence collection disciplines used concurrently, in parallel, or sequentially (based on target behavior or movement or change in target measurables and observables) to collect information against a specified target or set of targets.

MULTI-INTELLIGENCE COLLECTION MANAGEMENT Denotation of the application of multiple intelligence disciplines to the process of converting intelligence requirements into collection requirements, establishing priorities, tasking or coordinating with appropriate collection sources or agencies, monitoring results, and retasking as required.

MULTILEVEL SECURITY (MLS) Concept of processing information with different classifications and categories that simultaneously permits access by users with different security clearances and denies access to users who lack authorization.[61]

MURKY INTELLIGENCE Intelligence of questionable reliability or validity; information that cannot be placed in the context of typical routine analysis to determine its worth. For example, "United States Deputy Defense Secretary Paul Wolfowitz said the use of murky intelligence is justified in the war on terror if it prevents future attacks." Wolfowitz was interviewed by several U.S. television networks following a congressional report that concluded the September 11 attacks could have been prevented if security services shared and acted upon information. Wolfowitz stated "the lesson of 9/11 is that, if you're not prepared to act on the basis of murky intelligence, then you're going to have to act after the fact."[62] *See* ACTIONABLE INTELLIGENCE

MUTUAL LEGAL ASSISTANCE TREATIES (MLATS) Mutual Legal Assistance Treaties (MLATs) allow generally for the exchange of evidence and information in criminal and related matters. In money laundering cases, they can be extremely useful as a means of obtaining banking and other financial records from our treaty partners. MLATs are negotiated by the Department of State in cooperation with the Department of Justice to facilitate cooperation in criminal matters.[63]

MUTUAL SUSPICION Condition in which two information systems need to rely upon each other to perform a service, yet neither trusts the other to properly protect shared data.[64]

NOTES

1. Chairman of the Joint Chiefs of Staff, *National Military Strategic Plan for the War on Terrorism*. February 1, 2006, accessed September 12, 2015, http://www. strategicstudiesinstitute.army.mil/pdffiles/gwot.pdf. *A Glossary of Common Cybersecurity Terminology*. n.d., accessed March 5, 2015, http://niccs.us-cert.gov/glossary fense.gov/qdr/docs/2006-02-08-Strategic-Plan.pdf.

2. Center for Democracy and Technology. *Digital Search and Seizure: Updating Privacy Protections to Keep Pace with Technology*, February 2006, accessed July 27, 2015, http://www.cdt.org/publications/digital-search-and-seizure.pdf.

3. Nat Hentoff, "The FBI's Magic Lantern," *Village Voice*, May 28, 2002, accessed July 27, 2015, http://www.villagevoice.com/news/the-fbis-magic-lantern-6413591.

4. Office of Management and Budget. *Management of Federal Information Resources*. Circular A-130, revised. November 28, 2000, accessed February 10, 2015, http://www.whitehouse.gov/omb/circulars_a130_a130trans4/.

5. Committee for National Security Systems (CNSS). Instruction 4009, *National Information Assurance Glossary*. April 2010, accessed January 30, 2015, http://www. ncix.gov/publications/policy/docs/CNSSI_4009.pdf.

6. *Presidential Policy Directive/PPD-20. U.S. Cyber Operations Policy*. October 2012, accessed February 17, 2015, https://www.fas.org/irp/offdocs/ppd/ppd-20.pdf.

7. National Initiative for Cybersecurity Education. *A Glossary of Common Cybersecurity Terminology*. n.d., accessed September 12, 2015, https://niccs.us-cert. gov/glossary.

8. National Initiative for Cybersecurity Education. *A Glossary of Common Cybersecurity Terminology*. n.d., accessed September 12, 2015, https://niccs.us-cert. gov/glossary.

9. U.S. Department of Justice. *Declassification Frequently Asked Questions*, accessed January 27, 2015, http://www.justice.gov/open/declassification/declassification-faq.

10. Kristin Adair and Catherine Nielsen, *Effective FOIA Requesting for Everyone, Chapter 4: Another Way, Mandatory Declassification Review*. National Security

Archive, 2009, accessed January 27, 2015. http://www2.gwu.edu/~nsarchiv/nsa/foia/foia_guide/foia_guide_chapter4.pdf.

11. Defense Intelligence Agency, Office of Counterintelligence. *CI Glossary—Terms & Definitions of Interest for DoD CI Professionals.* July 2014, accessed January 30, 2015, https://www.hsdl.org/?view&did=699056.

12. House of Lords, *Surveillance: Citizens and the State*, Volume 1, February 6, 2009, Stationary Office, accessed February 2, 2016, http://www.publications.parliament.uk/pa/ld200809/ldselect/ldconst/18/18.pdf.

13. U.S. Department of Defense. *Department of Defense Dictionary of Military and Associated Terms.* JP 1-02, 08 November 2010, as Amended through 15 January 2016. Accessed January 26, 2016, http://www.dtic.mil/doctrine/new_pubs/jp1_02.pdf.

14. Committee for National Security Systems (CNSS). Instruction 4009. *National Information Assurance Glossary.* April 2010, accessed January 25, 2015. http://www.ncix.gov/publications/policy/docs/CNSSI_4009.pdf.

15. Department of the Army. *Open-Source Intelligence.* ATP 2-22.9, July 10, 2012, accessed January 31, 2015. http://fas.org/irp/doddir/army/atp2-22-9.pdf.

16. U.S. Department of Defense. *Dictionary of Military and Associated Terms.* JP 1-02, 08 November 2010, as Amended through 15 January 2015. Washington, DC: Joint Chiefs of Staff.

17. National Security Agency and Central Security Service. *Medical Pattern of Life.* SIGNIT Development Conference, June 2010, accessed July 27, 2015, https://www.documentcloud.org/documents/2085557-medical-pattern-of-life-targeting-high-value.html.

18. National Information Standards Organization. *Understanding Metadata.* 2004, accessed January 18, 2015, http://www.niso.org/publications/press/Understanding-Metadata.pdf.

19. Office of the Director of National Intelligence. *Writing for Maximum Utility.* Intelligence Community Directive 208, December 17, 2008, accessed January 24, 2015, http://www.dni.gov/files/documents/ICD/icd_208.pdf.

20. Department of Homeland Security, Risk Steering Committee. *DHS Risk Lexicon.* September 2010, accessed February 14, 2015, http://www.dhs.gov/dhs-risk-lexicon.

21. Federal Bureau of Investigation. *Minimum Criminal Intelligence Training Standards for Law Enforcement and Other Criminal Justice Agencies in the United States.* October 2007, accessed January 28, 2015, https://it.ojp.gov/gist/108/Minimum-Criminal-Intelligence-Training-Standards.

22. Department of the Army. Marine Corps Combat Development Command. Department of the Navy. *Operational Terms and Graphics.* FM 1-02 (FM 101-5), September 21, 2004, accessed July 3, 2015. http://www.udel.edu/armyrotc/current_cadets/cadet_resources/manuals_regulations_files/FM%201-02%20-%20Operational%20Terms%20&%20Graphics.pdf.

23. Department of the Army. Marine Corps Combat Development Command. Department of the Navy. *Operational Terms and Graphics.* FM 1-02 (FM 101-5). September 21, 2004, accessed January 11, 2015, http://www.udel.edu/armyrotc/

current_cadets/cadet_resources/manuals_regulations_files/FM%201-02%20-%20 Operational%20Terms%20&%20Graphics.pdf.

24. Security Service (MI-5). *Who We Are*, accessed March 11, 2015, https://www.mi5.gov.uk/home/about-us/who-we-are.html.

25. Security Intelligence Service (MI-6). *Who We Are*, accessed March 11, 2015, https://www.sis.gov.uk/about-us/who-we-are.html.

26. Federal Bureau of Investigation. *Minimum Criminal Intelligence Training Standards for Law Enforcement and Other Criminal Justice Agencies in the United States.* October 2007, accessed January 22, 2015, https://it.ojp.gov/gist/108/Minimum-Criminal-Intelligence-Training-Standards.

27. United States Department of Defense. *Foreign Humanitarian Assistance.* JP 3-29, January 3, 2014, accessed March 7, 2015, http://www.dtic.mil/doctrine/new_pubs/jp3_29.pdf.

28. Jennifer K. Elsea, "The Military Commissions Act of 2009 (MCA 2009): Overview and Legal Issues." *CRS Report for Congress* R41163, August 4, 2014, accessed February 20, 2015, https://www.fas.org/sgp/crs/natsec/R41163.pdf.

29. U.S. Department of Defense. *Department of Defense Dictionary of Military and Associated Terms.* JP 1-02, 08 November 2010, as Amended through 15 January 2016. Accessed January 26, 2016, http://www.dtic.mil/doctrine/new_pubs/jp1_02.pdf.

30. Jan Goldman, *Intelligence Warning Terminology*, Joint Military Intelligence College, October 2001, accessed July 3, 2015. https://archive.org/details/JMICIntelligencelwarnterminology.

31. North Atlantic Treaty Organization. *NATO Glossary of Terms and Definitions.* NATO Standardization Agency, 2008, accessed July 2, 2015, https://fas.org/irp/doddir/other/nato2008.pdf.

32. U.S. Department of Defense. *Standard Practice System Safety, Military Standard (MIL-STD) 882E.* May 11, 2012, accessed July 27, 2015, http://www.systemsafety.org/Documents/MIL-STD-882E.pdf.

33. Chairman of the Joint Chiefs of Staff. *National Military Strategic Plan for the War on Terrorism.* February 1, 2006, accessed September 12, 2015, http://www.strategicstudiesinstitute.army.mil/pdffiles/gwot.pdf.

34. Louis Fisher, "Military Tribunals: A Sorry History," *Presidential Studies Quarterly* 33, no. 3 (2003): 484–508.

35. 50 U.S. Code § 1801(h) "Definitions" (Current through Pub. L. 113-234), accessed February 10, 2015, http://www.law.cornell.edu/uscode/text/50/1801; also see *Exhibit B: Minimization Procedures used by the National Security Agency in Connection with Acquisitions of Foreign Intelligence Information Pursuant to Section 702 of the Foreign Intelligence Surveillance Act of 1978, Amended*, accessed January 28, 2015, https://www.aclu.org/files/assets/minimization_procedures_used_by_nsa_in_connection_with_fisa_sect_702.pdf.

36. U.S. Department of Defense. Center for Development of Security Excellence. *Glossary of Security Terms and Definitions.* November 2012, accessed February 16, 2015, http://www.cdse.edu/documents/cdse/Glossary_Handbook.pdf.

37. U.S. Department of Defense. Center for Development of Security Excellence. *Glossary of Security Terms and Definitions.* November 2012, accessed February 16, 2015, http://www.cdse.edu/documents/cdse/Glossary_Handbook.pdf.

38. Ladislas Fargo, *The Broken Seal: The Story of "Operation Magic" and the Pearl Harbor Disaster* (New York: Random House, 1967), 284.

39. U.S. Department of State. Bureau of International Information Programs. *Definitions.* January 14, 2005. Wayback Machine, accessed February 24, 2015, http://wayback.archive.org/web/20080213085231/http://usinfo.state.gov/media/Archive/2005/Jan/26-288268.html.

40. Edgar M. Bottoms, *The Missile Gap* (Rutherford, NJ: Fairleigh Dickenson University Press, 1971), 155.

41. U.S. Department of State. "Definitions of Diplomatic Security Terms," *Foreign Affairs Manual.* 12FAM090. November 12, 2014, accessed January 28, 2015, http://www.state.gov/documents/organization/88330.pdf.

42. Office of the Director of National Intelligence. *Competency Directories for the Intelligence Community Workforce.* Intelligence Community Directive 610, October 4, 2010, accessed March 2, 2015, http://www.dni.gov/files/documents/ICD/ICD_610.pdf.

43. Department of Homeland Security, Risk Steering Committee, *DHS Risk Lexicon*, September 2010, accessed November 4, 2015, http://www.dhs.gov/dhs-risk-lexicon.

44. John A. Gentry, "Complex Civil-Military Operations: A US Military-Centric Perspective," *Naval War College Review* 53, no. 4 (2000): 57–76.

45. Defense Intelligence Agency. *Defense Intelligence Report: Lexicon of Hardened Structure Definitions and Terms.* Washington, DC: 2000.

46. Deputy Secretary of Defense. *Directive-Type Memorandum (DTM) 12-005, Implementing Guidelines for Periodic Review of Detainees Held at Guantanamo Bay per Executive Order 13567.* May 9, 2012 (November 4, 2012), accessed January 22, 2015, http://fas.org/irp/doddir/dod/dtm-12-005.pdf.

47. *Presidential Policy Directive/PPD-8: National Preparedness.* March 30, 2011, accessed February 15, 2011, http://www.dhs.gov/presidential-policy-directive-8-national-preparedness.

48. Department of Homeland Security, Risk Steering Committee. *DHS Risk Lexicon.* September 2010, accessed February 14, 2015, http://www.dhs.gov/dhs-risk-lexicon.

49. National Initiative for Cybersecurity Education. *A Glossary of Common Cybersecurity Terminology.* n.d., accessed September 12, 2015, https://niccs.us-cert.gov/glossary.

50. U.S. Department of Defense. *Department of Defense Dictionary of Military and Associated Terms.* JP 1-02, 08 November 2010, as Amended through 15 January 2016. Accessed January 26, 2016, http://www.dtic.mil/doctrine/new_pubs/jp1_02.pdf.

51. Department of Homeland Security, Risk Steering Committee. *DHS Risk Lexicon.* September 2010, accessed February 14, 2015, http://www.dhs.gov/dhs-risk-lexicon.

52. Chairman of the Joint Chiefs of Staff. National Military Strategic Plan for the War on Terrorism. February 1, 2006, accessed September 12, 2015, http://www.strategicstudiesinstitute.army.mil/pdffiles/gwot.pdf.

53. U.S. Department of Defense. *Joint and National Intelligence Support to Military Operations.* JP 2-01. January 5, 2012, accessed February 26, 2015, http://www.dtic.mil/doctrine/new_pubs/jp2_01.pdf.

54. U.S. Department of the Treasury. *Money Laundering.* Accessed January 28, 2015, http://www.treasury.gov/resource-center/terrorist-illicit-finance/Pages/Money-Laundering.aspx.

55. Andrée Rose, Howard Timm, Corrie Pogson, Jose Gonzalez, Edward Appel, and Nancy Kolb, *Developing a Cybervetting Strategy for Law Enforcement.* Defense Personnel Security Research Center, U.S. Department of Defense, December 2010, accessed January 17, 2015, http://www.dhra.mil/perserec/reports/pp11-02.pdf.

56. Kim Zetter, "Meet Monstermind, the NSA Bot that Could Wage Cyberwar Autonomously," *Wired*, August 13, 2014, accessed July 27, 2015, http://www.wired.com/2014/08/nsa-monstermind-cyberwarfare/.

57. *All Ali Bin Ali Ahmed, et al v. Barack H. Obama, et al., Respondents*, United States District Court for the District of Columbia, Civil Action No. 05-1678, May 11, 2009, accessed January 27, 2015, https://ccrjustice.org/files/2009-05-11%20Ahmed%20Unclassified%20Opinion.pdf. Also see David Cozen, "The Mosaic Theory, National Security, and the Freedom of Information Act," *Yale Law Journal* 115, no. 3 (2005), accessed January 27, 2015, http://newspaperwomen/sol3/paperless?abstract_id=820326.

58. FAS Intelligence Resource Program. *Mossad: The Institute for Intelligence and Special Tasks*, accessed July 27, 2015, http://fas.org/irp/world/israel/mossad/.

59. Michael Dewar, *The Art of Deception in Warfare* (New York: David & Charles Publisher, 1989).

60. Office of the Director of National Intelligence. *National Intelligence Program FY 2009 Congressional Budget Justification Book.* Vol. XII, February 2008, accessed January 17, 2015, http://www.fas.org/irp/dni/cbjb-2009.pdf.

61. Committee for National Security Systems (CNSS). Instruction 4009. *National Information Assurance Glossary.* April 2010, accessed January 25, 2015, http://www.ncix.gov/publications/policy/docs/CNSSI_4009.pdf.

62. "Wolfowitz Justifies 'Murky Intelligence.'" *BBC News*, July 28, 2003, accessed March 9, 2015, http://news.bbc.co.uk/1/hi/world/middle_east/3102409.stm.

63. U.S. Department of State. *2012 International Narcotics Control Strategy Report (INCSR).* March 7, 2012, accessed January 28, 2015, http://www.state.gov/j/nil/rls/nrcrpt/2012/vol2/184110.htm.

64. Committee for National Security Systems (CNSS). Instruction 4009. *National Information Assurance Glossary.* April 2010, accessed January 25, 2015, http://www.ncix.gov/publications/policy/docs/CNSSI_4009.pdf.

N

NARCO-SUPPORTED TERRORISM Coined in 1983 by Former president Belaunde Terry of Peru, who used the term to describe terrorist-type attacks against his nation's anti-narcotics police. "Narco-driven terrorism" are drug trafficking organizations that use terrorist tactics (high-profile violence and intimidation) to advance or protect their drug trafficking activities. The modern definition is narco-supported terrorism, those terrorist/insurgent organizations that use drug trafficking proceeds to advance their political agenda.[1]

NATIONAL A citizen of the United States or a person who, though not a citizen of the United States, owes permanent allegiance to the United States.[2]

NATIONAL AGENCY CHECK A Personnel Security Investigation (PSI) consisting of a records review of certain national agencies, including a technical fingerprint search of the files of the Federal Bureau of Investigation (FBI).[3]

NATIONAL AGENCY CHECK PLUS WRITTEN INQUIRIES (NACI) A personnel security investigation conducted by the Defense Investigative Service (DIS) for access to SECRET information consisting of a National Agency Check (NAC), credit bureau check, and written inquires to current and former employers, covering a 5-year scope.[4]

NATIONAL AGENCY CHECK WITH LOCAL AGENCY CHECKS AND CREDIT CHECK (NACLC) A Personnel Security Investigation (PSI) covering the past 5–7 years and consisting of a National Agency Check (NAC), financial review, verification of date and place of birth, and Local Agency Checks (LACs).[5]

NATIONAL ASSET DATABASE A list of critical assets, but rather as a national asset inventory providing the "universe" from which various lists of critical assets are produced. As such, the Department maintains that it represents just the first step in DHS's risk management process outlined in the

National Infrastructure Protection Plan. DHS has developed, apparently from the National Asset Database, a list of about 600 assets that it has determined are critical to the nation. Also, while the National Asset Database has been used to support federal grant-making decisions, according to a DHS official, it does not drive those decisions.[6] *See* CRITICAL INFRASTRUCTURE

NATIONAL BIODEFENSE ANALYSIS AND COUNTERMEASURES CENTER The Department of Homeland Security's Science and Technology Directorate is proud to have NBACC as the first laboratory built for DHS—a national resource to understand the scientific basis of the risk posed by biological threats and to attribute their use in bioterror or bio-crime events. The president and Congress have charged NBACC with research and development of technologies to protect the American public from bioterrorism. In November 2002, Congress passed the Homeland Security Act in part to coordinate and advance homeland security research and development activities across the federal government. President Bush issued government-wide directives on biodefense research and development in April 2004.[7]

NATIONAL CAPITAL REGION (NCR) A geographic area encompassing the District of Columbia and eleven local jurisdictions in the State of Maryland and the Commonwealth of Virginia.[8]

NATIONAL CLANDESTINE SERVICE (NCS) Agency within the CIA that coordinates U.S. HUMINT (human intelligence) efforts; intended to make the CIA director "national HUMINT manager" for all 15 intelligence agencies, to improve cooperation among the spy agencies, as well as streamline the flow of information to elected officials. The 9/11 Commission also recommended that the director emphasize rebuilding the CIA's analytic capabilities; transforming the clandestine service by building its human intelligence capabilities; developing a stronger language program, with high standards and sufficient financial incentives; renewing emphasis on recruiting diversity among operations officers so they can blend more easily in foreign cities; ensuring a seamless relationship between human source collection and signals collection at the operational level; and stressing a better balance between unilateral and liaison operations.[9]

NATIONAL COMMISSION ON TERRORIST ATTACKS UPON THE UNITED STATES (9/11 COMMISSION) The National Commission on Terrorist Attacks Upon the United States (also known as the 9/11 Commission), an independent, bipartisan commission created by congressional legislation and the signature of President George W. Bush in late 2002, is chartered to prepare a full and complete account of the circumstances surrounding the September 11, 2001, terrorist attacks, including preparedness for and the immediate response to the attacks. The Commission is also mandated to provide recommendations designed to guard against future attacks.[10]

NATIONAL COMMUNICATION SYSTEM Connects the president, National Security Council, director of the Office of Science and Technology Policy, and director of the Office of Management and Budget in the implementation of the telecommunications functions and responsibilities, and the coordination of the planning for and provision of national security and emergency preparedness communications for the federal government under crisis or emergency situations.

NATIONAL CONSORTIUM FOR THE STUDY OF TERRORISM AND RESPONSES TO TERRORISM (START) A university-based research and education center comprised of an international network of scholars committed to the scientific study of the causes and human consequences of terrorism in the United States and around the world. Headquartered at the University of Maryland, START supports the research efforts of leading social scientists at more than 50 academic and research institutions.[11]

NATIONAL COUNTERINTELLIGENCE STRATEGY The product of an intensive consultation process across the Intelligence Community. It sets forth strategic objectives for the counterintelligence community, and it does so consistent with statutory requirements. The strategy will guide the organizational, programmatic, and budgetary priorities of all counterintelligence elements of the U.S. government. It will do so consistent with the president's *National Security Strategy*, the DNI's *National Intelligence Strategy*, and other applicable guidance. Essential strategic goals do not and should not change every year; yet the process of risk management requires that the counterintelligence community continually assess challenges, opportunities, and vulnerabilities. The NCIX will therefore review this strategy every year and, supported by the National Counterintelligence Policy Board, will make adjustments as circumstances require.[12]

NATIONAL COUNTERTERRORISM CENTER The Intelligence Reform and Terrorism Prevention Act (IRTPA) of 2004 established NCTC in law, and mandated the Center serve as the "central and shared knowledge bank on known and suspected terrorists and international terror groups."[13] NCTC serves as the primary organization in the U.S. government for integrating and analyzing all intelligence pertaining to terrorism possessed or acquired by the

U.S. government (except purely domestic terrorism); serves as the central and shared knowledge bank on terrorism information; provides all-source intelligence support to government-wide counterterrorism activities; establishes the information technology (IT) systems and architectures within the NCTC and between the NCTC and other agencies that enable access to, as well as integration, dissemination, and use of, terrorism information. NCTC serves as the principal advisor to the DNI on intelligence operations and analysis relating to counterterrorism, advising the DNI on how well U.S. intelligence activities, programs, and budget proposals for counterterrorism conform to priorities established by the president.[14] *See* TERRORIST THREAT INTEGRATION CENTER

NATIONAL CRIME INFORMATION CENTER (NCIC) Helps criminal justice professionals apprehend fugitives, locate missing persons, recover stolen property, and identify terrorists. It also assists law enforcement officers in performing their official duties more safely and provides them with information necessary to aid in protecting the general public. About the records: the NCIC database currently consists of 21 files. There are seven property files containing records of stolen articles, boats, guns, license plates, parts, securities, and vehicles. There are 14 persons files, including Supervised Release; National Sex Offender Registry; Foreign Fugitive; Immigration Violator; Missing Person; Protection Order; Unidentified Person; U.S. Secret Service Protective; Gang; Known or Appropriately Suspected Terrorist; Wanted Person; Identity Theft; Violent Person; and National Instant Criminal Background Check System (NICS) Denied Transaction. The system also contains images that can be associated with NCIC records to help agencies identify people and property items. The Interstate Identification Index, which contains automated criminal history record information, is accessible through the same network as NCIC.[15]

NATIONAL CRIMINAL INTELLIGENCE SHARING PLAN (NCISP) A formal intelligence sharing initiative, supported by the U.S. Department of Justice, Office of Justice Programs, that securely links local, state, tribal, and federal law enforcement agencies, facilitating the exchange of critical intelligence information. The Plan contains model policies and standards and is a blueprint for law enforcement administrators to follow when enhancing or building an intelligence function. It describes a nationwide communications capability that will link all levels of law enforcement personnel, including officers on the street, intelligence analysts, unit commanders, and police executives.[16] Developed by the Global Intelligence Working Group that addresses the security and intelligence needs recognized after September 11, 2001. It describes a nationwide communications capability to link together all levels of law enforcement personnel, including officers on the streets, intelligence analysts, unit commanders, and police executives for the purpose of sharing critical data.[17]

NATIONAL CYBER INVESTIGATIVE JOINT TASK FORCE In 2008, the U.S. president mandated the NCIJTF to be the focal point for all government agencies to coordinate, integrate, and share information related to all domestic cyber threat investigations. The FBI is responsible for developing and supporting the joint task force, which includes 19 intelligence agencies and law enforcement, working side by side to identify key players and schemes. Its goal is to predict and prevent what's on the horizon and to pursue the enterprises behind cyber attacks.[18]

NATIONAL CYBER RISK ALERT LEVEL SYSTEM (NCRAL) The National Cyber Risk Alert Level (NCRAL) system operates as a national-level alert and warning system that conveys the current level of cyber risk to critical infrastructure and key resources (CIKR) critical functions. The system utilizes the common operational picture from the National Cybersecurity and Communications Integration Center (NCCIC) and works with NCCIC partners to examine risk to cybersecurity systems across CIKR sectors and across the nation. When risk to critical systems is determined, it will be communicated through four alert levels (Guarded, Elevated, Substantial, Severe) and will be accompanied by additional, more detailed information as described in the Alert Levels.[19]

NATIONAL CYBERSECURITY AND COMMUNICATIONS INTEGRATION CENTER (NCCIC) A 24/7 cyber situational awareness, incident response, and management center that is a national nexus of cyber and communications integration for the federal government, intelligence community, and law enforcement. The NCCIC shares information among the public and private sectors to provide greater understanding of cybersecurity and communications situation awareness of vulnerabilities, intrusions, incidents, mitigation, and recovery actions.[20]

NATIONAL DATA EXCHANGE (N-DEx) The only national investigative information-sharing system enabling local, state, tribal, and federal criminal justice agencies to search, link, and analyze information across jurisdictional boundaries. Records in N-DEx span the criminal justice lifecycle, including information related to cases, arrests, missing persons, service calls, bookings, holdings, incarcerations, pre-trial and pre-sentencing proceedings, warrants, supervised releases, citations/tickets, and field contacts/field interviews. All of this information promotes safety at an initial patrol stop, during the effective supervision of an offender, and in the efforts to promote victim safety. The N-DEx connects many regional and local information-sharing systems and leverages their collective power to provide access to more than 228 million records from over 5,000 agencies. N-DEx connects users to a number of federal agencies in addition to the FBI, including the Drug Enforcement Administration; Bureau of Alcohol, Tobacco, Firearms and Explosives (ATF); U.S. Marshals Service; the Department of Defense; and the Department of Homeland Security.[21]

NATIONAL DEFENSE INFORMATION (NDI) 1. Espionage statutes . . . may make criminal nearly all acquisitions by newspapers of "national defense" information, a term defined so broadly by the courts that it comprehends most properly classified information.[22] 2. (Former CIA officer John) Kiriakou was charged with one count of violating the Intelligence Identities Protection Act for allegedly illegally disclosing the identity of a covert officer and two counts of violating the Espionage Act for allegedly illegally disclosing national defense information to individuals not authorized to receive it. Kiriakou was also charged with one count of making false statements for allegedly lying to the Publications Review Board of the CIA in an unsuccessful attempt to trick the CIA into allowing him to include classified information in a book he was seeking to publish.[23]

NATIONAL DEFENSE STRATEGY (NDS) National defense strategy articulates the ends that the Department of Defense will pursue to help execute the national security strategy, together with the ways and means that DoD will use to do so. Requirement: Title 10, U.S. Code, §118 requires that the QDR process "delineate a national defense strategy" and that the QDR report include a "comprehensive discussion of the national defense strategy of the United States." There is no separate statutory mandate for an NDS. Contents of the mandate: §118 requires that the NDS—as part of the QDR report—be submitted to Armed Services Committees every four years, no later than the president's budget submission. There is no statutory description of the discrete contents of defense strategy, but §118 requires that it be consistent with the most recent NSS.[24] *See* NATIONAL SECURITY STRATEGY; QUADRENNIAL DEFENSE REVIEW

NATIONAL DETAINEE REPORTING CENTER (NDRC) The national-level center that accounts for all persons who pass through the care, custody, and control of the Department of Defense and that obtains and stores information concerning detainees and their confiscated personal property.[25]

NATIONAL DISASTER An emergency situation posing significant danger to life and property that results from a natural cause.[26]

NATIONAL DISASTER MEDICAL SYSTEM (NDMS) The National Disaster Medical System (NDMS) is a cooperative asset-sharing program that augments local medical care when an emergency exceeds the scope of a community's hospital and healthcare resources. The emergency resources—which include some 8,000 medical and support personnel—come from federal, state and local governments, the private sector and civilian volunteers. The Federal Emergency Management Agency, now part of the Department of Homeland Security (DHS), coordinates all components of NDMS.[27]

NATIONAL DISCLOSURE POLICY (NDP-1) 1. A document that promulgates national policy and procedures in the form of specific disclosure criteria and limitations, definition of terms, release arrangements, and other guidance required by U.S. departments and agencies having occasion to disclose classified information to foreign governments and international organizations. NDP-1 establishes and provides for management of interagency mechanisms and procedures required for effective implementation of the national policy.[28] 2. Promulgates national policy and procedures in the form of specific disclosure criteria and limitations, definitions of terms, release arrangements, and other guidance required by U.S. departments and agencies having occasion to release classified U.S. information. In addition, it establishes and provides for the management of an interagency mechanism and procedures that are required for the effective implementation of the policy.[29]

NATIONAL DRUG INTELLIGENCE CENTER Established by the Department of Defense Appropriations Act, 1993 (Public Law 102-396) signed into law on October 6, 1992. Placed under the direction and control of the Attorney General, NDIC was established to "coordinate and consolidate drug intelligence from all national security and law enforcement agencies, and produce information regarding the structure, membership, finances, communications, and activities of drug trafficking organizations." In 2012, NDIC was abolished with staff and duties moved into the Drug Enforcement Administration.[30]

NATIONAL EMERGENCY A condition declared by the president or the Congress by virtue of powers previously vested in them that authorize certain emergency actions to be undertaken in the national interest.[31]

NATIONAL ESSENTIAL FUNCTIONS (NEFS) 1. That subset of government functions that are necessary to lead and sustain the nation during a catastrophic emergency and that, therefore, must be supported through COOP and COG capabilities.[32] 2. "National essential functions" means that subset of government functions that are necessary to lead and sustain the nation during a catastrophic emergency.[33] *See* CATASTROPHIC EVENT

NATIONAL EXERCISE PROGRAM (NEP) As a component of the NPS (National Preparedness System), the National Exercise Program (NEP) serves to test and validate core capabilities. Participation in exercises, simulations or other activities, including real-world incidents, helps organizations validate their capabilities and identify shortfalls. Exercises also help organizations see their progress toward meeting their preparedness objectives. The Capstone Exercise, formerly titled the National Level Exercise (NLE), is conducted every two years as the final component of each NEP progressive exercise cycle.[34] *See* NATIONAL PREPAREDNESS GOAL; NATIONAL PREPAREDNESS SYSTEM

NATIONAL FOREIGN INTELLIGENCE BOARD Consists of the most senior officials of all U.S. Intelligence agencies. In effect, this acts as a "Board of Directors" for U.S. Intelligence and is chaired by the Director of National Intelligence. Members include representatives from all 16 agencies of the intelligence community. *See* INTELLIGENCE COMMUNITY

NATIONAL GANG INTELLIGENCE CENTER (NGIC) Integrates gang intelligence from across federal, state, and local law enforcement on the growth, migration, criminal activity, and association of gangs that pose a significant threat to the United States. It supports law enforcement by sharing timely and accurate information and by providing strategic/tactical analysis of intelligence. Located just outside Washington, DC, the NGIC is manned by analysts from multiple federal agencies. The databases of each component agency are available to the NGIC, as are other gang-related databases, permitting centralized access to information. In addition, the NGIC provides operational and analytical support for investigations.[35] *See* NATIONAL GANG UNIT; OPERATION COMMUNITY SHIELD

NATIONAL GANG UNIT A critical part of ICE's Immigration and Customs Enforcement mission to bring the fight to transnational criminal gangs. The NGU identifies and develops intelligence on gang membership, associations, activities and international movements. It also deters, disrupts gang operations by tracing and seizing cash, weapons and other assets derived from illicit activities.[36] *See* NATIONAL GANG INTELLIGENCE CENTER; OPERATION COMMUNITY SHIELD

NATIONAL INCIDENT-BASED REPORTING SYSTEM (NIBRS)
Implemented to improve the overall quality of crime data collected by law enforcement, captures details on each single crime incident—as well as on separate offenses within the same incident—including information on victims, known offenders, relationships between victims and offenders, arrestees, and property involved in the crimes. As compared to UCR's (*Uniform Crime Reports*) traditional Summary Reporting System currently used in the annual Crime in the United States report—which is an aggregate monthly tally of crimes—the NIBRS is a more comprehensive accounting of crime occurring in a law enforcement agency's jurisdiction. When used to its full potential, the NIBRS can identify with precision when and where crime takes place, the form it takes, and the characteristics of its victims and perpetrators.[37]

NATIONAL INCIDENT MANAGEMENT SYSTEM (NIMS) A national crisis response system that provides a consistent, nationwide approach for federal, state, local, and tribal governments; the private sector; and non-governmental organizations to work effectively and efficiently together to prepare for, respond to, and recover from domestic incidents, regardless of cause, size, or complexity.[38]

NATIONAL INDUSTRIAL SECURITY PROGRAM (NISP) A partnership between the federal government and private industry to safeguard classified information. Executive Order 12829, as amended, "National Industrial Security Program," was established to achieve cost savings and protect classified information held by contractors, licensees, and grantees of the U.S. government. The Order was signed by President Bush in January of 1993. Redundant, overlapping, or unnecessary requirements impede the technological and economic interests of the U.S. government. Executive Order 12829 calls for a single, integrated, cohesive system for safeguarding classified information held by industry. Consistent with the goal of achieving greater uniformity in security requirements for classified contracts, the four major tenets of the NISP are:

- Achieving uniformity in security procedures.
- Implementing the reciprocity principle in security procedures, particularly with regard to facility and personnel clearances.
- Eliminating duplicative or unnecessary requirements, particularly agency inspections.
- Achieving reductions in security costs.

The NISP affects all executive branch agencies. The major signatories to the program are the Department of Energy, the Nuclear Regulatory Commission, the Department of Defense, and the Central Intelligence Agency.[39]

NATIONAL INFORMATION EXCHANGE MODEL (NIEM) A partnership of the U.S. Department of Justice, Department of Homeland Security, and Department of Health and Human Services. It is designed to develop, disseminate and support enterprise-wide information exchange standards and processes that can enable jurisdictions to effectively share critical information in emergency situations, as well as support the day-to-day operations of agencies throughout the nation. NIEM enables information sharing, focusing on information exchanged among organizations as part of their current or intended business practices. The NIEM exchange development methodology results in a common semantic understanding among participating organizations and data formatted in a semantically consistent manner. NIEM will standardize content (actual data exchange standards), provide tools, and manage processes.[40] *See* GLOBAL JUSTICE INFORMATION SHARING INITIATIVE

NATIONAL INFORMATION INFRASTRUCTURE (NII) The nationwide interconnection of communications networks, computers, databases, and consumer electronics that makes vast amounts of information available to users. The NII encompasses a wide range of equipment, including cameras, scanners, keyboards, fax machines, computers, switches, CDs, video and audio tape, cable, wire, satellites, fiber-optic transmission lines, networks of all types, televisions, monitors, printers, and much more. The transmitted information constitutes a critical component of the national information infrastructure.[41] *See* GLOBAL INFORMATION INFRASTRUCTURE; INFORMATION

NATIONAL INFRASTRUCTURE COORDINATING CENTER Dedicated 24/7 coordination and information-sharing operations center that maintains situational awareness of the nation's critical infrastructure for the federal government. When an incident or event affecting critical infrastructure occurs and requires coordination between the Department of Homeland Security and the owners and operators of our nation's infrastructure, the NICC serves as that information sharing hub to support the security and resilience of these vital assets. The NICC is part of the National Protection and Programs Directorate/Office of Infrastructure Protection and the DHS National Operations Center.[42]

NATIONAL INFRASTRUCTURE PROTECTION PLAN (NIPP) 1. Pursuant to Presidential Policy Directive (PPD)-21, DHS is to coordinate the overall federal effort to promote the security and resilience of the nation's critical infrastructure from all hazards. DHS issued the National Infrastructure Protection Plan (NIPP) in 2006 to provide the overarching approach for integrating the nation's CI security and resilience activities into a single national effort. The NIPP, which was updated in 2009, and most recently in 2013, sets forth a risk management framework and outlines the roles and responsibilities of DHS with regard to CI security and resilience.[43] 2. Consistent with the Homeland Security Act of 2002, the Secretary shall produce a comprehensive, integrated National Plan for Critical Infrastructure and Key Resources Protection to outline national goals, objectives, milestones, and key initiatives within 1 year from the issuance of this directive.[44] *See* CRITICAL INFRASTRUCTURE

NATIONAL INFRASTRUCTURE SIMULATION AND ANALYSIS CENTER (NISAC) The National Infrastructure Simulation and Analysis Center (NISAC) is a modeling, simulation, and analysis program within the Department of Homeland Security (DHS) comprising personnel in the Washington, D.C., area, as well as from Sandia National Laboratories (SNL) and Los Alamos National Laboratory (LANL). Congress mandated that NISAC serve as a "source of national expertise to address critical infrastructure protection" research and analysis. NISAC prepares and shares analyses of critical infrastructure, including their interdependencies, vulnerabilities, consequences, and other complexities, under the direction of the Office of Infrastructure Protection (IP), Infrastructure Analysis and Strategy Division (IASD).[45] *See* CRITICAL INFRASTRUCTURE

NATIONAL INITIATIVE FOR CYBERSECURITY EDUCATION A nationally coordinated effort comprising over 20 federal departments and agencies, academia, and industry. The mission of this initiative is to enhance the overall cybersecurity posture of the United States by accelerating the availability of educational and training resources designed to improve the cyber behavior, skills, and knowledge of every segment of the population, enabling a safer cyberspace for all. The NICE initiative extends beyond the federal workplace to include private industry, those changing careers, and students in kindergarten through post-graduate school. NICE was established in support of the 2009 Cyberspace Policy review and expands upon the cyber education Initiative of the 2008 Comprehensive National Cybersecurity Initiative (CNCI).[46]

NATIONAL INSIDER THREAT TASK FORCE (NITTF) In October 2011, the president issued Executive Order (E.O.) 13587 establishing the National Insider Threat Task Force (NITTF), under joint leadership of the Attorney General and the Director of National Intelligence. The primary mission of the NITTF is to prevent, deter and detect compromises of classified information by malicious insiders. As part of the E.O., the president directed federal departments and agencies, with classified networks, to establish insider threat detection and prevention programs. The E.O. directs the NITTF to assist agencies in developing and implementing their insider threat programs, while ensuring the program standards do not erode civil liberties, civil rights, or privacy protections for government employees. In November 2012, following an extensive interagency coordination and vetting process, the president issued the National Insider Threat Policy and the Minimum Standards for Executive Branch Insider Threat Programs via a Presidential Memorandum.[47]

NATIONAL INSTANT CRIMINAL BACKGROUND CHECK SYSTEM (NICS) Mandated by the Brady Handgun Violence Prevention Act of 1993 and launched by the FBI on November 30, 1998, NICS is used by Federal Firearms Licensees (FFLs) to instantly determine whether a prospective buyer is eligible to buy firearms or explosives. Before ringing up the sale, cashiers call in a check to the FBI or to other designated agencies to ensure that each customer does not have a criminal record or isn't otherwise ineligible to make a purchase. More than 100 million such checks have been made in the last decade, leading to more than 700,000 denials. NICS is located at the FBI's Criminal Justice Information Services Division in Clarksburg, West Virginia. It provides full service to FFLs in 30 states, five U.S. territories, and the District of Columbia. Upon completion of the required Bureau of Alcohol, Tobacco, Firearms and Explosives (ATF) Form 4473, FFLs contact the NICS Section via a toll-free telephone number or electronically on the Internet through the NICS E-Check System to request a background check with the descriptive information provided on the ATF Form 4473.[48]

NATIONAL INSTITUTE OF STANDARDS AND TECHNOLOGY (NIST) A non-regulatory federal agency within the U.S. Department of Commerce that develops and promotes measurement, standards, and technology to enhance productivity, facilitate trade, and improve the quality of life. NIST's measurement and standards work promotes the well-being of the nation and helps improve, among many others things, the nation's homeland security.[49]

NATIONAL INTEGRATED TSCM COMMITTEE (NITC) The National Integrated TSCM (Technical Surveillance Countermeasures) Committee (NITC), charted by the DNI, shall provide policy, strategic, and procedural guidance on all TSCM matters involving the IC and its customers. The NITC shall meet at least quarterly. The NITC chair report annually to the DNI on IC compliance with this directive (ICD 702), compile TCSM programmatic and procedural recommendations, and submit a program and budget plan for consideration in coordination with the DNI Chief Financial Officer. The NITC shall be as inclusive as practical. NITC initiatives shall include the creation of a DNI funding mechanism that addresses TSCM issues of common concern.[50]

NATIONAL INTEGRATION CENTER This center will periodically review, and revise as appropriate, the National Incident Management System and the National Response Plan, including (A) establishing, in consultation with the Director of the Corporation for National and Community Service, a process to better use volunteers and donations; (B) improving the use of federal, state, local, and tribal resources and ensuring the effective use of emergency response providers at emergency scenes; and (C) revising the Catastrophic Incident Annex, finalizing and releasing the Catastrophic Incident Supplement to the National Response Plan, and ensuring that both effectively address response requirements in the event of a catastrophic incident.[51]

NATIONAL INTELLIGENCE 1. The collection, analysis, processing, and dissemination of intelligence that primarily supports the president, cabinet, and other national leaders. Most of this intelligence is strategic in nature and is done under the component programs of the National Intelligence Program. The term "national intelligence" applies to information gathered within or outside the United States that pertains to more than one U.S. government agency and that involves threats to the United States, its people, property, or interests; the development, proliferation, or use of weapons of mass destruction; or any other matter bearing on U.S. national homeland security.[52] 2. Intelligence produced by the CIA which bears on the broad aspects of U.S. national policy and national security. It is of concern to more than one department or agency.[53]

NATIONAL INTELLIGENCE ANALYSIS AND PRODUCTION BOARD (NIAPB) Chaired by the Deputy DNI for Analysis, with senior reps from all analytic components across the IC. Serves as the DDNI/A's board of directors advising on the direction of the analytic community.[54]

NATIONAL INTELLIGENCE AND INTELLIGENCE RELATED TO NATIONAL SECURITY Refers to all intelligence, regardless of the source from which derived and including information gathered within or outside the United States, that pertains, as determined consistent with any guidance issued by the president, to more than one U.S. government agency; and that involves threats to the United States, its people, property, or interests; the development, proliferation, or use of weapons of mass destruction; or any other matter bearing on U.S. national or homeland security.[55]

NATIONAL INTELLIGENCE BOARD Serves as the senior Intelligence Community advisory body to the Director of National Intelligence (DNI) on the analytic judgments and issues related to analysis of national intelligence; functions include: production, review, and coordination of national intelligence; interagency exchanges of national intelligence information; sharing of IC intelligence products with foreign governments; protection of intelligence sources and methods; activities of common concern and other matters as may be referred to it by the DNI.[56]

NATIONAL INTELLIGENCE COMMUNITY AWARDS (NICA) Established and granted by or on behalf of the Director of National Intelligence (DNI) in recognition of distinguished service or exceptional contribution to the IC and the United States.[57]

NATIONAL INTELLIGENCE COORDINATION CENTER (NIC-C) Established on October 1, 2007, and exemplifies the DNI's desire to work more collaboratively and efficiently across the Intelligence Community; and in this case across all intelligence collection activities in the entire U.S. government. The NIC-C was established in collaboration with the Department of Defense and several domestic agencies, and will for the first time give us a mechanism to coordinate, collaborate, assess, and efficiently deploy our nation's total array of intelligence collection capabilities.[58]

NATIONAL INTELLIGENCE COUNCIL (NIC) Established within the Office of the Director of Central Intelligence, the NIC is composed of senior analysts within the intelligence community and substantive experts from the public and private sector. The analysts are appointed by, report to, and serve at the pleasure of the director of central intelligence. The NIC produces national intelligence estimates for the government, including alternative views held by elements of the intelligence community. It also evaluates community-wide collection and production of intelligence by the intelligence community and the requirements and resources of such collection and production.[59] *See* NATIONAL INTELLIGENCE OFFICER FOR WARNING

NATIONAL INTELLIGENCE DAILY (NID) A top-secret summary of the main intelligence items from the previous days, with a very limited distribution.

NATIONAL INTELLIGENCE ESTIMATE (NIE) 1. A strategic estimate of the capabilities, vulnerabilities, and probable courses of action of foreign nations produced at the national level as a composite of the views of the intelligence community.[60] 2. A strategic estimate of capabilities, vulnerabilities, and probable courses of action of foreign nations.[61] *See* INTELLIGENCE ESTIMATE; SPECIAL NATIONAL INTELLIGENCE ESTIMATE

NATIONAL INTELLIGENCE OFFICER FOR WARNING (NIO/W) Principal point of contact between the director of central intelligence and intelligence consumers below the cabinet level; primary source of national-level substantive guidance to intelligence community planners, collectors, and resource managers; appointed by the director of central intelligence in consultation with the director of the Defense Intelligence Agency. The NIO/W is one of the 13 national intelligence officers of the National Intelligence Council.[62] *See* OFFICE OF NATIONAL ESTIMATES (ONE); NATIONAL INTELLIGENCE COUNCIL

NATIONAL INTELLIGENCE PRIORITIES FRAMEWORK (NIPF) 1. A planning framework used by the DNI to prioritize intelligence topics based on level of concern, relevance, and urgency. The NIPF is the DNI's sole mechanism for establishing national intelligence priorities. The NIPF is updated semi-annually with any ad-hoc adjustments to reflect current events and policy priorities. 2. The primary mechanism to establish, disestablish, manage, and communicate national intelligence priorities. The NIPF reflects customers' priorities for national intelligence support and ensures that enduring and emerging national intelligence issues are addressed. Guidance from the president and National Security advisor determines the overall priorities of top-level NIPF issues.[63]

NATIONAL INTELLIGENCE PROFESSIONAL AWARDS (NIPA) Established by the DNI and granted by or on behalf of IC Senior Program Executives (SPE) in recognition of distinguished service or exceptional contribution to a particular IC profession, function, or intelligence discipline.[64] *See* IC SENIOR PROGRAM EXECUTIVE

NATIONAL INTELLIGENCE PROGRAM (NIP) 1. The consolidation of the National Foreign Intelligence Program (NFIP) and other national intelligence programs into a single funding program providing the resources needed to develop and maintain intelligence capabilities supporting national priorities.[65] 2. All programs, projects and activities of the IC, as well as any other programs of the IC designated jointly by the DNI and the head of a U.S. department or agency or by the president. It does not include programs, projects or activities of the military departments to acquire intelligence solely for the planning and conduct of tactical military operations by U.S. armed forces.[66]

NATIONAL INTELLIGENCE RESERVE CORPS The director of National Intelligence may provide for the establishment and training of a National Intelligence Reserve Corps (in this section referred to as "National Intelligence Reserve Corps") for the temporary reemployment on a voluntary basis of former employees of elements of the intelligence community during periods of emergency, as determined by the director. (b) An individual may participate in the National Intelligence Reserve Corps only if the individual previously served as a full-time employee of an element of the intelligence community. (c) The director of National Intelligence shall prescribe the terms and conditions under which eligible individuals may participate in the National Intelligence Reserve Corps.[67]

NATIONAL INTELLIGENCE SCIENCE AND TECHNOLOGY COMMITTEE (NISTC) A committee consisting of the chief scientists and chief technology officers from the Intelligence Community, who provide scientific and technical advice to the Assistant DNI for Science and Technology. The committee coordinates the IC advanced research and development efforts in support of national security missions.[68]

NATIONAL INTELLIGENCE STRATEGY (NIS) The DNI's guidance to the IC for the accomplishment of the goals set forth in the president's National Security Strategy.[69]

NATIONAL INTELLIGENCE STRATEGY PERFORMANCE REVIEW (NISPR) The DNI's senior decision-making body to consider how well the IC is accomplishing the NIS.[70]

NATIONAL JOINT TERRORISM TASK FORCE (NJTTF) A group created in July 2002 by the FBI to complement the JTTFs around the country.[71] The NJTTF is composed of representatives from approximately 30 federal, state, and local agencies, and "provides a central fusion point for terrorism information and intelligence to the Joint Terrorism Task Forces," which include state and local law enforcement officers and federal agency officials.[72] *See* COUNTERTERRORISM CENTER; INFORMATION ANALYSIS AND INFRASTRUCTURE PROTECTION DIRECTORATE; JOINT TERRORISM TASK FORCE; TERRORIST THREAT INTEGRATION CENTER

NATIONAL LAW ENFORCEMENT TELECOMMUNICATION SYSTEM (NLETS) A broad-based information-sharing network servicing the justice community at the local, state, and federal levels. It is the pre-eminent interstate law enforcement network in the nation for the exchange of law enforcement and related justice information. The mission of NLETS is to provide, within a secure environment, an international justice telecommunications capability and information services that will benefit the safety, security, and preservation of human life and the protection of property. NLETS will assist those national and international governmental agencies and other organizations with similar missions that enforce or aid in enforcing local, state, or international laws or ordinances.[73]

NATIONAL MARITIME INTELLIGENCE CENTER (NMIC) The primary functions of the center will be the integration of maritime information and intelligence collection and analysis in support of national policy and decision makers, Maritime Domain Awareness objectives, and interagency operations, at all levels. It will also be the maritime intelligence interface for supporting such other national intelligence centers as the National Counterterrorism Center and the National Counterproliferation Center.[74]

NATIONAL MEDIA EXPLOITATION CENTER (NMEC) The National Media Exploitation Center (NMEC) is responsible for ensuring the rapid collection, processing, exploitation, dissemination and sharing of all acquired and seized media throughout the intelligence, counterintelligence, military and law enforcement communities. A Director of National Intelligence (DNI) Center composed of DIA, CIA, FBI, NSA, and Defense Cyber Crime Center (DCCC) as partner organizations; DIA is the Executive Agent. NMEC acts as a DOMEX [document and media exploitation] service of common concern and ensures prompt and responsive DOMEX support to meet the needs of intelligence, defense, homeland security, law enforcement, and other U.S. government consumers, to include provision of timely and accurate collection, processing, exploitation, and dissemination consistent with the protection of intelligence sources and methods.[75]

NATIONAL MILITARY STRATEGY (NMS) The National Defense Authorization Act (NDAA) for FY2004, P.L. 108-136, §903, introduced a permanent requirement for an NMS, codified in Title 10, U.S. Code, §153(b), as amended by the NDAAs for FY2012 and FY2013. The NMS is required to be consistent with the most recent NSS, the most recent QDR, and with "any other national security or defense strategic guidance issued by the President or the Secretary of Defense." Each NMS is required to address strategic challenges and opportunities; U.S. military objectives; the missions and activities required to accomplish those objectives; force planning and sizing; contributions from interagency and international partners and from contractors; and resource constraints that affect the strategy.[76] *See* NATIONAL SECURITY STRATEGY; QUADRENNIAL DEFENSE REVIEW

NATIONAL NOTIFIABLE DISEASES SURVEILLANCE SYSTEM (NNDSS) The National Electronic Disease Surveillance System (NEDSS) facilitates electronically transferring public health surveillance data from the healthcare system to public health departments. It is a conduit for exchanging information that supports NNDSS. Today, when states and territories voluntarily submit notifiable disease surveillance data electronically to CDC, they use data standards and electronic disease information systems and resources supported in part by NEDSS.[77]

NATIONAL OPERATIONS SECURITY PROGRAM A program created by the Reagan administration in which each department and agency assigned or supporting national security missions with classified or sensitive activities was to establish a formal Operations Security (OPSEC) program with the following common features:

- Specific assignment of responsibility for OPSEC direction and implementation.
- Specific requirements to plan for and implement OPSEC in anticipation of and, where appropriate, during department or agency activity.
- Direction to use OPSEC analytical techniques to assist in identifying vulnerabilities and to select appropriate OPSEC measures.
- Enactment of measures to ensure that all personnel commensurate with their positions and security clearances are aware of hostile intelligence threats and understand the OPSEC process.
- Annual review and evaluation of OPSEC procedures so as to assist the improvement of OPSEC programs.
- Provision for interagency support and cooperation with respect to OPSEC programs.

Agencies with minimal activities that could affect national security need not establish a formal OPSEC program; however, they must cooperate with other departments and agencies to minimize damage to national security when OPSEC problems arise.[78]

NATIONAL PALM PRINT SYSTEM 1. In 2013, the NGI System deployed the new NPPS which contains millions of palm prints that are now searchable on a nationwide basis. The NPPS and improvements in latent fingerprint search performance are providing powerful new and enhanced crime-solving capabilities for more than 18,000 local, state, tribal, and federal law enforcement agencies across the country. In addition, NGI has expanded criminal and civil searches against the Universal Latent File, potentially generating new investigative leads in unsolved and/or cold cases as well as latent enrollment and search enhancements.[79] 2. In May 2013 the NGI expanded beyond traditional finger and thumbprint capabilities to include palms, as the majority of prints left at crime scenes contain hand ridges and palm prints.[80] *See* NEXT GENERATION IDENTIFICATION

NATIONAL POLICY A broad course of action or statements of guidance adopted by the government at the national level in pursuit of national objectives.[81]

NATIONAL PREPAREDNESS The term "national preparedness" refers to the actions taken to plan, organize, equip, train, and exercise to build and sustain the capabilities necessary to prevent, protect against, mitigate the effects of, respond to, and recover from those threats that pose the greatest risk to the security of the nation.[82]

NATIONAL PREPAREDNESS GOAL Presidential Policy Directive 8 (PPD-8) describes the nation's approach to national preparedness. The National Preparedness Goal is the cornerstone for the implementation of PPD-8; identified within it are the nation's core capabilities across five mission areas: prevention, protection, mitigation, response, and recovery. The National Preparedness System is the instrument the nation will employ to build, sustain, and deliver those core capabilities in order to achieve the goal of a secure and resilient nation. The guidance, programs, processes, and systems that support each component of the National Preparedness System enable a collaborative, whole community approach to national preparedness that engages individuals, families, communities, private and nonprofit sectors, faith-based organizations, and all levels of government.[83] *See* NATIONAL EXERCISE PROGRAM; NATIONAL PREPAREDNESS SYSTEM

NATIONAL PREPAREDNESS SYSTEM An organized process for everyone in the whole community to move forward with their preparedness activities and achieve the National Preparedness Goal. The National Preparedness System has six parts: Identifying and Assessing Risk; Estimating Capability Requirements; Building and Sustaining Capabilities; Planning to Deliver Capabilities; Validating Capabilities; Reviewing and Updating.[84] *See* NATIONAL EXERCISE PROGRAM; NATIONAL PREPAREDNESS GOAL

NATIONAL SECURITY 1. A collective term encompassing both national defense and foreign relations of the United States with the purpose of gaining: a. a military or defense advantage over any foreign nation or group of nations; b. a favorable foreign relations position; or c. a defense posture capable of successfully resisting hostile or destructive action from within or without, overt or covert.[85] 2. U.S. national security is the ability of national institutions to prevent adversaries from using force to harm Americans or their national interests and the confidence of Americans in this capability. There are two dimensions of this definition: physical and psychological. The first is an objective measure based on the strength and military capacity of the nation to challenge adversaries successfully, including going to war if necessary. This also includes a more prominent role for intelligence, economics, and other nonmilitary measures as well as the ability to use them as political-military levers in dealings with other states. The psychological dimension is subjective, reflecting the opinion and attitudes of Americans on the nation's ability to remain secure relative to the external world. It affects the people's willingness to support government efforts to achieve national security goals. Underpinning this is that the majority of people have the knowledge and political will to support clear policies to achieve clear national security goals.[86]

NATIONAL SECURITY AGENCY SECURE TELEPHONE SYSTEM (NSTS) A stand-alone secure telephone system. IC entities call these phones by different names, such as gray, white, or green phones, although these colors do not always reflect the actual color of the telephone unit.

NATIONAL SECURITY ANALYSIS CENTER (NSAC) In 2006, the FBI identified unmet analytical and technical needs in its National Security Branch (NSB) and determined that the FTTTF (Foreign Terrorist Tracking Task Force) could fill this gap by establishing the Nation Security Analysis Center. As a result, the FTTTF incorporated the NSAC and expanded its role to support the NSB operational divisions in the detection, identification, and tracking of individuals or entities that pose threats to the United States and its interests.[87] *See* FOREIGN TERRORIST TRACKING TASK FORCE; NATIONAL SECURITY BRANCH

NATIONAL SECURITY AREA (NSA) An area established on nonfederal lands located within the United States, its possessions, or territories, for safeguarding classified and/or restricted data information, or protecting DoE equipment and/or material. Establishment of an NSA temporarily places such nonfederal lands under the control of the DoE and results only from an emergency event.[88]

NATIONAL SECURITY BRANCH (NSB) Through the use of intelligence, focused on defeating national security threats directed against the United States. The NSB's executives provide oversight for the FBI's Counterterrorism Division, Counterintelligence Division, Directorate of Intelligence, and Weapons of Mass Destruction Directorate, as well as the Terrorist Screening Center and the High-Value Detainee Interrogation Group. The NSB combines the missions, capabilities, and resources of these components into a single, unified branch. The NSB is also accountable for enterprise functions—such as cyber, training, technology, human resources, and security—that directly support the national security mission. The NSB was established by authority of a 2005 memorandum from the president directing the attorney general to implement the WMD Commission's recommendation for the FBI to establish a "National Security Service." The president instructed the attorney general to combine the missions, capabilities, and resources of the counterterrorism, counterintelligence, and intelligence elements of the FBI under the leadership of a senior FBI official. Congress approved the new structure in 2006.[89] *See* FOREIGN TERRORIST TRACKING TASK FORCE

NATIONAL SECURITY COORDINATION COUNCIL (NSCC) The Attorney General announced the creation of the NSCC on March 5, 2002, to provide a more coordinated effort to combat terrorism and address other national security challenges, both within the Department and in the Department's interaction with other law enforcement and intelligence agencies. By Attorney General Memorandum, the NSCC was formed to: centralize and coordinate policy, resource allocation, operations, and long-term planning of Department components regarding counterterrorism, counterespionage, and other major national security issues; monitor the implementation of Department policy to ensure that components are taking necessary and appropriate actions to prevent and disrupt the occurrence of terrorist attacks in the United States; provide an institutionalized Department forum for crises management; promote coordination and information-sharing within the Department, between the Department and other federal agencies and interagency bodies, and between the Department and state and local law enforcement authorities, to prevent, prepare for, and respond to terrorist attacks within the United States; frame national security issues for resolution by the Deputy Attorney General or the Attorney General; and ensure that positions advanced by the Deputy Attorney General on behalf of the Department at interagency meetings of the National Security Council, the Homeland Security Council, and other interagency forums reflect input from Department national security components.[90]

NATIONAL SECURITY COUNCIL (NSC) The National Security Council was established by the National Security Act of 1947 (PL 235 - 61 Stat. 496; U.S.C. 402), amended by the National Security Act Amendments of 1949 (63 Stat. 579; 50 U.S.C. 401 et seq.). Later in 1949, as part of the

Reorganization Plan, the Council was placed in the Executive Office of the president. The NSC is the highest executive-branch entity providing review of, guidance for, and direction to the conduct of all national foreign intelligence and counterintelligence activities. The statutory members of the NSC are the president, vice president, secretary of state, and secretary of defense. The director of national intelligence and the chair of the Joint Chiefs of Staff participate as advisers.[91]

NATIONAL SECURITY COUNCIL INTELLIGENCE DIRECTIVES
With each succeeding president, national security instruments of varying denominations and character evolved from the NSC policy papers. In general, they were not required to be published in the *Federal Register*, were usually security classified at the highest level of protection, and were available to the public after a great many years had elapsed, usually at the official library of the president who had approved them. Many of the more recent ones remain officially secret. The national security instruments of the past several administrations are briefly profiled.[92]

NATIONAL SECURITY CRIMES Crime(s) likely to impact upon the national security, defense, or foreign relations of the United States, including but not limited to espionage, spying, sabotage, treason, and sedition.[93]

NATIONAL SECURITY DIVISION Created in March 2006 by the USA PATRIOT Reauthorization and Improvement Act (Pub. L. No. 109-177). The creation of the NSD consolidated the Justice Department's primary national security operations: the former Office of Intelligence Policy and Review and the Counterterrorism and Counterespionage Sections of the Criminal Division. The new Office of Law and Policy and the Executive Office, as well as the Office of Justice for Victims of Overseas Terrorism (which previously operated out of the Criminal Division) complete the NSD. The NSD commenced operations in September 2006 upon the swearing in of the first Assistant Attorney General for National Security. The mission of the National Security Division is to carry out the Department's highest priority: to combat terrorism and other threats to national security.[94]

NATIONAL SECURITY EMERGENCY Any occurrence, including natural disaster, military attack, technological, or other emergency, that seriously degrades or threatens the national security of the United States.[95]

NATIONAL SECURITY EMERGENCY PREPAREDNESS TELECOMMUNICATIONS SERVICES Telecommunications services that are used to maintain a state of readiness or to respond to and manage any event or crisis (local, national, or international) that causes or could cause injury or harm to the population, damage to or loss of property, or degrade or threaten the national security or emergency preparedness posture of the United States.[96]

NATIONAL SECURITY ESTABLISHMENT A normative-analytical term referring to those responsible for national security decision making as well as a descriptive term that identifies a set of actors and processes that actually produce security policy outcomes. Often, however, the character and personality of the president lead to the creation of informal and parallel structures and processes for developing national security policy. This sets up a series of policy power clusters that form a national security network that drives the national security establishment and the formal policymaking process. The relationships among and within these power clusters and their actual powers are dependent upon the way the president exercises his leadership and views on how the national security establishment should function.[97]

NATIONAL SECURITY INFORMATION (NSI) 1. Data, nuclear and otherwise, classified under the authority of various presidential executive orders. Depending on the degree of harm that unauthorized disclosure could "reasonably be expected to cause," NSI can be classified as Top Secret, Secret, or Confidential. 2. Information that has been determined by Executive Order to require protection against unauthorized disclosure and is marked to indicate its classification status when in document form. NSI is referred to as "defense information" in the Atomic Energy Act. NSI includes information related to:[98]

- Military plans, weapons systems, or operations.
- Foreign government information.
- Intelligence activities (including special activities), intelligence sources or methods, or cryptology.
- Foreign relations or foreign activities of the United States, including confidential sources.
- Scientific, technological, or economic matters relating to the national security, which includes defense against transnational terrorism.
- U.S. government programs for safeguarding nuclear materials or facilities.
- Vulnerabilities or capabilities of systems, installations, infrastructures, projects, plans, or protection services relating to the national security, which includes defense against transnational terrorism.
- Weapons of mass destruction.

- Official information or material which requires protection against unauthorized disclosure in the interest of national defense or foreign relations of the United States.

A declaration of NSI requires prior approval from an authorized person.[99]

NATIONAL SECURITY INTELLIGENCE The collection and analysis of information concerned with the relationship and homeostasis of the United States with foreign powers, organizations, and persons with regard to political and economic factors as well as the maintenance of the United States' sovereign principles. It embodies both policy intelligence and military intelligence. *See* POLITICAL INTELLIGENCE

NATIONAL SECURITY INTERESTS The foundation for the development of valid national objectives that define U.S. goals or purposes.[100]

NATIONAL SECURITY LETTERS A type of administrative subpoena which may be issued independently by FBI field offices and not subject to judicial review unless a case comes to court. The USA PATRIOT Act authorizes FBI field agents to issue national security letters to obtain financial, bank, and credit records of individuals. In certain instances, under 18 U.S.C. 2709, it is possible for the FBI to require the production of records and information pertaining to wire or electronic communications through a National Security Letter, where the only requirement is for the agent of the FBI to certify that the records and information sought are "relevant to an authorized investigation."

NATIONAL SECURITY SPACE The space-related systems, services, capabilities, and associated information networks of the Department of Defense and the national intelligence community, or other space-related systems that the Secretary of Defense may designate as national security space systems in coordination with the system owner, that support U.S. national security and enable defense and intelligence operations during times of peace, crisis, or conflict.[101]

NATIONAL SECURITY STATE (NSS) The NSS is critically described by scholars as having the following elements: control of the public sphere, covert actions and the rise of secrecy regarding state actions, limiting or undermining individual rights, and organizing for war, Cold War, and limited war;[102] federal (and local) law enforcement metamorphosing into security enforcement and surveillance;[103] nuclear weapons are a key component of the NSS discourse.[104]

NATIONAL SECURITY STRATEGY (NSS) NSS documents are issued by the president and pertain to the U.S. government as a whole. The NSS was initially required by the Goldwater-Nichols Department of Defense Reorganization Act of 1986 (Goldwater-Nichols Act), P.L. 99-433, §603, and is codified in Title 50, U.S. Code, §3043. The NSS is a report "on the national security strategy of the United States" from the president to Congress. It is required to be submitted annually on the date the president submits his annual budget request, and in addition not more than 150 days from the date a new president takes office. It must be submitted in both classified and unclassified forms. The report must address U.S. interests, goals and objectives; the policies, worldwide commitments, and capabilities required to meet those objectives; and the use of elements of national power to achieve those goals; and it must provide an assessment of associated risk. The 2015 NSS proposed "a comprehensive national security agenda, allocate resources accordingly, and work with the Congress to end sequestration. Even so, our resources will never be limitless. Policy tradeoffs and hard choices will need to be made. In such instances, we will prioritize efforts that address the top strategic risks to our interests: catastrophic attack on the U.S. homeland or critical infrastructure; threats or attacks against U.S. citizens abroad and our allies; global economic crisis or widespread economic slowdown.[105] *See* NATIONAL MILITARY STRATEGY; QUADRENNIAL DEFENSE REVIEW

NATIONAL SECURITY SYSTEM Any information system (including any telecommunication system) used or operated by an agency, an agency contractor, or other organization on behalf of an agency, where the function, operation, or use of that system involves (i) intelligence activities, (ii) cryptologic activities related to national security, (iii) command and control of military forces, (iv) equipment that is an integral part of a weapon or weapon systems, or (v) critical to the direct fulfillment of military or intelligence missions; or is protected at all times by procedures established for information that have been specifically authorized under criteria established by an Executive Order or an Act of Congress to be kept classified in the interest of national defense or foreign policy. This definition excludes any system that is designed to be used for routine administrative and business applications such as payroll, finance, or logistics and personnel management applications.[106]

NATIONAL SIGNALS INTELLIGENCE OPERATIONS CENTER (NSOC) Located at the National Security Agency, this 24-hour watch center monitors incoming intelligence of national security value; not to be confused with NSOC, Navy Satellite Operations Center.

NATIONAL SPECIAL SECURITY EVENT (NSSE) A designated event that, by virtue of its political, economic, social, or religious significance, may be the target of terrorism or other criminal activity.[107]

NATIONAL STRATEGY The art and science of developing and using the diplomatic, economic, and informational powers of a nation, together with its armed forces, during peace and war to secure national objectives. Also called national security strategy or grand strategy.

NATIONAL STRATEGY FOR INFORMATION SHARING AND SAFEGUARDING National security depends on the ability to share the right information, with the right people, at the right time. This information-sharing mandate requires sustained and responsible collaboration between federal, state, local, tribal, territorial, private sector, and foreign partners . . . The 2012 *National Strategy for Information Sharing and Safeguarding* provides guidance for effective development, integration, and implementation of policies, processes, standards, and technologies to promote secure and responsible information sharing . . . Our responses to these challenges must be strategic and grounded in three core principles. First, in treating Information as a *National Asset*, we recognize departments and agencies have achieved an unprecedented ability to gather, store, and use information consistent with their missions and applicable legal authorities; correspondingly they have an obligation to make that information available to support national security missions. Second, our approach recognizes *Information Sharing and Safeguarding Requires Shared Risk Management.* In order to build and sustain the trust required to share with one another, we must work together to identify and collectively reduce risk, rather than avoiding information loss by not sharing at all. Third, the core premise *Information Informs Decision Making* underlies all our actions and reminds us better decision making is the purpose of sharing information in the first place.[108]

NATIONAL STRATEGY FOR TRUSTED IDENTITIES IN CYBER-SPACE (NSTIC) The National Strategy for Trusted Identities in Cyberspace (NSTIC or Strategy) charts a course for the public and private sectors to collaborate to raise the level of trust associated with the identities of individuals, organizations, networks, services, and devices involved in online transactions. The Strategy's vision is that individuals and organizations utilize secure, efficient, easy-to-use, and interoperable identity solutions to access online services in a manner that promotes confidence, privacy, choice, and innovation; the realization of this vision is the user-centric "Identity Ecosystem" described in this Strategy. It is an online environment where individuals and organizations will be able to trust each other because they follow agreed-upon standards to obtain and authenticate their digital identities—and the digital identities of devices. The Identity Ecosystem is designed to securely support transactions that range from anonymous to fully authenticated and from low to high value. The Identity Ecosystem, as envisioned here, will increase the following: privacy protections for individuals, who will be able trust that their personal data is handled fairly and transparently; convenience for individuals, who may choose to manage.

NATIONAL TECHNICAL MEANS (NTM) All data available to a nation from all sources and exploitation techniques, whether classified or unclassified, to use in assessing the actions and behavior of other nations. The term is frequently applied to compliance determinations, but can be used to assess threats emanating from hostile nations. NTM can include data from sensors/devices on the surface, under the surface, in the air, or in space, as well as data reported by individuals and groups. It also can include publicly available data from international inspectorates (such as the International Atomic Energy Agency and the Organization for the Prohibition of Chemical Weapons), commercial imaging satellites, defector reports, news media, and various sources on the Internet.[109]

NATIONAL TERRORISM ADVISORY SYSTEM (NTAS) NTAS replaced the color-coded Homeland Security Advisory System (HSAS) in April, 2011. The NTAS system effectively communicates information about terrorist threats by providing timely, detailed information to the public, government agencies, first responders, airports and other transportation hubs, and the private sector. It recognizes that Americans all share responsibility for the nation's security, and should always be aware of the heightened risk of terrorist attack in the United States and what they should do.[110]

NATIONAL THREAT IDENTIFICATION AND PRIORITIZATION ASSESSMENT (NTIPA) A strategic threat assessment produced by the Office of the National Counterintelligence Executive (ONCIX) that defines and prioritizes threats to the United States posed by traditional and emerging foreign intelligence activities. It is designed to assist senior policymakers and officials with CI responsibilities to focus on the current and emerging foreign intelligence threats that could cause unacceptable damage to U.S. national security. The NTIPA fulfills the reporting requirement outlined in the Counterintelligence Enhancement Act of 2002 (ONCIX).[111]

NATIONAL VEHICLE LOCATION SERVICE (NVLS) NVLS is a national data-sharing initiative started by Vigilant Solutions in 2008. The data in NVLS is made up from two primary sources: (1) data shared to NVLS from law enforcement and (2) commercial LPR, or "private" data harvested by Vigilant. Data shared to NVLS by law enforcement is available free of charge via a LEARN (Law Enforcement Archival and Reporting Network) account from Vigilant; sharing to NVLS by Vigilant LPR customers is up to the agency and can be changed at any time. The data remains the property of the agency and is governed by the data retention policy set by that agency. The data is accessible only to law enforcement users.[112] *See* LAW ENFORCEMENT ARCHIVAL AND REPORTING NETWORK (LEARN)

NATIONWIDE SUSPICIOUS ACTIVITY REPORTING (SAR) INITIATIVE (NSI) The NSI is a partnership among federal, state, local, tribal, and territorial law enforcement that establishes a national capacity for gathering, documenting, processing, analyzing, and sharing SAR information—also referred to as the SAR process—in a manner that rigorously protects the privacy and civil liberties of Americans. The ISE-SAR Functional Standard v. 1.5 defines *suspicious activity* as "observed behavior reasonably indicative of preoperational planning related to terrorism or other criminal activity." This definition was developed after critical input from several privacy, civil rights, and civil liberties advocacy groups, including the American Civil Liberties Union (ACLU). The SAR process is critical to sharing information about suspicious activity with a potential nexus to terrorism, which can help prevent terrorist attacks and other related criminal activity from occurring. In developing the standards and processes, the NSI leveraged the guidance and expertise provided by the Global Justice Information Sharing Initiative (Global), which serves as a Federal Advisory Committee and advises the U.S. Attorney General on justice information sharing and integration initiatives. This includes leveraging the National Information Exchange Model (NIEM), which allows the interoperability and seamless exchange of information.[113]

NATO WARNING TIME The time between recognition by a NATO strategic commander, or higher NATO authority, that an attack is impending and the start of the attack.[114] *See* WARNING TIME

NATURAL HAZARD Source of harm or difficulty created by a meteorological, environmental, or geological phenomenon or combination of phenomena.[115]

NAVAL NUCLEAR PROPULSION INFORMATION (NNPI) All classified and controlled unclassified information related to the naval nuclear propulsion program. This marking supplements existing classification and control systems and is not a separate category outside of the authorities provided under the AEA or Executive Order 12958 for, as an example, classified NNPI. The use of NNPI is an additional marking applied to some of the previously defined categories of information to indicate additional controls for protection or access.[116]

NCIC MIRROR IMAGE A mirror image copy of the NCIC (National Crime Information Center) Wanted Persons File that will be continuously updated. Initially the IMESA (Department of Defense Identity Management Capability Enterprise Services Application) will search for felony arrest warrants and misdemeanor arrest warrants for domestic violence. Subsequently, the file will expand the arrest warrant scope and bring on additional NCIC files, as applicable.[117]

NEAR REAL-TIME The reception of data and its analysis that has been processed and communicated in close duration to the actual event. *See* CURRENT INTELLIGENCE; REAL TIME

NEED FOR ACCESS A determination that an employee requires access to a particular level of classified information in order to perform or assist in a lawful and authorized governmental function.[118]

NEED-TO-KNOW 1. Need-to-know demands not merely that customers receive only what they need, but also that they receive all the information they need to carry out their missions. To effectively implement this directive, IC agencies must work cooperatively with customers to understand their requirements and ensure that they receive all applicable intelligence information while minimizing the risk of unauthorized disclosure. Customers, in turn, will be responsible for ensuring the application of need-to-know within their organizations.[119] 2. Requested information is pertinent and necessary to the requestor agency in initiating, furthering, or completing an investigation.[120]

NET ASSESSMENT Comparative review and analysis of opposing national strengths, capabilities, and vulnerabilities.

NETWORK ADDRESS TRANSLATION A service that allows computers on a private network to access the Internet without requiring their own publicly routable Internet Protocol address. NAT modifies outgoing network packets so that the return address is a valid Internet host, thereby protecting the private addresses from public view.[121]

NETWORK ANALYSIS *See* ASSOCIATION ANALYSIS

NETWORK DEFENSE Programs, activities, and the use of tools necessary to facilitate them (including those governed by NSPD-54/HSPD-23 and NSD-42) conducted on a computer, network, or information or communications system by the owner or with the consent of the owner and, as appropriate, the users for the primary purpose of protecting (1) that computer, network, or system; (2) data stored on, processed on, or transiting that computer, network, or system; or (3) physical and virtual infrastructure controlled by that computer, network, or system. Network defense does not involve or require accessing or conducting activities on computers, networks, or information or communications systems without authorization from the owners or exceeding access authorized by the owners.[122]

NETWORK FUSION Network fusion is an information sharing system that fuses information and intelligence from multiple sources to allow decision makers to better adapt to a changing threat environment. It leverages technology to improve awareness and collaboration across different disciplines by connecting voice, video, and data communications at classified and unclassified levels. Networks bridge gaps, strengthen relationships, and allow for innovation, speed, and flexibility in exchanging critical information. Through the use of collaborative technology, network fusion is a framework for linking multiple systems for pushing and pulling information and intelligence. It provides a platform for connecting disparate organizations and their unique viewpoints.[123]

NETWORK WARFARE/GLOBAL NETWORK OPERATIONS JOINT OPERATION CENTER The Network Warfare/Global Network Operations Joint Operation Center directs the operation and defense of the Global Information Grid to assure timely and secure Net-Centric capabilities across strategic, operational, and tactical boundaries in support of DoD's full spectrum of warfighting, intelligence, and business missions.[124]

NEW STRATEGIC ARMS REDUCTION TREATY (NEW START) The Treaty between the United States of America and the Russian Federation on Measures for the Further Reduction and Limitation of Strategic Offensive Arms. The treaty was signed on April 8, 2010, in Prague, and the Senate provided advice and consent to ratification on December 22, 2010. The New START Treaty replaces the original START Treaty, which expired on December 5, 2009.[125]

NEW TERRORISM Analyses point to the steady augmentation of traditional patterns of terrorism by new forms of the phenomenon, both as stand-alone threats and in the context of more conventional conflict (i.e., as an asymmetric strategy). This new terrorism is increasingly networked; more diverse in terms of motivations, sponsorship, and security consequences; more global in reach; and more lethal. As a result, much existing counterterrorism experience may be losing its relevance as network forms of organization replace the canonical terrorist hierarchies, or as state sponsorship becomes more subtle and difficult to expose.[126]

NEWLY DISCOVERED RECORDS Records that were inadvertently not reviewed prior to the effective date of automatic declassification because the Agency's Declassification Authority was unaware of their existence.[127]

NEXT GENERATION IDENTIFICATION (NGI) Developed over multiple years, it is an incremental replacement of the Integrated Automated Fingerprint Identification System (IAFIS) that provides new functionality and improves existing capabilities. The FBI's Criminal Justice Information Services (CJIS) Division operated and maintained IAFIS, which became the world's largest person-centric biometric database when it was implemented in July 1999. Since then, advancements in technology and the changing business needs of IAFIS's customers necessitated the next generation of identification services. To further advance biometric identification services, the CJIS Division, with guidance from the user community, established the vision for the Next Generation Identification.[128] *See* INTERSTATE PHOTO SYSTEM FACIAL RECOGNITION PILOT; NATIONAL PALM PRINT SYSTEM; RAP BACK SERVICE

NO FLY LIST 1. The safety of air travel, particularly after the terrorist attacks of September 11, 2001, is an important priority for the U.S. government. The Aviation and Transportation Security Act of 2001 created the Transportation Security Administration (TSA) and charged it with ensuring the security of all modes of transportation, including civil aviation. The TSA is responsible for prescreening all potential commercial airline travelers before they board an aircraft. Pursuant to this responsibility, TSA uses the "No Fly" list to identify individuals who pose a threat to aviation safety. Persons attempting to board an aircraft who are matched to an identity on the No Fly list are not allowed to board. Recent news reports claim that 47,000 people are currently on the No Fly list, including 800 Americans.[129] 2. A list that contains the names of individuals who are prohibited from boarding an aircraft "based on the totality of information, as representing a threat to commit an act of 'international terrorism' or 'domestic terrorism' (as defined in 18 U.S.C.

2331) to an aircraft (including threat or air piracy, or a threat to airline, passenger, or civil aviation security), or representing a threat to commit an act of domestic terrorism with respect to the homeland."[130] *See* SELECTEE LIST

NOFORN Document that is not to be seen by foreign eyes. *See* CLASSIFICATION MARKINGS

NOISE The quantity of extraneous, irrelevant, or inconsistent signals and signs that could lead to the misinterpretation or masking of a threat. For example, "signals announcing the Pearl Harbor attack were always accompanied by competing or contradictory signals, by all sorts of information useless for anticipating this particular disaster. We refer to these competing signals as noise. To understand the fact of surprise it is necessary to examine the characteristics of the noise as well as the signals that after the event are clearly seen to herald the attack. If it does nothing else, an understanding of the noise present in any signal system will teach us humility and respect for the job of the information analyst."[131] *See* PARADOX OF SILENCE

NON-ADAPTIVE RISK Category of risk that includes threats caused by natural and technological hazards. Threats from non-adaptive risks are caused by physical characteristics and dimensions.[132]

NON-BATTLE CASUALTY A person who is not a battle casualty, but who is lost to his organization by reason of disease or injury, including persons dying from disease or injury, or by reason of being missing where the absence does not appear to be voluntary or due to enemy action or to being interned.[133]

NON-COMPLIANT ACTORS Non-compliant actors are defined as individuals or groups which exhibit behavior which negatively affects coalition efforts to achieve goals/objectives in support of the host nation and/or international mandates. While irregular adversaries are a subgroup of non-compliant actors, their specific characteristic consists in their regular resort to armed violence.[134]

NONCRITICAL-SENSITIVE (NCS) Designation for a national security position where there is the potential for serious damage to national security.[135]

NONDISCLOSURE AGREEMENT A legally enforceable contract to protect sensitive information and expressly outline what information is not to be publicly released. The agreement serves as a document that classifies exclusive and confidential information. The U.S. government Classified Information Nondisclosure Agreement (Standard Form 312) is signed by every employee or contractor that holds any security clearance. According to documents that precede the agreement the "SF 312 is a contractual agreement between the U.S. Government and you, a cleared employee, in which you agree never to disclose classified information to an unauthorized person. Its primary purpose is to inform you of (1) the trust that is placed in you by providing you access to classified information; (2) your responsibilities to protect that information from unauthorized disclosure; and (3) the consequences that may result from your failure to meet those responsibilities."[136]

NON-GOVERNMENTAL AGENCIES (NGOs) Legally constituted organizations created by physical or legal persons with no participation or representation of any government. In the cases in which NGOs are funded totally or partially by governments, the NGO maintains its non-governmental status insofar as it excludes government representatives from membership in the organization. USAID refers to NGOs as private voluntary organizations.[137]

NON-OFFICIAL COVER Intelligence officers who pose as businessmen or employees of private companies to hide their real activities.[138] *See* COMMERCIAL COVER

NONPROLIFERATION Actions to prevent the acquisition of weapons of mass destruction by dissuading or impeding access to, or distribution of, sensitive technologies, material, and expertise.[139]

NON-PROLIFERATION TREATY (NPT) The Treaty on the Non-Proliferation of Nuclear Weapons, also known as the NPT, entered into force on March 5, 1970. The Treaty is designed to: prevent the spread of nuclear weapons; provide assurance, through international safeguards, that the peaceful nuclear activities of states which have not already developed nuclear weapons will not be diverted to making such weapons; promote, to the maximum extent consistent with the other purposes of the treaty, the peaceful uses of nuclear energy, to include the potential benefits of any peaceful application of nuclear explosion technology being made available to non-nuclear parties under appropriate international observation; and express the determination of the parties that the treaty should lead to further progress in comprehensive arms control and nuclear disarmament measures.[140]

NON-REPUDIATION 1. Assurance that the sender of data is provided with proof of delivery and the recipient is provided with proof of the sender's identity, so that neither can later deny having processed the data. Digital signatures are the current non-repudiation technique of choice for the National Information Infrastructure (NII).[141] 2. A property achieved through cryptographic methods to protect against an individual or entity falsely denying having performed a particular action related to data. Extended Definition: Provides the capability to determine whether a given individual took a particular action such as creating information, sending a message, approving information, and receiving a message.[142]

NON-SECURE INTERNET PROTOCOL ROUTER NETWORK (NI-PRNET) Used to exchange sensitive but unclassified information between "internal" users as well as provide users access to the Internet. The NIPRNET is composed of Internet Protocol (IP) routers owned by the Department of Defense. It was created by the Defense Information Systems Agency (DISA) to supersede the earlier Military Network.[143]

NON-STATE ACTOR, NONSTATE ACTOR Non-state actors are non-sovereign entities that exercise significant economic, political, or social power and influence at a national, and in some cases international, level. There is no consensus on the members of this category, and some definitions include trade unions, community organizations, religious institutions, ethnic groupings, and universities.[144]

NON-STATE ARMED GROUPS Groups that have the potential to employ arms in the use of force to achieve political, ideological or economic objectives; are not within the formal military structures of States, State-alliances or intergovernmental organizations; and are not under the control of the State(s) in which they operate.[145]

NON-TITLE 50 (NT50) Refers to those federal departments and organizations whose authorities derive from portions of *United States Code* other than Title 50, which addresses U.S. intelligence activities. NT50s are involved in many activities that affect national security, such as conducting foreign affairs; combating pandemic diseases; halting illicit trafficking; conducting scientific and medical research; regulating finance, commerce, and transportation; and protecting food, water and nuclear infrastructures.[146]

NON-U.S. PERSON Any person who falls outside the definition of "individual" as defined in the Privacy Act of 1974.[147]

NORMAL THEORY Projecting an adversary's objectives, capabilities, and propensity to risk based on problematic thinking and making the best possible estimates about numerous instances of behavior over time.[148] *See* EXCEPTIONAL THEORY

NORMALIZED RISK Measure of risk created by mathematically adjusting a value in order to permit comparisons. Typically, normalized risk divides the risk of each scenario by the sum of the risk across the set of scenarios under consideration. For example, if you are considering the expected number of fatalities from three different biological agents A, B and C, then the total risk posed by these biological agents is the sum of the risk posed by each of them. If agent A has expected fatalities of 10,000, Agent B has 7,000, and Agent C has 3,000, then the total risk is 20,000 fatalities and the normalized risks are 0.5 for Agent A, 0.35 for Agent B, and 0.15 for Agent C. This particular way of normalizing risk is commonly referred to as "normalizing to 1" because now the risk from all the scenarios in the considered set sums to 1.[149]

NORTH ATLANTIC TREATY ORGANIZATION (NATO) CLASSIFIED INFORMATION All classified information—military, political, and economic—circulated within the North Atlantic Treaty Organization (NATO), whether such information originated in NATO or is received from member nations or from international organizations.[150]

NOT RELEASABLE TO CONTRACTORS/CONSULTANTS (NO-CONTRACT) This marking may be used only on intelligence information that is provided by a source on the express or implied condition that it not be made available to contractors; or that, if disclosed to a contractor, would actually or potentially give him or her a competitive advantage, which could reasonably be expected to cause a conflict of interest with his or her obligation to protect the information.[151]

NOT RELEASABLE TO FOREIGN NATIONALS (NOFORN) This marking is used to identify intelligence information that may not be released in any form to foreign governments, foreign nationals, or non-U.S. citizens.[152]

NOTIONAL Fictitious, private commercial entities which exist on paper only. They serve as the ostensible employer of intelligence personnel, or as the ostensible sponsor of certain activities in support of clandestine operations.[153]

NOTORIOUS INDIVIDUAL Someone who is widely known and has an unfavorable public reputation.[154]

NOVEL INTELLIGENCE FROM MASSIVE DATA (NIMD) A program aimed at focusing analytic attention on the most critical information found within massive data, information that indicates the potential for strategic surprise; actionable information not previously known to the analyst or poli-cymakers. It gives the analyst new insight into a previously unappreciated or misunderstood threat. Massive data information has multiple dimensions that may cause difficulty, some of which include volume or depth, heterogeneity or breadth, and complexity.

NSANET The National Security Agency's internal classified computer net-work.

NUCLEAR BONUS EFFECTS Desirable damage or casualties produced by the effects from friendly nuclear weapons that cannot be accurately calcu-lated in targeting as the uncertainties involved preclude depending on them for a militarily significant result.[155]

NUCLEAR CLOUD A cloud of hot gases, smoke, dust and other particu-late matter from a nuclear weapon and its environment, that is carried aloft in conjunction with the rise of the fireball produced by the detonation of that weapon.[156]

NUCLEAR DAMAGE The damage effect from nuclear attack, categorized into three levels: (1) light damage, which does not prevent the immediate use of equipment or installations for which it was intended, although some repair by the user may be required to make full use of the equipment or installations; (2) moderate damage, which prevents the use of equipment or installations until extensive repairs are made; (3) severe damage, which prevents use of equipment or installations permanently.[157]

NUCLEAR INTELLIGENCE (NUCINT) *See* SOURCES OF INTELLI-GENCE

NUCLEAR MATERIALS INFORMATION PROGRAM (NMIP) The 2006 National Security Presidential Directive 48 (NSPD-48/HSPD-17) estab-lished the Nuclear Materials Information Program (NMIP). NMIP is an inter-agency effort managed by DOE to "consolidate information from all sources pertaining to worldwide nuclear materials holdings and their security status into an integrated and continuously updated information management sys-tem." From open sources, it is not clear that this data collection is complete at this time, or to what extent this inventory includes threat assessments.[158]

NUCLEAR SAFETY LINE A line selected, if possible, to follow well-defined topographical features and used to delineate levels of protective measures, degrees of damage or risk to friendly troops, and/or prescribe limits to which the effects of friendly weapons may be permitted to extend.[159]

NUCLEAR STRIKE WARNING A warning of impending friendly or suspected enemy nuclear attack.[160]

NUCLEAR VULNERABILITY ASSESSMENT The estimation of the probable effect on population, forces, and resources from a hypothetical nuclear attack. It is performed predominately in the pre-attack period; however, it may be extended to the trans-attack or post-attack periods.[161]

NUCLEAR WEAPON A complete assembly (i.e., implosion type, gun type, or thermonuclear type) in its intended ultimate configuration which, upon completion of the prescribed arming, fusing and firing sequence, is capable of producing the intended nuclear reaction and release of energy.[162]

NUCLEAR WEAPON DEBRIS The residue of a nuclear weapon after it has exploded; that is, materials used for the casing and other components of the weapon, plus unexpended plutonium or uranium, together with fission products.[163]

NOTES

1. Brian Dodd, *U.S. Drug Enforcement Administration: The Nexus between Drugs and Terrorism*. 2009, accessed March 11, 2015, http://www.dtic.mil/ndia/2010homeland/Dodd.pdf.

2. U.S. Department of Defense. Center for Development of Security Excellence. *Glossary of Security Terms and Definitions.* November 2012, accessed February 16, 2015, http://www.cdse.edu/documents/cdse/Glossary_Handbook.pdf.

3. U.S. Department of Defense. Center for Development of Security Excellence. *Glossary of Security Terms and Definitions.* November 2012, accessed February 16, 2015, http://www.cdse.edu/documents/cdse/Glossary_Handbook.pdf.

4. U.S. Department of Defense. Center for Development of Security Excellence. *Glossary of Security Terms and Definitions.* November 2012, accessed February 16, 2015, http://www.cdse.edu/documents/cdse/Glossary_Handbook.pdf.

5. U.S. Department of Defense. Center for Development of Security Excellence. *Glossary of Security Terms and Definitions.* November 2012, accessed February 16, 2015, http://www.cdse.edu/documents/cdse/Glossary_Handbook.pdf.

6. John Moteff, "Critical Infrastructure: the National Asset Database." *CRS Report for Congress*, September 14, 2006, accessed January 25, 2015, http://www.fas.org/sgp/crs/homesec/RL33648.pdf.

7. National Biodefense Analysis and Countermeasures Center. *Mission*. Accessed January 30, 2015, http://www.bnbi.org/BNBI.org/Home.html.

8. U.S. Department of Defense. *Defense Support of Civil Authorities.* JP 3-28, July 31, 2013, accessed January 26, 2015, http://www.dtic.mil/doctrine/new_pubs/jp3_28.pdf; John Moteff, "Critical Infrastructure: the National Asset Database." *CRS Report for Congress*, September 14, 2006, accessed January 25, 2015, http://www.fas.org/sgp/crs/homesec/RL33648.pdf.

9. National Commission on Terrorist Attacks Upon the United States. How to Dot (Chap. 13), accessed February 4, 2016, http://govinfo.library.unt.edu/911/report/index.htm.

10. National Commission on Terrorist Attacks Upon the United States. *About the Commission.* Accessed January 25, 2015, http://govinfo.library.unt.edu/911/about/index.htm.

11. START. *About START.* Accessed March 7, 2015, http://www.start.umd.edu/about/about-start.

12. National Counterintelligence Executive and National Counterintelligence Policy Board. *National Counterintelligence Strategy of the United States of America.* 2007, accessed February 27, 2015, http://www.ncix.gov/publications/strategy/docs/CIStrategy.pdf.

13. National Counterterrorism Center. *Terrorist Identities Datamart Environment (TIDE) Factsheet.* August 1, 2014, accessed February 9, 2015, http://www.nctc.gov/docs/tidefactsheet_aug12014.pdf.

14. Office of the Director of National Intelligence, National Counterterrorism Center. *Who We Are.* Accessed January 29, 2015, http://www.nctc.gov/whoweare.html.

15. Federal Bureau of Investigation. *NCIC.* Accessed January 29, 2015, http://www.fbi.gov/about-us/cjis/ncic/ncic.

16. Federal Bureau of Investigation. *Minimum Criminal Intelligence Training Standards for Law Enforcement and Other Criminal Justice Agencies in the United States.* October 2007, accessed January 22, 2015, https://it.ojp.gov/gist/108/Minimum-Criminal-Intelligence-Training-Standards.

17. Department of Justice, Bureau of Justice Assistance, *Global Intelligence Working Group: Intelligence Sharing Plan*, http://it.ojp.gov/topic.jsp?topic_id=93.

18. Federal Bureau of Investigation. *National Cyber Investigative Joint Task Force.* Accessed January 30, 2015, http://www.fbi.gov/about-us/investigate/cyber/ncijtf.

19. Department of Homeland Security. *National Cyber Incident Response Plan.* Interim version December 2010, accessed February 16, 2015, http://www.federalnewsradio.com/pdfs/NCIRP_Interim_Version_September_2010.pdf.

20. Department of Homeland Security. *About the National Cybersecurity and Communications Integration Center.* Accessed February 15, 2015, http://www.dhs.gov/about-national-cybersecurity-communications-integration-center.

21. U.S. Department of Justice, Criminal Justice Information Services Division. *Criminal Justice Information Services (CJIS) Annual Report, 2014.* Accessed Feb-

ruary 25, 2015, http://www.fbi.gov/about-us/cjis/annual-report-2014/cjis-annual-report-2014.

22. Edgar, Harold, and Benno C. Schmidt, "The Espionage Statutes and Publication of Defense Information," *Columbia Law Review* 73, no. 5 (1973): 929-1087, accessed February 1, 2016, https://www.fas.org/sgp/library/edgar.pdf and 18 U.S. Code § 793—"Gathering, transmitting or losing defense information," accessed February 1, 2016, https://www.law.cornell.edu/uscode/text/18/793.

23. U.S. Attorney's Office, *Former CIA Officer John Kiriakou Charged with Disclosing Covert Officer's Identity and Other Classified Information to Journalists and Lying to CIA's Publications Review Board*, January 23, 2012, accessed February 1, 2016, https://www.fbi.gov/washingtondc/press-releases/2012/former-cia-officer-john-kiriakou-charged-with-disclosing-covert-officers-identity-and-other-classified-information-to-journalists-and-lying-to-cias-publications-review-board.

24. Catherine Dale, *National Security Strategy: Mandates, Execution to Date, and Issues for Congress. CRS Report for Congress*, R43174. August 6, 2013, accessed February 9, 2015, http://www.fas.org/sgp/crs/natsec/R43174.pdf.

25. U.S. Department of Defense. *Detainee Operations*. JP 3-63. November 13, 2014, accessed February 26, 2015. http://www.dtic.mil/doctrine/new_pubs/jp3_63.pdf.

26. U.S. Department of Defense. *Foreign Humanitarian Assistance*. JP 3-29, January 3, 2014, accessed March 7, 2015, http://www.dtic.mil/doctrine/new_pubs/jp3_29.pdf.

27. Federal Emergency Management Agency, *National Disaster Medical System*, April 21, 2004, accessed February 3, 2016, https://www.fema.gov/news-release/2004/04/21/national-disaster-medical-system.

28. Defense Intelligence Agency, Office of Counterintelligence. *CI Glossary—Terms & Definitions of Interest for DoD CI Professionals*. July 2014, accessed January 30, 2015, https://www.hsdl.org/?view&did=699056.

29. Defense Acquisition University. *Glossary: Defense Acquisition Acronyms and Terms*. 13th ed. November 2009, accessed February 24, 2015. http://www.dau.mil/pubscats/pubscats/13th_edition_glossary.pdf.

30. U.S. Department of Justice, National Drug Intelligence Center. *About NDIC*. Accessed February 8, 2015, http://www.justice.gov/archive/ndic/about.htm and "Justice to Close Drug Intel Center, Offer Buyouts." *Federal Times*, February 13, 2012, accessed February 8, 2015, http://archive.federaltimes.com/article/20120213/AGENCY01/202130307/Justice-close-drug-intel-center-offer-buyouts.

31. U.S. Department of Defense. *Defense Support of Civil Authorities*. JP 3-28, July 31, 2013, accessed January 26, 2015, http://www.dtic.mil/doctrine/new_pubs/jp3_28.pdf.

32. National Security and Homeland Security Presidential Directive/NSPD-51/HSPD 20. *National Continuity Policy*. May 9, 2007, accessed February 27, 2015, http://fas.org/irp/offdocs/nspd/nspd-51.htm.

33. *Presidential Policy Directive/PPD-21. Critical Infrastructure Security and Resilience*. February 12, 2013, accessed January 22, 2015, http://www.whitehouse.gov/the-press-office/2013/02/12/presidential-policy-directive-critical-infrastructure-security-and-resil.

34. Federal Emergency Management Agency. *National Exercise Program (NEP)—Capstone Exercise 2014.* Accessed February 24, 2015, https://www.fema.gov/national-exercise-program-nep-capstone-exercise-2014.

35. Federal Bureau of Investigation. *National Gang Intelligence Center.* Accessed January 30, 2015, http://www.fbi.gov/about-us/investigate/vc_majorthefts/gangs/ngic; also see National Gang Intelligence Center. *2013 National Gang Report.* Accessed March 29, 2015, http://www.fbi.gov/stats-services/publications/national-gang-report-2013.

36. U.S. Immigration and Customs Service. *National Gang Unit.* Accessed April 6, 2015, https://www.ice.gov/national-gang-unit.

37. Federal Bureau of Investigation. *FBI Releases Expanded Crime Statistics for 2013 Latest Report from National Incident-Based Reporting System.* December 22, 2014, accessed January 30, 2015. http://www.fbi.gov/news/stories/2014/december/fbi-releases-2013-national-incident-based-reporting-system-statistics/fbi-releases-2013-national-incident-based-reporting-system-statistics.

38. U.S. Department of Defense. *Department of Defense Dictionary of Military and Associated Terms.* JP 1-02, 08 November 2010, as Amended through 15 January 2016. Accessed January 26, 2016, http://www.dtic.mil/doctrine/new_pubs/jp1_02.pdf.

39. Information Security Oversight Office. *National Industrial Security Program.* Accessed January 29, 2015, http://www.archives.gov/isoo/oversight-groups/nisp/.

40. U.S. Department of Justice, Office of Justice Programs. *National Information Exchange Model.* Accessed January 30, 2015, https://it.ojp.gov/default.aspx?area=nationalInitiatives&page=1012.

41. Director of Central Intelligence. *National Intelligence Warning Directive No. 1/5,* May 23, 1979, accessed July 27, 2015, http://fas.org/irp/offdocs/dcid1-5.html.

42. Department of Homeland Security. *National Infrastructure Coordinating Center.* Accessed February 15, 2015, http://www.dhs.gov/national-infrastructure-coordinating-center.

43. Government Accountability Office. *Critical Infrastructure Protection: DHS Action Needed to Enhance Integration and Coordination of Vulnerability Assessment Efforts.* GAO-14-507. September 2014, accessed January 24, 2015, http://www.gao.gov.

44. Homeland Security Presidential Directive 7: *Critical Infrastructure Identification, Prioritization, and Protection.* December 17, 2003, accessed February 14, 2015, http://www.dhs.gov/homeland-security-presidential-directive-7#1; also see Department of Homeland Security. *NIPP 2013 Partnering for Critical Infrastructure Security and Resilience.* Accessed February 14, 2015, http://www.dhs.gov/national-infrastructure-protection-plan.

45. National Infrastructure Simulation and Analysis Center. *NISAC.* Accessed February 14, 2015, http://www.sandia.gov/nisac/.

46. National Initiative for Cybersecurity Careers and Studies. *About the National Initiative for Cybersecurity Education.* n.d., accessed March 5, 2015, http://niccs.us-cert.gov/footer/about-national-initiative-cybersecurity-education.

47. National Counterintelligence and Security Center. *National Insider Threat Task Force: Our Mission.* Accessed February 14, 2015, http://www.ncix.gov/nittf/index.php.

48. Federal Bureau of Investigation. *NICS.* Accessed February 24, 2015, http://www.fbi.gov/about-us/cjis/nics.

49. Defense Forensics and Biometrics Agency. *DoD Biometrics Enterprise Architecture (Integrated) v2.0 Common Biometric Vocabulary.* April 2013, accessed January 30, 2015, http://www.biometrics.dod.mil/Files/Documents/References/common%20biometric%20vocabulary.pdf.

50. Office of the Director of National Intelligence. *Technical Surveillance Countermeasures.* Intelligence Community Directive 702, February 18, 2008, accessed March 2, 2015, http://www.dni.gov/files/documents/ICD/ICD_702.pdf.

51. 6 U.S. Code § 319(2)—"National Integration Center." (Current through Pub. L. 113-234), accessed February 20, 2015, http://www.law.cornell.edu/uscode/text/6/319.

52. United States Senate, Select Committee to Study Governmental Operations with Respect to Intelligence Activities (Church Committee). *Final Report.* Book 1. April 26, 1976, accessed February 7, 2015, https://archive.org/details/finalreportofsel01unit.

53. United States Senate, Select Committee to Study Governmental Operations with Respect to Intelligence Activities (Church Committee). *Final Report.* Book 1. April 26, 1976. Accessed February 7, 2015. https://archive.org/details/finalreportofsel01unit.

54. Office of the Director of National Intelligence. *National Intelligence Program FY 2009 Congressional Budget Justification Book.* Vol. XII, February 2008, accessed January 17, 2015, http://www.fas.org/irp/dni/cbjb-2009.pdf.

55. Office of the Director of National Intelligence. *Human Intelligence.* Intelligence Community Directive 304, July 9, 2009. Accessed March 2, 2015. http://www.dni.gov/files/documents/ICD/ICD%20304.pdf.

56. Office of the Director of National Intelligence. *National Intelligence Board.* ICD 202. July 16, 2007, accessed January 30, 2015, http://www.fas.org/irp/dni/icd/icd-202.pdf.

57. Office of the Director of National Intelligence. *National Intelligence Awards Program.* Intelligence Community Directive 655, February 9, 2012, accessed March 2, 2015, http://www.dni.gov/files/documents/ICD/ICD_655.pdf.

58. Office of the Director of National Intelligence. *National Intelligence Program FY 2009 Congressional Budget Justification Book.* Vol. XII, February 2008, accessed January 17, 2015, http://www.fas.org/irp/dni/cbjb-2009.pdf.

59. 50 U.S.C. 15, subchap. I, § 403-3, "War and National Defense," accessed July 27, 2015, http://www.law.cornell.edu/uscode.

60. U.S. Department of Defense. *Department of Defense Dictionary of Military and Associated Terms.* JP 1-02, 08 November 2010, as Amended through 15 January 2016. Accessed January 26, 2016, http://www.dtic.mil/doctrine/new_pubs/jp1_02.pdf.

61. Jan Goldman, *Intelligence Warning Terminology*, Joint Military Intelligence College, October 2001, accessed July 3, 2015. https://archive.org/details/JMICInteligencelwarnterminology.

62. Jan Goldman, *Intelligence Warning Terminology*, Joint Military Intelligence College, October 2001, accessed July 3, 2015. https://archive.org/details/JMICInteligencelwarnterminology.

63. Office of the Director of National Intelligence. *National Intelligence Priorities Framework*. Intelligence Community Directive 204, January 2, 2015, accessed January 30, 2015, http://www.dni.gov/files/documents/ICD/ICD%20204%20National%20Intelligence%20Priorities%20Framework.pdf.

64. Office of the Director of National Intelligence. *National Intelligence Awards Program*. Intelligence Community Directive 655, February 9, 2012, accessed March 2, 2015. http://www.dni.gov/files/documents/ICD/ICD_655.pdf.

65. Dan Elkins, *Managing Intelligence Resources*. (Alexandria, VA: DWE Press, 2004).

66. Office of the Director of National Intelligence. *Human Intelligence*. Intelligence Community Directive 304, July 9, 2009, accessed March 2, 2015, http://www.dni.gov/files/documents/ICD/ICD%20304.pdf.

67. *Intelligence Reform and Terrorism Prevention Act of 2004*. P.L.108-458 of December 17, 2004; 118 STAT. 3638, accessed January 29, 2015, http://www.dni.gov/index.php/about/organization/ic-legal-reference-book-2012/ref-book-irtpa.

68. Office of the Director of National Intelligence. *National Intelligence Program FY 2009 Congressional Budget Justification Book*. Vol. XII, February 2008, accessed January 17, 2015, http://www.fas.org/irp/dni/cbjb-2009.pdf.

69. Office of the Director of National Intelligence. *National Intelligence Program FY 2009 Congressional Budget Justification Book*. Vol. XII, February 2008, accessed January 17, 2015, http://www.fas.org/irp/dni/cbjb-2009.pdf.

70. Office of the Director of National Intelligence. *National Intelligence Program FY 2009 Congressional Budget Justification Book*. Vol. XII, February 2008, accessed January 17, 2015, http://www.fas.org/irp/dni/cbjb-2009.pdf.

71. U.S. Department of Justice. Office of the Inspector General. *The Federal Bureau of Investigation's Efforts to Improve the Sharing of Intelligence and Other Information*, Audit Report 04-10, December 2003, accessed July 27, 2015, https://oig.justice.gov/reports/FBI/a0410/final.pdf.

72. U.S. General Accountability Office. *Homeland Security Advisory System*, GAO-04-453R, March 11, 2004, accessed July 27, 2015, http://www.gao.gov/assets/100/92478.pdf.

73. National Law Enforcement Telecommunication System, *Who We Are*, accessed February 3, 2016, https://www.nlets.org/about/who-we-are.

74. Office of the Director of National Intelligence. Global *Maritime and Air Intelligence Integration*. Intelligence Community Directive 902, January 14, 2009, accessed January 24, 2015, http://www.dni.gov/files/documents/ICD/ICD_902.pdf.

75. Office of the Director of National Intelligence. *Document and Media Exploitation*. Intelligence Community Directive 302, July 6, 2007, accessed February 24, 2015, http://www.dtic.mil/whs/directives/corres/pdf/330003p.pdf.

76. Catherine Dale, *National Security Strategy: Mandates, Execution to Date, and Issues for Congress. CRS Report for Congress*, R43174. August 6, 2013, accessed February 9, 2015, http://www.fas.org/sgp/crs/natsec/R43174.pdf.

77. Centers for Disease Control, *NEDSS/NBS*, accessed February 3, 2016, http://wwwn.cdc.gov/nndss/nedss.html.

78. *National Security Decision Directive 298*, January 22, 1988, accessed February 3, 2016, http://www.fas.org/irp/offdocs/nsdd298.htm.

79. Federal Bureau of Investigation. *Next Generation Identification (NGI): Identification and Investigative Services*. Accessed February 11, 2015, http://www.fbi.gov/about-us/cjis/fingerprints_biometrics/ngi.

80. "FBI NGI Goes Live with New Biometric Capabilities," *Biometric Technology Today*, 2014, issue 10 (October 2014): 1–2.

81. U.S. Department of Defense. *Doctrine for the Armed Forces of the United States*. JP 1, March 25, 2013, accessed February 21, 2015, http://www.dtic.mil/doctrine/new_pubs/jp1.pdf.

82. *Presidential Policy Directive/PPD-8: National Preparedness*. March 30, 2011, accessed February 15, 2011, http://www.dhs.gov/presidential-policy-directive-8-national-preparedness.

83. Department of Homeland Security. *National Preparedness System*. November 2011. Accessed February 24, 2015, http://www.fema.gov/media-library-data/20130726-1855-25045-8110/national_preparedness_system_final.pdf.

84. Federal Emergency Management Agency. *National Preparedness System*. February 19, 2015. Accessed February 24, 2015, https://www.fema.gov/national-preparedness-system.

85. U.S. Department of Defense. *Doctrine for the Armed Forces of the United States*. JP 1, March 25, 2013. Accessed February 21, 2015, http://www.dtic.mil/doctrine/new_pubs/jp1.pdf.

86. Sam C. Sarkesian, John Allen Williams, and Stephen J. Cimbala, *U.S. National Security: Policymakers, Processes, and Politics*, 5th ed. (Boulder, CO: Lynne Rienner, 2013), 2.

87. U.S. Department of Justice. *The Federal Bureau of Investigation's Foreign Terrorist Tracking Task Force* (Office of the Inspector General, Audit Report 13-18, March 2013), 2, accessed July 27, 2015, https://oig.justice.gov/reports/2013/a1318r.pdf.

88. U.S. Department of Defense. *Nuclear Accident and Incident Public Affairs (PA) Guidance*. Directive 5230.16, December 20, 1993, Certified Current as of November 21, 2003, accessed July 27, 2015, http://fas.org/nuke/guide/usa/doctrine/dod/dodd-5230_16.htm and U.S. Department of Defense. *Nuclear Weapon Accident Response Procedures (NARP)*. Directive 3150.08, August 22, 2013, accessed July 27, 2015, http://www.dtic.mil/whs/directives/corres/pdf/315008m.pdf.

89. Federal Bureau of Investigation. *National Security Branch Frequently Asked Questions*. Accessed January 29, 2015, http://www.fbi.gov/about-us/nsb/faqs#established.

90. U.S. Department of Justice, Office of the Inspector General. *The Department of Justice's Terrorism Task Forces Evaluation and Inspections Report I-2005-007*.

June 2005, accessed February 15, 2015, http://www.justice.gov/oig/reports/plus/
e0507/background.htm#nscc.

91. The White House, National Security Council, accessed February 4, 2016,
https://www.whitehouse.gov/administration/eop/nsc.

92. Harold C. Relyea, Presidential Directives: Background and Overview," *CRS
Report for Congress* 98–611, November 26, 2008, accessed https://www.fas.org/sgp/
crs/misc/98-611.pdf. For select Truman and Eisenhower Directives, see Federation of
American Scientists. https://fas.org/irp/offdocs/direct.htm and the Office of the Historian, U.S. Department of State, *Foreign Relations of the United States, 1945–1950,
Emergence of the Intelligence Establishment*, accessed February 2, 2016, https://his-
tory.state.gov/historicaldocuments/frus1945-50Intel/ch9.

93. Defense Intelligence Agency, Office of Counterintelligence. *CI Glossary—
Terms & Definitions of Interest for DoD CI Professionals.* July 1, 2014, accessed
January 30, 2015, http://www.fas.org/irp/eprint/ci-glossary.pdf.

94. U.S. Department of Justice. *National Security Division.* Accessed February
20. 2015, http://www.justice.gov/nsd/about-division.

95. U.S. Department of Defense. *Assistant Secretary of Defense for Homeland
Defense and Americas' Security* Affairs (ASD(HD&ASA)). DoD Directive 5111.13,
January 16, 2009, accessed January 30, 2015, http://www.dtic.mil/whs/directives/
corres/pdf/511113p.pdf.

96. Committee for National Security Systems (CNSS). Instruction 4009. *National Information Assurance Glossary.* April 2010, accessed January 30, 2015,
http://www.ncix.gov/publications/policy/docs/CNSSI_4009.pdf.

97. Sam C. Sarkesian, John Allen Williams, and Stephen J. Cimbala, *U.S. National Security: Policymakers, Processes, and Politics,* 5th ed. (Boulder, CO: Lynne
Rienner, 2013), 16.

98. Executive Order 12065, *National Security Information,* June 28, 1978, accessed July 27, 2015, http://www.archives.gov/federal-register/executive-orders/
1978.html, and Executive Order 13292, *Further Amendment to Executive Order 12958, as Amended, Classified National Security Information,* March 25,
2003, accessed July 27, 2015, http://www.archives.gov/federal-register/executive-
orders/2003.html; also see Arvin S. Quist, *Security Classification of Information,*
accessed July 27, 2015, http://www.fas.org/sgp/library/quist2/chap_3.html; and
Alexander DeVolpi, Jerry Marsh, Ted Postol, and George Stanford, *Born Secret: The
H-Bomb, the Progressive Case, and National Security* (New York: Pergamon, 1981).

99. DOE, *Understanding Classification* (Washington, DC: DOE, Office of Classification, 1987); Carter, *Law Enforcement Intelligence.*

100. U.S. Department of Defense. *Doctrine for the Armed Forces of the United
States.* JP 1, March 25, 2013, accessed February 21, 2015, http://www.dtic.mil/doc-
trine/new_pubs/jp1.pdf.

101. U.S. Department of Defense. *Space Policy.* Directive Number DI3100.10.
October 18, 2012, accessed February 9, 2015, http://www.dtic.mil/whs/directives/
corres/pdf/310010p.pdf.

102. U.S. Department of Justice. *National Security Division.* Accessed February
20, 2015, http://www.justice.gov/nsd/about-division.

103. U.S. Department of Defense. *Assistant Secretary of Defense for Homeland Defense and Americas' Security* Affairs (ASD(HD&ASA)). DoD Directive 5111.13, January 16, 2009, accessed January 30, 2015, http://www.dtic.mil/whs/directives/corres/pdf/511113p.pdf.

104. Marcus G. Raskin and Carl A. LeVan, "The National Security State and the Tragedy of Empire," in *Democracy's Shadow: The Secret World of National Security*, edited by Marcus G. Raskin and A. Carl LeVan (New York: Nation Books, 2005), 3–42; Peter Raven-Hansen, "Security's Conquest of Federal Law Enforcement," In *Democracy's Shadow: The Secret World of National Security*, edited by Marcus G. Raskin and A. Carl LeVan (New York: Nation Books, 2005), 217–362.

105. Executive Office of the President. *National Security Strategy.* February 2015, accessed February 28, 2015, http://www.whitehouse.gov/the-press-office/2015/02/06/fact-sheet-2015–national-security-strategy; Anabel L. Dwyer and David J. Dwyer, "Courts and Universities as Institutions in the National Security State." In *Democracy's Shadow: The Secret World of National Security*, edited by Marcus G. Raskin and A. Carl LeVan (New York: Nation Books, 2005), 165–204.

106. National Security Presidential Directive-54 / Homeland Security Presidential Directive-23. *Cybersecurity Policy.* January 9, 2008, accessed February 14, 2015, http://www.fas.org/irp/offdocs/nspd/nspd-54.pdf.

107. U.S. Department of Defense. *Defense Support of Civil Authorities.* JP 3-28, July 31, 2013, accessed January 26, 2015, http://www.dtic.mil/doctrine/new_pubs/jp3_28.pdf.

108. Executive Office of the President. *National Strategy for Information Sharing and Safeguarding.* December 2012, accessed January 30, 2015, http://www.whitehouse.gov/sites/default/files/docs/2012sharingstrategy_1.pdf.

109. U.S. Department of State. "Bureau of Arms Control, Verification, and Compliance (AVC)." *Foreign Affairs Manual.* 1 FAM 440. May 9, 2013, accessed February 16, 2015, http://www.state.gov/documents/organization/156858.pdf.

110. U.S. Department of Homeland Security. *National Terrorism Advisory System.* Accessed January 23, 2015, http://www.dhs.gov/national-terrorism-advisory-system.

111. Defense Intelligence Agency, Office of Counterintelligence. *CI Glossary—Terms & Definitions of Interest for DoD CI Professionals.* July 1, 2014, accessed January 30, 2015, http://www.fas.org/irp/eprint/ci-glossary.pdf.

112. Vigilant Solutions, *National Vehicle Location Services*, accessed February 2, 2016, http://vigilantsolutions.com/products/nvls.

113. Nationwide SAR Initiative. *About the NSI.* Accessed January 24, 2015, http://nsi.ncirc.gov/about_nsi.aspx.

114. North Atlantic Treaty Organization. *NATO Glossary of Terms and Definitions.* NATO Standardization Agency, 2014, AAP-06, accessed July 27, 2015, http://nso.nato.int/nso/zPublic/ap/aap6/AAP-6.pdf.

115. Department of Homeland Security, Risk Steering Committee. *DHS Risk Lexicon.* September 2010, accessed February 14, 2015, http://www.dhs.gov/dhs-risk-lexicon.

116. Government Accountability Office. *Managing Sensitive Information: Actions Needed to Ensure Recent Changes in DOE Oversight Do Not Weaken an Effective*

Classification System. GAO-06-785, June 26, 2006, accessed January 30, 2015, http://www.gao.gov/new.items/d06785.pdf.

117. Undersecretary of Defense. 2015. *Directive-type Memorandum (DTM) 14-005—DoD Identity Management Capability Enterprise Services Application (IMESA) Access to FBI National Crime Information Center (NCIC) Files.* May 13, accessed June 6, 2015, http://www.dtic.mil/whs/directives/corres/pdf/DTM14005_2014.pdf.

118. U.S. Department of Defense. Center for Development of Security Excellence. *Glossary of Security Terms and Definitions.* November 2012, accessed February 16, 2015, http://www.cdse.edu/documents/cdse/Glossary_Handbook.pdf.

119. Director of Central Intelligence Directive 8/1, *Intelligence Community Policy on Intelligence Sharing*, June 4, 2004, accessed February 3, 2016, http://www.fas.org/irp/offdocs/dcid8-1.html.

120. David L. Carter. *Law Enforcement Intelligence: a Guide for State, Local, and Tribal Law Enforcement Agencies*, Dept. of Justice, Office of Community Oriented Policing Services, 2004, accessed February 5, 2016, http://www.cops.usdoj.gov/default.asp?Item=1404.

121. U.S. Department of Justice, Office of Justice Programs. *Investigations Involving the Internet and Computer Networks.* January 2007, accessed March 7, 2015, https://www.ncjrs.gov/pdffiles1/nij/210798.pdf.

122. *Presidential Policy Directive/PPD-20. U.S. Cyber Operations Policy.* October 16, 2012, accessed February 17, 2015, https://www.fas.org/irp/offdocs/ppd/ppd-20.pdf.

123. Joseph W. Pfeifer, "Network Fusion: Information and Intelligence Sharing for a Networked World." *Homeland Security Affairs* 8, Article 17 (October 2012), accessed February 15, 2015, https://www.hsaj.org/articles/232.

124. Department of Homeland Security. *National Cyber Incident Response Plan.* Interim version. December 2010, accessed February 20, 2015, http://www.federalnewsradio.com/pdfs/NCIRP_Interim_Version_September_2010.pdf.

125. U.S. Department of State. "Bureau of Arms Control, Verification, and Compliance (AVC)." *Foreign Affairs Manual.* 1 FAM 440, May 9, 2013, accessed February 20, 2015, http://www.state.gov/documents/organization/156858.pdf.

126. Ian O. Lesser, "Countering the New Terrorism: Implications for Strategy." In *Countering the New Terrorism*, edited by Ian O. Lesser, Bruce Hoffman, John Arquilla, David Ronfeldt, and Michele Zanini (Santa Monica, CA: RAND, 1999), 85–144, accessed March 11, 2015. http://www.nps.edu/academics/centers/ctiw/files/The%20New%20Terrorism.pdf.

127. U.S. Department of Defense. Center for Development of Security Excellence. *Glossary of Security Terms and Definitions.* November 2012, accessed February 15, 2015, http://www.cdse.edu/documents/cdse/Glossary_Handbook.pdf.

128. Federal Bureau of Investigation. *Next Generation Identification (NGI).* Accessed January 30, 2015, http://www.fbi.gov/about-us/cjis/fingerprints_biometrics/ngi.

129. Jared P. Cole, "Terrorist Databases and the No Fly List: Procedural Due Process and Hurdles to Litigation." *CRS Report for Congress*, R43730, April 2, 2015, accessed April 7, 2015, http://www.fas.org/sgp/crs/homesec/R43730.pdf; also see Adam Goldman, "More Than 1 Million People Are Listed in U.S. Terrorism Data-

base." *The Washington Post*, August 5, 2014, accessed April 7, 2015. http://www. washingtonpost.com/world/national-security/more-than-1-million-people-are-listed-in-us-terrorism-database/2014/08/05/a66de30c-1ccc-11e4-ab7b-696c295ddfd1_ story.html.

130. EPIC, "Documents Show Errors in TSA's 'No Fly' and 'Selectee' Watch Lists," March 23, 2006, accessed February 4, 2016, https://epic.org/privacy/airtravel/foia/watchlist_foia_analysis.html.

131. Roberta Wohlstetter, *Pearl Harbor: Warning and Decision* (Stanford, CA: Stanford University Press, 1962), 3.

132. Department of Homeland Security, Risk Steering Committee. *DHS Risk Lexicon.* September 2010. Accessed February 14, 2015. http://www.dhs.gov/dhs-risk-lexicon.

133. North Atlantic Treaty Organization. *NATO Glossary of Terms and Definitions.* NATO Standardization Agency, 2014, AAP-06, accessed July 27, 2015, http://nso.nato.int/nso/zPublic/ap/aap6/AAP-6.pdf.

134. Bundeswehr Transformation Centre. *Non-compliant Actors (NONCAS) Handbook.* Ottobrunn, Germany, sponsored by USJFCOM J9 Joint Concept Development and Experimentation, July 2010, accessed February 20, 2015, http://www.dtic. mil/dtic/tr/fulltext/u2/a561891.pdf.

135. Office of Personnel Management, *Investigations.* Accessed on January 20, 2016, https://www.opm.gov/investigations/background-investigations/position-designation-tool/oct2010.pdf.

136. Information Security Oversight Office. *Classified Information Nondisclosure Agreement (Standard Form 312) Briefing Booklet*, accessed July 22, 2015, http:// www.archives.gov/isoo/training/standard-form-312.html.

137. U.S. Central Command Assessment Team. *Annex I Command and Control Knowledge Management.* February 2009. Accessed January 25, 2015. http://cryptome.org/dodi/centcom-c2km.pdf.

138. Dreyfuss, Robert. *Mother Jones*, "The CIA Crosses Over." Accessed January 20, 2016. http://www.motherjones.com/politics/1995/01/cia-crosses-over.

139. United States Department of Defense. *Countering Weapons of Mass Destruction.* JP 3-40, October 31, 2014. Accessed March 7, 2015. http://www.dtic.mil/ doctrine/new_pubs/jp3_40.pdf.

140. U.S. Department of State. "Bureau of Arms Control, Verification, and Compliance (AVC)." *Foreign Affairs Manual.* 1 FAM 440, May 9, 2013, accessed February 20 2015, http://www.state.gov/documents/organization/156858.pdf.

141. U.S. Department of Defense. Center for Development of Security Excellence. *Glossary of Security Terms and Definitions.* November 2012, accessed February 15, 2015, http://www.cdse.edu/documents/cdse/Glossary_Handbook.pdf.

142. National Initiative for Cybersecurity Education. *A Glossary of Common Cybersecurity Terminology.* n.d., accessed March 5, 2015, http://niccs.us-cert.gov/ glossary.

143. U.S. Department of Defense. Center for Development of Security Excellence. *Glossary of Security Terms and Definitions.* November 2012, accessed February 15, 2015, http://www.cdse.edu/documents/cdse/Glossary_Handbook.pdf.

144. National Intelligence Council. *Nonstate Actors: Impact on International Relations and Implications for the United States.* Accessed March 6, 2015, http://www.dni.gov/files/documents/nonstate_actors_2007.pdf.

145. United Nations. *Guidelines on Humanitarian Negotiations with Armed Groups.* United Nations Office for the Coordination of Humanitarian Affairs (OCHA) in collaboration with members of the Inter-Agency Standing Committee (IASC), 2006, accessed March 5, 2015, http://www.unicef.org/emerg/files/guidelines_negotiations_armed_groups.pdf.

146. Defense Intelligence Agency, Office of Counterintelligence. *CI Glossary— Terms & Definitions of Interest for DoD CI Professionals.* July 1, 2014, accessed January 30, 2015, http://www.fas.org/irp/eprint/ci-glossary.pdf.

147. U.S. Department of State. "Classification of Web Based Documents." *Foreign Affairs Manual.* 5 FAM 760, October 14, 2011, accessed February 16, 2015, http://www.state.gov/documents/organization/85755.pdf.

148. Richard K. Betts, *Warning Dilemmas: Normal Theory vs. Exceptional Theory* (Pennsylvania, PA: Jai Press for the Foreign Policy Research Institute, 1983), 828–33.

149. Department of Homeland Security, Risk Steering Committee. *DHS Risk Lexicon.* September 2010. Accessed February 14, 2015. http://www.dhs.gov/dhs-risk-lexicon.

150. U.S. Department of Defense. Center for Development of Security Excellence. *Glossary of Security Terms and Definitions.* November 2012, accessed February 15, 2015, http://www.cdse.edu/documents/cdse/Glossary_Handbook.pdf.

151. U.S. Department of Defense. *National Industrial Security Program Operating Manual (NISPOM).* DoD 5220.22-M. February 28, 2006, accessed January 5, 2015, http://www.dss.mil/documents/odaa/nispom2006-5220.pdf.

152. U.S. Department of Defense. *National Industrial Security Program Operating Manual (NISPOM).* DoD 5220.22-M. February 28, 2006, accessed January 5, 2015, http://www.dss.mil/documents/odaa/nispom2006-5220.pdf.

153. United States Senate, Select Committee to Study Governmental Operations with Respect to Intelligence Activities (Church Committee). *Final Report.* Book 1. April 26, 1976, accessed February 24, 2015, https://archive.org/details/finalreportofsel01unit.

154. U.S. Department of Defense. *Defense Human Intelligence (HUMINT) and Related Intelligence Activities.* Instruction, Number S-5200.42, December 8, 2009, accessed February 26, 2015, http://www.dod.mil/pubs/foi/homeland_defense/intelligence/10_F_0682_DoD_Instruction_S_5200_42_Defense_Human_Intell.pdf.

155. North Atlantic Treaty Organization. *NATO Glossary of Terms and Definitions.* NATO Standardization Agency, 2008, AAP-06, accessed July 2, 2015, https://fas.org/irp/doddir/other/nato2008.pdf.

156. North Atlantic Treaty Organization. *NATO Glossary of Terms and Definitions.* NATO Standardization Agency, 2014, AAP-06, accessed July 27, 2015, http://nso.nato.int/nso/zPublic/ap/aap6/AAP-6.pdf.

157. North Atlantic Treaty Organization. *NATO Glossary of Terms and Definitions.* NATO Standardization Agency, 2008, AAP-06, accessed July 2, 2015, https://fas.org/irp/doddir/other/nato2008.pdf.

158. Mary Beth Nikitin, "Securing Nuclear Materials: The 2010 Summit and Issues for Congress." *CRS Report for Congress*, R41169. April 27, 2011, accessed January 30, 2015, https://www.fas.org/sgp/crs/nuke/R41169.pdf.

159. North Atlantic Treaty Organization. *NATO Glossary of Terms and Definitions*. NATO Standardization Agency, 2014, AAP-06, accessed July 27, 2015, http://nso.nato.int/nso/zPublic/ap/aap6/AAP-6.pdf.

160. North Atlantic Treaty Organization. *NATO Glossary of Terms and Definitions*. NATO Standardization Agency, 2008, AAP-06, accessed July 2, 2015, https://fas.org/irp/doddir/other/nato2008.pdf.

161. North Atlantic Treaty Organization. *NATO Glossary of Terms and Definitions*. NATO Standardization Agency, 2008, AAP-06, accessed July 2, 2015, https://fas.org/irp/doddir/other/nato2008.pdf.

162. North Atlantic Treaty Organization. *NATO Glossary of Terms and Definitions*. NATO Standardization Agency, 2014, AAP-06, accessed July 27, 2015, http://nso.nato.int/nso/zPublic/ap/aap6/AAP-6.pdf.

163. North Atlantic Treaty Organization. *NATO Glossary of Terms and Definitions*. NATO Standardization Agency, 2008, AAP-06, accessed July 2, 2015, https://fas.org/irp/doddir/other/nato2008.pdf.

OBJECTIVE AREA A defined geographical area within which is located an objective to be captured or reached. This area is defined by competent authority for purposes of command and control.[1]

OCCUPATIONAL STRUCTURE A Defense Civilian Intelligence Personnel System (DCIPS) grouping aligning mission categories and work categories with standardized, competency-based position descriptions (PDs), and competencies defined as measurable or observable knowledge, skills, abilities, behaviors, and other characteristics needed to perform a type of work or function.[2]

OFFENSIVE CYBER EFFECTS OPERATIONS (OCEO) Operations and related programs or activities—other than network defense, cyber collection, or DCEO—conducted by or on behalf of the U.S. government, in or through cyberspace, that are intended to enable or produce cyber effects outside U.S. government networks.[3]

OFFICE OF HOMELAND SECURITY The Office of Homeland Security (CT/HSMA/HS) serves as the principal point-of-contact for the (State) Department with the Department of Homeland Security (DHS) for the coordination of international counter-terrorism activities as they affect homeland security.[4]

OFFICE OF INCISIVE ANALYSIS The Office of Incisive Analysis focuses on maximizing insights from the massive, disparate, unreliable and dynamic data that are—or could be—available to analysts, in a timely manner. We are pursuing new sources of information from existing and novel data, and we are investigating innovative techniques that can be utilized in the processes of analysis. Our programs are in diverse technical disciplines but have common features: involve potential transition partners at all stages, beginning with the definition of success; create technologies that can earn the trust of the analyst user by providing the reasoning for results; address uncertainty and data provenance explicitly.[5] *See* AUTOMATED LOW-LEVEL ANALYSIS AND DESCRIPTION OF DIVERSE INTELLIGENCE VIDEO (ALADDIN)

OFFICE OF INTELLIGENCE AND ANALYSIS The Intelligence and Analysis (I&A) mission is to equip the Homeland Security Enterprise with the intelligence and information it needs to keep the homeland safe, secure, and resilient. I&A's mission is supported by four strategic goals: promote understanding of threats through intelligence analysis; collect information and intelligence pertinent to homeland security; share information necessary for action; manage intelligence for the homeland security enterprise. This Department of Homeland Security office, is a member of the Intelligence Community.[6]

OFFICE OF MANAGEMENT AND BUDGET The largest component of the Executive Office of the President. It reports directly to the president and helps a wide range of executive departments and agencies across the federal government to implement the commitments and priorities of the president. as the implementation and enforcement arm of presidential policy government-wide, OMB carries out its mission through five critical processes that are essential to the president's ability to plan and implement his priorities across the Executive Branch: 1. budget development and execution; 2. management—oversight of agency performance, federal procurement, financial management, and information/IT; 3. coordination and review of all significant federal regulations by executive agencies, to reflect presidential priorities and to ensure that economic and other impacts are assessed as part of regulatory decision-making, along with review and assessment of information collection requests; 4. legislative clearance and coordination; and 5. executive orders and presidential memoranda to agency heads and officials, the mechanisms by which the president directs specific government-wide actions by Executive Branch officials.[7]

OFFICE OF NATIONAL ESTIMATES (ONE) A CIA research office that was to be limited to economic intelligence when it was created in 1950 but in subsequent years began dealing with political intelligence. The National Intelligence Council replaced it in 1973.[8] *See* KOREAN WAR; NATIONAL INTELLIGENCE OFFICER FOR WARNING

OFFICE OF OPERATIONS COORDINATION AND PLANNING The Office of Operations Coordination and Planning is responsible for monitoring the security of the United States on a daily basis and coordinating activities within the Department and with governors, Homeland Security Advisors, law enforcement partners, and critical infrastructure operators in all 50 states and more than 50 major urban areas nationwide.[9]

OFFICE OF TAILORED ACCESS OPERATIONS The NSA's TAO hacking unit is considered to be the intelligence agency's top secret weapon. It maintains its own covert network, infiltrates computers around the world and even intercepts shipping deliveries to plant back doors in electronics ordered by those it is targeting.[10] *See* TAILORED ACCESS OPERATIONS

OFFICIAL DEPARTMENT OF DEFENSE INFORMATION All information that is in the custody and control of the Department of Defense (DoD), relates to information in the custody and control of the DoD, or was acquired by DoD employees as part of their official duties or because of their official status within the DoD.[11]

OFFICIAL INFORMATION Information that is owned by, produced for or by, or subject to the control of the U.S. government. All classified information is considered official information.

OFFICIAL SECRETS ACT The Official Secrets Act remains in effect in the United Kingdom. The Act makes it unlawful for British government employees and contractors to the British government to disclose information they have access to as a result of their employment, if such disclosure is deemed harmful to the national interest. This law has broader jurisdiction than any U.S. law regarding the protection of classified information and consequences of sharing such information with unauthorized third parties.[12]

OFFICIAL USE ONLY (OUO) A designation identifying certain unclassified but sensitive information that may be exempt from public release under the Freedom of Information Act.[13] A security classification marking used from July 18, 1949, through October 22, 1951.

OMBUDSMAN FOR POLITICIZATION The CIA created the position of Ombudsman for Politicization in 1992 to respond to alleged issues of politicization and analytic distortion. According to the Ombudsman's Charter, the position serves as an "independent, informal, and confidential counselor for those who have complaints about politicization, biased reporting, or the lack of objective analysis" (359).[14]

ONEIROMANCY The practice of predicting the future by interpreting dreams (not encouraged as a methodology for intelligence analysts). From Greek *oneiros* (dream). *See* FATIDIC

OPEN GOVERNMENT DIRECTIVE In the Memorandum on Transparency and Open Government, issued on January 21, 2009, the president instructed the Director of the Office of Management and Budget (OMB) to issue an Open Government Directive. This memorandum requires executive departments and agencies to take the following steps toward the goal of creating a more open government: 1. publish government information online; 2. improve the quality of government information; 3. create and institutionalize a culture of open government; 4. create an enabling policy framework for open government.[15]

OPEN GOVERNMENT INITIATIVE On his first day in office, President Obama signed the Memorandum on Transparency and Open Government, ushering in a new era of open and accountable government meant to bridge the gap between the American people and their government; on December 8, 2009, the White House issued an unprecedented Open Government Directive requiring federal agencies to take immediate, specific steps to achieve key milestones in transparency, participation, and collaboration. Agencies have set forth those steps in biennial Open Government Plans available on each agency's Open Government website; in 2011, the administration expanded its support of open government efforts when President Obama launched the Open Government Partnership at the UN General Assembly meeting with seven other heads of state. U.S. efforts with the Open Government Partnership are set forth in biennial Open Government National Action Plans that detail specific and measurable open government commitments.[16] See OPEN GOVERNMENT DIRECTIVE; OPEN GOVERNMENT NATIONAL ACTION PLAN; OPEN GOVERNMENT PARTNERSHIP

OPEN GOVERNMENT NATIONAL ACTION PLAN In September 2011, the United States released its first Open Government National Action Plan, setting a series of ambitious goals to create a more open government. As we developed a U.S. National Action Plan ("National Plan"), the federal government engaged in extensive consultations with external stakeholders, including a broad range of civil society groups and members of the private sector. We solicited input from the administration's own Open Government Working Group, comprised of senior-level representatives from executive branch departments and agencies. White House policymakers also engaged the public via a series of blog posts, requesting ideas about how to focus Open Government efforts on increasing public integrity, more effectively managing public resources, and improving public services. Initiatives include "We the People" (petition platform to give Americans a direct line to voice their concerns to the administration via online petitions); Whistleblower Protection;

Extractive Industries Transparency Initiative (EITI) to require governments to publicly disclose their revenues from oil, gas, and mining assets, and for companies to make parallel disclosures regarding payments. Other initiatives include expanding the use of technology to achieve greater efficiencies in Freedom of Information Act (FOIA) administration; overhauling the public participation interface on regulations.gov to help the public find, follow, and participate in federal rulemakings; and launching ExpertNet, a platform to communicate with citizens who have expertise on a pertinent topic.[17] See OPEN GOVERNMENT DIRECTIVE; OPEN GOVERNMENT INITIA-TIVE; OPEN GOVERNMENT PARTNERSHIP

OPEN GOVERNMENT PARTNERSHIP The Open Government Partnership is a multilateral initiative that aims to secure concrete commitments from governments to promote transparency, empower citizens, fight corruption, and harness new technologies to strengthen governance. In the spirit of multi-stakeholder collaboration, OGP is overseen by a Steering Committee including representatives of governments and civil society organizations. To become a member of OGP, participating countries must endorse a high-level Open Government Declaration, deliver a country action plan developed with public consultation, and commit to independent reporting on their progress going forward. The Open Government Partnership formally launched on September 20, 2011, when the 8 founding governments (Brazil, Indonesia, Mexico, Norway, the Philippines, South Africa, the United Kingdom and the United States) endorsed the Open Government Declaration, and announced their country action plans.[18] *See* OPEN GOVERNMENT DIREC-TIVE; OPEN GOVERNMENT INITIATIVE; OPEN GOVERNMENT NATIONAL ACTION PLAN

OPEN SKIES TREATY The essence of the Treaty is the right to observe any point on the territory of the states parties—from Vancouver to Vladivostok. The legitimate interests of the observed state party are taken into account by ensuring that the maximum ground resolution of the sensors to be used allows for the reliable identification of major weapon systems, but not for detailed analysis. The Treaty incorporates several innovations: it has a strong cooperative element, since flight preparation, execution and follow-up as well as aircraft certification are carried out by bilateral or multilateral teams. The imagery taken during observation flights is accessible to all states parties. Thus the Treaty places all states parties on an equal footing. It prevents a monopoly on information and ensures reciprocity of observation, in stark contrast to monitoring by reconnaissance satellites owned and operated by an individual state.[19]

OPEN SOURCE 1. Any person or group that provides information without the expectation of privacy—the information, the relationship, or both is not protected against public disclosure.[20] 2. Software in which the source code is available to the general public for use and/or modification from its original design.[21]

(DNI) OPEN SOURCE CENTER (OSC) The DNI OSC, created by the DNI under the ADDNI for Open Source on November 1, 2005, is the U.S. government's center for open source intelligence. The D/CIA serves as the Executive Agent for the DNI in managing the OSC. The OSC is charged with collecting, translating, producing, and disseminating open source information that meets the needs of policymakers, the military, state and local law enforcement, operations officers, and analysts throughout the U.S. government. The OSC produces over 2,300 products daily, including translations, transcriptions, analyses, reports, video compilations, and geospatial intelligence to address short-term needs and longer-term issues. Its products cover issues that range from foreign political, military, economic, and science and technology topics, to counter-terrorism, counter-proliferation, counter-narcotics, and other homeland security topics.[22]

OPEN SOURCE INFORMATION Information that any member of the public could lawfully obtain by request or observation as well as other unclassified information that has limited public distribution or access.[23]

OPEN-SOURCE INTELLIGENCE (OSINT) 1. Information of potential intelligence value that is available to the general public, such as from radio, television, newspapers, journals, and the Internet. 2. Publicly available information (e.g., any member of the public could lawfully obtain the information by request or observation), as well as other unclassified information that has limited public distribution or access; to include any information that may be used in an unclassified context without compromising national security or intelligence sources or methods. If the information is not publicly available, certain legal requirements relating to collection, retention, and dissemination might apply.[24] *See* SOURCES OF INTELLIGENCE

OPEN SOURCE WORKS Open Source Works, which was charged by the Director for Intelligence with drawing on language-trained analysts to mine open-source information for new or alternative insights on intelligence issues. Open Source Works' products, based only on open source information, do not represent the coordinated views of the Central Intelligence Agency.[25]

OPEN STORAGE Any storage of classified national security information outside of approved containers. This includes classified information that is resident on information systems media and outside of an approved storage container, regardless of whether or not that media is in use (i.e., unattended operations).[26]

OPENNET OpenNet is the Sensitive but Unclassified (SBU) network in the Department. It provides access to standard desktop applications, such as word processing, e-mail, and Internet browsing, and supports a battery of custom Department software solutions and database management system.[27]

OPERATING DIRECTIVE A document specifying the tailored long-term collection priorities of a specific HUMINT field element.[28]

OPERATING LOCATION A facility from which Defense HUMINT collectors conduct overt or clandestine operations.[29]

OPERATION A military or domestic action or the carrying out of a strategic, tactical, service, training, or administrative mission.

OPERATION BARBAROSSA A German surprise attack on Russia in World War II that was an example of Soviet intelligence failures. Although Soviet intelligence had uncovered German troop movements eastward and an increase in the number of German aerial surveillance flights over the Soviet Union, and even though U.S. intelligence had alerted Soviet intelligence about Hitler's plans to invade, the paranoid Soviet government was convinced that similar intelligence leaked to them by the British was really counterintelligence. Stalin ignored all these warnings and believed his own intelligence that Hitler would not dare try to fight a war on two fronts.

OPERATION COMMUNITY SHIELD In 2005, ICE (Immigration and Customs Enforcement) initiated Operation Community Shield, an international law enforcement initiative that combines Homeland Security Investigations' (HSI) expansive statutory and civil enforcement authorities to combat the growth and proliferation of transnational criminal street gangs, prison gangs and outlaw motorcycle gangs throughout the United States. With assistance from state, local, tribal and foreign law enforcement partners, the initiative helps HSI locate, investigate, prosecute, and where applicable, immediately remove gang members from our neighborhoods and ultimately from the United States.[30]

OPERATIONAL CHAIN OF COMMAND The chain of command established for a particular operation or series of continuing operations.

OPERATIONAL CHARACTERISTICS The specific qualities required for an item of equipment to enable it to meet an agreed operational need.

OPERATIONAL COMMAND The authority granted to a commander to assign missions or tasks to subordinate commanders, to deploy units, to reassign forces, and to retain or delegate operational and/or tactical control as may be deemed necessary. It does not of itself include responsibility for administration or logistics. May also be used to denote the forces assigned to a commander.

OPERATIONAL CONTROL The authority delegated to a commander to direct forces assigned so that the commander may accomplish specific missions or tasks which are usually limited by function, time, or location; to deploy units concerned; and to retain or assign tactical control of those units. It does not include authority to assign separate employment of components of the units concerned. Neither does it, of itself, include administrative or logistic control.[31]

OPERATIONAL INTELLIGENCE Information is evaluated and systematically organized on an active or potential target, such as groups of individual criminals, relevant premises, contact points, and methods of communication. This process is developmental in nature, wherein there are sufficient articulated reasons to suspect criminal activity. Intelligence activities explore the basis of those reasons and newly developed information in order to develop a case for arrest or indictment.[32]

OPERATIONAL INTERCHANGEABILITY Ability to substitute one item for another of different composition or origin without loss in effectiveness, accuracy, and safety of performance.

OPERATIONAL PLAN A plan for a single operation or series of connected operations to be carried out simultaneously or in succession. It is usually based on stated assumptions and is the form of directive employed by a higher authority to permit subordinate commanders to prepare supporting plans and orders. The designation plan is usually used instead of order in preparing for operations well in advance. An operation plan may be put into effect at a prescribed time or on signal and then becomes the operation order.

OPERATIONAL PROCEDURES The detailed methods by which head-quarters and units carry out their operational tasks.

OPERATIONAL READINESS Capability of a unit/formation, ship, weapon system, or equipment to perform the missions or functions for which it is organized or designed. This term may be used in a general sense or to express a level of readiness. *See* COMBAT READINESS

OPERATIONAL READINESS EVALUATION (ORE) An evaluation of the operational capability and effectiveness of a unit or equipment, or any portion thereof.[33]

OPERATIONAL RESERVE An emergency reserve of personnel and/or material established for the support of a specific operation.

OPERATIONAL RISK 1. Risk that has the potential to impede the successful execution of operations.[34] 2. The ability of the current force to execute strategy successfully within acceptable human, materiel, financial, and strategic costs. Consideration of operational risk requires assessing the Department's (DoD) ability to execute current, planned, and contingency operations in the near term.[35]

OPERATIONAL ROUTE A route by air, sea, or land allocated to a command for the conduct of a specific operation, derived from the corresponding basic route network.

OPERATIONAL TRAINING Training that develops, maintains, or improves the operational readiness of individuals or units.

OPERATIONAL WARNING Required for effectively countering any major military operation that would hinder the ability to execute those military operations needed to accomplish strategic objectives within theaters or areas of operations.

OPERATIONALLY CRITICAL THREAT, ASSET, AND VULNERABILITY EVALUATION (OCTAVE) An information system analysis tool designed for large organizations and sponsored by the U.S. Department of Defense.[36]

OPERATIONS OFFICER *See* CASE OFFICER

OPERATIONS SECURITY (OPSEC) 1. A process to deny potential adversaries information about capabilities and/or intentions by identifying, controlling, and protecting generally unclassified evidence of the planning and execution of sensitive activities. The process involves five steps: identification of critical information, analysis of threats, analysis of vulnerabilities, assessment of risks, application of appropriate countermeasures.[37] 2. Process of identifying critical information and subsequently analyzing friendly actions attendant to military operations and other activities to: (a) identify those actions that can be observed by adversary intelligence systems; (b) determine indicators adversary intelligence systems might obtain that could be interpreted or pieced together to derive critical information in time to be useful to adversaries; and (c) select and execute measures that eliminate or reduce to an acceptable level the vulnerabilities of friendly actions to adversary exploitation.[38]

OPERATIONS SECURITY PROTECTED INFORMATION Unclassified information concerning Centers for Disease Control mission, functions, operations, or programs that require protection in the national interest, security, or homeland defense as iterated in National Security Decision Directive 298, January 1988, which established a National Operations Security Program.[39]

OPINION A value judgment regarding a future course of action that cannot be directly observed; most heavily relied on for warning in lieu of factual data. *See* ANALYSIS; ASSESSMENT

OPTICAL INTELLIGENCE (OPTINT) *See* SOURCES OF INTELLIGENCE

ORAL/VISUAL DISCLOSURE To brief orally, to expose to view, or to permit use under United States (U.S.) supervision in order to permit the transfer of knowledge or information, but not to physically transfer documents, material, or equipment to a foreign government or its representatives.[40]

ORDER A communication, written, oral, or by signal, which conveys instructions from a superior to a subordinate.

ORDER OF BATTLE The identification, strength, command structure, and disposition of the personnel, units, and equipment of any unit whether it is military or nonmilitary.

ORIGINAL CLASSIFICATION Original classification is the initial decision that particular information requires protection in the interest of national security and could be expected to cause damage if subjected to unauthorized disclosure. It is a six-step process in which the classifier must answer specific questions at each step and make considerations and decisions before classifying information.[41]

ORIGINAL CLASSIFICATION AUTHORITY (OCA) 1. Original classification authorities, also called original classifiers, are those individuals designated in writing, either by the president, by selected agency heads, or by designated senior agency officials with Top Secret original classification authority, to classify information in the first instance. Only original classifiers are authorized to determine what information, if disclosed without authorization, could reasonably be expected to cause damage to national security. Original classifiers must be able to identify or describe the damage. Agencies reported 2,269 OCAs in FY 2013; a 2 percent decrease from the 2,326 reported in FY 2012.[42] 2. OCAs, also called original classifiers, include the president, vice president, secretary of defense, the secretaries of the military departments, and other officials within DoD who have been specifically delegated this authority in writing. When Original Classification Authority is granted, OCAs are delegated classification authority specific to a level of classification and cumulative downwards. For example, an OCA appointed with Top Secret classification authority may classify information at the Top Secret, Secret, and Confidential levels. An OCA appointed with Confidential classification authority may only classify information at the Confidential level. OCAs may only classify information that is under their area of responsibility, such as a specific project, program, or type of operation.[43] 3. There is no requirement for an OCA to identify or describe the damage to the national security that warrants a classification decision in a security classification guide beyond a reference to the category of national security information described by Section 1.4 of E.O. 12958, as amended. The ISOO's "Classified National Security Information Directive No. 1: Final Rule" underscores this deficiency in Section 2001.10, "Classification Standards," stating that an OCA must be able to support his/her decision in writing, including identifying or describing the potential damage that could result should the classification decision become the subject of a challenge or access demand.[44]

ORIGINATING AGENCY DETERMINATION REQUIRED (OADR) Declassification guidance for classified materials. Any material flagged Originating Agency Determination Required (OADR) requires that the agency which originally classified the material determine whether the information can be declassified.[45]

OUTLAW MOTORCYLE GANGS (OMGS) 1. Outlaw motorcycle gangs are sophisticated organizations who utilize their affiliation with a motorcycle club as a conduit for criminal activity. The nature of their activity is generally conspiratorial, and their goals are attained through use of violence and intimidation. Because of their expertise in sophisticated weaponry and their international intelligence networks, outlaw motorcycle gangs pose a formidable threat to society in general and specifically to law enforcement.[46] 2. Office of Strategic Intelligence and Information (OSII), Field Intelligence Support Branch, notes that particular OMGs and their support clubs continue to court active-duty military personnel and government workers, both civilians and contractors, for their knowledge, reliable income, tactical skills and dedication to a cause.[47]

OUTLINE PLAN A preliminary plan that outlines the salient features of principles of a course of action prior to the initiation of detailed planning.

OUTSIDE(R) THREAT An unauthorized entity outside the security domain that has the potential to harm an information system through destruction, disclosure, modification of data, and/or denial of service.[48]

OVERCLASSIFICATION, OVER-CLASSIFICATION The designation of information as classified when the information does not meet one or more of the standards for classification under section 1.1 of Executive Order (EO) 13526. In other words, over-classification is either treating unclassified information as if it were classified, or classifying information at a higher level of classification than is appropriate.[49]

OVERSEAS SECURITY POLICY BOARD (OSPB) An interagency group of security professionals from the foreign affairs and intelligence communities who meet regularly to formulate security policy for U.S. missions abroad. The OSPB is chaired by the Assistant Secretary for Diplomatic Security.[50]

OVERT 1. Activities that are openly acknowledged by or readily attributable to the U.S. government, and include activities designed to acquire information through legal and open means without concealment. Overt information may be collected by observation, elicitation, or from knowledgeable human sources.[51] 2. Refers to being in the open, without any attempt to deceive or mislead, with full knowledge of coordinating units or agencies; done without attempts to conceal.

OVERT COLLECTION The acquisition of information and intelligence via the public domain.[52]

OVERT INTELLIGENCE Information collected openly from public or open sources.[53]

OVERT OPERATION An operation conducted openly without concealment.[54]

NOTES

1. U.S. Department of Defense. *Department of Defense Dictionary of Military and Associated Terms.* JP 1-02, 08 November 2010, as Amended through 15 January 2016. Accessed January 26, 2016, http://www.dtic.mil/doctrine/new_pubs/jp1_02.pdf.

2. Defense Civilian Intelligence Personnel System, *FAQ,* accessed February 2, 2016, http://dcips.dtic.mil/faq.html#Q5.

3. *Presidential Policy Directive/PPD-20. U.S. Cyber Operations Policy.* October 16, 2012. Accessed February 17, 2015. https://www.fas.org/irp/offdocs/ppd/ppd-20.pdf.

4. U.S. Department of State. "Bureau of Counterrorism." *Foreign Affairs Manual.* 1 FAM 480. March 5, 2013. Accessed February 16, 2015. http://www.state.gov/documents/organization/205857.pdf.

5. Intelligence Advanced Research Projects Activity (IARPA). *Incisive Analysis.* Accessed January 25, 2015. http://www.iarpa.gov/index.php/about-iarpa/incisive-analysis.

6. Department of Homeland Security, *Office of Intelligence and Analysis*, July 23, 2015, accessed February 1, 2016, http://www.dhs.gov/office-intelligence-and-analysis.

7. Office of Management and Budget. *Mission and Structure of the Office of Management and Budget.* Accessed February 9, 2015. http://www.whitehouse.gov/omb/organization_mission/.

8. Central Intelligence Agency. "The First Year of the Office of National Estimates." *Sherman Kent and the Board of National Estimates: Collected Essays.* March 19, 2007. Accessed June 9, 2015. https://www.cia.gov/library/center-for-the-study-of-intelligence/csi-publications/books-and-monographs/sherman-kent-and-the-board-of-national-estimates-collected-essays/7year.html.

9. Department of Homeland Security. *About Office of Operations Coordination and Planning.* Accessed February 15, 2015. http://www.dhs.gov/about-office-operations-coordination-and-planning.

10. SPEIGEL Staff. "Inside TAO: Documents Reveal Top NSA Hacking Unit." *SPEIGEL Online,* December 29, 2013. Accessed February 16, 2015. http://www.spiegel.de/international/world/the-nsa-uses-powerful-toolbox-in-effort-to-spy-on-global-networks-a-940969-2.html.

11. U.S. Department of Defense. Center for Development of Security Excellence. *Glossary of Security Terms and Definitions.* November 2012. Accessed February 16, 2015. http://www.cdse.edu/documents/cdse/Glossary_Handbook.pdf.

12. Masse, Todd. "Domestic Intelligence in the United Kingdom: Applicability of the MI-5 Model to the United States." *CRS Report for Congress* RL31920, May 19, 2003. Accessed March 8, 2015. http://www.dtic.mil/dtic/tr/fulltext/u2/a455815.pdf; also see *The Official Secrets Act 1989* (with current amendments). Accessed March 7, 2015. http://www.legislation.gov.uk/ukpga/1989/6/section/1.

13. Department of Energy, Office of Safeguards and Security, *Safeguards and Security Glossary of Terms* (December 18, 1995), accessed October 28, 2015, http://www.directives.doe.gov/references/.

14. Senate Select Committee on Intelligence. *Report of the Select Committee on Intelligence on the U.S. Intelligence Community's Prewar Intelligence Assessments on Iraq.* Ordered July 7, 2004, 108th congress. Accessed November 22, 2015. https://fas.org/irp/congress/2004_rpt/ssci_iraq.pdf. Also see Hastedt, Glenn. "The Politics of Intelligence and the Politicization of Intelligence: The American Experience." *Intelligence and National Security* 28, no. 1 (2013): 5–31; Marrin, Stephen. "Rethinking Analytic Politicization." *Intelligence and National Security* 28, no. 1 (2013): 32–54.

15. Orszag, Peter R. *Memorandum for the Heads of Executive Departments and Agencies.* Office of Management and Budget, December 8, 2009. Accessed February 4, 2015. http://www.whitehouse.gov/sites/default/files/omb/assets/memoranda_2010/m10-06.pdf; also see OMB. *Office of Management and Budget: Open Government.* Accessed February 4, 2015. http://www.whitehouse.gov/omb/open.

16. Executive Office of the President. *About Open Government.* Accessed February 4, 2015. http://www.whitehouse.gov/open/about.

17. Executive Office of the President. *The United States Releases Its Open Government National Action Plan.* September 20, 2011. Accessed February 3, 2015. http://www.whitehouse.gov/blog/2011/09/20/united-states-releases-its-open-government-national-action-plan; also see the *Second Open Government National Action Plan for the United States of America.* December 5, 2013. http://www.whitehouse.gov/sites/default/files/docs/us_national_action_plan_6p.pdf.

18. Open Government Partnership. *About.* Accessed January 31, 2015. http://www.opengovpartnership.org/about.

19. Dunay, Pál, Krasznai, Márton, Spitzer, Hartwig, Spitzer, Wiemker, Rafael, and Wynn, William. *Open Skies: A Cooperative Approach to Military Transparency and Confidence Building.* United Nations Institute for Disarmament Research, 2004. Accessed February 20, 2015. http://www.unidir.org/files/publications/pdfs/open-skies-a-cooperative-approach-to-military-transparency-and-confidence-building-319.pdf.

20. Department of the Army. *Open-Source Intelligence.* ATP 2-22.9, July 10, 2012. Accessed January 31, 2015. http://fas.org/irp/doddir/army/atp2-22-9.pdf.

21. U.S. Department of State. "Definitions of Diplomatic Security Terms." *Foreign Affairs Manual.* 12FAM090. November 12, 2014. Accessed February 4, 2015. http://www.state.gov/documents/organization/88330.pdf.

22. Central Intelligence Agency. *Centers in the CIA.* Accessed February 2, 2015. https://www.cia.gov/library/publications/additional-publications/the-work-of-

a-nation/cia-director-and-principles/centers-in-the-cia.html. Also see Office of the Director of National Intelligence. *National Open Source Enterprise.* Intelligence Community Directive 301, July 11, 2006. Accessed February 2, 2015. https://fas.org/irp/dni/icd/icd-301.pdf.

23. U.S. Department of Defense. *Department of Defense Dictionary of Military and Associated Terms.* JP 1-02, 08 November 2010, as Amended through 15 March 2015. Accessed March 21, 2015. http://www.dtic.mil/doctrine/dod_dictionary/.

24. CIA Office of Public Affairs, A Consumer's Guide to Intelligence.

25. Central Intelligence Agency. *Russia: Security Concerns About Iran's Space Program Growing.* November 16, 2010. CIA-DI-10-04951. http://fas.org/irp/cia/product/iran-space.pdf. Also see "Charter of Open Source Org Is Classified, CIA Says." *Secrecy News*, December 12, 2011. Accessed February 12, 2015. http://fas.org/blogs/secrecy/2011/12/cia_osw/.

26. Committee for National Security Systems (CNSS). Instruction 4009. *National Information Assurance Glossary.* April 2010. Accessed January 30, 2015. http://www.ncix.gov/publications/policy/docs/CNSSI_4009.pdf.

27. U.S. Department of State. "Networks." *Foreign Affairs Manual.* 5 FAM 870. September 22, 2014. Accessed June 9, 2015. http://www.state.gov/documents/organization/205857.pdf.

28. U.S. Department of Defense. *Defense Human Intelligence (HUMINT) and Related Intelligence Activities.* Instruction, Number S-5200.42, December 8, 2009. Accessed February 26, 2015. http://www.dod.mil/pubs/foi/homeland_defense/intelligence/10_F_0682_DoD_Instruction_S_5200_42_Defense_Human_Intell.pdf.

29. U.S. Department of Defense. *Defense Human Intelligence (HUMINT) and Related Intelligence Activities.* Instruction, Number S-5200.42, December 8, 2009. Accessed February 26, 2015. http://www.dod.mil/pubs/foi/homeland_defense/intelligence/10_F_0682_DoD_Instruction_S_5200_42_Defense_Human_Intell.pdf.

30. U.S. Immigration and Customs Service. *National Gang Unit.* Accessed April 6, 2015. https://www.ice.gov/national-gang-unit.

31. North Atlantic Treaty Organization. *NATO Glossary of Terms and Definitions.* NATO Standardization Agency, 2014, AAP-06, accessed July 27, 2015, http://nso.nato.int/nso/zPublic/ap/aap6/AAP-6.pdf.

32. Federal Bureau of Investigation. *Minimum Criminal Intelligence Training Standards for Law Enforcement and Other Criminal Justice Agencies in the United States.* October 2007. Accessed January 31, 2015. https://it.ojp.gov/gist/108/Minimum-Criminal-Intelligence-Training-Standards.

33. North Atlantic Treaty Organization. *NATO Glossary of Terms and Definitions.* NATO Standardization Agency, 2014, AAP-06, accessed July 27, 2015, http://nso.nato.int/nso/zPublic/ap/aap6/AAP-6.pdf.

34. Department of Homeland Security, Risk Steering Committee. *DHS Risk Lexicon.* September 2010. Accessed February 14, 2015. http://www.dhs.gov/dhs-risk-lexicon.

35. U.S. Department of Defense. *Quadrennial Defense Review Report.* February 2010. Accessed February 11, 2015. http://www.defense.gov/qdr/qdr%20as%20of%2029jan10%201600.pdf.

36. Department of Homeland Security, Risk Steering Committee. *DHS Risk Lexicon.* September 2010. Accessed February 14, 2015. http://www.dhs.gov/dhs-risk-lexicon.

37. Office of the Director of National Intelligence. *Glossary of Security Terms, Definitions, and Acronyms.* Intelligence Community Standard (ICS) 700-1. April 4, 2008. Accessed June 5, 2015. https://fas.org/irp/dni/icd/ics-700-1.pdf.

38. U.S. Department of Defense. Center for Development of Security Excellence. *Glossary of Security Terms and Definitions.* November 2012. Accessed February 16, 2015. http://www.cdse.edu/documents/cdse/Glossary_Handbook.pdf.

39. Centers for Disease Control. *Manual Guide—Information Security CDC-02.* Office of Security and Emergency Preparedness "Sensitive But Unclassified Information." Part B. 07/22/2005. http://www.fas.org/sgp/othergov/cdc-sbu.pdf.

40. U.S. Department of Defense. Center for Development of Security Excellence. *Glossary of Security Terms and Definitions.* November 2012. Accessed February 15, 2015. http://www.cdse.edu/documents/cdse/Glossary_Handbook.pdf.

41. U.S. Department of Defense. Center for Development of Security Excellence. *Original Classification Authority Desktop Reference.* July 2012. Accessed January 31, 2015. http://www.cdse.edu/documents/cdse/oca-desktop-reference.pdf.

42. Information Security Oversight Office. *2013 Annual Report to the President.* Accessed January 31, 2015. http://www.archives.gov/isoo/reports/2013-annual-report.pdf.

43. U.S. Department of Defense. Center for Development of Security Excellence. *Original Classification Authority Desktop Reference.* July 2012. Accessed January 31, 2015. http://www.cdse.edu/documents/cdse/oca-desktop-reference.pdf.

44. Director of National Intelligence and Chief Information Officer, Intelligence Community Technology Governance. *Intelligence Community Classification Guidance: Findings and Recommendations Report.* January 2008, 11. Accessed February 11, 2015. https://www.fas.org/sgp/othergov/intel/class.pdf.

45. U.S. Department of Defense. Center for Development of Security Excellence. *Glossary of Security Terms and Definitions.* November 2012. Accessed February 16, 2015. http://www.cdse.edu/documents/cdse/Glossary_Handbook.pdf.

46. U.S. Department of Justice. *Outlaw Motorcycle Gangs: USA Overview.* National Institute of Justice and State of California, Bureau of Organized Crime and Criminal Intelligence, May 1991. Accessed June 9, 2015. https://www.ncjrs.gov/pdffiles1/Digitization/147691NCJRS.pdf.

47. U.S. Department of Justice. *Outlaw Motorcycle Gangs (OMGs) and the Military 2014.* ATF Office of Strategic Intelligence and Information. *The Intercept,* May 22, 2015. Accessed June 9, 2015. https://firstlook.org/theintercept/2015/05/22/atf-report-warned-military-government-membership-outlaw-motorcycle-gangs/.

48. Committee for National Security Systems (CNSS). Instruction 4009. *National Information Assurance Glossary.* April 2010. Accessed January 30, 2015. http://www.ncix.gov/publications/policy/docs/CNSSI_4009.pdf.

49. Information Security Oversight Office, quoted in U.S. Department of Justice. *Audit of the Department of Justice's Implementation of and Compliance with Certain*

Classification Requirements (Audit Report 13-40, September 2013). Accessed February 3, 2015. http://www.justice.gov/oig/reports/2013/a1340.pdf.

50. U.S. Department of State. "Definitions of Diplomatic Security Terms." *Foreign Affairs Manual.* 12FAM090. November 12, 2014. Accessed February 4, 2015. http://www.state.gov/documents/organization/88330.pdf.

51. Office of the Director of National Intelligence. *Human Intelligence.* Intelligence Community Directive 304, July 9, 2009. Accessed March 2, 2015. http://www.dni.gov/files/documents/ICD/ICD%20304.pdf.

52. U.S. Department of Defense. Center for Development of Security Excellence. *Glossary of Security Terms and Definitions.* November 2012. Accessed February 15, 2015. http://www.cdse.edu/documents/cdse/Glossary_Handbook.pdf.

53. United States Senate, Select Committee to Study Governmental Operations with Respect to Intelligence Activities (Church Committee). *Final Report.* Book 1. April 26, 1976. Accessed January 11, 2015. https://archive.org/details/finalreportof-sel01unit.

54. U.S. Department of Defense. Center for Development of Security Excellence. *Glossary of Security Terms and Definitions.* November 2012. Accessed February 17, 2015. http://www.cdse.edu/documents/cdse/Glossary_Handbook.pdf.

P

P5+1 The United States, United Kingdom, France, China, Russia plus Germany that formed in 2006 to address Iran's nuclear program through diplomatic channels.[1]

PALM-READING ASSESSMENT Mostly used as a pejorative term for estimates and forecasting based on qualitative or intuitive judgment. The term received widespread use among U.S. intelligence analysts and policymakers during the Vietnam War in the 1960s.[2] *See* BEAN-COUNTING ASSESSMENT

PARADOX OF COLLECTION As additional information is collected, the analyst becomes inundated with intelligence leading to ambiguity and uncertainty and thus making the person more ignorant. By collecting more intelligence, the analyst is exposed to more variables that can lead to more uncertainty.

PARADOX OF EXPERTISE The more a person becomes an expert in a particular area or field of study, the more likely that person will miss changes that would normally be detected by those with less knowledge or experience. The strengths of expertise can also be weaknesses, as reflected in the saying "He kept missing the forest for the trees."[3]

PARADOX OF SILENCE (SOUNDS OF SILENCE PARADOX) The lack of any communications by the enemy may actually be a signal that preparations for war are beginning; the enemy may use silence as noise to disguise activity. For example, prior to attacking Pearl Harbor, the Japanese fleet had engaged in radio silence, thus making U.S. electronic signal interceptors believe the fleet had not yet set sail when in fact it was about to attack. Similarly, a quiescent international environment may act as background noise which, by conditioning observers to a peaceful routine, actually covers preparations for war. *See* CREEPING NORMALCY; NOISE

PARADOX OF WARNING (WARNING PARADOX) Enemy counter-action based on friendly action taken as a result of a warning may alter the enemy's initially intended course of action. The warning thus appears to be wrong on the basis of the change in enemy action. *See* CRY-WOLF SYNDROME

PARAMILITARY OPERATIONS Operations undertaken by military forces separate from the regular armed forces of a nation. Often used in an effort to hide source of control, associated with covert operations. *See* CO-VERT OPERATIONS

PASSENGER NAME RECORD U.S. law requires airlines operating flights to, from, or through the United States to provide the Department of Homeland Security (DHS), U.S. Customs and Border Protection (CBP), with certain passenger reservation information, called Passenger Name Record (PNR) data, primarily for purposes of preventing, detecting, investigating, and prosecuting terrorist offenses and related crimes and certain other crimes that are transnational in nature. This information is collected from airline travel reservations and is transmitted to CBP prior to departure. Collection of this information from air carriers is authorized by 49 U.S.C.§ 44909(c)(3) and its implementing (interim) regulations at 19 CFR 122.49d. These statutory and regulatory authorities require each air carrier operating passenger flights in foreign air transportation to, from, or through the United States to provide CBP with electronic access to PNR data to the extent it is collected and contained in the air carrier's reservation and/or departure control systems.[4]

PASSIVE ACQUIESCENCE A term used in the policy, military, and intelligence communities to mean "the acceptance to do nothing." For example, "Over the past few months, with the demise of their safe haven in Afghanistan, some al Qaida operatives have relocated to Iraq. Baghdad's support for international terrorist organizations ranges from explicit and overt support to implicit and passive acquiescence."[5]

PASSIVE DECEPTION Measures designed to mislead a foreign power, organization, or person by causing an object or situation to appear non-threatening when a threat does exist; downplaying capabilities or intentions to look less threatening. "Passive deception is primarily based on secrecy and camouflage, on hiding and concealing one's intentions and/or capabilities from the adversary. Some experts view passive deception as inferior and not likely to succeed against any competent intelligence organization" (133).[6]

Most computer viruses use passive deception to enter a computer's operating system by hiding inside another program or e-mail. *See* A-TYPE DECEPTION; ACTIVE DECEPTION; DECEPTION; DENIAL AND DECEPTION; M-TYPE DECEPTION

PASSIVE WIRETAPPING The monitoring or recording of data while it is being transmitted over a communications link, without altering or affecting the data.[7]

PASSWORD A secret word or distinctive sound used to reply to a challenge. *See* COUNTERSIGN

PATTERN RECOGNITION An inductive process of recognizing a commonality or trend in an aggregate of indications from which a plausible explanation or model can be developed.

PAYLOAD 1. The sum of the weight of passengers and cargo that an aircraft can carry. 2. The warhead, its container, and activating devices in a military missile. 3. The satellite or research vehicle or a space probe or research missile. 4. The load (expressed in tons of cargo or equipment, gallons of liquid, or number of passengers) that the vehicle is designed to transport under specified conditions of operation, in addition to its unladen weight.

PEACEKEEPING Military operations undertaken with the consent of all major parties to a dispute, designed to monitor and facilitate implementation of an agreement (cease fire, truce, or other such agreement) and support diplomatic efforts to reach a long-term political settlement.[8]

PEACEMAKING The process of diplomacy, mediation, negotiation, or other forms of peaceful settlements that arranges an end to a dispute and resolves issues that led to it.[9]

PEARL HARBOR The Japanese attack on the U.S. base at Pearl Harbor, Hawaii, during World War II is regarded as the worst intelligence failure in U.S. history. In 1941, a task force of 33 Japanese ships stationed themselves 200 miles north of Oahu and launched two successive waves of air attack (350 planes) in which the United States lost 18 warships, 200 airplanes, and more than 2,000 personnel. Naval intelligence had believed that Japan might possibly attack Thailand about that time of year, although the United States lacked any specific human intelligence on Japan, despite intercepting Japanese diplomatic and espionage messages.

PEEKING The obvious action by someone to identify any surveillance coverage.

PEN REGISTER The term "pen register" means a device or process which records or decodes dialing, routing, addressing, or signaling information transmitted by an instrument or facility from which a wire or electronic communication is transmitted, provided, however, that such information shall not include the contents of any communication, but such term does not include any device or process used by a provider or customer of a wire or electronic communication service for billing, or recording as an incident to billing, for communications services provided by such provider or any device or process used by a provider or customer of a wire communication service for cost accounting or other like purposes in the ordinary course of its business.[10]

PENETRABILITY The measure of a structure's potential to resist penetration by munitions. A material's compressive strength and thickness largely determine its penetrability, but in the case of rock, the degree of weathering and jointing have significant influence. Penetrability is described in terms of an S-number.[11]

PERFORMANCE ELEMENTS The IC-common and component-specific behaviors that describe the manner in which work is to be performed. Performance elements are derived from 2 ICD 610 competencies developed in accordance with accepted legal, professional, and technical guidelines. ICDs 651 and 656 describe the performance elements common across the IC.[12]

PERIODIC REINVESTIGTION An investigation conducted every 5 years for the purpose of updating a previously completed background or special background investigation.[13]

PERMANENT RECORDS Any federal record that has been determined by the National Archives and Records Administration (NARA) to have sufficient value to warrant its preservation in the National Archives of the United States. Permanent records include all records accessioned by the NARA into the National Archives and later increments of the same records, and those for which the disposition is permanent on Standard Form (SF) 115s, Request for Records Disposition Authority, approved by the NARA on or after May 14, 1973.[14]

PERMANENT RESIDENT ALIEN Any alien lawfully admitted into the United States under an immigration visa for permanent residence.[15]

PERSEREC (DEFENSE PERSONNEL AND SECURITY RESEARCH CENTER) PERSEREC was established in response to a recommendation by the Department of Defense (DoD) Security Review Commission (known as the Stilwell Commission), set up in the wake of the very damaging Walker espionage case, to improve the department's personnel security system. In its 1985 report, the commission called for a personnel security research center to provide policymakers with an objective basis for policies and processes related to the security clearance system. Established in 1986, PERSEREC was located in Monterey, CA, because of its proximity to the Defense Manpower Data Center (DMDC) West and the Naval Postgraduate School (NPS), where there was already a nucleus of personnel security researchers. Our original directive included a sunset clause requiring that the organization cease to exist in 1990 unless DoD directed its continued existence. Based on a favorable review by DoD components of PERSEREC's performance, this clause was eliminated in 1992 and we became a permanent element within the DoD.[16]

PERSISTENT SURVEILLANCE Persistent surveillance, also known as persistent intelligence, surveillance, and reconnaissance (ISR); persistent stare; and pervasive knowledge of the adversary, is an often-used term to describe the need for and application of future ISR capabilities to qualitatively transform intelligence support to operational and tactical commands. The essence of persistent surveillance is to use enterprise systems to detect, collect, disseminate, and characterize activity in the battlespace (41–42).[17]

PERSONA NON GRATA (PNG) A Latin phrase meaning "unwelcome person." As a legal term, it refers to the practice of a state prohibiting a diplomat from entering the country as a diplomat, or censuring a diplomat already resident in the country for conduct unbecoming of the status of a diplomat.[18]

PERSONAL INDENTIFYING INFORMATION, PERSONALLY IDENTIFIABLE INFORMATION The information that permits the identity of an individual to be directly or indirectly inferred.[19] *See* PII

PERSONALLY IDENTIFIABLE INFORMATION (PII) The term "personally identifiable information" means—(A) if provided by an individual to the debtor in connection with obtaining a product or a service from the debtor primarily for personal, family, or household purposes—

1. the first name (or initial) and last name of such individual, whether given at birth or time of adoption, or resulting from a lawful change of name;

2. the geographical address of a physical place of residence of such individual;
3. an electronic address (including an e-mail address) of such individual;
4. a telephone number dedicated to contacting such individual at such physical place of residence;
5. a social security account number issued to such individual; or
6. the account number of a credit card issued to such individual; or

(B) if identified in connection with 1 or more of the items of information specified in subparagraph (A)—

1. a birth date, the number of a certificate of birth or adoption, or a place of birth; or
2. any other information concerning an identified individual that, if disclosed, will result in contacting or identifying such individual physically or electronically.[20] *See* PERSONAL INDENTIFYING INFORMATION; PII

PERSONNEL REACTION TIME The time required by personnel to take prescribed protective measures after receipt of a nuclear strike warning.

PERSONNEL SECURITY (PERSEC) A security discipline that assesses the loyalty, reliability and trustworthiness of individuals for initial and continued eligibility for access to classified information.[21]

PERSONNEL SECURITY CLEARANCE (PCL) An administrative determination that an individual is eligible, from a security viewpoint, for access to classified information at the same or lower category as the level of the personnel clearance being granted.[22]

PERSONNEL SECURITY DETERMINATION A discretionary security decision by appropriately trained adjudicative personnel of all available personal and professional information that bears on the individual's loyalty to the United States (U.S.), strength of character, trustworthiness, honesty, reliability, discretion and sound judgment, as well as freedom from conflicting allegiances and potential for coercion, and the willingness and ability to abide by regulations governing the use, handling, and protection of classified information and/or the execution of responsibilities of a sensitive position.[23]

PERSONNEL SECURITY INVESTIGATION (PSI) An investigation required for the purpose of determining the eligibility of Department of Defense (DoD) military and civilian personnel, contractor employees, consultants, and other persons affiliated with the DoD, for access to classified information, acceptance or retention in the Armed Forces, assignment or retention in sensitive duties, or other designated duties requiring such investigation. Personnel Security Investigations (PSIs) include investigations of affiliations with subversive organizations, suitability information, or hostage situations, conducted for the purpose of making personnel security determinations. PSIs also include investigations of allegations that arise subsequent to adjudicative action and require resolution to determine an individual's current eligibility for access to classified information or assignment or retention in a sensitive position.[24]

PHASES OF WARNING Stages of a surprise attack that can degrade a nation's defense. The three phases of warning are political, strategic, and tactical. Some analysts label these phases strategic, operational, and tactical. *See* POLITICAL WARNING; STRATEGIC WARNING; TACTICAL WARNING

PHISHING Tricking individuals into disclosing sensitive personal information through deceptive computer-based means.

PHOTO INTELLIGENCE (PHOTINT) *See* IMAGERY INTELLIGENCE; SOURCES OF INTELLIGENCE

PHOTOGRAPHIC SCALE The ratio of a distance measured on a photographic or mosaic to the corresponding distance on the ground, classified as follows:
Very large scale, 1:4,999 and larger; Large scale, 1:5,000 to 1:9,999; Medium scale, 1:10,000 to 1:24,999; Small scale, 1:25,000 to 1:49,999; Very small scale, 1:50,000 and smaller. *See* PRINCIPLE SCALE

PHYSICAL ACCESS CONTROL The process of physically controlling personnel and vehicular entry to installations, facilities, and resources. Access will be either unescorted or escorted.[25]

PHYSICAL DEFEAT Physical damage or destruction of an element or structure. This damage also may affect the intended mission of the facility.[26] *See* DEFEAT ASSESSMENT; FUNCTIONAL DEFEAT

PHYSICAL SECURITY 1. The security discipline concerned with physical measures designed to protect personnel; prevent unauthorized access to facilities, equipment, material, and documents; and defend against espionage, terrorism, sabotage, damage, and theft. 2. That part of security concerned with active and passive measures designed to prevent unauthorized access to personnel, equipment, installations, and information, and to safeguard them against espionage, sabotage, terrorism, damage, and criminal activity. Designed for prevention and provides the means to counter threats when preventive measures are ignored or bypassed.[27]

PIANO Clandestine radio.

PII Information that can be used to distinguish or trace an individual's identity, such as his or her name, social security number, date and place of birth, mother's maiden name, and biometric records, including any other personal information which is linked or linkable to a specific individual.[28] See PERSONALLY IDENTIFIABLE INFORMATION

PLAIN WRITING 1. Writing that is clear, concise, well organized, and follows other best practices appropriate to the subject or field and intended audience.[29] 2. Clear and simple communication has many benefits. Avoiding vagueness and unnecessary complexity makes it easier for members of the public to understand and to apply for important benefits and services for which they are eligible. Plain writing can also assist the public in complying with applicable requirements simply because people better understand what they are supposed to do.[30]

PLAINTEXT KEY An unencrypted cryptographic key.

PLAUSIBLE DENIAL 1. The ability to disown or deny any relationship one has with an intelligence agency. 2. Official disclaimer supported by a believable cover story.[31]

PLUMBING A term referring to the development of assets or services supporting the clandestine operations of CIA field stations—such as safehouses, unaccountable funds, investigative persons, surveillance teams.[32]

PMAT (POLITICAL MILITARY ACTION TEAM) A cell of officials devoted to providing 24-hour support for political-military affairs (within the U.S. State Department).[33]

POINTEE-TALKEE A language aid containing selected phrases in English opposite a translation in a foreign language. It is used by pointing to appropriate phrases.

POINTER SYSTEM OR INDEX A system that stores information designed to identify individuals, organizations, and/or crime methodologies with the purpose of linking law enforcement agencies that have similar investigative and/or intelligence interests in the entity defined by the system.[34]

POLICY The principles and values that guide the performance of a duty. A policy is not a statement of what must be done in a particular situation. Rather, it is a statement of guiding principles that should be followed in activities that are directed toward the attainment of goals.[35]

POLICY BIAS Development of analysis to fit established objectives in support of an existing policy or the implementation of a new policy; also known as "finding the facts to fit the conclusion." For example, "Neither camp can completely avoid the impact of policy bias when it comes to dealing with uncertainty. The intelligence side likes to pretend otherwise, but the manner in which it favors certain substantive assumptions over others has predictable implications for U.S. policy debates. The serious policy official recognizes the power of policy bias and has a powerful incentive to do all he or she can to insure against the influence of bias and wishful thinking during the working out of analytic assumptions. Policymakers want to succeed and cannot do so without sound assumptions."[36] *See* POLITICIZED INTELLIGENCE

POLICY INTELLIGENCE *See* POLITICAL INTELLIGENCE

POLITICAL INTELLIGENCE 1. Originally, arranging, coordinating and conducting covert operations so as to "plausibly" permit official denial of U.S. involvement, sponsorship or support. Later this concept evolved so that it was employed by high officials and their subordinates to communication without using precise language which would reveal authorization and involvement in certain activities and would be embarrassing and politically damning if publicly revealed.[37] 2. Pertaining to foreign and domestic policies of governments and the activities of political movements; intelligence concerned with threatening actions and activities. *See* NATIONAL SECURITY INTELLIGENCE

POLITICAL WARNING A forecast of increasing tensions between two or more countries that raises the possibility that deterrence can fail, leading to an unforeseen crisis; usually can range over a period of days or months. *See* PHASES OF WARNING; STRATEGIC WARNING; TACTICAL WARNING

POLITICIZED INTELLIGENCE Any intelligence or analysis that is developed to meet the conclusions or key judgments that have already been predetermined to support policy. *See* POLICY BIAS; POTOMAC FEVER

POLLYANNA One who sees and reports only positive outcomes from current indications, regardless of the message read into the same indications by less biased analysts. The term originates from the novel *Pollyanna* written in 1913 by Eleanor Porter.[38] *See* CASSANDRA

PORTFOLIO MANAGEMENT The act or process of exerting control over processes and resources of a designated group or set of functions to produce a degree of control, predictability, and order of that group or set of functions.

POSITIVE INTELLIGENCE Information gathered concerning a foreign power that is significant to national security, foreign relations, economic interest, and other plans and policies of a government.

POSSIBLE That which can occur, or may happen, or could come true. Sometimes confused with "probable," a statement of likelihood. For example, "Their having the capability is possible, but the estimate of an opponent's intention to use that capability is not probable." *See* PROBABLE

POST-SURPRISE MEASURES Planned methods and activities to deal with a sudden attack once it has taken place. *See* BASIC MEASURES OF MILITARY PREPAREDNESS; EMERGENCY MEASURES OF MILITARY PREPAREDNESS

POTENTIAL THREAT ELEMENT An individual or group for which there are allegations or information indicating a possibility of the unlawful use of force or violence in furtherance of a specific motivation or goal, possibly political or social in nature. An actual history of criminal activity increases a person's or group's "point scale" in a threat assessment.[39]

POTOMAC FEVER A pejorative term used to describe those who seek to provide intelligence or information they think senior-level leaders want; any analysis or assessment produced with the guiding principle to please as many and offend as few as possible; warning production used solely to further the ambition and career goals of an individual. The term is derived from the river that runs adjacent to the Pentagon. *See* POLITICIZED INTELLIGENCE

POWER INTANGIBLES Factors, such as ideology, a government's ability to mobilize resources, the maintenance of ruling coalitions, or a fear of domestic revolutions or opposition movements that have an independent impact on political intentions.

POWER PROJECTION The ability of a nation to apply all or some of its elements of national power—political, economic, informational, or military—to rapidly and effectively deploy and sustain forces in and from multiple dispersed locations to respond to crises, to contribute to deterrence, and to enhance regional stability.[40]

PRECISION ACQUISITION INTELLIGENCE Required intelligence needed to create a valid assessment in an environment of ambiguity and uncertainty in a given crisis situation or warning problem. For example, data collected on reserve military medical technicians with advanced training in chemical or biological warfare may be the precision acquisition intelligence needed to understand a nation's readiness for certain types of warfare. *See* PRECISION ATTACK/ENGAGEMENT

PRECISION ATTACK/ENGAGEMENT Any attack of a target by weapons employing guidance, with sufficient spatial and temporal accuracy, that seeks to achieve its required effect with minimum expenditure of munitions and a reduced risk of collateral damage. "It is a scalpel approach to all types of military operations using lethal or non-lethal, kinetic or non-kinetic force. In conventional warfighting, precision engagement is the ability to forgo brute force-on-force tactics and apply discriminate force precisely where required. One B-2 dropping 16 precision-guided weapons and destroying 16 key targets epitomizes precision engagement."[41] *See* DECAPITATION STRIKE; PRECISION ACQUISITION INTELLIGENCE; SALAMI TACTICS

PREDICTION A STATEMENT of the expected time, place, and/or magnitude of a future event. *See* ESTIMATE; FORECAST

PREDICTIVE INTELLIGENCE Fulfills the requirement of the need to know what will happen next.

PREEMPTIVE ATTACK An attack initiated first, in the belief that there will be no time to respond or retaliate as the victim of an opposing attack. *See* PREVENTIVE ATTACK

PREPARATION TIME The time between the receipt of authorization from NATO political authorities for major NATO commanders to implement military measures to counter an impending attack and the start of the attack.[42] See WARNING TIME

PREPAREDNESS Actions that involve a combination of planning, resources, training, exercising, and organizing to build, sustain, and improve operational capabilities. It is the process of identifying the personnel, training, and equipment needed for a wide range of potential incidents, and developing jurisdiction-specific plans for delivering capabilities when needed for an incident.[43]

PREPUBLICATION REVIEW 1. All persons with authorized access to Sensitive Compartmented Information (SCI) shall be required to sign a nondisclosure agreement as a condition of access to SCI and other classified information. All such agreements must include a provision for prepublication review to assure deletion of SCI and other classified information.[44] 2. The purpose of pre-publication review is to prevent unauthorized disclosure of information and ensure the mission of the ODNI and the foreign relations and security of the United States are not adversely affected by public disclosure. All information meant to be made available in a public forum must be submitted for review prior to release. The obligation applies to current and former ODNI staff, including cadre, detailees, and contractors, who have access to classified information. There are two categories of material that must be reviewed:

Non-Official: Anything published or presented in your personal capacity. Examples include resumes, books, op-eds, personal blogs.
Official: Anything created as part of your official duties on behalf of the ODNI. Examples include speeches, newsletters, official web pages, outreach documents, brochures.[45]

PRESIDENTIAL DECISION DIRECTIVE 56 (PDD-56) After several failed crisis interventions in Somalia, Rwanda, and Haiti, U.S. strategic planners had to improve techniques regarding participation in such missions. President Clinton signed this directive in 1997 to address the need to focus on complex emergencies. The directive orders the National Security Council to work with the National Defense University, Army War College, Pentagon, State Department, Central Intelligence Agency, and other agencies to develop and conduct a multiagency training and planning program focused on complex emergency issues.[46]

PRESIDENTIAL DIRECTIVES CFR Title 3 compilations for the 1938–1943 and 1943–1948 periods contain the texts of 12 presidential directives denominated as military orders. The first of these was issued on July 5, 1939, and the last on October 18, 1948. Ten of them bear the signature of President Roosevelt; the other two were signed by President Truman. These directives appear to have been issued by the president in conjunction with the execution of his duties as commander-in-chief and pertain to matters concerning armed forces administration and personnel. Shortly after the creation of the National Security Council (NSC) in 1947, supporting staff began producing four types of policy papers: basic comprehensive policy statements on a broad variety of national security problems, together with pertinent political, economic, and military implementation strategies; situation profiles of large geographic areas or specific countries; assessments of mobilization, arms control, atomic energy, and other functional matters; and organizational statements on NSC, foreign intelligence, and internal security structure and activities. The initial products in the series reportedly were of the geographical type; the first comprehensive policy statement was completed and given NSC approval in November 1948. By the time President Dwight D. Eisenhower took office, approximately 100 NSC papers mandated operative policy. With each succeeding president, national security instruments of varying denominations and character evolved from the NSC policy papers. In general, they were not required to be published in the *Federal Register*, were usually security classified at the highest level of protection, and were available to the public after a great many years had elapsed, usually at the official library of the president who had approved them. Many of the more recent ones remain officially secret. National security instruments have been given different names by presidential administrations:

- National Security Action Memoranda (NSAMs): Kennedy and Johnson
- National Security Decision Memoranda (NSDMs): Nixon and Ford
- Presidential Directives (PDs): Carter
- National Security Decision Directives (NSDDs): Reagan
- National Security Directives (NSDs): Bush
- Presidential Decision Directives (PDDs): Clinton
- National Security Presidential Directives (NSPDs): G. W. Bush
- Presidential Policy Directives (PPDs): Obama[47]

PRESIDENTIAL HISTORICAL MATERIALS AND RECORDS The papers or records of former presidents of the United States under the legal control of the Archivist pursuant to sections 2107, 2111, 2111 note, or 2203 of Title 44, United States Code, as defined at 44 USC 2111, 2111 note, and 2001.[48]

PRESIDENTIAL POLICY DIRECTIVE 8 (PPD-8) Facilitates an integrated, all-of-nation approach to national preparedness for the threats that pose the greatest risk to the security of the nation, including acts of terrorism, cyber attacks, pandemics, and catastrophic natural disasters; directs the federal government to develop a national preparedness system to build and improve the capabilities necessary to maintain national preparedness across the five mission areas covered in the PPD: prevention, protection, mitigation, response, and recovery.[49]

PRESIDENTIAL RECORDS ACT (PRA) Presidential documents are historical resources that capture each incumbent's conduct in presidential office. Pursuant to the Presidential Records Act ((PRA) 44 U.S.C. §§2201–2207), the National Archives and Records Administration (NARA) collects most records of presidents and vice presidents at the end of each administration. They are then disclosed to the public—unless the archivist of the United States, the incumbent president, or the appropriate former president requests the records be kept private. The PRA is the primary law governing the collection and preservation of, and access to, records of a former president. Although the PRA has remained relatively unchanged since enactment in 1978, successive presidential administrations have interpreted its meaning differently.

Additionally, it is unclear whether the PRA accounts for presidential record-keeping issues associated with increasing and heavy use of new and potentially ephemeral technologies—like email, Facebook, Twitter, and YouTube—by the president and his immediate staff.[50]

PRESIDENTIAL RESERVE CALL-UP Provision of a public law (Title 10, United States Code, Section 12304) that provides the president a means to activate, without a declaration of national emergency, not more than 200,000 members of the Selected Reserve and the Individual Ready Reserve (of whom not more than 30,000 may be members of the Individual Ready Reserve), for not more than 365 days to meet the requirements of any operational mission, other than for disaster relief or to suppress insurrection.[51]

PRESIDENT'S DAILY BRIEF (PDB) 1. The most exclusive and sensitive items that are summarized succinctly and sent to the president and a highly select list of leaders and White House aides. 2. In 1961, President John F. Kennedy's aides requested a more concise summary of all-source intelligence on key issues—something small enough to fit in the president's jacket pocket. Three days later, the *President's Intelligence Checklist* (PICL) was delivered to President Kennedy, who liked it immediately. From that point forward, the PICL remained essentially unchanged until the *President's Daily Brief*

(PDB), crafted to President Lyndon B. Johnson's specifications, replaced it in 1964. Today, the PDB is an IC product coordinated by ODNI's PDB staff in partnership with the CIA Directorate of Intelligence (DI)'s President's Analytic Support Staff. It is still all-source publication that the president relies upon heavily to inform his national security decisions, and CIA analysts remain primary contributors.[52]

PRESIDENT'S FOREIGN INTELLIGENCE ADVISORY BOARD (PFIAB) The PFIAB is composed of 16 members appointed by the president from among distinguished citizens outside of government. The board reviews the performance of government agencies engaged in the collection, evaluation, or production of intelligence in the execution of intelligence policy. The PFIAB is specifically charged to make recommendations for actions to improve and enhance the performance of the intelligence of the United States. President Kennedy renamed it the President's Foreign Intelligence Advisory Board (PFIAB) in 1961, and it has served every president except for President Carter, who abolished the Board in 1977. President Reagan reinstituted the PFIAB in 1981, and in 2008 President Bush renamed it the President's Intelligence Advisory Board to reflect the fact that national intelligence doesn't begin or end at our nation's borders.[53]

PRESIDENT'S INTELLIGENCE ADVISORY BOARD (PIAB) The President's Intelligence Advisory Board (PIAB), with its component Intelligence Oversight Board (IOB), is an independent element within the Executive Office of the President. The President's Intelligence Advisory Board exists exclusively to assist the president by providing the president with an independent source of advice on the effectiveness with which the Intelligence Community is meeting the nation's intelligence needs, and the vigor and insight with which the community plans for the future. The Board has access to all information needed to perform its functions and has direct access to the president.[54] *See* INTELLIGENCE OVERSIGHT BOARD; PRESIDENT'S FOREIGN INTELLIGENCE ADVISORY BOARD

PRESIDENT'S SURVEILLANCE PROGRAM In the weeks following the terrorist attacks of September 11, 2001, the president authorized the National Security Agency (NSA) to conduct a classified program to detect and prevent further attacks in the United States. As part of the NSA's classified program, several different intelligence activities were authorized in Presidential Authorizations, and the details of these activities changed over time. The program was reauthorized by the president approximately every 45 days, with certain modifications. Collectively, the activities carried out under these

Authorizations are referred to as the "President's Surveillance Program" or "PSP." One of the activities authorized as part of the PSP was the interception of the content of communications into and out of the United States where there was a reasonable basis to conclude that one party to the communication was a member of Al-Qa'ida or related terrorist organizations. This aspect of the PSP was publicly acknowledged and described by the president, the Attorney General, and other administration officials beginning in December 2005 following a series of articles published in the *New York Times.* The Attorney General subsequently publicly acknowledged the fact that other intelligence activities were also authorized under the same Presidential Authorization, but the details of those activities remain classified (1).[55] *See* WARRANTLESS SURVEILLANCE

PREVENTION 1. The term "prevention" refers to those capabilities necessary to avoid, prevent, or stop a threatened or actual act of terrorism. Prevention capabilities include, but are not limited to, information sharing and warning; domestic counterterrorism; and preventing the acquisition or use of weapons of mass destruction (WMD). For purposes of the prevention framework called for in this directive, the term "prevention" refers to preventing imminent threats.[56] 2. Actions to avoid an incident or to intervene to stop an incident from occurring. Prevention involves actions to protect lives and property that may include such countermeasures as: deterrence operations; heightened inspections; improved surveillance and security operations; investigations to determine the full nature and source of the threat; public health and agricultural surveillance and testing processes; immunizations, isolation, or quarantine; and, as appropriate, specific law enforcement operations aimed at deterring, preempting, interdicting, or disrupting illegal activity and apprehending potential perpetrators and bringing them to justice.[57] 3. In humanitarian situations, activities to provide outright avoidance of the adverse impact of hazards and means to minimize related environmental, technological, and biological disasters.[58]

PREVENTIVE ATTACK An attack initiated to seize the initiative when an armed confrontation is not imminent but is believed likely to occur at a later date. *See* PREEMPTIVE ATTACK

PREVENTIVE DIPLOMACY Diplomatic actions taken in advance of a predictable crisis to prevent or limit violence before it occurs. A nation may act with political and economic tools, in concert with others, to head off conflict before it reaches the threshold of mass violence or military intervention. "The UN mission in Macedonia has been used as a part of a strategy of preventive diplomacy, and it is perhaps best known within a range of different preventive efforts undertaken within a longer period."[59]

PREVENTIVE INTELLIGENCE Intelligence that can be used to interdict or forestall a crime or terrorist attack.[60]

PRIDE OF PREVIOUS POSITION Refers to when an analyst has already expressed a viewpoint and is extremely reluctant to change it for fear of admitting error.[61] *See* CLIENTITIS; DOUBLE BLIND

PRIMARY MISSION ESSENTIAL FUNCTIONS (PMEFS) PMEFs "means those Government Functions that must be performed in order to support or implement the performance of NEFs before, during, and in the aftermath of an emergency."[62]

PRINCIPAL CONCLUSIONS Those conclusions of a report or estimate that are emphasized to elicit a specific action, or that point to a clear understanding of a potential threat or action based on basic intelligence. If done poorly or with bias, they can have a disastrous effect. Prior to the Korean War in 1950, estimates by General MacArthur's G-2, Major General Charles Willoughby, were purposely slanted. "MacArthur did not want the Chinese to enter the war in Korea. Anything MacArthur wanted, Willoughby produced intelligence for. . . . In this case, Willoughby falsified the intelligence reports" (377).[63] *See* ASSESSMENT; KEY JUDGMENTS; KEY QUESTIONS

PRINCIPLE A comprehensive and fundamental rule or an assumption of central importance that guides how an organization or function approaches and thinks about the conduct of operations.[64]

PRINCIPLE SCALE In cartography, the scale of a reduced or generating globe representing the sphere or spheroid, defined by the fractional relation of their respective radii. *See* PHOTOGRAPHIC SCALE; SCALE

PRIORITY INTELLIGENCE REQUIREMENTS Those intelligence requirements for which a commander has an anticipated and stated priority in his or her task of planning and decision making. *See* INTELLIGENCE CYCLE

PRISM The PRISM program allows the NSA, the world's largest surveillance organization, to obtain targeted communications without having to request them from the service providers and without having to obtain individual court orders. With this program, the NSA is able to reach directly into the servers of the participating companies and obtain both stored communications as well as perform real-time collection on targeted users. The presentation claims PRISM was introduced to overcome what the NSA regarded as shortcomings of FISA warrants in tracking suspected foreign terrorists. It noted that the United States has a "home-field advantage" due to housing much of the internet's architecture. But the presentation claimed "FISA constraints restricted our home-field advantage" because FISA required individual warrants and confirmations that both the sender and receiver of a communication were outside the United States.[65] *See* FOREIGN INTELLIGENCE SURVEILLANCE ACT; TERRORIST SURVEILLANCE PROGRAM; WARRANTLESS SURVEILLANCE

PRIVACY (INFORMATION) The assurance that legal and constitutional restrictions on the collection, maintenance, use, and disclosure of personally identifiable information will be adhered to by criminal justice agencies, with use of such information to be strictly limited to circumstances in which legal process permits use of the personally identifiable information.[66] *See* PERSONALLY IDENTIFIABLE INFORMATION

PRIVACY (PERSONAL) 1. The assurance that legal and constitutional restrictions on the collection, maintenance, use, and disclosure of behaviors of an individual—including his/her communications, associations, and transactions—will be adhered to by criminal justice agencies, with use of such information to be strictly limited to circumstances in which legal process authorizes surveillance and investigation.[67] 2. The assurance that the confidentiality of, and access to, certain information about an entity is protected. Extended Definition: The ability of individuals to understand and exercise control over how information about themselves may be used by others.[68]

PRIVACY ACT The Privacy Act of 1974, 5 U.S.C. 552a, establishes a code of fair information practices that governs the collection, maintenance, use, and dissemination of personally identifiable information about individuals that is maintained in systems of records by federal agencies. A system of records is a group of records under the control of an agency from which information is retrieved by an individual's name or by some other identifier assigned to the individual. The Privacy Act requires that agencies provide public notice of their systems of records through publication in the *Federal Register*. The Privacy Act prohibits the disclosure of information from a system of records absent the written consent of the individual who is the subject of the information search, unless the disclosure is pursuant to one of 12 statutory exceptions. The Privacy Act also provides individuals with a means by which to seek access to and amend their records and sets forth various agency record-keeping requirements.[69]

PRIVACY AND CIVIL LIBERTIES OVERSIGHT BOARD In its 2004 report, the National Commission on Terrorist Attacks Upon the United States (known as the 9/11 Commission) recommended the creation of what is now the Privacy and Civil Liberties Oversight Board. The 9/11 Commission recognized concerns about "the shifting balance of power to the government" after the September 11 attacks, but found that "there is no office within the government whose job it is to look across the government at the actions we are taking to protect ourselves to ensure that liberty concerns are appropriately considered." To fill that gap, the Commission recommended establishing a board within the executive branch to oversee the government's adherence to the protection of civil liberties in its efforts to prevent terrorism. The Board today is in its third iteration. In response to the recommendation of the 9/11 Commission, President George W. Bush created the President's Board on Safeguarding Americans' Civil Liberties in 2004. The President's Board ceased to meet following the enactment later that year of the Intelligence Reform and Terrorism Prevention Act of 2004 (IRTPA), which created a Privacy and Civil Liberties Oversight Board within the Executive Office of the President. In 2007, the Implementing Recommendations of the 9/11 Commission Act reconstituted the Board in its current form, as an independent agency within the executive branch. The Board is comprised of four part-time members and a full-time chairman, each of whom is appointed by the president, with the advice and consent of the Senate, for staggered six-year terms.[70]

PRIVACY IMPACT ASSESSMENT (PIA) An analysis of how information is handled: (1) to ensure compliance with applicable legal, regulatory, and policy requirements regarding privacy; (2) to determine the risks and effects of collecting, maintaining and disseminating information in identifiable form; and (3) to examine and evaluate protections and alternative processes for handling information to mitigate potential privacy risks.[71]

PRIVATE INFORMATION 1. Data, facts, instructions, or other material intended for or restricted to a particular person, group, or organization.[72] 2. Any information relating to a person in relation to which that person has or may have a reasonable expectation of privacy. This includes information relating to a person's private, family or professional affairs. Private information includes information about any person, not just the subject(s) of an investigation.[73]

PRIVILEGED ACCESS Explicitly authorized access of a specific user, process, or computer to a computer resource.[74]

PRIVILEGED BELLIGERENT The term "privileged belligerent" means an individual belonging to one of the eight categories enumerated in Article 4 of the Geneva Convention Relative to the Treatment of Prisoners of War.[75]

PROACTIVE DISCLOSURES Proactive disclosures are records made publicly available by agencies without specific requests from the public. These disclosures are an integral part of the Freedom of Information Act. All federal agencies are required to affirmatively and continuously disclose records described by subsection (a)(2) of the FOIA, which applies to four categories of agency records that must routinely be made "available for public inspection and copying": (1) "final opinions [and] . . . orders" rendered in the adjudication of administrative cases; (2) specific agency policy statements; (3) certain administrative staff manuals; and (4) since March 31, 1997, records disclosed in response to a FOIA request that "the agency determines have become or are likely to become the subject of subsequent requests for substantially the same records."[76]

PROBABILISTIC RISK ASSESSMENT (PRA) Type of quantitative risk assessment that considers possible combinations of occurrences with associated consequences, each with an associated probability or probability distribution. (1) Probabilistic risk assessments are typically performed on complex technological systems with tools such as fault and event trees and Monte Carlo simulations to evaluate security risks and/or accidental failures. (2) For some types of risk, like those involving human volition, the probability of occurrence of an event may not be independent of the consequences and, in fact, may be a function of the consequences.[77]

PROBABILISTIC VETTING Data matching based on certain criteria, characteristics, or thresholds.[78]

PROBABILITY Numerical value between zero and one assigned to a random event (which is a subset of the sample space) in such a way that the assigned number obeys three axioms: (1) the probability of the random event "A" must be equal to, or lie between, zero and one; (2) the probability that the outcome is within the sample space must equal one; and (3) the probability that the random event "A" or "B" occurs must equal the probability of the random event "A" plus the probability of the random event "B" for any two mutually exclusive events.[79]

PROBABILITY OF DAMAGE The probability that damage will occur to a target, expressed as a percentage or as a decimal.

PROBABLE, LIKELY TO OCCUR OR PROVE TRUE; SUPPORTED GENERALLY BUT NOT Commonly confused with "possibility." According to a U.S. national warning estimate of 1966, "Intelligence is not likely to give warning of probable Soviet intent to attack until a few hours before the attack, if at all. Warning of increased Soviet readiness, implying a possible intent to attack, might be given somewhat earlier."[80] *See* POSSIBLE

PROBLEM PROFILE Identifies established and emerging crimes or incidents for the purpose of preventing or deterring further crime.

PROCESSING Development of collected raw information of possible intelligence value to make it useable for analysis and into a finished intelligence product. *See* FINISHED INTELLIGENCE; RAW INTELLIGENCE

PROCESSING AND EXPLOITATION In intelligence usage, the conversion of collected information into forms suitable to the production of intelligence.

PRODUCT The finished intelligence, which is disseminated to those who need it for decision making. *See* FINISHED INTELLIGENCE

PROFESSIONAL TRADECRAFT Competencies required for employees in one or more occupations within a particular mission category (e.g., Collection Management and Operations).[81]

PROFIENCY SCALE The labels used to describe competency proficiency levels ranging from basic/developmental to expert. The IC's proficiency scale has four levels.[82]

PROGRAM An endeavor consisting of several projects focused on creating a unique result meeting a specified objective; normally does not have a specified or designated end-state as seen with a project.

PROGRAM MANAGEMENT The overseeing of the planning, coordination, and integration of multiple projects as part of an overall construct to meet a specified objective according to established deadlines and budget achieving a desired result.

PROJECT A temporary endeavor undertaken to create a unique product, service, or result; has a definite beginning and a definite end.

PROJECT BIOSHIELD President Bush proposed Project BioShield in his 2003 State of the Union address. The 108th Congress considered this proposal and passed the Project BioShield Act of 2004 (P.L. 108-276, signed into law July 21, 2004). The Pandemic and All-Hazards Preparedness Act (PAHPA, P.L.109-417) and the Pandemic and All-Hazards Preparedness Reauthorization Act of 2013 (P.L. 113-5) modified some Project BioShield Act authorities and reauthorized appropriations through FY2018. The Project BioShield Act provides the federal government with authorities related to the development, acquisition, and use of medical countermeasures against CBRN attacks. Project BioShield creates a government-market guarantee by permitting the HHS Secretary to obligate funds to purchase countermeasures while they still need up to 10 more years of development. Another provision of the act establishes a process through which the HHS Secretary may temporarily allow the emergency use of countermeasures that lack Food and Drug Administration (FDA) approval (1–2). Project BioShield is only one piece of the federal efforts to develop and acquire medical countermeasures to protect against CBRN attacks. Homeland Security Presidential Directive 18 (HSPD-18), Medical Countermeasures Against Weapons of Mass Destruction, and Homeland Security Presidential Directive 21 (HSPD-21), Public Health and Medical Preparedness, provide the overall policy framework and strategy for federal efforts to develop and acquire CBRN countermeasures.[83] *See* HIGH-CONTAINMENT LABORATORIES

PROJECT MANAGEMENT The application of knowledge, skills, tools, and techniques to project activities to meet project requirements; accomplished through the application and integration of the project management processes consisting of initiating, planning, executing, monitoring, controlling, and closing.

PROJECT MANAGEMENT INSTITUTE (PMI) SPECIALTY A specialized position within a particular mission category or occupation, such as collection, analysis, finance. Specialties require specific expertise, skills sets, competencies, in addition to whatever may be required of the broader occupational group to which they belong.

PROLIFERATION SECURITY INITIATIVE (PSI) Proliferation Security Initiative is a response to the growing challenge posed by the proliferation of WMD, their delivery systems, and related materials worldwide. The

PSI builds on efforts by the international community to prevent proliferation of such items, including existing treaties and regimes. The PSI seeks to involve in some capacity all states that have a stake in non-proliferation and the ability and willingness to take steps to stop the flow of such items at sea, in the air, or on land. The PSI also seeks cooperation from any state whose ships, flags, ports, territorial waters, airspace, or land might be used for proliferation purposes by states and non-state actors of proliferation concern.[84]

PROMINENT INDIVIDUAL Someone who is widely known and has a favorable public reputation. The operational use of such individuals, if discovered, might have an adverse effect on U.S. foreign policy, DoD activities, or military operations, or might embarrass the United States, its allies, or the Department of Defense.[85]

PROOF The justification for an argument through the process of logical analysis. It involves analyzing the relationship between given facts (evidence) and a theory (hypothesis) with the claim that it explains these facts in terms of the observational data and context. Problems arise when the analyst has to reason from the known to the unknown or from probable, possible, hypothesized, or stipulated factual (evidence) to further inferred facts.[86] *See* EVIDENCE

PROPAGANDA Information, especially of a biased or misleading nature, used to promote a political cause or point of view.[87]

PROPRIETARIES A term used by CIA to designate ostensibly private commercial entities capable of doing business which are established and controlled by intelligence services to conceal governmental affiliation of intelligence personnel and/or governmental sponsorship of certain activities in support of clandestine operations.[88]

PROTECT AND SECURE The terms "protect" and "secure" mean reducing the vulnerability of critical infrastructure or key resources in order to deter, mitigate, or neutralize terrorist attacks.[89]

PROTECTED CRITICAL INFRASTRUCTURE INFORMATION (PCII) Protected Critical Infrastructure Information (PCII) is information voluntarily shared by critical infrastructure owners and operators with the government to analyze data, secure critical infrastructure, identify vulnerabilities, develop risk assessments, and enhance recovery preparedness measures. Under the Critical Infrastructure Information Act of 2002, all PCII is protected from disclosure from the Freedom of Information Act (FOIA); state, tribal, and local disclosure laws; use in regulatory actions; and use in civil litigation so that sensitive or proprietary data is not exposed. PCII is made available only to those federal, state, tribal, and local government employees and their contractors who: 1. are trained in the proper handling and safeguarding of PCII; 2. have homeland security responsibilities as specified in the Critical Infrastructure Information Act of 2002, the Final Rule, and the policies and procedures issued by the PCII Program; 3. have a need to know the specific information; and 4. sign a Non-Disclosure Agreement (non-federal employees).[90] *See* CRITICAL INFRASTRUCTURE INFORMATION

PROTECTED DISCLOSURE (a) A disclosure of information by the employee to a supervisor in the employee's direct chain of command up to and including the head of the employing agency, to the Inspector General of the employing agency or Intelligence Community Element, to the Director of National Intelligence, to the Inspector General of the Intelligence Community, or to an employee designated by any of the above officials for the purpose of receiving such disclosures, that the employee reasonably believes evidences (i) a violation of any law, rule, or regulation; or (ii) gross mismanagement, a gross waste of funds, an abuse of authority, or a substantial and specific danger to public health or safety; (b) any communication described by and that complies with subsection (a) (1), (d), or (h) of section BH of the Inspector General Act of 1978 (5 U.S.C. App.); subsection (d) (5) (A) of section 17 of the Central Intelligence Agency Act of 1949 (50 U.S.C. 403q); or subsection (k) (5) (A), (D), or (G), of section 103H of the National Security Act of 1947 (50 U.S.C. 403–3h); (c) the exercise of any appeal, complaint, or grievance with regard to the violation of Section A or B of this directive; (d) lawfully participating in an investigation or proceeding regarding a violation of Section A or B of this directive; or (e) cooperating with or disclosing information to an Inspector General, in accordance with applicable provisions of law in connection with an audit, inspection, or investigation conducted by the Inspector General.[91]

PROTECTED INFORMATION Includes sensitive, critical, and/or classified information.[92]

PROTECTION The term "protection" refers to those capabilities necessary to secure the homeland against acts of terrorism and manmade or natural disasters. Protection capabilities include, but are not limited to, defense against WMD threats; defense of agriculture and food; critical infrastructure protection; protection of key leadership and events; border security; maritime security; transportation security; immigration security; and cybersecurity.[93]

PROTECTION AGAINST INADVERTENT RELEASE OF RE-STRICTED DATA AND FORMERLY RESTRICTED DATA 1. Public Law 105-261, Section 3161 (*Strom Thurmond National Defense Authorization Act for Fiscal Year 1999*), Protection Against Inadvertent Release of Restricted Data and Formerly Restricted Data—Requires every government agency implementing the automatic declassification provisions of section 3.3 of Executive Order 12958 to follow procedures (i.e., a plan) to prevent the inadvertent release of records containing RD or FRD. 2. In a major setback to the successful declassification programs of recent years, Congress has adopted the following amendment to the 1999 Defense Authorization Act. It will have the effect of terminating all automatic declassification activity for at least several months, while a "plan to prevent the inadvertent release of records containing Restricted Data" is developed. This amendment was further amended in Section 1068 of the FY2000 Defense Authorization Act to require further review of previously declassified documents, yielding what became known as the "Kyl-Lott Amendment."[94]

PROTECTION FOR INTELLIGENCE *See* CLASSIFICATION LEVELS; CLASSIFICATION MARKINGS

PROTECTIVE MEASURES Those actions, procedures, or designs implemented to safeguard protected information.[95]

PROTOCOL (OF INTELLIGENCE COLLECTION) Information collection procedures employed to obtain verbal and written information, actions of people, and physical evidence required for strategic and tactical intelligence analysis.[96]

PROXY SERVER A server that acts as an intermediary between a workstation user and the Internet to facilitate security, administrative control, and caching services. A proxy server works as a gateway that separates a network from an outside network and as a firewall that protects the network from an outside intrusion.[97]

PSYCHOGRAPHICS Psychological characteristics of a target audience. These are internal psychological factors—attitudes, values, lifestyles, motivations, and opinions.[98]

PSYCHOLOGICAL CONSEQUENCE Effect of an incident, event, or occurrence on the mental or emotional state of individuals or groups resulting in a change in perception and/or behavior. In the context of homeland security, psychological consequences are negative and refer to the impact of an incident, event, or occurrence on the behavior or emotional and mental state of an affected population.[99]

PSYCHOLOGICAL CONSOLIDATION ACTIVITIES Planned psychological activities in peace and war directed at the civilian population located in areas under friendly control in order to achieve a desired behavior that supports the military objectives and the operational freedom of the supported commanders.

PSYCHOLOGICAL MEDIA The media, technical or nontechnical, which establish any kind of communication with a target audience.[100]

PSYCHOLOGICAL OPERATIONS (PSYOP) *See* MILITARY INFORMATION SUPPORT OPERATIONS

PSYCHOLOGICAL OPERATIONS APPROACH The technique adopted to induce a desired reaction on the part of the target audience.

PSYCHOLOGICAL OPERATIONS PROGRAM A Psychological Operations program that supports U.S. national policy and objectives and is approved by the Secretary of Defense through the interagency process. Approved Psychological Operations programs provide the framework for the execution of PSYOP in support of the range of military operations. Psychological Operations programs include PSYOP objectives, themes to stress, themes to avoid, potential target audiences, attribution posture, means of dissemination, a concept of operations, and funding sources. Also called PSYOP program.[101]

PSYCHOLOGICAL SITUATION The current emotional state, mental disposition, or other behavioral motivation of a target audience, basically founded on its national political, social, economic, and psychological peculiarities but also subject to the influence of circumstances and events.[102]

PSYCHOLOGICAL THEME An idea or topic on which a psychological operation is based.[103]

PUBLIC AFFAIRS GUIDANCE (PAG) Constraints and restraints established by proper authority regarding public communication activities.[104]

PUBLIC DIPLOMACY 1. Those overt international public information activities of the U.S. government designed to promote U.S. foreign policy objectives by seeking to understand, inform, and influence foreign audiences and opinion makers, and by broadening the dialogue between American citizens and institutions and their counterparts abroad. 2. In peace building, civilian agency efforts to promote an understanding of the reconstruction efforts, rule of law, and civic responsibility through public affairs and international public diplomacy operations.[105]

PUBLIC INFORMATION 1. Within public affairs, that information of a military nature, the dissemination of which is consistent with security and approved for release.[106] 2. Information that is released or published for the primary purpose of keeping the public fully informed, thereby gaining their understanding and support.

PUBLIC INTELLIGENCE Public intelligence is not a new phenomenon, but it is one that has risen in prominence due to several reinforcing changes in the complexion of American politics. By public intelligence we refer to secret intelligence that has become part of the societal debate over the conduct of American foreign policy (420).[107]

PUBLIC INTEREST DECLASSIFICATION BOARD The Public Interest Declassification Board (PIDB) is an advisory committee established by Congress in 2000, in order to promote the fullest possible public access to a thorough, accurate, and reliable documentary record of significant U.S. national security decisions and activities. The PIDB: 1. Advises and provides recommendations to the president and other executive branch officials on the systematic, thorough, coordinated, and comprehensive identification, collection, review for declassification, and release of declassified records and materials of archival value, including records and materials of extraordinary public interest. 2. Promotes the fullest possible public access to a thorough, accurate, and reliable documentary record of significant U.S. national security decisions and activities in order to: support the oversight and legislative functions of Congress; support the policymaking role of the executive branch; respond to the public interest on national security matters; and promote reliable historical analysis and new avenues of historical study in national security matters. 3. Advises the president and other executive branch officials on policies deriving from Executive Orders regarding the classification and declassification of national security information. 4. Reviews and makes recommendations to the president with respect to any congressional request, made by the committee of jurisdiction, to declassify certain records or to reconsider a rejection to declassify specific records.[108]

PUBLIC TRUST POSITIONS Positions designated at either the high, moderate, or low risk level as determined by the position's potential for adverse impact to the integrity and efficiency of the Service (see 5 CFR 731.106). Positions at the high or moderate risk levels are referred to as "public trust" positions and, generally, involve: policymaking, major program responsibility, public safety and health, law enforcement duties, fiduciary responsibilities, or other duties/responsibilities demanding a significant degree of public trust. "Public trust" positions also involve access to, operation of, or control of proprietary systems of information (e.g., financial or personal records), with a significant risk for causing damage to people, programs or an agency, or for realizing personal gain. The "low risk" positions are, generally, referred to as "non-sensitive" positions.[109]

PUBLICATIONS REVIEW BOARD In order to help avoid the damage to national security and to the Agency's mission that disclosing classified information would inflict, the CIA created the Publications Review Board (PRB) to preview materials produced by CIA personnel—former and current (both employees and contractors)—to determine if they contain such classified information before they are shared with publishers, blog subscribers, a TV audience, ghost-writers, co-authors, editors, family members, assistants, representatives, or anyone else not authorized to receive or review such classified information.[110]

PURGING The removal of data from an Information System (IS), its storage devices, or other peripheral devices with storage capacity in such a way that the data may not be reconstructed.[111]

NOTES

1. Arms Control Association. *History of Official Proposals on the Iranian Nuclear Issue*, January 2014, accessed February 2, 2016, http://www.armscontrol.org/fact-sheets/Iran_Nuclear_Proposals.

2. Adams, Sam. *War of Numbers: An Intelligence Memoir* (South Royalton, VT: Steerforth Press, 1994).

3. Camerer, Colin F. and Johnson, Eric J. "The Process-Performance Paradox in Expert Judgment: How Can Experts Know So Much and Predict So Badly?" In K. Anders Ericsson and Jacqui Smith (Eds.), *Toward a General Theory of Expertise: Prospects and Limited* (Cambridge: Cambridge University Press, 1991), 195–217.

4. Department of Homeland Security, U.S. Customs and Border Protection. *U.S. Customs and Border Protection: Passenger Name Record (PNR) Privacy Policy.* June 21, 2013. Accessed February 5, 2015. http://www.cbp.gov/sites/default/files/documents/pnr_privacy.pdf.

5. U.S. House of Representatives. *Testimony, General Richard B. Myers, Chair, Joint Chiefs of Staff.* Committee on Armed Services, September 18, 2002. 107–2, Washington: Government Printing Office.

6. Handel, Michael I. "Intelligence and Deception." *The Journal of Strategic Studies* 5, no. 1 (1982): 122–54.

7. Committee for National Security Systems (CNSS). Instruction 4009. *National Information Assurance Glossary.* April 2010. Accessed February 15, 2015. http://www.ncix.gov/publications/policy/docs/CNSSI_4009.pdf.

8. U.S. Department of Defense, *Peace Operations*, JP 3-07.3, August 1, 2012, accessed February 1, 2016, https://fas.org/irp/doddir/dod/jp3-07-3.pdf.

9. U.S. Department of Defense, *Peace Operations*, JP 3-07.3, August 1, 2012, accessed February 1, 2016, https://fas.org/irp/doddir/dod/jp3-07-3.pdf.

10. 18 U.S. Code § 3127—"Definitions for Chapter" (Current through Pub. L. 113-234). Accessed February 5, 2015. http://www.law.cornell.edu/uscode/text/18/3127.

11. Defense Intelligence Agency. *Defense Intelligence Report: Lexicon of Hardened Structure Definitions and Terms.* Washington, DC: 2000.

12. Office of the Director of National Intelligence. *Competency Directories for the Intelligence Community Workforce.* Intelligence Community Directive 610, October 4, 2010. Accessed March 2, 2015. http://www.dni.gov/files/documents/ICD/ICD_610.pdf.

13. U.S. Department of Defense. Center for Development of Security Excellence. *Glossary of Security Terms and Definitions.* November 2012. Accessed February 16, 2015. http://www.cdse.edu/documents/cdse/Glossary_Handbook.pdf.

14. U.S. Department of Defense. Center for Development of Security Excellence. *Glossary of Security Terms and Definitions.* November 2012. Accessed February 16, 2015. http://www.cdse.edu/documents/cdse/Glossary_Handbook.pdf.

15. U.S. Department of Defense. Center for Development of Security Excellence. *Glossary of Security Terms and Definitions.* November 2012. Accessed February 15, 2015. http://www.cdse.edu/documents/cdse/Glossary_Handbook.pdf.

16. Defense Personnel and Security Research Center (PERSEREC). *History.* Accessed February 5, 2015. http://www.dhra.mil/perserec/vision.html.

17. Pendall, David W. "Persistent Surveillance and Its Implications for the Common Operating Picture." *Military Review* 85, no. 6 (2005): 41.

18. U.S. Department of State. *Diplomatic Dictionary.* Accessed March 6, 2015. http://diplomacy.state.gov/discoverdiplomacy/references/169792.htm.

19. National Initiative for Cybersecurity Education. *A Glossary of Common Cybersecurity Terminology.* n.d. Accessed March 5, 2015. http://niccs.us-cert.gov/glossary.

20. 11 U.S. Code § 101—"Definitions" (Current through Pub. L. 113-234). Accessed February 5, 2015. http://www.law.cornell.edu/uscode/text/11/101.

21. U.S. Department of Defense. Center for Development of Security Excellence. *Glossary of Security Terms and Definitions.* November 2012. Accessed February 15, 2015. http://www.cdse.edu/documents/cdse/Glossary_Handbook.pdf.

22. U.S. Department of Defense. Center for Development of Security Excellence. *Glossary of Security Terms and Definitions.* November 2012. Accessed February 15, 2015. http://www.cdse.edu/documents/cdse/Glossary_Handbook.pdf.

23. U.S. Department of Defense. Center for Development of Security Excellence. *Glossary of Security Terms and Definitions.* November 2012. Accessed February 15, 2015. http://www.cdse.edu/documents/cdse/Glossary_Handbook.pdf.

24. U.S. Department of Defense. Center for Development of Security Excellence. *Glossary of Security Terms and Definitions.* November 2012. Accessed February 15, 2015. http://www.cdse.edu/documents/cdse/Glossary_Handbook.pdf.

25. Undersecretary of Defense. 2015. *Directive-type Memorandum (DTM) 14-005—DoD Identity Management Capability Enterprise Services Application (IMESA) Access to FBI National Crime Information Center (NCIC) Files.* May 13. Accessed June 6, 2015. http://www.dtic.mil/whs/directives/corres/pdf/DTM14005_2014.pdf.

26. Defense Intelligence Agency. *Defense Intelligence Report: Lexicon of Hardened Structure Definitions and Terms.* Washington, DC: 2000.

27. Undersecretary of Defense. 2015. *Directive-type Memorandum (DTM) 14-005—DoD Identity Management Capability Enterprise Services Application (IMESA) Access to FBI National Crime Information Center (NCIC) Files.* May 13. Accessed June 6, 2015. http://www.dtic.mil/whs/directives/corres/pdf/DTM14005_2014.pdf.

28. Undersecretary of Defense. 2015. *Directive-type Memorandum (DTM) 14-005—DoD Identity Management Capability Enterprise Services Application (IMESA) Access to FBI National Crime Information Center (NCIC) Files.* May 13. Accessed June 6, 2015. http://www.dtic.mil/whs/directives/corres/pdf/DTM14005_2014.pdf.

29. Plain Writing Act of 2010, P.L.111-274, October 13, 2010, https://www.gpo.gov/fdsys/pkg/PLAW-111publ274/pdf/PLAW-111publ274.pdf; also see http://www.plainlanguage.gov/plLaw/.

30. Sunstein, Cass R. *Final Guidance on Implementing the Plain Writing Act of 2010,* Office of Management and Budget, M-11-15, April 13, 2011. https://www.whitehouse.gov/sites/default/files/omb/memoranda/2011/m11-15.pdf.

31. Defense Intelligence Agency, Office of Counterintelligence. *CI Glossary—Terms & Definitions of Interest for DoD CI Professionals.* July 2014. Accessed January 17, 2015. https://www.hsdl.org/?view&did=699056.

32. United States Senate, Select Committee to Study Governmental Operations with Respect to Intelligence Activities (Church Committee). *Final Report.* Book 1. April 26, 1976. Accessed January 31, 2015. https://archive.org/details/finalreportof-sel01unit.

33. U.S. Department of State. "Political, Economic, and Intelligence Functional Bureaus." *Foreign Affairs Manual.* 1 FAM 400. July 31, 2013. Accessed February 16, 2015. http://www.state.gov/documents/organization/84192.pdf.

34. Federal Bureau of Investigation. *Minimum Criminal Intelligence Training Standards for Law Enforcement and Other Criminal Justice Agencies in the United States.* October 2007. Accessed February 6, 2015. https://it.ojp.gov/gist/108/Minimum-Criminal-Intelligence-Training-Standards.

35. Federal Bureau of Investigation. *Minimum Criminal Intelligence Training Standards for Law Enforcement and Other Criminal Justice Agencies in the United States.* October 2007. Accessed February 6, 2015. https://it.ojp.gov/gist/108/Minimum-Criminal-Intelligence-Training-Standards.

36. Davis, Jack. "The Challenge of Managing Uncertainty: Paul Wolfowitz on Intelligence Policy-Relations." *Studies in Intelligence* 39, no. 5 (1996). Accessed June 9, 2015. https://www.cia.gov/library/center-for-the-study-of-intelligence/csi-publications/csi-studies/studies/96unclass/davis.htm.

37. United States Senate, Select Committee to Study Governmental Operations with Respect to Intelligence Activities (Church Committee). *Final Report.* Book 1. April 26, 1976. Accessed January 11, 2015. https://archive.org/details/finalreportof-sel01unit.

38. Jan Goldman, *Intelligence Warning Terminology*, Joint Military Intelligence College, October 2001, accessed July 3, 2015. https://archive.org/details/JMICInteli-gencelwarnterminology.

39. Dreyfuss, Robert. "The Cops Are Watching You." *The Nation*, June 3, 2002.

40. U.S. Department of Defense. Joint Operational Access Concept (JOAC). January 17, 2012. Version 1.0. Accessed February 19, 2015. http://www.defense.gov/pubs/pdfs/JOAC_Jan%202012_Signed.pdf.

41. Baughman, Ronald. "The United States Air Force Perspective." *Rusi Journal* 145: 75–76.

42. North Atlantic Treaty Organization. *NATO Glossary of Terms and Definitions.* NATO Standardization Agency, 2008, Aap-06, accessed July 2, 2015. https://fas.org/irp/doddir/other/nato2008.pdf.

43. U.S. Department of Defense. Center for Development of Security Excellence. *Glossary of Security Terms and Definitions.* November 2012. Accessed February 15, 2015. http://www.cdse.edu/documents/cdse/Glossary_Handbook.pdf.

44. NSDD 84. *Safeguarding National Security Information.* March 11, 1983. Accessed June 9, 2015. https://www.fas.org/irp/offdocs/nsdd/nsdd-84.pdf.

45. Office of the Director of National Intelligence. *Pre-publication Review.* Accessed February 6, 2015. http://www.dni.gov/index.php/about/organization/chief-information-officer/prepublication-review; also see Office of the Director of National Intelligence. *Instruction 80.04. ODNI Pre-Publication Review of Information to be Publicly Released.* April 8, 2014. Accessed February 8, 2015. http://www.dni.gov/files/documents/CIO/Instr.%2080.04%20%20Pre-Publication%20Review%20of%20Information%20to%20be%20Publicly%20Relea.pdf.

46. PDD/NSC 56. *Managing Complex Contingency Operations.* May 1997. Accessed June 9, 2015. http://fas.org/irp/offdocs/pdd56.htm.

47. Relyea, Harold C. "Presidential Directives:Background and Overview." *CRS Report for Congress*, November 26, 2008. 8–9. Accessed February 8, 2015. http://fas.org/sgp/crs/misc/98-611.pdf and Intelligence Resource Program, Federation of American Scientists, *Presidential Directives and Executive Orders*, accessed February 8, 2015. http://fas.org/irp/offdocs/direct.htm.

48. U.S. Department of Defense. Center for Development of Security Excellence. *Glossary of Security Terms and Definitions.* November 2012. Accessed February 15, 2015. http://www.cdse.edu/documents/cdse/Glossary_Handbook.pdf.

49. Department of Homeland Security. *NIPP 2013: Partnering for Critical Infrastructure Security and Resilience.* Accessed February 15, 2015. http://www.dhs.gov/

sites/default/files/publications/NIPP%202013_Partnering%20for%20Critical%20Infrastructure%20Security%20and%20Resilience_508_0.pdf and *Presidential Policy Directive/ PPD-8: National Preparedness*. March 30, 2011. Accessed February 15, 2011. http://www.dhs.gov/presidential-policy-directive-8-national-preparedness.

50. Ginsberg, Wendy. "The Presidential Records Act: Background and Recent Issues for Congress." *CRS Report for Congress* R40238. December 31, 2014. Accessed February 20, 2015. https://www.fas.org/sgp/crs/secrecy/R40238.pdf.

51. U.S. Department of Defense. *Joint Mobilization Planning*. JP4-05. February 21, 2014. Accessed February 27, 2015. http://www.dtic.mil/doctrine/new_pubs/jp4_05.pdf.

52. Central Intelligence Agency. *The Evolution of the President's Daily Brief. 2014.* Accessed June 9, 2015. https://www.cia.gov/news-information/featured-story-archive/2014-featured-story-archive/the-evolution-of-the-presidents-daily-brief.html.

53. President's Foreign Intelligence Advisory Board and Intelligence Oversight Board. *History.* n.d. Accessed June 9, 2015. https://www.whitehouse.gov/administration/eop/piab/history.

54. Executive Order 13462. *President's Intelligence Advisory Board and Intelligence Oversight Board.* February 29, 2008. http://www.gpo.gov/fdsys/pkg/FR-2008-03-04/pdf/08-970.pdf and *President's Intelligence Advisory Board and Intelligence Oversight Board.* Accessed February 11, 2015. http://www.whitehouse.gov/administration/eop/piab.

55. Offices of Inspector Generals of the Department of Defense, Department of Justice, Central Intelligence Agency, National Security Agency, Office of Director of National Intelligence. *Unclassified Report on the President's Surveillance Program, Joint Inspector General Report.* July 10, 2009. Accessed February 18, 2015. http://www.fas.org/irp/eprint/psp.pdf.

56. *Presidential Policy Directive/PPD-8: National Preparedness*. March 30, 2011. Accessed February 15, 2011. http://www.dhs.gov/presidential-policy-directive-8-national-preparedness.

57. U.S. Department of Defense. Center for Development of Security Excellence. *Glossary of Security Terms and Definitions.* November 2012. Accessed February 15, 2015. http://www.cdse.edu/documents/cdse/Glossary_Handbook.pdf.

58. United Nations International Strategy for Disaster Reduction. *Terminology.* August 2007. Accessed June 9, 2015. http://www.unisdr.org/we/inform/terminology .

59. Vankovska-Cvetkovska, Biljana. "Between Preventive Diplomacy and Conflict Resolution: The Macedonian Perspective on the Kosovo Crisis." *International Studies Association 40th Annual Convention, Washington*. 1999, 17–20.

60. Federal Bureau of Investigation. *Minimum Criminal Intelligence Training Standards for Law Enforcement and Other Criminal Justice Agencies in the United States.* October 2007. Accessed February 6, 2015. https://it.ojp.gov/gist/108/Minimum-Criminal-Intelligence-Training-Standards.

61. Jan Goldman, *Intelligence Warning Terminology*, Joint Military Intelligence, October 2001, accessed July 3, 2015. https://archive.org/details/JMICInteligencel-warnterminology.

62. National Security and Homeland Security Presidential Directive/NSPD-51/HSPD 20. *National Continuity Policy.* May 9, 2007. Accessed February 27, 2015. http://fas.org/irp/offdocs/nspd/nspd-51.htm. Also see *Presidential Policy Directive/PPD-21. Critical Infrastructure Security and Resilience.* February 12, 2013. Accessed January 22, 2015. http://www.whitehouse.gov/the-press-office/2013/02/12/presidential-policy-directive-critical-infrastructure-security-and-resil.

63. Blair, Clay. *The Forgotten War: America in Korea, 1950–1953* (New York: Times Books, 1987).

64. Department of the Army. *Doctrine Primer.* September 9, 2014. ADP 1-01 http://armypubs.army.mil/doctrine/DR_pubs/dr_a/pdf/adp1_01.pdf.

65. Greenwald, Glenn and MacAskill, Ewen. "NSA Prism Program Taps in to User Data of Apple, Google and Others." *The Guardian*, June 7, 2013. Accessed February 18, 2015. http://www.theguardian.com/world/2013/jun/06/us-tech-giants-nsa-data. Also see *The Guardian.* "NSA Files Decoded." November 1, 2013. Accessed February 18, 2015. http://www.theguardian.com/world/interactive/2013/nov/01/snowden-nsa-files-surveillance-revelations-decoded#section/1; Gellman, Barton and Poitras, Laura. "U.S., British Intelligence Mining Data from Nine U.S. Internet Companies in Broad Secret Program." *The Washington Post*, June 7, 2013. Accessed February 25, 2015. http://www.washingtonpost.com/investigations/us-intelligence-mining-data-from-nine-us-internet-companies-in-broad-secret-program/2013/06/06/3a0c0da8-cebf-11e2-8845-d970ccb04497_story.html.

66. Federal Bureau of Investigation. *Minimum Criminal Intelligence Training Standards for Law Enforcement and Other Criminal Justice Agencies in the United States.* October 2007. Accessed February 6, 2015. https://it.ojp.gov/gist/108/Minimum-Criminal-Intelligence-Training-Standards.

67. Federal Bureau of Investigation. *Minimum Criminal Intelligence Training Standards for Law Enforcement and Other Criminal Justice Agencies in the United States.* October 2007. Accessed February 6, 2015. https://it.ojp.gov/gist/108/Minimum-Criminal-Intelligence-Training-Standards.

68. National Initiative for Cybersecurity Education. *A Glossary of Common Cybersecurity Terminology.* n.d. Accessed March 5, 2015. http://niccs.us-cert.gov/glossary.

69. Office of the Director of National Intelligence. *National Intelligence: A Consumer's Guide.* 2011. Accessed January 25, 2015. http://www.dni.gov/files/documents/IC_Consumers_Guide_2011.pdf.

70. Privacy and Civil Liberties Board. *About the Board.* Accessed February 7, 2015. http://www.pclob.gov/about-us.html.

71. U.S. Department of State. "The Privacy Act and Personally Identifiable Information." *Foreign Affairs Manual.* 5 FAM 460. October 1, 2014. Accessed February 14, 2015. http://www.state.gov/documents/organization/85694.pdf.

72. Department of the Army. *Open-Source Intelligence.* ATP 2-22.9, July 10, 2012. Accessed January 31, 2015. http://fas.org/irp/doddir/army/atp2-22-9.pdf.

73. Home Office. *Covert Surveillance and Property Interference: Revised Code of Practice Pursuant to Section 71 of the Regulation of Investigatory Powers Act.* The

Stationary Office, 2010. Accessed April 5, 2015. https://www.gov.uk/government/uploads/system/uploads/attachment_data/file/97960/code-of-practice-covert.pdf.

74. U.S. Department of Defense. Center for Development of Security Excellence. *Glossary of Security Terms and Definitions.* November 2012. Accessed February 16, 2015. http://www.cdse.edu/documents/cdse/Glossary_Handbook.pdf.

75. 50 U.S. Code § 1801(h) "Definitions" (Current through Pub. L. 113-234). Accessed February 30, 2015. http://www.law.cornell.edu/uscode/text/50/1801; *Convention (III) Relative to the Treatment of Prisoners of War.* Geneva, 12 August 1949. Accessed February 20, 2015. https://www.icrc.org/applic/ihl/ihl.nsf/7c4d08d9b287a42141256739003e63bb/6fef854a3517b75ac125641e004a9e68.

76. U.S. Department of Justice. *Proactive Disclosures.* July 29, 2014. Accessed February 8, 2015. http://www.justice.gov/oip/proactive-disclosures.

77. Department of Homeland Security, Risk Steering Committee. *DHS Risk Lexicon.* September 2010. Accessed February 14, 2015. http://www.dhs.gov/dhs-risk-lexicon.

78. Undersecretary of Defense. 2015. *Directive-type Memorandum (DTM) 14-005—DoD Identity Management Capability Enterprise Services Application (IMESA) Access to FBI National Crime Information Center (NCIC) Files.* May 13. Accessed June 6, 2015. http://www.dtic.mil/whs/directives/corres/pdf/DTM14005_2014.pdf.

79. Department of Homeland Security, Risk Steering Committee. *DHS Risk Lexicon.* September 2010. Accessed February 14, 2015. http://www.dhs.gov/dhs-risk-lexicon.

80. Grabo, Cynthia M. "Strategic Warning: The Problem of Timing," *Studies in Intelligence* 16, no. 2 (1972). Accessed June 9, 2015. https://www.cia.gov/library/center-for-the-study-of-intelligence/kent-csi/vol16no2/html/v16i2a07p_0001.htm.

81. Office of the Director of National Intelligence. *Competency Directories for the Intelligence Community Workforce.* Intelligence Community Directive 610, October 4, 2010. Accessed March 2, 2015. http://www.dni.gov/files/documents/ICD/ICD_610.pdf.

82. Office of the Director of National Intelligence. *Competency Directories for the Intelligence Community Workforce.* Intelligence Community Directive 610, October 4, 2010. Accessed March 2, 2015. http://www.dni.gov/files/documents/ICD/ICD_610.pdf.

83. Gottron, Frank. "The Project BioShield Act: Issues for the 113th Congress." *CRS Report for Congress.* R43607, June 18, 2014. Accessed April 1, 2015, http://fas.org/sgp/crs/terror/R43607.pdf.

84. Office of the Director of National Intelligence. *National Intelligence Program FY 2009 Congressional Budget Justification Book.* Vol. XII, February 2008. Accessed January 17, 2015. http://www.fas.org/irp/dni/cbjb-2009.pdf.

85. U.S. Department of Defense. *Defense Human Intelligence (HUMINT) and Related Intelligence Activities.* Instruction, Number S-5200.42, December 8, 2009. Accessed February 26, 2015. http://www.dod.mil/pubs/foi/homeland_defense/intelligence/10_F_0682_DoD_Instruction_S_5200_42_Defense_Human_Intell.pdf.

86. Frank J. Hughes and David A. Schum, "The Process of Intelligence Analysis." Joint Military Intelligence College, 2003.

87. North Atlantic Treaty Organization. *NATO Glossary of Terms and Definitions*. NATO Standardization Agency, 2014, AAP-06, accessed July 27, 2015, http://nso. nato.int/nso/zPublic/ap/aap6/AAP-6.pdf.

88. United States Senate, Select Committee to Study Governmental Operations with Respect to Intelligence Activities (Church Committee). *Final Report*. Book 1. April 26, 1976. Accessed January 11, 2015. https://archive.org/details/finalreportof-sel01unit.

89. Homeland Security Presidential Directive 7. *Critical Infrastructure Identification, Prioritization, and Protection*. December 17, 2003. Accessed February 11, 2015. http://www.dhs.gov/homeland-security-presidential-directive-7#1.

90. U.S. Department of Homeland Security. *PCII Protections from Disclosure*. Accessed February 7, 2015. http://www.dhs.gov/pcii-protections-disclosure#.

91. *Presidential Policy Directive/PPD-19: Protecting Whistleblowers with Access to Classified Information*. October 12, 2012. Accessed February 21, 2015. http://fas. org/irp/offdocs/ppd/ppd-19.pdf and Office of the Director of National Intelligence. *Intelligence Community Whistleblower Protection*. Intelligence Community Directive 120, March 20, 2014. Accessed February 21, 2015. http://www.dni.gov/files/documents/ICD/ICD%20120.pdf.

92. U.S. Department of Defense. Center for Development of Security Excellence. *Glossary of Security Terms and Definitions*. November 2012. Accessed February 16, 2015. http://www.cdse.edu/documents/cdse/Glossary_Handbook.pdf.

93. *Presidential Policy Directive/PPD-8: National Preparedness*. March 30, 2011. Accessed February 15, 2011. http://www.dhs.gov/presidential-policy-directive-8-national-preparedness.

94. U.S. Department of Energy. *Classification Policy, Guidance & Reports*. February 8, 2015. http://energy.gov/ehss/policy-guidance-reports/classification-policy-guidance-reports; Federation of American Scientists, Project on Government Secrecy. Accessed February 8, 2015. https://www.fas.org/sgp/congress/hr3616am. html; also see Aid, Matthew (ed.). *Declassification in Reverse: The U.S. Intelligence Community's Secret Historical Document Reclassification Program*. National Security Archive, February 21, 2006. Accessed February 8, 2015. http://www2.gwu. edu/~nsarchiv/NSAEBB/NSAEBB179/.

95. U.S. Department of Defense. Center for Development of Security Excellence. *Glossary of Security Terms and Definitions*. November 2012. Accessed February 16, 2015. http://www.cdse.edu/documents/cdse/Glossary_Handbook.pdf.

96. Federal Bureau of Investigation. *Minimum Criminal Intelligence Training Standards for Law Enforcement and Other Criminal Justice Agencies in the United States*. October 2007. Accessed February 6, 2015. https://it.ojp.gov/gist/108/Minimum-Criminal-Intelligence-Training-Standards.

97. U.S. Department of Justice, Office of Justice Programs. *Investigations Involving the Internet and Computer Networks*. January 2007. Accessed March 7, 2015. https://www.ncjrs.gov/pdffiles1/nij/210798.pdf.

98. Department of the Army. *Psychological Operations Process Tactics, Techniques, and Procedures*. FM 3-05.30, August 30, 2007. https://publicintelligence.net/ restricted-u-s-army-psyops-manual/.

99. Department of Homeland Security, Risk Steering Committee, *DHS Risk Lexicon*, September 2010, accessed November 4, 2015, http://www.dhs.gov/dhs-risk-lexicon.

100. North Atlantic Treaty Organization. *NATO Glossary of Terms and Definitions*. NATO Standardization Agency, 2014, AAP-06, accessed July 27, 2015, http://nso.nato.int/nso/zPublic/ap/aap6/AAP-6.pdf.

101. Department of the Army. *Psychological Operations Process Tactics, Techniques, and Procedures*. FM 3-05.30, August 30, 2007. https://publicintelligence.net/restricted-u-s-army-psyops-manual/.

102. North Atlantic Treaty Organization. *NATO Glossary of Terms and Definitions*. NATO Standardization Agency, 2014, AAP-06, accessed July 27, 2015, http://nso.nato.int/nso/zPublic/ap/aap6/AAP-6.pdf.

103. North Atlantic Treaty Organization. *NATO Glossary of Terms and Definitions*. NATO Standardization Agency, 2014, AAP-06, accessed July 27, 2015, http://nso.nato.int/nso/zPublic/ap/aap6/AAP-6.pdf.

104. U.S. Department of Defense. *Department of Defense Dictionary of Military and Associated Terms*. JP 1-02, 08 November 2010, as Amended through 15 January 2016. Accessed January 26, 2016, http://www.dtic.mil/doctrine/new_pubs/jp1_02.pdf.

105. U.S. Department of Defense. *Department of Defense Dictionary of Military and Associated Terms*. JP 1-02, 08 November 2010, as Amended through 15 January 2015. Accessed February 6, 2015. http://www.dtic.mil/doctrine/dod_dictionary/.

106. United States Air Force. *Public Affairs Operations*. Air Force Doctrine Document 3–6, 24 June 2005 Certified Current 20 August 2013 Incorporating Changes 1, 23 December 2010. Accessed February 14, 2015. http://static.e-publishing.af.mil/production/1/af_cv/publication/afdd3-61/afdd3-61.pdf.

107. Hastedt, Glenn. "Public Intelligence: Leaks as Policy Instruments—The Case of the Iraq War." *Intelligence and National Security* 20, no. 3 (2005): 419–39. Accessed June 9, 2015. http://dx.doi.org/10.1080/02684520500268897.

108. Public Interest Declassification Board (PIDB). *About the PIDB.* Accessed February 7, 2015. http://www.archives.gov/declassification/pidb/index.html.

109. U.S. Department of State. "Definitions of Diplomatic Security Terms," *Foreign Affairs Manual.* 12FAM090. November 12, 2014. Accessed February 27, 2015. http://www.state.gov/documents/organization/88330.pdf.

110. Central Intelligence Agency, *Keeping Secrets Safe: The Publications Review Board*, January 7, 2016, accessed February 2, 2016, https://www.cia.gov/about-cia/publications-review-board.

111. U.S. Department of Defense. Center for Development of Security Excellence. *Glossary of Security Terms and Definitions.* November 2012. Accessed February 16, 2015. http://www.cdse.edu/documents/cdse/Glossary_Handbook.pdf.

Q-LAT *See* STONEGHOST

Q-MESSAGE A classified message relating to navigational dangers, navigational aids, mined areas, and search or swept channels.

QUAD LINK *See* STONEGHOST

QUADRENNIAL DEFENSE REVIEW (QDR) 1. The Quadrennial Defense Review (QDR) is a legislatively mandated review of Department of Defense strategy and priorities. The QDR will set a long-term course for DoD as it assesses the threats and challenges that the nation faces and re-balances DoD's strategies, capabilities, and forces to address today's conflicts and tomorrow's threats.[1] 2. Quadrennial defense reviews are designed to formulate national defense strategy, and to determine the policies, approaches, and organization required to achieve that strategy, in broad support of national security strategy. *See* NATIONAL DEFENSE STRATEGY; NATIONAL MILITARY STRATEGY; NATIONAL SECURITY STRATEGY

QUADRENNIAL HOMELAND SECURITY REVIEW Section 707 of the Homeland Security Act of 2002 (P.L. 107-296), as amended by the Implementing Recommendations of the 9/11 Commission Act of 2007 (P.L. 110-53), includes the following requirement: each quadrennial homeland security review shall be a comprehensive examination of the homeland security strategy of the nation, including recommendations regarding the long term strategy and priorities of the nation for homeland security and guidance on the programs, assets, capabilities, budget, policies, and authorities of the Department.[2]

QUADRENNIAL INTELLIGENCE COMMUNITY REVIEW (QICR) The QICR does not have a statutory mandate, but Congress has shown interest in the possible creation of such a mandate. In its Report on the Intelligence Authorization Act for FY2006, the House Permanent Select Committee on Intelligence recommended that the Director of National Intelligence develop a "formalized, periodic, and structured" quadrennial intelligence review modeled on the QDR.[3]

QUALITATIVE RISK ASSESSMENT METHODOLOGY Set of methods, principles, or rules for assessing risk based on non-numerical categories or levels.[4]

QUANTITATIVE RISK ASSESSMENT METHODOLOGY A set of methods, principles, or rules for assessing risks based on the use of numbers where the meanings and proportionality of values are maintained inside and outside the context of the assessment.[5]

QUASI GOVERNMENT The quasi government, virtually by its name alone and the intentional blurring of the governmental and private sectors, is not easily defined. In general, the term is used in two ways: to refer to entities that have some legal relation or association, however tenuous, to the federal government; or to the terrain that putatively exists between the governmental and private sectors. For the most part, this report will use the term *quasi government* in the former context, referring to entities with some legal relationship to the federal government. The one common characteristic to this melange of entities in the quasi-government is that they are not agencies of the United States.[6]

QUERYING The exchange of information between analysts of different organizations with a common mission; requesting additional or amplifying information on specific collection activities.[7]

QUESTIONABLE INTELLIGENCE ACTIVITY 1. An intelligence activity, as defined in Reference (e.g., Executive Order 12333, "United States Intelligence Activities," December 4, 1981, as amended), that may be unlawful or contrary to E.O., presidential directive, or applicable DoD policy governing that activity.[8] 2. Questionable intelligence activities and significant or highly sensitive matters involving intelligence activities may have serious implications for the execution of DoD missions. It is DoD policy that senior leaders and policymakers within the government be made aware of events that may erode the public trust in the conduct of DoD intelligence operations . . . The Assistant to the Secretary of Defense for Intelligence Oversight (ATSD(IO)) is the principal staff assistant for intelligence oversight matters and shall serve as the conduit for all reporting to the IOB.[9]

NOTES

1. U.S. Department of Defense, *Quadrennial Defense Reviews*, accessed February 2, 2016, http://www.defense.gov/News/Special-Reports/QDR.

2. Dale, Catherine. *National Security Strategy: Mandates, Execution to Date, and Issues for Congress. CRS Report for Congress* R43174. August 6, 2013. Accessed February 9, 2015. http://www.fas.org/sgp/crs/natsec/R43174.pdf.

3. Dale, Catherine. *National Security Strategy: Mandates, Execution to Date, and Issues for Congress. CRS Report for Congress* R43174. August 6, 2013. Accessed February 9, 2015. http://www.fas.org/sgp/crs/natsec/R43174.pdf.

4. Department of Homeland Security, Risk Steering Committee. *DHS Risk Lexicon.* September 2010. Accessed February 14, 2015. http://www.dhs.gov/dhs-risk-lexicon.

5. Department of Homeland Security, Risk Steering Committee. *DHS Risk Lexicon.* September 2010. Accessed February 14, 2015. http://www.dhs.gov/dhs-risk-lexicon.

6. Kosar, Kevin R. "The Quasi Government: Hybrid Organizations with Both Government and Private Sector Legal Characteristics." *CRS Report for Congress* RL30533. Updated February 13, 2007. Accessed February 8, 2015. http://www.fas.org/sgp/crs/misc/RL30533.pdf.

7. Jan Goldman, *Intelligence Warning Terminology*, Joint Military Intelligence College, October 2001, accessed July 3, 2015. https://archive.org/details/JMICInteligencelwarnterminology.

8. U.S. Department of Defense. *Assistant to the Secretary of Defense for Intelligence Oversight.* Directive Number 5148.11, April 24, 2013. Accessed January 25, 2015. http://www.dtic.mil/whs/directives/corres/pdf/514811p.pdf.

9. U.S. Department of Defense. *DOD Guidance for Reporting Questionable Intelligence Activities and Significant or Highly Sensitive Matters.* DTM-08-052 6/17/2009, amended 10/1/2014. Accessed February 8, 2015. http://www.dtic.mil/whs/directives/corres/pdf/DTM08052.pdf.

R

RADAR CAMOUFLAGE The use of radar-absorbent or reflecting materials to change the radar-echoing properties of a surface of an object.

RADAR INTELLIGENCE (RADINT) *See* SOURCES OF INTELLIGENCE

RADAR PICKET Any ship, aircraft, or vehicle, stationed at a distance from the force protected, for the purpose of increasing the radar detection range.

RADICALIZATION PROCESS 1. The FBI assesses the radicalization process as four stages: pre-radicalization (e.g., motivation, conversion), identification (e.g., forge new social identity), indoctrination (e.g., intensified group bonds), and action (e.g., recruitment, financing). Each one is distinct, and a radicalized individual may never reach the final stage.[1] 2. The process through which an individual changes from a non-violent belief system to a belief system that includes the willingness to actively advocate, facilitate, or use violence as a method to effect societal or political change.[2] 3. The social and behavioral process whereby people adopt and embrace extremist attitudes, values or behaviors. It is a risk factor for involvement in terrorism, but involvement in terrorism does not always result from radicalization.[3] 4. Information obtained from generally reliable sources but not necessarily corroborated. It is deemed valid not only because of the sources but also because it coincides with other known information. It is usually time sensitive and its value is perishable in a relatively short period.[4] *See* FINISHED INTELLIGENCE

RADIO-TELEGRAPHY 1. The transmission of telegraphic codes by means of radio. 2. The transmission of speech by means of modulated radio waves.

RAID An operation, usually small scale, involving a swift penetration of hostile territory to secure information, confuse the enemy, or destroy installations. A raid ends with a planned withdrawal upon completion of the assigned mission.[5]

RAND CORPORATION 1. The RAND Corporation is a research organization that develops solutions to public policy challenges to help make communities throughout the world safer and more secure, healthier and more prosperous. RAND is nonprofit, nonpartisan, and committed to the public interest. RAND began in 1946 as a research project (Project RAND) backed by a single client, the U.S. Army Air Forces. The project was developed at the Douglas Aircraft Company in Santa Monica, California. It was on May 14, 1948, that Project RAND—an organization formed immediately after World War II to connect military planning with research and development decisions—separated from the Douglas Aircraft Company of Santa Monica, California, and became an independent, nonprofit organization; on November 1, 1948, the Project RAND contract was formally transferred from the Douglas Aircraft Company to the RAND Corporation. RAND operates three federally funded research and development centers (FFRDCs): the RAND Arroyo Center, which is sponsored by the U.S. Army; RAND Project AIR FORCE (PAF), sponsored by the U.S. Air Force; and the RAND National Defense Research Institute (NDRI), sponsored by a number of federal defense organizations. Because RAND operates these three FFRDCs, we do not accept funds (i.e., project sponsorship or philanthropic support) from firms or segments of firms whose primary business is that of supplying equipment, materiel, or services to the U.S. Department of Defense.[6] 2. Arthur E. Raymond of Douglas Aircraft suggested the name Project RAND, for research and development.[7]

RAP BACK SERVICE Provides authorized agencies with notification of criminal, and, in limited cases, civil activity of individuals that occurs after the initial processing and retention of criminal or civil transactions. Rap Back does not provide new authority to agencies, including the FBI, for collection of biometric and biographical information. It does, however, implement new response services to notify agencies of subsequent activity for individuals enrolled in the service. Including a more timely process of confirming suitability of those individuals placed in positions of trust and notification to users of criminal activity for those individuals placed on probation or parole. *See* NEXT GENERATION IDENTIFICATION PROGRAM

RAPID ANALYTIC SUPPORT AND EXPEDITIONARY RESPONSE (RASER) A program within the Office of the ADDNI/Analysis for Analytic Technology and Transformation that focuses on preparing select analysts, usually with less than five years of IC experience, to deploy rapidly in support of critical U.S. government missions at home and abroad. The program also tests innovative analytic tools, best practices, and tradecraft and explores whether younger analysts can be matured more quickly through intensified experiences and training.[8]

RAPID DNA INDEX SYSTEM The FBI's objective for Rapid DNA technology is to generate a CODIS (Combined DNA Index System)-compatible DNA profile and to search these arrestee DNA profiles within two hours against unsolved crime (forensic) DNA while an arrestee is in police custody. Rapid DNA technology has been designed for use within and outside the forensic DNA laboratory, as the Rapid DNA instruments are self-contained machines that require no human intervention beyond the loading of the DNA samples and analysis cartridges into the machines.[9]

RAW DATA Bits of collected data that individually convey little or no useful information and must be collated, aggregated, or interpreted to provide meaningful information.[10]

RAW INTELLIGENCE A colloquial term meaning collected intelligence information that has not yet been converted into finished intelligence.[11]

REACH-BACK CAPABILITY An organization's ability to provide additional detailed analysis to deployed units. For example, to help Russia rescue a sunken submarine, the U.S. Secretary of Defense said, "We have proposed having teams of experts who have a so-called reach-back capability to well-organized mission specific expertise."[12]

READINESS The level of capability within a predetermined time period with which an actor can adequately respond to an attack. Historically, readiness of U.S. military forces at the unit level has been measured using the Status of Resources and Training System (SORTS), under the sponsorship of the JCS. Under SORTS, units report their overall readiness status as well as the status of four resource areas (personnel, equipment and supplies on hand, equipment condition, and training). The readiness status of a unit is reported by assigning capability, or "C," ratings as follows:

C-1: Unit can undertake the full wartime missions for which it is organized or designed.
C-2: Unit can undertake the bulk of its wartime missions.
C-3: Unit can undertake major portions of its wartime missions.
C-4: Unit requires additional resources and/or training to undertake its wartime missions, but if the situation dictates, it may be required to undertake portions of the missions with resources on hand.

C-5: Unit is undergoing a service-directed resource change and is not prepared to undertake its wartime missions.

In addition, the secretary of defense and the JCS have established senior oversight groups to focus on readiness issues at a higher level and provide a more comprehensive assessment of readiness.[13]

REAL TIME Pertaining to the timeliness of data or information which has been delayed only by the time required for electronic communication. This implies that there are no noticeable delays.[14] *See* CURRENT INTELLIGENCE; NEAR REAL-TIME

REALPOLITIK A German term meaning the politics of the real, it refers to the realist's determination to treat politics as they really are and not as the idealist would wish them to be. "Machiavellianism" and *machtpolitik* or power politics are similar terms. Realpolitik is most commonly used in connection with foreign policy.[15]

REASONABLE SUSPICION When information exists that establishes sufficient facts to give a trained law enforcement or criminal investigative agency officer, investigator, or employee a basis to believe that there is a reasonable possibility that an individual or organization is involved in a definable criminal activity or enterprise.[16]

RECIPROCAL FEAR (OF SURPRISE ATTACK) 1. The strong incentive to initiate the first action or launch a preemptive attack because to not do so would cause irreparable vulnerability.[17] 2. The possibility that crisis conditions may trigger automatic mobilization responses, loss of control, and preemptive attacks, resulting in a self-fulfilling prophecy. "We fear they fear we fear they will strike; so they may strike . . . so we must."

RECIPROCITY Recognition and acceptance, without further processing of: (1) security background investigations and clearance eligibility determinations; (2) accreditations of information systems; and (3) facility accreditations. Reciprocity is obligatory in the Intelligence Community (IC) when there are no waivers, conditions, or deviations to the Director of National Intelligence.[18]

RECLASSIFICATION The term *reclassification* specifically refers to the classification of information after it has been declassified and released to the public under proper authority. Classified information that has been designated as unclassified without proper authority remains classified. Any subsequent public disclosure is unauthorized and constitutes a compromise of classified information.[19]

RECOGNITION The determination by any means of the friendly or enemy character or of the individuality of another, or of objectives such as aircraft, ships, or tanks, or of phenomena such as communications electronics patterns.[20]

RECOMMENDATIONS Suggestions for actions to be taken based on the findings of an analysis.[21]

RECONNAISSANCE A mission undertaken to obtain information about the activities, resources, or intention of a threat or potential threat.[22] *See* AIR RECONNAISSANCE

RECONNAISSANCE IN FORCE An offensive operation designed to discover and/or test the enemy's strength or to obtain other information.[23]

RECORDS CHECK The process whereby a Special Agent obtains relevant information about sources or subjects from the records and information holdings of military, civilian or government agencies, as well as certain commercial companies and vendors, during the conduct of an investigation or operation. Types include military agency checks (MACs), local agency checks (LACs) and national agency checks (NACs). Types of checks: Military Agency Check (MAC): a records or files check conducted at any military agency within the jurisdiction of the CI element conducting the check.[24]

RECRUITMENT 1. The deliberate and calculating effort to gain control of an individual and to induce him or her to furnish information or to carry out intelligence tasks for an intelligence or CI service.[25] 2. Also, authorized personnel establishing control over an foreign individual who, witting or unwitting of USG involvement, accepts tasking as a result of the established relationship; authorized personnel establishing control over a U.S. person who, fully aware of USG involvement, accepts tasking as a result of the established relationship. 3. Also, the acquisition of an individual's services who, witting or unwitting of U.S. government involvement, accepts directions and control thus obligating both parties to an act in a prescribed manner. 4. Also, the establishment of a degree of control over an individual who, witting or unwitting of U.S. government involvement, accepts tasking as a result of the relationship established. 5. Also, the process of enlisting an individual to work for an intelligence or counterintelligence service (FBI FCI Terms).[26]

RECRUITMENT IN PLACE (RIP) An official who overtly continues to work for his or her government and clandestinely provides information of intelligence value to a foreign government. Recruitment in place will in many instances be connected with a foreign government's intelligence service.[27]

RED TEAM ANALYSIS Understanding the behavior of an individual or group by modeling a replica of how this adversary would think about a particular issue; forecasting how a foreign leader or group may behave.

RED TEAMING Can mean role-playing the adversary, conducting a vulnerability assessment to determine weaknesses, or using analytical techniques to improve intelligence estimates and intelligence synchronization.[28]

RED TEAMS An organizational element comprised of trained and educated members that provide an independent capability to fully explore alternatives in plans and operations in the context of the operational environment and from the perspective of adversaries and others.[29]

REDACTION Redaction means the removal of classified information from copies of a document such that recovery of the information on the copy is not possible using any reasonably known technique or analysis.[30]

REDUNDANCY Additional or alternative systems, sub-systems, assets, or processes that maintain a degree of overall functionality in case of loss or failure of another system, sub-system, asset, or process.[31]

REDUNDANT EVIDENCE The association of two or more items of evidence that increasingly favor the same conclusion. There are two types: corroborative redundancy (e.g., when an item of evidence is repeatedly sent) and cumulative redundancy (e.g., when the value of two items for estimation is greater than either item alone).[32] *See* CONVERGENT EVIDENCE; DIVERGENT EVIDENCE

REFUGEE Any person who, owing to a well-founded fear of being persecuted for reasons of race, religion, nationality, membership of a particular social group or political opinion, is outside the country of his nationality and is unable, or owing to such fear, is unwilling to avail himself of the protection of that country; or who, not having a nationality and being outside the country of his former habitual residence as a result of such events, is unable or, owing to such fear, is unwilling to return to it.[33]

REGIONAL INFORMATION SHARING SYSTEM (RISS) RISS serves thousands of local, state, federal, and tribal criminal justice agencies in their effort to identify, detect, deter, prevent, and solve criminal and terrorist-related investigations. Through its RISS Secure Cloud (RISSNET™), information and intelligence-sharing resources, investigative support and analytical services, and deconfliction, RISS has enabled agencies and officers to increase their success exponentially. RISS supports efforts against organized and violent crime, gang activity, drug activity, terrorism, human trafficking, identity theft, and other regional priorities, while promoting officer safety. RISS offers full-service delivery from the beginning of an investigation to the ultimate prosecution and conviction of criminals.[34]

REGIONAL INTELLIGENCE CENTERS Multijurisdictional centers cooperatively developed within a logical geographical area that coordinate federal, state, and local law enforcement information with other information sources to track and assess criminal and terrorist threats that are operating in or interacting with the region.[35]

REGIONAL RESILENCY ASSESSMENT PROGRAM (RRAP) A cooperative, IP-led interagency assessment of specific CIKR and regional analysis of the surrounding infrastructure. The RRAP evaluates CIKR on a regional level to examine vulnerabilities, threats, and potential consequences from an all-hazards perspective to identify dependencies, interdependencies, cascading effects, resiliency characteristics, and gaps.[36] *See* CRITICAL INFRASTRUCTURE

REGISTERED MATTER Any classified matter registered, usually by number, and accounted for periodically.[37]

REGULATION OF INVESTIGATORY POWERS ACT 2000 (RIPA) 1. To make provision for and about the interception of communications, the acquisition and disclosure of data relating to communications, the carrying out of surveillance, the use of covert human intelligence sources and the acquisition of the means by which electronic data protected by encryption or passwords may be decrypted or accessed; to provide for commissioners and a tribunal with functions and jurisdiction in relation to those matters, to entries on and interferences with property or with wireless telegraphy and to the carrying out of their functions by the security service, the Secret Intelligence Service and the Government Communications Headquarters.[38] 2. Regulates the circumstances and methods by which public bodies may carry out covert surveillance; lays out a statutory framework to enable public authorities to carry out covert surveillance in compliance with the requirements of the Human Rights Act; defines five broad categories of covert surveillance—directed surveillance (includes photographing people); intrusive surveillance (includes bugging); the use of covert human intelligence sources (informants and undercover officers, including watching and following people); accessing communications data (record of emails sent, telephone calls made) and intercepting communications (i.e., reading content of emails, listening to calls)—allows the secretary of state to issue an interception warrant to examine the contents of letters or communications on the grounds of national security, and for the purposes of preventing or detecting crime, preventing disorder, public safety, protecting public health, or in the interests of the economic well-being of the United Kingdom. This is the only part of the act that requires a warrant; prevents the existence of interception warrants, and any and all data collected with them from being revealed in court; allows the police, intelligence services, HM Revenue and Customs (and several hundred more public bodies, including local authorities and a wide range of regulators) to demand telephone, Internet and postal service providers to hand over detailed communications records for individual users.[39] *See* SURVEILLANCE

RELATIVE RISK Measure of risk that represents the ratio of risks when compared to each other or a control. (1) The relative risk value of a scenario is meaningful only in comparison to other similarly constructed risk values. (2) Due to inherent uncertainties in risk analysis, relative risk may be more useful to decision makers than risk measured in expected annualized dollars lost or lives lost. (3) Using relative risk might convey the necessary meaning to decision makers while avoiding the disclosure of sensitive or classified information.[40]

RELIABILITY The determination of consistency and dependability of a source.[41]

RENDITION "The term 'rendition' in the counterterrorism context means nothing more than moving someone from one country to another, outside the formal process of extradition. For the CIA, rendition has become a key tool for getting terrorists from places where they're causing trouble to places where they can't. The problem is where these people are taken and what happens to them when they get there."[42] *See* EXTRAORDINARY RENDITION

RENEGADE A person who operates outside of conventional and approved procedures. Also defined by some as a person who has turned on his country in any of a variety of ways.

REPORTING Depending on the type of intelligence, the process of placing analyzed information into the proper form to ensure the most effective consumption.[43]

REPOSITORY FOR INDIVIDUALS OF SPECIAL CONCERN (RISC) The RISC will encompass a subset of NGI (Next Generation Identification) sensitive but unclassified data, consisting of records of known or appropriately suspected terrorists, wanted persons, registered sexual offenders, and (potentially) other categories of heightened interest warranting more rapid responses to inquiring criminal justice users. (Any additional categories proposed for inclusion, such as missing persons or protection order subjects that have associated biometrics currently in NGI could be considered for RISC. This PIA will be annotated to reflect the addition of any other categories of records.) The RISC will be queried by fingerprints (10 or fewer) electronically submitted by authorized NGI users, typically by first responder law enforcement officials in the course of their interaction with potential suspects or similar real-time encounters.[44]

REQUEST FOR INFORMATION (RFI) 1. Any specific time-sensitive ad hoc requirement for intelligence information or products to support an ongoing crisis or operation not necessarily related to standing requirements or scheduled intelligence production. 2. A term used by the National Security Agency/Central Security Service to state ad hoc signals intelligence requirements.[45]

REQUIREMENTS (INTELLIGENCE) The types of intelligence operational law enforcement elements need from the intelligence function within an agency or other intelligence-producing organizations in order for law enforcement officers to maximize protection and preventive efforts as well as identify and arrest persons who are criminally liable.[46]

RESEARCH DEVELOPMENT EXPERIMENTAL AND COLLABORATION (RDEC) RDEC is a program tasked with bringing together members of the intelligence community to explore the use of new, advanced analytical tools. RDEC excels in introducing new, advanced software tools that improve the efficiency and effectiveness of analysts' tasks to the Intel

Community. Allows rapid technology evaluation for consideration for operational transition.[47]

RESEARCH INTELLIGENCE An in-depth study of a specific issue.

RESETTLED PERSON A refugee or an internally displaced person wishing to return somewhere other than his or her previous home or land within the country or area of original displacement.[48]

RESIDUAL RISK Risk that remains after risk management measures have been implemented.[49]

RESILENCE 1. The ability to prepare for and adapt to changing conditions and withstand and recover rapidly from disruptions. Resilience includes the ability to withstand and recover from deliberate attacks, accidents, or naturally occurring threats or incidents.[50] 2. The term "resilience" refers to the ability to adapt to changing conditions and withstand and rapidly recover from disruption due to emergencies. Whether it is resilience toward acts of terrorism, cyber attacks, pandemics, and catastrophic natural disasters, our national preparedness is the shared responsibility of all levels of government, the private and nonprofit sectors, and individual citizens. The United States officially recognized resilience in national doctrine in the 2010 *National Security Strategy*, which states that we must enhance our resilience—the ability to adapt to changing conditions and prepare for, withstand, and rapidly recover from disruption. The U.S. Department of Homeland Security also recognized resilience in the 2014 Quadrennial Homeland Security Review, which established a series of goals and objectives in the areas of critical infrastructure, global movement and supply chain systems, and cyberspace. Further, one of the five QHSR missions is devoted to resilience: Mission 5—Strengthening National Preparedness and Resilience.[51]

RESPONSE The term "response" refers to those capabilities necessary to save lives, protect property and the environment, and meet basic human needs after an incident has occurred.[52]

RESTRICTED An active security classification marking used by some foreign governments and international organizations.[53]

RESULTS ANALYSIS An assessment of the effectiveness of police strategies and tactics as used to combat a particular crime problem which may include suggestions for changes to future policies and strategies.

RETURNEE A displaced person who has returned voluntarily to his or her former place of residence.[54]

REWARDS FOR JUSTICE Established by the 1984 Act to Combat International Terrorism, Public Law 98-533, the Program is administered by the U.S. Department of State's Bureau of Diplomatic Security. Under this program, the Secretary of State may authorize rewards for information that leads to the arrest or conviction of anyone who plans, commits, or attempts international terrorist acts against U.S. persons or property, that prevents such acts from occurring in the first place, that leads to the location of a key terrorist leader, or that disrupts terrorism financing. The Secretary is authorized to pay a reward greater than $25 million if he/she determines that a greater amount is necessary to combat terrorism or to defend the United States against terrorist acts.[55]

RIGHT TO BE FORGOTTEN Refers to the European Court of Justice ECJ case C 131/12, *Google Spain SL, Google Inc. v Agencia Española de Protección de Datos, Mario Costeja González*, where "According to Mr Costeja González and the Spanish and Italian Governments, the data subject may oppose the indexing by a search engine of personal data relating to him where their dissemination through the search engine is prejudicial to him and his fundamental rights to the protection of those data and to privacy—which encompass the 'right to be forgotten'—override the legitimate interests of the operator of the search engine and the general interest in freedom of information."[56]

RINT (RADIATION INTELLIGENCE-UNINTENTIONAL) *See* SOURCES OF INTELLIGENCE

RIOT CONTROL AGENT Any chemical, not listed in a schedule of the Convention on the Prohibition of the Development, Production, Stockpiling and Use of Chemical Weapons and on their Destruction that can produce rapidly in humans sensory irritation or disabling physical effects that disappear within a short time following termination of exposure.[57]

RISK 1. The probability that a particular threat will exploit a particular vulnerability of national security that will result in damage to the life, health, property, or the environment. 2. The probability of loss from an attack or adverse incident. It is a function of threat (adversaries' capabilities, intentions, and opportunities) and vulnerability (the inherent susceptibility to attack). Risk may be quantified and expressed in terms such as cost in loss of life, dollars, resources, or programmatic impact. 3. Potential for an unwanted outcome resulting from an incident, event, or occurrence, as determined by its likelihood and the associated consequences. Extended Definition: potential for an adverse outcome assessed as a function of threats, vulnerabilities, and consequences associated with an incident, event, or occurrence.[58]

RISK ACCEPTANCE Explicit or implicit decision not to take an action that would affect all or part of a particular risk. Risk acceptance is one of four commonly used risk management strategies, along with risk avoidance, risk control, and risk transfer.[59]

RISK ANALYSIS 1. Systematic examination of the components and characteristics of risk.[60] 2. The process of identifying the risks to system security and determining the likelihood of occurrence, the resulting impact, and the additional safeguards that mitigate this impact. Risk analysis is part of risk management and synonymous with risk assessment.

RISK ASSESSMENT 1. Product or process which collects information and assigns values to risks for the purpose of informing priorities, developing or comparing courses of action, and informing decision making.[61] 2. The appraisal of the risks facing an entity, asset, system, or network, organizational operations, individuals, geographic area, other organizations, or society, and includes determining the extent to which adverse circumstances or events could result in harmful consequences.[62]

RISK ASSESSMENT METHODOLOGY Set of methods, principles, or rules used to identify and assess risks and to form priorities, develop courses of action, and inform decision making.[63]

RISK ASSESSMENT PROCESS FOR INFORMED DECISION MAKING (RAPID) An RMA program aimed at developing a strategic-level process to gauge future risks across the full range of DHS responsibilities to inform the DHS's annual Planning, Programming, Budgeting, and Execution cycle of resource allocation decisions.[64]

RISK ASSESSMENT TOOL Activity, item, or program that contributes to determining and evaluating risks. Tools can include computer software and hardware, standard forms, or checklists for recording and displaying risk assessment data.[65]

RISK AVOIDANCE Strategies or measures taken that effectively remove exposure to a risk. Risk avoidance is one of a set of four commonly used risk management strategies, along with risk control, risk acceptance, and risk transfer.[66]

RISK-BASED DECISION MAKING Determination of a course of action predicated primarily on the assessment of risk and the expected impact of that course of action on that risk. Risk-based decision making uses the assessment of risk as the primary decision driver, while risk-informed decision making may account for multiple sources of information not included in the assessment of risk as significant inputs to the decision process in addition to risk information. Risk-based decision making has often been used interchangeably, but incorrectly, with risk-informed decision making.[67]

RISK COMMUNICATION Exchange of information with the goal of improving risk understanding, affecting risk perception, and/or equipping people or groups to act appropriately in response to an identified risk. Risk communication is practiced for both non-hazardous conditions and during incidents. During an incident, risk communication is intended to provide information that fosters trust and credibility in government and empowers partners, stakeholders, and the public to make the best possible decisions under extremely difficult time constraints and circumstances.[68]

RISK CONTROL Deliberate action taken to reduce the potential for harm or maintain it at an acceptable level. Risk control is one of a set of four commonly used risk management strategies, along with risk avoidance, risk acceptance, and risk transfer.[69]

RISK DATA Information on key components of risk that are outputs of or inputs to risk assessments and risk analyses.[70]

RISK EXPOSURE Contact of an entity, asset, system, network, or geographic area with a potential hazard.[71]

RISK GOVERNANCE Actors, rules, practices, processes, and mechanisms concerned with how risk is analyzed, managed, and communicated.[72]

RISK IDENTIFICATION Process of finding, recognizing, and describing potential risks.[73]

RISK INDICATOR Measure that signals the potential for an unwanted outcome as determined by qualitative or quantitative analysis.[74]

RISK-INFORMED DECISION MAKING Determination of a course of action predicated on the assessment of risk, the expected impact of that course of action on that risk, as well as other relevant factors. Risk-informed decision making may take into account multiple sources of information not included specifically in the assessment of risk as inputs to the decision process in addition to risk information, while risk-based decision making uses the assessment of risk as the primary decision driver.[75] Established rules developed to promote a workforce member's understanding of the importance of safeguarding personally identifiable information (PII), his or her individual role and responsibilities in protecting PII, and the consequences for failed compliance. All workforce members with access to PII in the performance of their official duties are required to comply with established rules.[76] *See* PERSONALLY IDENTIFIABLE INFORMATION

RISK MANAGEMENT 1. Process of identifying, analyzing, assessing, and communicating risk and accepting, avoiding, transferring or controlling it to an acceptable level considering associated costs and benefits of any actions taken. Effective risk management improves the quality of decision making. Risk management principles acknowledge that, while risk often cannot be eliminated, actions can usually be taken to control risk.[77] 2. The process of identifying, analyzing, assessing, and communicating risk and accepting, avoiding, transferring or controlling it to an acceptable level considering associated costs and benefits of any actions taken. Extended Definition: Includes: 1) conducting a risk assessment; 2) implementing strategies to mitigate risks; 3) continuous monitoring of risk over time; and 4) documenting the overall risk management program.[78] *See* ACCEPTABLE RISK; RISK; RISK ASSESSMENT

RISK MANAGEMENT ALTERNATIVES DEVELOPMENT Process of systematically examining risks to develop a range of options and their anticipated effects for decision makers. The risk management alternatives development step of the risk management process generates options for decision makers to consider before deciding on which option to implement.[79]

RISK MANAGEMENT ASSESSMENT TOOL (RMAT) A TSA agent–based computer simulation model for analyzing and informing decisions about risk reduction options based on threat, vulnerability, and consequence data.[80]

RISK MANAGEMENT-BASED INTELLIGENCE An approach to intelligence analysis that has as its object the calculation of the risk attributable to a threat source or acts threatened by a threat source; a means of providing strategic intelligence for planning and policymaking, especially regarding vulnerabilities and countermeasures designed to prevent criminal acts; a means of providing tactical or operational intelligence in support of operations against a specific threat source, capability, or modality; can be quantitative if a proper database exists to measure likelihood and impact and calculate risk; can be qualitative and subjective and still deliver a reasonably reliable ranking of risk for resource allocation and other decision making in strategic planning and for operations in tactical situations.[81]

RISK MANAGEMENT CYCLE Sequence of steps that are systematically taken and revisited to manage risk.[82]

RISK MANAGEMENT METHODOLOGY Set of methods, principles, or rules used to identify, analyze, assess, and communicate risk, and accept, avoid, transfer, or control it to an acceptable level considering associated costs and benefits of any actions taken.

RISK MANAGEMENT PLAN Definition: document that identifies risks and specifies the actions that have been chosen to manage those risks.[83]

RISK MANAGEMENT PRINCIPLES Three basic principles of risk management are: (1) while risk generally cannot be eliminated, it can be reduced by enhancing protection from validated and credible threats; (2) although many threats are possible, some are more likely to occur than others; and (3) all assets are not equally crucial.

RISK MANAGEMENT STRATEGY Course of action or actions to be taken in order to manage risks. Extended Definition: Proactive approach to reduce the usually negative impacts of various risks by choosing within a range of options that include complete avoidance of any risk that would cause harm or injury, accepting the risk, controlling the risk by employing risk mitigation options to reduce impacts, or transferring some or all of the risk to another entity based on a set of stated priorities.[84]

RISK MATRIX Tool for ranking and displaying components of risk in an array. A risk matrix is typically displayed in a graphical format to show the relationship between risk components.[85]

RISK MITIGATION Application of measure or measures to reduce the likelihood of an unwanted occurrence and/or its consequences.[86]

RISK MITIGATION OPTION Measure, device, policy, or course of action taken with the intent of reducing risk.[87]

RISK PERCEPTION Subjective judgment about the characteristics and/or severity of risk. Sample Usage: Fear of terrorist attacks may create a skewed risk perception. Risk perception may be driven by sense, emotion, or personal experience.[88]

RISK PROFILE Description and/or depiction of risks to an entity, asset, system, network, or geographic area. A risk profile can be derived from a risk assessment; it is often used as a presentation tool to show how risks vary across comparable entities.[89]

RISK REDUCTION Decrease in risk through risk avoidance, risk control, or risk transfer. (1) Risk reduction may be estimated during both the decision and evaluation phases of the risk management cycle. (2) Risk reduction can be accomplished by reducing vulnerability and/or consequences (damages).[90]

RISK SCENARIO Hypothetical situation comprised of a hazard, an entity impacted by that hazard, and associated conditions including consequences when appropriate. A scenario can be created and used for the purposes of training, exercise, analysis, or modeling as well as for other purposes. A scenario that has occurred or is occurring is an incident.[91]

RISK SCORE Numerical result of a semi-quantitative risk assessment methodology. The application of risk management alternatives may result in a change of risk score.[92]

RISK TOLERANCE 1. Degree to which an entity, asset, system, network, or geographic area is willing to accept risk.[93] 2. The level of risk an entity is willing to assume in order to achieve a potential desired result.

RISK TRANSFER Action taken to manage risk that shifts some or all of the risk to another entity, asset, system, network, or geographic area. Risk transfer is one of a set of four commonly used risk management strategies, along with risk control, risk acceptance, and risk avoidance.[94]

ROUTE CLASSIFICATION Classification assigned to a route using factors of minimum width, worst route type, and the least bridge, raft, or culvert military load classification and obstructions to traffic flow.

RULES OF BEHAVIOR Established rules developed to promote a workforce member's understanding of the importance of safeguarding personally identifiable information (PII), his or her individual role and responsibilities in protecting PII, and the consequences for failed compliance. All workforce members with access to PII in the performance of their official duties are required to comply with established rules.[95] *See* PERSONALLY IDENTIFIABLE INFORMATION

RULES OF ENGAGEMENT Directives issued by competent military authority which specify the circumstances and limitations under which forces will initiate and/or continue combat engagement with other forces encountered.[96]

NOTES

1. Dyer, Carol, McCoy, Ryan E., Rodriguez, Joel, and Van Duyn, Donald N. "Countering Violent Islamic Extremism: A Community Responsibility." *FBI Law Enforcement Bulletin* 76, no. 12 (2007): 3–9. Accessed February 8, 2015. http://leb.fbi.gov/2007-pdfs/leb-december-2007.

2. Department of Homeland Security. Office of Intelligence and Analysis. *Domestic Terrorism and Homegrown Violent Extremism Lexicon.* November 10, 2011. Accessed January 15, 2015. https://publicintelligence.net/domestic-terrorism-and-homegrown-violent-extremism-lexicon/.

3. Defense Science Board. *Predicting Violent Behavior: Final Report of the the Defense Science Board (DSB) Task Force (TF) on Predicting Violent Behavior.* August 2012. Accessed February 24, 2015. http://www.acq.osd.mil/dsb/reports/PredictingViolentBehavior.pdf.

4. Carter, David L. *Law Enforcement Intelligence*: *A Guide for State, Local, and Tribal Law Enforcement Agencies.* U.S. Dept. of Justice, Office of Community Oriented Policing Services, 2004.

5. North Atlantic Treaty Organization. *NATO Glossary of Terms and Definitions.* NATO Standardization Agency, 2014, AAP-06, accessed July 27, 2015, http://nso.nato.int/nso/zPublic/ap/aap6/AAP-6.pdf.

6. RAND Corporation. *Frequently Asked Questions.* Accessed February 8, 2015. http://www.rand.org/about/faq.html and RAND Corporation. *History and Mission* Accessed February 8, 2015. http://www.rand.org/about/history.html; also see Digby, James. *Strategic Thought at RAND 1948–1963: The Ideas, Their Origins, Their Fates.* RAND Note, June 1990. Accessed February 8, 2015. http://www.rand.org/content/dam/rand/pubs/notes/2009/N3096.pdf.

7. Abella, Alex. *Soldiers of Reason: The RAND Corporation and the Rise of American Empire.* Harcourt: New York, 2008.

8. Office of the Director of National Intelligence. *National Intelligence Program FY 2009 Congressional Budget Justification Book.* Vol. XII, February 2008. Accessed January 17, 2015. http://www.fas.org/irp/dni/cbjb-2009.pdf.

9. Hess, Amy S. (Executive Assistant Director, Science and Technology Branch Federal Bureau of Investigation) Statement Before the House Judiciary Committee, Subcommittee on Crime, Terrorism, Homeland Security, and Investigations. Washington, DC, June 18, 2015, accessed February 2, 2016, https://www.fbi.gov/news/testimony/fbis-plans-for-the-use-of-rapid-dna-technology-in-codis.

10. Office of the Director of National Intelligence, *U.S. National Intelligence: An Overview 2011*, accessed February 2, 2016, http://www.dni.gov/files/documents/IC_Consumers_Guide_2011.pdf.

11. Office of the Director of National Intelligence, *U.S. National Intelligence: An Overview 2011*, accessed February 2, 2016, http://www.dni.gov/files/documents/IC_Consumers_Guide_2011.pdf.

12. Suro, Robert. "Up in Arms: The Defense Department; Zeroing In on Zero Casualty Syndrome," *The Washington Post* August 20, 2000: A19.

13. Gebicke, Mark E. *Military Readiness: Improvements Still Needed in Assessing Military Readiness.* March 11, 1997, GAO/T-NSIAD-97-107. Accessed http://www.gao.gov/archive/1997/ns97107t.pdf.

14. Department of the Army. Marine Corps Combat Development Command. Department of the Navy. *Operational Terms and Graphics.* FM 1-02 (FM 101-5). September 21, 2004. Accessed July 3, 2015. http://www.udel.edu/armyrotc/current_cadets/cadet_resources/manuals_regulations_files/FM%201-02%20-%20Operational%20Terms%20&%20Graphics.pdf.

15. McLean, Iain and McMillan, Alistair. *The Concise Oxford Dictionary of Politics.* 3rd ed. New York: Oxford University Press, 2009.

16. Federal Bureau of Investigation. *Minimum Criminal Intelligence Training Standards for Law Enforcement and Other Criminal Justice Agencies in the United States.* October 2007. Accessed February 8, 2015. https://it.ojp.gov/gist/108/Minimum-Criminal-Intelligence-Training-Standards.

17. Jan Goldman, *Intelligence Warning Terminology*, Joint Military Intelligence College, October 2001, accessed July 3, 2015. https://archive.org/details/JMICIntelligencelwarnterminology.

18. U.S. Department of Defense. Center for Development of Security Excellence. *Glossary of Security Terms and Definitions.* November 2012. Accessed February 15, 2015. http://www.cdse.edu/documents/cdse/Glossary_Handbook.pdf.

19. Information Security Oversight Office. *Withdrawal of Records from Public Access at the National Archives and Records Administration for Classification Purpose.* Audit Report, April 26, 2006, 4. Accessed February 8, 2015. http://www2.gwu.edu/~nsarchiv/news/20060426/2006-audit-report.pdf.

20. U.S. Department of Defense. *Department of Defense Dictionary of Military and Associated Terms.* JP 1-02, 08 November 2010, as Amended through 15 January 2016. Accessed January 26, 2016, http://www.dtic.mil/doctrine/new_pubs/jp1_02.pdf.

21. Federal Bureau of Investigation. *Minimum Criminal Intelligence Training Standards for Law Enforcement and Other Criminal Justice Agencies in the United States.* October 2007. Accessed February 8, 2015. https://it.ojp.gov/gist/108/Minimum-Criminal-Intelligence-Training-Standards.

22. U.S. Department of Defense. *Department of Defense Dictionary of Military and Associated Terms.* JP 1-02, 08 November 2010, as Amended through 15 January 2016. Accessed January 26, 2016, http://www.dtic.mil/doctrine/new_pubs/jp1_02.pdf.

23. North Atlantic Treaty Organization. *NATO Glossary of Terms and Definitions.* NATO Standardization Agency, 2014, AAP-06, accessed July 27, 2015, http://nso.nato.int/nso/zPublic/ap/aap6/AAP-6.pdf.

24. Defense Intelligence Agency, Office of Counterintelligence. *CI Glossary— Terms & Definitions of Interest for DoD CI Professionals.* July 2014. Accessed January 17, 2015. https://www.hsdl.org/?view&did=699056.

25. Defense Intelligence Agency, Office of Counterintelligence. *CI Glossary— Terms & Definitions of Interest for DoD CI Professionals.* July 2014. Accessed January 17, 2015. https://www.hsdl.org/?view&did=699056.

26. Defense Intelligence Agency, Office of Counterintelligence. *CI Glossary— Terms & Definitions of Interest for DoD CI Professionals.* July 2014. Accessed February 8, 2015. https://www.hsdl.org/?view&did=699056.

27. Defense Intelligence Agency, Office of Counterintelligence. *CI Glossary— Terms & Definitions of Interest for DoD CI Professionals.* July 2014. Accessed January 17, 2015. https://www.hsdl.org/?view&did=699056.

28. Longbine, Davis F. *Red Teaming: Past and Present.* School of Advanced Military Studies, Fort Leavenworth, May 22, 2008. ADA485514. Accessed November 22, 2015. http://www.dtic.mil/get-tr-doc/pdf?AD=ADA485514.

29. U.S. Department of Defense. *Department of Defense Dictionary of Military and Associated Terms.* JP 1-02, 08 November 2010, as Amended through 15 January 2016. Accessed January 26, 2016, http://www.dtic.mil/doctrine/new_pubs/jp1_02.pdf.

30. 32 CFR Part 2001, *Classified National Security Information,* Subpart I "Reporting and Definitions," §2001.92, "Definitions." Accessed February 8, 2015. http://www.ecfr.gov/.

31. Department of Homeland Security, Risk Steering Committee. *DHS Risk Lexicon.* September 2010. Accessed February 14, 2015. http://www.dhs.gov/dhs-risk-lexicon.

32. Clark, Richard. *Intelligence Analysis: A Target-Centric Approach.* Washington, DC: CQ Press, 2004, 118–19.

33. North Atlantic Treaty Organization. *NATO Glossary of Terms and Definitions.* NATO Standardization Agency, 2014, AAP-06, accessed July 27, 2015, http://nso.nato.int/nso/zPublic/ap/aap6/AAP-6.pdf; also see *The Convention Relating to the Status of Refugees* (1951) and *Protocol Relating to the Status of Refugees* (1967). Accessed February 9, 2015. http://www.unhcr.org/3b66c2aa10.html.

34. Regional Information Sharing Systems, accessed February 4, 2016, http://www.riss.net/.

35. Federal Bureau of Investigation. *Minimum Criminal Intelligence Training Standards for Law Enforcement and Other Criminal Justice Agencies in the United States.* October 2007. Accessed February 8, 2015. https://it.ojp.gov/gist/108/Minimum-Criminal-Intelligence-Training-Standards.

36. Department of Homeland Security, Risk Steering Committee. *DHS Risk Lexicon.* September 2010. Accessed February 14, 2015. http://www.dhs.gov/dhs-risk-lexicon.

37. North Atlantic Treaty Organization. *NATO Glossary of Terms and Definitions.* NATO Standardization Agency, 2014, AAP-06, accessed July 27, 2015, http://nso.nato.int/nso/zPublic/ap/aap6/AAP-6.pdf.

38. *Regulation of Investigatory Powers Act 2000.* Accessed March 9, 2015. http://www.legislation.gov.uk/ukpga/2000/23/contents.

39. "Regulation of Investigatory Powers Act 2000." *The Guardian* (UK Civil liberties) January 19, 2009. Accessed March 9, 2015. http://www.theguardian.com/commentisfree/libertycentral/2009/jan/14/regulation-investigatory-powers-act.

40. Department of Homeland Security, Risk Steering Committee. *DHS Risk Lexicon.* September 2010. Accessed February 14, 2015. http://www.dhs.gov/dhs-risk-lexicon.

41. Federal Bureau of Investigation. *Minimum Criminal Intelligence Training Standards for Law Enforcement and Other Criminal Justice Agencies in the United States.* October 2007. Accessed February 8, 2015. https://it.ojp.gov/gist/108/Minimum-Criminal-Intelligence-Training-Standards.

42. Benjamin, Daniel. "Myths About Rendition (and That New Movie)." *The Washington Post*, October 19, 2007. Accessed June 8, 2015. http://www.washingtonpost.com/wp-dyn/content/article/2007/10/19/AR2007101900835.html.

43. Federal Bureau of Investigation. *Minimum Criminal Intelligence Training Standards for Law Enforcement and Other Criminal Justice Agencies in the United States.* October 2007. Accessed February 8, 2015. https://it.ojp.gov/gist/108/Minimum-Criminal-Intelligence-Training-Standards.

44. Federal Bureau of Investigation. *Privacy Impact Assessment Integrated Automated Fingerprint Identification System (IAFIS)/Next Generation Identification (NGI) Repository for Individuals of Special Concern (RISC).* n.d. Accessed February 2, 2016, https://www.fbi.gov/foia/privacy-impact-assessments/iafis-ngi-risc.

45. U.S. Department of Defense. *Joint Intelligence.* JP 2-0. October 22, 2013. Accessed February 15, 2015. http://www.dtic.mil/doctrine/new_pubs/jp2_0.pdf.

46. Federal Bureau of Investigation. *Minimum Criminal Intelligence Training Standards for Law Enforcement and Other Criminal Justice Agencies in the United States.* October 2007. Accessed February 8, 2015. https://it.ojp.gov/gist/108/Minimum-Criminal-Intelligence-Training-Standards.

47. Office of the Director of National Intelligence. *National Intelligence Program FY 2009 Congressional Budget Justification Book.* Vol. XII, February 2008. Accessed January 17, 2015. http://www.fas.org/irp/dni/cbjb-2009.pdf.

48. United States Department of Defense. *Foreign Humanitarian Assistance.* JP 3-29, January 3, 2014. Accessed March 7, 2015. http://www.dtic.mil/doctrine/new_pubs/jp3_29.pdf.

49. Department of Homeland Security, Risk Steering Committee. *DHS Risk Lexicon.* September 2010. Accessed February 14, 2015. http://www.dhs.gov/dhs-risk-lexicon.

50. *Presidential Policy Directive/PPD-21. Critical Infrastructure Security and Resilience.* February 12, 2013. Accessed January 22, 2015. http://www.whitehouse.gov/the-press-office/2013/02/12/presidential-policy-directive-critical-infrastructure-security-and-resil.

51. Department of Homeland Security. *Resilence.* Accessed January 27, 2015. http://www.dhs.gov/topic/resilience.

52. *Presidential Policy Directive/PPD-8: National Preparedness.* March 30, 2011. Accessed February 15, 2011. http://www.dhs.gov/presidential-policy-directive-8-national-preparedness.

53. Executive Order 10501 *Safeguarding Official Information in the Interests of the Defense of the United States.* November 3, 1953. Accessed June 8, 2015. http://www.archives.gov/federal-register/executive-orders/1953-eisenhower.html. This EO eliminated the Restricted category, leaving only Top Secret, Secret, and Confidential, and made a distinction between national security and national defense.

54. United States Department of Defense. *Foreign Humanitarian Assistance.* JP 3-29, January 3, 2014. Accessed March 7, 2015. http://www.dtic.mil/doctrine/new_pubs/jp3_29.pdf.

55. U.S. State Department, Rewards for Justice. *Program Overview.* Accessed February 9, 2015. http://www.rewardsforjustice.net/.

56. European Court of Justice. *Google Spain SL, Google Inc. v Agencia Española de Protección de Datos, Mario Costeja González.* ECJ case C 131/12. May 13, 2014. Accessed February 9, 2015. http://curia.europa.eu/. Court of Justice of the European Union Press Release No 70/14, *Judgment in Case C131/12.* Accessed February 9, 2015. http://curia.europa.eu/jcms/upload/docs/application/pdf/2014-05/cp140070en.pdf; also see European Commission. *Factsheet on the Right to Be Forgotten Ruling (C-131/12).* Accessed February 9, 2015. http://ec.europa.eu/justice/dataprotection/files/factsheets/factsheet_data_protection_en.pdf.

57. U.S. Department of Defense. *Joint and National Intelligence Support to Military Operations*, Joint Publication 2-01, January 5, 2012, accessed January 26, 2016, http://www.dtic.mil/doctrine/new_pubs/jp2_01.pdf.

58. Department of Homeland Security, Risk Steering Committee. *DHS Risk Lexicon.* September 2010. Accessed February 14, 2015. http://www.dhs.gov/dhs-risk-lexicon.

59. Department of Homeland Security, Risk Steering Committee. *DHS Risk Lexicon.* September 2010. Accessed February 14, 2015. http://www.dhs.gov/dhs-risk-lexicon.

60. Defense Intelligence Agency, Office of Counterintelligence. *CI Glossary— Terms & Definitions of Interest for DoD CI Professionals.* July 2014. Accessed January 17, 2015. https://www.hsdl.org/?view&did=699056.

61. Department of Homeland Security, Risk Steering Committee. *DHS Risk Lexicon.* September 2010. Accessed February 14, 2015. http://www.dhs.gov/dhs-risk-lexicon.

62. National Initiative for Cybersecurity Education. *A Glossary of Common Cybersecurity Terminology.* n.d. Accessed March 5, 2015. http://niccs.us-cert.gov/glossary.

63. Department of Homeland Security, Risk Steering Committee. *DHS Risk Lexicon.* September 2010. Accessed February 14, 2015. http://www.dhs.gov/dhs-risk-lexicon.

64. Department of Homeland Security, Risk Steering Committee. *DHS Risk Lexicon.* September 2010. Accessed February 14, 2015. http://www.dhs.gov/dhs-risk-lexicon.

65. Department of Homeland Security, Risk Steering Committee. *DHS Risk Lexicon.* September 2010. Accessed February 14, 2015. http://www.dhs.gov/dhs-risk-lexicon.

66. Department of Homeland Security, Risk Steering Committee. *DHS Risk Lexicon.* September 2010. Accessed February 14, 2015. http://www.dhs.gov/dhs-risk-lexicon.

67. Department of Homeland Security, Risk Steering Committee. *DHS Risk Lexicon.* September 2010. Accessed February 14, 2015. http://www.dhs.gov/dhs-risk-lexicon.

68. Department of Homeland Security, Risk Steering Committee. *DHS Risk Lexicon.* September 2010. Accessed February 14, 2015. http://www.dhs.gov/dhs-risk-lexicon.

69. Department of Homeland Security, Risk Steering Committee. *DHS Risk Lexicon.* September 2010. Accessed February 14, 2015. http://www.dhs.gov/dhs-risk-lexicon.

70. Department of Homeland Security, Risk Steering Committee. *DHS Risk Lexicon.* September 2010. Accessed February 14, 2015. http://www.dhs.gov/dhs-risk-lexicon.

71. Department of Homeland Security, Risk Steering Committee. *DHS Risk Lexicon.* September 2010. Accessed February 14, 2015. http://www.dhs.gov/dhs-risk-lexicon.

72. Department of Homeland Security, Risk Steering Committee. *DHS Risk Lexicon.* September 2010. Accessed February 14, 2015. http://www.dhs.gov/dhs-risk-lexicon.

73. Department of Homeland Security, Risk Steering Committee. *DHS Risk Lexicon.* September 2010. Accessed February 14, 2015. http://www.dhs.gov/dhs-risk-lexicon.

74. Department of Homeland Security, Risk Steering Committee. *DHS Risk Lexicon.* September 2010. Accessed February 14, 2015. http://www.dhs.gov/dhs-risk-lexicon.

75. Department of Homeland Security, Risk Steering Committee. *DHS Risk Lexicon.* September 2010. Accessed February 14, 2015. http://www.dhs.gov/dhs-risk-lexicon.

76. U.S. Department of State. "The Privacy Act and Personally Identifiable Information." *Foreign Affairs Manual.* 5 FAM 460. October 1, 2014. Accessed February 14, 2015. http://www.state.gov/documents/organization/85694.pdf.

77. Department of Homeland Security, Risk Steering Committee. *DHS Risk Lexicon.* September 2010. Accessed February 14, 2015. http://www.dhs.gov/dhs-risk-lexicon.

78. National Initiative for Cybersecurity Education. *A Glossary of Common Cybersecurity Terminology.* n.d. Accessed March 5, 2015. http://niccs.us-cert.gov/glossary.

79. Department of Homeland Security, Risk Steering Committee. *DHS Risk Lexicon.* September 2010. Accessed February 14, 2015. http://www.dhs.gov/dhs-risk-lexicon.

80. Department of Homeland Security, Risk Steering Committee. *DHS Risk Lexicon.* September 2010. Accessed February 14, 2015. http://www.dhs.gov/dhs-risk-lexicon.

81. Federal Bureau of Investigation. *Minimum Criminal Intelligence Training Standards for Law Enforcement and Other Criminal Justice Agencies in the United States.* October 2007. Accessed February 8, 2015. https://it.ojp.gov/gist/108/Minimum-Criminal-Intelligence-Training-Standards.

82. Department of Homeland Security, Risk Steering Committee. *DHS Risk Lexicon.* September 2010. Accessed February 14, 2015. http://www.dhs.gov/dhs-risk-lexicon.

83. Department of Homeland Security, Risk Steering Committee. *DHS Risk Lexicon.* September 2010. Accessed February 14, 2015. http://www.dhs.gov/dhs-risk-lexicon.

84. Department of Homeland Security, Risk Steering Committee. *DHS Risk Lexicon.* September 2010. Accessed February 14, 2015. http://www.dhs.gov/dhs-risk-lexicon.

85. Department of Homeland Security, Risk Steering Committee. *DHS Risk Lexicon.* September 2010. Accessed February 14, 2015. http://www.dhs.gov/dhs-risk-lexicon.

86. Department of Homeland Security, Risk Steering Committee. *DHS Risk Lexicon.* September 2010. Accessed February 14, 2015. http://www.dhs.gov/dhs-risk-lexicon.

87. Department of Homeland Security, Risk Steering Committee. *DHS Risk Lexicon.* September 2010. Accessed February 14, 2015. http://www.dhs.gov/dhs-risk-lexicon.

88. Department of Homeland Security, Risk Steering Committee. *DHS Risk Lexicon.* September 2010. Accessed February 14, 2015. http://www.dhs.gov/dhs-risk-lexicon.

89. Department of Homeland Security, Risk Steering Committee. *DHS Risk Lexicon.* September 2010. Accessed February 14, 2015. http://www.dhs.gov/dhs-risk-lexicon.

90. Department of Homeland Security, Risk Steering Committee. *DHS Risk Lexicon.* September 2010. Accessed February 14, 2015. http://www.dhs.gov/dhs-risk-lexicon.

91. Department of Homeland Security, Risk Steering Committee. *DHS Risk Lexicon.* September 2010. Accessed February 14, 2015. http://www.dhs.gov/dhs-risk-lexicon.

92. Department of Homeland Security, Risk Steering Committee. *DHS Risk Lexicon.* September 2010. Accessed February 14, 2015. http://www.dhs.gov/dhs-risk-lexicon.

93. Department of Homeland Security, Risk Steering Committee. *DHS Risk Lexicon.* September 2010. Accessed February 14, 2015. http://www.dhs.gov/dhs-risk-lexicon.

94. Department of Homeland Security, Risk Steering Committee. DHS Risk Lexicon. September 2010. Accessed February 14, 2015. http://www.dhs.gov/dhs-risk-lexicon.

95. U.S. Department of State. "The Privacy Act and Personally Identifiable Information." *Foreign Affairs Manual.* 5 FAM 460. October 1, 2014. Accessed February 14, 2015. http://www.state.gov/documents/organization/85694.pdf.

96. North Atlantic Treaty Organization. *NATO Glossary of Terms and Definitions.* NATO Standardization Agency, 2014, AAP-06, accessed July 27, 2015, http://nso.nato.int/nso/zPublic/ap/aap6/AAP-6.pdf.

S

SABOTAGE An act or acts with intent to injure, interfere with, or obstruct the national defense of a country by willfully injuring or destroying, or attempting to injure or destroy, any national defense or war materiel, premises, or utilities, to include human and natural resources.[1]

SAFEGUARD OFFICER A cleared person who watches classified diplomatic pouches while the courier is attending to other business.[2]

SAFEGUARDS Protective measures prescribed to meet the security requirements (i.e., confidentiality, integrity, and availability) specified for an information system. Safeguards may include security features, management constraints, personnel security, and security of physical structures, areas, and devices. Synonymous with security controls and countermeasures.[3]

SAFEHAVEN 1. A protected or reinforced area within an official facility or personal residence located overseas to which occupants can retreat during an emergency and remain until the situation returns to normal or outside help arrives. 2. A foreign country or protected area within a foreign country affording a hiding place or temporary asylum for persons evading hostile government elements. 3. Designated area(s) to which noncombatant evacuees of the U.S. government's responsibility and commercial vehicles and materiel may be evacuated during a domestic or other valid emergency.[4]

SAFEHOUSE An innocent-appearing house or premises established by an organization for the purpose of conducting clandestine or covert activity in relative security.[5]

SAFEKEEPING The transfer of custody of classified diplomatic pouches from a diplomatic courier for temporary storage in a secure area (such as an embassy vault). Safekeeping requires receipt of all items on a DS-7600 retained locally until custody is returned to the diplomatic courier.[6]

SALAFISM A movement comprised of Sunni extremists who believe they are the only correct interpreters of the Qur'an and consider moderate or mainstream Muslims to be infidels. Salafists seek to convert all Muslims and to ensure their own fundamentalist version of Islam will dominate the world. "Salafi" comes from the word "Salaf," which means ancestors in Arabic. This worldview holds that the Righteous Ancestors were the Prophet, his companions, and the Four Caliphs who succeeded him: Abu-Bakr, Umar, Uthman, and Ali (the nephew of the Prophet). This movement has influenced the rise of Wahhabism.[7]

SALAMI TACTICS The incremental attainment of an objective in a slow, methodical way by reducing capabilities in one location while increasing capabilities in another location. For example, "The selling of [President] George Bush's tax cut relies heavily on salami tactics—slicing away opposition a bit at a time. To understand how fundamentally misleading that sales pitch is, we must look at the whole salami."[8] *See* CREEPING NORMALCY; PRECISION ATTACK/ENGAGEMENT

SANCTIONS A form of hard power, these are coercive measures taken by one or more states to protest another state's actions and to force a change of behavior. Although sanctions may technically include military action, they usually refer to measures taken by diplomats in lieu of military action. Diplomatically, sanctions may include the breaking of formal relations or the removal of a country's embassy. Other forms include economic sanctions to ban certain types of trade, and sports sanctions to prevent a country's people and teams from competing in international events.[9]

SANITIZE The deletion or revision of a report or document so as to prevent identification of the intelligence sources and methods that contributed to or are dealt with in the report.[10]

SANITIZATION 1. The process of removing information from media such that information recovery is not possible. It includes removing all labels, markings, and activity logs. 2. The editing of intelligence to protect sources, methods, capabilities, and analytical procedures to permit wider dissemination.[11] *See* WRITE-TO-RELEASE

SCALE The ratio or fraction between the distance on a map, chart, or photograph and the corresponding distance on the surface of the earth. *See* PHOTOGRAPHIC SCALE

SCAME Acronym used to remember the steps in analyzing opponent propaganda. The letters stand for Source, Content, Audience, Media, Effects.

SCATTERED CASTLES The Intelligence Community (IC) security clearance repository and the Director of National Intelligence's (DNI) authoritative source for clearance and access information for all IC, military services, Department of Defense (DoD) civilians, and contractor personnel.[12]

SCENARIO A narrative, timeline estimate of one significant path or development that may be followed by opposing or friendly strategic forces, offering key indicators for intelligence and actionable threats or opportunities for supported decision makers. *See* THREAT SCENARIO

SCHEDULED RECORDS All records that fall under a National Archives and Records Administration (NARA)–approved records control schedule are considered scheduled records.[13]

SCIENTIFIC AND TECHNICAL INTELLIGENCE Information on foreign scientific advancements and technologies.[14] *See* COMBAT INTELLIGENCE; CURRENT OPERATIONAL INTELLIGENCE; ESTIMATIVE INTELLIGENCE; RESEARCH INTELLIGENCE; WARNING INTELLIGENCE

SCION (SENSITIVE COMPARTMENTED INFORMATION OPERATIONAL NETWORK) SCION ("S") is the FBI enterprise network for processing, transmitting, and storing information at the TS/SCI level. "S" connects the FBI to the rest of the U.S. government Intelligence Community (IC) through a connection to the Joint Worldwide Intelligence Communications System enabling the FBI National Security Professionals (NSP) to share information and coordinate with their counterparts throughout the IC. "S" provides the FBI NSP with access to multiple Communities of Interest such as the National Counter Terrorism Center OnLine and Intelink for Counter Intelligence. "S" hosts internal applications such as the FISA Management System, Proton, and Intrepid.[15]

SCOPE The time period to be covered and the sources of information to be contacted during the prescribed course of a personnel security investigation.

SCREENING In intelligence, the evaluation of an individual or a group of individuals to determine their potential to answer collection requirements or to identify individuals who match a predetermined source profile coupled with the process of identifying and assessing the areas of knowledge, cooperation, and possible approach techniques for an individual who has information of intelligence value.[16]

SCREENING OF PASSENGERS BY OBSERVATION TECHNIQUES (SPOT) According to TSA's strategic plan and other program guidance for the BDA program released in December 2012, the goal of the agency's behavior detection activities, including the SPOT program, is to identify high-risk passengers based on behavioral indicators that indicate "malintent." For example, the strategic plan notes that in concert with other security measures, behavior detection activities "must be dedicated to finding individuals with the intent to do harm, as well as individuals with connections to terrorist networks that may be involved in criminal activity supporting terrorism." TSA developed its primary behavior detection activity, the SPOT program, in 2003 as an added layer of security to identify potentially high-risk passengers through behavior observation and analysis techniques. The SPOT program's standard operating procedures state that BDOs are to observe and visually assess passengers, primarily at passenger screening checkpoints, and identify those who display clusters of behaviors indicative of stress, fear, or deception. The SPOT procedures list a point system BDOs are to use to identify potentially high-risk passengers on the basis of behavioral and appearance indicators, as compared with baseline conditions where SPOT is being conducted (8). TSA has taken several positive steps to validate the scientific basis and strengthen program management of BDA and the SPOT program, which has been in place for over 6 years at a total cost of approximately $900 million since 2007. Nevertheless, TSA has not demonstrated that BDOs can consistently interpret the SPOT behavioral indicators, a fact that may contribute to varying passenger referral rates for additional screening. The subjectivity of the SPOT behavioral indicators and variation in BDO referral rates raise questions about the continued use of behavior indicators for detecting passengers who might pose a risk to aviation security. Furthermore, decades of peer-reviewed, published research on the complexities associated with detecting deception through human observation also draw into question the scientific underpinnings of TSA's behavior detection activities (47).[17] *See* BEHAVIORAL DETECTION ANALYSIS PROGRAM

SEALING (RECORDS) Records are stored by an agency but cannot be accessed, referenced, or used without a court order or statutory authority based on a showing of evidence that there is a legitimate government interest to review the sealed information.[18]

SEARCH AND RESCUE The use of aircraft, surface craft, submarines, and specialized rescue teams and equipment to search for and rescue distressed persons on land or at sea in a permissive environment.[19]

SEARCH WARRANT An express authorization to search and seize issued by competent civilian authority. A search warrant is a court order authorizing law enforcement to search a specified location and seize evidence. Under the Fourth Amendment, searches must be reasonable and specific. The Fourth Amendment prohibits unreasonable searches and seizures (U.S. Constitution. Amendment, IV). Searches and seizures are presumptively unreasonable, unless they are conducted pursuant to a warrant issued by a neutral magistrate upon a sworn showing of probable cause (*Terry v. Ohio*, 393 U.S. 1, 20, 1968).[20]

SECRECY, SECRET, SECRETS 1. Consciously willed concealment.[21] 2. The compulsory withholding of knowledge, reinforced by the prospects of sanctions for disclosure.[22] 3. "[A] tampering of communications. Political and governmental secrecy consists of the process of secreting information about political entities, especially when that information has significant implications for rival entities of the general public."[23] 4. Anything that "is kept intentionally hidden, set apart in the mind of its keeper as requiring concealment. . . . Conflicts over secrecy . . . are conflicts over power: the power that comes through controlling the flow of information."[24] 5. Security classification that shall be applied to information, the unauthorized disclosure of which reasonably could be expected to cause serious damage to the national security that the original classification authority is able to identify or describe.[25]

Types of secrecy and secrets

CORE SECRETS: Any item, process, strategy, or element of information, in which the compromise of would result in unrecoverable failure.[26]

ESSENTIAL SECRECY: The condition achieved by denial of critical information to adversaries.[27]

OBJECTIVE SECRETS: *Objective* secrets are supposed to contrast with each of these qualities separately—they are supposed to be diffuse, technical, determinable, eternal, and long-lasting qua secrets. That is, they may be far from expressible in a few words (a theory of neutron diffusion involves integro-differential equations and takes volumes to express when it is put into useable form); they may not be understandable to anyone without a technical training (no untrained observer simply grasps the details of fluorocarbon chemistry); they are supposed to be determinable insofar as they can be deduced if the right question is posed (the number of neutrons emitted in uranium fission can be found with enough effort and equipment); and, finally, the objective secret is supposed to be in some sense unchangeable (in the limit case a law of nature but, if not that, then least as unchangeable as the finely articulated process of preparing equipment against the corrosive effects of uranium hexafluoride). As such, objective secrets are long-lasting secrets.[28]

STRUCTURAL SECRECY: The way that patterns of information, organizational structure, processes, and transactions, and the structure of regulatory relations systematically undermine the attempts to know and interpret situations in all organizations.[29]

SUBJECTIVE SECRETS: *Subjective* secrets are said by classifiers to display five key characteristics—they are compact, transparent, arbitrary, changeable, and perishable. Compact means they can be expressed very briefly; transparent that they are readily understandable ("two of the Abrams tanks are disabled"); changeable means that they typically can be revised ("the 101st Airborne will conduct its first drop at first light") and they are perishable (normally after some decent interval, once the 101st has landed the fact that they did so has lost its potency).[30]

TACIT SILENCE OR A PARTIAL SECRET: This type of secrecy is somewhere between deep concealment and full disclosure, and based on the philosophy that things are better left unsaid. Thompson writes, "Such secrets are not completely concealed because their content may be widely known or could be widely known. But their content is not made explicit, and its not being made explicit is necessary" for a policy's effectiveness. Thompson has identified three kinds of tacit silences/partial secrets: excuses and nonenforcement, compelled silence, political hypocrisy (3).[31]

TRADE SECRETS: "Trade secret" means information, including a formula, pattern, compilation, program, device, method, technique, or process, that: (1) derives independent economic value, actual or potential, from not being generally known to, and not being readily ascertainable by proper means by, other persons who can obtain economic value from its disclosure or use, and (2) is the subject of efforts that are reasonable under the circumstances to maintain its secrecy.[32]

SECRECY OATHS The House and Senate differ with regard to secrecy oaths for members and staff. Neither the full Senate nor any Senate panel apparently imposes a secrecy oath or affirmation on its Members or employees. The House, by comparison, has adopted such special procedures. Beginning with the 104th Congress, the House has required a secrecy oath (taken once per Congress) for each member, delegate, resident commissioner, officer, and employee of the chamber. Before any such person may have access to classified information, he or she must solemnly swear (or affirm) that "I will not disclose any classified information received in the course of my service with the House of Representatives, except as authorized by the House of Representatives or in accordance with its Rules." Previously, a similar oath was required only for members and staff of the House Permanent Select Committee on Intelligence. This requirement had been added in the 102nd Congress as part of the select committee's internal rules, following abortive attempts to establish it in public law. The oath is still in effect for the panel's members and staff: "I do solemnly swear (or affirm) that I will not disclose or cause to be disclosed any classified information received in the course of my service on the House Permanent Select Committee on Intelligence, except when authorized to do so by the Committee or the House of Representatives." At least one other panel has adopted a similar measure. The House Committee on Homeland Security requires an oath or affirmation from each committee member or staff seeking access to classified information, modeled after the one adopted by the House Intelligence Committee.[33]

SECRECY ORDERS Whenever publication or disclosure by the publication of an application or by the grant of a patent on an invention in which the government has a property interest might, in the opinion of the head of the interested government agency, be detrimental to the national security, the Commissioner of Patents upon being so notified shall order that the invention be kept secret and shall withhold the publication of the application or the grant of a patent therefore under the conditions set forth hereinafter. Whenever the publication or disclosure of an invention by the publication of an application or by the granting of a patent, in which the government does not have a property interest, might, in the opinion of the Commissioner of Patents, be detrimental to the national security, he shall make the application for patent in which such invention is disclosed available for inspection to the Atomic Energy Commission, the Secretary of Defense, and the chief officer of any other department or agency of the government designated by the president as a defense agency of the United States.[34]

SECRET AGENT A person secretly employed in espionage for a government. The term is mostly used in novels and movies. At the CIA, a "case officer" recruits "agents." At the FBI, a "special agent" or "agent" recruits "informants." At neither agency is the term "secret agent" used. *See* AGENT

SECRET-CLEARED U.S. CITIZEN A citizen of the United States who has undergone a background investigation by an authorized U.S. Government Agency and been issued a Secret security clearance, in accordance with Executive Orders 13526, and implementing guidelines and standards published in 32 CFR 147.[35]

SECRET DETENTION For the purpose of the present report, it is construed that a person is kept in secret detention if State authorities acting in their official capacity, or persons acting under the orders thereof, with the authorization, consent, support or acquiescence of the State, or in any other situation where the action or omission of the detaining person is attributable to the State, deprive persons of their liberty; where the person is not permitted any contact with the outside world ("incommunicado detention"); and when the detaining or otherwise competent authority denies, refuses to confirm or deny or actively conceals the fact that the person is deprived of his/her liberty hidden from the outside world, including, for example, family, independent lawyers or non-governmental organizations, or refuses to provide or actively conceals information about the fate or whereabouts of the detainee. In the present report, the term "detention" is used synonymously with "deprivation of liberty," "keeping in custody," or "holding in custody." 9. Secret detention does not require deprivation of liberty in a secret place of detention; in other words, secret detention within the scope of the present report may take place not only in a place that is not an officially recognized place of detention, or in an officially recognized place of detention, but in a hidden section or wing that is itself not officially recognized, but also in an officially recognized site. 10. Any detention facility may fall within the scope of the present study. It can be a prison, police station, governmental building, military base or camp, but also, for example, a private residence, hotel, car, ship or plane. 11. Incommunicado detention, where the detainees may only have contact with their captors, guards or co-inmates, would amount to secret detention also if the International Committee of the Red Cross (ICRC) is granted access by the authorities, but is not permitted to register the case, or, if it is allowed to register the case, is not permitted by the State to, or does not, for whatever reason, notify the next of kin of the detainee on his or her whereabouts.[36]

SECRET DIPLOMACY Negotiations in regard to which any number of the following is kept secret: (1) the content of the negotiations; (2) the fact that negotiations are going on; (3) the content of any agreement successfully negotiated ("secret treaties"); or (4) the fact that any agreement has been successfully negotiated. If secret diplomacy is defined as in sense 1, the term is nothing more than a pleonasm since serious negotiation is secret by definition.[37]

SECRET HOLDS Often used to stall action on legislation or nominations in order to extract concessions from other senators or the administration. They are also employed to "take hostages." Senators may delay bills or nominations, which they do not oppose, so they might gain political or procedural leverage to achieve other extraneous objectives. There have been times, said then-Senate GOP Leader Trent Lott, when holds have been applied to "every piece of a committee's legislation . . . by an individual or group of senators, not because they wish to be involved in consideration of those bills, but as a means of achieving unrelated purposes or leverage." From being a courtesy to keep senators informed about impending action on measures or matters, holds have evolved to become a parliamentary weapon for stalling or obstructing floor decision making" (2). For more than at least a quarter century, various senators have urged an end to secret holds. In 1984, for example, Senator James Exon lamented that "this Senator cannot even find out which Senator or the staff of which Senator has placed a hold on that bill."[38]

SECRET INTERNET PROTOCOL ROUTER NETWORK (SIPRNet) The Secret Internet Protocol Router Network (SIPRNet) is the Department of Defense network for the exchange of classified information and messages at the SECRET level. It supports the Global Command and Control System, the Defense Message System, and numerous other classified warfighting and planning applications. Although the SIPRNet uses the same communications procedures as the Internet, it has dedicated and encrypted lines that are separate from all other communications systems. It is the classified counterpart of the Unclassified but Sensitive Internet Protocol Router Network (NIPRNET), which provides seamless interoperability for unclassified combat support applications and controlled access to the Internet. Access to the SIPRNet requires a SECRET level clearance or higher and a need to have information that is available only on the SIPRNet. Because the SIPRNet is an obvious target for hostile penetration, a number of strict security procedures are applied. Appropriate credentials and two-factor authentication are required.[39]

SECRET SESSIONS OF THE HOUSE AND SENATE Secret, or closed, sessions of the House and Senate exclude the press and the public. They may be held for matters deemed to require confidentiality and secrecy—such as national security, sensitive communications received from the president, and Senate deliberations during impeachment trials. Although members usually seek advance agreement for going into secret session, any member of Congress may request a secret session without notice. When the House or Senate goes into secret session, its chamber and galleries are cleared of everyone except members and officers and employees specified in the rules or designated by the presiding officer as essential to the session. After the chamber is cleared, its doors are closed. Authority for the House and Senate to hold secret sessions appears in Article I, Section 5, of the Constitution: "Each House may determine the Rules of its Proceedings. . . . Each House shall keep a

Journal of its Proceedings, and from time to time publish the same, excepting such Parts as may in their judgment require Secrecy." Both chambers have implemented these constitutional provisions through rules and precedents.[40]

SECTOR-SPECIFIC AGENCY "Sector-Specific Agency" (SSA) means the federal department or agency designated under this directive to be responsible for providing institutional knowledge and specialized expertise as well as leading, facilitating, or supporting the security and resilience programs and associated activities of its designated critical infrastructure sector in the all-hazards environment.[41]

SECURE AND SECURITY The terms "secure" and "security" refer to reducing the risk to critical infrastructure by physical means or defense cyber measures to intrusions, attacks, or the effects of natural or manmade disasters.[42]

SECURE BORDERS AND OPEN DOORS A phrase that summarizes the goal of our federal government charged with interviewing, assessing, processing, analyzing, and welcoming hundreds of millions of international visitors while finding the small numbers of people—the needles in the haystack—intent on using our openness against us. It is also the name of our advisory committee tasked with advising the departments of homeland security and State in their mission to protect not only America's security but also our economic livelihood, ideals, image, and strategic relationships with the world.[43]

SECURE FLIGHT Since its implementation, in 2009, Secure Flight has changed from a program that identifies passengers as high risk solely by matching them against federal government watch lists—primarily the No Fly List, comprised of individuals who should be precluded from boarding an aircraft, and the Selectee List, composed of individuals who should receive enhanced screening at the passenger security checkpoint—to one that uses additional lists and risk-based criteria to assign passengers to a risk category: high risk, low risk, or unknown risk. In 2010, following the December 2009 attempted attack on a U.S.-bound flight, which exposed gaps in how agencies used watch lists to screen individuals, TSA began using risk-based criteria to create additional lists for Secure Flight screening. These lists are composed of high-risk passengers who may not be in the Terrorist Screening Database (TSDB) but who TSA has determined should be subject to enhanced screening procedures. Further, in 2011, TSA began screening passengers against additional identities in the TSDB that are not included on the No Fly or Selectee Lists. In addition, as part of TSA Pre™, a 2011 program through which TSA designates passengers as low risk for expedited screening, TSA began screening against several new lists of preapproved low-risk travelers. TSA also began conducting TSA Pre™ risk assessments, an activity distinct from matching against lists that uses the Secure Flight system to assign passengers scores based upon their travel-related data, for the purpose of identifying them as low risk for a specific flight.[44]

SECURE ROOM Any room with floor-to-ceiling, slab-to-slab construction of some substantial material—for example, concrete, brick, cinder block, plywood, or plaster board. Any window areas or penetrations of wall areas over 15.25 cm (96 square inches) must be covered with either grilling or substantial type material. Entrance doors must be constructed of solid wood, metal, or other secure material and be capable of holding a DS-approved three-way combination lock with interior extension.[45]

SECURE TELEPHONE UNIT (STU) A telephone that can carry secure conversations. STUs can also function as regular telephones when the crypto ignition is not inserted.

SECURE TERMINAL EQUIPMENT (STE) A telephone that can carry secure conversations. STEs are replacing Secure Telephone Units (STUs), although STUs are still in common use.

SECURE VOICE Systems in which transmitted conversations are encrypted to make them unintelligible to anyone except the intended recipient. Within the context of Department security standards, secure voice systems must also have protective features included in the environment of the systems terminals.[46]

SECURITY The term "security" refers to the protection of the nation and its people, vital interests, and way of life.[47]

SECURITY ANOMALY An irregularity possibly indicative of a security breach, an attempt to breach security, or of noncompliance with security standards, policy, or procedures.[48]

SECURITY CATEGORIZATION The characterization of information or an information system based on an assessment of the potential impact that a loss of confidentiality, integrity, or availability of such information or information system would have on organizational operations, organizational assets, or individuals.[49]

SECURITY CERTIFICATION A certification issued by competent national authority to indicate that a person has been investigated and is eligible for access for classified matter to the extent stated in the certification.

SECURITY CLASSIFICATION A category to which national security information and material is assigned to denote the degree of damage that unauthorized disclosure would cause to national defense or foreign relations of the United States and to denote the degree of protection required. There are three such categories: top secret, secret, and confidential.[50] There are classification levels: (1) "Top Secret" shall be applied to information, the unauthorized disclosure of which reasonably could be expected to cause exceptionally grave damage to the national security that the original classification authority is able to identify or describe. (2) "Secret" shall be applied to information, the unauthorized disclosure of which reasonably could be expected to cause serious damage to the national security that the original classification authority is able to identify or describe. (3) "Confidential" shall be applied to information, the unauthorized disclosure of which reasonably could be expected to cause damage to the national security that the original classification authority is able to identify or describe.[51] See CLASSIFICATION; CLASSIFICATION AND CONTROL MARKING SYSTEM; CLASSIFICATION MARKINGS; CUI REGISTRY

SECURITY CLEARANCE An administrative determination by competent authority that an individual is eligible for access to classified information.[52] *See* CLASSIFICATION; CLASSIFIED INFORMATION

SECURITY COUNTERMEASURES Actions, devices, procedures, and/or techniques to reduce security risks.[53]

SECURITY DETAINEE Those detainees who are not combatants, but who may be under investigation or pose a threat to U.S. forces if released.[54]

SECURITY DILEMMA Any action by a nation or a decision by that nation's leadership to enhance security that may also lead to a shift in a systemic power balance that could be perceived to endanger other nations.[55]

SECURITY ENVIRONMENT THREAT LIST (SETL) A list of countries with United States (U.S.) Diplomatic Missions compiled by the Department of State (DoS) and updated semi-annually. The listed countries are evaluated based on transnational terrorism; political violence; human intelligence; technical threats; and criminal threats. The following four threat levels are based on these evaluations: Critical: A definite threat to U.S. assets based on an adversary's capability, intent to attack, and targeting conducted on a recurring basis; High: A credible threat to U.S. assets based on knowledge of an adversary's capability, intent to attack, and related incidents at similar facilities; Medium: A potential threat to U.S. assets based on knowledge of an adversary's desire to compromise the assets and the possibility that the adversary could obtain the capability to attack through a third party who has demonstrated such a capability; Low: Little or no threat as a result of the absence of credible evidence of capability, intent, or history of actual or planned attack against U.S. assets.[56]

SECURITY GOALS In information technology, the five security goals are confidentiality, availability, integrity, accountability, and assurance.

SECURITY IMPACT ANALYSIS An analysis conducted by an agency official, often during the continuous monitoring phase of the security certification and accreditation process, to determine the extent to which changes to the information system have affected the security posture of the system.

SECURITY INCIDENT A knowing, willful, or negligent action resulting in the failure to safeguard materials appropriately. Security incidents may be judged as either security infractions or security violations.[57]

SECURITY INFRACTION A security incident that DS/IS/APD judges as not reasonably expected to result in an unauthorized disclosure of classified information. For example, at the end of the workday, an employee leaves a security container unlocked and unattended, containing classified information, in an area authorized for the storage of classified information (i.e., it meets 12 FAM 530 requirements), and there is no evidence of an unauthorized entry. DS/IS/APD likely would adjudicate an incident such as this infraction.[58]

SECURITY INTELLIGENCE Intelligence on the identity, capabilities, and intentions of hostile organizations or individuals who are or may be engaged in espionage, sabotage, subversion, or terrorism.[59] *See* COUNTERINTELLIGENCE; INTELLIGENCE, SURVEILLANCE, AND RECONNAISSANCE

SECURITY MARKING Human-readable indicators applied to a document, storage media, or hardware component to designate security classification, categorization and/or handling restrictions applicable to the information contained therein. For intelligence information, these could include compartment and sub-compartment indicators and handling restrictions. Human-readable information affixed to information system components, removable media, or output indicating the distribution limitations, handling caveats and applicable security markings.[60]

SECURITY POLICY A rule or set of rules that govern the acceptable use of an organization's information and services to a level of acceptable risk and the means for protecting the organization's information assets. Extended Definition: A rule or set of rules applied to an information system to provide security services.[61]

SECURITY REVIEW The process of reviewing information and products prior to public release to ensure the material will not jeopardize ongoing or future operations.[62]

SECURITY STATE The Security State gets its name from the fact that the chief drives of Americans' today appear to be the demands of the individual for economic and psychic security which are subsumed under the notion of the social-service or welfare principle of government, and the demands of people generally (for our purposes here, the State) for national security (self-preservation) . . . above, the Security State is the official institutionalization of a society which has as its aim the furtherance of the primordial value of security. Dual in nature, it includes programs designed to promote individual and national security. Individual security measures make up many of the fundamentally domestic goals of Americans, while national security measures constitute the external goals.[63] *See* NATIONAL SECURITY

SECURITY VIOLATION A security incident that DS/IS/APD judges as reasonably expected to result in an unauthorized disclosure of classified information. For example, if an employee transmits a classified document over an unclassified facsimile (FAX) machine, DS/IS/APD likely would adjudicate the incident as a violation, because electronic interception and transcription of the classified document is possible.[64]

SEGREGABLE NON-EXEMPT INFORMATION Section (b) of the FOIA, which contains the FOIA's nine statutory exemptions, also directs agencies to release to FOIA requesters any reasonably segregable, non-exempt information that is contained in those records. See 5 U.S.C. § 552(b) (sentence immediately following exemptions). As amended by the Open Government Act, the provision now reads:

Any reasonably segregable portion of a record shall be provided to any person requesting such record after deletion of the portions which are exempt under this subsection. The amount of information deleted, *and the exemption under which the deletion is made*, shall be indicated on the released portion of the record unless including that indication would harm an interest protected by the exemption in this subsection under which the deletion is made. If technically feasible, the amount of the information deleted, *and the exemption under which the deletion is made*, shall be indicated at the place in the record where such deletion is made. 5 U.S.C. § 552(b) (amended language in italics).[65]

SELECTEE LIST A list of individuals who do not meet the criteria to be placed on the No Fly List but meet the selectee criteria as members of a foreign or domestic terrorist organization or associated with terrorist activity. Individuals on the Selectee List may fly only after they and their checked and carry-on baggage have been subjected to additional screening. Originally maintained by TSA (and the FAA prior to 9/11), the No Fly and Selectee lists were transferred to the Terrorist Screening Center (TSC) in 2004. The TSC was established under the auspices of the FBI in an initiative under Homeland Security Presidential Directive 6.[66] *See* NO FLY LIST

SELF-RADICALIZATION 1. Significant steps an individual takes in advocating or adopting an extremist belief system for the purpose of facilitating ideologically based violence to advance political, religious, or social change. The self-radicalized individual has not been recruited by and has no direct, personal influence or tasking from other violent extremists. The self-radicalized individual may seek out direct or indirect (through the Internet for example) contact with other violent extremists for moral support and to enhance his or her extremist beliefs.[67] 2. The process whereby people seek out opportunities for involvement in terrorist activity absent a formal involvement in a terrorist group and/or recruitment by others.[68]

SEMI-QUANTITATIVE RISK ASSESSMENT METHODOLOGY Set of methods, principles, or rules to assess risk that uses bins, scales, or representative numbers whose values and meanings are not maintained in other contexts.[69]

SENIOR AGENCY INFORMATION SECURITY OFFICER (SAISO) Official responsible for carrying out the Chief Information Officer responsibilities under the Federal Information Security Management Act (FISMA) and serving as the Chief Information Officer's primary liaison to the agency's authorizing officials, information system owners, and information systems security officers.[70]

SENIOR OFFICIAL OF THE INTELLIGENCE COMMUNITY (SOIC)
The head of an agency, office, bureau, other intelligence element as identified in Section 3 of the National Security Act of 1947, as amended, 50 USC 401a(4), and Section 3.4(f) (1 through 6) of Executive Order 12333.[71] There are classification levels: (1) "Top Secret" shall be applied to information, the unauthorized disclosure of which reasonably could be expected to cause exceptionally grave damage to the national security that the original classification authority is able to identify or describe. (2) "Secret" shall be applied to information, the unauthorized disclosure of which reasonably could be expected to cause serious damage to the national security that the original classification authority is able to identify or describe. (3) "Confidential" shall be applied to information, the unauthorized disclosure of which reasonably could be expected to cause damage to the national security that the original classification authority is able to identify or describe.[72] *See* CLASSIFICATION; CLASSIFICATION AND CONTROL MARKING SYSTEM; CLASSIFICATION MARKINGS; CUI REGISTRY

SENSITIVE BUT UNCLASSIFIED INFORMATION (SBU) Information for which disclosure, loss, misuse, alteration, or destruction could adversely affect national security or governmental interests. National security interests are those unclassified matters that relate to the national defense or foreign relations of the U.S. government. Governmental interests are those related but not limited to the wide range of government or government-derived economic, human, financial, industrial, agriculture, technological, and law-enforcement information, as well as the privacy or confidentially of personal or commercial proprietary information provided to the U.S. government by its citizens.[73]

SENSITIVE BY AGGREGATION Refers to the fact that information on one site may seem unimportant, but when combined with information from other websites, it may form a larger and more complete picture that was neither intended nor desired. Similarly, the compilation of a large amount of information together on one site may increase the sensitivity of that information and make it more likely that site will be accessed by those seeking information that can be used against the government.[74]

SENSITIVE COMPARTMENTED INFORMATION 1. Information that requires restricted handling within the intelligence community, to include the programs used to collect the information and the intelligence that was produced. 2. Classified national intelligence concerning or derived from intelligence sources, methods, or analytical processes that is required to be protected within formal access control systems established and overseen by the director of national intelligence.[75]

SENSITIVE COMPARTMENTED INFORMATION FACILITY (SCIF) An accredited area, room, group of rooms, or installation where sensitive compartmented information may be stored, used, discussed, and/or electronically processed, where procedural and physical measures prevent the free access of persons unless they have been formally indoctrinated for the particular sensitive compartmented information authorized for use or storage within the sensitive compartmented information facility.[76] The information or material is subject to special intelligence community controls that indicate restricted handling for current and future intelligence collection programs and their end products.

SENSITIVE HOMELAND SECURITY INFORMATION (SHSI) Any information created or received by an agency or any local, county, state, or tribal government that the loss, misuse, unauthorized disclosure, modification of, or the unauthorized access to could reasonably be expected to impair significantly the capabilities and/or efforts of agencies and/or local, county, state, and tribal personnel to predict, analyze, investigate, deter, prevent, protect against, mitigate the effects of, or recover from acts that is: Classified as national security information (1) pursuant to Executive Order 12958, as amended, or any successor order; Designated by Executive Order 12951, any (2) successor order, or the Atomic Energy Act of 1954 (42 U.S.C. § 2011), to require protection against unauthorized disclosure; Protected Critical Infrastructure Information (PCII) (3) as defined in 6 *Code of Federal Regulations* (CFR) § 29.2; Sensitive Security Information (SSI) as defined 4. in 49 CFR Part 1520.[77]

SENSITIVE INFORMATION Information for which the loss, misuse, or unauthorized access to or modification of could adversely affect the national interest or the conduct of federal programs, or the privacy to which individuals are entitled under the Privacy Act, but which has not been specifically authorized under criteria established by an Executive Order or an Act of Congress to be kept secret in the interest of national defense or foreign policy.

SENSITIVE INTELLIGENCE INFORMATION Such intelligence information of which unauthorized disclosure would lead to counteraction: (1) Jeopardizing the continued productivity of intelligence sources or methods which provide intelligence vital to national security; or (2) Offsetting the value of intelligence vital to national security.[78]

SENSITIVE INVESTIGATIVE MATTER An investigative matter involving the activities of a domestic public official or political candidate (involving corruption or a threat to the national security), religious or political organization or individual prominent in such an organization, or news media, or any other matter which, in the judgment of the official authorizing an investigation, should be brought to the attention of FBI Headquarters and other Department of Justice officials.[79]

SENSITIVE MONITORING CIRCUMSTANCE Investigation of a member of Congress, a federal judge, a member of the Executive Branch at Executive Level IV or above, or a person who has served in such capacity within the previous two years; investigation of the governor, lieutenant governor, or attorney general of any state or territory, or a judge or justice of the highest court of any state or territory, concerning an offense involving bribery, conflict of interest, or extortion related to the performance of official duties; a party to the communication is in the custody of the Bureau of Prisons or the United States Marshals Service or is being or has been afforded protection in the Witness Security Program; or the attorney general, the deputy attorney general, or an assistant attorney general has requested that the FBI obtain prior approval for the use of consensual monitoring in a specific investigation.[80]

SENSITIVE PERSONALLY IDENTIFIABLE INFORMATION Personal information that specifically identifies an individual and, if such information is exposed to unauthorized access, may cause harm to that individual at a moderate or high impact level (see 5 FAM 1065.4 for the impact levels).[81]

SENSITIVE REVIEW BOARD (SRB) This board is responsible for ensuring appropriate personnel within their IC element obtain information that is relevant to their assigned mission need, which may include information exempted by the DNI from discovery by authorized IC personnel. SRB members' access is not limited to information made discoverable as a result of an IC integrated implementation plan.[82]

SENSITIVITY ANALYSIS Process to determine how outputs of a methodology differ in response to variation of the inputs or conditions. (1) When a factor considered in a risk assessment has uncertainty, sensitivity analysis examines the effect that the uncertainty has on the results. (2) A sensitivity analysis can be used to examine how individual variables can affect the outputs of risk assessment methodologies. (3) Alternatively, sensitivity analysis can show decision makers or evaluators the impact or predicted impact of risk management alternatives.[83]

SERE TECHNIQUES 1. Those techniques used by SERE (Survival, Evasion, Resistance and Escape) school instructors that are not authorized in Reference (i) for use as intelligence interrogation techniques (see U.S. Army Field Manual 2-22.3, "Human Intelligence Collector Operations," September 6, 2006).[84] 2. The CIA contracted with two psychologists to develop, operate, and assess its interrogation operations. The psychologists' prior experience was at the U.S. Air Force Survival, Evasion, Resistance and Escape (SERE) school. Neither psychologist had any experience as an interrogator, nor did either have specialized knowledge of al-Qa'ida, a background in counterterrorism, or any relevant cultural or linguistic expertise (11).[85]

SEVEN MEMBER RULE In 2001, seventeen Democrats and one Independent in the House invoked a seldom-used statute, first enacted in 1928, that requires executive agencies to furnish information if requested by seven members of the House Committee on Government Reform or five members of the Senate Committee on Governmental Affairs. They sought census data from the Commerce Department. After the administration challenged the constitutionality of this statutory provision, a federal district court ruled in favor of the lawmakers.[86]

SHADOW GOVERNMENT Governmental elements and activities performed by the irregular organization that will eventually take the place of the existing government. Members of the shadow government can be in any element of the irregular organization (underground, auxiliary, or guerrillas).[87]

SHARED SITUATIONAL AWARENESS The comprehensive, cross-network domain knowledge resulting from combining and synthesizing relevant, timely, and comprehensive situational awareness information, tailored to the needs of each organization, which enables a transformational improvement in their ability to operate, maintain, and defend their networks or perform their cybersecurity missions.[88]

SHEEP DIPPING The utilization of a military instrument (e.g., an airplane) or officer in clandestine operations, usually in a civilian capacity or under civilian cover, although the instrument or officer will covertly retain its or his military ownership or standing. The term is also applied to the placement of individuals in organizations or groups in which they can become active in order to establish credentials so that they can be used to collect information of intelligence interest on similar groups.[89]

SHELTER IN PLACE (SIP) Taking cover and remaining in the current location during a crisis (sometimes referred to as "stand fast") until either receiving an all-clear signal, instructions to change locations, or making a decision to leave the current location based on training, experience, and/or threat analysis. Instructions on when/how to decide to remain sheltering in place or to leave for a different location is a post Emergency Action Committee (EAC) decision and can be added to the Emergency Action Plan (EAP). SIP can also apply to residences.[90]

SIGNAL Information accurately interpreted as evidence that points to an adversary's future action or intention. *See* NOISE

SIGNAL FLAGS The Intelligence Community (IC) database containing information used to assist security and counterintelligence professionals conducting National Agency Checks (NACs) on individuals applying for positions with IC organizations.[91]

SIGNALS INTELLIGENCE (SIGINT) The collection of intelligence from nonpublic communications and other types of electromagnetic emissions such as radar and telemetry.[92] *See* SOURCES OF INTELLIGENCE

SIGNATURE A recognizable, distinguishing pattern associated with an attack, such as a binary string in a virus or a particular set of keystrokes used to gain unauthorized access to a system.

SIGNIFICANT CONSEQUENCES Loss of life, significant responsive actions against the United States, significant damage to property, serious adverse U.S. foreign policy consequences, or serious economic impact on the United States.[93]

SIGNIFICANT DEROGATORY INFORMATION Information that could justify an unfavorable administrative action, or prompt an adjudicator to seek additional investigation or clarification.[94]

SIGNIFICANT OR HIGHLY SENSITIVE MATTER A development or circumstance involving an intelligence activity or intelligence personnel that may or may not be unlawful or contrary to an executive order or presidential directive, but could impugn the reputation or integrity of a DoD intelligence components or otherwise call into question the propriety of an intelligence activity. Such matters might be manifested in or by an activity that involves congressional inquiries or investigations; may result in adverse media coverage; may impact on foreign relations or foreign partners; or is related to the unauthorized disclosure of classified or protected information, such as information identifying a sensitive source and method, but not including routine security violations.[95]

SIGNPOSTS Intermediate developments indicating that events may not be unfolding as expected; also known as indicators of change.[96] *See* INDICATION

SILK ROAD—SILK ROAD RELOADED An online market place, part of the dark Internet or Dark Web. Users browse anonymously through the Tor Onion Router (Tor); Silk Road Reloaded utilizes the I2P anonymity network.[97]

SIMULATION A model that behaves or operates like a given process, concept, or system when provided a set of controlled inputs.[98]

SINGAPORE INTELLIGENCE FAILURE A Japanese surprise attack against the British during World War II in 1942 that resulted in 130,000 well-equipped British, Australian, and Indian troops surrendering to 35,000 ill-equipped Japanese soldiers. The Singapore incident is considered one of Britain's greatest military defeats and intelligence failures.

SINGLE-DISCIPLINE The use of only one intelligence specialty in addressing issues and answering questions. *See* INTELLIGENCE-SPECIFIC; SINGLE-INTELLIGENCE

SINGLE-DISCIPLINE COLLECTION The method of using one intelligence collection discipline (usually specified or designated by a command authority) to answer a request for information and intelligence issue, or to cross-queue other intelligence collection disciplines' activities or operations against a predetermined target or set of targets.

SINGLE-INTELLIGENCE (SINGLE-INT) The use of only one intelligence discipline to address and answer an issue or request for information. *See* INTELLIGENCE-SPECIFIC; SINGLE-DISCIPLINE

SINGLE-POINT CONCLUSION A threat scenario that considers no other alternative. For example, U.S. intelligence has been criticized for developing all their weapons of mass destruction scenarios for Iraq on the assumption that Iraq had that capability.

SINGLE-SOURCE The use of only one resource or set of common resources.

SINGLE-SOURCE COLLECTION The use of only one intelligence collection resource to collect against, analyze and characterize, and report against a given target or set of targets.

SITUATION ASSESSMENT 1. An assessment produced by analyzing various indicators to provide a comprehensive projection of a current situation, with the understanding that additional or unknown variables can immediately change any outcomes from a situation assessment. 2. An assessment process based on the theory that comprehending the meaning or the quality and quantity of variables in the environment and the projection of their status into the near future will result in analysis of how various actions will occur in the future.[99]

SITUATIONAL AWARENESS 1. Within a volume of time and space, the perception of an enterprise's security posture and its threat environment; the comprehension/meaning of both taken together (risk); and the projection of their status into the near future.[100] 2. In cybersecurity, comprehending the current status and security posture with respect to availability, confidentiality, and integrity of networks, systems, users, and data, as well as projecting future states of these.[101]

SITUATIONAL INFORMATION A component of contextual data that describes the who, what, when, where, how, why, and more associated with an event and/or subject.[102]

SKYNET 1. Collaborative cloud research effort between five different organizations crossing three NSA Directorates. SKYNET applies complex combinations of geospatial, geotemporal, pattern-of-life and travel analytics to bulk DNR (dialed number activity) data to identify patterns of suspect activity.[103] 2. Skynet uses phone location and call metadata from bulk phone call records to detect suspicious patterns in the physical movements of suspects and their communication habits.[104]

SLEEPER An illegal or agent residing in a foreign country under orders to engage in no intelligence activities. The inactive status, which can endure for a considerable time, serves to strengthen the legend and permit access by a foreign power to an individual in position to be ready for action under certain circumstances should a specific need arise.

SLUR An open source, decentralized and anonymous marketplace for the selling of secret information in exchange for bitcoin. Slur is written in C and operates over the Tor network with bitcoin transactions through libbitcoin. Both buyers and sellers are fully anonymous, and there are no restrictions on the data that is auctioned. There is no charge to buy or sell on the Slur marketplace except in the case of a dispute, where a token sum is paid to volunteers.[105]

SMART POWER The flexible and combined use of hard power—military force or economic sanctions—and soft power—diplomatic and cultural influence—to overcome a foreign policy challenge.[106]

SNIFFER Software that monitors network packets and can be used to intercept data including passwords, credit card numbers, and more.[107]

SNOWDEN SURVEILLANCE ARCHIVE Our aim in creating this archive is to provide a tool that would facilitate citizen, researcher and journalist access to these important documents. Indexes, document descriptions, links to original documents and to related news stories, a glossary and comprehensive search features are all designed to enable a better understanding of state surveillance programs within the wider context of surveillance by the U.S. National Security Agency (NSA) along with its partners in the Five Eyes countries—U.K., Canada, Australia and New Zealand. The Snowden Archive is the result of a research collaboration between Canadian Journalists for Free Expression (CJFE) and the Politics of Surveillance Project at the Faculty of Information at the University of Toronto. Partners and supporters of this initiative include the Surveillance Studies Centre, Queen's University; the Digital Curation Institute, Faculty of Information, University of Toronto; and the Centre for Free Expression, Faculty of Communications and Design, Ryerson University.[108]

SOCIAL AMPLIFICATION OF RISK Distortion of the seriousness of a risk caused by public concern about the risk and/or about an activity contributing to the risk. 1) Describes the phenomenon by which hazards interact with psychological, social, institutional, and cultural processes in ways that may amplify or attenuate the public's perceived level of risk. 2) The social amplification of risk phenomenon is the subject of a field of study that seeks to systematically link the technical of risk with sociological perspectives of risk perception and risk-related behavior.[109]

SOCIAL MEDIA POLICY Guidelines that pertain to employees' interaction with social media websites. Employees are often encouraged to follow these guidelines, but in some cases employees are required to follow the guidelines or risk disciplinary action.[110]

SOCIAL RADAR A Social Radar needs to sense perceptions, attitudes, beliefs and behaviors (via indicators and correlation with other factors) and geographically and/or socially localize and track these to support the smart engagement of foreign populations and the assessment and replanning of efforts based on indicator progression. As a modern center of gravity, the perceptions, cognitions, emotions, and behaviors of populations encompass the hopes, fears, and dreams of many publics. Accordingly, a social radar needs to be not only sensitive to private and public cognitions and the amplifying effect of human emotions but also sensitive to cultural values as they can drive or shape behavior. Conventional radar requires signatures for different kinds of objects and events: it needs to be tuned to different environmental conditions to provide accurate and reliable information. Analogously, a social radar needs signatures, calibration, and correlation to sense, if not forecast, a broad spectrum of phenomena (e.g., political, economic, social, environmental, health) and potentially forecast changing trends in population perceptions and behaviors. For example, radar or sonar enable some degree of forecasting by tracking spatial and temporal patterns (e.g., they track and display how military objects or weather phenomena move in what clusters, in which direction(s) and at what speed). A user can thus project where and when objects will be in the future. Similarly, a social radar should enable us to forecast who will cluster with whom in a network, where, and when in what kinds of relationships.[111]

SOCIOCULTURAL ANALYSIS (SCA) The analysis of adversaries and other relevant actors that integrates concepts, knowledge, and understanding of societies, populations, and other groups of people, including their activities, relationships, and perspectives across time and space at varying scales.[112]

SOFT BIOMETRICS Soft biometric traits are characteristics that provide some identifying information about an individual, but lack the distinctiveness and permanence to sufficiently differentiate any two individuals. Examples of soft biometrics traits include a person's height, weight, gender, eye color, ethnicity, and SMT.[113]

SOFTWARE ASSURANCE Level of confidence that software is free from vulnerabilities, either intentionally designed into the software or accidentally inserted at any time during its lifecycle and that the software functions in the intended manner.[114]

SOUND MASKING SYSTEM An electronic system used to create background noise to mask conversations and counter audio-surveillance threats.[115]

SOUNDS OF SILENCE PARADOX *See* PARADOX OF SILENCE

SOURCE 1. A person, thing, or activity from which information is obtained; also known as an asset. 2. In clandestine activities, a person (agent), normally a foreign national, in the employ of an intelligence activity for intelligence purposes. 3. In interrogation activities, any person who furnishes information, either with or without the knowledge that the information is being used for intelligence purposes. In this context, a controlled source is in the employment or under the control of the intelligence activity and knows that the information is to be used for intelligence purposes. An uncontrolled source is a voluntary contributor of information and may or may not know that the information is to be used for intelligence purposes.[116] *See* AGENCY

SOURCE DESCRIPTOR An explanation of factors contained in the cited report or publicly available information that the producing organization assesses may affect the quality or reliability of the information in the specific report cited. These factors may include, but are not necessarily limited to, completeness, precisions or technical quality, context, or age/currency of information. In the case of human sources, this explanation may include information that describes the level of access, past reporting record, or potential biases (e.g., political, personal, professional, or religious affiliations).[117]

SOURCE DOCUMENT An existing document that contains classified information that is incorporated, paraphrased, restated, or generated in new form into a new document.[118]

SOURCE RELIABILITY A scale that reflects the reliability of information sources; often shown as A to D or A to E. It ranges from factual source to reliability unknown.[119]

SOURCE SUMMARY STATEMENT A brief statement describing factors affecting the overall quality and reliability of the source upon which the analytic judgments within a given disseminated analytic product are based.[120]

SOURCES AND METHODS Sources include: persons, images, signals, documents, databases, and communications media capable of providing intelligence information through collection and analysis programs (e.g., HUMINT, SIGINT, IMINT, etc.). Methods include: information collection and analysis strategies, tactics, operations, and technologies employed to produced intelligence products. If intelligence sources or methods are disclosed without authorization, their effectiveness may be substantially negated or impaired.[121]

SOURCES OF INTELLIGENCE The means or systems used to observe, sense, and record or convey information of conditions, situations, and events.[122] Sources of intelligence are categorized as primary, secondary, and tertiary. The primary source types are counterintelligence (CI), human intelligence (HUMINT), imagery intelligence (IMINT), measurement and signature intelligence (MASINT), open source intelligence (OSINT), signals intelligence (SIGINT), and technical intelligence (TECHINT). The secondary source types are acoustical intelligence (ACINT), communications intelligence (COMINT), electronic intelligence (ELINT), electro-optical intelligence (ELECTRO-OPTICAL), infrared intelligence (IRINT), nuclear intelligence (NUCINT), and radiation intelligence-unintentional (RINT). The tertiary source types under ELINT are foreign instrumentation and signals intelligence (FISINT), telemetry intelligence (TELINT), and radar intelligence (RADINT). *See* ATTRIBUTES OF INTELLIGENCE QUALITY

SOUSVEILLANCE To view from below. This is what is called inverse panopticon "sousveillance" from the French words for "sous" (below) and "veiller" to watch. Sousveillance is a form of "reflectionism," a term invented by Mann (1998) for a philosophy and procedures of using technology to mirror and confront bureaucratic organization.[123] *See* SURVEILLANCE

SPATIAL ANALYSIS The process of using a geographic information system in combination with crime-analysis techniques to assess the geographic context of offenders, crimes, and other law enforcement activity.[124] *See* GEOGRAPHIC ANALYSIS

SPECIAL ACTIVITY An activity or associated support function conducted in support of national foreign policy objectives abroad that is planned and executed so that the role of the government is neither apparent nor acknowledged publicly. Special activities are not intended to influence United States (U.S.) political processes, public opinion, policies, or media, and do not include diplomatic activities or the collection and production of intelligence or related support functions.[125]

SPECIAL AGENT IN CHARGE The Special Agent in Charge of an FBI field office (including an Acting Special Agent in Charge), except that the functions authorized for Special Agents in Charge by these guidelines may also be exercised by the Assistant Director in Charge or by any Special Agent in Charge designated by the Assistant Director in Charge in an FBI field office headed by an Assistant Director, and by FBI Headquarters officials designated by the Director of the FBI.[126]

SPECIAL BACKGROUND INVESTIGATION (SBI) A Personnel Security Investigation (PSI) consisting of all the components of a background investigation plus certain additional investigative requirements. The period of investigation for a Special Background Investigation (SBI) is the last 15 years or since the 18th birthday, whichever is shorter, provided that the last 2 full years are covered and that no investigation will be conducted prior to an individual's 16th birthday.[127]

SPECIAL COLLECTIONS SERVICE A "top secret" classified NSA document from the year 2010 shows that a unit known as the "Special Collection Service" (SCS) is operational in Berlin, among other locations. It is an elite corps run in concert by the U.S. intelligence agencies NSA and CIA. The secret list reveals that its agents are active worldwide in around 80 locations, 19 of which are in Europe—cities such as Paris, Madrid, Rome, Prague and Geneva. The SCS maintains two bases in Germany, one in Berlin and another in Frankfurt. That alone is unusual. But in addition, both German bases are equipped at the highest level and staffed with active personnel. The SCS teams predominantly work undercover in shielded areas of the American Embassy and Consulate, where they are officially accredited as diplomats and as such enjoy special privileges. Under diplomatic protection, they are able to look and listen unhindered. They just can't get caught. Wiretapping from an embassy is illegal in nearly every country. But that is precisely the task of the SCS, as is evidenced by another secret document. According to the document, the SCS operates its own sophisticated listening devices with which they can intercept virtually every popular method of communication: cellular signals, wireless networks and satellite communication.[128]

SPECIAL EVENTS ASSESSMENT RATING (SEAR) An Office of Operations Coordination effort to provide a single federal interagency resource to assess and categorize the risk to domestic special events that do not rise to the level of a National Special Security Event.[129] *See* NATIONAL SPECIAL SECURITY EVENT

SPECIAL EVENTS MANAGEMENT Planning and conduct of public events or activities whose character may make them attractive targets for terrorist attack.[130]

SPECIAL INVESTIGATIVE INQUIRY (SII) A supplemental Personnel Security Investigation (PSI) of limited scope conducted to prove or disprove relevant allegations that have arisen concerning a person upon whom a personnel security determination has been previously made and who, at the time of the allegation, holds a security clearance or otherwise occupies a position that requires a personnel security determination.[131]

SPECIAL NATIONAL INTELLIGENCE ESTIMATE (SNIE) Specific policy problems that need to be addressed in the immediate future. SNIEs are generally unscheduled and prepared more quickly than national intelligence estimates.[132] Some cynics of the intelligence process have said, "A SNIE is an NIE that was never written beforehand." *See* NATIONAL INTELLIGENCE ESTIMATE

SPECIAL OPERATIONS 1. Special Operations are military operations requiring unique modes of employment, tactical techniques, equipment, and training often conducted in hostile, denied, or politically sensitive environments and characterized by one or more of the following: time sensitive, clandestine, low visibility, conducted with and/or through indigenous forces, requiring regional expertise, and/or a high degree of risk. 2. Special Operations Forces (SOF) are those active and reserve component forces of the services designated by the Secretary of Defense and specifically organized, trained, and equipped to conduct and support special operations. The U.S. Special Operations Command (USSOCOM), headquartered at Mac Dill Air Force Base in Tampa, FL, is a functional combatant command responsible for training, doctrine, and equipping for all U.S. SOF units.[133]

SPECIAL SOURCE ORGANIZATION (SSO) The Edward Snowden documents show that the NSA runs these surveillance programs through "partnerships" with major U.S. telecom and Internet companies. Some of these relationships go back decades; others are more recent, in the wake of 9/11 and with the growth of the Internet. The division inside the NSA that deals with collection programs that focus on private companies is Special Source Operations, described by Snowden as the "crown jewels" of the NSA. In one top document, published here for the first time, SSO spelled out the importance of these commercial relationships, which come under the heading "Corporate Partner Access." In bald terms, it sets out its mission: "Leverage unique key corporate partnerships to gain access to high-capacity international fiber-optic cables, switches and/or routes throughout the world."[134]

SPECIALLY DESIGNATED NATIONALS LIST As part of its enforcement efforts, OFAC (Office of Foreign Assets Control) publishes a list of individuals and companies owned or controlled by, or acting for or on behalf of, targeted countries. It also lists individuals, groups, and entities, such as terrorists and narcotics traffickers designated under programs that are not country-specific. Collectively, such individuals and companies are called "Specially Designated Nationals" or "SDNs." Their assets are blocked and U.S. persons are generally prohibited from dealing with them.[135]

SPHERICAL ZONE OF CONTROL A volume of space in which un-cleared personnel must be escorted, which extends a specific distance in all directions from TEMPEST equipment processing classified information or from a shielded enclosure.[136] *See* TEMPEST

SPILLAGE Security incident that results in the transfer of classified or CUI information onto an information system not accredited (i.e., authorized) for the appropriate security level.[137]

SPLIT KNOWLEDGE Data or information separated into two or more parts, each part constantly kept under control of authorized individuals or teams so no one individual or team will know the whole data.[138]

SPOOFING Faking the sending address of a transmission to gain illegal [un-authorized] entry into a secure system. Extended Definition: The deliberate inducement of a user or resource to take incorrect action. Note: Impersonat-ing, masquerading, piggybacking, and mimicking are forms of spoofing.[139]

SPOOK A nickname for a person involved in undercover, clandestine, or covert operations.

SPOT REPORT 1. A timely method of keeping DS headquarters informed of fast breaking or significant events. It is a concise narrative of essential information and is afforded the most expeditious means of transmission consistent with requisite security.[140] 2. A brief narrative report of essential information covering events or conditions that may have an immediate and significant effect on current planning and operations. A spot report is ac-corded the fastest means of transmission to the watch officer.[141]

SPOTTER An agent or illegal assigned to locate and assess individuals in positions of value to an intelligence service.[142]

SPYWARE Software that is secretly or surreptitiously installed into an infor-mation system to gather information on individuals or organizations without their knowledge; a type of malicious code.[143]

STABILITY POLICE FORCE (SPF) A high-end police force that engages in a range of tasks such as crowd and riot control, special weapons and tactics (SWAT), and investigations of organized criminal groups. In its ability to operate in stability operations, it is similar to such European forces as the Italian *Carabinieri* and French *Gendarmerie*. Its focus on highend tasks makes it fundamentally different from UN or other civilian police, who deal with more routine law and order functions. It is also different from most military forces, which are generally not trained and experienced to conduct policing tasks in a civilian environment.[144]

STAKEOUT A surveillance point or location that has been employed (or laid out) with the benefit of prior planning. Usually meant to be occupied for an extended period of time.

STATE SPONSORS OF TERRORISM In order to designate a country as a State Sponsor of Terrorism, the Secretary of State must determine that the government of such country has repeatedly provided support for acts of international terrorism. Once a country has been designated, it continues to be a State Sponsor of Terrorism until the designation is rescinded in accordance with statutory criteria. A wide range of sanctions are imposed as a result of a State Sponsor of Terrorism designation, including: 1. A ban on arms-related exports and sales; 2. Controls over exports of dual-use items, requiring 30-day congressional notification for goods or services that could significantly enhance the terrorist-list country's military capability or ability to support terrorism; 3. Prohibitions on economic assistance; 4. Imposition of miscellaneous financial and other restrictions.[145]

STATELESS PERSON A person who is not considered as a national by any state under the operation of its law.[146]

STATIC INFORMATION/INTELLIGENCE Statistical and historical information on an enemy's capabilities; associated with "basic" intelligence. "[Prior to World War II,] the question of who sent what to the operating forces was of course partly a matter of prestige. The static information was dull, safe, old, long term and primarily based on public sources. Directives were usually based on top-secret sources that concerned either the intentions of the U.S. government or of the enemy and were usually exciting and up to the minute."[147]

STATISTICAL SYSTEM An organized means of collecting, processing, storing, and retrieving aggregate information for purposes of analysis, research, and reference. No individual records are stored in a statistical system.[148]

STATUS OF FORCE AGREEMENT (SOFA) An agreement, which defines the legal position of a visiting military force deployed in the territory of a friendly state.[149]

STEADY STATE The posture for routine, normal, day-to-day operations as contrasted with temporary periods of heightened alert or real-time response to threats or incidents.[150]

STEGANOGRAPHY The art, science, and practice of communicating in a way that hides the existence of the communication.[151]

STELLAR WIND (STELLARWIND) STELLAR WIND is a highly classified and strictly compartmented program of electronic surveillance within the United States that President Bush directed the Department of Defense to undertake on October 4, 2001, in response to the attacks of September 11, 2001. Specifically, the program is designed to counter the threat of further terrorist attacks on the territorial United States by detecting communications that will disclose terrorist operatives, terrorist plans, or other information that can enable the disruption of such attacks, particularly the identification of al Qaeda operatives within the United States. The president's initial directive to the Secretary of Defense authorized the STELLAR WIND program for 30 days. Since then, the president has periodically (roughly every 30 to 45 days) reauthorized the program.[152]

STERILIZE To remove from material to be used in covert and clandestine actions any marks or devices which can identify it as originating with the sponsoring organization or nation.[153]

STEWARD Steward (includes both Collection Steward and Analytic Production Steward): a. Collection Steward: An appropriately cleared employee of an IC element, who is a senior official, designated by the head of that IC element to represent a collection activity that the IC element is authorized by law or executive order to conduct, and to make determinations regarding the dissemination to or the retrieval by authorized IC personnel of information collected by that activity. b. Analytic Production Steward: An appropriately cleared employee of an IC element, who is a senior official, designated by the head of that IC element to represent the analytic activity that the IC element is authorized by law or executive order to conduct, and to make determinations regarding the dissemination to or the retrieval by authorized IC personnel of analysis produced by that activity.[154]

STONEGHOST 1. The classified network run by the DIA to facilitate information sharing and exchange with commonwealth partners. It is used by Australia. Canada, the United Kingdom, and the United States. This capability may also be referred to a "Q-Lat" or "Quad link." This network does not carry Intelink at the Top Secret level. 2. STONEGHOST is an encrypted communications network designed to support collaboration and intelligence sharing between the U.S. Defense IC and its Commonwealth allies during combat operations. Other allies have long-standing relationships with U.S. Services and intelligence agencies, but release of U.S.-produced intelligence is subject to review by the FDO. Many coalition partners have no established intelligence relationship with the United States and operate on a strict need to know and tear-line reporting basis for operational necessity.[155]

STOPLIGHT CHART A graphical representation depicting the different levels of warning or activity within a country or region. The term originates from the typical warning chart found in most military command headquarters. For example, countries that are color-coded green represent normal military activity within the country, yellow-coded countries represent unusual military activity within the country, and red-coded countries represent extremely unusual military activity that is occurring within a country. However, "the often-used but crude 'stoplight' charts—red-amber-green 'metrics' of easily observable variables—may be useless or even counterproductive if they oversimplify complex situations, inaccurately and incompletely measure key variables or address peripheral ones, or stimulate unwarranted confidence about how well the situation 'outside the wire' is understood" (71).[156]

STORAGE OBJECT A data object used in the system as a repository of information.[157]

STOVEPIPE WARNING An administrative process that transmits information through a predetermined set of guidelines and that does not allow the information to be shared outside the organization or within the organization among departments. For example, in response to NATO's accidental bombing of the Chinese Embassy in Belgrade, House Intelligence Committee Chair Porter Goss suggested the problem might be stovepiping. According to Goss, a former CIA employee, told the media, "In the intelligence community, everyone does his job and you don't share the information unless there is a need to know. This could be a case where the right compartments didn't talk to each other."[158] *See* BOOTLEGGING

STRATEGIC, MILITARY, AND POLITICAL RISK To create and maintain the right mix of forces and military capability, the Department must make hard, strategy-informed choices. To do so, it must determine where to invest additional resources and where to accept and manage a degree of operational, force management, institutional and future challenge risk over the near and longer term. These judgments inform our broader consideration of strategic, military, and political risks, as required by Title 10 legislation. In the 2010 QDR risk assessment, strategic risk constitutes the Department's ability to execute the defense priority objectives in the near term, midterm, and long term in support of national security. Military risk encompasses the ability of U.S. forces to adequately resource, execute, and sustain military operations in the near- to midterm, and the mid- to longer term. In the international context, political risk derives from the perceived legitimacy of our actions and the resulting impact on the ability and will of allies and partners to support shared goals. In the domestic context, political risk relates to public support of national strategic priorities and the associated resource requirements in the near term, midterm, and long term.[159]

STRATEGIC ANALYSIS PROGRAM The NIC's Strategic Analysis Program combines the National Intelligence Estimates, the Strategic Estimates Program, and Strategic Transnational Threats Analysis.[160]

STRATEGIC COMMUNICATION (SC) 1. Focused U.S. government efforts to understand and engage key audiences to create, strengthen, or preserve conditions favorable for the advancement of U.S. government interests, policies, and objectives through the use of coordinated programs, plans, themes, messages, and products synchronized with the actions of all instruments of national power.[161] 2. The transmission of integrated and coordinated U.S. government themes and messages that advance U.S. interests and policies through a synchronized interagency effort supported by public diplomacy, public affairs, and military information operations (IO), in concert with other political, economic, information and military actions.[162]

STRATEGIC COMMUNICATIONS By "strategic communication(s)" we refer to: (a) the synchronization of words and deeds and how they will be perceived by selected audiences, as well as (b) programs and activities deliberately aimed at communicating and engaging with intended audiences, including those implemented by public affairs, public diplomacy, and information operations professionals.[163]

STRATEGIC CONCEPT The course of action accepted as a result of the estimate of the strategic situation. It is a statement of what is to be done in broad terms sufficiently flexible to permit its use in framing the military, diplomatic, economic, psychological, and other measures that stem from it.[164]

STRATEGIC DEPTH The elements of space and time, which when accommodated by intelligence analysis provide a means for timely warning.[165]

STRATEGIC FORESIGHT Range of activities associated with longer-range planning and alternative futures analysis. Strategic foresight can be applied to activities such as scenario development, critical thinking and brainstorming about long-term trends, Delphi sessions, workshops, trend analysis and gaming (or "war-gaming").[166]

STRATEGIC HOMELAND INFRASTRUCTURE RISK ASSESSMENT (SHIRA) An annual collaborative process conducted in coordination with the infrastructure protection and intelligence communities to assess and analyze the risks to the nation's CIKR sectors from natural and man-made hazards.[167]

STRATEGIC INFORMATION AND OPERATIONS CENTER (SIOC) Located in the FBI headquarters building in Washington, D.C., this crisis center is the agency's worldwide connection to the Department of Defense, other governmental agencies, and the FBI's network of field offices in the United States and abroad. In operation since 1998, the center can handle four international crises at once.[168]

STRATEGIC INFORMATION WARFARE Intersection of information and strategic warfare.

STRATEGIC INTELLIGENCE 1. Evaluated and processed information about the power and intentions of foreign nations or other external phenomena of significance in decision-making councils. Most generally the term refers to the informational needs of national government officials, particularly foreign and defense policymakers. 2. Intelligence required for the formation of policy and military plans at national and international levels. Its components include such characteristics as biographic data, economic, sociological, transportation, telecommunications, geography, political, and scientific and technical intelligence.[169] 3. Related to the structure and movement of organized criminal elements, patterns of criminal activity, criminal trend projections, or projective planning.[170] *See* TACTICAL INTELLIGENCE

STRATEGIC INTELLIGENCE INTERROGATION An intelligence interrogation of any person who is in the custody or under the effective control

STRATEGIC WARNING • 535

of the DoD or under detention in a DoD facility, conducted at a theater-level detention facility.[171]

STRATEGIC PSYCHOLOGICAL ACTIVITIES Planned psychological activities in peace and war that normally pursue objectives to gain the support and cooperation of friendly and neutral countries and to reduce the will and the capacity of hostile or potentially hostile countries to wage war.

STRATEGIC RISK Risk that affects an entity's vital interests or execution of chosen strategy, whether imposed by external threats or arising from flawed or poorly implemented strategy. 1) Managing strategic risk is associated with the ability to recognize future trends, challenges, and threats and match these with appropriate operational concepts, capabilities, competencies, and capacity. 2) Strategic risk can arise from three basic sources. First, strategic risk can arise from the actions of adversaries, from natural hazards or from non-adversarial human actions, such as accidents. These can be thought of as imposed risks. Second, strategic risk can be created by the unintended consequences of the strategies we adopt in response to imposed risks. These can be thought of as self-imposed risks. Finally, strategic risk can arise from obstacles to successful implementation of an adopted strategy. These obstacles can be either imposed (e.g., the actions of an adaptive adversary to counter a security measure or to exploit an unintended vulnerability created by a security measure) or self-imposed (e.g., failure to adequately resource, or to prematurely abandon, a strategy or course of action that would otherwise be beneficial).[172]

STRATEGIC THREAT AND ACTION REPORT (STAR) The Strategic Threat and Action Report is a combined NCTC-DHS product that provides a risk-based analysis for the president and senior leadership of the federal government on the current threat, the vulnerabilities of the potential targets, and the actions taken to reduce, neutralize, or negate the threat.[173]

STRATEGIC WARNING 1. A forecast of a probable attack or a forecast that enemy-initiated hostilities may be imminent. The warning must be received early enough to permit decision makers to undertake countermeasures (military, political, or diplomatic) prior to actual hostilities. The time frame usually can range from a few weeks to several days. "For strategic warning, the key problem is not when attack may occur, but whether the enemy is preparing to attack at all. . . . Strategic warning is not a forecast of imminent attack. Strategic warning is a forecast of probable attack and it is this above all which the policy official and commander need to know."[174] 2. Intelligence information or intelligence regarding the threat of the initiation of hostilities against the United States or in which U.S. forces may become involved. It may be received at any time prior to the initiation of hostilities. It does not include tactical warning.[175] *See* PHASES OF WARNING; POLITICAL WARNING; TACTICAL WARNING

STRATEGIC WARNING LEAD TIME That time between the receipt of strategic warning and the beginning of hostilities. This time may include strategic warning pre-decision time and post-decision time.[176] *See* STRATEGIC WARNING POST-DECISION TIME; STRATEGIC WARNING PRE-DECISION TIME

STRATEGIC WARNING POST-DECISION TIME That time after a decision is made in response to strategic warning and the order is executed. This time ends with the start of hostilities or termination of the threat.[177] *See* STRATEGIC WARNING LEAD TIME; STRATEGIC WARNING PRE-DECISION TIME

STRATEGIC WARNING PRE-DECISION TIME That time which begins upon receipt of strategic warning and ends when a decision is ordered and executed. (See figure S.1.) *See* STRATEGIC WARNING LEAD TIME; STRATEGIC WARNING POST-DECISION TIME

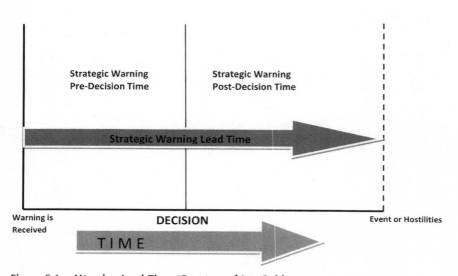

Figure S.1. Warning Lead Time (Courtesy of Jan Goldman)

STRUCTURED ANALYSIS A distinct form of intelligence analysis methodology that provides a step-by-step process for analyzing the kinds of incomplete, ambiguous, and sometimes deceptive information that analysts must deal with.[178]

STUDIES IN INTELLIGENCE Publication of the Central Intelligence Agency's Center for the Study of Intelligence. *Studies in Intelligence* has been published since 1955 in a classified and public version. Volumes have also been declassified.[179]

SUBJECT Generally an individual, process, or device causing information to flow among objects or change to the system state.[180]

SUBJECT MATTER EXPERT Individual with in-depth knowledge in a specific area or field.[181]

SUBJECT MATTER EXPERTISE/SPECIALTY Competencies required for employees in one or more occupations within a mission category, depending on a particular specialty or assignment. These competencies include substantive knowledge areas, such as intelligence topics and target countries, certifications, and intelligence disciplines (e.g., GEOINT, HUMINT, and SIGINT).[182]

SUBJECTIVE PROBABILITY Interpretation or estimate of probability as a personal judgment or "degree of belief" about how likely a particular event is to occur, based on the state of knowledge and available evidence.[183]

SUBSTANTIVE DUE PROCESS Guarantees persons against arbitrary, unreasonable, or capricious laws, and it acts as a limitation against arbitrary governmental actions so that no government agency may exercise powers beyond those authorized by the Constitution.[184]

SUBVERSION Actions designed to undermine the military, economic, political, psychological, or moral strength of a nation or entity. It can also apply to an undermining of a person's loyalty to a government or entity.[185]

SUICIDE ATTACKS Events where the "success" of the operation cannot occur without the death of the perpetrator, and he or she is apparently aware of this in advance . . . suicide attacks that are carried out by "terrorists," by which is meant nonstate actors whose goal is the threat or use of violence for political ends against noncombatant or civilian targets.[186]

SUPERTERRORISM In the past, terrorists have been ruthless opportunists, using a bloody, but relatively narrow, range of weapons to further clear political ends. The next fifteen years may well be the age of superterrorism, when terrorists gain access to weapons of mass destruction and show a new willingness to use them. Tomorrow's most dangerous terrorists will be motivated, not by an urge to further a political ideology but by fierce ethnic and religious hatreds. Their goal will not be political control, but rather the utter destruction of their chosen enemies. Biological and chemical weapons and improvised nuclear devices are ideal for their purpose. Increasingly, they will be joined by another variety of terrorist: criminals with the goal of maximizing profit, minimizing risk, and protecting their enterprises by intimidating or co-opting government officials.[187]

SURGE CAPABILITY The ability to move intelligence resources quickly to address immediate, usually ad-hoc, needs; augment existing resources from outside the intelligence community; and improve responsiveness of resources by building in more flexible options for collection and analysis. Taken together, these capabilities should provide for the development and maintenance of some level of knowledge on all countries and issues providing an intelligence base. This "surge" capability needs to be flexible, dynamic, and well planned—one that can be relied upon both day to day and during crises.[188]

SURPRISE DOSAGE ATTACK A chemical operation which establishes on target a dosage sufficient to produce the desired casualties before troops can mask or otherwise protect themselves.[189]

SURVEILLANCE 1. The observation of activities, behaviors, and associations of a LAWINT target (individual or group) with the intent to gather incriminating information, or "lead" information, that is used for the furtherance of a criminal investigation.[190] 2. The etymology of this word is from the French word "surveiller" which means "to watch over." Specifically, the word "surveillance" is formed from two parts: (1) the French prefix "sur" which means "over" or "from above," and (2) the French verb "veiller" which means "to watch." The closest English word is "oversight," although the latter has two meanings: (1) watching from above, as in "oversight committee" and (2) an omission or error, as in "that was an oversight on our part."[191] 3. The systematic observation of aerospace, surface, or subsurface areas, places, persons, or things by visual, aural, electronic, photographic, or other means. 4. Executive Order 12333 *United States Intelligence Activities* provides the Intelligence Community elements to collect, retain, or disseminate information concerning U.S. persons (USPs) only in accordance with procedures established by the head of the Intelligence Community element and approved by the attorney general in consultation with the director of national intelligence.[192] *See* COUNTERSURVEILLANCE; INTELLIGENCE, SURVEILLANCE, AND RECONNAISSANCE

SURVEILLANCE DEVICE A piece of equipment or mechanism used to gain unauthorized access to and removal of information.[193]

SWEEP To electronically and/or physically examine a room or area in order to detect any clandestine devices; a search for "bugs"—for example, concealed electronic listening devices at a specific location.

SWOT ANALYSIS (STRENGTHS, WEAKNESSES, OPPORTUNITIES, AND THREATS ANALYSIS) An analytic tool to assist in determining resource priorities, capitalizing on opportunities, thwarting enemy initiatives, identifying and exploiting advantages over the enemy, and shoring up defensive vulnerabilities and weaknesses. The SWOT analysis summarizes the most potent and essential knowledge about a situation in relation to the threat and environment in a relatively straightforward way to institutionalize knowledge so that it is readily accessible to others who have a need to know and who can help advance the quality of knowledge it imparts. SWOT has the effect of organizing critical thinking about a situation in a straightforward and simple manner.

SYNCHRONIZATION 1. The arrangement of military actions in time, space, and purpose to produce maximum relative combat power at a decisive place and time. 2. In the intelligence context, application of intelligence sources and methods in concert with the operation plan to answer intelligence requirements in time to influence the decisions they support.[194]

SYNTHESIS In intelligence usage, the examining and combining of processed information with other information and intelligence for final interpretation.[195]

SYSTEM Any combination of facilities, equipment, personnel, procedures, and communications integrated for a specific purpose.[196]

SYSTEM SECURITY PLAN Formal document that provides an overview of the security requirements for the information system and describes the security controls in place or planned for meeting those requirements.[197]

SYSTEMATIC DECLASSIFICATION REVIEW The review for declassification of classified information contained in records that have been determined by the archivist to have permanent historical value in accordance with Title 44, United States Code (U.S.C), Section 2103.[198]

SYSTEMWIDE HOMELAND ANALYSIS AND RESOURCE EXCHANGE (SHARE) NETWORK Agencies' current information-sharing efforts tend to focus on sharing data laterally and narrowly—federal agency to federal agency, law enforcement to law enforcement, and state government to state government. Work needs to be done to enable a network in which data moves across all the gaps, and analysis occurs at multiple nodes rather than only in a few centralized locations. The Systemwide Homeland Analysis and Resource Exchange (SHARE) Network we envision would have the following attributes: 1. no single points of failure; 2. loosely coupled architecture; 3. directory-based services; 4. support for real-time operations; 5. security and accountability to prevent abuse.[199] *See* TERRORIST THREAT INTEGRATION CENTER

NOTES

1. U.S. Department of Defense. *Department of Defense Dictionary of Military and Associated Terms.* JP 1-02, 08 November 2010, as Amended through 15 January 2016. Accessed January 26, 2016. http://www.dtic.mil/doctrine/new_pubs/jp1_02.pdf.

2. U.S. Department of State. "Definitions of Diplomatic Security Terms." *Foreign Affairs Manual.* 12FAM090. November 12, 2014. Accessed February 14, 2015. http://www.state.gov/documents/organization/88330.pdf.

3. U.S. Department of State. "Definitions of Diplomatic Security Terms." *Foreign Affairs Manual.* 12FAM090. November 12, 2014. Accessed February 14, 2015. http://www.state.gov/documents/organization/88330.pdf.

4. U.S. Department of Defense. *Department of Defense Dictionary of Military and Associated Terms.* JP 1-02, 08 November 2010, as Amended through 15 January 2016. Accessed January 26, 2016. http://www.dtic.mil/doctrine/new_pubs/jp1_02.pdf.

5. U.S. Department of Defense. *Department of Defense Dictionary of Military and Associated Terms.* JP 1-02, 08 November 2010, as Amended through 15 January 2016. Accessed January 26, 2016. http://www.dtic.mil/doctrine/new_pubs/jp1_02.pdf.

6. U.S. Department of State. "Definitions of Diplomatic Security Terms." *Foreign Affairs Manual.* 12FAM090. November 12, 2014. Accessed February 14, 2015. http://www.state.gov/documents/organization/88330.pdf.

7. Chairman of the Joint Chiefs of Staff. *National Military Strategic Plan for the War on Terrorism.* February 1, 2006. Accessed February 26, 2015. http://www.defense.gov/qdr/docs/2006-02-08-Strategic-Plan.pdf.

8. Krugman, Paul. "Reckonings: Slicing the Salami." *The New York Times*, February 11, 2001. Accessed June 5, 2015. http://www.nytimes.com/2001/02/11/opinion/reckonings-slicing-the-salami.html.

9. U.S. Department of State. *Diplomatic Dictionary.* Accessed March 6, 2015. http://diplomacy.state.gov/discoverdiplomacy/references/169792.htm.

10. United States Senate, Select Committee to Study Governmental Operations with Respect to Intelligence Activities (Church Committee). *Final Report.* Book 1. April 26, 1976. Accessed January 14, 2015. https://archive.org/details/finalreportof-sel01unit.

11. Office of the Director of National Intelligence. *Glossary of Security Terms, Definitions, and Acronyms.* Intelligence Community Standard (ICS) 700-1. April 4, 2008. Accessed June 5, 2015. https://fas.org/irp/dni/icd/ics-700-1.pdf.

12. U.S. Department of Defense. Center for Development of Security Excellence. *Glossary of Security Terms and Definitions.* November 2012. Accessed February 15, 2015. http://www.cdse.edu/documents/cdse/Glossary_Handbook.pdf.

13. U.S. Department of Defense. Center for Development of Security Excellence. *Glossary of Security Terms and Definitions.* November 2012. Accessed February 15, 2015. http://www.cdse.edu/documents/cdse/Glossary_Handbook.pdf.

14. U.S. Department of Defense. *Department of Defense Dictionary of Military and Associated Terms.* JP 1-02, 08 November 2010, as Amended through 15 January 2016. Accessed January 26, 2016. http://www.dtic.mil/doctrine/new_pubs/jp1_02.pdf.

15. U. S. Department of Justice. Exhibit 300: FBI Top Secret/Sensitive Compartmented Information Operational Network (SCION) (Revision 14). December 8, 2008. Accessed June 8, 2015. http://www.justice.gov/sites/default/files/jmd/legacy/2014/04/19/fbi-2011-scion.pdf.

16. U.S. Department of Defense. *Department of Defense Dictionary of Military and Associated Terms.* JP 1-02, 08 November 2010, as Amended through 15 January 2015. Accessed February 18, 2015. http://www.dtic.mil/doctrine/dod_dictionary/.

17. U.S. General Accountability Office. *Aviation Security: TSA Should Limit Future Funding for Behavior Detection Activities.* GAO-14-159, November 2013. Accessed February 15, 2015. http://www.gao.gov.

18. Federal Bureau of Investigation. *Minimum Criminal Intelligence Training Standards for Law Enforcement and Other Criminal Justice Agencies in the United States.* October 2007. Accessed February 18, 2015. https://it.ojp.gov/gist/108/Minimum-Criminal-Intelligence-Training-Standards.

19. U.S. Department of Defense. *Department of Defense Dictionary of Military and Associated Terms.* JP 1-02, 08 November 2010, as Amended through 15 January 2016. Accessed January 26, 2016. http://www.dtic.mil/doctrine/new_pubs/jp1_02.pdf.

20. Defense Intelligence Agency, Office of Counterintelligence. *CI Glossary— Terms & Definitions of Interest for DoD CI Professionals.* July 2014. Accessed February 18, 2015. https://www.hsdl.org/?view&did=699056.

21. Simmel, Georg. "The Sociology of Secrecy and Secret Societies." *American Journal of Sociology* 11, no. 4 (1906): 441–98.

22. Shils, Edward A. *The Torment of Secrecy: The Background and Consequences of American Security Policies* (Glencoe, IL: Free Press, 1956).

23. Friedrich, Carl. *The Pathology of Politics: Violence, Betrayal, Corruption, Secrecy, and Propaganda* (New York: Harper and Row, 1972).

24. Bok, Sissela. *Secrets* (New York: Vintage Books, 1989), 5, 19.

25. Executive Order 13526. *Classified National Security Information.* December 29, 2009. Accessed February 15, 2015. http://www.whitehouse.gov/the-press-office/executive-order-classified-national-security-information.

26. U.S. Department of Defense. Center for Development of Security Excellence. *Glossary of Security Terms and Definitions.* November 2012. Accessed February 16, 2015. http://www.cdse.edu/documents/cdse/Glossary_Handbook.pdf.

27. U.S. Department of Defense. Center for Development of Security Excellence. *Glossary of Security Terms and Definitions.* November 2012. Accessed February 16, 2015. http://www.cdse.edu/documents/cdse/Glossary_Handbook.pdf.

28. Galison, Peter. "Removing Knowledge." *Critical Inquiry* 31, no. 1 (2004): 229–43.

29. Vaughan, Diane. *The Challenger Launch Decision: Risky Technology, Culture, and Deviance at NASA.* Chicago: University of Chicago Press, 1996.

30. Galison, Peter. "Removing Knowledge." *Critical Inquiry* 31, no. 1 (2004): 229–43.

31. Thompson, Dennis F. "Democratic Secrecy." *Political Science Quarterly* 114, no. 2 (1999): 181–93.

32. National Conference of Commissioners on Uniform State Laws. *Uniform Trade Secrets Act.* Accessed February 25, 2015. http://www.uniformlaws.org/shared/docs/trade%20secrets/utsa_final_85.pdf; also see Yeh, Bruce H. "Protection of Trade Secrets: Overview of Current Law and Legislation." *CRS Report for Congress* R43714. September 4, 2014. Accessed February 25, 2015. http://fas.org/sgp/crs/secrecy/R43714.pdf.

33. Kaiser, Frederick M. "Protection of Classified Information by Congress: Practices and Proposals." *CRS Report for Congress* RS20748. August 31, 2011. Accessed February 15, 2015. https://www.fas.org/sgp/crs/secrecy/RS20748.pdf.

34. 35 U.S. Code § 181—"Secrecy of Certain Inventions and Withholding of Patent." (Current through Pub. L. 113-234). Accessed February 15, 2015. http://www.law.cornell.edu/uscode/text/35/181; also see United States Patent and Trademark Office. *120 Secrecy Orders [R-11.2013].* Accessed February 15, 2015. http://www.uspto.gov/web/offices/pac/mpep/s120.html.

35. U.S. Department of State. "Definitions of Diplomatic Security Terms." *Foreign Affairs Manual.* 12FAM090. November 12, 2014. Accessed February 14, 2015. http://www.state.gov/documents/organization/88330.pdf.

36. United Nations Human Rights Council. *Joint Study on Global Practices in Relation to Secret Detention in the Context of Countering Terrorism* (title truncated). A/HRC/13/42. February 19, 2010, 11–12. Accessed February 9, 2015. http://www2.ohchr.org/english/bodies/hrcouncil/docs/13session/A-HRC-13-42.pdf.

37. Berridge, G. R. and Lloyd, Lorna. (eds.) *Palgrave Macmillan Dictionary of Diplomacy*. 3rd ed. New York: Palgrave Macmillan, 2012.

38. Oleszek, Walter J. "Proposals to Reform 'Holds' in the Senate." *CRS Report for Congress* RL31685. August 31, 2011. Accessed February 15, 2015. http://fas.org/sgp/crs/misc/RL31685.pdf.

39. Defense Human Resources Activity. Using the SIPRNet. Accessed February 15, 2015. http://www.dhra.mil/perserec/osg/s1class/siprnet.htm. Borger, Julian and Leigh, David. "SIPRNet: Where America Stores its Secret Cables." *The Guardian*, November 28, 2010. Accessed February 15, 2015. http://www.theguardian.com/world/2010/nov/28/siprnet-america-stores-secret-cables.

40. Davis, Christopher M. *Secret Sessions of the House and Senate: Authority, Confidentiality, and Frequency*. R42106. December 30, 2014. Accessed February 15, 2015. http://fas.org/sgp/crs/secrecy/R42106.pdf.

41. *Presidential Policy Directive/PPD-21. Critical Infrastructure Security and Resilience*. February 12, 2013. Accessed January 22, 2015. http://www.whitehouse.gov/the-press-office/2013/02/12/presidential-policy-directive-critical-infrastructure-security-and-resil.

42. *Presidential Policy Directive/PPD-21. Critical Infrastructure Security and Resilience*. February 12, 2013. Accessed January 22, 2015. http://www.whitehouse.gov/the-press-office/2013/02/12/presidential-policy-directive-critical-infrastructure-security-and-resil.

43. Secure Borders and Open Doors Advisory Committee. *Secure Borders and Open Doors: Report of the Secure Borders and Open Doors Advisory Committee*. January 2008. Accessed March 7, 2015. http://www.dhs.gov/xlibrary/assets/hsac_SBODACreport508-compliant_version2.pdf.

44. U.S. General Accountability Office. *Aviation Security: TSA Has Taken Steps to Improve Oversight of Key Programs, but Additional Actions Are Needed*. Statement of Jennifer Grover, Director, Homeland Security and Justice. GAO-15-559T, May 13, 2015. Accessed June 5, 2015. http://www.gao.gov.

45. U.S. Department of State. "Definitions of Diplomatic Security Terms." *Foreign Affairs Manual*. 12FAM090. November 12, 2014. Accessed February 14, 2015. http://www.state.gov/documents/organization/88330.pdf.

46. U.S. Department of State. "Definitions of Diplomatic Security Terms." *Foreign Affairs Manual*. 12FAM090. November 12, 2014. Accessed February 14, 2015. http://www.state.gov/documents/organization/88330.pdf.

47. *Presidential Policy Directive/PPD-8: National Preparedness*. March 30, 2011. Accessed February 15, 2011. http://www.dhs.gov/presidential-policy-directive-8-national-preparedness.

48. U.S. Department of State. "Definitions of Diplomatic Security Terms." *Foreign Affairs Manual*. 12FAM090. November 12, 2014. Accessed February 14, 2015. http://www.state.gov/documents/organization/88330.pdf.

49. U.S. Department of State. "Definitions of Diplomatic Security Terms." *Foreign Affairs Manual*. 12FAM090. November 12, 2014. Accessed February 14, 2015. http://www.state.gov/documents/organization/88330.pdf.

50. U.S. Department of Defense. *Department of Defense Dictionary of Military and Associated Terms.* JP 1-02, 08 November 2010, as Amended through 15 January 2015. Accessed January 13, 2015. http://www.dtic.mil/doctrine/dod_dictionary/.

51. Executive Order 13526. *Classified National Security Information.* December 29, 2009. Accessed January 14, 2015. http://www.archives.gov/isoo/policy-documents/cnsi-eo.html.

52. U.S. Department of Defense. *Department of Defense Dictionary of Military and Associated Terms.* JP 1-02, 08 November 2010, as Amended through 15 January 2016. Accessed January 26, 2016. http://www.dtic.mil/doctrine/new_pubs/jp1_02.pdf.

53. Defense Intelligence Agency, Office of Counterintelligence. *CI Glossary— Terms & Definitions of Interest for DoD CI Professionals.* July 2014. Accessed January 17, 2015. https://www.hsdl.org/?view&did=699056.

54. Department of the Army. *Human Intelligence Collector Operations.* FM 2-22.3 (FM 34-52). September 2006. Accessed February 26, 2015. https://www.fas.org/irp/doddir/army/fm2-22-3.pdf.

55. This definition is expanded upon in Kenneth N. Waltz, *Theory of International Politics* (New York: Random House, 1979), and Joseph M. Grieco, *Cooperation among Nations: Europe, America, and Non-Tariff Barriers* (Ithaca, NY: Cornell University Press, 1990), 28–29.

56. U.S. Department of Defense. Center for Development of Security Excellence. *Glossary of Security Terms and Definitions.* November 2012. Accessed February 15, 2015. http://www.cdse.edu/documents/cdse/Glossary_Handbook.pdf.

57. U.S. Department of State. "Definitions of Diplomatic Security Terms." *Foreign Affairs Manual.* 12FAM090. November 12, 2014. Accessed February 14, 2015. http://www.state.gov/documents/organization/88330.pdf.

58. U.S. Department of State. "Definitions of Diplomatic Security Terms." *Foreign Affairs Manual.* 12FAM090. November 12, 2014. Accessed February 14, 2015. http://www.state.gov/documents/organization/88330.pdf.

59. North Atlantic Treaty Organization. *NATO Glossary of Terms and Definitions.* NATO Standardization Agency, 2014, AAP-06. Accessed July 27, 2015. http://nso.nato.int/nso/zPublic/ap/aap6/AAP-6.pdf.

60. Committee for National Security Systems (CNSS). Instruction 4009. *National Information Assurance Glossary.* April 2010. Accessed February 15, 2015. http://www.ncix.gov/publications/policy/docs/CNSSI_4009.pdf.

61. National Initiative for Cybersecurity Education. *A Glossary of Common Cybersecurity Terminology.* n.d. Accessed March 5, 2015. http://niccs.us-cert.gov/glossary.

62. United States Air Force. *Public Affairs Operations.* Air Force Doctrine Document 3–6, 24 June 2005 Certified Current 20 August 2013 Incorporating Changes 1, 23 December 2010. Accessed February 4, 2015. http://static.e-publishing.af.mil/production/1/af_cv/publication/afdd3-61/afdd3-61.pdf.

63. Miller, Arthur S. "The Constitutional Law of the 'Security State.'" *Stanford Law Review* (1958): 620–71.

64. U.S. Department of State. "Definitions of Diplomatic Security Terms." *Foreign Affairs Manual*. 12FAM090. November 12, 2014. Accessed February 14, 2015. http://www.state.gov/documents/organization/88330.pdf.

65. U.S. Department of Justice. *Segregating and Marking Documents for Release in Accordance with the Open Government Act*. September 24, 2014. Accessed February 15, 2015. http://www.justice.gov/oip/blog/foia-post-2008-oip-guidance-segregating-and-marking-documents-release-accordance-open.

66. Homeland Security Presidential Directive/HSPD-6, *Integration and Use of Screening Information*, September 16, 2003, accessed February 2, 2016, http://www.fas.org/irp/offdocs/nspd/hspd-6.html.

67. U.S. Department of Defense. *Counterintelligence Awareness and Reporting (CIAR)*. Directive (DoDD) 5240.06. May 17, 2011. Accessed February 17, 2015. http://www.dtic.mil/whs/directives/corres/pdf/524006p.pdf.

68. Defense Science Board. *Predicting Violent Behavior: Final Report of the the Defense Science Board (DSB) Task Force (TF) on Predicting Violent Behavior*. August 2012. Accessed February 24, 2015. http://www.acq.osd.mil/dsb/reports/PredictingViolentBehavior.pdf.

69. Department of Homeland Security, Risk Steering Committee. *DHS Risk Lexicon*. September 2010. Accessed February 14, 2015. http://www.dhs.gov/dhs-risk-lexicon.

70. Committee for National Security Systems (CNSS). Instruction 4009. *National Information Assurance Glossary*. April 2010. Accessed February 15, 2015. http://www.ncix.gov/publications/policy/docs/CNSSI_4009.pdf.

71. Director of Central Intelligence. *Directive 1/7 Security Controls on the Dissemination of Intelligence Information*. June 30, 1998. Accessed February 15, 2015. http://www.fas.org/irp/offdocs/dcid1-7.html.

72. Executive Order 13526. *Classified National Security Information*. December 29, 2009. Accessed January 14, 2015. http://www.archives.gov/isoo/policy-documents/cnsi-eo.html.

73. Department of Energy, Office of Safeguards and Security, *Safeguards and Security Glossary of Terms* (December 18, 1995), accessed February 2, 2016, http://www.directives.doe.gov/references/.

74. Centers for Disease Control. *Manual Guide—Information Security CDC-02*. Office of Security and Emergency Preparedness "Sensitive But Unclassified Information." Part B. 07/22/2005. http://www.fas.org/sgp/othergov/cdc-sbu.pdf.

75. Office of the Director of National Intelligence, *Glossary of Security Terms, Definitions, and Acronyms*, Intelligence Community Standard, 700-1, April 4, 2008, accessed February 2, 2016, https://fas.org/irp/dni/icd/ics-700-1.pdf.

76. U.S. Department of Defense. *Department of Defense Dictionary of Military and Associated Terms*. JP 1-02, 08 November 2010, as Amended through 15 January 2016. Accessed January 26, 2016. http://www.dtic.mil/doctrine/new_pubs/jp1_02.pdf.

77. Federal Bureau of Investigation. *Minimum Criminal Intelligence Training Standards for Law Enforcement and Other Criminal Justice Agencies in the United*

States. October 2007. Accessed February 8, 2015. https://it.ojp.gov/gist/108/Minimum-Criminal-Intelligence-Training-Standards.

78. U.S. Department of State. "Definitions of Diplomatic Security Terms." *Foreign Affairs Manual.* 12FAM090. November 12, 2014. Accessed February 14, 2015. http://www.state.gov/documents/organization/88330.pdf.

79. U.S. Department of Justice. *The Attorney General's Guidelines for Domestic FBI Operations.* 2008. Accessed February 25, 2015. http://www.justice.gov/sites/default/files/ag/legacy/2008/10/03/guidelines.pdf.

80. U.S. Department of Justice. *The Attorney General's Guidelines for Domestic FBI Operations.* 2008. Accessed February 25, 2015. http://www.justice.gov/sites/default/files/ag/legacy/2008/10/03/guidelines.pdf.

81. U.S. Department of State. "The Privacy Act and Personally Identifiable Information." *Foreign Affairs Manual.* 5 FAM 460. October 1, 2014. Accessed February 14, 2015. http://www.state.gov/documents/organization/85694.pdf.

82. Office of the Director of National Intelligence. *Intelligence Community Policy Guidance, ICPG 501.2: Sensitive Review Board and Information Sharing Dispute Resolution Process.* May 26, 2009. Accessed January 24, 2015. http://www.dni.gov/files/documents/ICPG/icpg_501_2.pdf.

83. Department of Homeland Security, Risk Steering Committee. *DHS Risk Lexicon.* September 2010. Accessed February 14, 2015. http://www.dhs.gov/dhs-risk-lexicon.

84. U.S. Department of Defense. *DoD Intelligence Interrogations, Detainee Debriefings, and Tactical Questioning.* Directive Number 3115.09, October 11, 2012 Incorporating Change 1, Effective November 15, 2013. Accessed February 26, 2015. http://fas.org/irp/doddir/dod/d3115_09.pdf. Department of the Army. *Human Intelligence Collector Operations.* FM 2-22.3 (FM 34-52). September 2006. Accessed February 26, 2015. https://www.fas.org/irp/doddir/army/fm2-22-3.pdf.

85. U.S. Department of Defense. *DoD Intelligence Interrogations, Detainee Debriefings, and Tactical Questioning.* Directive Number 3115.09, October 11, 2012 Incorporating Change 1, Effective November 15, 2013. Accessed February 26, 2015. http://fas.org/irp/doddir/dod/d3115_09.pdf. Department of the Army. *Human Intelligence Collector Operations.* FM 2-22.3 (FM 34-52). September 2006. Accessed February 26, 2015. https://www.fas.org/irp/doddir/army/fm2-22-3.pdf.

86. Senate Select Committee on Intelligence. *Committee Study of the Central Intelligence Agency's Detention and Interrogation Program.* Declassification revisions December 3, 2014. Accessed February 26, 2015. http://www.intelligence.senate.gov/study2014.html.

87. Fisher, Louis. *The Politics of Executive Privilege.* Durham, NC: Carolina Academic Press, 2004. Accessed February 15, 2015. http://www.loc.gov/law/help/usconlaw/pdf/fisher_politics_ch_08.pdf.

88. Department of the Army. *Army Special Operations Forces Unconventional Warfare.* FM 3-05.130, September 2008. Accessed February 9, 2015. http://fas.org/irp/doddir/army/fm3-05-130.pdf.

89. U.S. Department of Defense. Center for Development of Security Excellence. *Glossary of Security Terms and Definitions.* November 2012. Accessed February 15, 2015. http://www.cdse.edu/documents/cdse/Glossary_Handbook.pdf.

90. U.S. Department of State. "Definitions of Diplomatic Security Terms." *Foreign Affairs Manual.* 12FAM090. November 12, 2014. Accessed February 14, 2015. http://www.state.gov/documents/organization/88330.pdf.

91. U.S. Department of Defense. Center for Development of Security Excellence. *Glossary of Security Terms and Definitions.* November 2012. Accessed February 15, 2015. http://www.cdse.edu/documents/cdse/Glossary_Handbook.pdf.

92. U.S. Department of Defense. *Department of Defense Dictionary of Military and Associated Terms.* JP 1-02, 08 November 2010, as Amended through 15 January 2016. Accessed January 26, 2016. http://www.dtic.mil/doctrine/new_pubs/jp1_02.pdf.

93. *Presidential Policy Directive/PPD-20 U.S. Cyber Operations Policy*, October 16, 2012, accessed June 2, 2015, https://www.fas.org/irp/offdocs/ppd/ppd-20.pdf.

94. U.S. Department of Defense. Center for Development of Security Excellence. *Glossary of Security Terms and Definitions.* November 2012. Accessed February 15, 2015. http://www.cdse.edu/documents/cdse/Glossary_Handbook.pdf.

95. U.S. Department of Defense. *DoD Intelligence Interrogations, Detainee Debriefings, and Tactical Questioning.* Directive Number 3115.09, October 11, 2012 Incorporating Change 1, Effective November 15, 2013. Accessed February 26, 2015. http://fas.org/irp/doddir/dod/d3115_09.pdf.

96. Defense Intelligence Agency, Office of Counterintelligence. *CI Glossary—Terms & Definitions of Interest for DoD CI Professionals.* July 2014. Accessed January 17, 2015. https://www.hsdl.org/?view&did=699056.

97. Orf, Darren. "Silk Road Reloaded Ditches Tor for a More Anonymous Network." *Gizmodo*, January 11, 2015. Accessed February 15, 2015. http://gizmodo.com/silk-road-reloaded-ditches-tor-for-a-more-anonymous-net-1678839282.

98. Department of Homeland Security, Risk Steering Committee. *DHS Risk Lexicon.* September 2010. Accessed February 14, 2015. http://www.dhs.gov/dhs-risk-lexicon.

99. Based on Mica Endsley's definition in "Toward a Theory of Situation Awareness in Dynamic Systems." *Human Factors* 37, no. 1 (1995): 32–64.

100. Committee for National Security Systems (CNSS). Instruction 4009. *National Information Assurance Glossary.* April 2010. Accessed February 15, 2015. http://www.ncix.gov/publications/policy/docs/CNSSI_4009.pdf.

101. National Initiative for Cybersecurity Education. A Glossary of Common Cybersecurity Terminology. n.d. Accessed March 5, 2015. http://niccs.us-cert.gov/glossary.

102. Defense Forensics and Biometrics Agency. *DoD Biometrics Enterprise Architecture (Integrated) v2.0 Common Biometric Vocabulary.* April 2013. Accessed February 10, 2015. http://www.biometrics.dod.mil/Files/Documents/References/common%20biometric%20vocabulary.pdf.

103. The Intercept. *SKYNET: Applying Advanced Cloud-based Behavior Analytics.* 2012. Accessed June 15, 2015. https://firstlook.org/theintercept/document/2015/05/08/skynet-applying-advanced-cloud-based-behavior-analytics/.

104. Zetter, Kim. "So, the NSA Has an Actual Skynet Program." *Wired*, May 8, 2015. Accessed June 15, 2015. http://www.wired.com/2015/05/nsa-actual-skynet-program/.

105. Slur. Introducing *Slur.* Accessed February 11, 2015. http://slur.io/#what.

106. U.S. Department of State. *Diplomatic Dictionary.* Accessed March 6, 2015. http://diplomacy.state.gov/discoverdiplomacy/references/169792.htm.

107. U.S. Department of Justice, Office of Justice Programs. *Investigations Involving the Internet and Computer Networks.* January 2007. Accessed March 7, 2015. https://www.ncjrs.gov/pdffiles1/nij/210798.pdf.

108. Canadian Journalists for Free Expression. *Snowden Surveillance Archive.* Accessed March 6, 2015. https://snowdenarchive.cjfe.org/greenstone/cgi-bin/library.cgi.

109. Department of Homeland Security, Risk Steering Committee. *DHS Risk Lexicon.* September 2010. Accessed February 14, 2015. http://www.dhs.gov/dhs-risk-lexicon.

110. Rose, Andrée, Timm, Howard, Pogson, Corrie, Gonzalez, Jose, Appel, Edward, and Kolb, Nancy. *Developing a Cybervetting Strategy for Law Enforcement.* Defense Personnel Security Research Center, U.S. Department of Defense, December 2010. Accessed January 17, 2015. http://www.dhra.mil/perserec/reports/pp11-02.pdf.

111. Maybury, Mark. *Social Radar for Smart Power.* MITRE Corporation, 2010, 3. Accessed February 15, 2015. http://www.mitre.org/sites/default/files/pdf/10_0745.pdf.

112. U.S. Department of Defense. *Joint Intelligence.* JP 2-0. October 22, 2013. Accessed February 15, 2015. http://www.dtic.mil/doctrine/new_pubs/jp2_0.pdf.

113. Defense Forensics and Biometrics Agency. *DoD Biometrics Enterprise Architecture (Integrated) v2.0 Common Biometric Vocabulary.* April 2013. Accessed January 30, 2015. http://www.biometrics.dod.mil/Files/Documents/References/common%20biometric%20vocabulary.pdf.

114. Defense Forensics and Biometrics Agency. *DoD Biometrics Enterprise Architecture (Integrated) v2.0 Common Biometric Vocabulary.* April 2013. Accessed January 30, 2015. http://www.biometrics.dod.mil/Files/Documents/References/common%20biometric%20vocabulary.pdf.

115. Office of the Director of National Intelligence. *Glossary of Security Terms, Definitions, and Acronyms.* Intelligence Community Standard (ICS) 700-1. April 4, 2008. Accessed June 5, 2015. https://fas.org/irp/dni/icd/ics-700-1.pdf.

116. Defense Intelligence Agency, Office of Counterintelligence. *CI Glossary—Terms & Definitions of Interest for DoD CI Professionals.* July 2014. Accessed January 17, 2015. https://www.hsdl.org/?view&did=699056.

117. Committee for National Security Systems (CNSS). Instruction 4009. *National Information Assurance Glossary.* April 2010. Accessed February 15, 2015. http://www.ncix.gov/publications/policy/docs/CNSSI_4009.pdf.

118. Office of the Director of National Intelligence. *Sourcing Requirements for Disseminated Analytic Products.* Intelligence Community Directive 206, October 17, 2007. Accessed February 27, 2015. https://fas.org/irp/dni/icd/icd-206.pdf.

119. United States Department of Justice. *Law Enforcement Analytic Standard.* Global Justice Information Sharing Initiative and International Association of Law Enforcement Intelligence Analysts, Inc. 2nd ed. April 2012, accessed February

1, 2016, https://it.ojp.gov/documents/d/Law%20Enforcement%20Analytic%20Standards%2004202_combined_compliant.pdf.

120. Office of the Director of National Intelligence. *Sourcing Requirements for Disseminated Analytic Products.* Intelligence Community Directive 206, October 17, 2007. Accessed February 27, 2015. https://fas.org/irp/dni/icd/icd-206.pdf.

121. Office of the Director of National Intelligence. *Glossary of Security Terms, Definitions, and Acronyms.* Intelligence Community Standard (ICS) 700-1. April 4, 2008. Accessed June 5, 2015. https://fas.org/irp/dni/icd/ics-700-1.pdf.

122. U.S. Department of Defense. *Joint and National Intelligence Support to Military Operations*, Joint Publication 2-01, January 5, 2012. Accessed January 26, 2016, http://www.dtic.mil/doctrine/new_pubs/jp2_01.pdf.

123. Mann, Steve, Nolan, Jason, and Wellman, Barry. "Sousveillance: Inventing and Using Wearable Computing Devices for Data Collection in Surveillance Environments." *Surveillance & Society* 1, no. 3 (2003): 331–55. Accessed February 15, 2015. http://www.surveillance-and-society.org; also see Ali, Mir Adnan, and Steve Mann. "The Inevitability of the Transition from a Surveillance-Society to a Veillance-Society: Moral and Economic Grounding for Sousveillance." In *Technology and Society (ISTAS), 2013 IEEE International Symposium on Technology and Society*, 243–54.

124. Federal Bureau of Investigation. *Minimum Criminal Intelligence Training Standards for Law Enforcement and Other Criminal Justice Agencies in the United States.* October 2007. Accessed February 8, 2015. https://it.ojp.gov/gist/108/Minimum-Criminal-Intelligence-Training-Standards.

125. U.S. Department of Defense. Center for Development of Security Excellence. *Glossary of Security Terms and Definitions.* November 2012. Accessed February 15, 2015. http://www.cdse.edu/documents/cdse/Glossary_Handbook.pdf.

126. Federal Bureau of Investigation. *Minimum Criminal Intelligence Training Standards for Law Enforcement and Other Criminal Justice Agencies in the United States.* October 2007. Accessed February 8, 2015. https://it.ojp.gov/gist/108/Minimum-Criminal-Intelligence-Training-Standards.

127. U.S. Department of Defense. Center for Development of Security Excellence. *Glossary of Security Terms and Definitions.* November 2012. Accessed February 15, 2015. http://www.cdse.edu/documents/cdse/Glossary_Handbook.pdf.

128. U.S. Department of Justice. *The Attorney General's Guidelines for Domestic FBI Operations.* 2008. Accessed February 25, 2015. http://www.justice.gov/sites/default/files/ag/legacy/2008/10/03/guidelines.pdf.

129. Department of Homeland Security, Risk Steering Committee. *DHS Risk Lexicon.* September 2010. Accessed February 14, 2015. http://www.dhs.gov/dhs-risk-lexicon.

130. U.S. Department of Defense. Center for Development of Security Excellence. *Glossary of Security Terms and Definitions.* November 2012. Accessed February 15, 2015. http://www.cdse.edu/documents/cdse/Glossary_Handbook.pdf.

131. SPIEGEL Staff. "Embassy Espionage: The NSA's Secret Spy Hub in Berlin." *SPIEGEL Online*, October 27, 2013. Accessed February 15, 2015. http://www.spiegel.de/international/germany/cover-story-how-nsa-spied-on-merkel-cell-phone-from-berlin-embassy-a-930205.html.

132. Jan Goldman, *Intelligence Warning Terminology*, Joint Military Intelligence College, October 2001, accessed July 3, 2015. https://archive.org/details/JMICInteligencelwarnterminology.

133. Feickert, Andrew. "U.S. Special Operations Forces (SOF): Background and Issues for Congress." *CRS Report for Congress* RS21048, April 9, 2015. Accessed April 16, 2015. http://www.fas.org/sgp/crs/natsec/RS21048.pdf.

134. *The Guardian.* "NSA Files Decoded." November 1, 2013. Accessed February 18, 2015. http://www.theguardian.com/world/interactive/2013/nov/01/snowden-nsa-files-surveillance-revelations-decoded#section/1; also see Electronic Frontier Foundation. *Special Source Operations.* (slide). Accessed February 18, 2015. https://www.eff.org/document/20140618-dagbladet-special-source-operations.

135. U.S Department of the Treasury. *Specially Designated Nationals List (SDN).* January 1, 2016. Accessed February 2, 2016. https://www.treasury.gov/resource-center/sanctions/SDN-List/Pages/default.aspx.

136. U.S. Department of State. "Definitions of Diplomatic Security Terms." *Foreign Affairs Manual.* 12FAM090. November 12, 2014. Accessed February 14, 2015. http://www.state.gov/documents/organization/88330.pdf.

137. Committee for National Security Systems (CNSS). Instruction 4009. *National Information Assurance Glossary.* April 2010. Accessed January 30, 2015. http://www.ncix.gov/publications/policy/docs/CNSSI_4009.pdf.

138. Committee for National Security Systems (CNSS). Instruction 4009. *National Information Assurance Glossary.* April 2010. Accessed March 1, 2015. http://www.ncix.gov/publications/policy/docs/CNSSI_4009.pdf.

139. National Initiative for Cybersecurity Education. *A Glossary of Common Cybersecurity Terminology.* n.d. Accessed March 5, 2015. http://niccs.us-cert.gov/glossary.

140. U.S. Department of State. "Definitions of Diplomatic Security Terms." *Foreign Affairs Manual.* 12FAM090. November 12, 2014. Accessed February 14, 2015. http://www.state.gov/documents/organization/88330.pdf.

141. Jan Goldman, *Intelligence Warning Terminology*, Joint Military Intelligence College, October 2001, accessed July 3, 2015. https://archive.org/details/JMICInteligencelwarnterminology.

142. Defense Intelligence Agency, Office of Counterintelligence. *CI Glossary—Terms & Definitions of Interest for DoD CI Professionals.* July 2014. Accessed February 28, 2015. https://www.hsdl.org/?view&did=699056.

143. Defense Intelligence Agency, Office of Counterintelligence. *CI Glossary—Terms & Definitions of Interest for DoD CI Professionals.* July 2014. Accessed February 28, 2015. https://www.hsdl.org/?view&did=699056.

144. Kelly, Terrence, Jones, Seth G., Barnett II, James E., Crane, Keith, Davis, Robert C., and Jensen, Carl. *A Stability Police Force for the United States Justification and Options for Creating U.S. Capabilities.* Prepared for the U.S. Army. RAND, 2009. Accessed February 15, 2015. http://www.rand.org/content/dam/rand/pubs/monographs/2009/RAND_MG819.pdf.

145. U.S. Department of State, Office of the Coordinator for Counterterrorism. *Country Reports on Terrorism 2010, Chapter 3: State Sponsors of Terrorism.* August

18, 2011. Accessed February 10, 2015. http://www.state.gov/j/ct/rls/crt/2010/170260. htm.

146. United States Department of Defense. *Foreign Humanitarian Assistance.* JP 3-29, January 3, 2014. Accessed March 7, 2015. http://www.dtic.mil/doctrine/ new_pubs/jp3_29.pdf.

147. Wohlstetter, Roberta. *Pearl Harbor: Warning and Decision.* Stanford, CA: Stanford University Press, 318.

148. Federal Bureau of Investigation. *Minimum Criminal Intelligence Training Standards for Law Enforcement and Other Criminal Justice Agencies in the United States.* October 2007. Accessed February 8, 2015. https://it.ojp.gov/gist/108/Minimum-Criminal-Intelligence-Training-Standards.

149. Chairman of the Joint Chiefs of Staff. *National Military Strategic Plan for the War on Terrorism.* February 1, 2006. Accessed February 26, 2015. http://www. defense.gov/qdr/docs/2006-02-08-Strategic-Plan.pdf.

150. Department of Homeland Security, Risk Steering Committee. *DHS Risk Lexicon.* September 2010. Accessed February 14, 2015. http://www.dhs.gov/dhs-risk-lexicon.

151. Committee for National Security Systems (CNSS). Instruction 4009. *National Information Assurance Glossary.* April 2010. Accessed February 15, 2015. http://www.ncix.gov/publications/policy/docs/CNSSI_4009.pdf.

152. *Memorandum from Jack L. Goldsmith, III, Assistant Attorney General, to the Attorney General RE: Review of the Legality of the STELLAR WIND Program.* May 6, 2004. Obtained under FOIA by EPIC. Accessed February 15, 2015. https:// epic.org/privacy/nsa/foia/OLC-54-OCR.pdf. Also see Risen, James, and Lichtblau, Eric. "Bush Lets U.S. Spy on Callers Without Courts." *New York Times*, December 16, 2005. Accessed February 18, 2015. http://www.nytimes.com/2005/12/16/ politics/16program.html; Bamford, James. "The NSA Is Building the Country's Biggest Spy Center (Watch What You Say)." *Wired*, March 15, 2012. Accessed February 18, 2015. http://www.wired.com/2012/03/ff_nsadatacenter/all/1; and Nakashima, Ellen. "Legal Memos Released on Bush-era Justification for Warrantless Wiretapping." *Washington Post*, September 6, 2014. Accessed February 18, 2015. http://www.washingtonpost.com/world/national-security/legal-memos-released-on-bush-era-justification-for-warrantless-wiretapping/2014/09/05/91b86c52–356d-11e4 -9e92-0899b306bbea_story.html.

153. United States Senate, Select Committee to Study Governmental Operations with Respect to Intelligence Activities (Church Committee). *Final Report.* Book 1. April 26, 1976. Accessed January 14, 2015. https://archive.org/details/finalreportof-sel01unit.

154. Office of the Director for National Intelligence. *Discovery and Dissemination or Retrieval of Information within the Intelligence Community.* ICD 501, January 21, 2009, accessed February 2, 2016, http://www.dni.gov/index.php/intelligence-community/ic-policies-reports/intelligence-community-directives.

155. U.S. Department of Defense. *Joint and National Intelligence Support to Military Operations.* JP 2-01. January 5, 2012. Accessed February 26, 2015. http://www. dtic.mil/doctrine/new_pubs/jp2_01.pdf.

156. Gentry, John A. "Complex Civil-Military Operations: A US Military-Centric Perspective." *Naval War College Review* 53, no. 4 (2000): 57–76. Accessed June 8, 2015. Retrieved from https://www.usnwc.edu/NavalWarCollegeReviewArchives/20 00s/2000%20Autumn.pdf.

157. U.S. Department of State. "Definitions of Diplomatic Security Terms." *Foreign Affairs Manual.* 12FAM090. November 12, 2014. Accessed February 14, 2015. http://www.state.gov/documents/organization/88330.pdf.

158. Porter Goss, CNN interview, May 11, 1999.

159. U.S. Department of Defense. *Quadrennial Defense Review Report.* February 2010. Accessed February 11, 2015. http://www.defense.gov/qdr/qdr%20as%20 of%2029jan10%201600.pdf.

160. Office of the Director of National Intelligence. *National Intelligence Program FY 2009 Congressional Budget Justification Book.* Vol. XII, February 2008. Accessed January 17, 2015. http://www.fas.org/irp/dni/cbjb-2009.pdf.

161. U.S. Department of Defense. *Department of Defense Dictionary of Military and Associated Terms.* JP 1-02, 08 November 2010, as Amended through 15 March 2015. Accessed March 18, 2015. http://www.dtic.mil/doctrine/dod_dictionary/.

162. Chairman of the Joint Chiefs of Staff. *National Military Strategic Plan for the War on Terrorism.* February 1, 2006. Accessed February 26, 2015. http://www.defense.gov/qdr/docs/2006-02-08-Strategic-Plan.pdf.

163. The White House. *National Framework for Strategic Communication,* Pursuant to section 1055 of the Duncan Hunter National Defense Authorization Act for Fiscal Year 2009, March 16, 2010. Accessed March 20, 2015. http://fas.org/man/eprint/pubdip.pdf.

164. U.S. Department of Defense. *Department of Defense Dictionary of Military and Associated Terms.* JP 1-02, 08 November 2010, as Amended through 15 January 2016. Accessed January 26, 2016. http://www.dtic.mil/doctrine/new_pubs/jp1_02.pdf.

165. Jan Goldman, *Intelligence Warning Terminology,* Joint Military Intelligence College, October 2001, accessed July 3, 2015. https://archive.org/details/JMICIntelligencelwarnterminology.

166. Department of Homeland Security, Risk Steering Committee. *DHS Risk Lexicon.* September 2010. Accessed February 14, 2015. http://www.dhs.gov/dhs-risk-lexicon.

167. Department of Homeland Security, Risk Steering Committee. *DHS Risk Lexicon.* September 2010. Accessed February 14, 2015. http://www.dhs.gov/dhs-risk-lexicon.

168. Jan Goldman, *Intelligence Warning Terminology,* Joint Military Intelligence College, October 2001, accessed July 3, 2015. https://archive.org/details/JMICIntelligencelwarnterminology.

169. Jan Goldman, *Intelligence Warning Terminology,* Joint Military Intelligence College, October 2001, accessed July 3, 2015. https://archive.org/details/JMICIntelligencelwarnterminology.

170. United States Department of Justice. *Law Enforcement Analytic Standard.* Global Justice Information Sharing Initiative and International Association of Law

Enforcement Intelligence Analysts, Inc. 2nd ed. April 2012, accessed February 1, 2016, https://it.ojp.gov/documents/d/Law%20Enforcement%20Analytic%20Standards%2004202_combined_compliant.pdf.

171. U.S. Department of Defense. *DoD Intelligence Interrogations, Detainee Debriefings, and Tactical Questioning.* Directive Number 3115.09, October 11, 2012, Incorporating Change 1, Effective November 15, 2013. Accessed February 15, 2015. http://www.dtic.mil/whs/directives/corres/pdf/311509p.pdf.

172. Department of Homeland Security, Risk Steering Committee. *DHS Risk Lexicon.* September 2010. Accessed February 14, 2015. http://www.dhs.gov/dhs-risk-lexicon.

173. Office of the Director of National Intelligence. *National Intelligence Program FY 2009 Congressional Budget Justification Book.* Vol. XII, February 2008. Accessed January 17, 2015. http://www.fas.org/irp/dni/cbjb-2009.pdf.

174. Grabo, Cynthia M. "Strategic Warning: The Problem of Timing." *Studies in Intelligence* 16, no. 2 (1972). Accessed June 9, 2015. https://www.cia.gov/library/center-for-the-study-of-intelligence/kent-csi/vol16no2/html/v16i2a07p_0001.htm.

175. Central Intelligence Agency. *National Intelligence Warning.* DCI Directive No. 1/5, May 23, 1979. Accessed June 5, 2015. http://fas.org./irp/offdocs/dcid1-5.html.

176. Jan Goldman, *Intelligence Warning Terminology*, Joint Military Intelligence College, October 2001, accessed July 3, 2015. https://archive.org/details/JMICIntelligencelwarnterminology.

177. Jan Goldman, *Intelligence Warning Terminology*, Joint Military Intelligence College, October 2001, accessed July 3, 2015. https://archive.org/details/JMICIntelligencelwarnterminology.

178. Defense Intelligence Agency, Office of Counterintelligence. *CI Glossary—Terms & Definitions of Interest for DoD CI Professionals.* July 2014. Accessed February 18, 2015. https://www.hsdl.org/?view&did=699056.

179. Central Intelligence Agency, *Studies in Intelligence*, accessed February 2, 2016, https://www.cia.gov/library/center-for-the-study-of-intelligence/csi-publications/csi-studies/index.html.

180. U.S. Department of State. "Definitions of Diplomatic Security Terms." *Foreign Affairs Manual.* 12FAM090. November 12, 2014. Accessed February 14, 2015. http://www.state.gov/documents/organization/88330.pdf.

181. Department of Homeland Security, Risk Steering Committee. *DHS Risk Lexicon.* September 2010. Accessed February 14, 2015. http://www.dhs.gov/dhs-risk-lexicon.

182. Office of the Director of National Intelligence. *Competency Directories for the Intelligence Community Workforce.* Intelligence Community Directive 610, October 4, 2010. Accessed March 2, 2015. http://www.dni.gov/files/documents/ICD/ICD_610.pdf.

183. Department of Homeland Security, Risk Steering Committee. *DHS Risk Lexicon.* September 2010. Accessed February 14, 2015. http://www.dhs.gov/dhs-risk-lexicon.

184. Federal Bureau of Investigation. *Minimum Criminal Intelligence Training Standards for Law Enforcement and Other Criminal Justice Agencies in the United States.* October 2007. Accessed February 8, 2015. https://it.ojp.gov/gist/108/Minimum-Criminal-Intelligence-Training-Standards.

185. United States Senate, Select Committee to Study Governmental Operations with Respect to Intelligence Activities (Church Committee). *Final Report.* Book 1. April 26, 1976. Accessed January 15, 2015. https://archive.org/details/finalreportofsel01unit.

186. Cronin, Audrey Kurth. "Terrorists and Suicide Attacks." *CRS Report for Congress* RL32058, August 28, 2003. Accessed March 8, 2015. http://fas.org/irp/crs/RL32058.pdf.

187. Cetron, Marvin J. and Probst, Peter S. *Terror 2000: The Future Face of Terrorism.* June 24, 1994. Accessed February 28, 2015. http://www.dod.mil/pubs/foi/International_security_affairs/terrorism/951.pdf.

188. Permanent Select Committee on Intelligence. *IC21: The Intelligence Community in the 21st Century.* Staff Study Permanent Select Committee on Intelligence. June 5, 1996. Accessed June 9, 2015. http://www.gpo.gov/fdsys/pkg/GPO-IC21/content-detail.html.

189. North Atlantic Treaty Organization. *NATO Glossary of Terms and Definitions.* NATO Standardization Agency, 2014, AAP-06, accessed July 27, 2015, http://nso.nato.int/nso/zPublic/ap/aap6/AAP-6.pdf.

190. Federal Bureau of Investigation. *Minimum Criminal Intelligence Training Standards for Law Enforcement and Other Criminal Justice Agencies in the United States.* October 2007. Accessed February 8, 2015. https://it.ojp.gov/gist/108/Minimum-Criminal-Intelligence-Training-Standards.

191. Ali, Mir Adnan, and Mann, Steve. "The Inevitability of the Transition from a Surveillance-Society to a Veillance-Society: Moral and Economic Grounding for Sousveillance." In *Technology and Society (ISTAS), 2013 IEEE International Symposium on Technology and Society*, 243–54.

192. EO 12333, *United States Intelligence Activities*, December 4, 1981, accessed February 1, 2016, http://www.archives.gov/federal-register/codification/executive-order/12333.html. Also see Mark Jaycox, *A Primer on Executive Order 12333: The Mass Surveillance Starlet*, June 2, 2014, EFF, accessed February 2, 2016, https://www.eff.org/deeplinks/2014/06/primer-executive-order-12333-mass-surveillance-starlet, and Office of the Director of National Intelligence, *ODNI and DOJ Updated Guidelines for NCTC Access, Retention, Use, and Dissemination of Information in Datasets Containing Non-Terrorism Information*, March 22, 2012, accessed February 1, 2016, http://www.dni.gov/index.php/newsroom/press-releases/96-press-releases-2012/528-odni-and-doj-update-guidelines-for-nctc-access,-retention,-use,-and-dissemination-of-information-in-datasets-containing-non-terrorism-information.

193. U.S. Department of Defense. *Technical Surveillance Countermeasures.* Instruction, Number 5240.05. April 3, 2014. Accessed February 18, 2015. http://www.dtic.mil/whs/directives/corres/pdf/524005_2014.pdf.

194. U.S. Department of Defense. *Joint Intelligence.* JP 2-0. October 22, 2013. Accessed February 15, 2015. http://www.dtic.mil/doctrine/new_pubs/jp2_0.pdf.

195. U.S. Department of Defense. *Joint Intelligence*. JP 2-0. October 22, 2013. Accessed February 15, 2015. http://www.dtic.mil/doctrine/new_pubs/jp2_0.pdf.

196. U.S. Department of Defense. *Joint Intelligence*. JP 2-0. October 22, 2013. Accessed February 15, 2015. http://www.dtic.mil/doctrine/new_pubs/jp2_0.pdf.

197. U.S. Department of State. "Definitions of Diplomatic Security Terms." *Foreign Affairs Manual*. 12FAM090. November 12, 2014. Accessed February 14, 2015. http://www.state.gov/documents/organization/88330.pdf.

198. U.S. Department of Defense. Center for Development of Security Excellence. *Glossary of Security Terms and Definitions*. November 2012. Accessed February 15, 2015. http://www.cdse.edu/documents/cdse/Glossary_Handbook.pdf.

199. Markle Task Force. *Creating a Trusted Network for Homeland Security.* Second Report of the Markle Foundation Task Force. December 1, 2003. Accessed February 15, 2015. http://www.markle.org/publications/666-creating-trusted-network-homeland-security.

T

TACIT KNOWLEDGE Intangible, internal, intuitive knowledge that is undocumented and maintained in the human mind. Tacit knowledge has typically been characterized by intangible factors such as perception, belief, values, intuition, know-how, and gut feeling.[1] *See* EXPLICIT KNOWLEDGE

TACTICAL COLLECTION DEVICE A portable system used to capture data that represent biometric characteristics of an individual. The system provides the capability to collect, store, match, share, and manage biometric information and enable a decide/act capability.[2]

TACTICAL ENROLLMENT Biometric data on a subject that includes at least 2 fingerprints (indexes), 2 iris prints, and required text fields. The sample must be EBTS (Electronic Biometric Transmission Specification) compliant. Typically used when subject is not being detained, but a record of the encounter is required at an IED site, raid, humanitarian assistance, and more. It is an identification leading to an enrollment of a subject utilizing biometric data that includes at least 1 fingerprint or 1 iris and capture identification number.[3]

TACTICAL INTELLIGENCE Required for the planning and conduct of tactical operations. Essentially, tactical intelligence and strategic intelligence differ only in scope, point of view, and level of employment. TI seeks to gather and manage diverse information to facilitate a successful prosecution of the intelligence target. It is also used for specific decision making or problem solving to deal with an immediate situation or crisis.[4] *See* COMBAT INTELLIGENCE; CURRENT OPERATIONAL INTELLIGENCE; STRATEGIC INTELLIGENCE

TACTICAL QUESTIONING (TQ) Field-expedient initial questioning for information of immediate tactical value of a captured or detained person at or near the point of capture and before the individual is placed in a detention facility. Tactical questioning is generally performed by members of patrols, but can be done by any appropriately trained DoD personnel. Tactical questioning is limited to direct questioning.[5]

TACTICAL WARNING 1. Short-term warning that an attack is imminent or that forces are in motion; primarily intended for military commanders who must respond to it with usually no time to redeploy defensively; primarily the responsibility of operational forces. The process involves detection of the initial movements of the attack itself, before combat occurs. The time frame can range from minutes to hours depending on the distance from the ground force assembly area or missile launch site to target.[6] 2. Notification that the enemy has initiated hostilities. Such warning may be received at any time from the launching of the attack until it reaches its target.[7] See PHASES OF WARNING; POLITICAL WARNING; STRATEGIC WARNING

TAILORED ACCESS OPERATIONS (TAO) 1. NSA's top operative unit when normal access to a target is blocked. These on-call digital workers are involved in many sensitive operations conducted by American intelligence agencies. TAO's area of operations ranges from counterterrorism to cyberattacks to traditional espionage.[8] 2. Within TAO, different groups carry out a range of espionage and attack operations. One conducts surveillance to map out the computer networks of its targets and find their vulnerabilities. Another unit researches the latest hacking tools and techniques for penetrating secure computer networks. Another builds penetration tools tailored just for telecommunications networks. Within that group are hackers who develop tools for commandeering video cameras, particularly on laptop computers, and industrial control systems, devices that control and regulate power grids, nuclear reactors, dams, and other infrastructure. And yet another unit carries out computer network attacks in conjunction with a CIA group called the Technology Management Office, which helps the NSA break in to hard-to-reach networks where a person might be required to manually insert a virus or piece of spyware with, say, a USB thumb drive. TAO's offices are located in a secure building at Fort Meade, Maryland.[9] See OFFICE OF TAILORED ACCESS OPERATIONS

TAILORED TRUSTWORTHY SPACES (TTS) Provide flexible, adaptive, distributed trust environments that can support functional and policy requirements arising from a wide spectrum of activities in the face of an evolving range of threats. A TTS recognizes the user's context and evolves as the context evolves. A TTS enforces the user's chosen level of trust, ranging from a fully anonymous transaction to a trusted transaction with strong attribution and traceable authentication. The user is informed of the levels of trust available and chooses to accept the protections and risks of a particular tailored space. The attributes of each available trusted space must be expressible in an understandable way to support informed choice. The attributes must be made manifest and readily usable to support being customized, negotiated, adapted, and enforced. All parties to the transaction must agree on the level of trust enforced by the underlying infrastructure.[10]

TALLINN MANUAL *The Tallinn Manual on the International Law Applicable to Cyber Warfare* examines the international law governing "cyber warfare." As a general matter, it encompasses both the *jus ad bellum*, the international law governing the resort to force by States as an instrument of their national policy, and the *jus in bello*, the international law regulating the conduct of armed conflict (also labelled the law of war, the law of armed conflict, or international humanitarian law). Related bodies of international law, such as the law of State responsibility and the law of the sea, are dealt within the context of these topics. In short, this is not a manual on "cyber security" as that term is understood in common usage. Cyber espionage, theft of intellectual property, and a wide variety of criminal activities in cyberspace pose real and serious threats to all States, as well as to corporations and private individuals. An adequate response to them requires national and international measures. However, the Manual does not address such matters because application of the international law on uses of force and armed conflict plays little or no role in doing so. Such law is no more applicable to these threats in the cyber domain than it is in the physical world. The Tallinn Manual's emphasis is on cyber-to-cyber operations, *strictu sensu*. Examples include the launch of a cyber-operation against a State's critical infrastructure or a cyber-attack targeting enemy command and control systems. There are no treaty provisions that directly deal with cyber "warfare." Similarly, because State cyber practice and publicly available expressions of opinion are sparse, it is sometimes difficult to definitely conclude that any cyber-specific customary international law norm exists. This being so, any claim that every assertion in the Manual represents an incontrovertible restatement of international law would be an exaggeration.[11]

TANGIBLE THINGS 1. Subject to paragraph (3) (50 U.S. Code § 1861) the director of the Federal Bureau of Investigation or a designee of the director (whose rank shall be no lower than assistant special agent in charge) may make an application for an order requiring the production of any tangible things (including books, records, papers, documents, and other items) for an investigation to obtain foreign intelligence information not concerning a U.S. person or to protect against international terrorism or clandestine intelligence activities, provided that such investigation of a U.S. person is not conducted solely upon the basis of activities protected by the first amendment to the Constitution.[12] 2. FISA's (Foreign Intelligence Surveillance Act) tangible things provision is unusual in that it discriminates among federal agencies, referring specifically to the FBI rather than any other agency. It authorizes certain FBI officials to make the necessary application, and requires approval from a high-ranking FBI official if the tangible things sought are particularly sensitive (e.g., library patron lists). Its language also strongly suggests that the FBI will receive the tangible things pursuant to the FISA Court's order.[13]

TARGET 1. An entity or object that performs a function for the adversary considered for possible engagement or other action. 2. In intelligence usage, a country, area, installation, agency, or person against which intelligence operations are directed. 3. An area designated and numbered for future firing. 4. In gunfire support usage, an impact burst that hits the target.[14]

TARGET ACQUISITION The detection, identification, and location of a target in sufficient detail to permit the effective employment of weapons.[15]

TARGET ANALYSIS An examination of potential targets to determine military importance, priority of attack, and weapons required to obtain a desired level of damage or casualties.

TARGET AUDIENCE (TA) An individual or group selected for influence or attack by means of psychological operations.[16]

TARGET DATE The date on which it is desired that an action be accomplished or initiated.[17]

TARGET DISCRIMINATION The ability of surveillance or guidance systems to identify or engage any one target when multiple targets are present.[18]

TARGET OF OPPORTUNITY 1. A target identified too late, or not selected for action in time, to be included in deliberate targeting that, when detected or located, meets criteria specific to achieving objectives and is processed using dynamic targeting. 2. A target visible to a surface or air sensor or observer, which is within range of available weapons and against which fire has not been scheduled or requested.[19]

TARGET PROFILE A person- or organization-specific report providing everything known on the individual or organization that is useful as the investigation is initiated. Based on the data, a best course of action regarding the investigation may be recommended.[20]

TARGET STATUS BOARD A wall chart maintained by the air intelligence division of the joint operations center. It includes target lists, locations, priority, and status of action taken. It may also include recommended armament and fusing for destruction.[21]

TARGETED SURVEILLANCE Targeted surveillance is surveillance directed at particular individuals and can involve the use of specific powers by authorized public agencies. Targeted surveillance can be carried out overtly or covertly, and can involve human agents.[22]

TARGETED VIOLENCE Preconceived violence focused on individuals, groups, or locations where perpetrators are engaged in behaviors that precede and are related to their attacks. These perpetrators consider, plan and prepare before engaging in acts of violence and are often detectable, providing an opportunity for disruption of the intended violence.[23]

TARGETS In the NICE (National Initiative for Cybersecurity Education) Workforce Framework, where a person applies current knowledge of one or more regions, countries, non-state entities, and/or technologies.[24]

TASK FORCE A component of a fleet organized by the commander of a task fleet or higher authority for the accomplishment of a specific task or task.[25]

TASKING 1. The process of translating the allocation into orders, and passing these orders to the units involved. Each order normally contains sufficient detailed instructions to enable the executing agency to accomplish the mission successfully.[26] 2. Directing or requesting a source to perform in a specific manner to achieve an objective or conduct an activity; the process associated with acceptance of a validated collection requirement and assigning it to organic collection assets for action.[27]

TEAR LINE A physical line that appears on a message or document which separates information that has been approved for foreign/public disclosure and information which must not be released. Usually, the information below the tear line is releasable and that above the tear line remains classified and/or non-releasable. In a classified report, there may be a summary of critical information, without a description of sources and methods that is below a designated line, the tear line on the report. This portion is designated Sensitive but Unclassified (SBU) and may be disseminated to law enforcement personnel who do not have a security clearance as Law Enforcement Sensitive.[28]

TECHNICAL INFORMATION Relates to research, development, engineering, test, evaluation, production, operation, use and maintenance of munitions, and other military supplies and equipment.[29]

TECHNICAL INTELLIGENCE (TECHNIT) 1. Intelligence derived from the collection, processing, analysis, and exploitation of data and information pertaining to foreign equipment and materiel for the purposes of preventing technological surprise, assessing foreign scientific and technical capabilities, and developing countermeasures designed to neutralize an adversary's technological advantages.[30] 2. The post–Cold War political climate does not guarantee any army's arsenal to come from a single supplier state. S2's [intelligence officers] cannot template capabilities based on a single (normally Russian) model. Such diversity not only complicates Order of Battle study; it also provides opportunities for technological surprise. Technological surprise is the bogeyman for TECHINT [technical intelligence] analysis: the specter of U.S. commanders encountering optics, weapons ranges, or armor more sophisticated than they thought an opponent possessed. The key to preventing technological surprise is training soldiers ahead of time to look for, recognize, and report on new or modified weapons on the battlefield. The 203rd MI Battalion responds to such spot reports with a TECHINT Collection Team, which photographs and often retrieves the new systems off the battlefield for further study. This cycle of recognition, reporting, retrieval, and analysis is fundamental to avoiding technological surprise.[31] *See* SOURCES OF INTELLIGENCE

TECHNICAL RISK The risk that arises from activities related to technology, design and engineering, manufacturing, and the critical technical processes of test, production, and logistics.[32]

TECHNICAL SUPPORT WORKING GROUP (TSWG) The U.S. national forum that identifies, prioritizes, and coordinates interagency and international research and development (R&D) requirements for combating terrorism. The TSWG rapidly develops technologies and equipment to meet the high-priority needs of the combating terrorism community, and it addresses joint international operational requirements through cooperative R&D with major allies. The TSWG continues to focus its program development efforts to balance investments across the four pillars of combating terrorism.[33]

TECHNICAL SURVEILLANCE The act of establishing a technical penetration and intercepting information without authorization.[34]

TECHNOLOGICAL ASYMMETRY The unequal sophistication or distribution of technology within a country that could possibly lead to the overestimation of an enemy's capability. For example, country A has the ability to build a nuclear bomb but may lack the ability to weaponize it into a delivery system, which would result in technological asymmetry (assuming the country was seeking a nuclear missile capability).

TECHNOLOGICAL DEVELOPMENT Five stages are monitored to determine the threat capability of a real (or potential) enemy: basic research (to develop a theoretical understanding); item fabrication (translating a theory into practice by developing experimental confirmation); production prototype (to demonstrate feasibility); full production (item is available and could be mass produced); maturity (minor changes are made to production).

TECHNOLOGICAL SURPRISE The unilateral advantage gained by the introduction of a new weapon or by the use of a known weapon in an innovative way against an adversary who is either unaware of its existence or not ready with effective countermeasures.[35]

TECHNOLOGY CONTROL PLAN (TCP) The document that identifies and describes sensitive program information; the risks involved in foreign access to the information; the participation in the program or foreign sales of the resulting system; and the development of access controls and protective measures as necessary to protect the U.S. technological or operational advantage represented by the system.[36]

TECHNOLOGY CRITICAL Technologies that would make a significant contribution to the military potential of any country or combination of countries and that may prove detrimental to the security of the United States, consisting of arrays of design and manufacturing knowhow, including technical data; keystone manufacturing, inspection, and test equipment; keystone materials; goods accompanied by sophisticated operation, application, or maintenance know-how.[37]

TELEMETRY INTELLIGENCE (TELINT) Information derived from the intercept, processing, and analysis of foreign telemetry. *See* SOURCES OF INTELLIGENCE

TELEPHONE RECORD ANALYSIS/COMMUNICATION ANALYSIS
The review of records reflecting communications (telephone, e-mail, pager, text messaging, etc.) among entities that may be reflective of criminal associations or activity. The analysis may recommend steps to take to continue or expand the investigation or study.

TELEPHONY METADATA All call-detail records or "telephony metadata," defined as comprehensive communications routing information, including but not limited to session-identifying information (e.g., originating and terminating telephone number, communications device identifier, etc.), trunk identifier, and time and duration of call.[38] *See* METADATA

TEMPEST (TRANSIENT ELECTROMAGNETIC PULSE SURVEILLANCE TECHNOLOGY) Tempest is the unclassified short name referring to investigations and studies of compromising emanations. Compromising emanations are unintentional intelligence-bearing signals that, if intercepted and analyzed, will disclose classified information when they are transmitted, received, handled, or otherwise processed by any information processing equipment. Because the details of many Tempest issues are classified and controlled under strict conditions of need-to-know, unclassified discussions must be somewhat general.[39]

TEMPORA A key innovation of GCHQ's (the UK's Government Communications Headquarters) ability to tap into and store huge volumes of data drawn from fiber-optic cables for up to 30 days so that it can be sifted and analyzed. That operation, codenamed Tempora, has been running for some 18 months. For the 2 billion users of the world wide web, Tempora represents a window on to their everyday lives, sucking up every form of communication from the fiber-optic cables that ring the world.[40] The Snowden documents revealed the existence of Tempora, a program established in 2011 by GCHQ (the UK's Government Communications Headquarters) that gathers masses of phone and internet traffic by tapping into fiber-optic cables. GCHQ shares most of its information with the NSA.[41]

TEMPORARY RECORDS Federal records approved for disposal, either immediately or after a specified retention period.[42]

TERMS OF REFERENCE Elements that define the subject matter of a report or estimate, to include context, scope, and time frame. According to Sherman Kent, one of the standard bearers of intelligence analysis at the CIA, terms of reference "focus the forthcoming estimate on the new major points which were discerned as the principal concern of the requestor; aimed to ask the questions (irrespective of anyone's ability to supply factual answers) which would direct research and cogitation to the general area of these major points. In a word, it was a statement of precisely what was wanted and a polite message to the community's expert research analysts, telling what was wanted of them."[43]

TERRORISM 1. The calculated use of violence or threat of violence to inculcate fear; intended to coerce or to intimidate governments or societies in the pursuit of goals that are generally political, religious, or ideological.[44] 2. Whoever, involving conduct transcending national boundaries and in a circumstance described in subsection (b) (A) kills, kidnaps, maims, commits an assault resulting in serious bodily injury, or assaults with a dangerous weapon any person within the United States; or (B) creates a substantial risk of serious bodily injury to any other person by destroying or damaging any structure, conveyance, or other real or personal property within the United States or by attempting or conspiring to destroy or damage any structure, conveyance, or other real or personal property within the United States.[45]

TERRORISM INFORMATION The term "terrorism information"—(A) means all information, whether collected, produced, or distributed by intelligence, law enforcement, military, homeland security, or other activities relating to—(i) the existence, organization, capabilities, plans, intentions, vulnerabilities, means of finance or material support, or activities of foreign or international terrorist groups or individuals, or of domestic groups or individuals involved in transnational terrorism; (ii) threats posed by such groups or individuals to the United States, United States persons, or United States interests, or to those of other nations; (iii) communications of or by such groups or individuals; or (iv) groups or individuals reasonably believed to be assisting or associated with such groups or individuals; and (B) includes weapons of mass destruction information.[46] *See* WEAPONS OF MASS DESTRUCTION INFORMATION

TERRORISM INFORMATION AWARENESS A DoD program to integrate advanced collaborative and decision support tools; language translation; and data search, pattern recognition, and privacy protection technologies into a network focused on combating terrorism through better analysis and decision making. It is intended to provide advance actionable information and knowledge about terrorist planning and preparation activities that would aid in making informed decisions to prevent future international terrorist attacks against the United States at home or abroad. The aim is to use technology to help those working to "connect the dots" of terrorist-related activity.[47]

TERRORISM INFORMATION PREVENTION SYSTEM (OPERA-TION TIPS) An idea proposed as a Citizen Corps program that would create a national information-sharing system for specific industry groups to report suspicious, publicly observable activity that could be related to terrorism. The idea was based on programs such as Highway Watch and Coast Watch, which allow truckers and ship captains to report dangerous conditions along their routes. Under Operation TIPS, workers in specific industry groups would have a single phone number for reporting information to state, local, and federal law enforcement agencies about unusual activities that they might observe in the normal course of their daily routines. However, there was resistance to the idea, and the plan was scrapped: "Any and all activities of the federal government to implement the proposed component program of the Citizen Corps known as Operation TIPS (Terrorism Information and Prevention System) are hereby prohibited."[48]

TERRORIST EXTREMISTS An extremist that uses terrorism—the purposeful targeting of ordinary people—to produce fear to coerce or intimidate governments or societies in the pursuit of political, religious, or ideological goals. Extremists use terrorism to impede and undermine political progress, economic prosperity, the security and stability of the international state system, and the future of civil society.[49]

TERRORIST GROUP LOGOS Law enforcement officers should be on the watch for these emblems and/or named groups during traffic stops and other contacts. These emblems may be found on jewelry, documents, posters, or other material. Displaying them may indicate membership in these groups and/or financial or general support for them. All groups whose logos are displayed on these pages, with one exception, have been designated by the U.S. Department of State as either a Foreign Terrorist Organization or under Executive Order 13224.[50]

TERRORIST IDENTITIES DATABASE (TID) TTIC (Terrorist Threat Integration Center) will also establish and maintain the TID, which will be a repository for all-source information on known and suspected terrorists. The TID is envisioned as becoming the primary source for international terrorist data provided by TTIC to the TSC (Terrorist Screening Center). Such information will include names, aliases, dates and places of birth, identification and travel documents, unique and distinguishing physical features, biometric data, and individuals' past affiliation with terrorist acts or groups. In the past, much of this information was stored in disparate databases maintained by several agencies. Consolidating and expanding this data could remedy systemic weaknesses that in the past prevented intelligence analysts and investigators from positively identifying known and suspected terrorists (13–14).[51] *See* TERRORIST THREAT INTEGRATION CENTER

TERRORIST IDENTITIES DATAMART ENVIRONMENT (TIDE) 1. TIDE is that knowledge bank and supports the USG's various terrorist screening systems or "watchlists" and the U.S. Intelligence Community's overall counterterrorism mission. The TIDE database includes, to the extent permitted by law, all information the USG possesses related to the identities of individuals known or appropriately suspected to be or to have been involved in activities constituting, in preparation for, in aid of, or related to terrorism (with the exception of purely domestic terrorism information). This information is available to counterterrorism professionals throughout the Intelligence Community, including the Department of Defense, via the web-based, read-only "TIDE Online." As of December 2013, TIDE contained about 1.1 million persons, most containing multiple minor spelling variations of their names. U.S. Persons (including both citizens and legal permanent residents) account for about 25,000 of that total.[52] 2. The National Counterterrorism Center pulls terrorist intelligence data into the TIDE database "from more than 30 networks in an unprecedented effort to uncover and disrupt terrorist plots." Maintaining and updating the data fed into TIDE from the CIA, NSA, Department of State, and other intelligence sources on a daily basis as well as ensuring that only qualified terrorist intelligence is available to the government's counterterrorist analysts is a growing concern . . . There is no foolproof way to ensure that only good data gets into the TIDE database and unqualified data stays out. But the technical issues that hinder TIDE's ability to properly process, store, and search the data it does have is a major concern.[53]

TERRORIST SCREENING CENTER Created in 2003 in the aftermath of the 9/11 terrorist attacks by Homeland Security Presidential Directive-6 (HSPD-6) that directed the attorney general to establish an organization to consolidate the U.S. government's approach to terrorism screening. TSC is a multi-agency organization, administered by the FBI, that maintains a 24/7 operation center and manages and operates the U.S. government's consolidated Terrorist Screening Database (TSDB), often referred to as the "Terrorist Watchlist," and serves as a bridge between Law Enforcement, Homeland Security, the Intelligence Community and International Partners.[54] *See* CONSOLIDATED TERRORIST SCREENING DATABASE

TERRORIST SCREENING DATABASE (TSB, TSDB) 1. The U.S. Government's authoritative consolidated database that contains terrorist identifiers concerning individuals known or reasonably suspected to be or have been engaged in conduct constituting, in preparation for, in aid of, or related to terrorism or terrorist activities.[55] 2. The TSDB, commonly referred to as the Terrorist Watchlist, contains both international and domestic terrorist identity information. The procedure for submitting information on individuals for inclusion on the Terrorist Watchlist is referred to as the nomination process. The nomination process is the most fundamental and singularly important step in the watchlisting process. It is through this process that individuals are added to the Terrorist Watchlist. Nominations originate from credible information developed by our intelligence and law enforcement partners.[56]

TERRORIST SURVEILLANCE PROGRAM (TSP) An electronic surveillance program implemented by the National Security Agency (NSA) and part of the President's Surveillance Program. *The New York Times* disclosed the TSP on December 16, 2005. The following day, President George W. Bush confirmed the existence of a "terrorist surveillance program" in his weekly radio address.[57] *See* PRISM

TERRORIST THREAT INTEGRATION CENTER (TTIC) 1. Creation was announced by President Bush in his State of the Union address in January, began operations today. Earlier this week, TTIC Director Brennan briefed the president, the vice president, and senior administration officials on TTIC's mission and how it will serve as a hub for terrorist threat–related information collected domestically or abroad. TTIC officers are responsible for assessing, integrating, and expeditiously disseminating available threat information and analysis; maintaining an all-source database on known and suspected terrorists; and identifying collection requirements related to the terrorist threat. The doors to TTIC opened at CIA Headquarters today with over 50 officers from the Department of State, the Department of Defense, the Department of Justice, the FBI, the Department of Homeland Security, and the Intelligence Community. TTIC will gradually grow in size over the next several months, and it will have several hundred officers by the time it moves to a separate facility in May 2004.[58] 2. Sec. 1092 of the 2004 Intelligence Reform and Terrorism Prevention Act (IRTPA) transferred the TTIC to the National Counterterrorism Center "including all functions and activities discharged by the Terrorist Threat Integration Center or its successor entity as of the date of the enactment of this Act." In addition, IRTPA directed "The Director of the National Counterterrorism Center shall administer the Terrorist Threat Integration Center after the date of the enactment of this Act as a component of the Directorate of Intelligence of the National Counterterrorism Center under section 119(i) of the National Security Act of 1947, as added by section 1021(a) of this Act.[59] *See* NATIONAL COUNTERRORISM CENTER, SYSTEMWIDE HOMELAND ANALYSIS AND RESOURCE EXCHANGE (SHARE) NETWORK

TERRORIST WATCHLIST PERSON DATA EXCHANGE STANDARD (TWPDES) An Extensible Markup Language (XML)–based data exchange format for terrorist watchlist data that supports the Department of State, Department of Justice, Intelligence Community under the Director of Central Intelligence, and the Department of Homeland Security. It is designed to develop and maintain, to the extent permissible by law, the most thorough, accurate, and current information possible about individuals known or appropriately suspected to be or have been involved in activities constituting, in preparation for, in aid of, or related to terrorism.[60]

TERTIARY TARGETING Plans or attacks against parties with indirect links to the primary target of an organized campaign. Tertiary targets can include employees, customers, investors, and other participants in a company (the secondary target) that does business with or provides support services to the primary target; or parties who provide direct financial, logistic, or physical support to the secondary target.[61]

TET OFFENSIVE During the Tet holiday in January 1968, as part of the Vietnam War, North Vietnamese forces launched surprise attacks against U.S. troops in South Vietnam. The Tet Offensive represents another example of U.S. intelligence failures. Although considered a tactical military defeat for North Vietnam, it was a strategic political victory, since this led to public pressure for withdrawal of U.S. forces by the American public.

THEATER-LEVEL DETENTION FACILITY Any theater- or higher-level internment facility under the control of the DoD, including the Detention Facility in Parwan, Afghanistan; the DoD Detention Facility at the U.S. Naval Base, Guantanamo Bay, Cuba; and any successor internment facilities.[62]

THERMAL IMAGERY Imagery produced by sensing and recording the thermal energy emitted or reflected from the objects that are imaged.

THERMAL RADIATION 1. The heat and light produced by a nuclear explosion. 2. Electromagnetic radiations emitted from a heat or light source as a consequence of its temperature.[63]

THERMONUCLEAR WEAPON A weapon in which very high temperatures are used to bring about the fusion of light nuclei such as those of hydrogen isotopes (e.g., deuterium and tritium) with the accompanying release of energy. The high temperatures required are obtained by means of fission.[64]

THIRD-AGENCY RULE The rule that except as provided in section 102, National Security Act of 1947, classified information originating in one U.S. agency (e.g., DoD) will not be disseminated by another agency to which the information has been made available without the consent of the originating agency.[65]

THREAT 1. The extant military, economic, and political capability of a foreign country with aggressive intentions to use such capability to undertake any action whose consequences will be detrimental to another country.[66] 2. The culmination of a country's capabilities and intentions. 3. In the security technology context, the likelihood that attempts will be made to gain unauthorized access to information or facilities.[67] 4. Natural or man-made occurrence, individual, entity, or action that has or indicates the potential to harm life, information, operations, the environment, and/or property. Threat as defined refers to an individual, entity, action, or occurrence; however, for the purpose of calculating risk, the threat of an intentional hazard is generally estimated as the likelihood of an attack (that accounts for both the intent and capability of the adversary) being attempted by an adversary; for other hazards, threat is generally estimated as the likelihood that a hazard will manifest.[68] 5. The activities of foreign intelligence services, foreign adversaries, international terrorist organizations, or extremists that may pose a danger to the Army, DoD, or the United States; any person with access to soldiers, DoD installations, and facilities who may be positioned to compromise the ability of a unit to accomplish its mission where there is evidence to indicate that he may be acting on behalf of or in support of foreign intelligence, foreign adversaries, international terrorists, or extremist causes (insider threat).[69] *See* RISK; THREAT AWARENESS AND REPORTING PROGRAM

THREAT ANALYSIS 1. In antiterrorism, a continual process of compiling and examining all available information concerning potential terrorist activities by terrorist groups which could target a facility.[70] 2. Examination of information to identify the elements comprising a threat.[71]

THREAT AND HAZARD IDENTIFICATION AND RISK ASSESSMENT (THIRA) A four-step common risk assessment process that helps the whole community—including individuals, businesses, faith-based organizations, nonprofit groups, schools and academia and all levels of government—understand its risks and estimate capability requirements. The THIRA process helps communities map their risks to the core capabilities, enabling them to determine whole-community informed: desired outcomes; capability targets; resources required to achieve their capability targets. The outputs of this process inform a variety of emergency management efforts, including: emergency operations planning, mutual aid agreements, and hazard mitigation planning. Ultimately, the THIRA process helps communities answer the following questions: What do we need to prepare for? What shareable resources are required in order to be prepared? What actions could be employed to avoid, divert, lessen, or eliminate a threat or hazard?[72]

THREAT AND LOCAL OBSERVATION NOTICE (TALON) The Air Force Office of Special Investigations developed the TALON report format in 2001 for its Eagle Eye Program, a neighborhood watch program to detect and report suspicious activity of possible targeting of air force interests by terrorists. The TALON report program was instituted DoD-wide on May 2, 2003, by Deputy Secretary of Defense memorandum, "Collection, Reporting, and Analysis of Terrorist Threats to DoD Within the United States," because DoD had no formal mechanism to collect and share non-validated domestic threat information between intelligence, counterintelligence, law enforcement, and force protection entities and to analyze that information for indications of foreign terrorist activity. A TALON report consists of raw information reported by concerned citizens and military members about suspicious incidents. The memorandum also directs that TALON reports be provided to the DoD Counterintelligence Field Activity (CIFA) for incorporation into a database repository. The Counterintelligence Field Activity is a designated DoD law enforcement and counterintelligence organization and serves as the bridge between intelligence related to international terrorism information and domestic law enforcement information.[73]

THREAT ASSESSMENT 1. In antiterrorism, examining the capabilities, intentions, and activities, past and present, of terrorist organizations as well as the security environment within which friendly forces operate to determine the level of threat.[74] 2. A report that evaluates a natural or man-made occurrence, an individual, an entity, or an action which has harmed or could harm life, information, operations, the environment, and/or property. Assesses the present or future threat and recommends ways to lessen the impact.[75] 3. Product or process of identifying or evaluating entities, actions, or occurrences, whether natural or man-made, that have or indicate the potential to harm life, information, operations, and/or property.[76]

THREAT AWARENESS AND REPORTING PROGRAM (TARP)
DODI 5240.6 (Department of Defense Instruction) *Counterintelligence Awareness and Reporting* provides policy and responsibilities for threat awareness and education and establishes a requirement for DA personnel to report any incident of known or suspected espionage, international terrorism, sabotage, subversion, theft or diversion of military technology, information systems intrusions, and unauthorized disclosure of classified information, among others. This regulation applies to the active Army, the Army National Guard/Army National Guard of the United States, and the U.S. Army Reserve, unless otherwise stated. It also applies to the following: Department of the Army civilian personnel; DOD contractor personnel with security clearances for their briefing and reporting requirements as specified under EO 12829 and foreign nationals employed by the DA. The applicability of this regulation to local national employees and contractors employed by Army agencies in overseas areas will be governed by Status of Forces Agreements and applicable treaties between the United States and host countries. During mobilization or national emergency, this regulation remains in effect without change.[77] *See* THREAT

THREAT CONDITION (THREATCON) A designated scale used to convey a situation in a particular country or region as it pertains to terrorist activity. Threat conditions are measured by military commanders in the field based on intelligence reports and local conditions. There are five threat condition levels, each of which carries suggestions about vehicle inspections, personnel alerts, and identity checks. Local commanders decide what to do under each condition. The five levels of threat condition are:

Normal: No threat of terrorist activity is present.
Alpha: There is a general threat of possible terrorist activity against installations, building locations, and/or personnel, the nature and extent of which are unpredictable.
Bravo: There is an increased and more predictable threat of terrorist activity even though no particular target has been identified.
Charlie: An incident has occurred or intelligence has been received indicating some form of terrorist action is imminent.
Delta: A terrorist attack has occurred or intelligence has been received indicating that action against a specific location is likely.

After the terrorist attack on the USS *Cole*, Rear Admiral Craig Quigley told journalists that Threat Condition Delta is appropriate "if you really do have information that you think is specific and credible and presents a real possibility of danger to your forces at the local level."[78] *See* DEFENSE CONDITION; WATCH CONDITION

THREAT INVENTORY An information and intelligence-based survey within the region of a law enforcement agency to identify potential individuals or groups that pose a criminal or terrorist threat without a judgment of the kind of threat they pose. The inventory is simply to determine their presence.[79]

THREAT MANAGEMENT Provides warning of war and instability to support planning and the development of contingency measures to deter, avoid, deflect, and manage threats before they inflict damage on persons or a country's interests and to support early readiness measures so as to minimize the damage should deterrence fail; to provide warning support throughout the duration of the crisis management phases, through to the restoration of normal conditions.[80]

THREAT MONITORING The analysis, assessment, and review of Information System (IS) audit trails and other data collected for the purpose of searching out system events that may constitute violations or attempted violations of data or system security.[81]

THREAT MULTIPLIER Anything that has the ability to increase the potential for harm by making more harm. For example, as greenhouse gas emissions increase, sea levels are rising, average global temperatures are increasing, and severe weather patterns are accelerating. These changes, coupled with other global dynamics, including growing, urbanizing, more affluent populations, and substantial economic growth in India, China, Brazil, and other nations, will devastate homes, land, and infrastructure. Climate change may exacerbate water scarcity and lead to sharp increases in food costs. The pressures caused by climate change will influence resource competition while placing additional burdens on economies, societies, and governance institutions around the world. These effects are threat multipliers that will aggravate stressors abroad such as poverty, environmental degradation, political instability, and social tensions—conditions that can enable terrorist activity and other forms of violence.[82]

THREAT PERCEPTION An assessment derived from another nation's behavior that is a function of both estimated capabilities and intentions.[83]

THREAT SCENARIO A sequence of events that when completed represents an unambiguous threat; provides the basis for the formulation of an indicator list.[84] *See* SCENARIO

THREAT SCORE Perhaps the most controversial and revealing technology is the threat-scoring software Beware. Fresno is one of the first (police) departments in the nation to test the program. As officers respond to calls, Beware automatically runs the address. The searches return the names of residents and scans them against a range of publicly available data to generate a color-coded threat level for each person or address: green, yellow or red. Exactly how Beware calculates threat scores is something that its maker, Intrado, considers a trade secret, so it is unclear how much weight is given to a misdemeanor, felony or threatening comment on Facebook. However, the program flags issues and provides a report to the user.[85]

THREAT SHIFTING Response of adversaries to perceived countermeasures or obstructions, in which the adversaries change some characteristic of their intent to do harm in order to avoid or overcome the countermeasure or obstacle. (1) Threat shifting can occur in one or more of several domains: the time domain (e.g., a delay in attack or illegal entry to conduct additional surveillance, etc.), the target domain (selecting a different, less-protected target), the resource domain (adding resources to the attack in order to reduce uncertainty or overcome countermeasures), or the planning/attack method domain (changing the weapon or path, for example, of the intended attack or illegal entry). (2) Threat shifting is commonly cited as a reason for countermeasure failure or ineffectiveness—particularly in the case of target shifting. For example, when police occupy one street corner, the drug dealers simply go a few blocks away. This assumes that threat shifting is frictionless for the adversary, which frequently is the case. (3) However, threat shifting is not always frictionless for the adversary—and therefore can be of some value to the defenders. The adversaries may delay their attack, consume additional resources, undertake complexity, expose themselves to additional counter-surveillance and counter-terrorism scrutiny, and/or shift to a less consequential target. (4) Threat shifting can, in some cases, increase risk by steering an adversary to an attack that is more likely to succeed or of greater consequence.[86]

THREATS TO THE NATIONAL SECURITY This list includes international terrorism; espionage and other intelligence activities, sabotage, and assassination, conducted by, for, or on behalf of foreign powers, organizations, or persons; foreign computer intrusion; and other matters determined by the

Attorney General, consistent with Executive Order 12333 or a successor order.[87]

TIPOFF U.S. government's principal terrorist watch list database prior to HSPD-6. TIPOFF is a classified computer lookout system, which was maintained by the DoS's [Department of State, Bureau of Intelligence Research] INR to identify and watch-list known and suspected terrorists. Created in 1987, it originally consisted of 3x5 index cards in a shoe box. Beginning in 1987, the DoS [Department of State] began keeping watch list (lookout) records on known and suspected terrorists through a system as TIPOFF. While the DoS had maintained computerized visa records since 1965, including watch lists, the events surrounding the first World Trade Center bombing in 1993 prompted the CA to accelerate the development of the Consular Lookout and Security System (CLASS), so that, among other records, TIPOFF-generated terrorist watch list records could be more easily and efficiently searched by computer at U.S. consular posts and embassies abroad. Consular, intelligence, immigration, and law enforcement officers nominate individuals for inclusion in TIPOFF.[88]

TOKYO CONVENTION Officially known as the Convention on Offences and Certain Other Acts Committed On Board Aircraft was signed on September 14, 1963, and entered into force on December 4, 1969. The Convention governs international air navigation offenses that jeopardize aircraft safety or that of individuals aboard the aircraft. In 2014, a Diplomatic Conference was held to consider proposed revisions to the Convention to ensure that it is an effective deterrent to unruly behavior. The result was the Montreal Protocol 2014 which makes important changes to the original Tokyo Convention. The Protocol extends the jurisdiction over offence to the destination country of the flight in addition to the country of aircraft registration. This closes a loophole which allowed many serious offences to escape legal action. The agreed changes give greater clarity to the definition of unruly behavior (such as including the threat of or actual physical assault, or refusal to follow safety-related instructions). There are also new provisions to deal with the recovery of significant costs arising from unruly behavior.[89]

TOP SECRET U.S. CLEARED CITIZEN A citizen of the United States who has undergone a background investigation by an authorized U.S. Government Agency and been issued a Top Secret security clearance, in accordance with Executive Orders 13526, and implementing guidelines and standards published in 32 CFR 147.[90]

TOR The Tor network is a group of volunteer-operated servers that allows people to improve their privacy and security on the Internet. Tor's users employ this network by connecting through a series of virtual tunnels rather than making a direct connection, thus allowing both organizations and individuals to share information over public networks without compromising their privacy. Along the same line, Tor is an effective censorship circumvention tool, allowing its users to reach otherwise blocked destinations or content. Tor can also be used as a building block for software developers to create new communication tools with built-in privacy features. Individuals use Tor to keep websites from tracking them and their family members, or to connect to news sites, instant messaging services, or the like when these are blocked by their local Internet providers. Tor's hidden services let users publish websites and other services without needing to reveal the location of the site.[91]

TORTURE 1. An act committed by a person acting under the color of law specifically intended to inflict severe physical or mental pain or suffering (other than pain or suffering incidental to lawful sanctions) upon another person within his custody or physical control.[92] 2. As defined by Title 18, U.S. Code, Section 2340, it is any act committed by a person acting under color of law specifically intended to inflict severe physical or mental pain or suffering (other than pain or suffering incidental to lawful sanctions) upon another person within his custody or physical control. "Severe mental pain or suffering" means the prolonged mental harm caused by or resulting from: (a) the intentional infliction or threatened infliction of severe physical pain or suffering; (b) the administration or application, or threatened administration or application, of mind-altering substances or other procedures calculated to disrupt profoundly the senses or personality; (c) the threat of imminent death; or (d) the threat that another person will imminently be subjected to death, severe physical pain or suffering, or the administration or application of mind-altering substances or other procedures calculated to disrupt profoundly the senses or personality.[93]

TOTAL INFORMATION AWARENESS This project was to focus on three specific areas of research, anticipated to be conducted over five years, to develop technologies that would assist the detection of terrorist groups planning attacks against American interests, both inside and outside the country. The three areas of research and their purposes were described in a DoD Inspector General report as "language translation, data search with pattern recognition and privacy protection, and advanced collaborative and decision support tools. Language translation technology would enable the rapid analysis of foreign languages, both spoken and written, and allow analysts to quickly search the translated materials for clues about emerging threats. The data search, pattern recognition, and privacy protection technologies would permit analysts to search vast quantities of data for patterns that suggest terrorist activity while at the same time controlling access to the data, enforcing laws and policies, and ensuring detection of misuse of the information obtained. The collaborative reasoning and decision support technologies would allow analysts from different agencies to share data (2–3)." The Total Information Awareness was renamed the Terrorism Information Awareness Project in May 2003.[94] *See* TERRORISM INFORMATION AWARENESS

TRACE BIOINFORMATION Biological material left behind by an individual (for example, at a crime scene) from which information can be determined (such as a DNA profile).[95]

TRACK PRODUCTION A function of a surveillance organization in which the active and passive radar inputs are correlated into coherent position reports, together with historical positions, to identify height, strength, and direction.

TRACK SYMBOLOGY Symbols used to display tracks on a data display console or other display device.

TRACK TELLING The process of communicating air surveillance and tactical data information between command and control systems or between facilities within the systems. Telling may be classified into the following types:[96]

> *Back tell:* The transfer of information from a higher to a lower echelon of command.
> *Cross tell or Lateral tell:* The transfer of information between facilities at the same operational level.
> *Forward tell:* The transfer of information to a higher level of command.
> *Overlap tell:* The transfer of information to an adjacent facility concerning tracks detected in the adjacent facility's area of responsibility.
> *Relateral tell:* The relay of information between facilities through the use of a third facility. This type of telling is appropriate between automated facilities in a degraded communications environment.

TRACKING Precise and continuous position finding of targets by radar, optical, or other means.[97]

TRACKOGRAPHY When we access websites, third parties are able to track our online behavior. This is part of a larger business which can involve web analytics and user profiling. These activities are often geared towards aiding online marketing and advertising. Third party trackers can aggregate our data, link it to other data collected about us and subsequently create profiles. These profiles tell a story about us—which may or may not be true—and can include our political beliefs, gender, sexual orientation, economic status, habits, interests, affiliations and much more. And while this might all appear to be harmless, we largely have very little control over how and when our data is collected, how our profiles are created, whether they are accurate, who they are subsequently shared with, who has access to them, what they are used for and where they are stored and for how long. Trackography also shows that when we read the news online, our data is collected by companies we have not given our consent to and travels to servers located in foreign countries. Once our data is there it falls under the laws of the countries where such servers are based.[98]

TRADECRAFT 1. Specialized methods and equipment used in the organization and activity of intelligence organizations, especially techniques and methods for handling communications with agents. 2. Operational practices and skills used in the performance of intelligence-related duties.[99]

TRADECRAFT IDENTITY An identity used for the purpose of work-related interactions that may or may not be synonymous with an individual's true identity.[100]

TRADE-OFF Selection among alternatives with the intent of obtaining the optimal, achievable system configuration. Often a decision is made to opt for less of one parameter in order to achieve a more favorable overall system result.[101]

TRANSIENT ELECTROMAGNETIC PULSE SURVEILLANCE TECHNOLOGY *See* TEMPEST

TRANSNATIONAL GANGS There is no single definition of what characteristics constitute a transnational gang. Various definitions have cited one or more of the following characteristics in defining a transnational gang: (1) such gangs are criminally active and operational in more than one country; (2) criminal activities committed by gang members in one country are planned, directed, and controlled by gang leaders in another country; (3) such gangs tend to be mobile and adapt to new areas; and (4) the criminal activities of such gangs tend to be sophisticated and transcend borders. For a gang to be considered transnational, it would appear that the gang would have more than one of the aforementioned characteristics (2). Perhaps most disturbing for policymakers in a post-9/11 world, alarms have been sounded in some circles that international terrorist organizations like al-Qaeda could exploit alien and narcotics smuggling networks controlled by these gangs to infiltrate the United States. To date, however, no evidence suggests that these gangs and international terrorist groups are cooperating with one another (1).[102]

TRANSNATIONAL ORGANIZED CRIME Refers to those self-perpetuating associations of individuals who operate transnationally for the purpose of obtaining power, influence, monetary and/or commercial gains, wholly or in part by illegal means, while protecting their activities through a pattern of corruption and/or violence, or while protecting their illegal activities through a transnational organizational structure and the exploitation of transnational commerce or communication mechanisms. There is no single structure under which transnational organized criminals operate; they vary from hierarchies to clans, networks, and cells, and may evolve to other structures. The crimes they commit also vary. Transnational organized criminals act conspiratorially in their criminal activities and possess certain characteristics which may include, but are not limited to: in at least part of their activities they commit violence or other acts which are likely to intimidate, or make actual or implicit threats to do so.[103]

TRANSNATIONAL THREAT Any activity, individual, or group not tied to a particular country or region that operates across international boundaries and threatens U.S. national security or interests.[104]

TRANSPORTATION RISK ASSESSMENT AND VULNERABILITY EVALUATION TOOL (TRAVEL) A TSA (Transportation Safety Administration) tool that is used in facilitated, on-site assessments of transportation assets.[105]

TRANSPORTATION SECTOR SECURITY RISK ASSESSMENT (TSSRA) A TSA strategic-level risk assessment of terrorism-based risks facing the U.S. transportation sector. Comprised of attack scenarios and attack families, and based on the inputs of government and private sector transportation stakeholders, the TSSRA evaluates and compares threats, vulnerabilities, and consequences of selected terrorist attack scenarios across all modes of transportation (except maritime). It is intended to identify needs for more detailed analysis, inform planning and resource decisions, and establish a baseline for other periodic analyses and analytical activities related to transportation security.[106]

TRANSPORTATION SECURITY ADMINISTRATION OFFICE OF INTELLIGENCE (TSA-OI) The TSA has the responsibility for security in all modes of transportation: aviation, maritime, mass transit, highway and motor carrier, freight rail, and pipeline. TSA uses a threat-based, risk-management approach to the security task. Intelligence is a key driver in determining the level of security appropriate for the threat environment. The TSA intelligence function is centered in its Office of Intelligence (TSA-OI). The office consists of six divisions and an intelligence cell at the Transportation Security Operations Center (TSOC, also known as the "Freedom Center") in Herndon, Virginia.[107]

TRANSPORTATION SECURITY OPERATIONS CENTER (TSOC) The TSOC is an operations center open 24 hours a day, 7 days a week, that serves as TSA's main point of contact for monitoring security-related incidents or crises in all modes of transportation.[108]

TRAP AND TRACE DEVICE The term "trap and trace device" means a device or process which captures the incoming electronic or other impulses which identify the originating number or other dialing, routing, addressing, and signaling information reasonably likely to identify the source of a wire or electronic communication, provided, however, that such information shall not include the contents of any communication.[109]

TRASH COVER The intentional search of a specific person's trash (that is located at the place of collection), whether from a home or business, designed to find information relevant to an ongoing investigation when no reasonable expectation of privacy exists. A trash cover is a targeted effort to gather information regarding a particular person or entity by reviewing that person or entity's refuse.[110]

TREASON One who, owing allegiance to the United States, levies war against the United States or adheres to its enemies, giving them aid and comfort within the United States or elsewhere. It also includes one who, having knowledge of the commission of treason, conceals and does not, as soon possible, report.[111]

TRI-CAMERA PHOTOGRAPHY Obtained by simultaneous exposure of three cameras systematically disposed in an air vehicle at fixed overlapping angles relative to each other in order to cover a wide field.

TROJAN HORSE A computer program that appears to have a useful function, but also has a hidden and potentially malicious function that evades security mechanisms, sometimes by exploiting legitimate authorizations of a system entity that invokes the program.[112]

TRUST ANCHOR An established point of trust (usually based on the authority of some person, office, or organization) from which an entity begins the validation of an authorized process or authorized (signed) package. A "trust anchor" is sometimes defined as just a public key used for different purposes (e.g., validating a Certification Authority, validating a signed software package or key, validating the process (or person) loading the signed software or key).[113]

TRUSTED CHANNEL A channel where the endpoints are known and data integrity is protected in transit. Depending on the communications protocol used, data privacy may be protected in transit.[114]

TRUSTED PATH A mechanism by which a person at a terminal can communicate directly with the trusted computing base. This mechanism can only be activated by the person or the trusted computing base and cannot be imitated by untrusted software.[115]

TRUSTWORTHNIESS The attribute of a person or enterprise that provides confidence to others of the qualifications, capabilities, and reliability of that entity to perform specific tasks and fulfill assigned responsibilities.[116]

TSA OFFICE OF INTELLIGENCE (TSA-OI) The TSA intelligence function is centered in its Office of Intelligence (TSA-OI) and led by an assistant administrator for intelligence. The office consists of six divisions and an intelligence cell at the Transportation Security Operations Center (TSOC) (also known as the "Freedom Center") in Herndon, Virginia.[117]

TWILIGHT The periods of incomplete darkness following sunset and preceding sunrise. Twilight is designated as civil, nautical, or astronomical, as the darker limit occurs when the center of the sun is 6, 12, or 18 degrees, respectively, below the celestial horizon.[118]

TWITTER CRIME SCANNER 1. Dataminr (Twitter Crime Scanner) transforms the Twitter stream into actionable signals, identifying the most relevant information in real-time for clients in Finance, News and the Public Sector. Using powerful, proprietary algorithms, Dataminr instantly analyzes all public tweets and delivers the earliest warning for breaking news, real-world events, off-the-radar content and emerging trends.[119] 2. Bluejay (Twitter Crime Scanner) provides "access the full Twitter Firehose, Geofence and visualize tweet locations, Monitor keywords and users you select, Drill-down into specific user's activity."[120]

TWO-PERSON INTEGRITY Using two people to validate each other for either security or to confirm validity of information.[121]

TWO-WAY STREET Philosophy encouraging the United States to buy arms from, in addition to selling arms to, North Atlantic Treaty Organization (NATO) and other friendly nations.[122]

NOTES

1. Polanyi, Michael. *The Tacit Dimension.* Garden City, NY: Doubleday, 1966.

2. Defense Forensics and Biometrics Agency. *DoD Biometrics Enterprise Architecture (Integrated) v2.0 Common Biometric Vocabulary.* April 2013. Accessed February 25, 2015. http://www.biometrics.dod.mil/Files/Documents/References/common%20biometric%20vocabulary.pdf.

3. Defense Forensics and Biometrics Agency. *DoD Biometrics Enterprise Architecture (Integrated) v2.0 Common Biometric Vocabulary.* April 2013. Accessed February 25, 2015. http://www.biometrics.dod.mil/Files/Documents/References/common%20biometric%20vocabulary.pdf.

4. Carter, David L. *Law Enforcement Intelligence*: *A Guide for State, Local, and Tribal Law Enforcement Agencies.* U.S. Dept. of Justice, Office of Community Oriented Policing Services, 2004.

5. U.S. Department of Defense. *DoD Intelligence Interrogations, Detainee Debriefings, and Tactical Questioning.* Directive Number 3115.09, October 11, 2012 Incorporating Change 1, Effective November 15, 2013. Accessed February 26, 2015. http://fas.org/irp/doddir/dod/d3115_09.pdf.

6. Jan Goldman, *Intelligence Warning Terminology*, Joint Military Intelligence College, October 2001, accessed July 3, 2015. https://archive.org/details/JMICIntelligencelwarnterminology.

7. Central Intelligence Agency. *National Intelligence Warning.* DCI Directive No. 1/5, May 23, 1979. Accessed June 5, 2015. http://fas.org./irp/offdocs/dcid1-5.html.

8. SPIEGEL Staff. "Inside TAO: Documents Reveal Top NSA Hacking Unit." *SPIEGEL Online* December 29, 2013. Accessed March 29, 2015. http://www.spiegel.de/international/world/the-nsa-uses-powerful-toolbox-in-effort-to-spy-on-global-networks-a-940969.html.

9. Harris, Shane. *@WAR: The Rise of the Military-Internet Complex.* Boston: Houghton Mifflin Harcourt, 2014.

10. Executive Office of the President and National Science and Technology Council. *Trustworthy Cyberspace: Strategic Plan for the Federal Cybersecurity Research and Development Program.* December 2011. Accessed March 7, 2015. http://

www.whitehouse.gov/sites/default/files/microsites/ostp/fed_cybersecurity_rd_strategic_plan_2011.pdf.

11. Schmit, Michael N. (ed.). *Tallinn Manual on the International Law Applicable to Cyber Warfare.* Prepared by the International Group of Experts at the Invitation of The NATO Cooperative Cyber Defence Centre of Excellence. New York: Cambridge University Press, 2013. Accessed February 25, 2015. https://ccdcoe.org/multimedia/tallinn-paper-nature-international-law-cyber-norms.html.

12. 50 U.S. Code § 1861—"Access to Certain Business Records for Foreign Intelligence and International Terrorism Investigations" (Current through Pub. L. 113-234). Accessed February 25, 2015. https://www.law.cornell.edu/uscode/text/50/1861.

13. Kris, David S. "On the Bulk Collection of Tangible Things." *Lawfare Research Paper Series* 1, no. 4 (2013): 1–67. Accessed February 25, 2015. https://www.lawfareblog.com/david-kris-bulk-collection-tangible-things-lawfare-research-paper-series.

14. U.S. Department of Defense. *Department of Defense Dictionary of Military and Associated Terms.* JP 1-02, 08 November 2010, as Amended through 15 January 2016. Accessed January 26, 2016. http://www.dtic.mil/doctrine/new_pubs/jp1_02.pdf.

15. U.S. Department of Defense. *Department of Defense Dictionary of Military and Associated Terms.* JP 1-02, 08 November 2010, as Amended through 15 January 2016. Accessed January 26, 2016. http://www.dtic.mil/doctrine/new_pubs/jp1_02.pdf.

16. U.S. Department of Defense. *Department of Defense Dictionary of Military and Associated Terms.* JP 1-02, 08 November 2010, as Amended through 15 January 2016. Accessed January 26, 2016. http://www.dtic.mil/doctrine/new_pubs/jp1_02.pdf.

17. U.S. Department of Defense. *Department of Defense Dictionary of Military and Associated Terms.* JP 1-02, 08 November 2010, as Amended through 15 January 2016. Accessed January 26, 2016, http://www.dtic.mil/doctrine/new_pubs/jp1_02.pdf.

18. North Atlantic Treaty Organization. *NATO Glossary of Terms and Definitions.* NATO Standardization Agency, 2014, AAP-06, accessed July 27, 2015, http://nso.nato.int/nso/zPublic/ap/aap6/AAP-6.pdf.

19. U.S. Department of Defense. *Department of Defense Dictionary of Military and Associated Terms.* JP 1-02, 08 November 2010, as Amended through 15 January 2016. Accessed January 26, 2016, http://www.dtic.mil/doctrine/new_pubs/jp1_02.pdf.

20. United States Department of Justice. *Law Enforcement Analytic Standard.* Global Justice Information Sharing Initiative and International Association of Law Enforcement Intelligence Analysts, Inc. 2nd ed. April 2012, accessed February 1, 2016, https://it.ojp.gov/documents/d/Law%20Enforcement%20Analytic%20Standards%2004202_combined_compliant.pdf.

21. North Atlantic Treaty Organization. *NATO Glossary of Terms and Definitions.* NATO Standardization Agency, 2014, AAP-06, accessed July 27, 2015, http://nso.nato.int/nso/zPublic/ap/aap6/AAP-6.pdf.

22. As quoted in House of Lords, Select Committee on the Constitution. *Surveillance: Citizens and the State.* 2nd Report of Session 2008–09. Volume I: Report. The Stationary Office, February 9, 2009. Accessed February 15, 2015. http://www.publications.parliament.uk/pa/ld200809/ldselect/ldconst/18/18.pdf.

23. Defense Science Board. Predicting Violent Behavior: Final Report of the Defense Science Board (DSB) Task Force (TF) on Predicting Violent Behavior. August 2012. Accessed February 24, 2015. http://www.acq.osd.mil/dsb/reports/PredictingViolentBehavior.pdf.

24. National Initiative for Cybersecurity Education. *A Glossary of Common Cybersecurity Terminology.* n.d. Accessed March 5, 2015. http://niccs.us-cert.gov/glossary.

25. North Atlantic Treaty Organization. *NATO Glossary of Terms and Definitions.* NATO Standardization Agency, 2014, AAP-06, accessed July 27, 2015, http://nso.nato.int/nso/zPublic/ap/aap6/AAP-6.pdf.

26. North Atlantic Treaty Organization. *NATO Glossary of Terms and Definitions.* NATO Standardization Agency, 2014, AAP-06, accessed July 27, 2015, http://nso.nato.int/nso/zPublic/ap/aap6/AAP-6.pdf.

27. Defense Intelligence Agency, Office of Counterintelligence. *CI Glossary—Terms & Definitions of Interest for DoD CI Professionals.* July 2014. Accessed February 28, 2015. https://www.hsdl.org/?view&did=699056.

28. Carter, David L. *Law Enforcement Intelligence: A Guide for State, Local, and Tribal Law Enforcement Agencies.* U.S. Dept. of Justice, Office of Community Oriented Policing Services, 2004.

29. Defense Acquisition University. *Glossary: Defense Acquisition Acronyms and Terms.* 13th ed., November 2009. Accessed February 24, 2015. http://www.dau.mil/pubscats/pubscats/13th_edition_glossary.pdf.

30. U.S. Department of Defense. *Joint Intelligence.* JP 2-0. October 22, 2013. Accessed February 15, 2015. http://www.dtic.mil/doctrine/new_pubs/jp2_0.pdf.

31. Outzen, Richard H. M. "Technical Intelligence: Added Realism at the NTC." *Military Intelligence Professional Bulletin* 23, no. 3 (1997): 20. Accessed February 27, 2016, http://permanent.access.gpo.gov/lps1654/.

32. Defense Acquisition University. *Glossary: Defense Acquisition Acronyms and Terms.* 13th ed., November 2009. Accessed February 24, 2015. http://www.dau.mil/pubscats/pubscats/13th_edition_glossary.pdf.

33. Combating Terrorism Technical Support Office. *About CTTSO*, 2015. Accessed February 1, 2016, http://www.cttso.gov/?q=vendors_about.

34. U.S. Department of State. "Definitions of Diplomatic Security Terms." *Foreign Affairs Manual.* 12FAM090. November 12, 2014. Accessed February 24, 2015. http://www.state.gov/documents/organization/88330.pdf.

35. Jan Goldman, *Intelligence Warning Terminology*, Joint Military Intelligence College, October 2001, accessed July 3, 2015. https://archive.org/details/JMICIntelligencewarnterminology.

36. U.S. Department of Defense, Center for Development of Security Excellence. *Glossary of Security Terms and Definitions.* November 2012. Accessed February 26, 2015. http://www.cdse.edu/documents/cdse/Glossary_Handbook.pdf.

37. U.S. Department of Defense, Center for Development of Security Excellence. *Glossary of Security Terms and Definitions.* November 2012. Accessed February 26, 2015. http://www.cdse.edu/documents/cdse/Glossary_Handbook.pdf.

38. Lizza, Ryan. "The Metadata Program in Eleven Documents." *The New Yorker*, December 31, 2013. Accessed February 18, 2015. http://www.newyorker.com/news/daily-comment/the-metadata-program-in-eleven-documents; also see *ACLU, et al., v. James R. Clapper, et al.*, Memorandum and Order, 13 Civ. 3994. United States District Court Southern District of New York. December 27, 2013. Accessed February 18, 2015. https://www.aclu.org/files/assets/order_granting_governments_motion_to_dismiss_and_denying_aclu_motion_for_preliminary_injunction.pdf.

39. SANS Institute, Info Sec Reading Room: An Introduction to TEMPEST. Accessed July 9, 2015. https://www.sans.org/reading-room/whitepapers/privacy/introduction-tempest-981.

40. MacAskill, Ewen, Borger, Julian, Hopkins, Nick, Davies, Nick, and Ball, James. "Secret Document Detailing GCHQ's Ambition to 'Master the Internet.'" *The Guardian*, June 21, 2013. Accessed February 18, 2015. http://www.theguardian.com/uk/2013/jun/21/gchq-cables-secret-world-communications-nsa.

41. *The Guardian.* "NSA Files Decoded." November 1, 2013. Accessed February 18, 2015. http://www.theguardian.com/world/interactive/2013/nov/01/snowden-nsa-files-surveillance-revelations-decoded#section/1.

42. U.S. Department of Defense, Center for Development of Security Excellence. *Glossary of Security Terms and Definitions.* November 2012. Accessed February 26, 2015. http://www.cdse.edu/documents/cdse/Glossary_Handbook.pdf.

43. Kent, Sherman. "The Law and Custom of the National Intelligence Estimate." *DCI Miscellaneous Studies*, MS-12 (February 1976). Accessed June 6, 2015. https://www.cia.gov/library/center-for-the-study-of-intelligence/csi-publications/books-and-monographs/sherman-kent-and-the-board-of-national-estimates-collected-essays/5law.html.

44. U.S. Department of Defense, Center for Development of Security Excellence. *Glossary of Security Terms and Definitions.* November 2012. Accessed February 26, 2015. http://www.cdse.edu/documents/cdse/Glossary_Handbook.pdf.

45. 18 U.S. Code § 2332b—"Acts of Terrorism Transcending National Boundaries" (Current through Pub. L. 113-234). Accessed February 26, 2015. https://www.law.cornell.edu/uscode/text/18/2332b.

46. *Intelligence Reform and Terrorism Prevention Act* P.L.108-458, 118 STAT. 3638. December 17, 2004. Accessed February 15, 2015. http://www.gpo.gov/fdsys/pkg/PLAW-108publ458/pdf/PLAW-108publ458.pdf.

47. DARPA, Report to Congress regarding the Terrorism Information Awareness Program. Accessed on July 9, 2015. http://www.globalsecurity.org/security/library/report/2003/tia-exec-summ_20may2003.pdf.

48. A good resource on this program is at the American Library Association, http://www.ala.org/offices/oif/ifissues/terrorisminformationprevention.

49. Chairman of the Joint Chiefs of Staff. *National Military Strategic Plan for the War on Terrorism.* February 1, 2006. Accessed February 26, 2015. http://archive.defense.gov/pubs/pdfs/2006-01-25-Strategic-Plan.pdf.

50. National Counterterrorism Center. *Terrorist Group Logos.* Accessed February 9, 2015. http://www.nctc.gov/site/groups/index.html.

51. Krous, William J. "Terrorist Identification, Screening, and Tracking Under Homeland Security Presidential Directive 6." *CRS Report for Congress*, RL32366. April 21, 2004. Accessed February 15, 2015. http://www.fas.org/irp/crs/RL32366.pdf.

52. National Counterterrorism Center. *Terrorist Identities Datamart Environment (TIDE) Factsheet.* August 1, 2014. Accessed February 9, 2015. http://www.nctc.gov/docs/tidefactsheet_aug12014.pdf.

53. Chairman Brad Miller, Subcommittee on Investigations and Oversight, Committee on Science and Technology, House of Representatives, August 21, 2008, to Edward Maquire, Inspector General, Office of the Director of National Intelligence. Wayback Machine. Accessed February 9, 2015. http://wayback.archive.org/web/20100408015942/http://democrats.science.house.gov/Media/File/AdminLetters/bm_InspectorGeneralMaquire_terrorwatchlist_8.21.08.pdf.

54. Federal Bureau of Investigation. *About the Terrorist Screening Center.* Accessed February 15, 2015. http://www.fbi.gov/about-us/nsb/tsc/about-the-terrorist-screening-center; also see *Homeland Security Presidential Directive 6: Directive on Integration and Use of Screening Information to Protect against Terrorism.* September 6, 2003. Accessed February 15, 2015. http://www.fas.org/irp/offdocs/nspd/hspd-6.html.

55. Undersecretary of Defense. 2015. *Directive-type Memorandum (DTM) 14-005—DoD Identity Management Capability Enterprise Services Application (IMESA) Access to FBI National Crime Information Center (NCIC) Files.* May 13. Accessed June 6, 2015. http://www.dtic.mil/whs/directives/corres/pdf/DTM14005_2014.pdf.

56. Christopher M. Piehota, Director, Terrorist Screening Center, FBI. *Statement Before the House Homeland Security Committee, Subcommittee on Transportation Security.* September 18, 2014. Accessed June 19, 2015. https://www.fbi.gov/news/testimony/tscs-role-in-the-interagency-watchlisting-and-screening-process.

57. Risen, James, and Lichtblau, Eric. "Bush Lets US Spy on Callers without Courts." *The New York Times* 16 (2005): A1. Accessed February 25, 2015. http://www.nytimes.com/2005/12/16/politics/16program.html. *ACLU v. NSA.* United States Court of Appeals for the Sixth Circuit. Argued January 31, 2007, Decided and Filed: July 6, 2007. Accessed February 25, 2015. http://www.ca6.uscourts.gov/opinions.pdf/07a0253p-06.pdf. *The President's Radio Address*, December 17, 2005. Accessed February 25, 2015. http://georgewbush-whitehouse.archives.gov/news/releases/2005/12/20051217.html.

58. Central Intelligence Agency. *Terrorist Threat Integration Center Begins Operations.* May 1, 2003. Accessed February 15, 2015. https://www.cia.gov/news-information/press-releases-statements/press-release-archive-2003/pr05012003.html.

59. *Intelligence Reform and Terrorism Prevention Act* P.L.108-458, 118 STAT. 3638. December 17, 2004. Accessed February 15, 2015. http://www.gpo.gov/fdsys/pkg/PLAW-108publ458/pdf/PLAW-108publ458.pdf.

60. Defense Forensics and Biometrics Agency. *DoD Biometrics Enterprise Architecture (Integrated) v2.0 Common Biometric Vocabulary.* April 2013. Accessed

February 25, 2015. http://www.biometrics.dod.mil/Files/Documents/References/common%20biometric%20vocabulary.pdf; also see the National Information Exchange Model. *Terrorist Watchlist Person Data Exchange Standard (TWPDES) Version 3.0 Biometric Data and Minor TWPDES Core Changes Information Exchange Package Documentation (IEPD)*. December 2009. Accessed February 24, 2015. https://www.niem.gov/documentsdb/Documents/Technical/TWPDES3.0-Biometric-TWPDESCore-IEPD.pdf.

61. Department of Homeland Security. Office of Intelligence and Analysis. *Domestic Extremism Lexicon*. March 26, 2009. Accessed January 15, 2015. http://www.fas.org/irp/eprint/lexicon.pdf.

62. U.S. Department of Defense. *DoD Intelligence Interrogations, Detainee Debriefings, and Tactical Questioning*. Directive Number 3115.09, October 11, 2012 Incorporating Change 1, Effective November 15, 2013. Accessed February 26, 2015. http://fas.org/irp/doddir/dod/d3115_09.pdf.

63. U.S. Department of Defense. *Department of Defense Dictionary of Military and Associated Terms*. JP 1-02, 08 November 2010, as Amended through 15 January 2016. Accessed January 26, 2016. http://www.dtic.mil/doctrine/new_pubs/jp1_02.pdf.

64. North Atlantic Treaty Organization. *NATO Glossary of Terms and Definitions*. NATO Standardization Agency, 2014, AAP-06, accessed July 27, 2015, http://nso.nato.int/nso/zPublic/ap/aap6/AAP-6.pdf.

65. Department of the Army, *Investigative Records Repository*, AR381-45, August 25, 1989, accessed February 2, 2016, http:// www.army.mil/usapa/epubs/pdf/r381_45.pdf and National Security Act of 1947, http://global.oup.com/us/companion.websites/9780195385168/resources/chapter10/nsa/nsa.pdf.

66. Jan Goldman, *Intelligence Warning Terminology*, Joint Military Intelligence College, October 2001, accessed July 3, 2015. https://archive.org/details/JMICInteligencelwarnterminology.

67. U.S. Department of State. *Foreign Affairs Manual*. Accessed September 29, 2015. http://www.state.gov/m/a/dir/regs/fam/.

68. Department of Homeland Security, Risk Steering Committee. *DHS Risk Lexicon*. September 2010. Accessed February 14, 2015. http://www.dhs.gov/dhs-risk-lexicon.

69. Department of the Army. *Threat Awareness and Reporting Program*. Army Regulation 381-12, October 4, 2010. Accessed February 24, 2015. http://www.apd.army.mil/pdffiles/r381_12.pdf.

70. U.S. Department of Defense. *Department of Defense Dictionary of Military and Associated Terms*. JP 1-02, 08 November 2010, as Amended through 15 January 2016. Accessed January 26, 2016. http://www.dtic.mil/doctrine/new_pubs/jp1_02.pdf.

71. Committee for National Security Systems (CNSS). Instruction 4009. *National Information Assurance Glossary*. April 2010. Accessed January 11, 2015. http://www.ncix.gov/publications/policy/docs/CNSSI_4009.pdf.

72. Federal Emergency Management Agency. *About the Threat and Hazard Identification and Risk Assessment (THIRA)*. Accessed February 15, 2015. https://www.fema.gov/threat-and-hazard-identification-and-risk-assessment.

73. U.S. Department of Defense. Office of the Inspector General. *Threat and Local Observation Notice (TALON) Report Program.* June 27, 2007. Report No. 07—INTEL-09. Accessed February 24, 2015. http://www.dodig.mil/pubs/documents/07-INTEL-09.pdf.

74. U.S. Department of Defense. *Department of Defense Dictionary of Military and Associated Terms.* JP 1-02, 08 November 2010, as Amended through 15 January 2016. Accessed January 26, 2016. http://www.dtic.mil/doctrine/new_pubs/jp1_02.pdf.

75. United States Department of Justice. *Law Enforcement Analytic Standard.* Global Justice Information Sharing Initiative and International Association of Law Enforcement Intelligence Analysts, Inc. 2nd ed. April 2012, accessed February 1, 2016, https://it.ojp.gov/documents/d/Law%20Enforcement%20Analytic%20Standards%2004202_combined_compliant.pdf.

76. Department of Homeland Security, Risk Steering Committee. *DHS Risk Lexicon.* September 2010. Accessed February 14, 2015. http://www.dhs.gov/dhs-risk-lexicon.

77. Department of the Army. *Threat Awareness and Reporting Program.* Army Regulation 381-12, October 4, 2010. Accessed February 24, 2015. http://www.apd.army.mil/pdffiles/r381_12.pdf.

78. Starr, Barbara. "U.S. Military on High Alert." ABCNews.com, October 23, 2000. Accessed June 15, 2015. http://abcnews.go.com/International/story?id=82296.

79. Federal Bureau of Investigation. *Minimum Criminal Intelligence Training Standards for Law Enforcement and Other Criminal Justice Agencies in the United States.* October 2007. Accessed February 28, 2015. https://it.ojp.gov/gist/108/Minimum-Criminal-Intelligence-Training-Standards.

80. Jan Goldman, *Intelligence Warning Terminology*, Joint Military Intelligence College, October 2001, accessed July 3, 2015. https://archive.org/details/JMICInteligencelwarnterminology.

81. U.S. Department of Defense, Center for Development of Security Excellence. *Glossary of Security Terms and Definitions.* November 2012. Accessed February 26, 2015. http://www.cdse.edu/documents/cdse/Glossary_Handbook.pdf.

82. U.S. Department of Defense. *Quadrennial Defense Review Report.* 2014. Accessed February 21, 2015. http://www.defense.gov/pubs/2014_Quadrennial_Defense_Review.pdf.

83. Joint Military Intelligence College. *Intelligence Warning Terminology.* October 2001. Accessed July 3, 2015. https://archive.org/details/JMICInteligencelwarnterminology.

84. Jan Goldman, *Intelligence Warning Terminology*, Joint Military Intelligence College, October 2001, accessed July 3, 2015. https://archive.org/details/JMICInteligencelwarnterminology.

85. Justin Jouvenal, "The New Way Police Are Surveilling You: Calculating Your Threat 'Score,'" *Washington Post*, January 10, 2016, accessed February 2, 2016, https://www.washingtonpost.com/local/public-safety/the-new-way-police-are-surveilling-you-calculating-your-threat-score/2016/01/10/e42bccac-8e15-11e5-baf4-bdf37355da0c_story.html.

86. Department of Homeland Security, Risk Steering Committee. *DHS Risk Lexicon.* September 2010. Accessed February 14, 2015. http://www.dhs.gov/dhs-risk-lexicon.

87. U.S. Department of Justice. *The Attorney General's Guidelines for Domestic FBI Operations.* 2008. Accessed February 25, 2015. http://www.justice.gov/sites/default/files/ag/legacy/2008/10/03/guidelines.pdf.

88. Krouse, William J. "Terrorist Identification, Screening, and Tracking Under Homeland Security Presidential Directive 6." *CRS Report for Congress* RL32366. April 21, 2004. Accessed February 24, 2015. http://www.fas.org/irp/crs/RL32366.pdf.

89. Convention on Offences and Certain Other Acts Committed On Board Aircraft, 1969. Accessed March 11, 2015. http://www.icao.int/Meetings/LC35/Refererences/Tokyo%20Convention.EN.FR.SP.pdf. International Air Transport Association. *Unruly Passengers.* Accessed March 11, 2015. http://www.iata.org/policy/pages/tokyo-convention.aspx.

90. U.S. Department of State. "Definitions of Diplomatic Security Terms." *Foreign Affairs Manual.* 12FAM090. November 12, 2014. Accessed February 24, 2015. http://www.state.gov/documents/organization/88330.pdf.

91. Tor Project, *Tor: Overview*, accessed February 3, 2016, https://www.torproject.org/about/overview.html.en, and Snowden files, "Tor Stinks" presentation, accessed February 3, 2016, http://www.theguardian.com/world/interactive/2013/oct/04/tor-stinks-nsa-presentation-document.

92. U.S. Department of Defense. *DoD Intelligence Interrogations, Detainee Debriefings, and Tactical Questioning.* Directive Number 3115.09, October 11, 2012 Incorporating Change 1, Effective November 15, 2013. Accessed February 15, 2015. http://www.dtic.mil/whs/directives/corres/pdf/311509p.pdf.

93. U.S. Department of Defense. *Department of Defense Dictionary of Military and Associated Terms.* JP 1-02, 08 November 2010, as Amended through 15 March 2015. Accessed March 28, 2015. http://www.dtic.mil/doctrine/new_pubs/jp1_02.pdf.

94. Seifert, Jeffrey W. "Datamining: An Overview." *CRS Report for Congress* RL31798. December 16, 2004. Accessed February 24, 2015. http://fas.org/irp/crs/RL31798.pdf. Also see Steven, Gina Marie. "Privacy: Total Information Awareness Programs and Related Information Access, Collection, and Protection Law." *CRS Report for Congress*, RL31730. March 21, 2003. Accessed February 24, 2015. http://fas.org/irp/crs/RL31730.pdf.

95. Nuffield Council on Bioethics. *The Forensic Use of Bioinformation: Ethical Issues.* September 2007. Accessed February 15, 2015. http://nuffieldbioethics.org/project/bioinformation/.

96. North Atlantic Treaty Organization (NATO) Standardization Agency 2008, accessed July 15, 2015, https://fas.org/irp/doddir/other/nato2008.pdf.

97. U.S. Department of Defense. *Department of Defense Dictionary of Military and Associated Terms.* JP 1-02, 08 November 2010, as Amended through 15 January 2016. Accessed January 26, 2016. http://www.dtic.mil/doctrine/new_pubs/jp1_02.pdf.

98. Tactical Tech. *Me and My Shadow: Trackography*. Accessed February 11, 2015. https://myshadow.org/learn-about-trackography.

99. U.S. Department of Defense. *Department of Defense Dictionary of Military and Associated Terms.* JP 1-02, 08 November 2010, as Amended through 15 January 2016. Accessed January 26, 2016, http://www.dtic.mil/doctrine/new_pubs/jp1_02. pdf; and Defense Intelligence Agency, Office of Counterintelligence. *CI Glossary—Terms & Definitions of Interest for DoD CI Professionals.* July 2014. Accessed January 17, 2015. https://www.hsdl.org/?view&did=699056.

100. Committee for National Security Systems (CNSS). Instruction 4009. *National Information Assurance Glossary.* April 2010. Accessed February 25, 2015. http://www.ncix.gov/publications/policy/docs/CNSSI_4009.pdf.

101. Defense Acquisition University. *Glossary: Defense Acquisition Acronyms and Terms*. 13th ed., November 2009. Accessed February 24, 2015. http://www.dau. mil/pubscats/pubscats/13th_edition_glossary.pdf.

102. Franco, Celinda. "The MS-13 and 18th Street Gangs: Emerging Transnational Gang Threats?" *CRS Report for Congress* RL34233, January 30, 2008. Accessed April 6, 2015. http://www.fas.org/sgp/crs/row/RL34233.pdf.

103. National Security Council. *Strategy to Combat Transnational Organized Crime: Addressing Converging Threats to National Security.* July 25, 2011. Accessed February 25, 2015. http://www.whitehouse.gov/administration/eop/nsc/transnational-crime.

104. U.S. Department of Defense. *Counterterrorism*. JP 3-26. October 24, 2014. Accessed February 24, 2015. http://www.dtic.mil/doctrine/new_pubs/jp3_26.pdf.

105. Department of Homeland Security, Risk Steering Committee. *DHS Risk Lexicon.* September 2010. Accessed February 14, 2015. http://www.dhs.gov/dhs-risk-lexicon.

106. Department of Homeland Security, Risk Steering Committee. *DHS Risk Lexicon.* September 2010. Accessed February 14, 2015. http://www.dhs.gov/dhs-risk-lexicon. Also see U.S. General Accountability Office. *Aviation Security: TSA Should Limit Future Funding for Behavior Detection Activities.* GAO-14-159, November 2013. Accessed February 15, 2015. http://www.gao.gov/products/GAO-14-159.

107. P.L. 107-71, 19 November 2001. Now codified as 49 U.S.C. 114; 49 U.S.C. 114(d).

108. Transportation Security Administration, *TSA Transportation Security Operations Center: Still on Watch*, May 7, 2014, accessed February 1, 2016, http://blog.tsa. gov/2014/05/tsa-transportation-security-operations.html.

109. 18 U.S. Code § 3127—"Definitions for Chapter" (Current through Pub. L. 113-234). Accessed February 5, 2015. http://www.law.cornell.edu/uscode/ text/18/3127.

110. Federal Bureau of Investigation. *Domestic Investigations and Operations Guide.* October 15, 2011. Accessed February 25, 2015. http://vault.fbi.gov/.

111. 18 U.S. Code § 2381 "Treason" (Current through Pub. L. 113-234). Accessed February 8, 2015. http://www.law.cornell.edu/uscode/text/18/2381.

112. Committee for National Security Systems (CNSS). Instruction 4009. *National Information Assurance Glossary.* April 2010. Accessed February 25, 2015. http://www.ncix.gov/publications/policy/docs/CNSSI_4009.pdf.

113. Committee for National Security Systems (CNSS). Instruction 4009. *National Information Assurance Glossary.* April 2010. Accessed February 25, 2015. http://www.ncix.gov/publications/policy/docs/CNSSI_4009.pdf.

114. Committee for National Security Systems (CNSS). Instruction 4009. *National Information Assurance Glossary.* April 2010. Accessed February 25, 2015. http://www.ncix.gov/publications/policy/docs/CNSSI_4009.pdf.

115. Committee for National Security Systems (CNSS). Instruction 4009. *National Information Assurance Glossary.* April 2010. Accessed February 25, 2015. http://www.ncix.gov/publications/policy/docs/CNSSI_4009.pdf.

116. U.S. Department of Defense, Center for Development of Security Excellence. *Glossary of Security Terms and Definitions.* November 2012. Accessed February 26, 2015. http://www.cdse.edu/documents/cdse/Glossary_Handbook.pdf.

117. Mark A. Randol, "The Department of Homeland Security Intelligence Enterprise: Operational Overview and Oversight Challenges for Congress," R40602, March 19, 2010, accessed February 1, 2016, https://www.fas.org/sgp/crs/homesec/R40602.pdf.

118. *Oxford Essential Dictionary of the U.S. Military* (New York: Oxford University Press, 2001).

119. Dataminr. *About.* Accessed February 25, 2015. https://www.dataminr.com/.

120. Brightplanet. *Bluejay.* Accessed March 6, 2015. http://brightplanet.com/bluejay/.

121. Brightplanet. *Bluejay.* Accessed March 6, 2015. http://brightplanet.com/bluejay/.

122. Defense Acquisition University. *Glossary: Defense Acquisition Acronyms and Terms.* 13th ed., November 2009. Accessed February 24, 2015. http://www.dau.mil/pubscats/pubscats/13th_edition_glossary.pdf.

U

UBERVEILLANCE An omnipresent electronic surveillance facilitated by technology that makes it possible to embed surveillance devices in the human body.[1]

UNACCEPTABLE RISK Level of risk at which, given costs and benefits associated with further risk reduction measures, action is deemed to be warranted at a given point in time.[2]

UNACKNOWLEDGED SAP 1. The existence of the Special Access Program (SAP) is protected as special access and the details, technologies, materials, techniques, and more, of the program are classified as dictated by their vulnerability to exploitation and the risk of compromise. Program funding is often unacknowledged, classified, or not directly linked to the program. The four Congressional Defense Committees normally have access to the unacknowledged SAP.[3] 2. A SAP having protective controls ensuring the existence of the program is not acknowledged, affirmed, or made known to any person not authorized for such information.[4]

UNAUTHORIZED ACCESS 1. Occurs when a person gains logical or physical access without permission to a network, system, application, data, or other resource. 2. Occurs when a user, legitimate or unauthorized, accesses a resource that the user is not permitted to use.

UNAUTHORIZED DISCLOSURE 1. An event involving the exposure of information to entities not authorized for access to the information. 2. A communication or physical transfer of classified information to an unauthorized recipient. 3. The compromise of classified information by communication or physical transfer to an unauthorized recipient. It includes the unauthorized disclosure of classified information in a newspaper, journal, or other publication where such information is traceable to an agency because of a direct quotation or other uniquely identifiable fact.[5]

UNAUTHORIZED PERSON A person not authorized to have access to specific classified information.[6]

UNCERTAINTY A condition, event, outcome, or circumstance of which the extent, value, or consequence is not predictable. State of knowledge about outcomes in a decision such that it is not possible to assign probabilities in advance. Some techniques for coping with this problem are *a fortiori* analysis (making use of conclusions inferred from another reasoned conclusion or recognized fact), contingency analysis, and sensitivity analysis.[7]

UNCLASSIFIED CONTROLLED NUCLEAR INFORMATION (UCNI) Unclassified Controlled Nuclear Information (UCNI) under jurisdiction of the Department of Energy (DoE) includes unclassified facility design information, operational information concerning the production, processing, or utilization of nuclear material for atomic energy defense programs, safeguards and security information, nuclear material, and declassified controlled nuclear weapon information once classified as Restricted Data (RD). Department of Defense (DoD) UCNI is unclassified information on security measures (including security plans, procedures and equipment) for the physical protection of DoD Special Nuclear Material (SNM), equipment, or facilities. Information is designated UCNI only when it is determined that its unauthorized disclosure could reasonably be expected to have a significant adverse effect on the health and safety of the public or the common defense and security by significantly increasing the likelihood of the illegal production of nuclear weapons or the theft, diversion, or sabotage of SNM, equipment, or facilities.[8]

UNCLASSIFIED INTELLIGENCE 1. Information, a document, or material that has been determined not to be classified or that has been declassified by a proper authority. 2. A limited distribution category applied to the wide range of unclassified types of official information, not requiring protection as national security information, but limited to official use and not publicly releasable. *See* OPEN SOURCE INTELLIGENCE (OSINT); UNCLASSIFIED MATTER

UNCLASSIFIED INTERNET PROTOCOL ROUTER NETWORK Used to exchange sensitive but unclassified information between "internal" users as well as providing users access to the Internet. The Unclassified Internet Protocol Router Network is composed of Internet Protocol routers owned by the United States Department of Defense (DoD). It was created by the Defense Information Systems Agency (DISA) to supersede the earlier Military Network.[9]

UNCLASSIFIED MATTER Official matter that does not require the application of security safeguards but the disclosure of which may be subject to control for other reasons. *See* CLASSIFIED MATTER; UNCLASSIFIED INTELLIGENCE

UNCLASSIFIED SENSITIVE For computer applications, this term refers to any information, which the loss, misuse, unauthorized access to, or modification of could adversely affect the national interest or the conduct of a federal program, or the privacy to which individuals are entitled under the section 552a of Title 5, United States Code (U.S.C), "Privacy Act," but which has not been specifically authorized under the criteria established by an Executive Order (EO) or an act of Congress to be kept secret in the interest of national defense or foreign policy.[10]

UNCONTROLLED ACCESS AREA (UAA) The space in and around a building where no personnel access controls are exercised.[11]

UNCONTROLLED MOSAIC A mosaic composed of uncorrected photographs, the details of which have been matched without ground control or other orientation. Accurate measurement and direction cannot be accomplished.

UNCONVENTIONAL WARFARE A broad spectrum of military and paramilitary operations, normally of long duration, predominantly conducted through, with, or by indigenous or surrogate forces who are organized, trained, equipped, supported, and directed in varying degrees by an external source. It includes, but is not limited to, guerrilla warfare, subversion, sabotage, intelligence activities, and unconventional assisted recovery. Operations conducted by, with, or through irregular forces in support of a resistance movement, an insurgency, or conventional military operations.[12]

UNDERCOVER A covert or clandestine person, objective, or operation.

UNDERGROUND The element of the irregular organization that conducts operations in areas normally denied to the auxiliary and the guerrilla force.[13]

UNFAVORABLE PERSONNEL SECURITY DETERMINATION Any one or a combination of the following scenarios: denial/revocation of clearance for access to classified information; denial/revocation of access to classified information; denial/revocation of a Special Access Authorization (AA), including access to Sensitive Compartmented Information (SCI);

non-appointment/non-selection for appointment to a sensitive position; non-appointment/non-selection for any other position requiring trustworthiness; reassignment to a position of lesser sensitivity or to a non-sensitive position; non-acceptance for or discharge for the armed forces when any of the foregoing actions are based on derogatory information of personnel security significance.[14]

UNGOVERNED SPACE Territory lacking effective, organized, and/or responsible governance, affording secure sanctuary for illicit criminal organizations, terrorist network(s), and/or antigovernment paramilitaries. Includes under-governed areas within a country with a functioning government. Government may be witting or unwitting.[15]

UNIFORM CODE OF MILITARY JUSTICE (UCMJ) 1. The criminal code governing the armed services of the United States. 2. The Uniform Code of Military Justice is the foundation of military law in the United States. The UCMJ applies to all members of the uniformed services of the United States: the Air Force, Army, Coast Guard, Marine Corps, Navy, National Oceanic and Atmospheric Administration Commissioned Corps, and Public Health Service Commissioned Corps.[16]

UNIFORM CRIME REPORTING (UCR) With the participation of more than 18,000 agencies nationwide, the FBI's UCR Program provides crime statistics for use in law enforcement administration, operation, and management. These statistics are shared annually in four high-profile reports which include Crime in the United States, a comprehensive collection of crime offenses, clearances, arrests, and police employment information; Hate Crime Statistics, a report focused on bias-motivated crimes; Law Enforcement Officers Killed and Assaulted (LEOKA), a statistical perspective detailing information on local, state, tribal, and federal law enforcement officers killed and assaulted in the line of duty; and NIBRS, a compilation of data from the National Incident-Based Reporting System.[17]

UNIT 1. Any military element whose structure is prescribed by competent authority. 2. An organization title of a subdivision of a group in a task force. 3. A standard or basic quantity into which an item of supply is divided, issued, or used. Also called unit of issue. 4. With regard to Reserve Component of the Armed Forces, a selected reserve unit organized, equipped, and trained for mobilization to serve on active duty as a unit or to augment or be augmented by another unit.[18]

UNITED NATIONS SECURITY COUNCIL RESOLUTION 1540 Imposes binding obligations on all States to adopt legislation to prevent the proliferation of nuclear, chemical and biological weapons, and their means of delivery, and establish appropriate domestic controls over related materials to prevent their illicit trafficking. It also encourages enhanced international cooperation on such efforts. The resolution affirms support for the multilateral treaties whose aim is to eliminate or prevent the proliferation of WMDs and the importance for all States to implement them fully; it reiterates that none of the obligations in resolution 1540 (2004) shall conflict with or alter the rights and obligations of States Parties to the Treaty on the Non-Proliferation of Nuclear Weapons, the Chemical Weapons Convention, or the Biological Weapons Convention or alter the responsibilities of the IAEA and OPCW.[19]

UNITED STATES CITIZEN (NATIVE BORN) A person born in one of the 50 United States (U.S.), Puerto Rico, Guam, American Samoa, Northern Mariana Islands, U.S. Virgin Islands, or Panama Canal Zone, if the father, mother, or both, was or is a citizen of the United States.[20]

UNITED STATES COMPUTER EMERGENCY READINESS TEAM (US-CERT) It is mission is improve the nation's cybersecurity posture, coordinate cyber information sharing, and proactively manage cyber risks to the nation while protecting the constitutional rights of Americans. US-CERT strives to be a trusted global leader in cybersecurity—collaborative, agile, and responsive in a dynamic and complex environment. US-CERT leverages the Protected Critical Infrastructure Information (PCII) Program to prevent inappropriate disclosure of proprietary information or other sensitive data. Established in response to the Critical Infrastructure Information Act of 2002 (CII Act), the PCII Program enables members of the private sector to voluntarily submit confidential information regarding the nation's critical infrastructure to DHS with the assurance that the information will be protected from public disclosure.[21]

UNITED STATES CYBER COMMAND (USCYBERCOM) This command plans, coordinates, integrates, synchronizes and conducts activities to: direct the operations and defense of specified Department of Defense information networks and; prepare to, and when directed, conduct full-spectrum military cyberspace operations in order to enable actions in all domains, ensure U.S./Allied freedom of action in cyberspace and deny the same to our adversaries. The Command has three main focus areas: defending the DoDIN (Department of Defense Information Network), providing support to combatant commanders for execution of their missions around the world, and strengthening our nation's ability to withstand and respond to cyber attack. The Command unifies the direction of cyberspace operations, strengthens DoD cyberspace capabilities, and integrates and bolsters DoD's cyber expertise.[22]

UNITED STATES GOVERNMENT MANUAL Known as the Official handbook of the federal government. This annual resource provides comprehensive information on the agencies of the legislative, judicial, and executive branches, as well as quasi-official agencies, international organizations in which the United States participates, boards, commissions, and committees. Each agency's description consists of a list of principal officials; a summary statement of the agency's purpose and role in the federal government; a brief history of the agency, including its legislative or executive authority; and a description of consumer activities, contracts and grants, employment, and publications. A typical agency description includes a list of principal officials, a summary statement of the agency's purpose and role in the federal government, a brief history of the agency, including its legislative or executive authority, a description of its programs and activities, and a "Sources of Information" section. This last section provides information on consumer activities, contracts and grants, employment, publications, and many other areas of public interest.[23]

UNITED STATES NATIONAL A citizen of the United States (U.S.) or a person who, though not a citizen of the United States, owes permanent allegiance to the United States (e.g., a lawful permanent resident of the United States). Categories of persons born in and outside the United States or its possessions who may qualify as nationals of the United States are listed in 8 United States Code 1101(a) and 8 United States Code 1401; subsection (a) paragraphs (1) through (7). Legal counsel should be consulted when doubt exists as to whether or not a person can qualify as a national of the United States. NOTE: A U.S. national shall not be treated as a foreign person except when acting as a foreign representative.[24]

UNITED STATES PERSON 1. Any U.S. citizen or permanent resident alien, a group or organization that is an unincorporated association substantially composed of U.S. citizens or permanent resident aliens, or a corporation incorporated in the United States, except for a corporation directed and controlled by a foreign government or governments. 2. A citizen of the United States, an alien lawfully admitted for permanent residence (as defined in section 1101 (a)(20) of title 8), an unincorporated association a substantial number of members of which are citizens of the United States or aliens lawfully admitted for permanent residence, or a corporation which is incorporated in the United States, but does not include a corporation or an association which is a foreign power, as defined in subsection (a)(1), (2), or (3) of this section.[25]

UNITED STATES STRATEGIC COMMAND (USSTRATCOM) Responsible for directing the operation and defense of the Global Information Grid (GIG) to assure timely and secure net-centric capabilities across strategic, operational, and tactical boundaries in support of the Department of Defense's (DoD) full spectrum of warfighting, intelligence, and business missions.[26]

UNIVERSAL TIME 1. A measure of time that conforms, within a close approximation, to the mean diurnal rotation of the Earth and serves as the basis of civil timekeeping. Also called ZULU time.[27] 2. Mostly used in the military to designate Greenwich Mean Time. The Department of the Navy serves as the country's official timekeeper, with the Master Clock facility at the U.S. Naval Observatory, Washington, D.C. Specifically, the U.S. Navy, as well as civil aviation, uses the letter "Z" (phonetically "Zulu") to refer to the time at the prime meridian. The U.S. time zones are Eastern ["R," "Romeo"]; Central ["S," "Sierra"]; Mountain ["T," "Tango"]; Pacific ["U," "Uniform"]; Alaska ["V," "Victor"], and Hawaii ["W," "Whiskey"].

UNKNOWN 1. A code meaning "information not available." 2. An unidentified target. An aircraft or ship that has not been determined to be hostile, friendly, or neutral using identification friend or foe and other techniques, but that must be tracked by air defense or naval engagement systems. 3. An identity applied to an evaluated track that has not been identified.[28]

UNKNOWN SUBJECT (UNSUB) The subject of an investigation, whose identity has not been determined, commonly referred to as an "UNSUB."[29]

UNLIMITED RIGHTS Rights to use, modify, reproduce, display, release, or disclose technical data (TD) in whole or in part, in any manner, and for any purpose whatsoever, and to have or authorize others to do so.[30]

UNPRIVILEGED ENEMY BELLIGERENT 1. An individual (other than a privileged belligerent) who: "(A) has engaged in hostilities against the United States or its coalition partners"; "(B) has purposefully and materially supported hostilities against the United States or its coalition partners"; or "(C) was a part of al Qaeda at the time of the alleged offense under this chapter."[31] 2. In general, journalists are civilians. However, journalists may be members of the armed forces, persons authorized to accompany the armed forces, or unprivileged belligerents (4.24).[32]

UNSOLICITED CORRESPONDENCE Requests for information from a person which may range from direct inquiries by phone, e-mail, fax, or letter in which the recipient is asked to provide seemingly innocuous data. Typical requests include solicitation of research papers, requests for additional information after a public presentation, suggestions for mutual research, requests for survey participation, and so forth; correspondence where the actual purpose may be to identify by name and position any individual who might be targeted later by a foreign intelligence service, and to elicit targeted information not readily obtainable by other means.[33]

UNWARNED EXPOSED The vulnerability of friendly forces to nuclear weapon effects. In this condition, personnel are assumed to be standing in the open at burst time but have dropped to a prone position by the time the blast wave arrives. They are expected to have areas of bare skin exposed to direct thermal radiation, and some personnel may suffer dazzle. *See* WARN EXPOSED; WARN PROTECTED

UPGRADING The determination that certain classified information requires, in the interests of national security, a higher degree of protection against unauthorized disclosure than currently provided, coupled with a changing of the classification designation to reflect the higher degree.[34]

U.S. CONTROLLED SPACE Room or floor within a facility that is not a U.S.-controlled facility, access to which is physically controlled by U.S. individuals who are authorized U.S. government or U.S. government contractor employees. Keys or combinations to locks controlling entrance to U.S.-controlled spaces must be under the exclusive control of U.S. individuals who are U.S. government or U.S. government contractor employees.[35]

U.S. HOMELAND The physical territory of the United States: the 50 states, District of Columbia, U.S. territories and territorial waters; significant infrastructure linked to the United States; and major commercial air, land and sea corridors into the country.[36]

U.S. NATIONAL INTERESTS Matters of vital interest to the United States to include national security, public safety, national economic security, the safe and reliable functioning of "critical infrastructure," and the availability of "key resources."[37]

U.S. PERSONS (USPERS; USP) A U.S. citizen; an alien known by the DoD intelligence component concerned to be a permanent resident alien; an unincorporated association substantially composed of U.S. citizens or permanent resident aliens; a corporation incorporated in the United States, except for a corporation directed and controlled by a foreign government or governments. A corporation or corporate subsidiary incorporated abroad, even if partially or wholly owned by a corporation incorporated in the United States, is not a U.S. person. A person or organization outside the United States shall be presumed not to be a U.S. person unless specific information to the contrary is obtained. An alien in the United States shall be presumed not to be a U.S. person unless specific information to the contrary is obtained. A permanent resident alien is a foreign national lawfully admitted into the United States for permanent residence.[38] *See* UNITED STATES PERSON

U.S. VISIT/IDENT (USVISIT) The United States Visitor and Immigrant Status Indicator Technology (USVISIT) Automated Biometric Identification System (IDENT) is a Department of Homeland Security (DHS)–wide system for the storage and processing of biometric and limited biographic information for DHS national security, law enforcement, immigration, intelligence, and other DHS mission-related functions.[39]

U.S. VISITOR AND IMMIGRANT STATUS INDICATOR TECHNOLOGY (US-VISIT) The office of US-VISIT supplies a continuum of security measures that begins overseas, at the Department of State's visa-issuing posts, and continues through arrival and departure from the United States of America. Using biometrics, such as digital, inkless finger-scans and digital photographs, the identity of visitors requiring a visa is now matched at each step to ensure that the person crossing the U.S. border is the same person who received the visa. For visa-waiver travelers, the capture of biometrics first occurs at the port of entry to the United States. By checking the biometrics of a traveler against its databases, US-VISIT verifies whether the traveler has previously been determined inadmissible, is a known security risk (including having outstanding wants and warrants), or has previously overstayed the terms of a visa.[40]

USA FREEDOM ACT The USA FREEDOM Act, P.L. 114-23 was signed into law on June 2, 2015. The new law contains eight titles, spanning a range of national security topics from reauthorizing expired investigative authorities under the Foreign Intelligence Surveillance Act of 1978 (FISA) to enhancing criminal prohibitions against maritime and nuclear terrorism. But the legislative history and debate surrounding the Act indicate that the principal focus of the legislation was to address the bulk collection of telephone metadata by the National Security Agency (NSA) under Section 215 of the USA PATRIOT Act. The USA FREEDOM Act will generally prohibit the use of Section 215 for collection activities, such as bulk collection, that are not limited "to the greatest extent reasonably practicable" by a "specific selection term" (SST), defined as "a term that specifically identifies a person, account, address, or personal device, or any other specific identifier." The Act also expressly prohibits orders under Section 215 that are limited only by broad geographic terms (such as a state or zip code) or named communications service providers (such as Verizon or AT&T). A slightly relaxed standard can be used under the amended Section 215 to obtain telephone metadata in furtherance of international terrorism investigations. Similar SST-requirements are also added to other provisions of FISA and national security letter statutes in order to prevent those authorities from being used for bulk collection.[41]

USA PATRIOT ACT 1. The Uniting and Strengthening America by Providing Appropriate Tools Required to Intercept and Obstruct Terrorism (USA PATRIOT) Act of 2001, P.L. 107-56 is part of the congressional response to September 11. It is the merger of two similar bills. S.1510 passed the Senate on October 11 (2001) and H.R.2975 passed the House on October 12 (2001) after substituting the language of H.R.3108 for its text. Having informally resolved their differences, the House enacted the measure in final form on October 24 (2011) and the Senate on October 25 (2001). The Act consists of ten titles which, among other things: give federal law enforcement and intelligence officers greater authority to gather and share evidence particularly with respect to wire and electronic communications; amend federal money laundering laws, particularly those involving overseas financial activities; create new federal crimes, increase the penalties for existing federal crimes, and adjust existing federal criminal procedure, particularly with respect to acts of terrorism; modify immigration law; authorize appropriations to enhance the capacity of immigration, law enforcement, and intelligence agencies to more effectively respond to the threats of terrorism.[42] 2. The USA PATRIOT Act modified many major U.S. intelligence, communications, and privacy laws, including: The Electronic Communications Privacy Act (EPCA), which modifies Title III of the Omnibus Crime Control and Safe Streets Act (the Wiretap Act); the Foreign Intelligence Surveillance Act of 1978 (FISA); and the Communications Act of 1934. The Act was reauthorized in 2005, amended and reauthorized in 2006, and in 2011, four-year extensions of the "lone wolf," definition and authorization of "roving wiretaps" and "request for production business records" search authority occurred.[43]

USERS Any person who interacts directly with an Automated Information System (AIS) or a network system. This includes both those persons who are authorized to interact with the system and those people who interact without authorization (e.g., active/passive wiretapping).[44]

UTILITY State or quality of being useful militarily or operationally. Designed for or possessing a number of useful or practical purposes rather than a single, specialized one.[45]

NOTES

1. Michael, M. G. *On the '"Birth" of Uberveillance.* February 14, 2012. Accessed February 15, 2015. http://uberveillance.com/blog/2012/2/15/on-the-birth-of-uberveillance.html.

2. Department of Homeland Security, Risk Steering Committee. *DHS Risk Lexicon.* September 2010. Accessed February 14, 2015. http://www.dhs.gov/dhs-risk-lexicon.

3. U.S. Department of Defense, Center for Development of Security Excellence. *Glossary of Security Terms and Definitions.* November 2012. Accessed February 27, 2015. http://www.cdse.edu/documents/cdse/Glossary_Handbook.pdf.

4. U.S. Department of Defense. *Special Access Program (SAP) Policy.* DoD Directive Number 5205.07, July 1, 2010. Accessed March 1, 2015. http://www.dtic.mil/whs/directives/corres/pdf/520507p.pdf.

5. White House, Office of the Press Secretary, *Executive Order 13292, as Amended To Executive Order 12958, Classified National Security Information.* Accessed on July 1, 2015, http://www.fas.org/sgp/bush/eoamend.html.

6. U.S. Department of Defense, Center for Development of Security Excellence. *Glossary of Security Terms and Definitions.* November 2012. Accessed February 27, 2015. http://www.cdse.edu/documents/cdse/Glossary_Handbook.pdf.

7. Defense Acquisition University. *Glossary: Defense Acquisition Acronyms and Terms.* 13th ed., November 2009. Accessed February 27, 2015. http://www.dau.mil/pubscats/pubscats/13th_edition_glossary.pdf.

8. U.S. Department of Defense, Center for Development of Security Excellence. *Glossary of Security Terms and Definitions.* November 2012. Accessed February 27, 2015. http://www.cdse.edu/documents/cdse/Glossary_Handbook.pdf.

9. U.S. Department of Defense, Center for Development of Security Excellence. *Glossary of Security Terms and Definitions.* November 2012. Accessed February 27, 2015. http://www.cdse.edu/documents/cdse/Glossary_Handbook.pdf.

10. U.S. Department of Defense, Center for Development of Security Excellence. *Glossary of Security Terms and Definitions.* November 2012. Accessed February 27, 2015. http://www.cdse.edu/documents/cdse/Glossary_Handbook.pdf.

11. U.S. Department of Defense, Center for Development of Security Excellence. *Glossary of Security Terms and Definitions.* November 2012. Accessed February 27, 2015. http://www.cdse.edu/documents/cdse/Glossary_Handbook.pdf.

12. Department of the Army. *Army Special Operations Forces Unconventional Warfare*. FM 3-05.130, September 2008. Accessed February 9, 2015. http://fas.org/irp/doddir/army/fm3-05-130.pdf.

13. Department of the Army. *Army Special Operations Forces Unconventional Warfare*. FM 3-05.130, September 2008. Accessed February 9, 2015. http://fas.org/irp/doddir/army/fm3-05-130.pdf.

14. U.S. Department of Defense, Center for Development of Security Excellence. *Glossary of Security Terms and Definitions*. November 2012. Accessed February 27, 2015. http://www.cdse.edu/documents/cdse/Glossary_Handbook.pdf.

15. Chairman of the Joint Chiefs of Staff. *National Military Strategic Plan for the War on Terrorism*. February 1, 2006. Accessed February 26, 2015. http://archive.defense.gov/pubs/pdfs/2006-01-25-Strategic-Plan.pdf.

16. *Uniform Code of Military Justice*. "About." Accessed February 26, 2015. http://www.ucmj.us/about-the-ucmj.

17. U.S. Department of Justice, Criminal Justice Information Services Division. *Criminal Justice Information Services (CJIS) Annual Report, 2014*. Accessed February 25, 2015. http://www.fbi.gov/about-us/cjis/annual-report-2014/cjis-annual-report-2014.

18. U.S. Department of Defense. *Department of Defense Dictionary of Military and Associated Terms*. JP 1-02, 08 November 2010, as Amended through 15 January 2016. Accessed January 26, 2016, http://www.dtic.mil/doctrine/new_pubs/jp1_02.pdf.

19. United Nations. *1540 Committee*. Accessed February 20, 2015. http://www.un.org/en/sc/1540/.

20. U.S. Department of Defense, Center for Development of Security Excellence. *Glossary of Security Terms and Definitions*. November 2012. Accessed February 27, 2015. http://www.cdse.edu/documents/cdse/Glossary_Handbook.pdf.

21. United States Computer Emergency Readiness Team. *About Us*. Accessed February 14, 2015. https://www.us-cert.gov/about-us.

22. U.S. Strategic Command. *U.S. Cyber Command*. January 15, 2015. Accessed February 27, 2015. http://www.stratcom.mil/factsheets/2/Cyber_Command/.

23. U.S. Government Publishing Office. *United States Government Manual*. Accessed February 16, 2015. http://bookstore.gpo.gov/products/sku/069-000-00216-1; also see the *Manual* online at http://www.usgovernmentmanual.gov/.

24. U.S. Department of Defense, Center for Development of Security Excellence. *Glossary of Security Terms and Definitions*. November 2012. Accessed February 27, 2015. http://www.cdse.edu/documents/cdse/Glossary_Handbook.pdf.

25. 50 U.S. Code § 1801(i)—"Definitions" (Current through Pub. L. 113-234). Accessed February 10, 2015. http://www.law.cornell.edu/uscode/text/50/1801.

26. U.S. Department of Defense, Center for Development of Security Excellence. *Glossary of Security Terms and Definitions*. November 2012. Accessed February 27, 2015. http://www.cdse.edu/documents/cdse/Glossary_Handbook.pdf; also see U.S. Strategic Command. *Mission*. Accessed February 27, 2015. http://www.stratcom.mil/mission/.

27. U.S. Department of Defense. *Department of Defense Dictionary of Military and Associated Terms.* JP 1-02, 08 November 2010, as Amended through 15 January 2016. Accessed January 26, 2016, http://www.dtic.mil/doctrine/new_pubs/jp1_02.pdf.

28. U.S. Department of Defense. *Department of Defense Dictionary of Military and Associated Terms.* JP 1-02, 08 November 2010, as Amended through 15 January 2016. Accessed January 26, 2016, http://www.dtic.mil/doctrine/new_pubs/jp1_02.pdf.

29. Defense Intelligence Agency, Office of Counterintelligence. *CI Glossary— Terms & Definitions of Interest for DoD CI Professionals.* July 2014. Accessed February 28, 2015. https://www.hsdl.org/?view&did=699056.

30. Defense Acquisition University. *Glossary: Defense Acquisition Acronyms and Terms.* 13th ed., November 2009. Accessed February 27, 2015. http://www.dau.mil/pubscats/pubscats/13th_edition_glossary.pdf.

31. 10 U.S. Code § 948a—"Definitions" (Current through Pub. L. 113-234). Accessed February 20, 2015. http://www.law.cornell.edu/uscode/text/10/948a.

32. U.S Department of Defense. *Law of War Manual,* Office of General Counsel, June 2015, accessed February 3, 2016, http://www.defense.gov/Portals/1/Documents/pubs/Law-of-War-Manual-June-2015.pdf.

33. Department of the Army. *Threat Awareness and Reporting Program.* Army Regulation 381-1. October 4, 2010. Accessed February 8, 2015. http://www.apd.army.mil/pdffiles/r381_12.pdf.

34. Center for Development of Security Excellence. *Marking Classified Information: Job Aid.* Accessed on July 1, 2015, http://www.cdse.edu/documents/cdse/Marking_Classified_Information.pdf.

35. Committee for National Security Systems (CNSS). Instruction 4009. *National Information Assurance Glossary.* April 2010. Accessed February 27, 2015. http://www.ncix.gov/publications/policy/docs/CNSSI_4009.pdf.

36. Defense Intelligence Agency, Office of Counterintelligence. *CI Glossary— Terms & Definitions of Interest for DoD CI Professionals.* July 2014. Accessed February 28, 2015. https://www.hsdl.org/?view&did=699056.

37. *Presidential Policy Directive/PPD-20. U.S. Cyber Operations Policy.* October 16, 2012. Accessed February 17, 2015. https://www.fas.org/irp/offdocs/ppd/ppd-20.pdf.

38. U.S. Department of Defense. *DoD Intelligence Interrogations, Detainee Debriefings, and Tactical Questioning.* Directive Number 3115.09, October 11, 2012 Incorporating Change 1, Effective November 15, 2013. Accessed February 15, 2015. http://www.dtic.mil/whs/directives/corres/pdf/311509p.pdf.

39. Defense Forensics and Biometrics Agency. *DoD Biometrics Enterprise Architecture (Integrated) v2.0 Common Biometric Vocabulary.* April 2013. Accessed February 27, 2015. http://www.biometrics.dod.mil/Files/Documents/References/common%20biometric%20vocabulary.pdf.

40. Defense Forensics and Biometrics Agency. *DoD Biometrics Enterprise Architecture (Integrated) v2.0 Common Biometric Vocabulary.* April 2013. Accessed

February 27, 2015. http://www.biometrics.dod.mil/Files/Documents/References/common%20biometric%20vocabulary.pdf.

41. Congressional Research Service. *Legal Sidebar USA FREEDOM Act Reinstates Expired USA PATRIOT Act Provisions but Limits Bulk Collection.* June 4, 2015. Accessed June 15, 2015. http://www.fas.org/sgp/crs/intel/usaf-rein.pdf.

42. Doyle, Charles. "Terrorism: Section by Section Analysis of the USA PATRIOT Act." *CRS Report for Congress* RL3120, December 10, 2001. Accessed March 8, 2015. http://fpc.state.gov/documents/organization/7952.pdf.

43. U.S. Department of Justice, Office of Justice Programs. *Uniting and Strengthening America by Providing Appropriate Tools Required to Intercept and Obstruct Terrorism (USA PATRIOT) Act of 2001.* Accessed March 7, 2015. https://it.ojp.gov/default.aspx?area=privacy&page=1281.

44. U.S. Department of Defense, Center for Development of Security Excellence. *Glossary of Security Terms and Definitions.* November 2012. Accessed February 27, 2015. http://www.cdse.edu/documents/cdse/Glossary_Handbook.pdf.

45. Defense Acquisition University. *Glossary: Defense Acquisition Acronyms and Terms.* 13th ed. November 2009. Accessed February 27, 2015. http://www.dau.mil/pubscats/pubscats/13th_edition_glossary.pdf.

VALIDATION OF INFORMATION Procedures governing the periodic review of criminal intelligence information to assure its continuing compliance with system submission criteria established by regulation or program policy.[1]

VALIDITY 1. The determination that the information actually represents a true and accurate representation. 2. Asks the question, "Does the information actually represent what we believe it represents?"[2]

VALUE ADDED Additional analysis or commentary in a report that significantly redirects or confirms an assessment for a warning effort. For example, an individual who has lived in a target country recently may have input that would impart value added to current intelligence operations.[3]

VALUE OF STATISTICAL LIFE (VSL) The amount people are willing to pay to reduce risk so that on average one less person is expected to die from the risk.[4]

VARIABLE Any characteristic on which individuals, groups, items, or incidents differ.[5]

VEILLANCE (WATCHING) One can be in favor of more surveillance (safety) or less surveillance (privacy), or one can be merely conducting studies, in an allegedly objective manner, as "surveillance studies." But in all 3 cases, one would be against sousveillance. All three approaches are part of the problem: considering only one side of the argument (one side of the square box below). Those who only consider the surveillance side of the space are inherently biased—that is, looking at the world from a one-sided point of view. We must consider all the veillances—various combinations of surveillance and sousveillance.[6] *See* SOUSVEILLANCE; SURVEILLANCE

VERIFY To accept a statement as true based on confirmation by an independent and authoritative source. For example, the birth certificate on file at the

Bureau of Vital Statistics would be used to verify the date and place of birth claimed on an official form.[7] *See* CORROBORATE

VET To subject a proposal, work product, or concept to an appraisal by command personnel and/or experts to ascertain the product's accuracy, consistency with philosophy, and/or feasibility before proceeding.[8]

VETTING An evaluation of an applicant's or a card holder's character and conduct for approval, acceptance, or denial for the issuance of a physical access control credential.[9]

VIOLATION Any knowing, willful, or negligent action that could reasonably be expected to result in an unauthorized disclosure of classified information; or, any knowing, willful, or negligent action to classify or continue the classification of information contrary to the requirements of Executive Order (EO) 13526, "Classified National Security Information," or its implementing directives; or, any knowing, willful, or negligent action to create or continue a special access program contrary to the requirements of EO 13526.[10]

VIOLENT CRIMINAL APPREHENSION PROGRAM (VICAP) A nationwide data information center operated by the FBI's National Center for the Analysis of Violent Crime, designed to collect, collate, and analyze specific crimes of violence.[11]

VIOLENT EXTREMISM The FBI defines violent extremists as persons who engage in, encourage, endorse, condone, justify, or support in any way the commission of a violent act against either the U.S. government, its citizens, or its allies to achieve political, social, or economic changes or against others who may possess opinions contrary to their own radicalized ideology.[12]

VIOLENT GANG AND TERRORIST ORGANIZATION FILE The Violent Gang and Terrorist Organization File is the FBI's lookout system for known or appropriately suspected terrorists, as well as gang groups and members. The file is part of the FBI's National Crime Information Center database, which is accessible by federal, state, and local law enforcement officers and other criminal justice agencies for screening in conjunction with arrests, detentions, and other criminal justice purposes. A subset of the Violent Gang and Terrorist Organization file consists of TSC's (Terrorist Screening Center) records to be used to screen for possible terrorist links.[13]

VIOLENT NON-STATE ACTORS (VNSA) The VNSA as an organism can be understood in terms of several key characteristics, which directly relate to the system of violence examined earlier. First, the VNSA imports some form of energy from the environment. The Revolutionary Armed Forces of Colombia (Fuerzas Armadas Revolucionarias di Colombia-FARC), for example, imports recruits as well as guns, training (urban tactic training since 1998) and drug monies. Second, the FARC converts, or transforms, the input into a trained guerrilla. Third, the reorganized input is exported to the environment; the FARC recruit joins a unit and conducts attacks on Colombian armed forces. Fourth, this pattern of activity is cyclic; the attacks generate new inputs, recruits, resources, governmental responses, and more. In a clear rejection of the closed system approach, the VNSA seeks negative entropy. That is, it seeks to arrest the entropic process of inevitable disorganization and death by importing more energy (recruits, guns, funds) than it expends, acquiring the negative entropy that allows it to survive crisis. Fifth, the energy inputs are also informative, providing the VNSA with intelligence about its environment. Defeat in combat provides the negative feedback often required to drive a fundamental shift in tactics as we saw with Al Qaeda after the pitched battle of Tora Bora.[14]

VISUAL INFORMATION Various visual media with or without sound. Generally, visual information includes still and motion photography, audio video recording, graphic arts, visual aids, models, display, and visual presentations.[15]

VOICE IN THE WILDERNESS A forecast or warning given within the context of receptive ambiguity, negligence, or denial by the consumer; an assessment or report that is contradictory to an overwhelming consensus.[16]

VULNERABILITIES Indicators of an organization's planning or operational procedures that, when detected by hostile intelligence collection resources, could be exploited to jeopardize the success of the plan or operation. Such indicators include requests for maps of a certain area, a change in volume of radio traffic, and an increase in reconnaissance or logistic activity.

VULNERABILITY 1. Physical feature or operational attribute that renders an entity, asset, system, network, or geographic area open to exploitation or susceptible to a given hazard. Extended Definition: characteristic of design, location, security posture, operation, or any combination thereof, that renders an entity, asset, system, network, or geographic area susceptible to disruption, destruction, or exploitation.[17] 2. The susceptibility of a nation or military force to any action by any means through which its war potential or combat effectiveness may be reduced or its will to fight diminished.[18] 3. In information operations, a weakness in information system security design, procedures, implementation, or internal controls that could be exploited to gain unauthorized access to information or an information system.[19]

VULNERABILITY (DEGREE) Qualitative or quantitative expression of the level to which an entity, asset, system, network, or geographic area is susceptible to harm when it experiences a hazard. In calculating risk of an intentional hazard, the common measurement of vulnerability is the likelihood that an attack is successful, given that it is attempted.[20]

VULNERABILITY ASSESSMENT 1. Product or process of identifying physical features or operational attributes that render an entity, asset, system, network, or geographic area susceptible or exposed to hazards.[21] 2. An assessment of possible criminal or terrorist group targets within a jurisdiction integrated with an assessment of the target's weaknesses, likelihood of being attacked, and ability to withstand an attack.[22] *See* ASSESSMENT

VULNERABILITY ASSESSMENT AND MANAGEMENT In the NICE (National Initiative for Cybersecurity Education) Workforce Framework, cybersecurity work where a person: Conducts assessments of threats and vulnerabilities, determines deviations from acceptable configurations, enterprise or local policy, assesses the level of risk, and develops and/or recommends appropriate mitigation countermeasures in operational and non-operational situations.[23]

VULNERABLE CAPTURED PERSON An individual who by reason of mental or other disability, age or illness, is or may be unable to take care of him/herself or unable to protect him/herself against significant harm or exploitation, and is dependent on others for assistance in the performance of basic physical functions.[24]

NOTES

1. Judicial Administration, 28 CFR 23, http://www.gpoaccess.gov/CFR/index.html.

2. Federal Bureau of Investigation. *Minimum Criminal Intelligence Training Standards for Law Enforcement and Other Criminal Justice Agencies in the United States.* October 2007. Accessed February 28, 2015.

3. Jan Goldman, *Intelligence Warning Terminology*, Joint Military Intelligence College, October 2001, accessed July 3, 2015. https://archive.org/details/JMICIntelligencelwarnterminology.

4. Department of Homeland Security, Risk Steering Committee. *DHS Risk Lexicon.* September 2010. Accessed February 14, 2015. http://www.dhs.gov/dhs-risk-lexicon.

5. Federal Bureau of Investigation. *Minimum Criminal Intelligence Training Standards for Law Enforcement and Other Criminal Justice Agencies in the United States.* October 2007. Accessed February 28, 2015. https://it.ojp.gov/gist/108/Minimum-Criminal-Intelligence-Training-Standards.

6. Mann, Steve. "The Sousveillance Scenarios." Presented at *Identity, Privacy Security by ReDesign,* October 22, 2012. Accessed February 15, 2015. http://eyetap. blogspot.com/2012/10/the-sousveillance-scenarios.html.

7. Federal Bureau of Investigation. *Minimum Criminal Intelligence Training Standards for Law Enforcement and Other Criminal Justice Agencies in the United States.* October 2007. Accessed February 28, 2015. https://it.ojp.gov/gist/108/Minimum-Criminal-Intelligence-Training-Standards.

8. U.S. Department of Defense, Center for Development of Security Excellence. *Glossary of Security Terms and Definitions.* November 2012. Accessed February 27, 2015. http://www.cdse.edu/documents/cdse/Glossary_Handbook.pdf.

9. Undersecretary of Defense. 2015. *Directive-type Memorandum (DTM) 14-005—DoD Identity Management Capability Enterprise Services Application (IMESA) Access to FBI National Crime Information Center (NCIC) Files.* May 13. Accessed June 6, 2015. http://www.dtic.mil/whs/directives/corres/pdf/DTM14005_2014.pdf.

10. Federal Bureau of Investigation. *Minimum Criminal Intelligence Training Standards for Law Enforcement and Other Criminal Justice Agencies in the United States.* October 2007. Accessed February 28, 2015.

11. Dyer, Carol, McCoy, Ryan E., Rodriguez, Joel, and Van Duyn, Donald N. "Countering Violent Islamic Extremism: A Community Responsibility." *FBI Law Enforcement Bulletin* 76, no. 12 (2007): 3–9. Accessed February 8, 2015. http://leb. fbi.gov/2007-pdfs/leb-december-2007.

12. U.S. General Accountability Office. *Terrorist Watch Screening: Recommendations to Promote a Comprehensive and Coordinated Approach to Terrorist-Related Screening.* GAO-08-253T. November 8, 2007. Accessed February 25, 2015. http://www.gao.gov/products/GAO-08-253T.

13. Federal Bureau of Investigation. Minimum Criminal Intelligence Training Standards for Law Enforcement and Other Criminal Justice Agencies in the United States. October 2007. Accessed February 28, 2015. https://it.ojp.gov/gist/108/Minimum-Criminal-Intelligence-Training-Standards.

14. Casebeer, William and Thomas, Troy. *Strategic Insight: Deterring Violent Non-State Actors in the New Millennium.* Naval Postgraduate School Center for Contemporary Conflict, Monterey, CA, December 2, 2002. Accessed March 5, 2015. http://www.dtic.mil/dtic/tr/fulltext/u2/a525955.pdf.

15. U.S. Department of Defense. *Department of Defense Dictionary of Military and Associated Terms.* JP 1-02, 08 November 2010, as Amended through 15 March 2015. Accessed March 18, 2015. http://www.dtic.mil/doctrine/dod_dictionary/.

16. Jan Goldman, *Intelligence Warning Terminology*, Joint Military Intelligence College, October 2001, accessed July 3, 2015. https://archive.org/details/JMICInteligencelwarnterminology.

17. Department of Homeland Security, Risk Steering Committee. *DHS Risk Lexicon.* September 2010. Accessed February 14, 2015. http://www.dhs.gov/dhs-risk-lexicon.

18. U.S. Department of Defense. *Department of Defense Dictionary of Military and Associated Terms.* JP 1-02, 08 November 2010, as Amended through 15 January 2016. Accessed January 26, 2016, http://www.dtic.mil/doctrine/new_pubs/jp1_02.pdf.

19. U.S. Department of Defense. *Department of Defense Dictionary of Military and Associated Terms.* JP 1-02, 08 November 2010, as Amended through 15 January 2016. Accessed January 26, 2016, http://www.dtic.mil/doctrine/new_pubs/jp1_02.pdf.

20. Department of Homeland Security, Risk Steering Committee. *DHS Risk Lexicon.* September 2010. Accessed February 14, 2015. http://www.dhs.gov/dhs-risk-lexicon.

21. Department of Homeland Security, Risk Steering Committee. *DHS Risk Lexicon.* September 2010. Accessed February 14, 2015. http://www.dhs.gov/dhs-risk-lexicon.

22. Federal Bureau of Investigation. *Minimum Criminal Intelligence Training Standards for Law Enforcement and Other Criminal Justice Agencies in the United States.* October 2007. Accessed February 28, 2015. https://it.ojp.gov/gist/108/Minimum-Criminal-Intelligence-Training-Standards.

23. National Initiative for Cybersecurity Education. *A Glossary of Common Cybersecurity Terminology.* n.d. Accessed March 5, 2015. http://niccs.us-cert.gov/glossary.

24. Ministry of Defense. *Captured Persons (CPERS).* Joint Doctrine Publication 1-10, 3rd edition, January 2015. Accessed February 3, 2016. https://www.gov.uk/government/uploads/system/uploads/attachment_data/file/455589/20150820-JDP_1_10_Ed_3_Ch_1_Secured.pdf.

W

WAIVED SPECIAL ACCESS PROGRAM (SAP) 1. An unacknowledged Special Access Program (SAP) to which access is extremely limited in accordance with the statutory authority of Section 119e of 10 United States Code (U.S.C), Reference b. The unacknowledged SAP protections also apply to Waived SAPs. Only the chairman, senior minority member, and, by agreement, their staff directors of the four Congressional Defense Committees normally have access to program material.[1] 2. A SAP for which the Secretary of Defense has waived applicable reporting in accordance with Reference (c; Section 119 of title 10, United States Code) following a determination of adverse effect to national security. An unacknowledged SAP that has more restrictive reporting and access controls.[2]

WALK-IN AGENT (WALK-IN) A person who on his or her own initiative makes contact with a representative of a foreign country and volunteers intelligence information and/or requests asylum in exchange for information.[3]

WAR CRIME "War crime" means any conduct—(1) defined as a grave breach in any of the international conventions signed at Geneva 12 August 1949, or any protocol to such convention to which the United States is a party; (2) prohibited by Article 23, 25, 27, or 28 of the Annex to the Hague Convention IV, Respecting the Laws and Customs of War on Land, signed 18 October 1907; (3) which constitutes a grave breach of common Article 3 (as defined in subsection (d)) when committed in the context of and in association with an armed conflict not of an international character; or (4) of a person who, in relation to an armed conflict and contrary to the provisions of the Protocol on Prohibitions or Restrictions on the Use of Mines, Booby-Traps and Other Devices as amended at Geneva on 3 May 1996 (Protocol II as amended on 3 May 1996), when the United States is a party to such Protocol, willfully kills or causes serious injury to civilians.[4]

WAR POWERS RESOLUTION The War Powers Resolution P.L. 93-148 was passed over the veto of President Nixon on November 7, 1973, to provide procedures for Congress and the president to participate in decisions to send

U.S. Armed Forces into hostilities. Section 4(a)(1) requires the president to report to Congress any introduction of U.S. forces into hostilities or imminent hostilities. When such a report is submitted, or is required to be submitted, Section 5(b) requires that the use of forces must be terminated within 60 to 90 days unless Congress authorizes such use or extends the time period. Section 3 requires that the "President in every possible instance shall consult with Congress before introducing" U.S. Armed Forces into hostilities or imminent hostilities . . . The reports submitted by the president since enactment of the War Powers Resolution cover a range of military activities, from embassy evacuations to full-scale combat military operations, such as the Persian Gulf conflict, and the 2003 war with Iraq, the intervention in Kosovo, and the anti-terrorism actions in Afghanistan.[5]

WARDEN SYSTEM An informal method of communication used to pass information to U.S. citizens during emergencies.[6]

WARHEAD That part of a missile, projectile, torpedo, rocket, or other munition that contains either the nuclear or thermonuclear system, high-explosive system, chemical or biological agents, or inert materials intended to inflict damage.[7]

WARN EXPOSED Vulnerability of friendly forces to nuclear weapon effects in which personnel are assumed to be in a position that all skin is covered with minimal thermal protection provided by a "two-layer summer uniform." However, the term has been used as a pejorative to indicate a victim's false sense of security and insulation from a perceived threat.[8] *See* UNWARNED EXPOSED; WARN PROTECTED

WARN PROTECTED Vulnerability of friendly forces to nuclear weapon effects in which personnel are assumed to be in a position protected against heat, blast, and radiation afforded in closed armored vehicles or crouched in foxholes with improvised overhead shielding. However, the term has been used as a pejorative to indicate a victim's false sense of security and insulation from a perceived threat.[9] *See* UNWARNED EXPOSED; WARN EXPOSED

WARNING A notification of impending activities that may adversely affect U.S. national security interests or military forces. For the U.S. intelligence community, it is those measures taken, and the intelligence information produced, by the intelligence community to avoid surprise to the president, the NSC, and the armed forces of the United States by foreign events of major importance to the security of the United States. It includes strategic but not tactical warning.[10]

WARNING OF ATTACK A warning to national policymakers that an adversary not only is preparing its armed forces for war but also intends to launch an attack in the near future. According to Presidential Decision Directive 63, which discusses the newly formed National Infrastructure Protection Center (NIPC), "All executive departments and agencies shall cooperate with the NIPC and provide such assistance, information and advice that the NIPC may request, to the extent permitted by law. All executive departments shall also share with the NIPC information about threats and warning of attacks and about actual attacks on critical government and private sector infrastructures, to the extent permitted by law."[11] *See* WARNING OF WAR

WARNING OF WAR A warning to national policymakers that a state or alliance intends war or is on a course that substantially increases the risks of war and is taking steps to prepare for war. "The 1938 Nazi Party Congress put the might of Hitler's fearsome Wehrmacht on full display to the world and made clear what a forceful hold the Fuhrer had on his people. Delivering his fiery speeches to the well-rehearsed formations, he gave Europe an implicit warning of war which would erupt one year later."[12] *See* WARNING OF ATTACK

WARRANTLESS SURVEILLANCE Electronic surveillance without a court order.[13] *See* PRESIDENT'S SURVEILLANCE PROGRAM

WARNING CENTER A site where strategic intelligence assessments are made in support to, and as a part of, a larger warning system.[14] *See* ALERT CENTER; INDICATIONS CENTER; WATCH CENTER

WARNING DAY (W-DAY) The day on which the intelligence community judges that a potential adversary's preparations (political, economic, and military) suggest that a decision to initiate hostilities occurred. This term may also be used to designate a specific day when conditions represent a growing threat.[15]

WARNING FAILURE An unanticipated action, event, or decision by a foreign leader that results in detrimental consequences to another nation's national security; often related to the failure to forecast events before they happen. Not all warning failures are solely the responsibility of the intelligence community. Intelligence is used to influence decisions that may result in a specific action. Although a policymaker may receive intelligence that a specific act will likely occur, the policymaker may not implement preventative action. In 1997, concerned about proposed cuts in the National Weather Service budget, a group of meteorologists noted: "While nobody can specifically identify when and where a warning will fail, we can say, with assurance, that the risk of warning failure is now substantially increased. As maintenance of critical equipment degrades because of a lack of personnel and spare parts, the chances of failure increase. As meteorologists and other professionals are eliminated, or positions remain vacant, the forecast and warning load on those that remain becomes excessive."[16] *See* INTELLIGENCE FAILURE

WARNING INTELLIGENCE 1. Notice that something urgent might happen that may require immediate attention; an intelligence product on which to base a notification of impending activities on the part of foreign powers, including hostilities, which may adversely affect military forces or security interests.[17] 2. Those intelligence activities intended to detect and report time-sensitive intelligence information on foreign developments that forewarn of hostile actions or intention against U.S. entities, partners, or interests.[18] *See* COMBAT INTELLIGENCE; CURRENT INTELLIGENCE; ESTIMATIVE INTELLIGENCE; RESEARCH INTELLIGENCE; SCIENTIFIC AND TECHNICAL INTELLIGENCE

WARNING INTELLIGENCE APPRAISAL 1. An in-depth analysis and assessment prepared, printed, and disseminated on an urgent basis whenever a short assessment of imminent development is of considerable interest to high-level officials. 2. An alerting document on a developing intelligence and warning situation.[19]

WARNING JUDGMENT A forecast of the anticipated course of action that a threat will take; an appraisal of a future course of anticipated events or estimate of the likelihood (probability) of occurrence of a current or potential threat.[20]

WARNING LEAD TIME (WLT) 1. A point in time deemed necessary to adequately prepare prior to an attack or an outbreak of hostilities.[21] 2. The time between the receipt of warning and the beginning of hostilities. This time may include two action periods: warning pre-decision time and warning post-decision time. *See* STRATEGIC WARNING LEAD TIME; STRATEGIC WARNING POST-DECISION TIME; STRATEGIC WARNING PRE-DECISION TIME

WARNING NET A communications system established for the purpose of disseminating warning information of enemy movements to all affected commands.[22]

WARNING ORDER A preliminary notice of an order or an action that is to follow; designed to give subordinates time to make the necessary plans and preparations; commonly referred to as a "heads up" notice. According to some Department of Defense documents, this term may also refer to "a crisis action planning directive" issued by the chair of the Joint Chiefs of Staff that "initiates the development and evaluation of courses of action by a supported commander and requests that a commander's estimate be submitted."[23]

WARNING PARADOX *See* PARADOX OF WARNING

WARNING PROBLEM An identified potential threat that when translated into threat scenarios postulates a sequence of events that, when this process is completed, represents an unambiguous threat.[24]

WARNING SYNTHESIS 1. The building of a plausible threat model from specific (indications intelligence) facts and opinions and the development of a warning judgment based on this threat model.[25] 2. An inductive process wherein the warning judgment on the threat model is refined as new intelligence becomes available or when the validity of existing intelligence options is upgraded.

WARNING SYSTEMS Arrangements to rapidly disseminate information concerning imminent disaster threats to government officials, institutions, and the population at large in the areas at immediate risk.[26]

WARNING THRESHOLD A level of activity, specific actions, or decisions by key personnel that result in the implementation of a heightened sense of awareness and action.[27]

WARNING TIME 1. The time between the receipt of a warning and the beginning of hostilities.[28] 2. In NATO usage, the time between recognition by a major NATO commander or higher NATO authority that an attack is impending and the start of the attack.[29] *See* PREPARATION TIME; WARNING LEAD TIME

WASH FAX A secure fax system intended for use within the Washington, DC, Beltway.

WATCH CENTER A location for the review of all incoming intelligence information and which possesses, or has access to, extensive communications for alerting local intelligence personnel and contacting appropriate external reporting sources and other nodes in the indications and warning system.[30] *See* ALERT CENTER; INDICATIONS CENTER; WARNING CENTER

WATCH CONDITION (WATCHCON) 1. An operational and intelligence alerting mechanism and shorthand expression of the reporting organization's degree of intelligence concern regarding a particular warning problem. Often confused with defense condition (DEFCON) and threat condition (THREAT-CON).[31] 2. Intelligence interest and concern relative to the potential outlined in a warning problem. A warning problem for a country or region is a set of detectable events that might lead to a crisis and threaten U.S. citizens, interests, and operating forces. WATCHCON IV is defined as a "potential threat," WATCHCON III is "increased threat," WATCHCON II is "significant threat," and WATCHCON I is "clear immediate threat." For example, "Both DIA and CENTCOM had established the Iraq regional warning problem and assumed watch condition (WATCHCON) level IV in April 1990. DIA raised its WATCHCON to level III on 21 July and to level II on 24 July based on the concentration of Iraqi troops on the Kuwaiti border and the failure of diplomatic initiatives. DIA declared WATCHCON level I on 1 August, the first time any command or agency had assumed this highest level watch condition in advance of a conflict."[32] *See* DEFENSE CONDITION; THREAT CONDITION

WATCH LIST A list of words—such as names, entities, or phrases—which can be employed by a computer to select out required information from a mass of data.[33]

WATCH OFFICER A person in the command's intelligence element trained to identify indications of hostilities and to cope with other intelligence that requires immediate attention; a senior officer who is the duty representative of the commander in intelligence matters.[34]

WEAPONEERING The process of determining the quantity of a specific type of lethal or nonlethal weapon required to achieve a specific level of damage to a given target. It considers target vulnerability, weapon effect, munitions, delivery accuracy, damage criteria, probability of kill, and weapon reliability.[35]

WEAPONS OF MASS DESTRUCTION (WMD) 1. Any nuclear, biological, or chemical weapons. 2. Under U.S. law, any weapons or devices that are intended, or have the capability, to cause death or serious bodily injury to a significant number of people through the release, dissemination, or impact of toxic or poisonous chemicals or their precursors, a disease organism, or radiation or radioactivity.[36]

WEAPONS OF MASS DESTRUCTION INFORMATION The term "weapons of mass destruction information" means information that could reasonably be expected to assist in the development, proliferation, or use of a weapon of mass destruction (including a chemical, biological, radiological, or nuclear weapon) that could be used by a terrorist organization against the United States, including information about the location of any stockpile of nuclear materials that could be exploited for use in such a weapon that could be used by a terrorist or a terrorist organization against the United States.[37] *See* TERRORISM INFORMATION

WEAPONS OF MASS DESTRUCTION OR EFFECT (WMD/E) WMD/E relates to a broad range of adversary capabilities that pose potentially devastating impacts. WMD/E includes chemical, biological, radiological, nuclear, and enhanced high-explosive weapons as well as other, more asymmetrical "weapons." They may rely more on disruptive impact than destructive kinetic effects. For example, cyberattacks on U.S. commercial information systems or attacks against transportation networks may have a greater economic or psychological effect than a relatively small release of a lethal agent.[38]

WEAPONS OF MASS DESTRUCTION PROLIFERATION The transfer of weapons of mass destruction or related materials, technology, and expertise from suppliers to state or non-state actors.[39]

WEB PRESENCE Any information available on the Internet about an individual which is also under the control of that individual.[40]

WHITE LIST The identities and locations of individuals who have been identified as being of intelligence or counterintelligence interest and are expected to be able to provide information or assistance in existing or new intelligence areas of interest.[41]

WHITE TEAM 1. The group responsible for refereeing an engagement between a Red Team of mock attackers and a Blue Team of actual defenders of their enterprise's use of information systems. In an exercise, the White Team acts as the judges, enforces the rules of the exercise, observes the exercise, scores teams, resolves any problems that may arise, handles all requests for information or questions, and ensures that the competition runs fairly and does not cause operational problems for the defender's mission.

The White Team helps to establish the rules of engagement, the metrics for assessing results and the procedures for providing operational security for the engagement. The White Team normally has responsibility for deriving lessons learned, conducting the post engagement assessment, and promulgating results. 2. Can also refer to a small group of people who have prior knowledge of unannounced Red Team activities. The White Team acts as observers during the Red Team activity and ensures the scope of testing does not exceed a pre-defined threshold.[42]

WHOLE COMMUNITY An approach to emergency management that reinforces the fact that FEMA is only one part of our nation's emergency management team. We must leverage all of the resources of our collective team in preparing for, protecting against, responding to, recovering from and mitigating against all hazards; and collectively we must meet the needs of the entire community in each of these areas.[43]

WILLINGNESS-TO-ACCEPT Amount a person is willing to accept to forgo a benefit.[44]

WILLINGNESS-TO-PAY Amount a person would be willing to pay, sacrifice, or exchange for a benefit.[45]

WISDOM WARFARE A cognitive process that has three main components: knowledge, which includes systems that collect raw data, organize it into useful information, analyze it to create intelligence, and assimilate it to gain knowledge; wisdom contains those systems that allow humans to interact with the knowledge to exercise wisdom, which includes modeling and simulation tools; Human System Integration, or HIS, contains all of the systems necessary to assist decision makers in getting the information needed in the form desired. Once the decision makers understand the information, they can apply experience to make the best decisions.[46]

WORK CATEGORIES Common types of work (i.e., Technician/Administrative Support, Professional, and Supervision/Management). ICD 652 (*Occupational Structure for the Intelligence Community Civilian Workforce*, April 28, 2008) describes work categories for the IC.[47]

WORK LEVELS General standards that define work in terms of increasing complexity, span of authority/responsibility, level of supervision (received or exercised), scope and impact of decisions, and work relationships associated with a particular work category. ICD 652 (*Occupational Structure for the*

Intelligence Community Civilian Workforce, April 28, 2008) describes work levels for the IC.[48]

WORKING FILES (WORKING PAPERS) Documents such as rough notes, calculations, or drafts assembled or created and used to prepare or analyze other documents.[49]

WORKING PAPERS *See* WORKING FILES

WORM A self-replicating, self-propagating, self-contained computer program that uses networking mechanisms to spread itself.

WOUNDED IN ACTION A battle casualty other than "killed in action" who has incurred an injury due to an external agent or cause. The term encompasses all kinds of wounds and other injuries incurred in action: penetrating or perforated wounds, contused wounds, fractures, burns, blast concussions, effects of biological and chemical warfare agents, effects of exposure to ionizing radiation or any other destructive weapon or agent.

WRITE FOR MAXIMUM UTILITY (WMU) An approach that guides the way that intelligence organizations conceive, format, produce, and disseminate intelligence products in order to increase their usability for the intended customers. Utility is maximized when customers receive or are able to expeditiously discover and pull or request intelligence, information, and analysis in a form they are able to easily use and able to share with their colleagues, subordinates, and superiors. WMU ensures intelligence, information, and analysis are produced in a manner to facilitate reuse—either in its entirety or in coherent portions—thereby enabling wider dissemination and enhancing its usability. WMU shares certain goals as well as techniques with previous and ongoing IC WTR efforts. WMU and WTR do, however, differ in important ways. WMU goes farther than WTR in linking knowledge of the customer's operating environment to the intelligence production effort. The resulting effort is not "one size fits all" or production of all intelligence products at the lowest classification, but products tailored to best meet a customer's requirements. This may mean producing the definitive assessment on a given topic area based on all available intelligence, regardless of classification.[50]

WRITE-PROTECT A term used to indicate that there is a machine hardware capability which may be manually used to protect some storage media from accidental or unintentional overwrite by inhibiting the write capability of the system.[51]

WRITE-TO-RELEASE 1. A general approach whereby intelligence reports are written in such a way that sources and methods are disguised so that the report can be distributed to customers or intelligence partners at lower security levels. In essence, write-to-release is proactive sanitization that makes intelligence more readily available to a more diverse set of customers. The term encompasses a number of specific implementation approaches, including sanitized leads and tearline reporting.[52] 2. Refers to writing intelligence reports to disguise sources and methods in order to enable distribution to customers or intelligence partners at lower security levels. It is a proactive sanitization that makes intelligence more readily available to a more diverse set of customers.[53] *See* SANITIZATION; TEAR LINE

NOTES

1. U.S. Department of Defense, Center for Development of Security Excellence. *Glossary of Security Terms and Definitions.* November 2012. Accessed March 1, 2015. http://www.cdse.edu/documents/cdse/Glossary_Handbook.pdf.

2. U.S. Department of Defense. *Special Access Program (SAP) Policy.* DoD Directive Number 5205.07, July 1, 2010. Accessed March 1, 2015. http://www.dtic.mil/whs/directives/corres/pdf/520507p.pdf.

3. Defense Intelligence Agency, Office of Counterintelligence. *CI Glossary— Terms & Definitions of Interest for DoD CI Professionals.* July 2014. Accessed February 28, 2015. https://www.hsdl.org/?view&did=699056.

4. 18 U.S. Code § 2441—"War Crimes" (Current through Pub. L. 113-234). https://www.law.cornell.edu/uscode/text/18/2441.

5. Weed, Matthew C. "The War Powers Resolution: Concepts and Practice." *CRS Report for Congress* R42699, April 3, 2015. Accessed April 15, 2015. http://www.fas.org/sgp/crs/natsec/R42699.pdf.

6. U.S. Department of Defense. *Dictionary of Military and Associated Terms.* JP 1-02, 08 November 2010, as Amended through 15 March 2015. Accessed June 4, 2015. http://www.dtic.mil/doctrine/dod_dictionary/.

7. North Atlantic Treaty Organization. 2005. *NATO Intelligence, Surveillance and Reconnaissance Interoperability Architecture.* Accessed June 5, 2015. http://www.nato.int/structur/ac/224/standard/aedp2/aedp2_documents/aedp-02v1.pdf.

8. Jan Goldman, *Intelligence Warning Terminology*, Joint Military Intelligence College, October 2001, accessed July 3, 2015. https://archive.org/details/JMICIntelligencelwarnterminology.

9. Jan Goldman, *Intelligence Warning Terminology*, Joint Military Intelligence College, October 2001, accessed July 3, 2015. https://archive.org/details/JMICIntelligencelwarnterminology.

10. Central Intelligence Agency. *National Intelligence Warning.* DCI Directive No. 1/5, May 23, 1979. Accessed June 5, 2015. http://fas.org./irp/offdocs/dcid1-5.html.

11. Dick, Ronald L. *Issue of Intrusions into Government Computer Networks.* Testimony, House Energy and Commerce Committee, Oversight and Investigation Subcommittee, April 5, 2001. Accessed June 5, 2015. http://www.fbi.gov/news/testimony/issue-of-intrusions-into-government-computer-networks.

12. World War II Nazi Rally photograph (quotation), Electric Library Plus, as cited in Jan Goldman, *Intelligence Warning Terminology*, Joint Military Intelligence College, October 2001, accessed July 3, 2015. https://archive.org/details/JMICInteligencelwarnterminology.

13. 50 U.S. Code § 1802—"Electronic Surveillance Authorization without Court Order" (Current through Pub. L. 113-234). Accessed February 18, 2015. http://www.law.cornell.edu/uscode/text/50/1802. Bazan, Elizabeth B. and Elsea, Jennifer K. "Presidential Authority to Conduct Warrantless Electronic Surveillance to Gather Foreign Intelligence Information." *Congressional Research Memorandum.* January 5, 2006. Accessed February 18, 2015. http://www.fas.org/sgp/crs/intel/m010506.pdf.

14. Jan Goldman, *Intelligence Warning Terminology*, Joint Military Intelligence College, October 2001, accessed July 3, 2015. https://archive.org/details/JMICInteligencelwarnterminology.

15. Jan Goldman, *Intelligence Warning Terminology*, Joint Military Intelligence College, October 2001, accessed July 3, 2015. https://archive.org/details/JMICInteligencelwarnterminology.

16. Atlas, David, et al. "Past Presidents of AMS Voice Concern about Cuts in the National Weather Service Budget." *American Meteorological Society Newsletter* 18, no. 4 (1997): 1. Accessed June 5, 2015. http://wayback.archive.org/web/20000311070340/http://atm.geo.nsf.gov/AMS/newsltr/nl_4_97.html#PAST.

17. Watson, Bruce W., Watson, Susan, and Hopple, Gerald W. *United States Intelligence: An Encyclopedia.* New York: Garland, 1990. 594.

18. U.S. Department of Defense. *Joint Intelligence.* JP 2-0. October 22, 2013. Accessed February 15, 2015. http://www.dtic.mil/doctrine/new_pubs/jp2_0.pdf.

19. Watson, Bruce W., Watson, Susan, and Hopple, Gerald W. *United States Intelligence: An Encyclopedia* (New York: Garland, 1990), 594.

20. Jan Goldman, *Intelligence Warning Terminology*, Joint Military Intelligence College, October 2001, accessed July 3, 2015. https://archive.org/details/JMICInteligencelwarnterminology.

21. Jan Goldman, *Intelligence Warning Terminology*, Joint Military Intelligence College, October 2001, accessed July 3, 2015. https://archive.org/details/JMICInteligencelwarnterminology.

22. Jan Goldman, *Intelligence Warning Terminology*, Joint Military Intelligence College, October 2001, accessed July 3, 2015. https://archive.org/details/JMICInteligencelwarnterminology.

23. Jan Goldman, *Intelligence Warning Terminology*, Joint Military Intelligence College, October 2001, accessed July 3, 2015. https://archive.org/details/JMICInteligencelwarnterminology.

24. Jan Goldman, *Intelligence Warning Terminology*, Joint Military Intelligence College, October 2001, accessed July 3, 2015. https://archive.org/details/JMICInteligencelwarnterminology.

25. Jan Goldman, *Intelligence Warning Terminology*, Joint Military Intelligence College, October 2001, accessed July 3, 2015. https://archive.org/details/JMICInteligencelwarnterminology.

26. Jan Goldman, *Intelligence Warning Terminology*, Joint Military Intelligence College, October 2001, accessed July 3, 2015. https://archive.org/details/JMICInteligencelwarnterminology.

27. Jan Goldman, *Intelligence Warning Terminology*, Joint Military Intelligence College, October 2001, accessed July 3, 2015. https://archive.org/details/JMICInteligencelwarnterminology.

28. Jan Goldman, *Intelligence Warning Terminology*, Joint Military Intelligence College, October 2001, accessed July 3, 2015. https://archive.org/details/JMICInteligencelwarnterminology.

29. North Atlantic Treaty Organization. *N2-02 NATO Intelligence Course*. Accessed June 5, 2015. http://www.natoschool.nato.int/Academics/Resident-Courses/Course-Catalogue/Course-description?ID=3.

30. Jan Goldman, *Intelligence Warning Terminology*, Joint Military Intelligence College, October 2001, accessed July 3, 2015. https://archive.org/details/JMICInteligencelwarnterminology.

31. Jan Goldman, *Intelligence Warning Terminology*, Joint Military Intelligence College, October 2001, accessed July 3, 2015. https://archive.org/details/JMICInteligencelwarnterminology.

32. Shellum, Brian G. *Defense Intelligence Crisis Response Procedures and the Gulf War*. Defense Intelligence Agency. Accessed June 5, 2015. http://nsarchive.gwu.edu/NSAEBB/NSAEBB39/document14.pdf.

33. United States Senate, Select Committee to Study Governmental Operations with Respect to Intelligence Activities (Church Committee). *Final Report.* Book 1. April 26, 1976. Accessed February 24, 2015. https://archive.org/details/finalreportof-sel01unit.

34. Jan Goldman, *Intelligence Warning Terminology*, Joint Military Intelligence College, October 2001, accessed July 3, 2015. https://archive.org/details/JMICInteligencelwarnterminology.

35. U.S. Department of Defense. *Dictionary of Military and Associated Terms.* JP 1-02, 08 November 2010, as Amended through 15 March 2015. Accessed June 4, 2015. http://www.dtic.mil/doctrine/dod_dictionary/.

36. 50 U.S. Code § 2302—"Definitions." Accessed June 5, 2015. https://www.law.cornell.edu/uscode/text/50/2302.

37. *Intelligence Reform and Terrorism Prevention Act* P.L.108-458, 118 STAT. 3638. December 17, 2004. Accessed February 15, 2015. http://www.gpo.gov/fdsys/pkg/PLAW-108publ458/pdf/PLAW-108publ458.pdf.

38. Chairman of the Joint Chiefs of Staff. *National Military Strategic Plan for the War on Terrorism.* February 1, 2006. Accessed February 26, 2015. http://www.defense.gov/qdr/docs/2006-02-08-Strategic-Plan.pdf.

39. United States Department of Defense. *Countering Weapons of Mass Destruction.* JP 3-40, October 31, 2014. Accessed March 7, 2015. http://www.dtic.mil/doctrine/new_pubs/jp3_40.pdf.

40. Rose, Andrée, Timm, Howard, Pogson, Corrie, Gonzalez, Jose, Appel, Edward, and Kolb, Nancy. *Developing a Cybervetting Strategy for Law Enforcement.* Defense Personnel Security Research Center, U.S. Department of Defense, December 2010. Accessed January 17, 2015. http://www.dhra.mil/perserec/reports/pp11-02.pdf.

41. Defense Intelligence Agency, Office of Counterintelligence. *CI Glossary—Terms & Definitions of Interest for DoD CI Professionals.* July 2014. Accessed February 28, 2015. https://www.hsdl.org/?view&did=699056.

42. Committee for National Security Systems (CNSS). Instruction 4009. *National Information Assurance Glossary.* April 2010. Accessed March 1, 2015. http://www.ncix.gov/publications/policy/docs/CNSSI_4009.pdf.

43. Department of Homeland Security. *Threat and Hazard Identification and Risk Assessment Guide Comprehensive Preparedness Guide (CPG).* 2nd ed., August 2013. Accessed March 5, 2015. http://www.fema.gov/media-library-data/8ca0a9e54dc8b03 7a55b402b2a269e94/CPG201_htirag_2nd_edition.pdf.

44. Department of Homeland Security, Risk Steering Committee. *DHS Risk Lexicon.* September 2010. Accessed February 14, 2015. http://www.dhs.gov/dhs-risk-lexicon.

45. Department of Homeland Security, Risk Steering Committee. *DHS Risk Lexicon.* September 2010. Accessed February 14, 2015. http://www.dhs.gov/dhs-risk-lexicon.

46. Murphy, Edward F., Bender, Gary C., Schaefer, Larry J., Shepard, Michael M. and Williamson, Charles W., III. *Information Operations: Wisdom Warfare For 2025: A Research Paper Presented to Air Force 2025.* April 1996. Accessed June 5, 2015. http://www.fas.org/spp/military/docops/usaf/2025/v1c1/v1c1-1.htm#CONTENTS.

47. Office of the Director of National Intelligence. *Competency Directories for the Intelligence Community Workforce.* Intelligence Community Directive 610, October 4, 2010. Accessed March 2, 2015. http://www.dni.gov/files/documents/ICD/ICD_610.pdf.

48. Office of the Director of National Intelligence. *Competency Directories for the Intelligence Community Workforce.* Intelligence Community Directive 610, October 4, 2010. Accessed March 2, 2015. http://www.dni.gov/files/documents/ICD/ICD_610.pdf.

49. Department of Energy. *Records Management Definitions.* Accessed June 5, 2015. https://www.emcbc.doe.gov/msd/definitions.php#W.

50. Office of the Director of National Intelligence. *Writing for Maximum Utility.* Intelligence Community Directive 208, December 17, 2008. Accessed January 24, 2015. http://www.dni.gov/files/documents/ICD/icd_208.pdf.

51. U.S. Department of Defense, Center for Development of Security Excellence. *Glossary of Security Terms and Definitions.* November 2012. Accessed March 1, 2015. http://www.cdse.edu/documents/cdse/Glossary_Handbook.pdf.

52. Central Intelligence Agency. *Intelligence Community Policy on Intelligence Sharing.* Director of Central Intelligence Directive 8/1, June 4, 2004. Accessed June 5, 2015. http://fas.org/irp/offdocs/dcid8-1.html.

53. Office of the Director of National Intelligence. *Glossary of Security Terms, Definitions, and Acronyms.* Intelligence Community Standard (ICS) 700-1. April 4, 2008. Accessed June 5, 2015. https://fas.org/irp/dni/icd/ics-700-1.pdf.

XKEYSCORE A top secret National Security Agency program allows analysts to search with no prior authorization through vast databases containing emails, online chats and the browsing histories of millions of individuals, according to documents provided by whistleblower Edward Snowden. XKeyscore, the documents boast, is the NSA's "widest reaching" system developing intelligence from computer networks—what the agency calls Digital Network Intelligence (DNI). One presentation claims the program covers "nearly everything a typical user does on the internet," including the content of emails, websites visited and searches, as well as their metadata.[1]

X-SCALE On an oblique photograph, the scale along a line parallel to the true horizon.[2] *See* Y-SCALE; Z-SCALE

NOTES

1. Greenwald, Glenn. "XKeyscore: NSA Tool Collects 'Nearly Everything a User Does on the Internet.'" *The Guardian*, July 31, 2013. Accessed February 18, 2015. http://www.theguardian.com/world/2013/jul/31/nsa-top-secret-program-online-data.
2. North Atlantic Treaty Organization. *NATO Glossary of Terms and Definitions*. NATO Standardization Agency, 2014, AAP-06, accessed July 27, 2015, http://nso.nato.int/nso/zPublic/ap/aap6/AAP-6.pdf.

Y-SCALE On an oblique photograph, the scale along the line of the principal vertical, or any other line inherent or plotted, which, on the ground, is parallel to the principal vertical.[1] *See* X-SCALE; Z-SCALE

YANKEE WHITE A rigorous, special security investigation and background check for military personnel working with the president. The 89 U.S. Air Force Security Police Squadron administers the Yankee White clearance program.[2]

YES/NO WARNING A theoretical system that would provide a clear understanding for intelligence services to tell them that there will either be an attack or not, so that appropriate counter-mobilization actions can be taken or not taken. However, a warning system that removes all uncertainty from the decision-making process is not realistic. While there will inevitably be indications of an enemy's intention to attack, these can be lost in the noise of contrary or ambiguous indications. Mostly, successful surprise attacks occur "not out of the blue, but out of a murky grey which did not fit well into the Yes/No warning model."[3]

YOM KIPPUR WAR (ARAB-ISRAELI WAR) On October 6, 1973, which was Yom Kippur, a day of fasting and the holiest day in the Jewish calendar, Egypt and Syria opened a coordinated surprise attack against Israel. On the Golan Heights, approximately 180 Israeli tanks faced 1,400 Syrian tanks; fewer than 500 Israeli troops were attacked by 80,000 Egyptians along the Suez Canal. Israel mobilized its reserves and eventually defended itself by taking the war deep into Syria and Egypt. The Arab states were resupplied by sea and air from the Soviet Union, which rejected U.S. efforts to work toward an immediate cease-fire. As a result, the United States belatedly began its own airlift to Israel. Two weeks later, Egypt was saved from a disastrous defeat by UN Security Council Resolution 338 calling for "all parties to the present fighting to cease all firing and terminate all military activity immediately." For many participants, the war was a diplomatic and military failure as well as an intelligence failure.

NOTES

1. North Atlantic Treaty Organization. *NATO Glossary of Terms and Definitions.* NATO Standardization Agency, 2014, AAP-06, accessed July 27, 2015, http://nso. nato.int/nso/zPublic/ap/aap6/AAP-6.pdf.

2. Global Security.org. *Weapons of Mass Destruction: The Football.* Accessed June 5, 2015. http://www.globalsecurity.org/wmd/systems/nuclear-football.htm.

3. Brody, Richard. "The Limits of Warning." *Washington Quarterly* 6, no. 3 (1983): 40–48.

Z

Z-SCALE On an oblique photograph, the scale used in calculating the height of an object; the name given to this method of height determination.[1] *See* X-SCALE; Y-SCALE

ZOMBIE A computer program that is installed on a system to cause it to attack other systems.

ZONE OF ACTION A tactical subdivision of a larger area, the responsibility of which is assigned to a tactical unit; generally applied to offensive action.

ZONING A method of surveillance in which the surveillance area is divided into zones, and surveillants are assigned to cover a specific zone.

ZULU TIME *See* UNIVERSAL TIME

NOTE

1. North Atlantic Treaty Organization. *NATO Glossary of Terms and Definitions*. NATO Standardization Agency, 2014, AAP-06, accessed July 27, 2015, http://nso.nato.int/nso/zPublic/ap/aap6/AAP-6.pdf.

Bibliography

Aftergood, Steven. "A Growing Body of Secret Intelligence Law." *Secrecy News*, May 4, 2015. Accessed January 11, 2016. https://fas.org/blogs/secrecy/2015/05/secret-intel-law/.

Almond, Gabriel A. "Public Opinion and National Security Policy." *Public Opinion Quarterly* 20, no. 2 (1956): 371–78.

Bagehot, Walter. *The English Constitution and Other Political Essays.* New York: Appleton and Company, 1895.

Barley, Stephen R., and Pamela S. Tolbert. "Institutionalization and Structuration: Studying the Links between Action and Institution." *Organization Studies* 18, no. 1 (1997): 93–117.

Behavioural Insights Team. *About Us.* Cabinet Office, 2016. Accessed February 2, 2016. http://www.behaviouralinsights.co.uk/about-us/.

Berger, Peter and Thomas Luckmann. *The Social Construction of Reality: A Treatise in the Sociology of Knowledge.* New York: Anchor Books, 1967.

Blau, Peter M., and Marshall W. Meyer. *Bureaucracy in Modern Society.* New York: Random House, 1971.

Bolinger, Dwight. *Language, the Loaded Weapon: The Use and Abuse of Language Today.* New York: Longman, 1980.

Braman, Sandra. "Defining Information Policy." *Journal of Information Policy* 1 (2011): 1–5.

Braman, Sandra. "Horizons of the State: Information Policy and Power." *Journal of Communication* 45, no. 4 (1995): 4–24.

Brubaker, Rogers. *The Limits of Rationality: An Essay on the Social and Moral Thought of Max Weber.* Boston: Allen & Unwin, 1984.

Butcher, David, and Sally Atkinson. "Stealth, Secrecy and Subversion: The Language of Change." *Journal of Organizational Change Management* 14, no. 6 (2001): 554–69.

Carus, W. Seth. *Defining Weapons of Mass Destruction.* National Defense University, Center for the Study of Weapons of Mass Destruction, ADA577317, 2012. Accessed December 15, 2015. http://oai.dtic.mil/oai/oai?verb=getRecord&metadataPrefix=html&identifier=ADA577317.

Commission on Protecting and Reducing Government Secrecy. *Report of the Commission on Protecting and Reducing Government Secrecy: Pursuant to Public Law 236, 103rd Congress.* Washington, DC: Government Printing Office,

1997. Accessed December 29, 2015. http://www.gpo.gov/fdsys/pkg/GPO-CDOC-105sdoc2/content-detail.html.

Conley, John M., and William M. O'Barr. *Just Words: Law, Language, and Power.* Chicago: University of Chicago Press, 2005.

Cowan, Geoffrey, and Nicholas J. Cull. "Preface: Public Diplomacy in a Changing World." *Annals of the American Academy of Political and Social Science* 616 (2008): 6–8.

Cripp, Robert. "Introduction: Parapolitics, State Governance, and Criminal Sovereignty." In *Government of the Shadows: Parapolitics and Criminal Sovereignty*, edited by Eric Wilson, 1–9. New York: Pluto Press, 2009.

De Beaugrande, Robert. "Critical Discourse Analysis from the Perspective of Ecologism: The Discourse of the 'New Patriotism' for the 'New Secrecy.'" *Critical Discourse Studies* 1, no. 1 (2004): 113–45.

Defense Security Service, Center for Security Excellence. *Glossary of Security Terms, Definitions, and Acronyms.* November 2012. Accessed November 29, 2015. http://www.cdse.edu/documents/cdse/Glossary_Handbook.pdf.

Department of Homeland Security, Risk Steering Committee. *DHS Risk Lexicon.* September 2010. Accessed February 14, 2016. http://www.dhs.gov/dhs-risk-lexicon.

DeVolpi, A., G. E. Marsh, T. A. Postol, and G. S. Stanford. *Born Secret: The H-Bomb, the Progressive Case and National Security.* New York: Pergamon Press, 1981.

Domestic Council Committee on the Right of Privacy. *National Information Policy: Report to the President of the United States.* National Commission on Libraries and Information Science. Washington, DC: Government Printing Office, 1976.

Dryzek, John S. *The Politics of the Earth: Environmental Discourses.* New York: Oxford University Press, 2005.

Easton, David. *A Framework for Political Analysis.* Englewood Cliffs, NJ: Prentice-Hall, 1965.

Executive Order 10290. *Prescribing Regulations Establishing Minimum Standards for the Classification, Transmission, and Handling, by Departments and Agencies of the Executive Branch, of Official Information Which Requires Safeguarding in the Interest of the Security of the United States.* September 24, 1951. Accessed November 29, 2015. http://www.presidency.ucsb.edu/ws/index.php?pid=78426.

Executive Order 13526. *Classified National Security Information.* December 29, 2009. Accessed July 15, 2015. https://www.whitehouse.gov/the-press-office/executive-order-classified-national-security-information.

Feldman, Martha S., and James G. March. "Information in Organizations as Signal and Symbol." *Administrative Science Quarterly* 26, no. 2 (1981): 171–86.

Fleming, Matthew H., Samuel J. Brannen, Andrew G. Mosher, Bryan Altmire, Andrew Metrick, Meredith Boyle, and Richard Say. *Unmanned Systems in Homeland Security.* Center for Strategic and International Studies and Homeland Security Studies and Analysis Institute, January 2015. Accessed January 29, 2016. http://www.anser.org/Unmanned_Systems.

Flood, Dana. "How the Space Community Must Change Language and Perspective to Achieve Cross-Domain Integration and Dominance." *High Frontier* 4, no. 4 (2008): 31–34.

Foucault, Michel. *Archaeology of Knowledge and the Discourse on Language.* New York: Pantheon Books, 1972.

Foucault, Michel. *History of Sexuality: An Introduction* (vol. 1). New York: Pantheon Books, 1978.

Foucault, Michel. "Politics and the Study of Discourse." In *The Foucault Effect: Studies in Governmentality,* edited by Graham Burchell, Colin Gordon, and Peter Miller, 53–72. Chicago: University of Chicago Press, 1991.

Foucault, Michel. *Power/Knowledge: Selected Interviews and Other Writings, 1972–1977.* Pantheon, 1980.

Gibson, Walker, and William Gibson. *Doublespeak: A Brief History, Definition, and Bibliography, with a List of Award Winners, 1974–1990.* NCTE Concept Paper Series. Concept Paper No. 2. ED337802. Accessed January 29, 2016. http://eric. ed.gov/?id=ED337802.

Giddens, Anthony. *Politics, Sociology and Social Theory: Encounters with Classical and Contemporary Social Thought.* Stanford: Stanford University Press, 1995.

Glennon, Michael J. *National Security and Double Government.* New York: Oxford University Press, 2015.

Goitein, Elizabeth. "Secret Law Isn't the Public's Fault." *Just Security,* November 9, 2015. Accessed November 10, 2015. https://www.justsecurity.org/27484/secret-law-isnt-publics-fault.

Goldman, Jan. *Words of Intelligence: An Intelligence Professional's Lexicon for Domestic and Foreign Threats.* 2nd ed. Lanham, MD: Scarecrow Press, 2011.

Gouldner, Alvin W. "Contexts: Bureaucrats and Agitators." In *Studies in Leadership: Leadership and Democratic Action,* edited by Alvin W. Gouldner, 53–66. New York: Harper, 1950.

Gray, Chris Hables. *Peace, War, and Computers.* New York: Routledge, 2005.

Haas, Peter M. "Introduction: Epistemic Communities and International Policy Coordination." *International Organization* 46, no. 1 (1992): 1–35.

Halchin, L. Elaine. "The Intelligence Community and Its Use of Contractors: Congressional Oversight Issues." *CRS Report for Congress* R44157, August 18, 2015. Accessed January 11, 2016. https://www.fas.org/sgp/crs/intel/R44157.pdf.

Hall, Stuart. "Foucault, Power, Knowledge, and Discourse." In *Discourse Theory and Practice: A Reader,* edited by Margaret Wetherell, Stephanie Taylor, and Simeon J. Yates, 72–81. Thousand Oaks, CA: SAGE, 2001.

Hock, George H., Jr., "Joint Terminology: At the Heart of Doctrine." *Joint Force Quarterly* 62 (2011): 139–40. ADA546454.

Intelligence Reform and Terrorism Prevention Act of 2004, P.L.108–458, 118 STAT. 3638. December 17, 2004. Accessed February 15, 2015. http://www.gpo.gov/fdsys/pkg/PLAW-108publ458/pdf/PLAW-108publ458.pdf.

IQT. *About IQT.* Accessed February 3, 2016. https://www.iqt.org/about-iqt/.

Jackson, Henry M. "Organizing for Survival." *Foreign Affairs* 38, no. 3 (1960): 446–56.

Jenkins, Richard. "Disenchantment, Enchantment and Re-Enchantment: Max Weber at the Millennium." *Max Weber Studies* 1 (2010): 11–32.

Johnson, Loch K. *A Season of Inquiry: The Senate Intelligence Investigation.* Lexington: University Press of Kentucky, 1985.

Johnston, Rob. *Analytic Culture in the U.S. Intelligence Community: An Ethnographic Study.* Washington, DC: Center for the Study of Intelligence, Central Intelligence Agency, Government Printing Office, 2005. Accessed January 29, 2016. https://www.cia.gov.

Kent, Sherman. *Strategic Intelligence for American World Policy.* Princeton, NJ: Princeton University Press, 1950.

Keohane, Robert O. "International Institutions: Two Approaches." *International Studies Quarterly* 32, no. 4 (1988): 379–96.

Kosar, Kevin R. "Classified Information Policy and Executive Order 13526." *CRS Reports for Congress* R41528, December 10, 2010. Accessed December 15, 2015. http://fas.org/sgp/crs/secrecy/R41528.pdf.

Lecercle, Jean-Jacques. *The Violence of Language.* New York: Routledge, 1990.

Longbine, Davis F. *Red Teaming: Past and Present.* School of Advanced Military Studies, Fort Leavenworth, May 22, 2008. ADA485514. Accessed November 22, 2015. http://www.dtic.mil/get-tr-doc/pdf?AD=ADA485514.

Luhmann, Niklas. *Ecological Communication.* Translated by John Bednarz Jr. Chicago: University of Chicago Press, 1989.

Luhmann, Niklas. *Social Systems.* Translated by John Bednarz Jr. and Dirk Baecker. Stanford: Stanford University Press, 1995.

Maret, Susan. "Introduction." In *Government Secrecy, Research in Social Problems and Public Policy,* edited by Susan Maret, xi–xxx. Howard House, UK: Emerald Group Publishing, 2011.

Maret, Susan. *On Their Own Terms: A Lexicon with an Emphasis on Information-Related Terms Produced by the U.S. Federal Government.* 6th ed. 2015. Accessed February 14, 2016. http://www.fas.org/sgp/library/maret.pdf.

McCarthy, E. Doyle. *Knowledge as Culture: The New Sociology of Knowledge.* New York: Routledge, 1996.

McClure, Charles R. "Libraries and Federal Information Policy." *Journal of Academic Librarianship* 22, no. 3 (1996): 214–18.

Merton, Thomas. "War and the Crisis of Language." In *Passion for Peace: The Social Essays,* edited by William H. Shannon, 300–314. New York: Crossroad Publishing, [1969], 1995.

Mills, C. Wright. "Methodological Consequences of the Sociology of Knowledge." *American Journal of Sociology* 46, no. 3 (1940): 316–30.

Mommsen, Wolfgang T. *The Age of Bureaucracy: Perspectives on the Political Sociology of Max Weber.* New York: Harper and Row, 1974.

Morgenthau, Hans J. *The Decline of Democratic Politics (Politics in the Twentieth Century,* volume 1). Chicago: University of Chicago Press, 1962.

Mueller, Claus. *The Politics of Communication.* New York: Oxford University Press, 1973.

Nee, Victor. "Sources of the New Institutionalism." In *New Institutionalism in Sociology*, edited by Mary C. Brinton and Victor Nee, 1–16. New York: Russell Sage Foundation, 1998.

Nolan, Bridget Rose. *Information Sharing and Collaboration in the United States Intelligence Community: An Ethnographic Study of the National Counterterrorism Center*. Ph.D. diss., University of Pennsylvania, 2013.

Office of the Director of National Intelligence. *Appointment of Highly Qualified Experts*. Intelligence Community Directive 623, October 16, 2008. Accessed November 29, 2015. http://www.dni.gov/files/documents/ICD/ICD_623.pdf.

Office of the Director of National Intelligence. *Critical Information (CRITIC)*. Intelligence Community Directive 190, February 3, 2015a. Accessed July 29, 2015. http://www.dni.gov/files/documents/ICD/ICD%20190.pdf.

Office of the Director for National Intelligence. *Principles of Intelligence Transparency for the Intelligence Community Implementation Plan*. October 27, 2015b. Accessed November 19, 2015. http://www.dni.gov/index.php/newsroom/reports-and-publications/207–reports-publications-2015/1274–principles-of-intelligence-transparency-implementation-plan.

Office of the Director for National Intelligence. *Write for Maximum Utility*. Intelligence Community Directive 208, December 17, 2008. Accessed November 29, 2015. http://www.dni.gov/files/documents/ICD/icd_208.pdf.

Omand, David. "How Many Schlesingers Would It Take to Change a Light-Bulb?" *Intelligence and National Security* 24, no. 3 (2009): 418–21.

Peters, B. Guy. *Institutional Theory in Political Science: The "New Institutionalism."* New York: Continuum, 2005.

Powell, Walter W., and Paul J. DiMaggio (eds.). *The New Institutionalism in Organizational Analysis*. Chicago: University of Chicago Press, 1991.

President's Commission on Critical Infrastructure Protection. *Critical Foundations: Protecting America's Infrastructures: The Report of the President's Commission on Critical Infrastructure Protection*. Washington, DC: Government Printing Office, 1997. Accessed April 25, 2015. http://permanent.access.gpo.gov/lps15260/PCCIP_Report.pdf.

Program Manager Information Sharing Environment. *Annual Report to Congress on the Information Sharing Environment*. December 30, 2014. Accessed March 25, 2015. http://www.ise.gov/annual-report/ise-annual-report-congress-2014.

Public Interest Declassification Board. n.d. *Functions of the PIDB*. Accessed January 25, 2016. http://www.archives.gov/declassification/pidb/.

Quist, Arvin S. *Security Classification of Information: Volume 1. Introduction, History, and Adverse Impacts*. September 2002. Accessed January 11, 2016. https://www.fas.org/sgp/library/quist/index.html.

Raskin, Marcus G., and Carl A. LeVan, eds. *Democracy's Shadow: The Secret World of National Security*. New York: Nation Books, 2005.

Robertson, David Brian. "Historical Institutionalism, Political Development, and the Study of American Bureaucracy." In *The Oxford Handbook of American Bureaucracy*, edited by Robert F. Durant, 25–51. Oxford: Oxford University Press, 2010.

Sarangi, Srikant, and Stefaan Slembrouck. *Language, Bureaucracy, and Social Control.* New York: Longman, 1996.

Schneier, Bruce. "The Rise of Political Doxing." *Motherboard*, October 28, 2015. Accessed October 31, 2015. http://motherboard.vice.com/read/the-rise-of-political-doxing.

Scott, Peter Dale. *Deep Politics and the Death of JFK.* Berkeley: University of California Press, 1996.

Segre, Sandro. "Understanding Lived Experience: Max Weber's Intellectual Relationship to Simmel, Husserl, James, Starbuck, and Jaspers." *Max Weber Studies* 4, no. 1 (2004): 77–99.

Selznick, Philip. "Institutionalism 'Old' and 'New.'" *Administrative Science Quarterly* (1996): 270–77.

Selznick, Philip. *Leadership in Administration: A Sociological Interpretation.* New York: Harper & Row, 1957.

Senate Select Committee on Intelligence. *Report of the Select Committee on Intelligence on the U.S. Intelligence Community's Prewar Intelligence Assessments on Iraq.* Ordered July 7, 2004, 108th Congress. Accessed January 11, 2016. https://fas.org/irp/congress/2004_rpt/ssci_iraq.pdf.

Senate Select Committee on Intelligence. *Report of the Senate Select Committee on Intelligence Committee Study of the Central Intelligence Agency's Detention and Interrogation Program, Together with Foreword by Chairman Feinstein and Additional and Minority Views.* Washington, DC: Government Printing Office, 2014. Accessed January 11, 2016. http://www.gpo.gov/fdsys/pkg/CRPT-113srpt288/pdf/CRPT-113srpt288.pdf.

Shuy, Roger W. *Bureaucratic Language in Government and Business.* Washington, DC: Georgetown University Press, 1998.

Simmel, Georg. "The Sociology of Secrecy and of Secret Societies." *The American Journal of Sociology* 11, no. 4 (1906): 441–98.

Smith, Dorothy E. "Textually Mediated Social-Organization." *International Social Science Journal* 36, no. 1 (1984): 59–75.

Smoot, Dan. *The Invisible Government.* Dallas: Dan Smoot Report, 1962.

Spillman, Lynn. "Culture." In *The Concise Encyclopedia of Sociology*, edited by George Ritzer and J. Michael Ryan, 112–14. Malden, MA: Wiley-Blackwell, 2011.

Starr, Steven, Robin Collins, Robert Green, and Ernie Regehr. "New Terminology to Help Prevent Accidental Nuclear War." *Bulletin of the Atomic Scientists*, September 29, 2015. Accessed December 29, 2015. http://thebulletin.org/new-terminology-help-prevent-accidental-nuclear-war8773.

Stewart, Joseph, David M. Hedge, and James P. Lester. *Public Policy: An Evolutionary Approach.* Boston: Wadsworth Thomson Learning, 2008.

Subcommittee on National Policy Machinery. *Organizing for National Security.* Senate Committee on Government Operations. Interim Report Pursuant to S. Res. 115, 86th Cong. Senate Report 1026. Washington, DC: Government Printing Office, 1960.

Subcommittee on the Constitution of the Committee on the Judiciary. *Secret Law and the Threat to Democratic and Accountable Government: Hearing before the*

Subcommittee on the Constitution of the Committee on the Judiciary, United States Senate, 110–2, April 30, 2008. Washington: Government Printing Office, 2008.

Turner, Stephen. "The Continued Relevance of Weber's Philosophy of Social Science." *Max Weber Studies* 7, no. 1 (2007): 37–62.

United Kingdom Cabinet Office. *National Intelligence Machinery Booklet*. National Security and Intelligence, November 2010. Accessed December 15, 2015. https://www.gov.uk/government/publications/national-intelligence-machinery.

United Nations Office for Disaster Risk Reduction. *Our Mandate*. n.d. Accessed December 29, 2015. https://www.unisdr.org/who-we-are/mandate.

United Nations Office for Disaster Risk Reduction. *Terminology*. 2009. Accessed December 29, 2009. https://www.unisdr.org/we/inform/terminology.

U.S. Department of Defense. *Dictionary of Military and Associated Terms*. JP 1-02. 12 April 2001 as Amended through 17 October 2008. Accessed December 15, 2015. http://www.bits.de/NRANEU/others/jp-doctrine/jp1_02%2810–08%29.pdf.

U.S. Department of Defense. *Dictionary of Military and Associated Terms*. JP 1-02. 08 November 2010, as amended through 15 December 2015. Accessed December 30, 2015. https://web.archive.org/web/20151017194029/ http://www.dtic.mil/doctrine/new_pubs/jp1_02.pdf.

U.S. Department of Defense. *Doctrine for the Armed Forces of the United States*. JP 1, March 25, 2013. Accessed February 21, 2016. http://www.dtic.mil/doctrine/new_pubs/jp1.pdf.

U.S. Department of Defense. *Use of Animals in DoD Programs*. Instruction No. 3216.01, September 13, 2010. Accessed December 15, 2015. http://www.dtic.mil/whs/directives/corres/pdf/321601p.pdf.

U.S. State Department. (n.d.a). *Advisory Committee on Historical Diplomatic Documentation*. Office of the Historian. Accessed December 15, 2015. https://history.state.gov/about/hac.

U.S. State Department. (n.d.b). *Historical Documents: Foreign Relations of the United States*. Office of the Historian. Accessed December 15, 2015. http://history.state.gov/historicaldocuments.

Weaver, William G., and Robert M. Pallitto. "*The Law:* 'Extraordinary Rendition' and Presidential Fiat." *Presidential Studies Quarterly* 36, no. 1 (2006): 102–16.

Weber, Max. "Characteristics of Bureaucracy." In *From Max Weber: Essays in Sociology*, translated, edited, and with an introduction by Hans H. Gerth and C. Wright Mills, 196–240. New York: Oxford University Press, 1946.

Weber, Max. *Economy and Society: Essays in Interpretive Philosophy*. Edited by Guenther Roth and Claus Wittich. Berkeley: University of California Press, 1978.

Whittaker, Alan G., Smith, Frederick C., and McKune, Elizabeth. *The National Security Policy Process: The National Security Council and Interagency System*. Research Report, August 15, Annual Update. Washington, DC: Industrial College of the Armed Forces, National Defense University, U.S. Department of Defense, 2011. Accessed July 29, 2015. http://www.dtic.mil/get-tr-doc/pdf?AD=ada502949.

Williams, Raymond. *Culture and Society, 1780–1950*. New York: Columbia University Press, [1958], 1960.

Williams, Raymond. *Keywords: A Vocabulary of Culture and Society*. New York: Oxford University Press, 1976.

Wilson, Eric. "The Concept of the Parapolitical." In *The Dual State: Parapolitics, Carl Schmitt and the National Security Complex*, edited by Eric Wilson, 1–28. Burlington, VT: Ashgate, 2013.

Wilson, Eric. "Deconstructing the Shadows." In *Government of the Shadows: Parapolitics and Criminal Sovereignty*, edited by Eric Wilson, 13–55. New York: Pluto Press, 2009.

Wise, David, and Thomas B. Ross. *The Invisible Government*. New York: Bantam Books, 1964.

Workman, Samuel, Bryan D. Jones, and Ashley E. Jochim. "Policymaking, Bureaucratic Discretion, and Overhead Democracy." In *The Oxford Handbook of American Bureaucracy*, edited by Robert F. Durant, 612–37. Oxford: Oxford University Press, 2010.

Zegart, Amy B. "Agency Design and Evolution." In *The Oxford Handbook of American Bureaucracy*, edited by Robert F. Durant, 207–30. Oxford: Oxford University Press, 2010.

Zegart, Amy B. *Flawed by Design: The Evolution of the CIA, JCS, and NSC*. Stanford: Stanford University Press, 1999.

About the Authors

Dr. Jan Goldman is associate professor of intelligence and national security at Tiffin University. He is a practitioner and educator with over thirty years of experience in the intelligence community. He is the founding editor of a series of textbooks on intelligence and national security, the founding editor of an academic journal on ethics and intelligence, and a co-founder of a non-profit international intelligence professional organization. He has organized several international conferences on ethics and national security held at Johns Hopkins University, Georgetown University, and Oxford University.

He is the author or editor of dozens of publications to include *The Central Intelligence Agency: An Encyclopedia of Covert Operations, Intelligence Gathering, and Spies* (2 vols., 2016). His recent publications include *Handbook of Warning Intelligence—Complete and Declassified Edition* (2015), and *War on Terror Encyclopedia: From the Rise of Al Qaeda to 9/11 and Beyond* (2014). Additionally, Dr. Goldman sits on numerous international academic and professional boards, and he is a consultant to a series of children's books on the history of spying.

Dr. Susan Maret is a lecturer at the School of Library and Information Science, San Jose State University, where she teaches a course titled "Information Secrecy and Freedom of Information." She holds a MLS from the University of Arizona and a PhD in critical information studies from the Union Institute and University. Dr. Maret is the author of *On Their Own Terms: A Lexicon with an Emphasis on Information-Related Terms Produced by the U.S. Government* (3rd edition, 2006).

Front Cover Description

The cover photograph shows President Harry S. Truman and members of the National Security Council (NSC) on August 19, 1948.[1] The NSC was established by the National Security Act of 1947 (Public Law 80-253, Sec. 101) on July 26, 1947. This photograph captures the dynamic fusion of information and security in the post–World War II era.

The NSC is "the President's principal forum for function is to advise the President with respect to the integration of domestic, foreign, and military policies relating to the national security."[2] The members who attended the August 19 meeting include (left to right and clockwise around the table) Assistant Secretary of the Air Force Cornelius Vanderbilt Whitney; Secretary of the Army Kenneth Royall; Executive Secretary of the National Security Council Sidney Souers; National Security Resources Board Chairman Arthur M. Hill; Director of Central Intelligence (Rear Admiral) Roscoe Hillenkoetter; Secretary of Defense James Forrestal; Secretary of State George C. Marshall; President Truman; and Under-Secretary of the Navy W. John Kenney. At the far back in the photo are Major General A. M. Gruenther, director of the Joint Chiefs of Staff (left), and Robert Blum, foreign affairs specialist in the Department of Defense (right).

The topics on the August 19 agenda included "Situation with Respect to Berlin," "Internal Security of the United States," "Interim Terms of Reference of SANACC" (State-Army-Navy-Air Force Coordinating Committee), "Office of Special Projects," "Situation with Respect to Palestine," "United States Objectives with Respect to Russia," "Review of the World Situation," and "NSC Status of Projects."

NOTES

1. The black and white photograph is in the public domain from the Harry S. Truman Library and Museum (https://wwwtrumanlibrary.org), Accession Number 73-2703.

2. Truman Library and Museum. *Papers of Harry S. Truman Staff Member and Office Files: National Security Council, 1947–1953*. Accessed January 4, 2016. https://www.trumanlibrary.org/hstpaper/nsc.htm.